Principles of Marketing

Version 5.0

Jeff Tanner and Mary Anne Raymond

FlatWorld

978-1-4533-3920-6

Principles of Marketing
Version 5.0

Jeff Tanner and Mary Anne Raymond

Published by:

FlatWorld
292 Newbury Street
Suite #282
Boston, MA 02115-2832

Gen: 202303091235

Brief Contents

Contents

About the Authors

Jeff Tanner

John F. (Jeff) Tanner, Jr., is the former Dean of the Strome College of Business, Old Dominion University and Professor Emeritus of Marketing, Baylor University. He is the author or coauthor of fifteen books, including best-selling textbooks such as *Selling: Building Partnerships* and several books for practitioners, most recently *Analytics & Dynamic Customer Strategy: Big Profits from Big Data*. His books have been translated into several languages and distributed in over thirty countries.

Source: ODU, used with permission.

Dr. Tanner spent eight years in marketing and sales with Rockwell International and Xerox Corporation. In 1988, he earned his PhD from the University of Georgia and joined the faculty at Baylor University. In 2015, he joined Old Dominion University's Strome College of Business as Dean. Dr. Tanner has taught executives and business students around the world, including in Colombia, India, Mexico, Canada, France, Ireland, Australia, Malawi, and Trinidad.

In addition to writing and research, Dr. Tanner maintains an active consulting and training practice. Recent clients include Cativa, Teradata, EMC, and others. He is the founder and a partner in JK Tanner Inc., an investment firm and Bienestar, a consultancy supporting sustainability and growth for non-profits. He serves on the board of VersAbility, a $60m organization that supports and employs people with disabilities, as well as the Commonwealth of Virginia's Horse Racing Commission.

Mary Anne Raymond

Mary Anne Raymond is the Thomas F. Chapman Leadership Distinguished Professor of Leadership, a Professor of Marketing, and the Director of the Thomas F. Chapman Leadership Scholars program at the Wilbur O. and Ann Powers College of Business at Clemson University. Prior to joining the faculty at Clemson, she served on the faculty at American University in Washington, DC, as Interim Director of the Graduate Marketing Program at Johns Hopkins University, and as an invited Fulbright Professor of Marketing at Seoul National University in Seoul, Korea. In addition to teaching marketing in Korea for two years, Dr. Raymond taught in France and helped develop marketing programs in Spain, England, and Denmark.

Dr. Raymond received her PhD from the University of Georgia. She has extensive industry experience doing strategic planning and acquisition analysis, marketing research, and investment analysis for Holiday Inns, Inc.; Freeport Sulphur; and Howard, Weil, Labouisse, Friedrichs. Dr. Raymond also does consulting, seminars, and marketing training for multinational companies, which have included organizations such as Merit Communications in Seoul, Korea; the Conference Center and Inn at Clemson University; and Ssangyong Group.

Her research focuses on strategy in domestic and international markets, public policy issues, and social marketing. Recently, she served as one of the Principal Investigators for a grant with the Department of Defense focused on "Facilitating Necessary Mental Health Treatment for Soldiers." Dr. Raymond has published over one hundred papers appearing in journals such as the *Journal of International Marketing, International Marketing Review, Journal of Advertising Research, Journal of Advertising, Journal of Business Research, Personal Selling and Sales Management*, and the *Journal of Public Policy and Marketing*. Dr. Raymond has received numerous teaching and research awards including the Professor of the Year Award from Clemson University Panhellenic Association, the Undergraduate Teaching Excellence Award from the College of Business and Behavioral Science at Clemson three times, the Eli Lilly Faculty Excellence Awards for Outstanding Research and Outstanding Teaching, the Eli Lilly Partnership Award, and recognition for Leadership in Student Development from the Dow Chemical Company. Dr. Raymond was also recently awarded the coveted Axcess-Capon Distinguished Teaching Award.

Acknowledgments

The authors would like to expressly thank Jeffrey E. Anderson, PhD, California State University Los Angeles for his invaluable work updating the supplements to accompany this version of the text, as well as providing feedback for the revision.

The authors would also like to thank the following reviewers for their feedback, which helped shape the fifth edition:

- Dr. Polly Bashore, Baker College
- Nicole Toro, College of Mount Saint Vincent

The authors would like to thank the following reviewers for their feedback, which helped shape the fourth edition:

- CherylAnn Farrell, Colorado State University—Global Campus
- Dennis Hill, Southern New Hampshire University
- Dr. David C. Kimball, Elms College
- Ronald Kustek, Cabrillo College
- Dr. Tammie Lang, Bellevue University
- Greg Luce, Bucks County Community College
- Judith E. Orfao, MBA, Middlesex Community College
- Dr. Carla Patalano, New England College of Business
- Jeff W. Totten, McNeese State University
- Barbara Ross Wooldridge, University of Texas at Tyler

Preface

The field of marketing is changing at a breakneck pace. Most other principles of marketing textbooks are doing their best to keep up with changes, but often they fall short. Although it's been some time since our last revision, we believe that *Principles of Marketing* v5.0 contains the most-up-to-date information on what's going on in the field of marketing today—as well as how to do it. For example, Chapter 12, which was an entirely new chapter on digital marketing in 3.0, has been significantly updated to current trends in digital marketing.

What's New in Version 5.0

The following offers a glimpse into what's new in version 5.0 of *Principles of Marketing*. Updates include, but are not limited to, new corporate cases, many chapters feature new profiles of marketing professionals, and new videos showcasing marketing trends and examples.

Chapter 3

- Added a discussion on how the COVID-19 pandemic has affected consumer behavior along with a new table.
- Updated new types of payment methods consumers are using.
- Updated table of companies with top brand values.

Chapter 4

- Added a discussion of VARS (value-added resellers).
- Added an expanded discussion of B2B content marketing.
- Expanded the discussion on B2B marketing using social media networks.
- Added a new video on how to set up a virtual tradeshow.

Chapter 8

- Added a discussion on market development (co-op funds).
- Added a discussion of connected TV (CTV) ads.
- Included the rise of livestreaming as a marketing channel during the pandemic.

Chapter 10

- Added a Key Term definition for CDP (customer data platform).
- Added a discussion of privacy concerns and the controversy surrounding Meta Platform's use of facial recognition software.
- Added information on digital ethnographies.

Chapter 12

- Updated the statistics on the use of various social media sites by different demographics.

Supplements

Test Item Files

A robust test bank for each chapter allows you to assign easily self-scoring quizzes, midterms, and final exams. The questions span the full range of topics covered in each chapter so that you can test for comprehension. Questions are in a range of formats, too, from term matching to multiple choice to short essay, allowing for engaging variety no matter what the test.

Test Generator—Powered by Cognero

FlatWorld is pleased to provide a computer-generated test program powered by the leading assessment provider, Cognero, to assist instructors with selecting, randomizing, formatting, loading online, or printing exams. Please contact your local FlatWorld representative or FlatWorld support (support@flatworld.com) for more information or to request the program.

PowerPoint Slides

Present concepts easily to your students using the attractive, modern slide decks for each chapter. Decks include all of the topics and key concepts on separate slides so that you can customize to the topics you're teaching. Visuals are matched with the text graphics, allowing for concept reinforcement. You can mix and match these slide decks with your own or use them as is in your lectures.

Instructor's Manual

The instructor's manual (IM) includes learning objectives, an outline, key takeaways, interactive activities, and key terms with definitions for each chapter.

FlatWorld Homework

Accompanying FlatWorld Homework for this text is provided in an easy-to-use interface. Multiple choice, fill-in-the-blank, matching, and other question types are available for use and are all autogradable. Students who utilize the homework questions should see their performance improve on examinations that are given using the Test Item File questions provided to adopters via Word documents or LMS packages.

Sample Syllabi

Sample syllabi based on either 16-week or 10-week terms provide useful templates that help new adopters transition from their current course textbook to *Principles of Marketing*. Faculty can download the syllabi from the FlatWorld website or they can be obtained by contacting your local FlatWorld representative or FlatWorld support (support@flatworld.com).

Online Quizzes and Flashcards

Autograded Quiz questions and Flashcards for student self-evaluation are organized by chapter and section and embedded in the online version of the book. Students can use the Quizzes and Flashcards to test their comprehension by section as they read and learn, once they have completed a chapter, or for test review.

CHAPTER 1
What Is Marketing?

What makes a business idea successful? Do you have to be first to the market? If so, then explain how Nike became so successful; after all, they didn't invent the athletic shoe.

Or does it take capital? IBM had more capital than Apple but lost several battles a long time ago and sold out of the PC market and never got close to the smartphone market. Did Apple just have a better idea? If so, what made it possible for them to execute on that idea?

These examples may seem like ancient history to you; after all, Nike and Apple seem to be pretty well entrenched, maybe even bulletproof. Yet consumer tastes change, and suddenly or slowly, other brands can take over.

Better marketing isn't always the reason some companies outperform others, but bad marketing will kill a good idea. No matter what type of business you go into, marketing is important to understanding your customers, making sure you have what they want, and shaping how they view you and your competitors so that you become their preferred choice.

1.1 Defining Marketing

Learning Objective

1. Define marketing and outline its components.

Marketing is defined by the American Marketing Association as "the activity, set of institutions, and processes for creating, communicating, delivering, and exchanging offerings that have value for customers, clients, partners, and society at large."[1] If you read the definition closely, you see that there are four activities, or components, of marketing:

1. **Creating.** The process of collaborating with suppliers and customers to create offerings that have value.
2. **Communicating.** Broadly, describing those offerings, as well as learning from customers.
3. **Delivering.** Getting those offerings to the consumer in a way that optimizes value.
4. **Exchanging.** Trading value for those offerings.

marketing

"The activity, set of institutions, and processes for creating, communicating, delivering, and exchanging offerings that have value for customers, clients, partners, and society at large."

However, the traditional way of viewing the components of marketing, which emerged in the early 1950s, is based on the following four Ps:

1. **Product.** Goods and services (creating offerings).
2. **Promotion.** Communication.
3. **Place.** Getting the product to a point at which the customer can purchase it (delivering).
4. **Price.** The monetary amount charged for the product (exchanging).

marketing mix

The balance of product, price, promotion, and place decisions that makes up a marketing plan.

The four Ps are called the **marketing mix**, meaning that a marketing plan is a mix of these four components. If the four Ps are the same as creating, communicating, delivering, and exchanging, you might be wondering why there was a change. The answer is that they are *not* exactly the same. Product, price, place, and promotion are nouns. As such, these words fail to capture all the activities of marketing. For example, exchanging requires mechanisms for a transaction, which consist of more than simply a price or place. Exchanging requires, among other things, the transfer of ownership. For example, when you buy a car, you sign documents that transfer the car's title from the seller to you. That's part of the exchange process but not clear in the four Ps.

FIGURE 1.1 The Four Ps

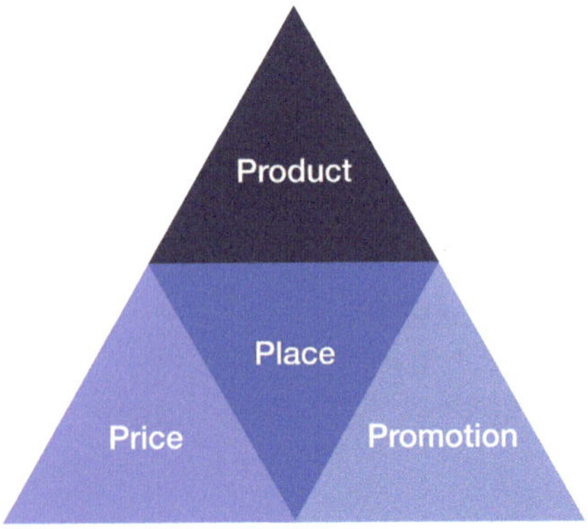

Even the term *product*, which seems pretty obvious, is limited. Does the product include services that come with your new car purchase (such as free maintenance for a certain period of time on some models)? Or does the product mean only the car itself? Finally, none of the four Ps describes particularly well what marketing people do. However, one of the goals of this book is to focus on exactly what it is that marketing professionals do, partly so that you can see if you want to pursue a marketing career, but also so you can understand how your organization engages in creating communicating, delivering, and exchanging value.

Value

Value lies at the center of everything marketing does (Figure 1.2). Marketing is composed of four activities centered on customer value: creating, communicating, delivering, and exchanging value. What does value mean?

FIGURE 1.2 Value: The Center of Marketing

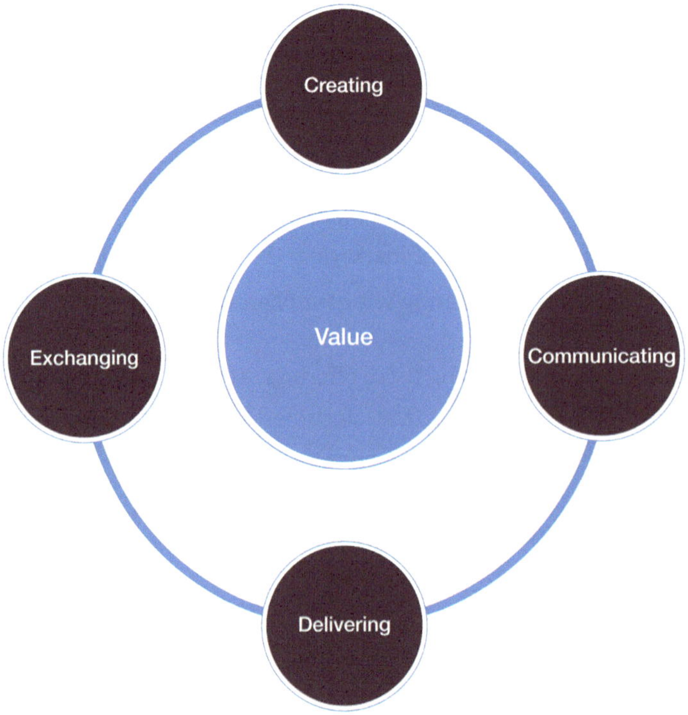

When we use the term **value**, we mean the benefits buyers receive that meet their needs. In other words, value is what the customer gets by purchasing and consuming a company's offering. So, although the offering is created by the company, the value is determined by the customer.

Furthermore, our goal as marketers is to create a profitable exchange for consumers. By profitable for your customer, we mean that the consumer's personal value equation is positive. The **personal value equation** is

$$\text{value} = \text{benefits received} - (\text{price} + \text{hassle})$$

Hassle is the time and effort the consumer puts into the shopping process. The equation is a personal one because how each consumer judges the benefits of a product will vary, as will the time and effort they put into shopping. Value, then, varies for each consumer.

One way to think of value is to think of a meal in a restaurant. If you and three friends go to a restaurant and order the same dish, each of you will like it more or less depending on your own personal tastes. Yet the dish was exactly the same, priced the same, and served exactly the same way. Because your tastes varied, the benefits you received varied. Therefore the value varied for each of you. That's why we call it a *personal* value equation.

Value varies from customer to customer based on each customer's needs. The **marketing concept**, a philosophy underlying all that marketers do, requires that marketers seek to satisfy customer wants and needs. Firms operating with that philosophy are said to be **market oriented**. At the same time, market-oriented firms recognize that exchange must be profitable for the company to be successful. A marketing orientation is not an excuse to fail to make profit; otherwise, there would be no company!

Firms didn't always embrace the marketing concept and a market orientation. Beginning with the Industrial Revolution in the late 1800s, companies were **production oriented**. They believed that the best way to compete was by reducing production costs. In other words, companies thought that good products would sell themselves. Perhaps the best example of such a product was Henry Ford's Model A automobile, the first product of his production line innovation. Ford's production line made the automobile cheap and affordable for just about everyone. The **production era** lasted until the 1920s, when production-capacity growth began to outpace demand growth and new strategies were called for. There are, however, companies that still focus on production as the way to compete.

value

Total sum of benefits received that meet a buyer's needs. See personal value equation.

personal value equation

The net benefit a consumer receives from a product less the price paid for it and the hassle or effort expended to acquire it.

The Great Depression forced companies to push products through strong selling, but they also developed low cost products like everyone's favorite, Kraft Macaroni & Cheese.

Source: TonelsonProductions/Shutterstock.com

marketing concept

A philosophy underlying all that marketers do, driven by satisfying customer wants and needs.

market oriented

The degree to which a company follows the marketing concept.

production oriented

A belief that the way to compete is a function of product innovation and reducing production costs, as good products appropriately priced sell themselves.

production era

A period beginning with the Industrial Revolution and concluding in the 1920s in which production-orientation thinking dominated the way in which firms competed.

selling oriented

A philosophy that products must be pushed through selling and advertising in order for a firm to compete successfully.

selling era

A period running from the 1920s to until after World War II in which the selling orientation dominated the way firms competed.

product orientation

A philosophy that focuses on competing through product innovation.

marketing era

From 1950 to at least 1990 (see service-dominant logic era, value era, and one-to-one era), the dominant philosophy among businesses is the marketing concept.

value era

From the 1990s to the present, some argue that firms moved into the value era, competing on the basis of value; others contend that the value era is simply an extension of the marketing era and is not a separate era.

one-to-one era

From the 1990s to the present, the idea of competing by building relationships with customers one at a time and seeking to serve each customer's needs individually.

transformative era

A time in which companies are transformed into new companies because marketing is driving the company to change to meet customer needs more completely, resulting in new product categories and ways of selling.

From the 1920s until after World War II, companies tended to be **selling oriented**, meaning they believed it was necessary to push their products by heavily emphasizing advertising and selling. Consumers during the Great Depression and World War II did not have as much money, so the competition for their available dollars was stiff. The result was this push approach during the **selling era**. Companies like the Fuller Brush Company and Hoover Vacuum began selling door to door, and the vacuum-cleaner salesman (they were always men) was created. Just as with production, some companies still operate with a push focus.

At the same, you should also know that the selling era did not mean that the production orientation completely disappeared. Again, because of the Great Depression, companies tried to squeeze dollars out of production costs so that they could reduce prices and compete more effectively. This period was also the golden age of processed food, when Kraft Macaroni and Cheese and Spam were created as ways to feed more people for less money—a value-based offer even then.

In the post–World War II environment, demand for goods increased as the economy soared. Some products, limited in supply during World War II, were now plentiful to the point of surplus. Companies believed that a way to compete was to create products different from the competition, so many focused on product innovation. This focus on product innovation is called the **product orientation**. Companies like Procter & Gamble created many products that served the same basic function but with a slight twist or difference in order to appeal to a different consumer, and as a result products proliferated. But as consumers had many choices available to them, companies had to find new ways to compete. Which products were best to create? Why create them? The answer was to create what customers wanted, leading to the development of the marketing concept. During this time the marketing concept was developed, and from about 1950 to 1990, businesses operated in the **marketing era**.

So what era would you say we're in now? Some call it the **value era**: a time when companies emphasize creating value for customers. Is that really different from the marketing era, in which the emphasis was on fulfilling the marketing concept? Or the selling era, when Kraft Macaroni and Cheese and Spam were invented? Maybe not. Others call today's business environment the **one-to-one era**, meaning that the way to compete is to build relationships with customers one at a time and seek to serve each customer's needs individually. For example, the longer you are customer of Amazon, the more details they gain in your purchasing habits and the better they can target you with offers of new products. With the advent of social media and the empowerment of consumers through ubiquitous information that includes consumer reviews, there is clearly greater emphasis on meeting customer needs. Yet is that substantially different from the marketing concept?

Still others call this the **transformative era**: a time when marketing is transforming complete companies into new forms and core products because of the drive to serve customers more completely.[2] For example, Mars Petcare, maker of Pedigree and Whiskas pet foods, now also sells a Fitbit-type product for dogs and sells new services through channels such as vet clinics. One aspect driving transformation is the ability to deliver one-to-one marketing through better use of technology and data, but new ways to reach consumers and business models (such as sharing models like Uber, GrubHub, and VRBO) are also changing companies.

Danielle Johnson, House of MKTG

Source: Danielle Johnson, used with permission.

Danielle Johnson graduated from college in 2019 and started her own marketing firm that same year. In only two years, she had to hire ten employees in order to manage the firm's growth. "One of my favorite things about marketing is that it's constantly evolving. If you want to stand out, you have to get creative. In an industry that's so saturated, I love finding unique opportunities to help businesses express their value in a way they've never done before."

Whatever era we're in now, most historians would agree that defining and labeling it is difficult. Value and one-to-one are both natural extensions of the marketing concept, so we may still be in the marketing era; some have argued that is also true about the transformative era. To make matters more confusing, not all companies adopt the philosophy of the era. For example, in the 1800s Singer and National Cash Register adopted strategies rooted in sales, so they operated in the selling era forty years before it existed. Some companies are still in the selling era. Recently, many considered automobile manufacturers to be in the trouble they were in because they work too hard to sell or push product and not hard enough on delivering value.

Creating Offerings That Have Value

Marketing creates those goods and services that the company offers at a price to its customers or clients. That entire bundle, consisting of the tangible good, the intangible service, and the price, is the company's **offering**.[3] When you compare one car to another, for example, you can evaluate each of these dimensions—the tangible, the intangible, and the price—separately. However, you can't buy one manufacturer's car, another manufacturer's service, and a third manufacturer's price when you actually make a choice. Together, the three make up a single firm's offer.

offering

The entire bundle of a tangible good, intangible service, and price that composes what a company offers to customers.

Marketing people do not create the offering alone. For example, when the iPhone 12 was created, Apple's engineers were also involved in its design. Apple's financial personnel had to review the costs of producing the offering and provide input on how it should be priced. Apple's operations group needed to evaluate the manufacturing requirements the product would need. The company's logistics managers had to evaluate the cost and timing of getting the offering to retailers and consumers. Even suppliers were involved, as they also helped design the product and made sure that it could be produced at a certain price in sufficient quantities. Marketing, however, has the biggest responsibility because it is marketing's responsibility to ensure that the new product delivers value.

Communicating Offers

communicating

In marketing, a broad term meaning describing the offering and its value to potential customers, as well as learning from customers.

Communicating is a broad term in marketing that means describing the offering and its value to your potential and current customers, as well as learning from customers what it is they want and like. Sometimes communicating means educating potential customers about the value of an offering, and sometimes it means simply making customers aware of where they can find a product. Communicating also means that customers get a chance to tell the company what they think. Most marketers separate communicating into promotion and research, promotion (including selling) being communicating to customers and research involving listening to customers.

A Hermès purse like this can cost nearly $60,000. But why is it worth so much more than other brands? What makes up the complete offering that creates more value?

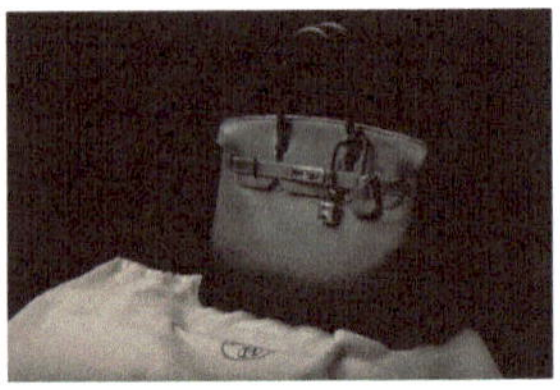

Source: Camera Rules/ Shutterstock.com

Today companies are finding that to be successful, they need a more interactive dialogue with their customers. In other words, firms need to *engage* customers so they are more than just passive buyers of their products. Marketers want to make their customers fans of their products, talk about the products on social media and elsewhere. As part of the effort, companies are also trying to tap into what customers want and what can be improved. For example, Apple and Nike partnered to create the Apple Watch NikePlus Run Club, an online community of runners. Both companies listen to what customers are saying on the platform, as well as use data collected by the watch and website, to create better offerings.

Mobile devices like ismartphones and watches make mobile marketing possible, too. For example, consumers can allow stores to send coupons and other offers directly to their phones and tablets when those consumers are near the store. Similarly, digital signs can be equipped with WiFi to connect to your phone and, with your permission, customize offerings for you in the store.

Companies use many forms of communication, including advertising on the web or television, on billboards or in magazines, through product placements in movies, and through salespeople. Other forms of communication include attempting to have news media cover the company's actions, which is part of public relations (PR): participating in special events such as the annual International Consumer Electronics Show in which Apple and other companies introduce their newest gadgets; and sponsoring special events like the Susan G. Komen Race for the Cure. Packaging provides another important way that companies can communicate with their customers.

Delivering Offerings

delivering

In marketing, as in delivering value, a broad term that means getting the product to the consumer and making sure that the user gets the most out of the product and service.

supply chain

All of the organizations that participate in the production, promotion, and delivery of a product or service from the producer to the end consumer.

logistics

The physical flow of materials in the supply chain.

Marketing can't just promise value, it also has to deliver value. **Delivering** an offering that has value is much more than simply getting the product into the hands of the user; it is also making sure that the user understands how to get the most out of the product and is taken care of if service is required later. Value is delivered in part through a company's supply chain. The **supply chain** includes a number of organizations and functions that mine or farm, make, assemble, or deliver materials and products from a manufacturer to consumers. The actual group of organizations can vary greatly from industry to industry, and include wholesalers, transportation companies, and retailers. **Logistics**, or transportation and storage of materials and products, is the primary component of supply chain management, but there are other aspects of supply chain management that we will discuss later.

Technology, though, is changing the nature of how some offerings are delivered. For example, the Apple Watch NikePlus offering is a combination of the Apple Watch and the NikePlus shoe insert. Runners with a NikePlus join a community where, with the insert, they can track their running activities, compete or work out with friends, and engage in other ongoing interactions. As Apple and Nike continue to add services to the Watch and NikePlus website, the offering's value is increased. So just handing over the watch or the insert doesn't end the delivery—delivery continues through the digital platform across a number of transactions.[4] This ongoing value creation and delivery is different from physical logistics but requires a robust delivery system nonetheless.

Exchanging Offerings

In addition to creating an offering, communicating its benefits to consumers, and delivering the offering, there is the actual transaction, or **exchange**, that has to occur. In most instances, we consider the exchange to be cash for products and services. However, if you were to fly to Louisville, Kentucky, for the Kentucky Derby, you could pay for your airline tickets using frequent-flier miles. You could also use Hilton Honors points to pay for your hotel, and cash-back points on your credit card to pay for meals. None of these transactions would actually require cash. Other exchanges, such as information about your preferences gathered through surveys, might not involve cash.

exchange

The transaction of value, usually economic, between a buyer and seller.

When consumers acquire, consume (use), and dispose of products and services, exchange occurs, including during the consumption phase. For example, via Apple's "One-to-One" program, you can pay a yearly fee in exchange for additional periodic product training sessions with an Apple professional. So each time a training session occurs, another transaction takes place. A transaction also occurs when you are finished with a product. For example, you might sell your old iPhone to a friend, trade in a car, or ask the Salvation Army to pick up your old refrigerator.

Disposing of products has become an important ecological issue. Batteries and other components of cell phones, computers, and high-tech appliances can be very harmful to the environment, and many consumers don't know how to dispose of these products properly. Some companies, such as Office Depot, have created recycling centers to which customers can take their old electronics.

Apple has a web page where consumers can fill out a form, print it, and ship it along with their old cell phones to Apple. Apple then pulls out the materials that are recyclable and properly disposes of those that aren't. By lessening the hassle associated with disposing of products, Office Depot and Apple add value to their product offerings.

Key Takeaway

- The focus of marketing has changed from emphasizing the product, price, place, and promotion mix to one that emphasizes creating, communicating, delivering, and exchanging value. Value is a function of the benefits an individual receives and consists of the price the consumer paid and the time and effort the person expended making the purchase.

Review Questions

1. What is the marketing mix?
2. How has marketing changed from the four Ps approach to the more current value-based perspective?
3. What is the personal value equation?

1.2 Who Does Marketing?

Learning Objective

1. Describe how the various institutions and entities that engage in marketing use marketing to deliver value.

The short answer to the question of who does marketing is *everybody*! But that answer is a bit glib and not too useful. Let's take a moment and consider how different types of organizations engage in marketing.

For-Profit Companies

The obvious answer to the question, "Who does marketing?" is for-profit companies like McDonald's, Procter & Gamble (the makers of Tide detergent and Crest toothpaste), and Walmart. For example, McDonald's creates a new spicy chicken sandwich for $1.99 (the offering), launches a social media campaign (communicating), makes the sandwiches available on certain dates (delivering), and then sells them in its stores (exchanging). When Procter & Gamble (or P&G for short) creates a new Crest tartar control toothpaste, it launches a direct mail campaign in which it sends information and samples to dentists to offer to their patients. P&G then sells the toothpaste through retailers like Walmart, which has a panel of consumers sample the product and provide feedback through an online community. These are all examples of marketing activities.

One interesting marketing job has to be Chris Pantoya's, who is the Chief Strategy Officer for Fan Controlled Football. She knows most of the players, owners, and coaches personally, people like Joe Montana. The professional arena football league where the fans call the plays, Fan Controlled Football was a start-up when she joined, and while it sounds like a lot of fun, Chris has revenue targets that she has to hit, revenue based on advertising, sponsorships, tickets, and other streams. Like she says, "It's not all fun and games, but it is fun!"

For-profit companies can be defined by the nature of their customers. A B2C (business-to-consumer) company like Chris Pantoya's Fan Controlled Football or P&G sells products and services to be used by consumers like you, while a B2B (business-to-business) company sells products to be used within another company's operations, as well as by government agencies and entities. To be sure, P&G sells toothpaste to other companies like Walmart (and probably to the military, prisons, and other government agencies) in a B2B way, but the end user is an individual person.

Other ways to categorize companies that engage in marketing is by the functions they fulfill. P&G is a manufacturer, Walmart is a retailer, and Grocery Supply Company is a wholesaler of grocery items that buys from companies like P&G in order to sell to small convenience store chains. Though they have different functions, all these types of for-profit companies engage in marketing activities. Walmart, for example, advertises to consumers. Grocery Supply Company salespeople will call on convenience store owners and take orders, as well as build in-store displays. P&G might help Walmart or Grocery Supply Company with templates for advertising or special cartons to use in an in-store display, but all three of the companies are using marketing to help sell P&G's toothpaste.

Similarly, all of these companies engage in dialogues with their customers in order to understand what to sell. For Walmart and Grocery Supply, the dialogue may result in changing what they buy and sell; for P&G, such customer feedback may yield a new product or a change in pricing strategy.

Nonprofit Organizations

Nonprofit organizations also engage in marketing. When the American Heart Association (AHA) created a heart-healthy diet for people with high blood pressure, it bound the diet into a small book, along with access to a special website that people can use to plan their meals and record their health-related activities. The AHA then sent copies of the diet to doctors to give to patients. When does an exchange take place, you might be wondering? And what does the AHA get out of the transaction?

From a monetary standpoint, the AHA does not directly benefit. Nonetheless, the organization is meeting its mission, or purpose, of getting people to live heart-healthy lives, and considers the marketing campaign a success when doctors give the books to their patients, and when patients actually use the book. The point is that the AHA is engaged in the marketing activities of creating, communicating, delivering, and exchanging. This won't involve the same kind of exchange as a for-profit company, but it is marketing. When a nonprofit organization engages in marketing activities, this is called **nonprofit marketing**. Some schools offer specific courses in nonprofit marketing, and many marketing majors begin their careers with nonprofit organizations.

Nonprofits use marketing to promote their services, such as this food bank, in order to get people to take advantage of those services.

Source: Ringo Chiu/Shutterstock.com

nonprofit marketing

Marketing activities conducted to meet the goals of nonprofit organizations.

Government entities also engage in marketing activities. For example, when the U.S. Army advertises to parents of prospective recruits, sends brochures to high schools, or brings a Bradley Fighting Vehicle to a state fair, the army is engaging in marketing. The U.S. Army also listens to its constituencies, as evidenced by recent research aimed at understanding how to serve military families more effectively. One result was advertising aimed at parents and improving their responses to their children's interests in joining the Army; another was a program aimed at encouraging spouses of military personnel to access counseling services when their spouse is serving overseas.

Similarly, the Environmental Protection Agency (EPA) runs a number of advertising campaigns designed to promote environmentally friendly activities. One such campaign promoted the responsible disposal of motor oil instead of simply pouring it on the ground or into a storm sewer.

There is a difference between these two types of activities. When the Army is promoting the benefits of enlisting, it hopes young men and women will join the Army. By contrast, when the EPA runs commercials about how to properly dispose of motor oil, it hopes to change people's attitudes and behaviors so that social change occurs. Marketing conducted in an effort to achieve certain social objectives can be done by government agencies, nonprofit institutions, religious organizations, and others and is called **social marketing**. Convincing people that global warming is a real threat via advertisements and commercials is social marketing, as is the example regarding the EPA's campaign to promote responsible disposal of motor oil.

social marketing

Marketing conducted in an effort to achieve social change.

Individuals

If you create a résumé, are you using marketing to communicate the value you have to offer prospective employers? Is it digital marketing if you create a LinkedIn page? If you sell yourself in an interview, is that marketing? When Kylie Jenner sends a tweet about where she is and what she had for lunch, is that marketing? In other words, can individuals market themselves and their ideas?

Some marketing professionals say "no." But today, more marketing professionals are saying "yes," and that self-promotion is a form of marketing. Ultimately it may not matter what you are marketing, even if it's yourself or another person. If, as a result of reading this book, you learn how to more effectively create value, communicate and deliver it to the receiver, and get something in exchange for it, then we've achieved our purpose.

Key Takeaway

- Marketing can be thought of as a set of business practices that for-profit organizations, non-profit organizations, government entities, and even individuals can utilize. When a nonprofit organization engages in marketing activities, this is called *nonprofit marketing*. Marketing conducted in an effort to achieve certain social objectives is called *social marketing*.

Review Questions

1. What types of companies engage in marketing?
2. What is the difference between nonprofit marketing and social marketing?
3. What can individuals do for themselves that would be considered marketing?

1.3 Why Study Marketing?

Learning Objective

1. Explain the role marketing plays in individual firms and society as a whole.

Marketing Enables Profitable Transactions to Occur

Products don't, contrary to popular belief, sell themselves. Long ago, Ralph Waldo Emerson wrote, "Build a better mousetrap and the world will be a path to your door," but generally, the "build it and they will come" philosophy doesn't work. Good marketing educates customers so that they can find the products they want, make better choices about those products, and extract the most value from them. In this way, marketing helps facilitate exchanges between buyers and sellers for the mutual benefit of both parties. Likewise, good social marketing provides people with information and helps them make healthier decisions for themselves and for others.

Many people think of professional sports as one of the easiest ticket sales to make, but as Todd Pollock, VP of Ticketing and Suites for the Vegas Golden Knights of the NHL, knows, sales depend heavily on how well the team is doing. He joined the Golden Knights nearly two years before they ever dropped a puck in Las Vegas, and skeptics wondered if a hockey team could survive in the desert. "Some sales were easy because people wanted to say they were in there at the beginning," says Pollock. "But when we made that incredible run to the Stanley Cup Finals, sales were much easier." Then came competition in the form of the NFL team, the Raiders. Todd leveraged the strong hometown fanbase (most tickets are sold to local residents, not to Vegas visitors), and the arena continues to sell out, but Pollock still has a job to do. "For our premium seat holders, we create a number of special fan experiences, such as opportunities to skate with the team during warm-ups at a practice or fan nights. These can be revenue generators, but are also important in creating fans for life, much more important to us now that we have competition."

Of course, all business students should understand all functional areas of the firm, including marketing. There is more to marketing, however, than simply understanding its role in the business. Marketing has tremendous impact on society.

Marketing Delivers Value

Not only does marketing deliver value to customers, but also that value translates into the value of the firm as it develops a reliable customer base and increases its sales and profitability. So when we say that marketing delivers value, marketing delivers value to both the customer and the company. Franklin D. Roosevelt, the U.S. president with perhaps the greatest influence on our economic system, once said, "If I were starting life over again, I am inclined to think that I would go into the advertising business in preference to almost any other. The general raising of the standards of modern civilization among all groups of people during the past half century would have been impossible without the spreading of the knowledge of higher standards by means of advertising."[5] Roosevelt referred to advertising, but advertising is an important component of marketing for delivering value. Marketing completes the job by ensuring that what is delivered is valuable.

Marketing Benefits Society

Marketing benefits society in general by improving people's lives in two ways. First, as we mentioned, it facilitates trade. As you have learned, or will learn, in economics, being able to trade makes people's lives better. Otherwise people wouldn't do it. In addition, because better marketing means more successful companies, jobs are created. This generates wealth for people, who are then able to make purchases, which, in turn, creates more jobs.

The second way in which marketing improves the quality of life is based on the value delivery function of marketing, but in a broader sense: When you add all the marketers together who are trying to deliver offerings of greater value to consumers and are effectively communicating that value, consumers are able to make more informed decisions about a wider array of choices. From an economic perspective, more choices and smarter consumers are indicative of a higher quality of life.

Marketing Costs Money

Marketing can sometimes be the largest expense associated with producing a product. In the flavored water business, marketing expenses account for about one-third of a product's price—about the same as the ingredients used to make the soft drink itself. Some people argue that society does not benefit from marketing when it comprises such a huge chunk of a product's final price. In some cases, that argument is justified. Yet when marketing results in more informed consumers receiving a greater amount of value, then the cost is justified.

Marketing Offers People Career Opportunities

Marketing is the interface between producers and consumers. In other words, it is the one function in the organization in which the entire business comes together. Being responsible for both making money for your company and delivering satisfaction to your customers makes marketing a great career. In addition, because marketing can be such an expensive part of a business and is so critical to its success, companies actively seek good marketing people. As you will learn, there's a great variety of jobs available in the marketing profession. These positions represent only a few of the opportunities available in marketing.

- **Marketing research.** Personnel in marketing research are responsible for studying markets and customers in order to understand what strategies or tactics might work best for firms.
- **Merchandising.** In retailing, merchandisers are responsible for developing strategies regarding what products wholesalers should carry to sell to retailers such as Target and Walmart.
- **Sales.** Salespeople meet with customers, determine their needs, propose offerings, and make sure that the customer is satisfied. Sales departments can also include sales support teams who work on creating the offering.
- **Advertising.** Whether it's for an advertising agency or inside a company, some marketing personnel work on advertising. Television commercials and print ads are only part of the advertising mix. Many people who work in advertising spend all their time creating advertising for electronic media, such as websites and their pop-up ads, podcasts, and the like.
- **Product development.** People in product development are responsible for identifying and creating features that meet the needs of a firm's customers. They often work with engineers or other technical personnel to ensure that value is created.
- **Customer insights or marketing analytics.** In today's information technology and social media world, a great deal of data exists about consumers and markets. Marketing analysts or customer insights analysts are the professionals who analyze the data and provide insights to other members of the marketing team, from product development to merchandising, to sales and advertising.
- **Direct marketing.** Professionals in direct marketing communicate directly with customers about a company's product offerings via channels such as email, chat lines, telephone, or direct mail.
- **Digital marketing.** Digital marketing professionals combine advertising, direct marketing, and other areas of marketing to communicate directly with customers via social media, the web, and mobile media (including texts). They also work with statisticians to determine which consumers receive which message and with IT professionals to create the right look and feel of digital media.
- **Event marketing.** Some marketing personnel plan special events, orchestrating face-to-face conversations with potential and current customers in a special setting.
- **Nonprofit marketing.** Nonprofit marketers often don't get to do everything listed previously, as nonprofits typically have smaller budgets. But their work is always very important as they try to change behaviors without having a product to sell.

Carly Stephens, Integrity 9 Sports & Entertainment

Source: Photo courtesy of Kevin J. Hamm

A career in marketing can begin in a number of ways. Entry-level positions for new college graduates are available in many of the positions previously mentioned. Carly Stephens, a 2014 graduate of the University of Missouri in Columbia, initially majored in broadcast journalism, but found herself yearning for more opportunities to satisfy her creative side and work with creative people. So Stephens switched her major to strategic communication. Immediately after graduation, she went to work for a promotion agency in Dallas, working for accounts like Taco Bueno. She then worked for Genesco Sports, handling the Frito Lay account. Today she's director of marketing for Integrity 9 Sports & Entertainment. How does she like her job? "As an account executive, I am a part of the process from the beginning, so seeing how an amazing idea can come to life is something I will never get tired of," she says. "Which brings me to the most rewarding thing about my job: the end product. When my client is happy about the work we did and my team is proud of the work we did, nothing is better than that."

A growing number of CEOs are people with marketing backgrounds; in fact, more than one out of four CEOs now come out of marketing.[6] Some successful business leaders you may have heard of include Mark Cuban, Gina Rometty (IBM), and Howard Schultz (Starbucks).

Criticisms of Marketing

Marketing is not without its critics. False advertising and deceptive marketing practices, even by seemingly reputable companies, are an ongoing concern. Volkswagen was sued in 2016 for false claims regarding its cars' emissions record; even Red Bull was sued because, in spite of advertising saying "Red Bull gives you wings," one plaintiff said he had not sprouted wings![7]

Yet another criticism of marketing is that it fuels *consumerism*, which is the tendency of consumers to want more and more products and services they don't really need. Fashion marketing creates demand for high-dollar jeans when much less expensive jeans can fulfill the same basic function. Taken to the extreme, consumers may take on significant amounts of credit card debt to satisfy the wants created by marketing. The critics of consumerism also argue that the demand for products creates leads to more manufacturing and pollution than is necessary, which harms the environment.

societal marketing orientation

A marketing orientation that states that in addition to selling products to customers and delivering profits to shareholders, a company's marketing efforts should be aimed at improving the well-being of society and the world in general.

Concerns such as these are persuading more companies to take a **societal marketing orientation**, which holds that a company's marketing efforts should not be aimed only at delivering products to customers and profits to shareholders but ultimately improve the well-being of society and the world in general.

The outdoor-clothing maker Patagonia has a societal marketing orientation. To draw attention to the problem of consumerism, Patagonia actually ran ads showing one of its jackets with a headline that read "Don't Buy This Jacket." The company was trying to actually persuade people *not* to consume products—even its own products—if they don't need them. The ad campaign received a lot of attention, in part because people were who saw it wondered why a company would want to *not* sell its products. Ironically, instead of Patagonia's sales falling, they climbed as a result of the ad campaign.[8]

Part of the reason Patagonia's sales climbed is that people are looking more favorably on companies that have a societal marketing orientation. The Fair Trade Certification movement emerged in response to people wanting to do business with firms that consider the good of society when making and selling products. To have their products Fair Trade Certified, firms have to meet certain criteria. The criteria include, among other things, ensuring that the factories and production methods used to produce their products meet certain environmental goals, that the facilities are safe, and that people who work in them are paid fair wages and provided with good working conditions.

Key Takeaway

- By facilitating transactions, marketing delivers value to both consumers and firms. At the broader level, this process creates jobs and improves the quality of life in a society. Marketing can be costly, so firms need to hire good people to manage their marketing activities. Being responsible for both making money for your company and delivering satisfaction to your customers makes marketing a great career. Marketing has its critics, though. False and deceptive advertising has long been a problem people are concerned about. Other people believe marketing simply increases the price people have to pay for products. Still other people are concerned marketing leads to consumerism, which is the tendency of consumers to want more and more products and services they don't really need. For reasons such as these, more companies today are pursuing a societal marketing orientation. In addition to delivering products to their customers and profits to their shareholders, these companies actively strive to improve the well-being of society and the world in general.

Review Questions

1. How does marketing provide value?
2. Why does marketing cost so much? Is it worth it?

1.4 Themes and Organization of This Book

Learning Objective

1. Understand and outline the elements of a marketing plan as a planning process.

Marketing's Role in the Organization

We previously discussed marketing as a set of activities that all organizations do. Marketing is also a functional area in companies, just like operations and accounting are. Within a company, marketing might be the title of a department, but some marketing functions, such as sales, might be handled by another department. Marketing activities do not occur separately from the rest of the company, however.

As we have explained, pricing an offering, for example, will involve a company's finance and accounting departments in addition to the marketing department. Similarly, a marketing strategy is not created solely by a firm's marketing personnel. Instead, it flows from the company's overall strategy. For example, Starbucks has committed to an aggressive growth strategy.[9] Key elements include digital strategies that will reshape the company's interaction with customers. Those digital strategies will take capital investment into technology, which isn't marketing, but there will be marketing implications for the company's strategy. Once a company sets an overall strategy, marketing then creates the marketing plan to support it. We'll discuss strategy much more completely in Chapter 2.

Everything Starts with Customers

Most organizations start with an idea of how to serve customers better. Chris Pantoya at Fan Controlled Football plays an integral role in the design of services and fan experiences because she is very concerned with creating a customer experience that makes customers want to return. Her work, though, doesn't stop when the season starts—she continues to talk with and listen to customers so that she can improve the customer experience on every platform.

Many companies think about potential markets and customers when they first launch their businesses. John Deere, for example, founded his farm equipment company on the principle of serving customers. When admonished for making constant improvements to his products even though farmers would take whatever they could get, Deere reportedly replied, "They haven't got to take what we make and somebody else will beat us, and we will lose our trade."[10] He recognized that if his company failed to meet customers' needs, someone else would. Today the John Deere Company's strategy, or mission statement, is as follows:

> For those who cultivate and harvest the land. For those who transform and enrich the land. For those who build upon the land. John Deere is committed to your success.

John Deere Company started as a plow maker, but now makes many products, all because the company's founder realized early that his company had to continuously develop new products or other companies would take his customers away.

Source: jjvxphotography/Shutterstock.com

The following are a few mission or value statements from other companies. Note that they all refer to their customers, either directly or by making references to relationships with them. Notice, too, that the statements are written to inspire employees and others who interact with the companies.

IBM

IBM will be driven by these values:

- Dedication to every client's success.
- Innovation that matters, for our company and for the world.
- Trust and personal responsibility in all relationships.[11]

Coca-Cola Company

Our roadmap starts with our mission, which is enduring. It declares our purpose as a company and serves as the standard against which we weigh our actions and decisions

- To refresh the world . . .
- To inspire moments of optimism . . .
- To create value and make a difference . . .[12]

The Dow Chemical Company

- To constantly improve what is essential to human progress by mastering science and technology.[13]
- Working closely with our customers we deliver products and solutions that create value and competitive advantage while positively impacting the world we live in. Collectively, our efforts have lasting results, creating higher performance for our customers and reshaping the world around us to build a better future for everyone.[14]

Not all companies create mission statements that reflect a marketing orientation. Steve Jobs, the legendary co-founder of Apple, believed that meeting customers' needs wasn't enough because, he contended, they often don't know what products they want or need until they are made available to them. Instead, Apple's mission statement initially was product oriented. It was based on the premise that a company's success is due to great products and that simply supplying them will lead to demand for them.

But how exactly does a company create a "great" product without thinking too much about the customer's wants and needs? Apple, and for that matter, many other companies, fell prey to thinking that they knew what a great product was without asking their customers. In fact, Apple's first attempt at a graphic user interface (GUI) was the LISA computer, a dismal failure. Today, Apple's mission statement is more customer oriented than it was in the past, "bringing the best user experience to its customers through its innovative hardware, software, and services."[15]

The Marketing Plan

The **marketing plan** is the strategy for implementing the components of marketing: creating, communicating, delivering, and exchanging value. Once a company has decided what business it is in and expressed that in a mission statement, the firm then develops a corporate strategy. Marketing strategists subsequently use the corporate strategy and mission and combine that with an understanding of the market to develop the company's marketing plan. This is the focus of Chapter 2. Figure 1.3 shows the steps involved in creating a marketing plan.

marketing plan

A document that is designed to communicate the marketing strategy for an offering. The purpose of the plan is to influence executives, suppliers, distributors, and other important stakeholders of the firm so they will invest money, time, and effort to ensure the plan is a success.

Understanding the customer's wants and needs; how the customer wants to acquire, consume, and dispose of the offering; and what makes up their personal value equation are three important goals. Marketers want to know their customers—who they are and what they like to do—so as to uncover this information. Generally, learning about customers requires marketing researchers to collect sales and other related customer data and analyze it.

FIGURE 1.3 Steps in Creating a Marketing Plan

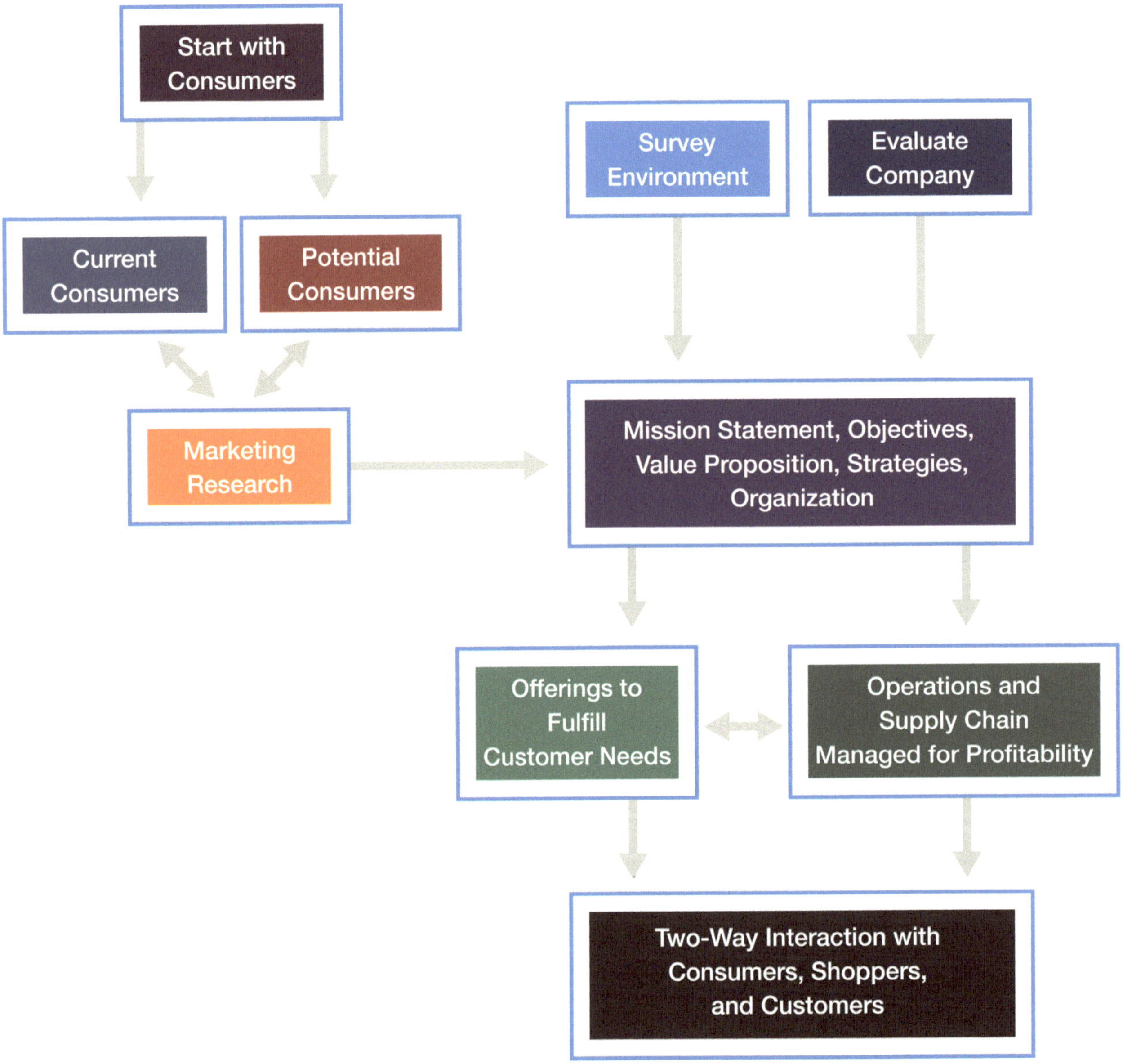

Once this information is gathered and digested, the planners can then work to create the right offering. Products and services are developed, bundled together at a price, and then tested in the market. Decisions have to be made as to when to alter the offerings, add new ones, or drop old ones. These decisions are the focus of the next set of chapters and are the second step in marketing planning.

Following the material on offerings, we explore the decisions associated with building the value chain. Once an offering is designed, the company has to be able to make it and then be able to get it to the market. This step, planning for the delivery of value, is the third step in the marketing plan.

The fourth step is creating the plan for communicating value. How does the firm make consumers aware of the value it has to offer? How can it help them recognize that value and decide that they should purchase products? These are important questions for marketing planners.

Once a customer has decided that her personal value equation is likely to be positive, then she will decide to purchase the product. That decision still has to be acted on, however, which is the exchange. The details of the exchange are the focus of the last few chapters of the book. As exchanges occur, marketing planners then refine their plans based on the feedback they receive from their customers, what their competitors are doing, and how market conditions are changing.

The Changing Marketing Environment

At the beginning of this chapter, we mentioned that the view of marketing has changed from a static set of four Ps to a dynamic set of processes that involve marketing professionals as well as many other employees in an organization. The way business is being conducted today is changing, too, and marketing is changing along with it. There are several themes, or important trends, that you will notice throughout this book.

- **Digital information and big data.** If you are like most people, many times a day you check your mobile phone or tablet to look at your email, search the internet, and scan social media. You might also play games with other people online, own a fitness tracker that automatically uploads your exercise statistics to the web, and use a GPS app to find your way around. All of these activities leave a digital trail of information. This information, along with the purchasing and other types of data companies have traditionally collected about consumers, is resulting in an information explosion that is being referred to as *big data*. Big data is allowing companies to create highly detailed profiles of customers like they never could before. That might sound scary for consumers, but it's vital for marketers. Being able to figure out who your customers are, where they congregate, what they want, and how to engage them is more important than ever. Why? Because there are so many more different types of media available to consumers today, all of which are competing for their attention. This has made the process of marketing more complex than in the past. In the past, it was much easier for companies to reach consumers through just a handful of media, such as radio, print, and TV ads.
- **Ethics and social responsibility.** Businesses exist only because customers and society allow them to. When businesses begin to fail their customers and society, they can find themselves in peril. The crackdown on companies in the subprime mortgage-lending industry is one example. These companies created and sold loans (products) that could only be paid back under ideal circumstances, and when consumers couldn't pay these loans back, the entire economy suffered greatly. Scandals such as these illustrate how society responds to unethical business practices. However, whereas ethics require that you only do no harm, the concept of **social responsibility** requires that you must actively seek to improve the lot of others, not just in terms of how you market and sell products but in all aspects of what you do as a company, including how you treat your employees and the public, and respond to crises. Today, people are demanding businesses take a proactive stance in terms of social responsibility, and businesses are being held to ever-higher standards of conduct.
- **Sustainability** is an example of social responsibility and involves engaging in practices that diminish the earth's resources to the least extent possible. Coca-Cola, for example, is working with governments in Africa to ensure clean water availability, not just for manufacturing Coke products, but for all consumers in that region. Further, the company seeks to engage American consumers in participating by offering opportunities to contribute to clean water programs. Right now, companies do not *have* to engage in these practices, but because firms really represent the people behind them (their owners and employees), forward-thinking executives are seeking ways to reduce the impact their companies are having on the planet.
- **Service-dominant logic.** You might have noticed that we use the word *offering* a lot instead of the term *product*. That's because of service-dominant logic, the approach to business that recognizes that consumers want value no matter how it is delivered—whether through a tangible product or through intangible services. That emphasis on value is what drives the functional approach to value that we've taken—that is, creating, communicating, delivering, and exchanging value.

social responsibility

The idea that companies should manage their businesses not just to earn profits but to advance the well-being of society.

sustainability

Engaging in practices that diminish the earth's resources to the least extent possible.

- **Metrics and analytics.** Technology has not only increased the amount of information available to decision makers but the number of statistical and other cutting-edge methods available to "crunch" or analyze it. The new technologies, availability of data, and improved analytical tools are allowing firms to develop new metrics, or benchmarks, they can use to fine-tune their marketing practices and ad campaigns, make better decisions, and ultimately improve how well their companies perform. For example, Amazon uses data from consumer transactions and search patterns to determine optimal order of presentation of products when you search for a product.
- **A global environment.** Every business is influenced by global issues. The price of oil, for example, is a global concern that affects everyone's prices and even the availability of some offerings. We already mentioned Coke's concern for clean water. But Coke also has to be concerned with distribution systems in areas with poor or nonexistent roads, myriad government policies and regulations, the availability of workers with the right skills, and so many different issues in trying to sell and deliver Coke around the world. Even companies with smaller markets source some or all their offerings from companies in other countries, or else face some sort of direct competition from companies based in other countries. Every business professional, whether marketing or otherwise, has to have some understanding of the global environment in which companies operate.

Key Takeaway

- A company's marketing plan flows from its strategic plan. Both begin with a focus on customers. The essential components of the plan are understanding customers, creating an offering that delivers value, communicating the value to the customer, exchanging with the customer, and evaluating the firm's performance. A marketing plan should be influenced by the recurring themes we emphasize in this text: social responsibility, sustainability, service-dominant logic, the increased availability of data and effective metrics and analytics, and the global nature of the business environment.

Review Questions

1. Why does everything start with customers? Or is it only marketing that starts with customers?
2. What are the key parts of a marketing plan?
3. What is the relationship between social responsibility, sustainability, service-dominant logic, and the global business environment? How do digital information, big data, and metrics and analytics fit into this relationship?

1.5 Discussion Questions and Activities

Discussion Questions

1. Compare and contrast a four Ps approach to marketing versus the value approach (creating, communicating, delivering, and exchanging value). What would you expect to be the same and what would you expect to be different between two companies that apply one versus the other approach?
2. During the pandemic, some companies managed to survive while their competitors did not. Apply concepts from this chapter to explain what you think the survivors did differently.
3. Assume you are about to graduate. How would you apply marketing principles to your job search? In what ways would you be able to create, communicate, deliver, and exchange value as a potential employee, and what would that value be, exactly? How would you prove that you can deliver that value?
4. When should government agencies use marketing? Why should they?
5. How do the activities of marketing for value fulfill the marketing concept for the market-oriented organization?
6. This chapter introduces the personal value equation. How would the PVE apply to someone buying components to be used in the manufacturing of cars for Tesla? How would the PVE apply to Chris Pantoya's efforts to market Fan Controlled Football?
7. This chapter addresses several reasons why marketing is an important area of study. Should marketing be required for all college students, no matter their major? Why or why not?
8. Of the four marketing functions, where does it look like most of the jobs are? What are the specific positions? How are the other marketing functions conducted through those job positions, even though in a smaller way?
9. What is the difference between a need and a want? How do marketers create wants? Provide several examples.
10. The marketing concept emphasizes satisfying customer needs and wants. How does marketing satisfy your needs as a college student? Are certain aspects of your life influenced more heavily by marketing than others? Provide examples.
11. The value of a product offering is determined by the customer and varies accordingly. How would you compare the value of a Coke to a Pepsi?

Activities

1. One of your friends is contemplating opening a vintage clothing shop near your college campus. She seeks your advice about size of the prospective customer base and how to market the business according to the concepts presented in the chapter. What strategies can you share with your friend to assist in launching the business?
2. You are considering working for the American Heart Association upon graduation, but your roommate wants to work for the Texas Rangers Major League Baseball team. Explain the marketing goals, strategies, and markets for the two organizations.
3. Compare and contrast the two personal value equations for shopping at Walmart.com (their online store) to shopping in a physical Walmart store.
4. Marketing can benefit organizations, customers, and society. Pick one of the organizations whose mission statement is described in the chapter and explain how it benefits the community in which it operates, as well as society at large. You may need to look up their website to see what they do and how they do it.

1.6 Case Study: Signet

Have you ever heard of Signet? Chances are that you haven't, but you have heard of Kay Jewelers ("Every kiss begins with Kay"), Jared, Zales, and Piercing Pagoda, all of which are jewelry stores owned and operated by Signet. In fact, walk through just about any mall and you'll find at least three of their brands represented. While the company experienced a dip in sales during 2020, sales roared back in 2021, in part due to the fact that weddings were allowed to happen again.

But the future of malls looks pretty dim. In fact, one study estimated that one out of every four malls will close completely over the next five years. In 2019 and 2020, before that five-year period, Signet actually closed 467 stores, or a little more than 1 in 8. To get ready for a decline in malls, Signet bought the company Rocksbox, an online jewelry rental company. Of course, if you like a piece that you rent, you can also buy it. In addition to Rocksbox, the company also rolled out significant marketing tools that allow customers to talk with consultants across the brands. In the first quarter alone, over 450,000 online conversations took place, though the company won't disclose how those affected sales figures. But they did say that overall online sales more than doubled during that same period.

Signet's diversified brands is also a challenge. They know that buyers who favor one brand, such as Zales, over another, such as Kay, are motivated differently. Consumers who prefer Zales tend to buy for themselves while Kay buyers are more likely to buy for someone else and to mark important life milestones. These differences don't just affect advertising for the brands, they also affect product mix. You can only find Serena Williams' line of jewelry at Zales, for example.

As malls change to meet the changing demands of consumers, so must stores. Signet's investment in online merchandising is impressive, but they haven't quite figured out how their traditional in-mall stores will change, other than perhaps changing some of the in-store advertising and decor to match changing tastes and fashions.

Case Study Questions

1. Does Signet really need four or more different store brands in the same mall? Why not put Jared, Kay, Zales, and Piercing Pagoda in one store and treat it like a department store for jewelry?
2. Is Signet late to the online market? Pick one of the brands (Jared, Kay, etc.) and describe how you would morph the brand to meet future shopping trends. What should the in-store shopping experience be and how would that interact with online shopping?
3. What Signet has done by creating separate retail store brands has been done by others in other areas. For example, Gap owns Gap stores but also Athleta, Banana Republic, and Old Navy. What is unique about the challenges facing Signet and what challenges do they share with companies like Gap? Is there a particular retailer you think is getting it right, at least in terms of combining online and physical stores?

Endnotes

1. American Marketing Association (2017), "Definition of Marketing," www.ama.org.
2. V. Kumar (2018), "Transformative Marketing: The Next 20 Years," *Journal of Marketing 82*(4), 1-12.
3. Venkat Ramaswamy and Kerimcan Ozcan (2018), "Offering as Digitalized Interactive Platforms: A Conceptual Framework and Implications," *Journal of Marketing 82*(4), 19-31.
4. Venkat Ramaswamy and Kerimcan Ozcan (2018), "Offerings as Digitalized Interactive Platforms: A Conceptual Framework and Implications," *Journal of Marketing 82*(4), 19-31.
5. Famous Quotes and Authors, "Franklin D. Roosevelt Quotes and Quotations," http://www.famousquotesandauthors.com/authors/franklin_d__roosevelt quotes.html.
6. Will Trevor (March 16, 2017), "Aiming for the C-Suite? A Recent Study Shows 25% of CEOs have a Marketing Background," http://nymarketing.org/2017/aiming-c-suite-recent-study-shows-25-ceos-marketing-background/.
7. Will Heilpern, (March 31, 2016), "18 False Advertising Scandals that Cost Some Brands Millions," www.businessinsider.com/false-advertising-scandals-2016-3.
8. Tim Nudd (November 28, 2011), "Patagonia: Ad of the Day," *Adweek*, http://www.adweek.com/news/advertising-branding/ad-day-patagonia-136745.
9. "Starbucks Outlines Vision for the Future and Reaffirms Strategy for Continued Growth at Scale," https://stories.starbucks.com/press/2020/starbucks-outlines-vision-for-the-future-and-reaffirms-strategy-for-continued-growth-at-scale/.
10. John Deere, *John Deere: A Biography*, http://www.deere.com/en_US/compinfo/history/johndeere2.html.
11. "About IBM," IBM, http://www.ibm.com/ibm/values/us/.
12. "Mission, Vision & Values," The Coca-Cola Company, https://www.coca-colacompany.com/our-company/mission-vision-values.
13. "Dow's Mission and Values | Workforce.com," https://www.workforce.com/news/dows-mission-and-values.
14. "The Human Element at Work," https://www.dow.com/en-us.
15. Apple Mission Statement 2021 | Apple Mission & Vision Analysis, https://mission-statement.com/apple.

CHAPTER 2

Strategic Planning

Have you ever wondered how an organization decides which products and services to develop, price, promote, and sell? Organizations typically develop plans and strategies that outline how they want to go about this process. Such a plan must take into account a company's current internal conditions, such as its resources, capabilities, technology, and so forth. The plan must also take into account conditions in the external environment, such as the economy, competitors, and government regulations that could affect what the firm wants to do. Organizations must also offer value to customers, and employees must provide value to their employers. As such, the value proposition becomes the basis for developing strategies. Given its importance for both organizations and students, we begin with the value proposition and then discuss the strategic planning process.

Just as your personal plans—such as what you plan to major in or where you want to find a job—are likely to change, organizations also have contingency plans. Individuals and organizations both must develop long-term (longer than a year) strategic plans, match their strengths and resources to available opportunities, and adjust their plans to changing circumstances as necessary.

2.1 The Value Proposition

Learning Objectives

1. Explain the meaning of a value proposition.
2. Understand why a company may develop different value propositions for different target markets.
3. Understand the importance of a personal value proposition.

What Is a Value Proposition?

Individual buyers and organizational buyers both evaluate products and services to see if they provide desired benefits. For example, when you're exploring your vacation options, you want to know the benefits of each destination and the value you will get by going to each place. Before you (or a firm) can develop a strategy or create a strategic plan, you (or the firm) must first develop a value proposition. A **value proposition** is a thirty-second "elevator speech" stating the specific benefits a product or service offering provides a buyer. It shows why the product or service is superior to competing offers. The value proposition answers the questions, "Why should I buy from you, do business with you, or hire you?" As such, the value proposition becomes a critical component in shaping strategy.[1]

value proposition

A statement that summarizes the key benefits or value for target customers. It explains why customers should buy a product, why stakeholders should donate, or why prospective employers may want to hire someone for their organization.

Many students have an Apple iPhone. The company knows their customers want a phone that is easy to use, yet durable with security features. They like to stream, take clear pictures, make great videos, store a lot of information, and want a long battery life. However, rather than focusing on on any feature or features that competitors may also have, Apple's value proposition states, "The Experience IS the Product," focusing on the experience of using the phone.[2]

"The Experience IS the Product"

Source: Urbanscape/ Shutterstock.com

Note that although a value proposition will hopefully lead to profits for a firm, when the firm presents its value proposition to its customers, it doesn't mention its own profits. That's because the goal is to focus on the external market or what customers want. Shopify's value proposition, "The ecommerce platform made for you. Whether you sell online, on social media, in store, or out of the trunk of your car, Shopify has you covered," encourages people to do business with them. Uber's value proposition, "The Smartest Way to Get Around," provides consumers a clear benefit. Uber's competitor Lyft states a value proposition for consumers, "Rides in Minutes," as well as a value proposition for potential drivers, "Take the Wheel." Slack, a productivity and messaging app, states their value proposition as, "Be More Productive at Work with Less Effort."[3]

Firms typically segment markets and then identify different **target markets**, or groups of customers, they want to reach when they are developing their value propositions. Target markets will be discussed in more detail in Chapter 5. For now, be aware that companies sometimes develop different value propositions for different target markets (such as Lyft does), just as individuals may develop a different value proposition for different employers. The value proposition tells each group of customers (or potential employers) why they should buy a product or service, vacation to a particular destination, donate to an organization, hire you, and so forth.

target market

The group of customers toward which an organization directs its marketing efforts.

Like many companies, Amazon has different value propositions for different target markets. For example, for Prime, the value prop is "Anything you want, quickly delivered." For business owners on Marketplace, the value proposition is "Sell more, sell better," which provides business owners an opportunity to reach more potential customers.

amazon

Source: By Amazon.com, Inc. - Amazon, Public Domain, https://commons.wikimedia.org/w/index.php?curid=50514840

Once the benefits of a product or service are clear, the firm must develop strategies that support the value proposition. The value proposition serves as a guide for this process. In the case of a sales consulting firm whose value proposition states, "Our clients grow their business, large or small, typically by a minimum of 30–50 percent over the previous year," their strategies must help clients improve their sales by 30–50 percent. Likewise, if a company is an "online, everything store," such as Amazon, they must have all types of products at competitive prices as a key part of their strategy. Looking at Amazon's logo and different value propositions, with a focus on "wide selection of products, fast delivery and low prices," or in other words "convenience" for different target markets, one can easily see how Amazon has been so successful.[4]

Individuals and students should also develop their own personal value propositions. Tell companies why they should hire you or why a graduate school should accept you. Show the value you bring to the situation. A value proposition will help you in different situations. Think about how your internship experience and/or study abroad experience may help a future employer. For example, you should explain to the employer the benefits and value of going abroad. Perhaps your study abroad experience helped you understand customers that buy from Company X, and your customer service experience during your internship increased your ability to generate sales, which improved your employer's profit margin. Thus, you may be able to quickly contribute to Company X, something that they might very much value.

Bruce Platzman, Co-Founder and CEO of AIS

Source: Bruce Platzman, photo used with permission

Bruce Platzman, co-founder and CEO of AIS, has over thirty years experience in the furniture industry, beginning as a salesperson and later, as a general manager for a dealership. Bruce spearheaded the growth of AIS from a small re-manufacturer of office furniture to a leading manufacturer of full line workplace solutions with sales over $200M, serving customers across North America. Bruce's engagement and hands-on management style has been apparent since day one, exemplifying the company's collaborative approach to leadership and ensuring that its growth outpaced the industry every single year. While Bruce has led all aspects of the business—from customer service to marketing, cost controls to production, product development to sales—he's never forgotten it's all about the people and the communities AIS serves, making him stand out. Making business easy for customers is crucial, and fearlessly embracing accountability set Bruce and AIS apart. His leadership and the diverse + talented teams he's led over the years ensured success for AIS. Bruce graduated from Babson College and is passionate about giving back to the community on a local and national stage—as well as on a personal and professional level. He gives his time and energy freely, striving to make positive impacts through his leadership. Philanthropy is a key ingredient in the corporate social responsibilities of Bruce and the people of AIS.

Learn more about AIS at https://spaces.hightail.com/receive/AOlncZ4v1b.

Key Takeaway

- A value proposition is a thirty-second "elevator speech" stating the specific value a product or service provides to a target market. Firms may develop different value propositions for different groups of customers. The value proposition shows why the product or service is superior to competing offers and why the customer should buy it or why a firm should hire you.

Review Questions

1. What is a value proposition?
2. You are interviewing for an internship. Create a value proposition for yourself that you may use as your thirty-second "elevator speech" to get the company interested in hiring you or talking to you more.

2.2 Components of the Strategic Planning Process

Learning Objectives

1. Explain how a mission statement helps a company with its strategic planning.
2. Describe how a firm analyzes its internal environment.
3. Describe the external environment a firm may face and how it is analyzed.

strategic planning process

A process that helps an organization allocate its resources under different conditions to accomplish its objectives, deliver value, and be competitive in a market-driven economy.

Strategic planning is a process that helps an organization allocate its resources to capitalize on opportunities in the marketplace. Typically, it is a long-term process. The **strategic planning process** includes conducting a situation analysis and developing the organization's mission statement, objectives, value proposition, and strategies. Figure 2.1 shows the components of the strategic planning process. Let's now look at each of these components.

FIGURE 2.1 The Strategic Planning Process

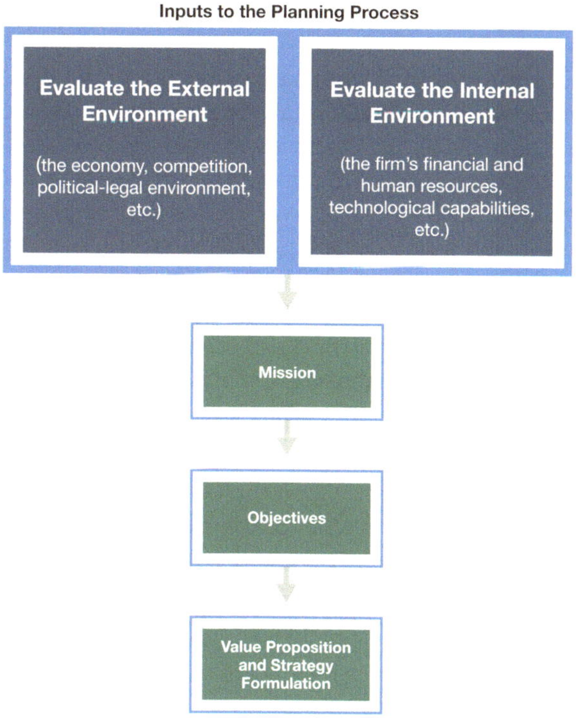

Conducting a Situation Analysis

As part of the strategic planning process, a **situation analysis** must be conducted before a company can decide on specific actions. A situation analysis involves analyzing both the external (macro and micro factors outside the organization) and the internal (company) environments. Figure 2.1 and Figure 2.2 show examples of internal and external factors and a SWOT analysis. The firm's internal environment—such as its financial resources, technological resources, and the capabilities of its personnel and their performance—has to be examined. It is also critical to examine the external macro and micro environments the firm faces, such as the economy, its competitors, and other uncontrollable factors. The external environment significantly affects the decisions a firm makes, and thus must be continuously evaluated. For example, during the COVID-19 pandemic, supply chain problems caused many product shortages and increased costs. Demand for many services and products decreased drastically, which caused some businesses to close and others to pivot in order to remain profitable. Restaurants began offering curbside pickup and delivery, prices of paper products and sanitizers increased, shipping costs increased, and the sale of fitness and office products for remote and isolated people increased. While a business cannot control factors such as the pandemic, the economy, changes in demographic trends, or what competitors do, it must decide what actions to take to remain competitive—actions that depend in part on their internal environment.

situation analysis

An assessment of an organization's internal and external environments.

Conducting a SWOT Analysis

SWOT analysis

An acronym for strengths, weaknesses, opportunities, and threats, the SWOT analysis is a tool that frames the situational analysis.

Based on the situation analysis, organizations analyze their **S**trengths, **W**eaknesses, **O**pportunities, and **T**hreats, or conduct what's called a **SWOT analysis**. Strengths and weaknesses are internal factors and are somewhat controllable. For example, an organization's strengths might include its brand name, efficient distribution network, reputation for great service, and strong financial position. A firm's weaknesses might include lack of awareness of its products in the marketplace, a lack of human resources talent, and a poor location. Opportunities and threats are factors that are external to the firm and largely uncontrollable. Opportunities might entail the international demand for the type of products the firm makes, few competitors, and favorable social trends, such as people living longer. Threats might include a bad economy, high interest rates that increase a firm's borrowing costs, and strong competitors take control of the market share.

You can conduct a SWOT analysis of yourself to help determine your competitive advantage. Perhaps your strengths include strong leadership abilities and communication skills, whereas your weaknesses include a lack of organization. Opportunities for you might exist in specific careers and industries; however, the economy and other people competing for the same position might be threats. Moreover, a factor that is a strength for one person (say, strong accounting skills) might be a weakness for another person (poor accounting skills). The same is true for businesses. See Figure 2.2 for an illustration of some of the factors examined in a SWOT analysis.

FIGURE 2.2 Elements of a SWOT Analysis

The easiest way to determine if a factor is external or internal is to take away the company, organization, or individual and see if the factor still exists. Internal factors such as strengths and weaknesses are specific to a company or individual, whereas external factors such as opportunities and threats affect multiple individuals and organizations in the marketplace. For example, if you are doing a situation analysis on PepsiCo (or any company) and are looking at the weak economy, take PepsiCo (company) out of the picture and see what factors remain. If the factor—the weak economy—is still there, it is an external factor and affects many companies.

Assessing the Internal Environment

As we have indicated, when an organization evaluates which factors are its strengths and weaknesses, it is assessing its internal environment. Once companies determine their strengths, they can use those strengths to capitalize on opportunities and develop their competitive advantage. For example, strengths for PepsiCo are its "flagship, iconic" brands, the twenty-three brands that individually generate over $1 billion in sales. These global brands are also designed to contribute to PepsiCo's environmental and social responsibilities.[5]

PepsiCo's brand awareness, profitability, and strong presence in global markets are also strengths. Especially in foreign markets, the loyalty of a firm's employees can be a major strength, which can provide it with a competitive advantage. Loyal and knowledgeable employees are easier to train and tend to develop better relationships with customers. This helps organizations pursue more opportunities.

Although the brand awareness for PepsiCo's products is strong, smaller companies often struggle with weaknesses such as low brand awareness, low financial reserves, and poor locations. When organizations assess their internal environments, they must look at factors such as performance and costs as well as brand awareness and location. Managers need to examine both the past and current strategies of their firms and determine what strategies succeeded and which ones failed. At the same time, companies must refer to their mission statement and objectives (see Section 3) as well as external factors such as social trends and competitors to better understand consumers, develop their future actions, and improve the odds they will be successful. For example, despite increased sales of orange juice during the pandemic, profitability was not as strong as other products for companies such as PepsiCo and did not fit current strategies due to the high sugar content. PepsiCo is selling their juice brands in North America and Europe to concentrate on healthier products such as plant-based snacks, sparkling and hydrating water (Frutly, which ironically contains fruit juice), Zero Sugar products, and products better for the planet. Before and during the pandemic, many companies focused on their most profitable products and sold, discontinued, or cut production of products not doing as well. Planter's was sold to Hormel, the Nestlé candy business was sold, and Coca-Cola discontinued its Odwalla brand.[6]

PepsiCo Introduces Frutly

Pepsi's release of Frutly was aimed at teenagers.

View in the online reader

Nestlé candy bars including Baby Ruth, Butterfinger, and Nestlé Crunch are now owned by Ferrero.

Source: © Shutterstock, Inc.

Individuals are also wise to look at the strategies they have tried in the past to see which ones failed and which ones succeeded. Have you ever done poorly on an exam? Was it the instructor's fault, the strategy you used to study, or did you decide not to study? See which strategies work best for you and perhaps try the same type of strategies for future exams. If a strategy did not work, see what went wrong and change it. Doing so is similar to what organizations do when they analyze their internal environments.

Assessing the External Environment

Analyzing the external environment involves tracking conditions in the macro and micro marketplace that, although largely uncontrollable, affect the way an organization does business. The macro environment includes economic factors, demographic trends, cultural and social trends, political and legal regulations, technological changes, and the price and availability of natural resources. The micro environment includes competition, suppliers, marketing intermediaries (retailers, wholesalers), the public, the company, and customers. Competition as well as each factor in the macro environment is discussed in the next section. Customers, including the public, will be the focus of Chapter 3, and marketing intermediaries and suppliers will be discussed in Chapter 8 and Chapter 9.

When firms globalize, analyzing the environment becomes more complex because they must examine the external environment in each country in which they do business. Regulations, competitors, technological development, and the economy may be different in each country and will affect how firms do business. To see how factors in the external environment such as technology may change education and lives of people around the world, watch the video "Did You Know," which provides information on social media sites compared to populations in the world. Originally created in 2006, the video has been updated multiple times and translated into other languages. With technology advancing rapidly, digital transformation is critical for businesses and organizations. A look at two additional videos shows not only how digital transformation is changing the world and the way people communicate and conduct business, but also emphasizes the importance of analytics and metrics.

Did You Know?

Information affects strategies.

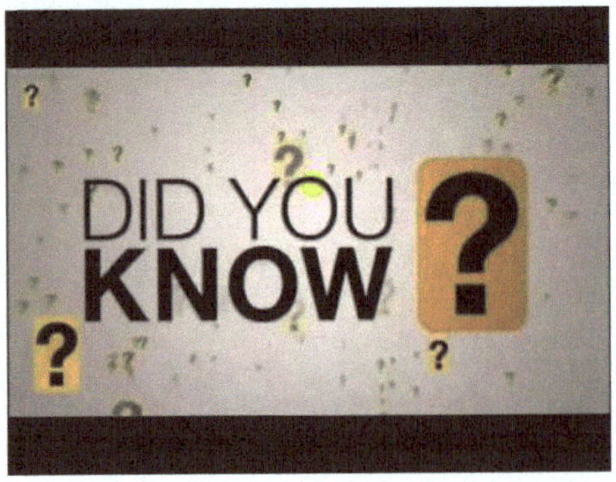

View in the online reader

Digital Transformation in the Intelligent World

New connectivity, new computing, new platform, new ecosystem: this is the foundation of the intelligent world 2030.

View in the online reader

Digital Transformation and Technological Changes

Many technologies will change. Cyber security, the Cloud, data analytics, and AI are critical.

View in the online reader

Although the external environment affects all organizations, companies must focus on factors that are relevant for their operations. For example, government regulations on food packaging will affect PepsiCo but not Goodyear. Similarly, students currently getting a business degree don't need to focus on job opportunities for registered nurses.

The Competitive Environment

All organizations must consider their competition, whether it is direct or indirect competition vying for the consumer's dollar. Both nonprofit and for-profit organizations compete for customers' resources. Coke and Pepsi are direct competitors in the soft drink industry, Hilton and Marriott are competitors in the hospitality industry, and organizations such as United Way and the American Cancer Society compete for resources in the nonprofit sector. However, hotels must also consider other options (substitutes) that people have when selecting a place to stay, such as hostels, dorms, bed and breakfasts, or rental homes.

A group of competitors that provide similar products or services form an industry and compete for market share. Michael Porter, a professor at Harvard University and a leading authority on competitive strategy, developed an approach for analyzing industries. Called the five forces model and shown in Figure 2.3,[7] the framework helps organizations understand their current competitors and substitutes as well as organizations that could become competitors (potential entrants) in the future. The perceptions of customers also represent a critical force as well as suppliers who are struggling to meet demand with COVID-19 and its variants. As such, firms must examine all factors to find the best way to defend their position in the industry.

FIGURE 2.3 Five Forces Model[8]

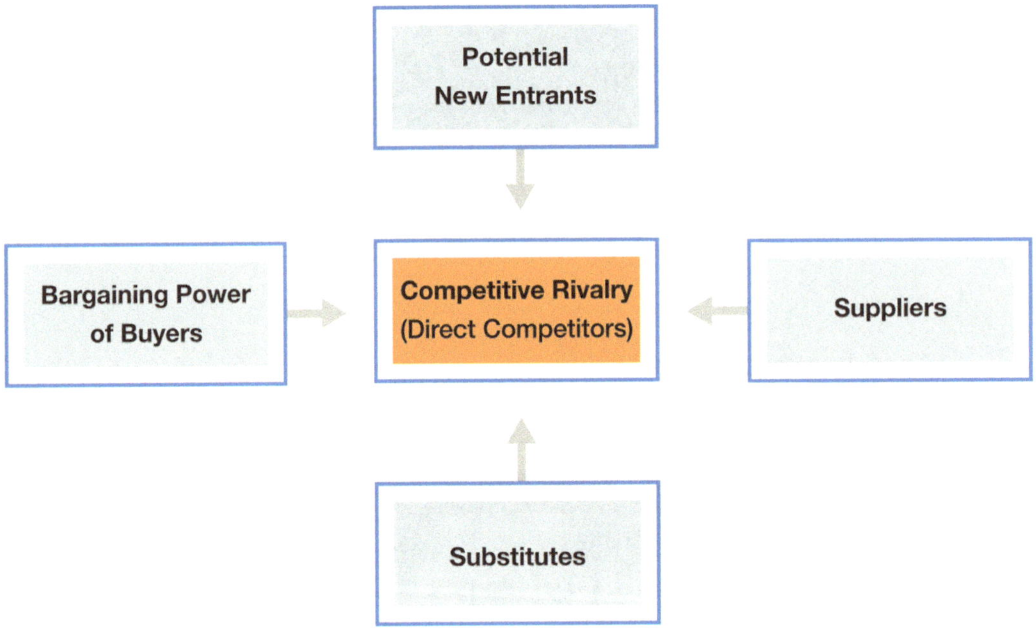

Competitive Analysis

mystery shopper

A person who is paid to shop at a firm's establishment or one of its competitors' to observe the level of service, cleanliness of the facility, and so forth, and report his or her findings to the firm.

When a firm conducts a competitive analysis, it tends to focus on direct competitors and tries to determine a firm's strengths and weaknesses, its image, and its resources. Doing so helps the firm figure out how much money a competitor may be able to spend on things such as research, new product development, promotion, and new locations. Competitive analysis involves looking at any information (annual reports, financial statements, news stories, observation details obtained on visits, etc.) available on competitors. Another means of collecting competitive information utilizes **mystery shoppers**, or people who act like customers. Mystery shoppers might visit competitors to learn about their customer service and their products. Imagine going to a competitor's restaurant and studying the menu and the prices and watching customers to see what items are popular and then changing your menu to better compete, or walking through a competitor's grocery store to examine prices, displays, and in-store specials. Competitors battle for the customer's dollar, and they must know what other firms are doing. Individuals and teams also compete for jobs, titles, and prizes and must figure out the competitors' weaknesses and plans in order to take advantage of their strengths and have a better chance of winning.

According to Porter, in addition to their direct competitors (competitive rivals), organizations must consider the strength and impact the following could have:[9]

- substitute products
- potential entrants (new competitors) in the marketplace

- the bargaining power of suppliers
- the bargaining power of buyers

When any of these factors change, companies may have to respond by changing their strategies. For example, because buyers are consuming fewer soft drinks these days, companies such as Coke and Pepsi developed new, substitute offerings such as vitamin water, sparkling water, hydrating drinks, and sports drinks. Coke and Pepsi both focused on zero sugar drinks in hopes of increasing sales. However, other bottled water companies may be potential entrants in the flavored water market. When you select a hamburger fast food chain, you also have the option of substitutes, such as getting food at the grocery or going to a pizza place. When computers entered the market, they were a substitute for typewriters. Most students may not have ever used or even seen a typewriter.

Suppliers, the companies that supply ingredients as well as packaging materials to other companies, must also be considered. If a company cannot get the supplies it needs, it's in trouble. Also, sometimes suppliers see how lucrative their customers' markets are and decide to enter them. During the pandemic, many suppliers suffered due to material shortages, price increases, and logistic challenges shipping supplies. Companies who stockpiled supplies may have created a competitive advantage, at least in the short term.

Remote learning during the pandemic became common with students seeing their instructor on their computer.

Source: © Shutterstock, Inc.

Buyers, who are the focus of marketing and strategic plans, must also be considered because they have bargaining power and must be satisfied. If a buyer is large enough, and doesn't purchase a product or service, it can affect a selling company's performance. Walmart, for instance, is a buyer with a great deal of bargaining power. Firms that do business with Walmart must be prepared to make concessions to them if they want their products on the company's store shelves.

Lastly, the world is becoming "smaller" and more of a global marketplace. Companies everywhere are finding that no matter what they make, numerous firms around the world are producing the same "widget" or a similar offering (substitute) and are eager to compete with them. Employees are in the same position. The internet has made it easier than ever for customers to find products and services and for workers to find the best jobs available, even if they are abroad. Companies are also acquiring foreign firms. Working remotely during the pandemic changed the way many companies do business and the requirement for face-to-face interactions. These factors all have an effect on the strategic decisions companies make.

The Political and Legal Environment

All organizations must comply with government regulations and understand the political and legal environments in which they do business. Different government agencies enforce the numerous regulations that have been established to protect both consumers and businesses. For example, the Sherman Act (1890) prohibits U.S. firms from restraining trade by creating monopolies and cartels. The regulations related to the act are enforced by the Federal Trade Commission (FTC), which also regulates deceptive advertising. The U.S. Food and Drug Administration (FDA) regulates the labeling of consumable products, such as food and medicine. One organization that has been extremely busy is the Consumer Product Safety Commission, the group that sets safety standards for consumer products. Unsafe sleep products for infants have concerned parents for years. Beginning in mid-2022, enforcement of a federal safety standard for "infant sleepers" will ensure the safety of the products. Choking hazards for infants and small children have presented problems for years. Children's products with small parts must include warning about choking hazard. Use of personal data remains a sensitive issue. While General Data Protection Regulation (GDPR) is not a law in the United States, companies with websites visited by people in the European Union (EU) must comply. Enactment of GDPR in 2018 protects both the processing and movement of personal data for all individuals in the European Union.[10]

The infant pulled the eye off the bear creating a choking hazard.

Source: © Shutterstock, Inc.

Boppy Infant Pillows Recalled

Millions of Boppy pillows were recalled following infant deaths.

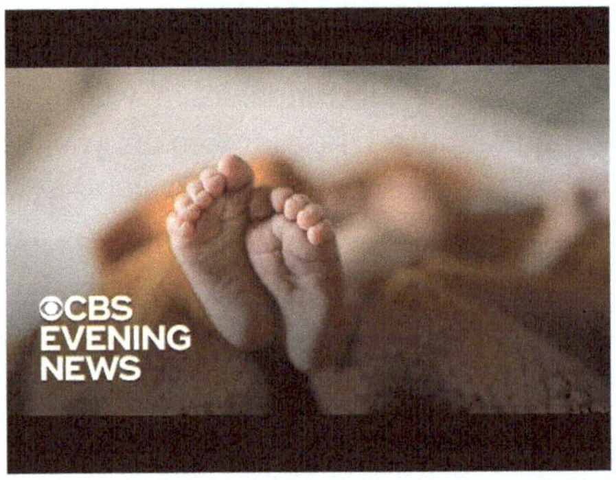

View in the online reader

When organizations conduct business in multiple markets, they must understand that regulations vary across countries and across states. Many states and countries have different laws that affect strategy. For example, suppose you are opening up a new factory because you cannot keep up with the demand for your products. If you are considering opening the factory in France (perhaps because the demand in Europe for your product is strong), you need to know that it is illegal for employees in that country to work more than thirty-five hours per week.

The Economic Environment

The economy has a major impact on spending by both consumers and businesses, which, in turn, affects the goals and strategies of organizations. Economic factors include variables such as inflation, unemployment, interest rates, and whether the economy is in a growth period or a recession. Inflation occurs when the cost of living continues to rise, eroding the purchasing power of money. When this happens, you and other consumers and businesses need more money to purchase goods and services. Interest rates often rise when inflation rises. Recessions can also occur when inflation rises, because higher prices sometimes cause low or negative growth in the economy.

During a recessionary period, it is possible for both high-end and low-end products to sell well. Consumers who can afford luxury goods may continue to buy them, while consumers with lower incomes tend to become more value conscious. Other goods and services, such as products sold in traditional department stores, may suffer as well as the stores themselves. In the face of a severe economic downturn, even the sales of luxury goods can suffer. Economic downturns affect consumers and businesses at all levels worldwide. Consumers reduce their spending, holiday sales drop, financial institutions may go bankrupt, the mortgage industry suffers, and automobile manufacturers often increase purchase incentives.

The Demographic and Social and Cultural Environments

The demographic and social and cultural environments—including social trends, such as people's attitudes toward fitness and nutrition; demographic characteristics, such as people's age, income, marital status, education, and occupation; and culture, which relates to people's beliefs and values—are constantly changing in the global marketplace. Fitness, nutrition, and health trends affect the product offerings of many firms. For example, PepsiCo produces vitamin water, sports drinks, and offers "hydrating drinks" products such as Frutly waters targeted to teens. More women are working, which has led to a rise in the demand for services such as house cleaning and daycare. U.S. baby boomers are reaching retirement age, sending their children to college, and trying to care for their aging parents, all at the same time. Firms are responding to the time constraints their buyers face by creating products that are more convenient, such as frozen meals and nutritious snacks.

Many food products appeal to the rapidly growing Latinx market.

Source: © Shutterstock, Inc.

The composition of the population is also constantly changing. Hispanics are the fastest-growing minority in the United States. Consumers in this group and other diverse groups prefer different types of products and brands. In many cities, stores and media cater specifically to Hispanic customers.

Technology

The technology available in the world is changing the way people communicate and the way firms do business. Everyone is affected by technological changes. Artificial intelligence (AI), digital technology, more self-scanners in stores, and mobile phones are a few examples of how technology continues to affect businesses and consumers. Many consumers get information, read the news, use text messaging, and shop online frequently using mobile devices. As a result, marketers have begun allocating more of their promotion budgets to digital technologies including social media platforms, online ads, and mobile marketing rather than focusing on traditional print media such as newspapers and magazines. Apps for telephones and electronic devices are changing the way people obtain information and shop, allowing customers to comparison shop without having to visit multiple stores. As you saw in "Did You Know?" videos, technology and social media are changing people's lives. Many young people may rely more on electronic books, streaming services, and news and depend on mobile devices for most of their information needs. Organizations must adapt to new technologies in order to succeed.

Natural Resources

Natural resources are scarce commodities, and consumers are becoming increasingly aware of this fact. Today, many firms are doing more to engage in "sustainable" practices that help protect the environment and conserve natural resources. **Green marketing** involves marketing environmentally safe products and services in a way that is good for the environment. Water shortages often occur in the summer months, so many restaurants now only serve patrons water upon request. Hotels voluntarily conserve water by not washing guests' sheets and towels every day unless they request it. Reusing packages (refillable containers); developing sustainable packaging as well as products; and reducing the amount of packaging, paper, energy, and water in the production of goods and services are becoming key considerations for many organizations, whether they sell their products to other businesses or to final users (consumers). Construction companies are using more energy-efficient materials and often have to comply with green building regulations. Green marketing not only helps the environment but also saves the company, and ultimately the consumer, money. Sustainability, ethics (doing the right things), and social responsibility (helping society, communities, and other people) influence an organization's planning process and the strategies they implement.

green marketing

Marketing environmentally safe products and services in a way that is good for the environment.

Although environmental conditions change and must be monitored continuously, the situation analysis is a critical input to an organization's or an individual's strategic plan. Let's look at the other components of the strategic planning process.

The Mission Statement

mission statement

Defines the purpose of the organization and answers the question of how a company defines its business.

The firm's **mission statement** states the purpose of the organization and why it exists. Both profit and nonprofit organizations have mission statements, which they often publicize. The following are examples of mission statements:

PepsiCo's Mission Statement

"Our mission is to provide consumers around the world with delicious, affordable, convenient, and complementary foods and beverages from wholesome breakfasts to healthy and fun daytime snacks and beverages to evening treats. We are committed to investing in our people, our company, and the communities where we operate to help position the company for long-term, sustainable growth."[11]

LinkedIn's Mission Statement

"Connect the world's professionals to make them more productive and successful."[12]

The United Way's Mission Statement

"United Way improves lives by mobilizing the caring power of communities around the world to advance the common good."[13]

strategic business units (SBUs)

Businesses or product lines within an organization that have their own competitors, customers, and profit centers.

Sometimes companies have multiple **strategic business units (SBUs)**, which have their own mission statement, competitors, objectives, and strategies. For example, at PepsiCo different global divisions (e.g., North America Beverages, Latin America, and Asia, Middle East, and North Africa) might each develop a different mission statement.

Key Takeaway

- A firm must analyze factors in the external and internal environments it faces throughout the strategic planning process. These factors are inputs to the planning process. As they change, the company must be prepared to adjust its plans. Different factors are relevant for different companies. Once a company has analyzed its internal and external environments, managers can begin to set objectives given the firm's mission statement. The mission is the organization's purpose and helps guide development of objectives.

Review Questions

1. What factors in the external environment affect automobile manufacturers in the United States and how did the pandemic affect them?
2. What are some examples of Walmart's strengths?
3. Suppose you work for a major hotel chain. Using Porter's Five Forces model, explain what you need to consider with regard to each force.

2.3 Developing Organizational Objectives and Formulating Strategies

Learning Objectives

1. Explain how companies develop the objectives driving their strategies.
2. Describe the different types of product strategies and market entry strategies that companies pursue.

Developing Objectives

Objectives are what organizations want to accomplish—the end results they want to achieve in a given time frame. In addition to being accomplished within a certain time frame, objectives should be realistic (achievable) and measurable, if possible. "To increase return on investment by 10 percent by the end of the year" is an example of an objective an organization might develop. You have probably set objectives for yourself that you want to achieve in a given time frame. For example, your objectives might be to maintain a certain grade point average and get work experience or an internship before you graduate.

objectives
What organizations want to accomplish (the end results) in a given time frame.

Objectives help guide and motivate a company's employees and give its managers reference points for evaluating the firm's marketing actions. Although many organizations publish their mission statements, most for-profit companies typically do not publish their objectives. Accomplishments at each level of the organization have helped PepsiCo meet its corporate objectives over the course of the past few years. PepsiCo's business units (divisions) have increased the number of their facilities to grow their brands and enter new markets. PepsiCo's beverage and snack units have gained market share by developing healthier products and products that are more convenient to use.

A firm's marketing objectives should be consistent with the company's objectives at other levels, such as the corporate level and business level. An example of a marketing objective for PepsiCo might be "to increase by 4 percent the market share of Gatorade by the end of the year." The way firms analyze their different divisions or businesses will be discussed later in the chapter.

Formulating Strategies

strategies

The means to an end, or what the firm will do to achieve its objectives.

tactics

Actions taken to execute strategies.

As discussed at the beginning of the chapter, firms and individuals must determine their value propositions before developing strategies or completing a strategic plan. **Strategies** are the means to the ends, the game plan, or what a firm is going to do to achieve its objectives. Successful strategies help organizations establish and maintain a competitive advantage that competitors cannot imitate easily. **Tactics** include specific actions, such as coupons, television commercials, banner ads, buy one–get one free, and so on, taken to execute the strategy. PepsiCo attempts to sustain its competitive advantage by constantly developing new products and innovations, including "mega brands," which include twenty-three individual brands that generate over $1 billion in sales each.[14]

"Great plan. Could we get some more details?"

Source: © Shutterstock, Inc.

Firms often use multiple strategies to accomplish their objectives and capitalize on marketing opportunities. For example, in addition to pursuing a low cost strategy (selling products inexpensively), Walmart has simultaneously pursued a strategy of opening new stores around the world as well as smaller "neighborhood markets." Many companies develop marketing strategies as part of their general, overall business plans. Other companies prepare separate marketing plans. We'll look at marketing plans here and discuss them more completely in Chapter 16.

marketing plan

A document that is designed to communicate the marketing strategy for an offering. The purpose of the plan is to influence executives, suppliers, distributors, and other important stakeholders of the firm so they will invest money, time, and effort to ensure the plan is a success.

A **marketing plan** is a strategic plan at the functional level that provides a firm's marketing group with direction. It is a road map that improves the firm's understanding of its competitive situation. The marketing plan also helps the firm allocate resources and divvy up the tasks that employees need to do for the company to meet its objectives. The different components of marketing plans will be discussed throughout the book and then put together at the end of the book. Next, let's take a look at the different types of basic market strategies firms pursue before they develop their marketing plans.

FIGURE 2.4 Product and Market Entry Strategies

The different types of product and market entry strategies a firm can pursue in order to meet their objectives.

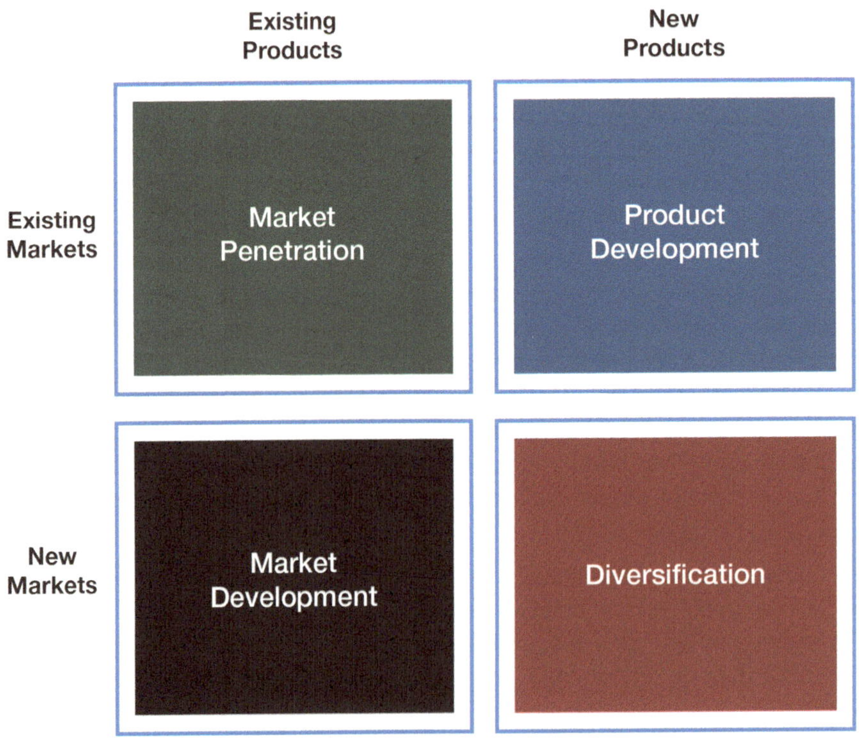

Market penetration strategies focus on increasing a firm's sales of its existing products to its existing customers. Companies often offer consumers special promotions or low prices to increase their usage and encourage them to buy products. When manufacturers such as Procter & Gamble distribute money-saving coupons to customers or offer them discounts to buy multiple packages of products, the company is utilizing a penetration strategy. The Campbell Soup Company gets consumers to buy more soup by providing easy recipes using their soup as an ingredient for cooking quick meals.

market penetration strategies

Selling more of existing products and services to existing customers.

Product development strategies involve creating new products for existing customers. A new product can be a totally new innovation, a product line extension, or a product with enhanced value, such as one with an improved feature. The iPhone 13 and other new cell phones with features such as better cameras and longer-lasting batteries are examples of products with enhanced value. A new product can also be one that comes in different variations, such as new flavors, colors, different packaging, and/or a changed ingredient. In August 2021, Coca-Cola rolled out a new package and taste for Coke Zero.[15]

Coca-Cola Zero Sugar is now in a classic red can.

Source: © Shutterstock, Inc.

Market development strategies focus on entering new markets with existing products. For example, when most business travel was halted, hotel occupancy was extremely low, and people worked remotely during the COVID-19 pandemic, some hotels around the world including Marriott, Hilton, and Hyatt, decided to go after a different market. Hotel rooms and public spaces provided workspace for remote workers as a way to generate revenue. People could purchase day passes as an option to working from home. Hotels also offered deals for longer stays where families could be in a separate room.[16]

product development strategies

Creating new products or services for existing markets.

New markets can include any new groups of customers, such as different age groups, new geographic areas, or international markets. Many companies, including PepsiCo and Hyundai, have entered—and been successful in—rapidly emerging markets such as Russia, China, and India. Decisions to enter foreign markets are based on a company's resources as well as the complexity of factors such as the political environment, economic conditions, competition, customer knowledge, and probability of success in the desired market. As Figure 2.4 shows, there are different ways, or strategies, by which firms can enter international markets. The strategies vary in the amount of risk, control, and investment that firms face. Firms can simply **export**, or sell their products to buyers abroad, which is the least risky and least expensive method but also offers the least amount of control. Many small firms export their products to foreign markets.

market development strategies

Selling existing products or services to new customers. Foreign markets often present opportunities for organizations to expand. Exporting, licensing, franchising, joint ventures, and direct investment are methods that companies use to enter international markets.

Firms can also **license**, or sell the right to use some aspect of their production processes, trademarks, or patents to individuals or firms in foreign markets. Licensing is a popular strategy, but firms must figure out how to protect their interests if the licensee decides to open its own business and void the license agreement. The French luggage and handbag maker Louis Vuitton faced this problem when it entered China. Competitors started illegally putting the Louis Vuitton logo on different products, which cut into Louis Vuitton's profits. Note that licensing is also used when companies may want to use a brand name or apparel or branded good, such as a Spiderman lunchbox or a Barbie backpack.

export

Sell products to buyers in foreign markets.

license

Sell the right to use some aspect of the production process, trademark, or patent to individuals in foreign markets.

The front of a KFC franchise in Asia may be much larger than KFC stores in the United States. Selling franchises is a popular way for firms to enter foreign markets.

Source: © Shutterstock, Inc.

franchising

Granting an independent operator the right to use your company's business model, techniques, and trademarks for a fee.

contract manufacturing

When companies hire manufacturers to produce their products in another country.

joint venture

An entity that is created when two parties agree to share their profits, losses, and control with one another in an economic activity they jointly undertake.

direct investment

Owning a company or facility overseas.

Franchising is a longer-term (and thus riskier) form of licensing that is extremely popular with service firms, such as restaurants like McDonald's and Subway, hotels like Holiday Inn Express, and cleaning companies like Stanley Steemer. Franchisees pay a fee for the franchise and must adhere to certain standards; however, they benefit from the advertising and brand recognition the franchising company provides.

Contract manufacturing allows companies to hire manufacturers to produce their products in another country. The manufacturers are provided specifications for the products, which are then manufactured and sold on behalf of the company that contracted the manufacturing. Contract manufacturing may provide tax incentives and may be more profitable than manufacturing the products in the home country. Examples of products in which contract manufacturing is often used include cell phones, computers, and printers.

Joint ventures combine the expertise and investments of two companies and help companies enter foreign markets. The firms in each country share the risks as well as the investments. Some countries such as China often require companies to form a joint venture with a domestic firm in order to enter the market. After entering the market in a partnership with a domestic firm and becoming established in the market, some firms may decide to separate from their partner and become their own business. Fuji Xerox Co., Ltd. is an example of a joint venture between the Japanese Fuji Photo Film Co. and the American document management company Xerox. Another example of a joint venture is Sony Ericsson. The venture combined the Japanese company Sony's electronic expertise with the Swedish company Ericsson's telecommunication expertise. With investment by both companies, joint ventures are riskier than exporting, licensing, franchising, and contract manufacturing but also provide more control to each partner.

Direct investment (owning a company or facility overseas) is another way to enter a foreign market, providing the most control but also having the most risk. For example, InBev, the Dutch maker of Beck's beer, was able to capture market share in the United States by purchasing St. Louis-based Anheuser-Busch. A direct investment strategy involves the most risk and investment but offers the most control. Other companies such as advertising agencies may want to invest and develop their own businesses directly in international markets rather than trying to do so via other companies.

FIGURE 2.5 Market Entry Methods

Diversification strategies involve entering new markets with new products or doing something outside a firm's current businesses. Firms that have little experience with different markets or different products often diversify their product lines by acquiring other companies. Diversification can be profitable, but it can also be risky if a company does not have the expertise or resources it needs to successfully implement the strategy. Google's acquisition of Motorola as an attempt to develop high quality mobile phones failed due to poor quality and low profitability.[17]

diversification strategy

Offering products that are unrelated to other existing products produced by the organization.

Key Takeaway

- The strategic planning process includes a a situation analysis, company's mission (purpose), objectives (end results desired), value proposition, and strategies (means). Sometimes the different SBUs of a firm have different mission statements. A firm's objectives should be realistic (achievable) and measurable. The different product market strategies firms pursue include market penetration, product development, market development, and diversification.

Review Questions

1. How do product development strategies differ from market development strategies?
2. Explain why some strategies work for some companies but not others.
3. What factors do firms entering foreign markets need to consider?
4. How do franchising and licensing strategies differ?

2.4 Where Strategic Planning Occurs within Firms

Learning Objectives

1. Identify the different levels at which strategic planning may occur within firms.
2. Understand how strategic planning that occurs at multiple levels in an organization helps a company achieve its overall corporate objectives.

corporate-level plans

Plans developed for the corporation as a whole take place at the corporate level.

business-level plans

Plans developed for each strategic business unit typically have their own mission statement.

As previously mentioned, strategic planning is a long-term process that helps an organization allocate its resources to take advantage of different opportunities. In addition to marketing plans, strategic planning may occur at different levels within an organization. For example, in large organizations top executives will develop strategic plans for the corporation as a whole. These are **corporate-level plans**. In addition, many large firms have different divisions, or businesses, called strategic business units. A strategic business unit (SBU) is a business or product line within an organization that has its own competitors, customers, and profit center for accounting purposes. A firm's SBUs may also have their own mission statement (purpose) and will generally develop strategic plans for themselves. These are called **business-level plans**. The different departments, or functions (accounting, finance, marketing, and so forth) within a company or SBU, might also develop strategic plans. For example, a company may develop a marketing plan or a financial plan, which are functional-level plans.

Figure 2.6 shows an example of different strategic planning levels that can exist within an organization's structure. The number of levels can vary, depending on the size and structure of an organization. Not every organization will have every level or have every type of plan. An overview of the marketing (or functional) plan will be discussed in detail in Chapter 16, so you can see how the information discussed throughout the text may be used in developing a marketing plan.

FIGURE 2.6 Strategic Planning Levels in an Organization

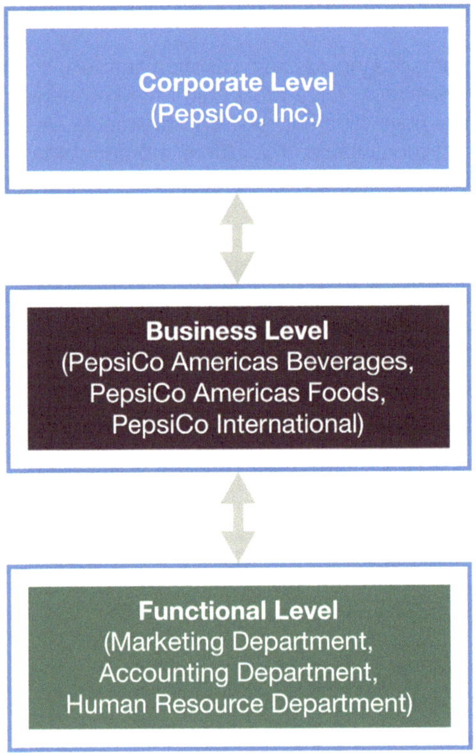

The strategies and actions implemented at the functional (department) level must be consistent with and help an organization achieve its objectives at both the business and corporate levels and vice versa. The SBUs at the business level must also be consistent with and help an organization achieve its corporate-level objectives. For example, if a company wants to increase its profits or return on investment (ROI) at the corporate level and owns multiple business units, each unit might develop strategic plans to increase its own profits and thereby the firm's profits as a whole. At the functional level, a firm's marketing department might develop strategic plans to increase sales and market share of the firm's most profitable products, which will increase profits at the business level and help the corporation's profitability and ROI. Both business-level and functional plans should help the firm increase its profits, so the company's corporate-level strategic objectives can be met.

Many consumers recognize the Goodyear blimp. Goodyear's strategic business units are North American Tire; Latin American Tire; Asia Pacific Tire; and Europe, Middle East, and Africa Tire. Goodyear's SBUs are set up to satisfy customers' needs in different worldwide markets.[18]

Source: Karl R. Martin/Shutterstock.com

For example, take PepsiCo, which has committed itself to achieving business and financial success while leaving a positive imprint on society. PepsiCo identifies its seven global divisions (business units) as (1) North America Beverages, which is responsible for products such as Pepsi soft drinks, Aquafina waters, and Gatorade products; (2) Frito Lay North Americas Food; (3) Quaker Foods North America; (4) Latin America, which includes beverage, food, and snacks; (5) Europe; (6) Africa, Middle East, and Asia, which includes beverage, food, and snacks; and (7) Asia Pacific, Australia/New Zealand, and China, which includes beverage, food, and snacks.[19] To support PepsiCo's overall corporate strategy, all seven business units must develop strategic plans to profitably produce offerings while demonstrating that they are committed to society and the environment.

At the functional (marketing) level, to increase PepsiCo's profits, employees responsible for different products or product categories such as beverages or foods might focus on developing healthier products and making their packaging more environmentally friendly so the company captures more market share. For example, the Aquafina bottle uses less plastic and has a smaller label, which helps the environment by reducing the amount of waste.

The Aquafina bottle uses less plastic and has a smaller label, reducing waste and helping the environment.

Source: © Shutterstock, Inc.

Organizations can utilize multiple methods and strategies at different levels in the corporation to accomplish their various goals, just as you may use different strategies to accomplish your goals. However, the basic components of the strategic planning process are the same at each of the different levels.

Key Takeaway

- Strategic planning can occur at different levels (corporate, business, and functional) in an organization. The number of levels may vary. However, if a company has multiple planning levels, the plans must be consistent, and all must help achieve the overall goals of the corporation.

Review Questions

1. What different levels of planning can organizations utilize?
2. Give an example and explain how a corporation that wants to help protect the environment can do so at its corporate, business, and functional levels.

2.5 Strategic Portfolio Planning Approaches

Learning Objectives

1. Explain how SBUs are evaluated using the Boston Consulting Group matrix.
2. Explain how businesses and the attractiveness of industries are evaluated using the General Electric approach.

portfolio

A group of business units owned by a single firm.

portfolio planning approach

An approach to analyzing various businesses relative to one another.

When a firm has multiple strategic business units like PepsiCo does, it must decide what the objectives and strategies for each business are and how to allocate resources among them. A group of businesses can be considered a **portfolio**, just as a collection of artwork or investments compose a portfolio. In order to evaluate each business, companies sometimes utilize what's called a portfolio planning approach. A **portfolio planning approach** involves analyzing a firm's entire collection of businesses relative to one another. Two of the most widely used portfolio planning approaches include the Boston Consulting Group (BCG) matrix and the General Electric (GE) approach.

The Boston Consulting Group Matrix

FIGURE 2.7 The Boston Consulting Group (BCG) Matrix

The **Boston Consulting Group (BCG) matrix** helps companies evaluate each of its strategic business units based on two factors: (1) the SBU's market growth rate (i.e., how fast the unit is growing compared to the industry in which it competes), and (2) the SBU's relative market share (i.e., how the unit's share of the market compares to the market share of its competitors). Because the BCG matrix assumes that profitability and market share are highly related, it is a useful approach for making business and investment decisions. However, the BCG matrix is subjective and managers should also use their judgment and other planning approaches before making decisions. Using the BCG matrix, managers can categorize their SBUs (products) into one of four categories, as shown in Figure 2.7.

Boston Consulting Group (BCG) matrix

A portfolio-planning approach that examines strategic business units based on their relative market shares and growth rates. Businesses are classified as stars, cash cows, question marks (problem children), or dogs.

Stars

Everyone wants to be a star. A **star** is a product with high growth and a high market share. To maintain the growth of their star products, a company may have to invest money to improve them and distribute them as well as promote them. Due to its brand equity and high market share, Aquafina may be considered a star.

star

Business or offering with high growth and a high market share.

Cash Cows

A **cash cow** is a product with low growth and a high market share. Cash cows have a large share of a shrinking market. Although they generate a lot of cash, they do not have a long-term future. For example, an Apple iPhone, when each new version is released, may be an example of a cash cow product. Companies with cash cows need to manage them so that they continue to generate revenue to fund star products or help grow question marks into stars.

cash cow

Business or offering with a large share of a shrinking market.

Question Marks or Problem Children

Did you ever hear an adult say they didn't know what to do with a child? The same question or problem arises when a product has a low share of a high-growth market. Managers classify these products as **question marks or problem children**. They must decide whether to invest in them and hope they become stars or gradually eliminate or sell them. For example, when sales of Mattel's Barbie doll fell, Mattel had to decide whether to continue to invest in the Barbie brand, since she was their "problem child." Mattel decided to invest in Barbie, but unfortunately did not pay attention and lost their Princess dolls to Hasbro.[20]

question marks or problem children

Businesses or offerings with a low share of a high-growth market.

Dogs

In business, it is not good to be considered a dog. A **dog** is a product with low growth and low market share. Dogs do not make much money and do not have a promising future. Companies often get rid of dogs. However, some companies are hesitant to classify any of their products as dogs. As a result, they keep producing products and services they shouldn't or invest in dogs in hopes they'll succeed.

dog

Business or offering with low growth and a low market share.

The BCG matrix helps managers make resource allocation decisions once different products are classified. Depending on the product, a firm might decide on a number of different strategies for it. One strategy is to build market share for a business or product, especially a product that might become a star. Many companies invest in question marks because market share is available for them to capture. The success sequence is often used as a means to help question marks become stars. With the success sequence, money is taken from cash cows (if available) and invested into question marks in hopes of them becoming stars.

harvest

When a firm lowers investment in a product or business.

divest

When a firm drops or sells a product or business.

Holding market share means the company wants to keep the product's share at the same level. When a firm pursues this strategy, it only invests what it has to in order to maintain the product's market share. When a company decides to **harvest** a product, the firm lowers its investment in it. The goal is to try to generate short-term profits from the product regardless of the long-term impact on its survival. If a company decides to **divest** a product, the firm drops or sells it. Many consumer package goods (CPG) companies such as Kraft Heinz and Mondelez decided to divest low performing brands in 2020 when the pandemic affected supply chains and manufacturing capabilities.[21] While firms may divest dogs, other companies divest products because they want to focus on other brands in their portfolio.

As competitors enter the market, technology advances, and consumer preferences change, the position of a company's products in the BCG matrix is also likely to change. The company has to continually evaluate the situation and adjust its investments and product promotion strategies accordingly. The firm must also keep in mind that the BCG matrix is just one planning approach and that other variables can affect the success of products.

The General Electric Approach

General Electric (GE) approach

A portfolio-planning approach that examines a business's strengths and the attractiveness of industries.

Another portfolio planning approach that helps a business determine whether to invest in opportunities is the **General Electric (GE) approach**. The GE approach examines a business' strengths and the attractiveness of the industry in which it competes. As we have indicated, a business' strengths are factors internal to the company, including strong human resources capabilities (talented personnel), strong technical capabilities, and the fact that the firm holds a large share of the market. The attractiveness of an industry can include aspects such as whether or not there is a great deal of growth in the industry, whether the profits earned by the firms competing within it are high or low, and whether or not it is difficult to enter the market. For example, the automobile industry is not attractive in times of economic downturn such as the recession in 2009, so many automobile manufacturers don't want to invest more in production. They want to cut or stop spending as much as possible to improve their profitability. Hotels and airlines face similar situations.

FIGURE 2.8 The General Electric (GE) Approach

Companies evaluate their strengths and the attractiveness of industries as high, medium, and low. The firms then determine their investment strategies based on how well the two correlate with one another. As Figure 2.8 shows, the investment options outlined in the GE approach can be compared to a traffic light. For example, if a company feels that it does not have the business strengths to compete in an industry and that the industry is not attractive, this will result in a low rating, which is comparable to a red light. In that case, the company should harvest the business (slowly reduce the investments made in it), divest the business (drop or sell it), or stop investing in it, which is what happened with many automotive manufacturers.

Although many people may think a yellow light means "speed up," it actually means caution. Companies with a medium rating on industry attractiveness and business strengths should be cautious when investing and attempt to hold the market share they have. If a company rates itself high on business strengths and the industry is very attractive (also rated high), this is comparable to a green light. In this case, the firm should invest in the business and build market share. During bad economic times, many industries are not attractive. However, when the economy improves, businesses must reevaluate opportunities.

Key Takeaway

- A group of businesses is called a portfolio. Organizations that have multiple business units must decide how to allocate resources to them and decide what objectives and strategies are feasible for them. Portfolio-planning approaches help firms analyze the businesses relative to each other. The BCG and GE approaches are two or the most common portfolio-planning methods. Both approaches are subjective.

Review Questions

1. How would you classify a product that has a low market share in a growing market?
2. What does it mean to hold market share?
3. What factors are used as the basis for analyzing businesses and brands using the BCG and the GE approaches?

2.6 Discussion Questions and Activities

Discussion Questions

1. Explain how a marketing objective differs from a marketing strategy. How are they related?
2. Explain how an organization like Coach can use licensing to create value for the brand.
3. How has Coca-Cola employed a product development strategy?
4. Discuss how conducting a SWOT (strengths, weaknesses, opportunities, threats) analysis helps a firm (or an individual) develop its strategic plan.
5. Describe the value propositions the social networking sites YouTube and Facebook offer web users.

Activities

1. Outline a strategic plan for yourself to begin planning for a job after graduation. Include your value proposition, targeted organizations, objectives, strategies, and the internal and external factors that may affect your plans.
2. Assume you have an interview for an entry-level sales position. Write a value proposition emphasizing why you are the best candidate for the position relative to other recent college graduates.
3. A mission statement outlines an organization's purpose and answers the question of how a company defines its business. Write a mission statement for a campus organization.
4. The website My M&Ms allows customers to personalize M&M candies with words, faces, and colors and select from multiple packaging choices. Identify and explain the product market or market development strategies Mars pursued when it introduced personalized M&Ms.

5. Explain how changing demographics and the social and cultural environment have impacted the health care industry. Identify new venues for health care that didn't exist a decade ago. (Hint: Emergency care services are available outside a hospital's emergency room today.)
6. Select an organization for which you would like to work. Look up its mission statement. What do you think the organization's objectives and strategies are? What macro and micro environmental and internal factors might affect its success?
7. Break up into teams. Come up with as many real-world examples as you can of companies that pursued market penetration, market development, product development, or diversification strategies. Explain what the company did and how successful you think each strategy will be.

2.7 Case Study: The Importance of Leadership and Culture for Corporate Success

As one of the largest furniture manufacturers in the United States, AIS's corporate culture (set of beliefs and actions) guides how management and employees interact and handle external business transactions. Their culture can be defined by aspects such as passion to succeed as a company financially, commitment to give back through philanthropic efforts, diversity and equality, supporting "Made in USA" initiatives, growing the local economy through regional business support, creativity, strategy, doing more with less, a customer service focus, always going above and beyond, rewarding results, and providing a work environment that provides a sense of pride to be part of the organization. The culture at AIS played a critical role during the COVID-19 pandemic.

COVID-19 and the delta variant have affected people, companies, and industries across the country and around the world. Many retail businesses, especially local businesses closed and had unemployed workers. Corporate owners felt great losses as they dealt with unprecedented economic problems. Companies big and small changed strategies and/or pivoted to help both local companies as well as people in need. Bruce Platzman, CEO of AIS, did both.

Mr. Platzman spearheaded a pivot from AIS's manufacturing lines to make high-quality facemasks to help fight COVID-19, launching a nationwide initiative called Sew The Masks. Using materials provided by AIS and engaging 1,000 volunteers from forty-five states, the company donated over 600,000 facemasks to first responders, frontline workers, and people in need across the USA. (Watch Sew The Masks video.)

Knowing the pandemic had taken its toll on the businesses and people around the country and that the Northeast was hit especially hard, AIS began driving the *ReNEW England* initiative. Reinforcing the premise that buying locally and regionally can accelerate the rebound of the region's economy, Mr. Platzman is sharing his company's dedication to sourcing as much material as possible from neighbors while encouraging other businesses in New England to do the same. When everyone commits to supporting each other, the local communities will benefit and the overall economic health of the area will improve more rapidly. Link to white paper here: http://aisinsidesales.blob.core.windows.net/files/AIS ReNEWEngland White Paper July 2021.pdf.

Case Study Questions

1. How important do you think having a corporate culture like AIS is to a business's success?
2. What strategies would you suggest local businesses in your hometown implement to support the local economy and drive economic health in the area?
3. What are two examples of pivot strategies that companies from your hometown did or could implement during the COVID-19 pandemic?
4. Philanthropy is a key part of being a good citizen, both individually and as part of an organization. Regardless of their financial means, what can organizations and individuals do to be more philanthropic?
5. What factors make Mr. Platzman and AIS so successful?

Endnotes

1. Newman, Casey (2021), "What is a Value Proposition? Plus 6 Great Examples and 3 Common Mistakes," https://www.kunocreative.com/blog/good-value-proposition-examples, February 17, 2021.
2. Shewan, Dan (2021), "7 of the Best Value Proposition Examples We've Ever Seen," https://www.wordstream.com/blog/ws/2016/04/27/value-proposition-examples, April 4.
3. Shewan, Dan (2021), "7 of the Best Value Proposition Examples We've Ever Seen," https://www.wordstream.com/blog/ws/2016/04/27/value-proposition-examples, April 4.
4. Pereria, Daniel (2021), "Amazon Business Modell," https://businessmodelanalyst.com/amazon-business-model/#Value_Proposition_of_Amazon (July 21); De Ternay, Guerric (2021), "Amazon Value Proposition in a Nutshell," https://fourweekmba.com/amazon-value-proposition/.
5. "About the Company," (2021), https://www.pepsico.com/about/about-the-company.
6. Poinski, Megan (2021), "PepsiCo to sell Tropicana, other juice brands for $3.3B," https://www.fooddive.com/news/pepsico-to-sell-tropicana-other-juice-brands-for-33-billion/604347/ (August 3); http://www.pepsico.com/live/story/trop50-innovation-shakes-up-the-orange-juice-market082920131115.
7. Michael E. Porter (1980), *Competitive Strategy,* New York: The Free Press, 3–33.
8. Michael E. Porter (1980), *Competitive Strategy,* New York: The Free Press, 4.
9. Michael E. Porter (1980), *Competitive Strategy*, New York: The Free Press, 3–33.
10. "CPSC Approves Major New Federal Safety Standard for Infant Sleep Products," (2021), https://www.cpsc.gov/Newsroom/News-Releases/2021/CPSC-Approves-Major-New-Federal-Safety-Standard-for-Infant-Sleep-Products, (June 2); "GDPR in the USA/GDPR Compliance in the USA/ GDPR and PII," (2020), https://www.cookiebot.com/en/gdpr-usa/, July 7.
11. http://www.pepsico.com/sustainability.
12. Linked In Corporation (2021), https://about.linkedin.com/.
13. "Mission," The United Way, http://www.unitedway.org/our-impact/mission.
14. "About the Company," (2021), https://www.pepsico.com/about/about-the-company.
15. Kirk, Alexander (2021), "New Recipe, new packaging of Coke Zero Debuts Nationwide," https://www.9news.com/article/money/coke-zero-sugar-new-look-taste/73-a82c1689-447f-41bb-8504-8c3a13044486, (August 10).
16. Fung, Ester (2020), "Hotels Attract Remote Workers with Daytime Rates," *Wall Street Journal*, (November 4), B1, B5.
17. Global Expansion (2021), "5 Largest Historical Mergers and Acquisitions that Failed," https://www.globalexpansion.com/blog/largest-historical-mergers-and-acquisitions-that-failed, January 17.
18. Goodyear Tire & Rubber Company, https://corporate.goodyear.com/us/en/about/our-brand-and-products.htmL.
19. "About the Company," (2021) https://www.pepsico.com/about/about-the-company.
20. Claire Suddath (January 2016), "How Hasbro Stole Disney's Dolls from Mattel," *Business Week*, 40–44.
21. Crawford, Elizabeth (2021), "CPG Giants Reshape Portfolios with Significant Divestitures, Limited Acquisitions," https://www.foodnavigator-usa.com/Article/2021/02/18/CPG-giants-reshape-portfolios-with-significant-divestitures-limited-acquisitions (February 18).

CHAPTER 3

Consumer Behavior: How People Make Buying Decisions

Why do you buy the things you do? How did you decide to go to the college you're attending? Where and how do you like to shop? Do your friends shop on the same websites and at the same places or different ones? How much more likely are you to buy a product if people "like" it on social media sites?

Marketing professionals with answers to those questions will have a much better chance of creating, communicating about, and delivering value-added products and services you and people like you want to buy. That's what the study of consumer behavior is all about. **Consumer behavior** considers the many reasons—personal, situational, psychological, and social—why people shop for products, buy and use them, sometimes become loyal customers, and then dispose of them.

consumer behavior

The study of when, where, and how people buy things and then dispose of them.

Companies spend billions of dollars annually studying what makes consumers "tick." Google and Meta (Facebook's parent company), among other organizations, monitor what you buy and where as well as your web patterns—the sites you search, the devices and apps you use to do so, and even how you search. (Do you use voice technology to search for products, for example?) Companies that pay for **search advertising**, or ads that appear on the web pages you pull up after doing online searches, want to find out what kind of things interest you and the best ways to reach you. Doing so allows these companies to send you emails, ads, and coupons you might actually be interested in instead of ads for things you aren't interested in.

search advertising

Advertising that appears on web pages pulled up when online searches are conducted.

Sellers also track consumers both online and physically in stores via cameras and also sometimes via their mobile phones. Seeing where consumers dwell, or spend more time either physically or digitally, can, among things, help a company place its more profitable items and attract more customers.[1]

Researchers even look at people's brains by having people lie in scanners and asking them questions about different products. What people *say* about the products is then compared to what their brain scans show—that is, what people are really thinking. Scanning people's brains for marketing purposes might sound extreme, but maybe not when you consider the fact that eight out of ten new consumer products fail, even when they are test marketed. Could it be that what people say about potential new products and what they think about them are different? Marketing professionals want to find out.[2]

Studying people's buying habits isn't just for big companies, though. Small businesses and entrepreneurs can study the behavior of their customers with great success. By figuring out what zip codes their customers are in, a business might determine where to locate an additional store. Small businesses such as restaurants often use coupon codes. For example, coupons sent out in newspapers are given one code. Those sent out via the web are given another. When the coupons are redeemed, the restaurants can tell which marketing avenues are having the biggest effect on their sales. Moreover, businesses large and small are using an array of social networks and tools to both gather information about their customers and disseminate information to them at a low cost.

Environmental factors (such as the economy and technology) and marketing actions taken to create, communicate about, and deliver products and services (such as marketing campaigns, sale prices, coupons, and websites) also affect the behavior of consumers. A consumer's situation, personal factors, and culture also influence what, when, and how they buy products. We'll look at those factors in Section 1. Section 2 focuses on different types of buying decisions and the stages consumers may go through when making purchase decisions.

3.1 Factors That Influence Consumers' Buying Behavior

Learning Objectives

1. Describe the personal and psychological factors that influence what consumers buy and when they buy it.
2. Explain what marketing professionals can do to influence the behavior of consumers.
3. Explain how looking at lifestyle information helps firms understand what consumers want to purchase.
4. Explain how Maslow's hierarchy of needs works.
5. Explain how culture, subcultures, social classes, families, and reference groups affect consumers' buying behavior.

You've been a consumer with purchasing power for much longer than you probably realize—since the first time you were asked which cereal or toy you wanted. Over the years, you've developed rules of thumb, or mental shortcuts, that provide you with a systematic way to choose among alternatives, even if you aren't aware of it. Other consumers follow a similar process, but different people, no matter how similar they are, make different purchasing decisions. You might be interested in a Tesla Model Y, but your best friend might want to buy a Ford F-150 truck. What factors influenced your decision, and what factors influenced your friend's decision?

What's hot and what's not online? Individuals and businesses can go to Google Trends, a free resource, to find out.

Source: © Shutterstock, Inc.

As we mentioned earlier in the chapter, consumer behavior is influenced by many things, including environmental and marketing factors, the situation, personal and psychological factors, family, and culture. Businesses try to figure out *trends* so they can reach the people most likely to buy their products in the most cost-effective way possible. The move to more organic products and less-processed foods is an example. McDonald's replaced nonorganic Minute Maid apple juice in its Happy Meals with Honest Kids Appley Ever After, which is organic and contains more water. Why? Because parents want their children to drink organic beverages with fewer calories and grams of sugar.[3]

Businesses also often try to influence a consumer's behavior with things they can control, such as the way in which they design their websites, apps, the layout of their stores, music, lighting, grouping of products, pricing, and advertising. While some influences may be temporary and others are long-lasting, different factors can affect how buyers behave—whether they influence you to make a purchase, buy additional products, or buy nothing at all. Let's now look at some of the influences on consumer behavior in more detail.

Shaping the Behavior of Consumers: Social Distancing

Can businesses "shape" the behavior of customers? The Maryland restaurant and bar Fish Tales did just that. Fish Tales found a unique way to both promote social distancing during the COVID-19 pandemic and get a lot of publicity and business too.

View in the online reader

Situational Factors

Have you ever been in a department store and couldn't find your way out? No, you aren't necessarily directionally challenged. Marketing professionals take physical factors such as a store's design and layout into account when they are designing their facilities. Presumably, the longer you wander around a facility, the more you will spend. Grocery stores frequently place bread and milk products on the opposite ends of the stores because people often need both types of products. To buy both, customers have to walk around an entire store, which of course, is loaded with other items they might see and buy.

Store locations also influence behavior. Starbucks does a good job in terms of locating its stores. It has the process down to a science; you can scarcely drive a few miles down the road without passing a Starbucks. You can also buy cups of Starbucks coffee at many grocery stores, airports, cruise ships, and even in the Tower of London—virtually any place where there is foot traffic.

Physical factors firms can control, such as the layout of a store, music played at stores, the lighting, temperature, and even the smells you experience are called **atmospherics**. Research shows that "strategic fragrancing" results in customers staying in stores longer, buying more, and leaving with better impressions of the quality of stores' services and products. Different hotels have their own distinct smells to establish their brands. If you put the scent for a W Hotel in a Westin Hotel, it would feel out of place, says one hotel brand manager.[4]

atmospherics

The physical aspects of the selling environment retailers try to control.

Mirrors near hotel elevators are another example. Hotel operators have found that when people are busy looking at themselves in the mirrors, they don't feel like they are waiting as long for their elevators. Likewise, airports have discovered that installing windows that automatically darken when it's sunny out leads to dramatically higher alcohol sales at airport bars.[5]

Not all physical factors are under a company's control, however. Take weather, for example. Rainy weather can be a boon to some companies, like umbrella makers such as Totes, but a problem for others. Beach resorts, outdoor concert venues, and golf courses suffer when it is raining heavily. Businesses such as automobile dealers also have fewer customers. Who wants to shop for a car in the rain?

Vending Machines

Carvana and Vroom are online car sellers that allow you to pick out your car online as if you were choosing a soda from a vending machine.

View in the online reader

Firms often attempt to deal with adverse physical factors such as bad weather by offering specials during unattractive times. For example, many resorts offer consumers discounts to travel to beach locations during hurricane season. Similarly, during the COVID-19 pandemic, resorts, hotels, and other vacation venues found themselves without guests. To deal with the downturn, resorts, hotels, and other vacation venues offered "workcation" packages to people who could work remotely and wanted to get out of their homes.

Crowding is another situational factor. Have you ever left a store and not purchased anything because it was just too crowded? This became another issue for sellers during the pandemic. Businesses dealt with it by offering everything from curbside pickup to virtual shopping events and fitting rooms.

Some studies have shown that consumers feel better about retailers that attempt to prevent overcrowding in their stores. However, other studies have shown that to a certain extent, crowding can have a positive impact on a person's buying experience. Crowding can make a people clamor to buy a product before others do and it is sold out. The phenomenon is often referred to as "herd behavior."[6]

Social Situation

The social situation you're in can significantly affect your purchase behavior. Perhaps you have seen Girl Scouts selling cookies outside grocery stores and other retail establishments and purchased nothing from them. But what if your neighbor's daughter is selling the cookies? Are you going to turn her down or be a friendly neighbor and buy a box (or two)?

Social Situations

Are you going to turn down cookies from this cute Girl Scout? What if she's your neighbor's daughter? Please serve me up some of those cookies with my DQ Blizzard!

View in the online reader

Companies like Pampered Chef that sell their products at parties understand that the social situation makes a difference. When you're at a friend's Pampered Chef party, you don't want to look cheap or disappoint your friend by not buying any cooking products. Certain social situations can also make you less willing to buy products. You might spend quite a bit of money each month eating at fast food restaurants like McDonald's and Subway, but would you take someone to one of those restaurants for your first date? Some people might. Other people would choose a more upscale restaurant. Likewise, if you have turned down a drink or dessert on a date because you were worried about what the person you were with might have thought, your consumption was affected by your social situation.[7]

Time

The time of day, time of year, and how much time consumers feel they have to shop affect what they buy. Researchers have even discovered that whether someone is a "morning person" or "evening person" affects the person's shopping patterns. Have you ever gone to the grocery store when you were hungry or after payday, when you had cash in your pocket? When you are hungry or have cash, you may purchase more than you would at other times.

Companies worldwide are aware of people's lack of time and are finding ways to accommodate them. Amazon is a "prime" example, pardon the pun. The site makes it easy to buy a lot of products fast. Americans aren't the only people who are "time starved." South Koreans work very long hours and are extremely pressed for time. In that country, marketers place electronic billboards in subway stations showing products and their prices. Commuters use their mobile phones to scan the products' barcodes on their way to work, and the products are delivered to their doors when they return home.

Reason for the Purchase

The reason you are shopping also affects the amount of time you will spend shopping. Are you making an emergency purchase? What if you need some items for an important dinner or a project and only have an hour to get everything? Are you shopping for a gift or for a special occasion? Are you buying something to complete a task or project and need it quickly? In recent years, emergency clinics have sprung up in strip malls all over the country. Convenience is one reason. The other is sheer necessity. If you cut yourself and you are bleeding badly, you're probably not going to shop around much to find the best clinic. You will go to the one that's closest to you.

Purchasing a gift might not be an emergency situation, but you might not want to spend much time shopping for it either. Gift certificates and cards you can buy online or easily pick up at a grocery or drugstore while you're shopping for something else are popular for this reason. That's why the cards are generally placed near checkout stands: grab and go. By contrast, suppose you need to buy an engagement ring. Sure, you could buy one online in a jiffy, but you probably wouldn't do that. What if the diamond were fake? What if your significant other turned you down and you had to return the ring? How hard would it be to get back online and return the ring?[8]

Mood

Some coffee shop and restaurant owners have found that WiFi can actually have a negative effect on sales if patrons stay too long, and don't ask for anything other than free coffee refills.

Source: © Shutterstock, Inc.

Have you ever felt like going on a shopping spree? At other times, wild horses couldn't drag you out to shop. People's moods temporarily affect their spending patterns.[9] People in a good moods are likely to linger longer in a store, buy more, and even pay more. One study found that relaxed shoppers are willing to pay up to 15 percent more for goods than less-relaxed shoppers. The clothing brand and retailer Tommy Bahama found that offering free appetizers and mimosas at its stores during the holidays was a major sales booster.

Another study found that Americans have doubled their spending online in the past few years while "drunk shopping." Gen Xers spend more money than millennials, and men spend about double what women do while soused.[10] Companies are responding by offering more online deals during late night binge-shopping hours.

Offering people places to sit down and free WiFi are other ways to get shoppers to relax. Maverick, an upscale Western-wear store in Fort Worth, Texas, has a full bar on one side of its store where one's spouse or shopping companions can take a break while the other(s) shops. Likewise, some restaurants put computer tablets on tables to keep antsy or cranky kids entertained and stressed-out patrons happy while looking at food offerings until their waiters are able to help them.

Economic Situation

People's economic situations definitely affect what they will buy and how much of it. For example, during economic downturns, many people reduce their spending. Stores with lower-priced merchandise like Costco and Walmart tend to fare better during these periods than higher-end stores such as Saks Fifth Avenue and Nordstrom.

To get buyers in the shopping mood during an economic downturn, companies resort to different measures, such as introducing more lower-priced brands. During the COVID-19 pandemic, packaged foods makers like Nestlé and Kellogg experimented with smaller, more affordable package sizes to lure economically strapped customers.[11] Studying customer's loyalty cards to figure out ways to persuade customers to purchase nonfood items with higher profit margins is another strategy.

Downturns can be downright good for some companies though. Dollar stores such as Dollar Tree and Dollar General saw double-digit increases in their sales during the pandemic. So did seed sellers and tractor supply-type companies as people began planting their own gardens to save money on food. Table 3.1 shows how people's consuming behaviors generally changed as a result of the pandemic.[12]

TABLE 3.1 Changes in the Demand for Various Products During the Pandemic

Increased Demand (+)	Decreased Demand (–)
drive-throughs	indoor dining
videogames	amusement parks
Peleton bikes/home gyms	public gyms
home delivery/curb-side pickup	in-store shopping
home office equipment and spaces	commercial office equipment and space
online gambling	in-person gambling
take-out liquor	bars
teleconferencing	in-person conferences and conventions
recreational vehicles	vacation and resort rentals
live-streamed concerts	public concerts

Personal Factors

Personality and Self-Concept

Personality describes a person's disposition, helps explain why people are different, and encompasses a person's unique traits. The "Big Five" personality traits psychologists discuss frequently include *openness* or how open you are to new experiences, *conscientiousness* or how diligent you are, *extraversion* or how outgoing or shy you are, *agreeableness* or how easy you are to get along with, and *neuroticism* or how prone you are to negative mental states.

personality

An individual's disposition as other people see it.

Do personality traits predict people's purchasing behavior? Can companies successfully target certain products to people based on their personalities? How do you find out what personalities consumers have? Are extroverts wild spenders and introverts penny pinchers?

The link between people's personalities and their buying behavior is somewhat unclear. Some research studies have shown that "sensation seekers," or people who seek out thrilling, dangerous, or unusual experiences, are more likely to respond well to advertising that's violent and graphic. The problem for firms is figuring out "who's who" in terms of their personalities.

Marketers have had better luck linking people's self-concepts to their buying behavior. Your **self-concept** is how you see yourself—be it positive or negative. Your **ideal self** is how you would *like* to see yourself—whether it's prettier, more popular, or more eco-conscious. How you think others see you also influences your purchasing behavior. Marketing researchers believe people buy products to enhance how they feel about themselves—to get themselves closer to their ideal selves, in other words.

self-concept

How a person sees himself or herself.

ideal self

How a person would like to view himself or herself.

The slogan "Be All That You Can Be," which for years was used by the U.S. Army to recruit soldiers, is an attempt to appeal to the self-concept. Presumably, by joining the U.S. Army, you will become a better version of yourself, which will, in turn, improve your life. Many beauty products and cosmetic procedures are advertised in a way that appeals to the ideal self people seek.

Gender, Age, and Stage of Life

Men and women need and buy different products. They also shop differently and in general, have different attitudes about shopping. You know the old stereotypes. Men see what they want and buy it, but women "try on everything and shop 'til they drop."

There's some truth to the stereotypes. That's why you see so many advertisements directed at one sex or the other—beer commercials that air on ESPN and commercials for household products that air on Lifetime. Research shows that women make more household product purchases, whereas men buy more alcoholic beverages. Women also spend more time in stores, whereas men want to get in and out of them quickly and tend to buy fewer items at a time.

The shopping differences between men and women seem to be changing, though. Younger, well-educated men are less likely to believe grocery shopping is a woman's job. Other men actually like shopping and consider it relaxing. Men today are also more likely to buy diapers as well as change them. As a result, a number of companies have begun selling neutral and camouflage diaper bags that look a lot like army gear.

Diaper Bags

Can a "manly" diaper bag turn a dad into a sex symbol? Tactical Baby Gear, a maker of such bags, would like you to think so.

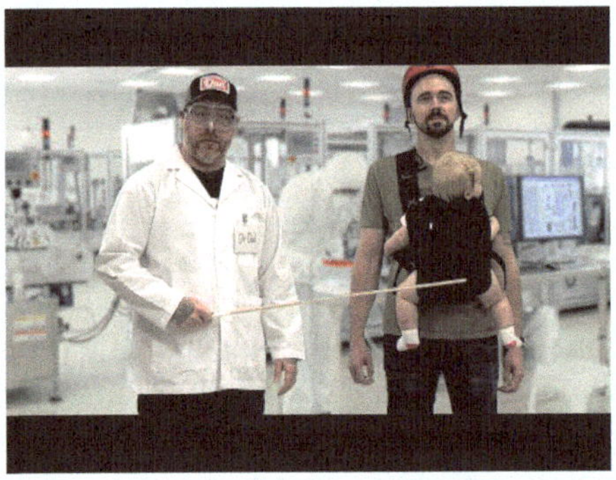

View in the online reader

One study by Resource Interactive, a technology research firm, found that when shopping online, men prefer sites that save them time and money and have lots of products. That way, the men don't have to navigate to other sites. Women prefer to browse more diverse sites and see products in a lifestyle context—say, a lamp in a living room. Women are also twice as likely as men to use viewing tools such as the zoom and rotate buttons and links that allow them to change the colors of products.

More businesses today are taking greater pains to figure out "what men want." Does a guy want a six-shooter or a four-poster canopy bed (a bed with tall posts on each corner and drapes around it)? Believe it or not, some men today *do* want four-poster beds. But instead of them being made of ornate wood and fancy curtains, men want them to be masculine and modern looking, and say, made from iron or steel posts. Ralph Lauren Home and Anthropologie are among the companies obliging these male shoppers.

Marketers are also targeting women in ways they haven't in the past. The maker of Johnnie Walker now has a brand of whiskey for women called "Jane Walker." Similarly, flasks for liquor used to be almost exclusively for men. Today, brightly colored flasks decked out with rhinestones have become popular among women.

Highlighting Differences

Check out this funny Heineken commercial, which highlights the stereotypical differences between "what women want" and "what men want."

View in the online reader

You have probably noticed that the things you buy have changed as you age. Think about what you wanted and how you spent your money when you were a child versus a teenager and an adult. When you were a child, the last thing you probably wanted as a gift was clothing. As you became a teen, cool clothes probably became a bigger priority. Don't look now, but depending on the stage of life you're currently in, baby diapers and wrinkle cream might be just around the corner!

If you're single and working after graduation, you probably spend your money differently than a newly married couple does. How do you think spending patterns change when someone has a young child, teenager, or student in college? Diapers and daycare, orthodontia, tuition, and electronics—affect the spending patterns of families. Once children graduate from college and their parents are empty nesters, their spending patterns change again.

You're only as old as you feel—and the goods and services you buy.

Source: © Shutterstock, Inc.

Your **chronological age**, or actual age in years, is one thing. Your **cognitive age**, or how old you perceive yourself to be, is another. A person's cognitive age affects his or her activities and sparks interests consistent with his or her perceived age. Cognitive age is a significant predictor of consumer behaviors, including dining out, watching television, going to bars and dance clubs, playing online games, and shopping.[13]

chronological age

A person's age in years.

cognitive age

The age a buyer perceives himself or herself to be.

Companies have found that many consumers feel younger than their chronological ages and are not receptive to products that feature "old folks" in ads because they can't identify with these people. If you watch network TV news, you'll notice that the commercials often feature products designed for older audiences because these people are more likely to watch the broadcasts than younger ones. However, the people shown using the products in the ads appear to be barely over age forty.

Lifestyle

People's lifestyles can differ radically, even when by all outward appearances the individuals seem very similar. To better understand and connect with consumers based on their lifestyles, companies interview or ask people to complete questionnaires about factors that relate to their lifestyles, such as their *activities, interests, and opinions* (which are often referred to as AIO statements). Consumers are not only asked about products they like, where they live, and what their genders are, but also about what they do—that is, how they spend their time and what their priorities, values, opinions, and general outlooks on the world are. Where do they go other than work? Whom do they like to talk to? What do they talk about? To find out, researchers hired by Procter & Gamble have gone so far as to follow women around for weeks as they shop, run errands, and socialize with one another.[14] Other companies pay people to keep daily journals of their activities and routines.

psychographics

Measuring the attitudes, values, lifestyles, and opinions of consumers using demographics.

A number of research organizations examine lifestyle and psychographic characteristics of consumers. **Psychographics** combines the lifestyle traits of consumers and their personality styles with an analysis of their attitudes, activities, and values to identify groups of consumers with similar characteristics. One of the most widely used systems to classify people based on psychographics is the VALS (Values, Attitudes, and Lifestyles) framework. Using VALS to combine psychographics with demographic information, such as people's marital statuses, education levels, and incomes provides a better understanding of consumers.

Psychological Factors

Motivation

motivation

The inward drive people have to get what they need.

Motivation is the inward drive we have to get what we need. In the mid-1900s, Abraham Maslow, an American psychologist, developed the hierarchy of needs shown in Figure 3.1.

FIGURE 3.1 Maslow's Hierarchy of Needs

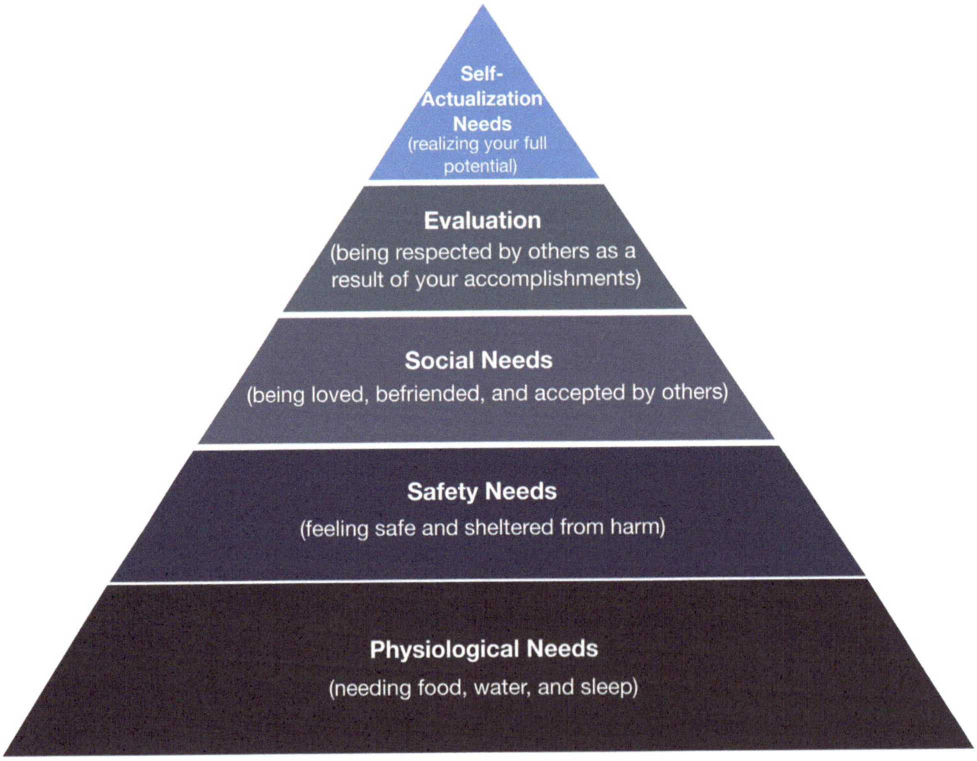

Maslow theorized that people have to fulfill their basic needs—for food, water, and sleep—before they can begin fulfilling higher-level needs. Have you ever gone shopping when you were tired or hungry? Even if you were shopping for something that would make you the envy of your friends (maybe a new car), you probably wanted to sleep or eat even more. (Forget the car. Just give me a nap or a snack.) The need for food is recurring. Other needs, such as shelter, clothing, and safety, tend to be enduring.

Still other needs arise at different points in time in a person's life. For example, during grade school and high school, your *social* needs probably rose to the forefront. You wanted to have friends and get a date. Perhaps this prompted you to buy certain types of clothing or electronic devices. After high school, you began thinking about how people would view you in your "station" in life, so you decided to pay for college and get a professional degree, thereby fulfilling your need for *esteem*. If you're lucky, at some point you will realize Maslow's state of *self-actualization*. You will believe you have become the person in life that you feel you were meant to be.

While achieving self-actualization may be a goal for many individuals in the United States, consumers in Eastern cultures may focus more on belongingness and group needs. Marketers look at cultural differences like these in addition to individual needs. The importance of groups affects advertising (using groups versus individuals) and product decisions.

Perception

Perception is how you interpret the world around you and make sense of it. You do so via stimuli that affect your different senses—sight, hearing, touch, smell, and taste. How you combine these senses also makes a difference. For example, in one study, consumers were blindfolded and asked to drink a new brand of clear beer. Most of them said the product tasted like regular beer. However, when the blindfolds came off and they drank the beer, many of them described it as "watery" tasting.[15]

perception

How people interpret the world around them.

Consumers are bombarded with messages on their phones, television, radio, magazines, the internet, and even bathroom walls. According to the American Marketing Association, a consumer can be exposed to as many as 10,000 advertisements per day. Consumers are surfing the internet, watching television, gaming, and checking their mobile phones simultaneously. Moreover, they are switching between screens as many as twenty-one times an hour.[16] Some, but not all, information makes it into our brains.

Have you ever read or thought about something and then started noticing ads and information about it popping up everywhere? Many people are more perceptive to advertisements for products they need. **Selective attention** is the process of filtering out information based on how relevant it is to you. It's been described as a "suit of armor" that helps you filter out information you *don't* need.

selective attention

The process whereby a person filters information based on how relevant it is to them.

At other times, people forget information, even if it's quite relevant to them, which is called **selective retention**. Often the information contradicts the person's belief. An example is a longtime chain smoker who forgets much of the information communicated during a commercial for an anti-smoking medication. To be sure their advertising messages get through to you and you remember them, companies use repetition. Some marketers believe that a consumer needs to see an advertisement between seven and twenty times before taking action.[17] Using surprising stimuli or shock advertising is also a technique that works. The Centers for Disease Control has used shock advertising to try to convince Americans of the terrible toll smoking has on people's health.

selective retention

The process whereby a person retains information based on how well it matches their values and beliefs.

The research on shock advertising is mixed, however. Some studies have found that it's becoming so commonplace that consumers are less affected by it; other studies that utilized brain scans have shown that such stimuli can have an effect on the behavior of consumers.[18]

Shock Ads

Shock ads like this one run by the Centers for Disease Control have convinced more than 2 million people to stop smoking.

View in the online reader

subliminal advertising

Advertising that is not apparent to consumers but is thought to be perceived subconsciously by them.

Subliminal advertising is the opposite of shock advertising and involves exposing consumers to marketing stimuli such as photos, ads, and messages by stealthily embedding them in movies, ads, and other media. Although there is no evidence that subliminal advertising works, years ago the words *Drink Coca-Cola* were flashed for a millisecond on a movie screen. Consumers were thought to perceive the information subconsciously and to be influenced to buy the products shown. Many people considered the practice to be subversive, and in 1974, the Federal Communications Commission banned it. However, much of the original research on subliminal advertising, conducted by a researcher trying to drum up business for his market research firm, was fabricated.[19]

Another offbeat technique marketers are using today to get your attention is ASMR (autonomous sensory meridian response). ASMR is the tingling feeling you get down your scalp and spine when you hear certain certain sounds, such as a whisper. Often used for meditative techniques, companies are now using it in their ads. During a Super Bowl, Anheuser-Busch ran a commercial that featured actress Zoe Kravitz whispering and tapping her nails on a glass of beer. People took notice.

Offbeat Techniques

Normally Super Bowl ads are super loud. This one wasn't.

View in the online reader

Different consumers also perceive information differently. You might be captivated by an ad that utilizes ASMR, but your friend might find it annoying. Similarly, one person might see an ad for a luxurious Gucci purse, but another person may see the ad as hype for an overpriced bag to hold one's keys and makeup.[20] The goal for companies is to figure out whom they are most likely to sell their products to, how to capture the attention of these people, build interest in their products, ultimately sell to them, and retain them as future customers.

Learning

Learning refers to the process by which consumers change their behavior after they gain information or experience. It's the reason you don't buy a bad product twice. Learning doesn't just affect what you buy; it affects how you shop. People with limited experience about a product or brand generally seek out more information than people who have used the product before.

learning

The process by which consumers change their behavior after they gain information or experience with a product.

Companies try to get consumers to learn about their products in different ways. Car dealerships offer test drives. Pharmaceutical representatives leave samples and brochures at doctors' offices. You have probably eaten free food samples in a grocery store. Although sampling is an expensive strategy, it gets consumers to try a product, and many customers end up buying it.

Another kind of learning is **operant or instrumental conditioning**, which is what occurs when researchers are able to get a mouse to run through a maze for a piece of cheese or a dog to salivate just by ringing a bell. In other words, operative conditioning occurs as a result of a repetitive behavior that has positive or negative consequences. Companies engage in operant conditioning by rewarding consumers, which causes them to repeat their purchasing behaviors. Prizes and toys that come in Cracker Jacks boxes and McDonald's Happy Meals, a free sandwich after a certain number of purchases, and free car washes when you fill up your car with a tank of gas are examples.

operant or instrumental conditioning

A type of behavior that's repeated when it's rewarded.

Gamification works along the same lines as operant conditioning. In a marketing context, **gamification** is a strategy of building a game component into a product to encourage consumers to buy a product or use it more. Peleton's exercise bike is an example. It features a digital leader board that lets you compete against your friends to see who is winning the exercise war.

gamification

A strategy of building a game component into a product to encourage consumers to use it or use it more.

Attitude

attitudes

"Mental positions" or emotional feelings, favorable or unfavorable evaluations, and action tendencies people have about products, services, companies, ideas, issues, or institutions.

Attitudes are "mental positions" or emotional feelings, favorable or unfavorable evaluations, and action tendencies people have about products, services, companies, ideas, issues, or institutions.[21] Attitudes tend to be enduring and hard to change because they are based on people's values and beliefs. Companies want people to have positive feelings about their offerings. As we mentioned, consumers are demanding food that's healthier and less processed. As a result, fast-casual restaurants like Panera Bread that use fresher ingredients have flourished. Rivals like McDonald's are finding it hard to compete against them. To compete, McDonald's, Taco Bell, and a number of other restaurant chains have hired dietitians and are now using fresher ingredients. But even though these companies have advertised that they are doing so, they are finding it hard to change people's attitudes about their offerings.

Societal Factors

Situational factors, personal factors, and psychological factors influence what you buy, but only on a temporary basis. Societal factors are a bit different. The culture you live in and the social class you were born into are examples of societal factors. They are more outward and have broader influences on your beliefs and the way you do things. Societal factors depend on the world around you and how it works.

Culture

culture

The shared beliefs, customs, behaviors, and attitudes that characterize a society used by people to cope with their world and with one another.

Culture refers to the shared beliefs, customs, behaviors, and attitudes that characterize a society. Culture is a handed-down way of life and is often considered the broadest influence on a consumer's behavior. Your culture prescribes how you should live and has a huge effect on the things you purchase. For example, in Beirut, Lebanon, women can often be seen wearing miniskirts. However, if you're a woman in Afghanistan wearing a miniskirt, you could face bodily harm or death. In Afghanistan, women commonly wear *burqas*, which cover them completely from head to toe.

Even cultures that share many of the same values can be quite different. Germans tend to use credits cards significantly less than people in many other countries. They prefer cash or PayPal to running up debt.[22] In contrast, people in the United States rely heavily on credit cards, even when they pay their balances every month. As a result, credit card companies such as Visa, American Express, and MasterCard must understand people's cultural perceptions about credit.

Subcultures

A **subculture** is a group of people within a culture who are different from the dominant culture but have something in common with one another such as common interests, vocations or jobs, religions, ethnic backgrounds, sexual orientations, and geographic locations.

Hispanics continue to account for more of the nation's overall population growth than any other race or ethnicity, but their growth rate has slowed.[23] Companies and marketers pay close attention to subcultural (and cultural) changes because they create opportunities to develop and market new products people want. Marketing products based on the ethnicity of consumers is useful but may become harder to do in the future because the boundaries between ethnic groups are blurring. Quick quiz: What do people in the United States buy more of: ketchup or salsa? The answer: salsa, by a 2-to-1 margin. Consequently, if you were marketing salsa, it wouldn't be a good idea to aim the product solely at the Hispanic market.

Subcultures can develop in response to people's interests, similarities, and behaviors. These characteristics allow marketing professionals to design specific products for them. People in the LGBTQ+ community, hip-hoppers, single people with pets, and gamers are examples of people who belong to subcultures.

The number of people in China who are single, live in cities, and own pets is increasing. The makers of pet food and pet-related products are eager to market to this subculture.

Source: © Shutterstock, Inc.

subculture

A group of people within a culture who are different from the dominant culture but have something in common with one another, such as common interests, vocations or jobs, religions, ethnic backgrounds, or sexual orientations.

Social Class

A **social class** is a group of people who have the same social, economic, or educational status in society.[24] While income helps define social class, the primary variable determining social class is occupation. To *some* degree, consumers in the same social class exhibit similar purchasing behaviors. That said, have you ever been surprised to find out that someone you know who is wealthy drives a beat-up old car or wears clothes and shoes purchased at thrift stores? Or that someone who isn't wealthy owns a Mercedes or other upscale vehicle? Although some products may appeal to people in a certain social class, you can't assume people are in that class because they either own or don't own certain products or brands.

Table 3.2 shows seven classes of American consumers along with the types of car brands they might buy. When asked, people tend to say they are middle class, which is not always the case but, rather, how they view themselves. Keep in mind that the U.S. market is just a fraction of the world market. The rise of the middle classes in India, China, and Brazil are creating opportunities for many companies to successfully sustain their products. For example, China—not the United States—is now the world's largest auto market as well as the world's largest producer of automobiles, which are increasingly electric.[25]

social class

A group of people who have the same social, economic, or educational status in society.

TABLE 3.2 An Example of Social Classes and Buying Patterns

Class	Type of Car	Definition of Class
Upper-Upper Class	Rolls-Royce	People with inherited wealth and aristocratic names (the Rockefellers, Kennedys, Vanderbilts, etc.)
Lower-Upper Class	Mercedes	Professionals such as CEOs, doctors, and lawyers
Upper-Middle Class	Lexus	College graduates and managers
Middle Class	Toyota	Both white-collar and blue-collar workers
Working Class	Chevrolet	Blue-collar workers
Lower but Not the Lowest	Used vehicle	People who are working but not on welfare
Lowest Class	No vehicle*	People on welfare

*Note: Assuming a car is purchased. There are adults in all categories who do not want or need a car.

The whiskey brand Johnnie Walker has managed to expand its market share without cheapening the brand by producing a few lower-priced versions of the whiskey and putting them in bottles with different labels.

Source: © Shutterstock, Inc.

The makers of upscale brands want their customer bases to be as large as possible yet don't want to risk "cheapening" their brands. For example, some brands, such as Louis Vuitton and Gucci, have refused to sell their products on Amazon for this reason—even during the pandemic when government lockdowns forced some of the brands' stores to close. The brands are also concerned that Amazon struggles to keep imitation, or knockoff products, off its site.[26]

Some companies, such as Johnnie Walker, have managed to capture market share by introducing "lower echelon" brands without damaging their luxury brands. For example, Johnnie Walker whiskeys come in bottles with red, green, blue, black, and gold labels. The blue label is the company's best product. Each blue-label bottle has its own serial number and is sold in a silk-lined box, which also contains a certificate of the whiskey's authenticity.

Reference Groups, Opinion Leaders, and Influencers

reference groups

Groups a consumer identifies with and wants to join.

Reference groups are groups (social groups, work groups, family, or close friends) a consumer identifies with and may want to join. They influence consumers' attitudes and behaviors. If you have ever dreamed of being a professional player of basketball or another sport, you have an *aspirational reference group*. That's why Nike hires celebrities such as LeBron James to pitch the company's products. *Dissociative reference groups* are groups a consumer does not want to be associated with. Perhaps you have declined to purchase something because it seemed like an item people who aren't "cool" are purchasing.

opinion leaders

People with expertise in certain areas. Consumers respect these people and often ask their opinions before they buy goods and services.

Opinion leaders are people with expertise in certain areas. Consumers respect these people and often ask their opinions before they buy goods and services. An information technology (IT) specialist with a great deal of knowledge about computer brands is an example. These people's purchases often lie at the forefront of leading trends. The IT specialist is probably a person who has the latest and greatest tech products, and her opinion of them is likely to carry more weight with you than any sort of advertisement.

In consumer markets, **influencers** are people who aren't necessarily celebrities or experts but who have a significant amount of influence over what people purchase, often because of what they post online about products. Bloggers are an example. Companies often try to develop relationships with bloggers who are influencers to keep them aware of their products in the hopes that they will talk positively about them online. People with large numbers of subscribers on their TikToK and YouTube channels are also influencers. So, for example, to build interest in its products, a company might provide a skateboarder who has a great YouTube channel with free skateboarding products the firm hopes the person will show in upcoming videos.

influencers

People who aren't necessarily celebrities or experts but who have a great deal of influence over what people purchase, often because of what they post online about products.

Companies also directly pay influencers to promote their products on the web. Rather than paying Pinterest to post, or "pin," products on the social networking site, Tommy Hilfiger and the paint-maker Benajamin Moore found it more cost-effective to hire influencers to post their products for them. Keep in mind that to prevent consumers from being misled, the U.S. Federal Trade Commission (FTC) requires paid influencers to prominently disclose in their posts the fact that they are being compensated by the maker of the products discussed in the posts. See the following video for good advice on how not to run afoul of the FTC if you are, or want to be, an influencer.[27]

Advice for Social Media Influencers from the FTC

Do you recommend or endorse things on social media? If so, this video has tips to help influencers like you comply with the law.

View in the online reader

Marketing professionals refer to celebrities, opinion leaders, and influencers who actively promote a company's products by letting others know how much they like them as "brand ambassadors." Firms use different techniques, including tools to mine social networking sites so as to reach these people in an effort to turn them into brand ambassadors. The Followerwonk tool on Twitter is an example. Followerwonk ranks opinion leaders by the number of followers they have. Explains Valdis Krebs, who specializes in finding influencers: "Pharmaceutical firms [for example] want to identify who the key opinion leaders are. They don't want to sell a new drug to everyone. They want to sell to the sixty key oncologists."

Of course, not all opinion leaders, influencers, and celebrities (unless they are hired to do so) end up being brand ambassadors. If they don't like a firm or its products, these people can negatively impact a brand by what they say about it.

Family

Most market researchers consider a person's family to be one of the most important influences on their buying behavior. Like it or not, you are more like your parents than you think, at least in terms of your consumption patterns. Many of the things you buy and don't buy are a result of what your parents bought when you were growing up. Products such as the brand of soap and toothpaste your parents bought and used, and even the "brand" of politics they leaned toward (Democratic or Republican) are examples.

Companies are interested in which family members have the most influence over certain purchases. Children have a great deal of influence over many household purchases. IKEA has used this knowledge to design its showrooms. The children's bedrooms feature fun beds with fashion-forward comforters so children will be prompted to identify and ask for what they want.[28]

To be sure, figuring out what kids want is a science. For example, Epic, a digital reading website for kids, tracks what kids search for when they go on Epic's website. The company then uses the information to create new books. Epic's researchers have found that children prefer owls to chickens or hedgehogs and search for unicorns on the site almost twice as often as mermaids.[29]

Critics of marketing to children accuse companies of deliberately manipulating kids to nag their parents for certain products. For example, even though tickets to see an Ariana Grande concert can cost as much as a few hundred dollars, the concerts are often still sold out. However, as one writer put it, exploiting "pester power" is not always ultimately in the long-term interests of advertisers if it alienates kids' parents.[30]

In addition, different local, state, and national laws restrict how children can legally be marketed to. For example, in the United States, the Children's Online Privacy Protection Act (COPPA) requires websites that collect or use personal information about children under the age of thirteen to obtain verifiable parental consent.

Key Takeaways

- Situational influences are temporary conditions that affect how buyers behave. They include physical factors such as a store's buying locations, layout, music, lighting, and even scent. Companies try to make the physical factors in which consumers shop as favorable as possible. If they can't, they utilize other tactics such as discounts. The consumer's social situation, time factors, the reason for their purchases, and their moods also affect their buying behavior.
- Your personality describes your disposition as other people see it. Market researchers believe people buy products to enhance how they feel about themselves. Your gender also affects what you buy and how you shop. Women shop differently than men. However, there's some evidence that this is changing. Younger men and women are beginning to shop more alike. People buy different things based on their ages and life stages. A person's cognitive age is how old one "feels" oneself to be. To further understand consumers and connect with them, companies have begun looking more closely at their lifestyles (what they do, how they spend their time, what their priorities and values are, and how they see the world).
- Psychologist Abraham Maslow theorized that people have to fulfill their basic needs—like the need for food, water, and sleep—before they can begin fulfilling higher-level needs. Perception is how you interpret the world around you and make sense of it in your brain. To be sure their advertising messages get through to you, companies often resort to repetition. Learning is the process by which consumers change their behavior after they gain information about or experience with a product. Consumers' attitudes are the "mental positions" people take based on their values and beliefs. Attitudes tend to be enduring and are often difficult for companies to change.
- Culture prescribes the way in which you should live and affects the things you purchase. A subculture is a group of people within a culture who are different from the dominant culture but have something in common with one another—common interests, vocations or jobs, religions, ethnic backgrounds, sexual orientations, and so forth. To some degree, consumers in the same social class exhibit similar purchasing behaviors. Most market researchers consider a person's family to be one of the biggest determinants of buying behavior. Reference groups are groups that a consumer identifies with and wants to join. Companies often hire celebrities to endorse their products to appeal to people's reference groups. Opinion lead-

ers are people with expertise in certain areas. Consumers respect these people and often ask their opinions before they buy goods and services. Influencers are people who aren't necessarily celebrities or experts but who have a great deal of influence over what people purchase, often because of what they post online about products.

Review Questions

1. Explain what physical factors, social situations, time factors, and/or moods have affected your buying behavior for different products.
2. Explain how someone's personality differs from his or her self-concept. How does the person's ideal self-concept come into play in a consumer behavior context?
3. Describe how buying patterns and purchase decisions may vary by age, gender, and stage of life.
4. Why are companies interested in consumers' cognitive ages and lifestyle factors?
5. How does the process of perception work, and how can companies use it to their advantage in their marketing?
6. How do Maslow's hierarchy of needs and learning affect how companies market to consumers?
7. Why do people's cultures and subcultures affect what they buy?
8. How do subcultures differ from cultures? Can you belong to more than one culture or subculture?
9. How are companies trying to reach opinion leaders?

3.2 Low-Involvement Versus High-Involvement Buying Decisions, and the Customer's Decision-Making Process

Learning Objectives

1. Distinguish between low-involvement and high-involvement buying decisions.
2. Understand what the stages of the buying process are and what happens in each stage.

Sometimes you make quick purchase decisions. At other times you need to get information and be more involved in the decision process. Your *level of involvement* reflects how personally important or interested you are in consuming a product and how much information you need to make a decision.

routine response behavior

When consumers make automatic purchase decisions based on limited information or information they have gathered in the past.

Consumers often engage in **routine response behavior** when they make low-involvement decisions—that is, they make automatic purchase decisions based on limited information or information they have gathered in the past. For example, if you always order a Diet Coke at lunch, you're engaging in routine response behavior. You may not even think about other drink options at lunch because your routine is to order a Diet Coke, and you simply do it. Similarly, if you run out of Diet Coke at home, you will probably put it on your grocery list without searching for other options.

impulse buying

Purchases that occur with no planning or forethought.

Some low-involvement purchases are made with no planning or previous thought whatsoever. These buying decisions are called **impulse buying**. While you're waiting to check out at the grocery store, perhaps you see a magazine with Taylor Swift on the cover and buy it on the spot simply because you want it. You might see a roll of tape at a check-out stand and remember you need one or you might see a bag of chips and realize you're hungry or just want them. These too are items that are typically low-involvement decisions. **Low-involvement decisions** aren't necessarily products purchased on impulse, although they can be.

low-involvement decisions

Products that carry a low risk of failure or have a low price tag for a specific individual or group making the decision.

By contrast, **high-involvement decisions** create higher risks for buyers, particularly if the products fail, are complex, and/or have high price tags. A computer, car, house, and an insurance policy are examples. These items are purchased less regularly. Buyers don't engage in routine response behavior when purchasing high-involvement products. Instead, consumers engage in what's called **extended problem solving**, where they spend a lot of time comparing different aspects such as the features of the products, prices, and warranties.

high-involvement decisions

Products that carry a high price tag or high level of risk to the individual or group making the decision.

High-involvement decisions can cause buyers a great deal of anxiety if they are unsure about their purchases or if they had a difficult time deciding between two alternatives. Companies that sell high-involvement products are aware that this can be a problem. Frequently, they try to offer consumers a lot of information about their products, including why they are superior to competing brands and how they won't let the consumer down. Salespeople may be utilized to answer questions and do a lot of customer "hand-holding."

extended problem solving

Purchasing decisions in which a consumer gathers a significant amount of information before making a decision.

Keep in mind that what is a high-involvement decision for one person may not be to another. The first car a person buys is likely to be a high-involvement decision for the consumer. But for someone who has purchased many cars over the years, it may not be.

Limited problem solving falls somewhere between low-involvement (routine) and high-involvement (extended problem solving) decisions. Consumers engage in **limited problem solving** when they already have some information about a good or service but continue to search for a little more information. Suppose you need a new backpack for a hiking trip. You may be familiar with backpacks, but you are also aware that since you purchased your last one, new features and materials are available for them, such as USB charging ports and anti-theft features. So, you're going to spend some time looking at and deciding what features you want. You might do a little research online and come to a decision relatively quickly. You might consider the choices available at your favorite retail outlet, but not look at every backpack at every outlet before making a decision. Or you might rely on the advice of a person you know who's knowledgeable about backpacks or online reviews of them. In some way you shorten or limit your involvement and the decision-making process.

Allstate's "You're in Good Hands" ads are designed to convince consumers that the insurance company won't let them down.

Source: © Shutterstock, Inc.

limited problem solving

Purchasing decisions made based on consideration of some outside information.

Companies that market products such as chewing gum, which is likely to a be low-involvement purchase for many consumers, often use advertising such as commercials and coupons to reach many consumers at once. Firms such as these also try to sell products such as gum in as many locations as possible so people can just grab the products and go without much thought. In contrast, companies that sell products such as home insurance, which is typically a high-involvement purchase, may use more personal selling to answer consumers' questions.

Brand names can also be very important, regardless of the consumer's purchasing involvement. Consider a low- versus high-involvement decision—say, purchasing a tube of toothpaste versus a new car. You might routinely buy your favorite brand of toothpaste, not thinking much about the purchase (engage in routine response behavior), but not be willing to switch to another brand either. Having a brand you like saves you "search time" and eliminates the evaluation period because you know what you're getting.

When it comes to the car, you might engage in extensive problem solving but, again, only be willing to consider a certain brand or brands. For example, in the 1970s, American-made cars had such a poor reputation for quality that buyers joked that a car that's "not Jap [Japanese made] is crap." The quality of American cars is very good today, but you get the picture. If you're purchasing a high-involvement product, a good brand name is probably going to be very important to you. That's why the manufacturers of products that are typically high-involvement decisions can't become complacent about the value of their brands. Products with better brand names also generally sell for higher prices. Brand names are so important, that accountants actually put a dollar value on them and they affect what a company is worth.

FIGURE 3.2 Top 15 Companies in 2021

Top fifteen companies in terms of the value of their brand names.

Rank	Logo	Brand	Country of Origin	Sector	Brand Value ($m)	Change in Brand Value
1		Apple	United States	Technology	408,251	+26%
2	amazon	Amazon	United States	Retail	249,249	+24%
3	Microsoft	Microsoft	United States	Technology	210,191	+27%
4	Google	Google	United States	Technology	196,811	+19%
5	SAMSUNG	Samsung	South Korea	Technology	74,635	+20%
6	Coca-Cola	Coca-Cola	United States	Beverages	57,488	+1%
7		Toyota	Japan	Automotive	54,107	+5%
8		Mercedes-Benz	Germany	Automotive	50,866	+3%
9	M	Mcdonald's	United States	Restaurants	45,865	+7%
10	Disney	Disney	United States	Media	44,183	+8%
11		Nike	United States	Sporting Goods	42,538	+24%
12		BMW	Germany	Automotive	41,631	+5%
13	LOUIS VUITTON	Louis Vuitton	France	Retail	36,766	+16%
14	TESLA	Tesla	United States	Automotive	36,270	+184%
15	facebook	Facebook	United States	Media	36,248	+3%

Source: Data from Interbrand, Inc.

Stages in the Buying Process

Figure 3.3 outlines the buying stages consumers go through. At any given time, you're probably in a buying stage for a product or service. You're thinking about the different types of things you want or need to eventually buy, how you are going to find the best ones at the best price, and where and how you will buy them. Meanwhile, there are other products you have already purchased that you're evaluating. Some might be better than others. Will you discard them, and if so, how? Then what will you buy? Where does that process start?

FIGURE 3.3 Stages in the Consumer's Purchasing Process

Stage 1. Need Recognition

Recognizing a need may involve something as simple as running out of bread or milk or realizing that you must get a new backpack or a car after you graduate to commute to a job you have been offered. Marketers try to show consumers how their products and services add value and help satisfy needs and wants they didn't know they had. Movie previews are an example. How many times have you have heard about a movie and had no interest in seeing it—until you saw the preview? Afterward, you felt like you had to see it. Similarly, do you think it's a coincidence that Gatorade, Powerade, and other beverage makers locate their machines in gymnasiums so you see them after a long, tiring workout?

Stage 2. Search for Information

For products such as milk and bread, you may simply recognize the need, go to the store, and buy more. However, if you are purchasing a car for the first time or need a particular type of backpack, you may need to get information about different alternatives. Maybe you have owned several backpacks and know what you like and don't like about them. Or there might be a particular brand that you've purchased in the past that you liked and want to purchase in the future. This is a great position for the company that owns the brand to be in—something firms strive for. Why? Because it often means you will limit your search and simply buy the firm's brand again.

If what you already know about backpacks doesn't provide you with enough information, you'll probably continue to gather information from various sources. Frequently people ask their friends, family, and neighbors and individuals they have become acquainted with on social media about their experiences with products. Checking out product reviews on Amazon or a source such as *Consumer Reports* (which is considered an objective source of information about many consumer products) might also help. The same is true of cars. People prefer "independent" sources such as this when they are looking for product information. However, they also often consult non-neutral sources of information, such as advertisements, brochures, company websites, and salespeople.

Stage 3. Product Evaluation

Obviously, there are hundreds of different backpacks and cars available. It's not possible for you to examine all of them. In fact, good salespeople and marketing professionals know that providing you with too many choices can be so overwhelming that you might not buy anything at all. Consequently, buyers often use *heuristics*, or "rules of thumb," that provide them with mental shortcuts in the decision-making process. Assuming a high-priced product is well-made and immediately rejecting the cheapest backpacks you see on the shelf as a result is an example of your using heuristics.

The grocer Aldi knows that too many choices can overwhelm shoppers. So it carefully tests products and only puts the best ones in its stores. Doing so also helps keep the company's profit margins higher.

Source: © Shutterstock, Inc.

In addition to heuristics (quick rules), you are also likely to use other evaluative criteria to help you narrow down your choices. **Evaluative criteria** are certain characteristics that are important to you, such as the price of the backpack, its weight, number of compartments, whether or not it has a USB charging port, and the backpack's color. Some of these characteristics are more important than others. For example, the weight and price might be more important to you than the color—unless, say, the color is pink and you hate pink. You must decide what criteria are most important and how well different alternatives meet the criteria. Backpacks that meet your initial criteria will determine the set of brands you'll consider for purchase.

evaluative criteria

Certain characteristics of products consumers consider when they are making buying decisions.

Companies want to convince you that the evaluative criteria you are considering reflect the strengths of their products. For example, you might not have thought about the weight or durability of the backpack you want to buy. However, a backpack manufacturer such as Osprey might remind you through magazine ads, packaging information, and its website that you should pay attention to these features—features that happen to be key selling points of its backpacks. The company also has a "Packfinder" feature on its website that asks consumers questions about themselves and the features they are looking for in a backpack. Based on their answers, the site suggests different backpacks for them.

Stage 4. Product Choice and Purchase

With low-involvement purchases, consumers may go straight from recognizing a need to purchasing the product. However, for backpacks and cars, you decide which one to purchase after you have evaluated different alternatives. In addition to which backpack or which car, you are probably also making other decisions at this stage, including where and how to purchase the backpack (or car) and on what terms. Maybe the backpack was cheaper at one store than another, but the salesperson there was rude. Or maybe you decide to order online because you're too busy to travel to a store.

Will Alexa pay your bills for you in the future? Currently she can pay your utility bill and as well as the gas you pump at some Exxon and Mobil stations across the United States.

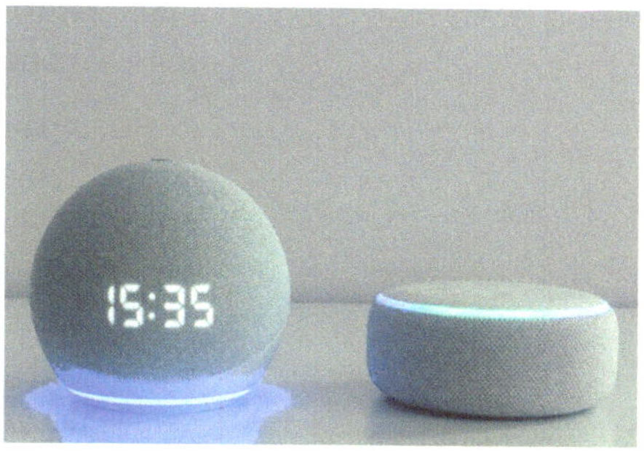

Source: © Shutterstock, Inc.

Other decisions related to the purchase, particularly those related to big-ticket items, are made at this stage as well. For example, if you're buying a high-definition television, you might look for a store that will offer you credit or a warranty. How people are able to pay for a product can have a huge impact on where and what they purchase.

To encourage large purchases, companies like Amazon and Best Buy have programs that allow consumers to pay for big-ticket items over a period of time without paying interest. The retailers do so by signing buyers up for credit cards underwritten by major banks. For low-income consumers or those on fixed budgets, this is a huge selling point. Small firms that aren't able to partner with major banks to offer customers credit cards can sign up with an online payment service such as PayPal Credit, which provides buyers with similar payment terms.

To make a mobile purchase at KFC in China, just smile—and facial recognition software processes your payment.

Source: © Shutterstock, Inc.

The ease with which busy consumers are able to pay also has an impact on what and where people buy products. Amazon, eBay, and Uber are among the companies that have attracted attention and customers by making it faster and easier to buy products using their computers or mobile devices. Google, Pinterest, and Instagram have done the same by adding buy buttons to their platforms so sellers can easily post and sell products on these websites. Companies have also enabled customers to buy products using third-party apps like Apple Pay, Google Pay, PayPal, Zelle, Venmo, and other "contactless" payment systems that don't require you to take out a card and swipe it.

Moreover, Amazon's research found that 44 percent of the consumers they surveyed are likely to use voice commands at least some part of their shopping journey in the next three years, including to make payments. Why? Because people can speak much faster and more easily than they can type or push buttons.[31]

quick response (QR) codes

Codes with black-and-white squares that contain payment and other product information that can be read with cameras and scanners.

Ideally, sellers would be able to offer their customers all of the options we've discussed. Barring that, studying the preferences of people you are selling to in a market is essential. Mobile Pay and Klarna are apps favored in Denmark. In China, where mobile payment systems are the most popular, customers prefer different payment apps, such as Alipay and WeChat Pay. Although they have raised privacy issues in the United States and other countries, facial recognition apps and software are commonly used in China to process customers' payments. **quick response (QR) codes**, which consist of black-and-white squares that contain payment and other product information that can be read with cameras and scanners, were widely used to pay for everything from street snacks to rental bikes in China, before becoming more commonplace in the United States and elsewhere. In Argentina, enabling customers to pay in installments will greatly increase your chances of making a sale. New digital currencies you have probably heard about, such as dogecoin and bitcoin, may not be far behind.

Stage 5. Postpurchase Use and Evaluation

postpurchase dissonance

Situations that occur when experiences do not match expectations and consumers rethink their decisions after purchasing products and wonder if they made the best decision.

At this point in the process you decide whether the backpack you purchased is everything it was cracked up to be. Hopefully, it is. If it's not, you're likely to suffer what's called **postpurchase dissonance**, or buyer's remorse. Typically, dissonance occurs when a product or service does not meet your expectations. You want to feel good about your purchase, but you don't. You begin to wonder whether you should have waited to get a better price, purchased something else, or gathered more information first.

Consumers are more likely to experience dissonance with products that are relatively expensive and that are purchased infrequently. If you don't feel good about what you've purchased, you might return the item and never purchase anything from that seller again. Or, worse yet, you might tell everyone you know how bad the product was.

Companies do various things to try to prevent buyer's remorse. For smaller items, they might offer a money back guarantee or they might encourage their salespeople to tell you what a great purchase you made. (If you have tried on clothes in a store, you have perhaps heard a salesperson say, "That outfit looks so great on you!") For larger items, companies might offer a warranty, along with instruction booklets, and a toll-free troubleshooting line to call, or they might have a salesperson call you to see if you need help with the product. Automobile companies may offer loaner cars when you bring your car in for service. Companies may also try to set expectations in order to satisfy customers. Service companies such as restaurants do this frequently. A hostess may tell you that your table will be ready in fifteen minutes, and then seat you in five minutes, in which case you will be much happier.

Stage 6. Disposal of the Product

There was a time when neither manufacturers nor consumers thought much about how products got disposed of, so long as people bought them. But that's changed. How products are being disposed of is becoming extremely important to consumers and society in general. Computers and batteries, which leach chemicals into landfills, are a huge problem. Plastics take between five hundred and one thousand years to decompose naturally.

The "Great Pacific Garbage Patch" is a plastic garbage island twice the size of Texas that floats between Hawaii and California.

Source: © Shutterstock, Inc.

Consumers don't want to degrade the environment if they don't have to, and companies are becoming more aware of this fact. For example, instead of buying new bottles of Windex to clean your windows all of the time, you can purchase a concentrate and add water. Many restaurants have stopped using plastic straws.

Other companies are less concerned about conservation than they are about **planned obsolescence**. Planned obsolescence is a deliberate effort by companies to make their products obsolete, or unusable, after a period of time. The goal is to improve a company's sales by reducing the amount of time between the repeat purchases consumers make of products.

planned obsolescence

A deliberate effort by companies to make their products obsolete, or unusable, after a period of time.

Making products with cheaper plastic parts that break more easily than those with more-expensive metal parts is one way to build planned obsolescence into products. Vacuum cleaners are an example. In decades past they were made largely of metal and lasted a long time. Not anymore. How many vacuum cleaners have you or your family owned over the years? Probably a lot.

Products that are deliberately disposable after one use or a short period of time are another way in which firms have managed to reduce the amount of time between purchases. Disposable lighters are an example. Do you know anyone today who owns a nondisposable lighter? Believe it or not, prior to the 1960s, scarcely anyone could have imagined using a cheap disposable lighter. There are many more disposable products today than there were in years past—including everything from bottled water and individually wrapped snacks to single-use eye drops and chopsticks.

Newer versions of software (that sometimes aren't better than older ones) are other examples. In 2017, Apple deliberately slowed down older phones. The company says it did so to prolong their aging batteries from shutting the phones down unexpectedly. "People shouldn't be forced to 'upgrade' to the newest model every time a replaceable part on their smartphone or home appliance breaks," says Mark Murray, executive director of Californians Against Waste, a group that is trying to make companies help people get their electronic devices repaired.

The Customer's Journey

We've talked about the various stages of the customer's decision. It can get interrupted, take much longer than the seller expects, or end at any time with no purchase. In recent years marketers have rethought the stages. Are they just a process people go through, or is there something more to it? Instead of a process, marketers have begun to rethink a buyer's purchase decision as a journey—that is, the *customer's journey.*

For example, why do some customers "travel" with a company for the long haul? (Apple customers are a good example of people who tend to stick with the company's products.) Why do other customers wander off to other places—and companies—midstream? What companies provide the best product "tour guides," so to speak, to keep customers coming back for more trips? Can that information be analyzed?

To answer questions such as these, companies are developing customer journey "maps" to walk a mile in their customers' shoes. The goal is to find out where the journey gets hard or breaks down for customers. A company also wants to get an idea of the emotions customers experience at each stage when they do business with it. Are they delighted? Disappointed? Or somewhere in between?

For example, if a customer switches devices, do they lose information, which creates frustration and ends the buying process? The goal of customer journey maps is to see what roadblocks consumers run into when they do business with a company and what "signs" or "maps" keep them engaged and having a great experience as they move through the sales process, and, hopefully, buy another product from the company later.[32]

Customer Journey Mapping

This video explains the basic idea behind customer journey mapping.

View in the online reader

Key Takeaways

- Consumer behavior looks at the many reasons why people buy things and later dispose of them. Consumers go through distinct buying phases when they purchase products: (1) realizing the need or wanting something, (2) searching for information about the item, (3) evaluating different products, (4) choosing a product and purchasing it, (5) using and evaluating the product after the purchase, and (6) disposing of the product.
- A consumer's level of involvement is how interested they are in buying and consuming a product. Low-involvement products are usually inexpensive and pose a low risk to the buyer if they make a mistake by purchasing them. High-involvement products carry a high risk to the buyer if they fail, are complex, or have high price tags. Limited-involvement products fall somewhere in between.
- Instead of a process, marketers have begun to rethink a buyer's purchase decision as journey—that is, the customer's journey. More companies are going so far as to develop customer "maps" to find out where the journey gets hard or breaks down for customers, and how to move them from merely being aware of a product to being a loyal customer.

Review Questions

1. How do low-involvement decisions differ from high-involvement decisions in terms of relevance, price, frequency, and the risks their buyers face? Name some products in each category that you've recently purchased.
2. What stages do people go through in the buying process for high-involvement decisions? How do the stages vary for low-involvement decisions?
3. What is postpurchase dissonance and what can companies do to reduce it?

3.3 Discussion Questions and Activities

Discussion Questions

1. Why do people in different cultures buy different products? Discuss with your class the types of vehicles you have seen in other countries. Why are they different, and how do they better meet buyers' needs in those countries? What types of cars do you think should be sold in the United States today?
2. What is your opinion of companies that gather information about your browsing patterns? What advantages and drawbacks does this pose for consumers? If you were a business owner, what kinds of information would you gather on your customers, and how would you use it?
3. Are there any areas in which you consider yourself an opinion leader or an influencer? What are they? How are companies getting information about opinion leaders?
4. What purchasing decisions have you been able to influence in your family and why? Is marketing to children a good idea? If not, what if one of your competitors were successful in doing so? Would it change your opinion?

5. Name some products that have led to postpurchase dissonance on your part. Then categorize them as high- or low-involvement products.
6. Describe the decision process for impulse purchases at the retail level. Would they be classified as high- or low-involvement purchases?
7. How do you think the manufacturers of products sold through infomercials reduce postpurchase dissonance?
8. Explain the relationship between extensive, limited, and routine decision making relative to high- and low-involvement decisions. Identify examples of extensive, limited, and routine decision making based on your personal consumption behavior.
9. Why is understanding consumer behavior so important for companies? Think of examples where you do not think companies understood their consumers.

Activities

1. Go to http://www.ospreypacks.com and click on the "Expert Advice" link. Does it make you more or less inclined to purchase an Osprey backpack?
2. Select three advertisements and describe the needs identified by Abraham Maslow that each ad addresses. Find an international version of an advertisement for one of the products. What differences do you detect in the international version of the ad?
3. Break up into groups and visit an ethnic part of your town that differs from your own ethnicity(ies). Walk around the neighborhood and its stores. What types of marketing and buying differences do you see? Write a report of your findings.
4. Using Maslow's hierarchy of needs, identify a list of popular advertising slogans that appeal to each of the five levels.
5. Identify how McDonald's targets both users (primarily children) and buyers (parents, grandparents, etc.). Provide specific examples of strategies used by the fast food marketer to target both groups. Make it a point to incorporate Happy Meals into your discussion.

3.4 Video Case Study: Coke Life

Coke Life

Using consumer psychology to understand buyer behavior.

View in the online reader

Case Study Questions

1. How did the Coca-Cola Company try to bridge the gap between people's real selves and their ideal selves with Coke Life?
2. Coke Life did not sell well and was discontinued in 2017. Can older companies reinvent themselves with newer products like Coke Life? Name a company that succeeded by doing so and one that did not.
3. In 2020, the Coca-Cola Company launched an energy drink called Coca-Cola Energy. It was designed to compete with Red Bull and Monster energy drinks, but it failed too in the United States. What factors do you think could have resulted in its failure, and what do they tell us about the behavior of consumers?

Endnotes

1. Marianne Wilson, "Blue Dot: Five Key Trends, Predictions for 2021," *Chain Store Age,* December 16, 2020, https://www.retailsensing.com/people-counting/retail-dwell-time-metric/.
2. Eben Harrell, "Neuromarketing: What You Need to Know," *Harvard Business Review,* January 23, 2019, https://hbr.org/2019/01/neuromarketing-what-you-need-to-know.
3. Danny Klein, "McDonald's Happy Meals are Still Getting Healthier," *QSR,* October, 2020, https://www.qsrmagazine.com/fast-food/mcdonalds-happy-meals-are-still-getting-healthier.
4. Scott McCartney (November 9, 2017), "How Should a Holiday Inn Smell?" *Wall Street Journal,* A12.
5. Justin Bachman (April 17, 2018), "Airports Are Using 'Smart Glass' to Make you Spend More," *Bloomberg,* https://www.bloomberg.com/news/articles/2018-04-17/airports-are-using-smart-glass-to-make-you-spend-more.
6. Mary Loxton, Robert Truskett, Brigitte Scarf, Laura Sindone, George Baldry, Yinong Zhao, 2020. "Consumer Behavior during Crises: Preliminary Research on How Coronavirus Has Manifested Consumer Panic Buying, Herd Mentality, Changing Discretionary Spending and the Role of the Media in Influencing Behavior," *Journal of Risk Financial Management,* 13 (8) 166. https://doi.org/10.3390/jrfm13080166.
7. Anna S. Matilla and Jochen Wirtz (2008), "The Role of Store Environmental Stimulation and Social Factors on Impulse Purchasing," *Journal of Services Marketing 22*(7), 562–567.
8. Jacob Hornik and Giulia Miniero (2009), "Synchrony Effects on Customers' Responses and Behaviors," *International Journal of Research in Marketing 26*(1), 34–40.
9. Charlene Y. Chen and Michel Tuan Phamm (2019), "Affect Regulation and Consumer Behavior," *Consumer Psychology Review,* https://doi.org/10.1002/arcp.1050.
10. Kenneth Kiesnoski (March 5, 2018), "Get Blasted, Go Broke," *CNBC,* https://www.cnbc.com.
11. Saabira Chaudhuri, "Companies Retool Offerings to Lure Frugal Consumers," *Wall Street Journal,* May 14, 2020, B1–2.
12. Beth Timmins, "Coronavirus: Seed Sales Soar as More of Us Become Budding Gardeners," BBC News, May 7, 2020, https://www.bbc.com/news/business-52544317.
13. George P. Moschis, Anil Mathur, and Thuckavadee Sthienrapapayut (2020), "Gerontographics and Consumer Behavior in Later life: Insights from the Life Course Paradigm," *Journal of Global Scholars of Marketing Science,* 30:1, 18-33, DOI: 10.1080/21639159.2019.1613908.
14. David Crockett, Samantha Cross, Samantha, and Steven Chen (2017), "Ethnography for Marketing and Consumer Research. Foundations and Trends," Marketing. 10. 61–151. 10.1561/1700000043; Robert Berner (May 1, 2006), "Detergent Can Be So Much More," *BusinessWeek,* 66–68.
15. Laura Ries (2009), *In the Boardroom: Why Left-Brained Management and Right-Brain Marketing Don't See Eye-to-Eye,* New York: HarperCollins.
16. Joshua Saxon, "Why Your Customer's Attention is the Scarcest Resource in 2017," American Marketing Association, https://www.ama.org.
17. Ibid.
18. Adam E. Green, Darren Mays, Emily B. Falk, Donna Vallone, Natalie Gallagher, Amanda Richardson, Kenneth P. Tercyak, David B. Abrams, and Raymond S. Niaura, "Young Adult smokers' Neural Response to Graphic Cigarette Warning Labels," *Addictive Behaviors Reports,* 2016; DOI: 10.1016/j.abrep.2016.02.001.
19. Cynthia Crossen (November 5, 2007), "For a Time in the '50s, A Huckster Fanned Fears of Ad 'Hypnosis,'" *Wall Street Journal,* eastern edition, B1.
20. James Chartrand, "Why Targeting Selective Perception Captures Immediate Attention," http://www.copyblogger.com/selective-perception.
21. "Dictionary of Marketing Terms," http://www.allbusiness.com/glossaries/marketing/4941810-1.html.
22. Henk Esselink and Lola Hernández (November 24, 2017), "The Use of Cash by Households in the Euro Area," *European Central Bank Occasional Paper Series.*
23. Luis Noe-Bustamante, Mark Hugo Lopez, and Jens Manuel Krogstad (July 7, 2020), "U.S. Hispanic Population Surpassed 60 Million in 2019, but Growth Has Leveled Off," *Pew Research Center,* http://www.pewresearch.org.
24. Princeton University, "WordNet," http://wordnetweb.princeton.edu/perl/webwn?s=social+class&sub=Search+Word-Net&o2=&o0=1&o7=&o5=&o1 =1&o6=&o4=&o3=&h=.
25. Russell Mitchell (February 05, 2018), "China Wants to Enter the U.S. Car Market, But a Rough Road Lies Ahead," *Los Angeles Times,* http://www.latimes.com.
26. Renata Geraldo, "Amazon Struggles to Lure Luxury Brands," *Wall Street Journal,* November 2, 2020, B3.
27. Joshn Constine, "FTC Votes to Review Influencer Marketing Rules and Penalties," (February 12, 2020), *TechCrunch,* https://techcrunch.com/2020/02/12/ftc-influencer-marketing-law/.
28. (2003), "Teen Market Profile," *Mediamark Research,* http://www.magazine.org/content/files/teenprofile04.pdf.
29. Ellen Gamerman, "Goodnight Ninja? Knuffle Blobfish? Children's Books Get the Algorithm Treatment," http://wsj.com, March 24, 2021.
30. Ray Waddell (June 27, 2009), "Miley Strikes Back," *Billboard,* 7–8.
31. Anna Maria Andriotis and Laura Stevens (April 7–8, 2018), "Amazon Voices Payment Strategy," *Wall Street Journal,* B12; https://pay.amazon.com/blog/embrace-voice-as-an-integral-part-of-your-commerce-strategy.
32. Paul Boag (Jan 28, 2018), "Customer Journey Mapping: Everything You Need to Know," Sailthru.com [blog], https://www.sailthru.com.

CHAPTER 4

Business Buying Behavior

In the last chapter, we talked about the buying behavior of consumers—people like you and me who buy products for our own personal use. However, many businesses don't offer their goods and services to individual consumers at all. Instead, their customers are other businesses, institutions, or government organizations. These are the business-to-business (B2B) markets we talked about in Chapter 1.

4.1 The Characteristics of Business-to-Business (B2B) Markets

Learning Objectives

1. Identify the ways in which business-to-business (B2B) markets differ from business-to-consumer (B2C) markets.
2. Explain why business buying is acutely affected by the behavior of consumers.

Business-to-business (B2B) markets differ from business-to-consumer (B2C) markets in many ways. For one, the number of products sold in business markets dwarfs the number sold in consumer markets. Suppose you buy a $1,500 computer from Dell. The sale amounts to a single transaction for you. But think of all the transactions Dell had to go through to sell you that one computer. Dell had to purchase many parts from many computer component makers. It also had to purchase equipment and facilities to assemble the computers, hire and pay employees, pay to warehouse its products, maintain its online operations and advertise, and buy insurance and accounting and financial services to keep its operations running smoothly. In other words, many purchase transactions had to happen before you could purchase your computer.

Each of those transactions needed a salesperson. Each of those companies has a marketing department. Thus, a lot more college marketing graduates go to work selling B2B products than B2C products, which is reason enough to spend some time studying the subject.

Business products can be very complex. Some need to be custom built or retrofitted for buyers. The products include everything from high-dollar construction equipment to commercial real estate and buildings, military equipment, and billion-dollar cruise liners used in the tourism industry. In some instances, the complexity is greater because what is purchased has to fit into an existing system. For example, a piece of equipment used to cut wood that is later turned into a bookcase or bed frame has to be hooked up into an existing manufacturing line.

Moreover, in B2B markets a single customer can account for a huge amount of business. If you manufacture diesel locomotives for the U.S. market, for example, almost all of your business is likely to be concentrated on perhaps a half-dozen railroad companies, such as CSX, Norfolk Southern, BNSF Railway, and Union Pacific.

Not only can business markets be concentrated in a few companies, but the buying dynamics of organizations can be complex and long. Many people within an organization can be part of the buying process and have a say in ultimately what gets purchased, how much of it, and from whom. Having different people involved makes business marketing much more complicated. And because of the quantities each business customer is capable of buying, the stakes are high. For some organizations, losing a big account can be financially devastating and winning one can be a financial bonanza.

How high are the stakes? Table 4.1 shows a recent ranking of the top five corporations in the United States in terms of the sales they generate annually. Believe it or not, these companies earn more in a year than all the businesses of some countries do. Imagine the windfall you could gain as a seller by landing an exclusive account with any one of them.

TABLE 4.1 Top Five U.S. Corporations in Terms of Their Revenues

Company	Sales (Billions of Dollars)
Walmart	559
Amazon	386
Apple	274
CVS Health	268
ExxonMobil	264

Data from *Fortune*, 2020.

Generally, the more high-dollar and complex the item being sold is, the longer it takes for the sale to be made. The sale of a new commercial jet to an airline company can take years to be completed. Purchases such as these are risky for companies. The buyers are concerned about many factors, such as the product's safety, reliability, and efficiency of the planes. The buyers also generally want the jets customized in some way. Consequently, a lot of time and effort is needed to close these deals.

Unlike many consumers, most business buyers demand that the products they buy meet strict standards. Take, for example, the Five Guys burger chain, based in Virginia. The company taste-tested eighteen different types of mayonnaise before settling on the one it uses. Would you be willing to taste eighteen different brands of mayonnaise before buying one? Probably not.

Another characteristic of B2B markets is the level of personal selling that goes on. Salespeople personally call on business customers to a far greater extent than they do consumers. Most of us have had door-to-door salespeople call on us occasionally. However, businesses often have multiple salespeople call on them in person daily. Some businesses even provide office space for their key vendors' salespeople. Table 4.2 outlines the main differences between B2C and B2B markets.

TABLE 4.2 Business-to-Consumer Markets versus Business-to-Business Markets: How They Compare

Consumer Market	Business Market
Many customers, geographically dispersed	Fewer customers, often geographically concentrated, with a small number accounting for most of a company's sales
Smaller total dollar amounts due to fewer transactions	Larger dollar amounts due to more transactions
Shorter decision cycles	Longer decision cycles
More reliance on mass marketing via advertising on TV, radio, websites, social media, and mobile phones	More reliance on personal selling
Less-rigid product standards	More-rigid product standards

The Demand for B2B Products

Even though they don't sell their products to individual consumers, B2B sellers carefully watch general economic conditions to anticipate consumer buying patterns. The firms do so because the demand for business products is based on derived demand. **Derived demand** is demand that springs from, or is derived from, a source other than the primary buyer of a product. When it comes to B2B sales, that source is consumers. If consumers aren't demanding the products produced by businesses, the firms that supply products to these businesses are in big trouble.

derived demand

Demand that springs from, or is derived from, a secondary source other than the primary buyer of the product.

Fluctuating demand is another characteristic of B2B markets. In other words, a small change in demand by consumers can have a big effect throughout the chain of businesses that supply all the goods and services that produce the product. Often a bullwhip type of effect occurs. If you have ever held a whip, you know that a slight shake of the handle will result in a big snap of the whip at its tip. Essentially, consumers are the handle, and businesses along the chain comprise the whip—hence the need to keep tabs on end consumers. They are a powerful purchasing force.

fluctuating demand

Demand that fluctuates sharply in response to a change in consumer demand.

For example, Cisco is a company that makes computer routers. If Google uses 50,000 routers and replaces 10 percent of them each year, that means Google usually buys 5,000 routers in a given year. But what happens if Google's ad sales fall by 10 percent in a given year, as do Google searches because people start using a different search engine? Then Google may need only 4,500 routers. Google's demand for servers therefore becomes zero in that year.

Suppose the following year the situation returns to normal, and Google recaptures its market share. Google now needs to replace the 5,000 routers it didn't buy a year ago plus the 500 it needs to replace this year. So in year two, Cisco's sales to Google go from zero to 10,000, or twice normal. As a result, Cisco experiences a significant bullwhip effect in terms of its sales, whereas Google's ad sales varied by only 10 percent.

Because consumers are such a powerful force, some companies try to increase their B2B sales by directly influencing consumers, even though they don't sell their products to them. Intel is a classic case. Do you really care what type of microprocessing chip gets built into your computer or phone? Intel would like you to, which is why for many years it ran "Intel Inside" commercials on TV. The commercials weren't likely to directly persuade a computer manufacturer to buy Intel's chips. But manufacturer might have been persuaded to buy them if the chips were important to consumers like you. Derived demand is also the reason why Intel required the buyers of its chips put a little "Intel Inside" sticker on each computer they made—so consumers got to know Intel and demand its products.

Intel Inside

Does this funny commercial featuring LeBron James make you want to buy a computer with an Intel chip? Intel hopes so.

View in the online reader

joint demand

When the demand for one product increases the demand for another.

B2B buyers also keep tabs on consumers to look for patterns that can create joint demand. **Joint demand** occurs when the demand for one product increases the demand for another. For example, when a new video console like the PlayStation 5 comes out, it creates demand for a whole new crop of video games.

Key Takeaway

- B2B markets differ from B2C markets in many ways. There are more transactions in B2B markets and more high-dollar transactions because business products are often costly and complex. There are also fewer buyers in B2B markets, but they spend much more than the typical consumer does and have more-rigid product standards. The demand for business products is based on derived demand. Derived demand is demand that springs from, or is derived from, a secondary source other than the primary buyer of a product. For businesses, this source is consumers. Fluctuating demand is another characteristic of B2B markets. A small change in demand by consumers can have a big effect throughout the chain of businesses that supply all the goods and services that produce it.

Review Questions

1. Why are there more transactions in B2B markets than B2C markets? Why are there fewer buyers?
2. Explain what derived demand is.
3. Why do firms experience a bullwhip effect in the demand for their products when consumers demand changes?

4.2 Types of B2B Buyers

Learning Objectives

1. Describe the major categories of business buyers.
2. Explain why finding decision makers in business markets is challenging for sellers.

Business buyers can be either not-for-profit or for-profit businesses. To help you get a better idea of the different types of business customers in B2B markets, we've put them into four basic categories: producers, resellers, governments, and institutions.

Producers

Producers are companies that purchase goods and services they transform into other products. This category includes both manufacturers and service providers. Procter & Gamble, McDonald's, Dell, Delta Airlines, and Tesla are examples. So are restaurants, your dentist, your doctor, and local tattoo parlors.

All these businesses have to buy certain products to produce the goods and services they create. For example, Tesla needs steel, lithium batteries, and hundreds of thousands of other products to produce cars. McDonald's needs beef and buns. Your dentist needs drugs such as Novocain, oral tools, and X-ray machines. Your local tattoo parlor needs special inks and needles and a bright neon sign that flashes "open" in the middle of the night.

Your local tattoo parlor is a producer.

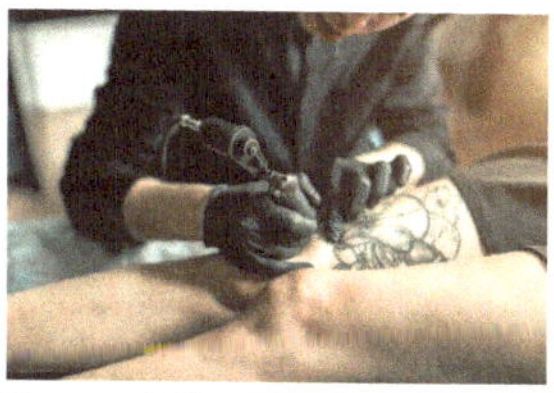

Source: © Shutterstock, Inc.

producers

Companies that purchase goods and services that they transform into other products.

Resellers

Resellers are companies that sell goods and services produced by other firms without materially changing them. This category of buyers includes wholesalers, brokers, and retailers. Walmart and Target are two big resellers. If you can get them to buy your products, you can increase your sales exponentially. Every day resellers flock to Walmart's corporate headquarters in Bentonville, Arkansas, to try to hawk their products.

Value-added resellers (VARS) are companies that buy finished products from other companies, customize them in some way, and then sell them at higher prices. That can include making modification to the products, and/or providing the buyer's personnel with training to use the product, among other things. The goal is to make the products a better "fit" for the buyer. A company in the information technology sector that buys computers and adapts them for special purposes, such as cloud-computing is an example of a VAR. So is an automobile dealer that customizes cars. By providing value-added services, VARs hope to develop better relationships with their customers and get repeat business from them.

resellers

Companies that sell goods and services produced by other firms without materially changing them.

value-added resellers (VARS)

Companies that buy finished products from other companies, customize them in some way, and then sell them at higher prices.

Governments

business-to-government (B2G) markets

Markets in which local, state, and federal governments buy products.

Can you guess who is the biggest purchaser of goods and services in the world? It is the U.S. government. It purchases everything you can imagine, from paper to tanks and weapons, buildings, toilets for NASA (the National Aeronautics and Space Administration), highway construction services, and medical and security services. State and local governments buy enormous amounts of products, too. They contract with companies that provide citizens with all kinds of services, from transportation to garbage collection. (So do foreign governments, provinces, and localities, of course.) **Business-to-government (B2G) markets**, that is, markets in which companies sell to local, state, and federal governments, represent a major selling opportunity even for smaller sellers. In fact, many government entities specify that their agencies must award a certain amount of business to small businesses, minority- and women-owned businesses, and businesses owned by veterans who are disabled. In addition, the U.S. government now requires even small businesses to pay their employees at least $15 per hour if the want to do business with the federal government.

There is no one central department or place in which all of the products purchased by governments are bought and sold. Companies that want to sell to the U.S. government should first register with the System for Award Management. They should then consult the General Services Administration (GSA) website. The GSA helps more than two hundred federal agencies buy a wide variety of products purchased routinely. The products can include office supplies, information technology services, repair services, vehicles, and many other products purchased by agencies on a regular basis. Consequently, the GSA is a good starting point. However, the GSA won't negotiate a contract for the NASA toilet or a fighter jet. It sticks to routine types of purchases.

The website for the General Services Administration (GSA) is a good starting point for companies that want to do business with the federal government. The U.S. Small Business Administration (SBA) also offers sellers a great deal of information on marketing to the government, including online courses that explain how to do it.

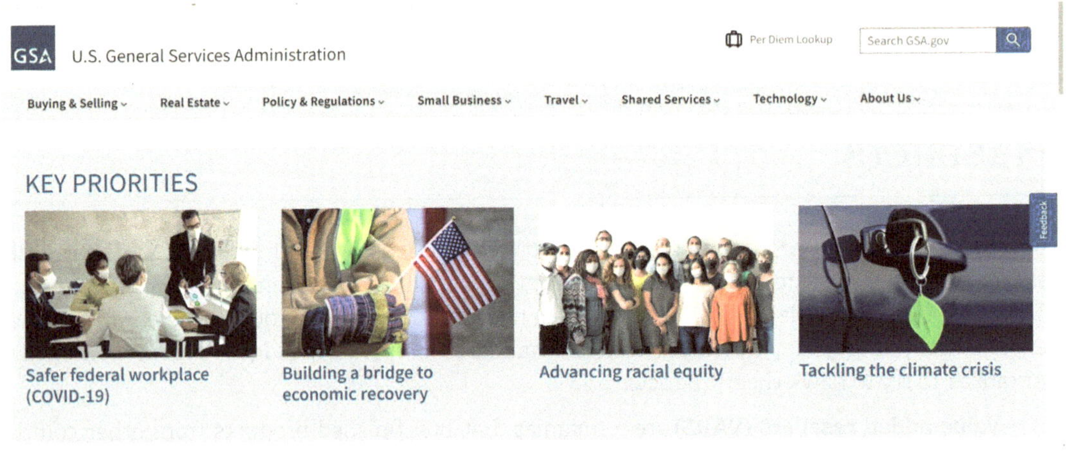

Source: www.gsa.gov

The existence of the GSA doesn't mean the agencies it works with don't have any say over what is purchased for them. The agencies themselves have a big say, so B2B sellers need to contact them and aggressively market their products to them. After all, agencies don't buy products, people do. Fortunately, every agency posts on the internet a forecast of its budget, that is, what it is planning on spending money on in the coming months. The agencies also list the contact information of the people responsible for purchasing decisions. Many federal agencies are able to purchase as much as $25,000 of products at a time by simply using a government credit card. This fact makes the agencies a good target for small businesses.

It's not unusual for each agency or department to have its own procurement policies that must be followed. Would-be sellers are often asked to submit sealed bids that contain the details of what they are willing to provide the government and at what price. But contrary to popular belief, it's not always the lowest bid that's accepted. Would the United States want to send its soldiers to war in the cheapest planes and tanks, bearing the lowest-cost armor? Probably not. Like other buyers, government buyers look for the best value.

Yet selling to the government is not always easy. The GSA has its own "red tape," as does each government division. In addition, many purchases come with additional regulations or specifications written into the legislation that funded them. Because many purchases can be rather large, decision cycles can be very long and involve large buying centers. Some businesses avoid selling to the government because the perceived hassle is too great to warrant the effort. Other businesses, though, realize that learning the ins and outs of government purchases can result in a sustainable competitive advantage.

Selling to the government can be big business. An F-35 fighter jet for the military can cost as much as $80–$100 million.

Source: © Shutterstock, Inc.

Institutions

Institutional markets include not-for-profit organizations such as the American Red Cross, churches, hospitals, charitable organizations, private colleges, civic clubs, and so on. Like government and for-profit organizations, they buy a huge quantity of products and services. Holding costs down is especially important to these organizations. The lower their costs are, the more people they can provide their services to.

institutional markets

Nonprofit organizations such as the American Red Cross, churches, hospitals, charitable organizations, private colleges, and civic clubs.

The businesses and products we have mentioned so far are broad generalizations to help you think about the various markets in which products can be sold. However, not all products a company buys are high dollar or complex. Businesses buy huge quantities of inexpensive products, too. McDonald's, for example, buys a lot of toilet paper, napkins, paper bags, employee uniforms, and so forth. Many products consumers use are also used for one or more business purposes. Mobile phones and mobile-phone services, various types of food products, and office supplies are examples. Likewise, some individuals own real estate, and so do many businesses. But very few of us own many of the other products businesses sell to one another: cranes, raw materials such as steel, fiber-optic cables, and so forth.

A smart B2B marketer will look at all of the markets we have mentioned to see if they represent potential opportunities. The Red Cross will have no use for a fighter jet. However, a company that manufactures toilet paper might be able to market it to both the Red Cross and the U.S. government. B2B opportunities abroad and online B2B markets can also be successfully pursued. We will discuss these topics later in the chapter.

Who Makes the Purchasing Decisions in Business Markets?

Figuring out who exactly in B2B markets is responsible for what gets purchased and when often requires some detective work for marketing professionals and the salespeople they work with. Think about the college textbooks you buy. Who decides which ones ultimately are purchased by the students at your school? Do publishers send you emails about certain books they want you to buy? Do you see unsolicited ads on the web or TV for different types of chemistry or marketing books you have never heard of? Generally, you do not. The reason is that even though you buy the books, the publishers know that professors ultimately decide which textbooks are going to be used in the classroom. Consequently, B2B sellers largely concentrate their selling efforts on these people.

That's not to say that to some extent the publishers don't target you. They may offer you a good deal by packaging an online study tool with your text or other sort of learning supplement online you can purchase. They might also offer your bookstore manager a discount for buying a certain number of textbooks. However, a publishing company that focused on selling its textbooks directly to you or to a bookstore manager would likely go out of business. The company knows the true revenue generators are professors.

The question is, which professors? Some professors choose their own books. Adjunct professors often don't have a choice—their books are chosen by a course coordinator or the dean or chair of the department. Still other decisions are made by groups of professors, some of whom have more say over the final decision than others. Are you getting the picture? Figuring out where to start in B2B sales can be a little bit like a scavenger hunt.

Matt Harrell, FI Navigator Corporation

Source: Photo courtesy of Tonya Harrell

Matt Harrell is a marketing expert who works for FI Navigator Corporation. FI Navigator delivers actionable digital insights on any financial institution's profits, growth, risks, and offerings.

A seasoned B2B marketer, Harrell is familiar with segmenting and targeting the right decision makers. That includes segmenting customers based on everything from a person's geography, job title, seniority and/or common challenges they face. "B2B marketers work backwards from the product we're looking to promote to identify the right mix of targeting criteria that align with our campaign objectives," says Harrell.

Key Takeaway

- Business buyers can be either not-for-profit or for-profit businesses. There are four basic categories of business buyers: producers, resellers, governments, and institutions. Producers are companies that purchase goods and services that they transform into other products. They include both manufacturers and service providers. Resellers are companies that sell goods and services produced by other firms without materially changing them. They include wholesalers, brokers, and retailers. Value-added resellers (VARS) are companies that buy finished products from other companies, customize them in some way, and then sell them at higher prices. Local, state, and national governments purchase large quantities of goods and services. Institutional markets include not-for-profit organizations such as the American Red Cross, churches, hospitals, charitable organizations, private colleges, civic clubs, and so on. Holding costs down is especially important to them because it enables them to provide their services to more people. Figuring out who exactly in B2B markets is responsible for what gets purchased and when often requires some detective work by marketing professionals and the salespeople they work with.

Review Questions

1. What sorts of products do producers buy?
2. What role do resellers and value-added resellers play in B2B markets? Why are they important to sellers?
3. How do sellers find government buyers? Institutional buyers?
4. Why is it difficult to figure out whom to call on in business markets?

4.3 Buying Centers

Learning Objectives

1. Explain what a buying center is.
2. Explain who the members of buying centers are and describe their roles.
3. Describe the duties of professional buyers.
4. Describe the personal and interpersonal dynamics that affect the decisions buying centers make.

Professional Buyers

The professors who form a committee at your school to choose textbooks are acting like a buying center. **Buying centers** are groups of people within organizations who make purchasing decisions. Large organizations often have permanent departments that consist of the people who, in a sense, shop for a living. They are professional buyers, in other words. Their titles vary. In some companies, they are simply referred to as *buyers*. In other companies, they are referred to as *purchasing agents*, *purchasing managers*, or *procurement officers*. Retailers often refer to their buyers as *merchandisers*. Most of the people who do these jobs have Bachelor of Science degrees. Some undergo additional industry training to obtain advanced purchasing certification designations.[1]

buying centers

Groups of people within organizations who make purchasing decisions.

Buyers can have a large impact on the expenses, sales, and profits of a company. The purchasing agent for the home goods retailer World Market literally comb the entire globe looking for products the company's customers want most. What happens if the products the purchasing agents pick don't sell? World Market's sales fall, and employees get fired or laid off. This doesn't happen in B2C markets. If you pick out the wrong comforter for your bed, you don't get fired. Your bedroom just looks crummy.

Consequently, professional buyers are shrewd. They have to be because their jobs depend on it. Their jobs depend on their choosing the best products at the best prices from the best vendors. Professional buyers are also well informed and less likely to buy a product on a whim than consumers. The following sidebar outlines the tasks professional buyers generally perform.

The Duties of Professional Buyers

- Considering the availability of products, the reliability of the products' vendors, and the technical support they can provide
- Studying their company's sales records and inventory levels
- Identifying suppliers and obtaining bids from them
- Negotiating prices, delivery dates, and payment terms for goods and services
- Keeping abreast of changes in the supply and demand for goods and services their firms need
- Staying informed of the latest trends so as to anticipate consumer buying patterns
- Determining the media (social media, TV, the internet, newspapers, and so forth) in which to buy ads
- Tracking advertisements and other media to check competitors' sales activities

Increasingly, purchasing managers have become responsible for buying not only products but also functions their firms want to outsource. The functions aren't limited to manufacturing. They also include product innovation and design services, customer service and order fulfillment services, and information technology and networking services, to name a few. Purchasing agents responsible for finding offshore providers of goods and services often take trips abroad to inspect the facilities of providers to get a better sense of their capabilities.

Other Players

Purchasing agents don't make all the buying decisions in their companies, though. As we explained, other people in the organization often have a say, as well they should. Purchasing agents frequently need their feedback and help to buy the best products and choose the best vendors. The people who provide their firms' buyers with input generally fall into one or more of the following groups.

Initiators

Initiators are the people within an organization who first see the need for a product. But they don't stop there; whether they have the ability to make the final decision about what to buy or not, they get the process going. Sometimes they initiate a purchase by simply notifying their firm's purchasing agents about what is needed; at other times initiators have to lobby the executives within their firms to agree to purchase the items they think their firms need. The executives, such as a firm's CEO, are also often initiators because they choose new business paths for their firms to pursue. Of course, doing so often requires purchasing new and different types of products than a company did in the past.

initiators

People within the organization who first see the need for a product and, depending on their ability to make the final decision, either notify the purchasing agents of what is needed or lobby executives to consider making a change.

Users

Users are the people and groups within the organization who actually use the product. Frequently, one or more users serve as initiators in an effort to improve what a firm produces or how it is produced. Consequently, they are responsible for implementing what is purchased. Users often have certain specifications in mind for products and how they want them to perform. An example of a user might be a professor at your school who wants to use a new online textbook and integrate it into her online class.

users

The people and groups within the organization that actually use the product.

Influencers

Influencers in B2B markets are people in the firm who may or may not use the product but have experience or expertise that can help improve the buying decision. For example, an engineer may prefer a certain vendor's product platform and try to persuade others in her organization that it is the best choice.

influencers

People who may or may not use the product but actively participate in the purchasing process in order to secure a decision they consider favorable.

Gatekeepers

If you want to sell a product to a large company like Walmart, you can't just walk into its corporate headquarters and demand to see a purchasing agent. You will first have to get past a number of **gatekeepers**, or people who will decide if and when you get access to members of the buying center. These are people such as buying assistants, personal assistants, and other individuals who have some say about which sellers are able to get a foot in the door.

Gatekeepers often need to be courted as hard as prospective buyers do. They generally have a lot of information about what's going on behind the scenes at a business and have a certain amount of informal power. If they like you, you're in a good position as a seller. If they don't, your job is going to be *much* harder. In the case of textbook sales, the gatekeepers are often faculty department managers. They know in advance which instructors will be teaching which courses and the types of books they will need. It is not uncommon for faculty department managers to screen textbook sales representatives trying to call on faculty members.

Warning: Do not be rude to or otherwise anger the department managers at your college. This is good advice for salespeople and students as well as faculty members.

Source: © Shutterstock, Inc.

gatekeepers

People who decide if and when a salesperson gets access to members of the buying center.

Deciders

The **decider** is the person who makes the final purchasing decision. The decider might or might not be the purchasing manager. Purchasing managers are generally solely responsible for deciding on routine purchases and small purchases. However, the decision to purchase a large, expensive product that will have a major impact on a company is likely to be made by or with the help of other people in the organization and perhaps even the CEO. The decision may be made by a single decider, or there may be a few deciders who reach a consensus. Deciders also usually utilize the input of all of the other participants: the users, influencers, and so forth. Sellers, of course, pay special attention to what deciders want. "Who makes the buying decision?" is a key question B2B sales and marketing personnel are trained to quickly ask potential customers.

decider

The person who makes the final purchasing decision.

The Interpersonal and Personal Dynamics of B2B Marketing

We made it a point earlier in our discussion to explain how rational and calculating business buyers are. So would it surprise you to learn that sometimes the dynamics that surround B2B marketing don't lead to the best purchasing decisions? Interpersonal factors among the people making a buying decision often have an impact on the products chosen, good or bad. (You can think of this phenomenon as "office politics.") For example, one person in a buying unit might wield a lot of power and greatly influence the purchasing decision. However, other people in the unit might resent the power the person wields and insist on a different offering, even if doesn't best meet the organization's needs. Savvy B2B marketers are aware of these dynamics and try their best to influence the outcome.

Personal factors also play a part. B2B buyers are overwhelmed with choices, features, benefits, information, data, and metrics. They often have to interview dozens of potential vendors and ask them hundreds of questions. No matter how disciplined they are when it comes to their buying procedures, they will often find a way to simplify their decision making, either consciously or subconsciously. For example, a buyer deciding upon multiple vendors running neck and neck in competition with one another might decide to simply choose the vendor whose sales representative she likes the most.

Factors such as these can be difficult for a company to control. However, branding—how successful a company is at marketing its brands—*is* a factor under a company's control, says Kevin Randall, who leads the global brand strategy at UL, the world's safety science leader. Sellers can use their brands to their advantage to help business buyers come to the conclusion that their products are the best choice. IBM has has a strong brand name when it comes to business products. The company's reputation was so solid that for years the catchphrase "Nobody ever got fired for buying IBM" was often repeated among purchasing agents—and by IBM salespeople of course![2]

In short, B2B marketing is very strategic. Selling firms try to gather as much information about their customers as they can and use that information to their advantage. As an analogy, imagine if you were interested in asking out someone you had seen on campus. Sure, you could simply try to show up at a party or somewhere on campus hoping to meet the person. But if you were thinking strategically, you might try to find out everything you could about the person, what they like to do and so forth, and then try to arrange a meeting. That way, when you did meet the person, you would be better able to strike up a conversation and develop a relationship with them. B2B selling is similarly strategic. Little is left to chance.

Key Takeaway

- Buying centers are groups of people within organizations who make purchasing decisions. The buying centers of large organizations employ professional buyers who, in a sense, shop for a living. They don't make all the buying decisions in their companies, though. The other people who provide input are users, or the people and groups within the organization that actually use the product; influencers, or people who may or may not use the product but have experience or expertise that can help improve the buying decision; gatekeepers, or people who will decide if and when a seller gets access to members of the buying center; and deciders, or the people who make the final purchasing decision. Interpersonal dynamics between the people in a buying center will affect the choices the center makes. Personal factors, such as how likable a seller is, play a part because buyers are often overwhelmed with information and will find ways to simplify their decision making.

Review Questions

1. Which people do you think have the most influence on the decisions a buying center makes? Why?
2. Describe the duties of professional buyers. What aspects of their jobs seem attractive? Which aspects seem unattractive to you?
3. How do personal and interpersonal dynamics affect the decisions buying centers make?

4.4 Stages in the B2B Buying Process and B2B Buying Situations

Learning Objectives

1. Outline the stages in the B2B buying process.
2. Explain the scorecard process of evaluating proposals.
3. Describe the different types of B2B buying situations and how they affect sellers.

Stages in the B2B Buying Process

Next, let's look at the stages in the B2B buying process. They are similar to the stages in the consumer's buying process.

1. **A need is recognized.** Someone recognizes that the organization has a need that can be solved by purchasing a good or service. Users often drive this stage, although others can serve the role of initiator. In the case of a digital textbook, the initiator could be, for example, the professor assigned to teach a department's online course. However, it could be the dean or chairman of the department in which the course is taught who is the initiator.
2. **The need is described and quantified.** Next, the buying center, or group of people brought together to help make the buying decision, work to put some parameters around what needs to be purchased. In other words, they describe what they believe is needed, the features it should have, how much of it is needed, where, and so on. For more technical or complex products the buyer will define the product's technical specifications. Will an off-the-shelf product do, or must it be customized?

Users and influencers come into play here. In the case of the e-book, the professor who teaches the online course, the person's teaching assistants, and the college's information technology staff would try to describe the type of book best suited for the course. Should the book be online, as this book is? Should it be downloadable? Maybe it should be compatible with Amazon's Kindle or Barnes and Noble's Nook. Figure 4.1 shows the specifications developed for a janitorial services purchase by the state of Kentucky.

FIGURE 4.1 An Example of Product Specifications Developed for a B2B Purchase

Who: Division of Building Services

What: Janitorial Services for State Office Building at High and Mero Streets, Frankfort, Kentucky

Background:

Past experience with various contractors indicates that not all vendors are prepared to handle buildings the size of the State Office Building. Building Services indicated that staff and materials supported by a quality review program have been the common elements of the more successful vendors.

- Gross area: 384,586 sq. ft
- Total area to be cleaned: 322,585 sq. ft
- Restroom areas: 7,801 sq. ft
- Carpeted areas: 126,304 sq. ft
- Basement areas: 22,734 sq. ft
- Computer areas: 1,104 sq. ft
- Stairways: 4 sets
- Passenger elevators: 6
- Freight elevators: 1

Specifications:

- Daily cleaning for waste baskets, ashtrays, trash can liners, glass partitions, floor (sweep, mop, and buff), carpets (vacuum), and restrooms
- All cleaning conducted after hours
- Sign-in sheets and identification on badges for contractor's employees
- Current insurance

DIVISION OF PURCHASES

3. **Potential suppliers are searched for.** At this stage, the people involved in the buying process seek out information about the products they are looking for and the vendors that can supply them. Most buyers look online first to find vendors and products, then attend industry trade shows and conventions, and call or email the suppliers with whom they have relationships. The buyers might also consult trade publications and the blogs of industry experts, and perhaps attend webinars or tune into podcasts or watch videos created by vendors or visit their facilities.

Purchasing agents often play a key role when it comes to deciding which vendors, are the most qualified. Are they reliable and financially stable? Will they be around in the future? Do they need to be located near the organization, or can they be in another region of the country or in another country? The vendors that don't make the cut are then quickly eliminated from the running.

request for proposal (RFP)
An invitation to submit a bid to supply the good or service.

4. **Qualified suppliers are asked to complete responses to requests for proposals (RFPs).** Each vendor that makes the cut is sent a **request for proposal (RFP)**, which is an invitation to submit a bid to supply the good or service. An RFP outlines what the vendor is able to offer in terms of its product—its quality, price, financing, delivery, after-sales service, whether it can be customized or returned, and even the product's disposal, in some cases. Good sales and marketing professionals do more than just provide basic information to potential buyers in RFPs. They focus on the buyer's problems and how to adapt their offers to solve those problems.

Oftentimes the vendors formally present their products to the people involved in the buying decision. If the good is a physical product, the vendors generally provide the purchaser with samples, which are then inspected and sometimes tested. They might also ask satisfied customers to make testimonials or initiate a discussion with the buyer to help the buyer get comfortable with the product and offer advice on how best to use it.

However, after the COVID-19 pandemic struck, in-person visits by B2B salespeople were sharply curtailed. This created a massive shift to virtual events and trade shows, which required B2B marketers to alter their tactics sharply. Marketers scrambled to line up online attendees, keynote speeches, live Webinars, and virtual Q&A and networking sessions, among other things.

How to Create a Virtual Trade Show

What do you need to do to set up a virtual trade show? This video will give you an idea about the basic tasks.

View in the online reader

5. **The proposals are evaluated and supplier(s) selected.** During this stage, the RFPs are reviewed and the vendor or vendors selected. RFPs are best evaluated if the members agree on the criteria being evaluated and the importance of each. Different organizations will weigh different parts of a proposal differently, depending on their goals and the products they purchase. The price might be very important to some sellers, such as discount and dollar stores. Other organizations might be more focused on top-of-the-line goods and the service a seller provides. Still other factors include the availability of products and the reliability with which vendors can supply them. Reliability of supply is extremely important. Why? Because delays in the supply chain can shut down a company's production of goods and services and cost the firm its customers and reputation.

For high-priced, complex products, after-sales service is likely to be important. A fast food restaurant might not care too much about the after-sales service for the paper napkins it buys—just that they are inexpensive and readily available. However, if the restaurant purchases a new drive-through ordering system, it wants to be assured that the seller will be available to repair the system if it breaks down and probably train its personnel to use it.

A scorecard approach can help a company rate the RFPs. Table 4.3 is a simple example of a scorecard completed by one member of a buying team. The scorecards completed by all the members of the buying team can then be tabulated to help determine the vendor with the highest rating.

TABLE 4.3 A Scorecard Used to Evaluate RFPs

Reviewer: Jose Martinez	Vendor A			Vendor B		Vendor C	
Criteria	**Weight**	**Score (scale of 1–3)**	**Points (score x weight)**	**Score (scale of 1–3)**	**Points (score x weight)**	**Score (scale of 1–3)**	**Points (score x weight)**
Product Performance	3	1	3	3	9	2	6
Product Durability	3	3	9	2	6	3	9
Price	3	3	9	2	6	2	6
On-Time Delivery	3	3	9	2	6	2	6
Customer Service	3	2	6	2	6	2	6
Returns Policy	2	2	6	2	6	2	6
SCORE			42		39		39

Sometimes organizations select a single supplier to provide the good or service. This can help streamline a company's paperwork and other buying processes. With a single supplier, instead of negotiating two contracts and submitting two purchase orders to buy a particular offering, the company only has to do one of each. Plus, the more the company buys from one vendor, the bigger the volume discount it gets.

However, single sourcing can be risky because it leaves a firm at the mercy of a sole supplier. What if the supplier doesn't deliver the goods, goes out of business, or increases its prices sharply? Many firms prefer to do business with more than one supplier to avoid problems such as these. Doing business with multiple suppliers also keeps them on their toes. If suppliers know their customers can easily switch their business over to another supplier, they are likely to compete harder to keep the business.

6. **An order routine is established.** This is the stage in which the actual order is put together. The order includes the agreed-upon price, payment terms, quantities, expected time of delivery, return policies, warranties, and any other terms of negotiation. The order can be made on paper, online, or sent electronically directly from the buyer's computer system to the seller's. It can also be a one-time order or consist of multiple orders that are made periodically as the company needs a good or service. Some buyers order products continuously by having their vendors electronically monitor their inventories for them and ship replacement items as the buyers need them. (We'll talk more about inventory management in Chapter 9.)
7. **A postpurchase evaluation is conducted and the feedback provided to the vendor.** Just as consumers go through an evaluation period after they purchase goods and services, so do businesses. The buying unit might survey users of the product to see how satisfied they were with it. Cessna Aircraft Company, a small U.S. airplane maker, routinely surveys the users of the products it buys so they can voice their opinions on a supplier's performance.

Some buyers establish on-time performance, quality, customer satisfaction, and other measures for their vendors to meet, and provide those vendors with the information regularly via what are called *supplier scorecards.* A scorecard contains trend reports that show if a supplier's performance is improving, remaining the same, or worsening.[3] (The process is similar to a performance evaluation you might receive as an employee.) The grocery chain Food Lion shares a wide variety of daily retail data and performance calculations with its suppliers in exchange for their commitment to closely collaborate with the grocery store chain.

Keep in mind that a supplier with a poor performance record might not be entirely to blame. The purchasing company might play a role, too. For example, if the U.S. Postal Service contracts with FedEx to help deliver its holiday packages on time, but a large number of the packages are delivered late, FedEx may or may not be to blame. Perhaps a large number of loads the U.S. Postal Service delivered to FedEx were late, weather played a role, or shipping volumes were unusually high. Companies need to collaborate with their suppliers to look for ways to improve their joint performance. Some companies hold annual symposiums with their suppliers to facilitate cooperation among them and to honor their best suppliers.[4]

Types of B2B Buying Situations

To some extent, the stages an organization goes through and the number of people involved depend on the buying situation. Is this the first time the firm has purchased the product or the fiftieth? If it's the fiftieth time, the buyer is likely to skip the search and other phases and simply make a purchase. A **straight rebuy** is a situation in which a purchaser buys the same product in the same quantities from the same vendor. Nothing changes, in other words. Postpurchase evaluations are often skipped, unless the buyer notices an unexpected change in the offering, such as a deterioration of its quality or delivery time.

straight rebuy

When a purchaser buys the same product in the same quantities from the same vendor.

Sellers like straight rebuys because the buyer doesn't consider any alternative products or search for new suppliers. The result is a steady, reliable stream of revenue for the seller. Consequently, the seller doesn't have to spend a lot of time on the account and can concentrate on capturing other business opportunities. Nonetheless, the seller cannot ignore the account. The seller still has to provide the buyer with topnotch, reliable service or the straight-rebuy situation could be jeopardized.

If an account is especially large and important, the seller might go so far as to station personnel at the customer's place of business to be sure the customer is happy and the straight-rebuy situation continues. IBM and the management consulting firm Accenture station employees all around the world at their customers' offices and facilities.

By contrast, a **new-buy** selling situation occurs when a firm purchases a product for the first time. Generally speaking, with a new buy all the buying stages we described in the last section occur. New buys are the most time-consuming for both the purchasing firm and the firms selling to them. If the product is complex, many vendors and products will be considered, and many RFPs will be solicited.

new-buy

When a firm purchases a product for the first time.

New-to-an-organization buying situations rarely occur. What is more likely is that a purchase is new to the people involved. For example, a school district owns buildings. But when a new high school needs to be built, there may not be anyone in management who has experience building a new school. That purchase situation is a new buy for those involved.

A **modified rebuy** occurs when a company wants to buy the same type of product it has in the past but make some modifications to it. Maybe the buyer wants different quantities, packaging, or delivery, or the product customized slightly differently. For example, your instructor might have initially adopted this textbook "as is" from its publisher, FlatWorld, but then decided to customize it later with additional questions, problems, or content that they created or that was available from FlatWorld.

modified rebuy

When a company wants to buy the same type of product it has in the past but make some modifications to it.

A modified rebuy doesn't necessarily have to be made with the same seller, however. Your instructor may have taught this course before using a different publisher's book. The high cost of the textbook, the inability of your instructor to customize it, and other factors may have led to the person's dissatisfaction. In this case, she might have visited with some other textbook suppliers to see what they have to offer.

Some buyers routinely solicit bids from other sellers when they want to modify their purchases in order to get sellers to compete for their business. Likewise, savvy sellers look for ways to turn straight rebuys into modified buys so they can get a shot at the business. They do so by regularly visiting with customers and seeing if they have unmet needs or problems a modified product might solve.

Key Takeaway

- The stages in the B2B buying process are as follows: Someone recognizes that the organization has a need that can be solved by purchasing a good or service. The need is described and quantified. Qualified suppliers are searched for, and each qualified supplier is sent a request for proposal (RFP), which is an invitation to submit a bid to supply the good or service. The proposals suppliers submit are evaluated, one or more supplier(s) selected, and an order routine with each is established. A postpurchase evaluation is later conducted and the feedback provided to the suppliers. The buying stages an organization goes through often depend on the buying situation—whether it's a straight rebuy, new buy, or modified rebuy.

Review Questions

1. What buying stages do buying centers typically go through?
2. Why should business buyers collaborate with the companies they buy products from?
3. Explain how a straight rebuy, new buy, and modified rebuy differ from one another.

4.5 B2B E-Commerce and Social Media Marketing

Learning Objectives

1. Explain e-commerce's effect on buying firms, the companies they do business with, where they are located, and the prices they charge.
2. Outline the different types of e-commerce sites and what each type of site is used for.
3. Describe how B2B firms use social media, and explain what content marketing is.

B2B E-Commerce

As you will learn in the next section, B2B firms often locate near one another. But not all B2B buyers and sellers are cozying up to one another location-wise today. Part of the reason why is e-commerce. **E-commerce** consists of transactions conducted electronically rather than face-to-face. The transactions can be conducted between two computers directly connected to one another—say, the computer of a businesses and the computer of its supplier—via phone, or over the internet, or using email.

e-commerce

Transactions conducted electronically rather than face-to-face.

Companies have developed sophisticated e-commerce systems that allow their customers to do many things for themselves electronically without having to ever contact a seller's employees directly. For example, does your business want to ship your products cheaply across the country via rail? You can sign up online for an account with a railroad like Union Pacific (UP), reserve some railcars on UP's site, and choose the route you want them to travel. Later, after you ship the goods, you can check your account balance on the website and track the railcars online, like when packages are shipped with FedEx and UPS.

That said, B2B sales can often be very complex. A survey conducted by the research firm Gartner found that more than three out of four people said their latest B2B purchase was extremely complicated.[5] But according to Gartner, buyers spend only 17 percent of their time actually meeting face-to-face with sellers. This underscores the importance of making the e-commerce "journey" as easy for B2B customers as it is for B2C customers.[6]

Types of B2B Websites

FIGURE 4.2 An Example of a Sell-Side B2B Website

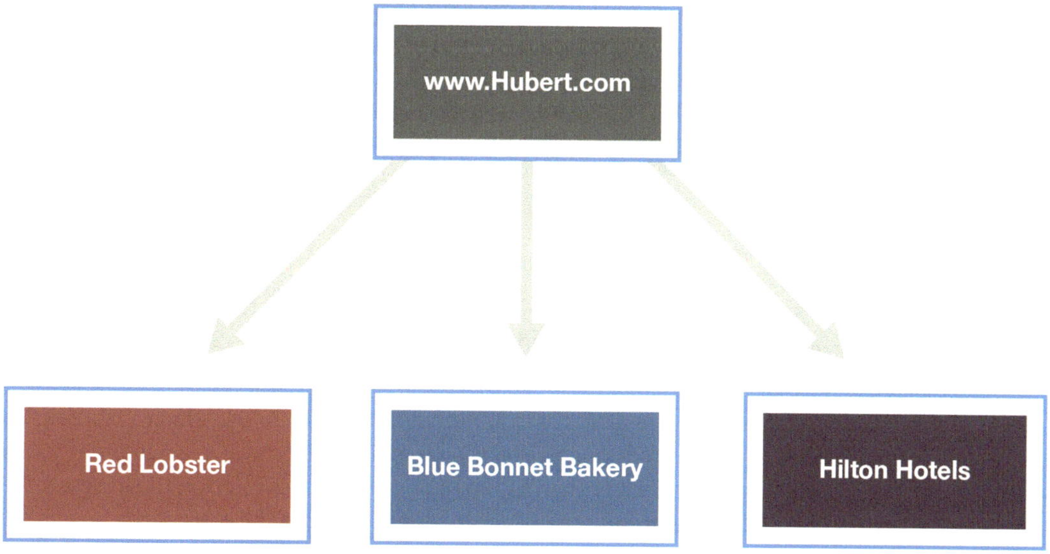

sell-side site

A website in which a single seller sells products to many different buyers.

buy-side site

A site in which a business buys products from multiple sellers that go there to do business with the firm.

B2B exchanges

E-commerce websites where multiple buyers and sellers go to find and do business with one another.

A **sell-side site** is a site in which a single seller sells products to many different buyers. Figure 4.2 shows the direction of the sale of goods and services sold on a sell-side site, such as the Hubert Company has. But there are buy-side e-commerce sites as well. A **buy-side site** is a site in which a business buys products from multiple sellers that go there to do business with the firm. Some government agencies have buy-side sites.

B2B exchanges are e-commerce sites where multiple buyers and sellers go to find and do business with one another. You can think of the exchanges as being somewhat like Craigslist but composed solely of business buyers and sellers. B2B exchanges make money by charging buyers and sellers a fee when they conduct transactions with one another. One of the most successful and largest exchanges is Alibaba.com, a trading platform for small and medium manufacturers to sell their products.[7] ChemNet.com is a global exchange where companies go to buy and sell chemicals of all kinds. The homepage for ChemNet is shown in Figure 4.3. (Ammonium, sodium, or potassium, anyone?)

FIGURE 4.3 Global Exchanges

Need chemicals? You can find them on the B2B exchange website ChemNet.

Source: www.chemnet.com

B2B auctions

Web-based auctions that occur between businesses.

reverse auction

When the buyer lists what they want to buy and also states how much they are willing to pay. The reverse auction is finished when at least one firm is willing to accept the buyer's price.

B2B auctions are web-based auctions that occur between businesses. The auctions can be either sell-side or buy-side. An example of a sell-side auction is a B2B auction that occurs on eBay or a site like Asset-sales.com, where surplus industrial equipment is sold. Sell-side auctions are sometimes referred to as forward auctions.

Buy-side auctions, by contrast, reverse the traditional auction formula, which is to help the seller get the highest price for the product. Instead, the buyer initiates the auction in order to find the cheapest supplier of a product. Sellers then bid against one another, offering the lowest prices they can for their products, in order to get the buyer's business. Because the roles of the buyers and sellers are reversed in buy-side auctions, they are often referred to as **reverse auctions**.

Not all companies use an intermediary like eBay or Asset-sales.com to conduct their auctions, though. Some companies conduct their own auctions on their websites so they don't have to pay a fee to an intermediary. For example, General Motors auctions off reconditioned vehicles to auto dealers on its own website.

Pricing in B2B E-Commerce Markets

B2B customers can easily shop around online, watch online product demonstrations, and read reviews and blogs about them from industry experts and other people. That's what buyers generally do before they get on the phone or personally meet with sellers. It's also easy for buyers to compare prices online. The cheapest price often attracts the most attention.

The result is that B2B sellers (and B2C sellers) can find their ability to raise prices is limited. The problem is more acute when products are very similar to one another (commodities) and B2B auctions and exchanges are utilized. If you are a buyer of chemicals looking for a supplier on ChemNet, do you want to pay more for one brand of a chemical that has the same molecular formula as every other brand? Maybe not.

However, if you believe you can get better service from one company than from another, you might pay more. "Everything has become much more of a commodity, meaning that it's basically more and more about price," says Bart Kohler, the former president of Hubert, a restaurant supply company that does a robust amount of e-commerce in the United States and around the globe. Kohler says his challenge today in his new role as a B2B consultant is to constantly find new ways to try to create value for Hubert's and his other clients' customers. When he is able to find a new way to create value for buyers than other companies can, the decision becomes less about price, and his clients can compete more effectively.

To avoid online price wars, some companies refuse to sell their products directly on the internet or put prices on them. Snapper products are an example. Go to Snapper.com, and you will find a lot of information about Snapper mowers and snowblowers online and dealers where you can buy them. But you won't see any prices listed. Nor can you buy a product directly from the website.

B2B Social Media Marketing

Most companies have figured out ways to use social networks to sell business products, reach and maintain relationships with their current customers, foster new ones, and amplify the word-of-mouth about their offerings. However, like other firms, B2B companies still face a continual learning curve in terms of figuring out how to use social networks to drive and close business because different social networks are constantly emerging and others are waning in popularity. What should you post, and where?

The process may be easier than you might think. The first step is to do what all great salespeople do: Listen to one's customers. What new trends are they interested in? How can your company help them do their jobs better, grow their businesses, and be successful? Keep in mind that the interaction occurring between individuals on social networks is basically a big online conversation that's generally not centered around hawking products. Just as you wouldn't have much luck breaking into conversation with a group of people by immediately talking about yourself, you won't get much traction by immediately talking about how great your company and products are on social networks. In other words, remember that when you are interacting with people on a social network, that's it's not about you. It's about them.

content marketing

A strategic marketing approach focused on creating and distributing valuable, relevant, and consistent content to attract and retain a clearly-defined audience—and, ultimately, to drive profitable customer action.

artificial intelligence (AI)

The ability of machines and computers to do things commonly associated with intelligent beings.

Another way companies are engaging buyers online and elsewhere without beating them over the heads with sales messages is with content marketing. **Content marketing** is a strategic marketing approach focused on creating and distributing valuable, relevant, and consistent content to attract and retain a clearly defined audience—and, ultimately, to drive profitable customer action.[8] Content marketing lends itself perfectly to B2B marketing on social networks. Why? Because businesspeople online are not only looking to network and socialize with one another; they are looking for valuable information and experts who can help them get a leg up on the competition.

To get an idea of how content marketing works, consider **artificial intelligence (AI)**, which is the ability of machines and computers to do things commonly associated with intelligent beings, such as the ability to reason, discover meaning, generalize, and learn from past experiences. Virtual assistants such as Siri for iPhones and Alexa, an Amazon product, are examples. Many businesses large and small want to better understand how to utilize AI and leverage it to their advantage.

An example of B2B seller that engages in content marketing is IBM. IBM's "Journey to AI Blog" features case studies, podcasts, animations, and clients' stories about how AI is helping them—all of which can be easily shared via social media. This is helping IBM position itself as a a go-to source not only for information about AI but other product solutions for business buyers. (No hard-sell tactics required.)

Social Network Choices

Finding out *what* your customers want to hear about isn't enough to drive a social media campaign. You also have to figure out *where* they want to hear it. This can be done by having online or offline conversations with your customers about what social networks they use and where they go on the web to find information.

Surveys show that LinkedIn is the social network most B2B companies utilize. Unlike networks such as Facebook, Instagram, and others where people go largely to socialize casually with one another and entertain themselves, LinkedIn was initially designed to facilitate communication among businesspeople. Consequently, it's easier to break into the conversation and target specific buyers by joining certain LinkedIn groups—such as groups for CEOs, technical and salespeople, or whomever you are trying to do business with.

LinkedIn also allows companies to run paid marketing campaigns that are even more highly targeted. The bank HSBC used a content-marketing campaign on LinkedIn designed to provide companies with information about to how to do business internationally. Spokespeople for HSBC say that the effort has gained it thousands of followers and business customers.

Other social networks are increasingly tweaking their offerings to help B2B marketers target customers with products that are comparable to those offered by LinkedIn—Workplace by Facebook and Twitter for Business are examples. Companies of all types large and small use Twitter to point B2B customers to information they might be interested in, including blog posts, announcements, industry-wide news and statistics, and information about upcoming events such as webinars, seminars, and trade shows.

YouTube is becoming more widely used by B2B companies, including manufacturing companies, to explain their products, offer business buyers information about how to use them, and just plain develop buzz about them. Volvo doesn't make its industrial trucks for the consumer market. Nonetheless, Volvo generated a lot of buzz and views by making a series of stunt videos it put on YouTube featuring the trucks. One of them shows the action star Jean-Claude Van Damme gradually doing the splits between two Volvo semi-trucks as they drive backward. The video has been viewed tens of million of times.

Volvo Generates Buzz

Volvo's video featuring Jean-Claude Van Damme went viral on YouTube.

View in the online reader

Parody Videos

The Jean-Claude Van Damme video also spawned a lot of funny parody videos like this one on YouTube.

View in the online reader

Ultimately, what social media sites and combinations of them a business will use to market its products to other businesses will vary depending on the type of product being sold and which social networks tend to work better than others. All of the networks, as well as independent firms and websites, provide users with metrics to monitor a site's traffic, "likes," number of retweets, and so forth. Tweriod is a product that can be used to determine the best time to send tweets and how many of them to send. Hootsuite is a tool people and firms can use to monitor the metrics for all of their social media campaigns at a glance.

By examining the data, a manufacturer might find YouTube ideal for presenting technical information, and Instagram a good place for posting pictures of its employees to give people a sense of the firm's corporate culture. In contrast, a fashion merchandiser might find that Instagram, which is photo-oriented, is superior to Twitter. We will talk more about how companies measure the results of their social media efforts later in the book when we talk about social media marketing in B2C markets.

Key Takeaway

- E-commerce, or commerce conducted electronically such as over the internet, makes locating near buyers less important for business-to-business sellers and enables them to sell their products around the world. However, e-commerce also leads to more competition and makes it difficult for sellers to raise their prices. Many companies have sophisticated e-commerce systems, including sell-side and buy-side websites, exchanges, and B2B auction sites. Most major B2B companies have figured out ways to use social networks to market their products. Content marketing is usually a part of the strategy. However, like other firms, B2B companies still face a learning curve in terms of figuring out how to use social networks. Ultimately the combinations will vary depending on the type of product being sold and which social networks work better than others for various purposes.

Review Questions

1. How do B2B exchange sites differ from B2B auction sites?
2. How can firms that sell their products on the internet prevent their prices from being driven down by competitors?
3. What type of content marketing might not take place on the internet?
4. Think about a business you or one of your have friends have considered starting. Which social network do you think would be best for promoting the business? Explain your answer.

4.6 International B2B Markets and Ethics in B2B Markets

Learning Objectives

1. Describe the reasons why firms in the same industries are often located in the same geographic areas.
2. Explain how the ethical dilemmas B2B marketers face differ from the ethical dilemmas B2C marketers face.
3. Outline the measures companies take to encourage their employees and executives to act in ethical ways.

International B2B Markets

A characteristic of B2B markets that you may or may not have noticed or thought about is that firms in the same industry tend to cluster in the same geographic areas around the world. In the United States, many banks and financial companies are located on or near Wall Street in New York City. Many film and television companies operate out of Hollywood. Is it just by chance that this has occurred? No.

The clustering occurs because the resources these firms need—both human and natural—are located in some areas and not others. For example, the Gulf of Mexico is rich with oil deposits. As a result, many oil companies and facilities are located along or near the Gulf in cities such as Houston. Likewise, many high-tech companies are located in Silicon Valley (California). One reason is that nearby Stanford University is one of the top computer science schools in the country, and the firms want to hire graduates from the school.

Bollywood, which refers to the film industry in India, has become one of the largest film centers in the world. It's growing faster than Hollywood and is beginning to rival its size.

Source: © Shutterstock, Inc.

But these are not the only reasons why businesses in the same industry cluster together. Another reason is that sellers want to be close to their buyers. Bentonville, Arkansas, the world headquarters of Walmart, used to be a sleepy little rural town. As Walmart grew, so have the number of companies moving into the area to do business with Walmart. Since 1990, the size of the town has grown five-fold.

Why do companies want to be near their buyers? Let's go back to our date analogy. Suppose you hit it off with the person you're interested in, and you become "an item." You probably wouldn't want to be half the world away from the person for a long period of time because you would miss the person and wouldn't want a rival moving in on your turf! The same is true for sellers. Buyers also want to be close to their suppliers because that can help them get inventory more quickly. Many of Dell's suppliers are located right next to the company's assembly plants. And, as you have learned, some companies actually locate their personnel on their customers' sites.

Ethics in B2B Markets

It's likely that every topic we have talked about so far in this chapter has an ethical dimension to it. Take procurement, for example: unlike B2C markets, offering customers free dinners, golf games, and so forth is very common in B2B settings. In many foreign countries, business and government buyers not only expect perks such as these but actually demand bribes be paid to do business with them. And firms pay them, even though some countries prohibit the practice. (The United States is one such country.)

Walmart came under fire by the U.S. government when it was discovered that for years its Mexico division had achieved rapid growth by bribing public officials to expedite the building permits and zoning approvals for its stores, among other things. The company spent more than a billion dollars in legal fees and fines to settle the case.[9]

Or take, for example, the straight-rebuy situation we discussed earlier. Recall that in a straight rebuy, buyers repurchase products automatically. Dean Foods, which formerly manufactured the Silk brand of soy milk, experienced a lot of negative press after the company changed the word "organic" to "natural" on the labels of its milk and quietly switched to conventional soybeans, which are often grown with pesticides. But Dean didn't change the barcode for the product, the packaging of the product, or the price much. So stores kept ordering what they thought was the same product—making it a straight rebuy—but it wasn't. After it came to light what Dean Foods was doing, many stores and consumers felt as though they had been duped. Some grocers dropped the entire Silk line of products, and Dean Foods later sold the brand to another company.[10]

And remember Intel's strategy to increase the demand for its chips by insisting that PC makers put "Intel Inside" stickers on computers? Intel later paid a competitor more than a billion dollars to settle a court case contending that it strong-armed PC makers into doing business exclusively with Intel. (Does that make you feel less warm and fuzzy about the "Intel Inside" campaign?)[11]

What Dean Foods and Intel did might strike you as being wrong. However, what is ethical and what is not is often not clear-cut. Is it fair to prohibit U.S. companies from offering bribes when their foreign competitors can? Walmart has a reputation for using its market power to squeeze its suppliers for the best deals possible, in some cases putting them out of business. Is that ethical? What about companies that hire suppliers abroad, putting U.S. companies and workers out of business? Is that wrong? It depends on whom you ask. Some economists believe Walmart's ability to keep costs low has benefited consumers far more than it has hurt the suppliers of products.

Clearly, people have very different ideas about what's ethical and what's not. So how does a business get all of its employees on the same page in terms of how they behave? Laws and regulations—state, federal, and international—are an obvious starting point for companies, their executives, and employees wanting to do the right thing. The U.S. Federal Trade Commission (FTC) often plays a role when it comes to B2B laws and regulations. The FTC regulates companies in an effort to prevent them from engaging in unfair and harmful trade practices that hamper competition. Companies that sell to the government must, by law, follow very strict ethical guidelines.

chief ethics officers

Top-level executives responsible for ensuring ethics are properly implemented within their organizations.

Most major companies have ethics codes that provide general guidelines about how their employees should behave and require them to go through ethics training so they know what to do when they face tricky ethical dilemmas. **Chief ethics officers** in these organizations are responsible for ensuring ethics are properly implemented within their organizations. Walmart has overhauled its ethics and compliance programs and appointed chief ethics and compliance officers and anti-corruption directors within each of its markets. An executive vice president oversees the unit, which employs 2,300 people.[12]

At some companies, purchasing agents aren't allowed to accept a lunch, dinner, golf game, or so much as a cup of coffee from potential vendors. The firms ban the practices because (1) they realize that perks such as these drive up product costs, and (2) they don't want their buyers making decisions based on what they personally can get out of them rather than what's best for the company.

All things equal, companies want to do business with firms that are responsible. They don't want to be associated with firms that are not. Why is this important? Because that's what consumers are increasingly demanding. Nike and a number of other apparel makers were lambasted when it came to light that the factories they contracted with were using child labor and keeping workers toiling for long hours under terrible conditions. Nike didn't own the factories, but it still got a bad rap. Apple came under scrutiny when it was discovered that at FoxConn, a Chinese factory that makes the company's iPhones, workers were so poorly treated they were jumping out of the factory's windows to commit suicide.[13]

Apple has since cracked down on suppliers such as these or stopped doing business with them. Nike now uses a "balanced scorecard" when evaluating suppliers. The sports-apparel maker looks at their labor code compliance along with measures such as price, quality, delivery time, and their impact on the environment.[14] Nike does so because its customers are becoming more conscious of workers' rights and environmental damage.

Likewise, because consumers are concerned about global warming, companies ranging from Loreal to Colgate-Palmolive are looking to add "carbon footprint" labels to their products based on the carbon emissions used to make them. Although tracking the carbon emissions related to a product can be a difficult task, consumers may begin demanding the information, just like they do calorie information.[15] Of course, worker and environmental abuses continue to occur and present ethical and other problems for companies and society.

The maker of Quorn, a meat substitute, includes carbon labels on its packages.

Source: https://www.quorn.co.uk/

That's not to say the problems are solved. Worker and environmental abuses continue to occur and present ethical and other problems for companies and society.

Key Takeaway

- Firms in the same industry tend to cluster in the same geographic areas because the resources these firms need—both human and natural—are located in some areas and not others. Sellers also want to be close to their buyers. Ethics come into play in almost all business settings. Business-to-business markets are no different. For example, unlike B2C markets, offering customers perks is very common in B2B settings. In many foreign countries, buyers demand bribes be paid if a company wants to do business with them. Understanding the laws and regulations that apply to their firms is an obvious starting point for companies, their executives, and employees in terms of knowing how to act ethically. Companies also adopt ethics codes that provide general guidelines about how their employees should behave, require their employees to go through ethics training, and hiring chief ethics officers. Companies want to do business with firms that are responsible. They don't want to be associated with firms that are not. Why? Because they know ethics are important to consumers and that they are increasingly demanding firms behave responsibly.

Review Questions

1. Name some other industries you're aware of in which companies tend to cluster geographically. Why are the companies in these industries located near one another?
2. Name some of the types of ethical dilemmas facing firms in B2B markets.
3. Why is it difficult for employees and firms to know what's considered to be ethical behavior and what is not?

4.7 Discussion Questions and Activities

Discussion Questions

1. Assume your company makes shop towels, hand-washing stations, and similar products. Make a list of all the companies that could be potential customers of your firm. Then identify all the markets from which their demand is derived. (Who are their customers and their customers' customers?) What factors might influence the success or failure of your business in these markets?
2. How might a buying center be different for a company that is considering building a new plant versus choosing a new copier?
3. Imagine you are a salesperson for a company that sells maintenance items used in keeping a manufacturing plant running. There is a large plant in your territory that buys 60 percent of its products from one competitor and the other 40 percent from another competitor. What could you do to try to make a sale in that plant if it has never purchased from you before? How would your answer change if you were the 40 percent vendor and wanted to increase your share of the buyer's business? Would your answer change if you were the other vendor? Why or why not?
4. When your family makes a major purchase, such as choosing a vacation destination or buying furniture, does it resemble a buying center? If so, who plays what roles?
5. Katie is a forklift operator who is tired of her forklift breaking down. She points out to her boss, the plant supervisor, that her forklift is broken down at least 20 percent of the time, and it is beginning to impact production. The plant supervisor tells the purchasing agent that a new forklift is needed and asks the purchasing agent to get three bids on new ones with similar features. The purchasing agent calls three companies and gets bids, which the plant supervisor uses to narrow it down to two. He then has Katie test drive the two, and since she liked the Yamamatsu best, he decides to purchase that one. What roles do the supervisor and Katie play in this firm's buying center? Does the process followed resemble the process outlined in the chapter? If not, why not?
6. Someone who works in a company is also a consumer at home. You have already learned about how consumers buy. How does what you already know about how consumers buy relate to what you would expect those same people to do at work when making a purchase?
7. A major office equipment manufacturer and an airline once teamed up to offer a special deal: Buy a copier/printer and get a free round-trip ticket anywhere in the United States where the airline flies. The promotion didn't last long—buyers complained it was unethical. What about it was unethical? Who was really doing the complaining?
8. Congratulations, you just made a sale! For the first time in five years, the Humongo Corporation purchased from your company. How do you turn this into a straight rebuy? What product characteristics might make this goal easier to accomplish? What buyer characteristics might make it more difficult to accomplish?
9. Consider a company where marketing and sales are two different departments. Their customers are other businesses. Using both the buying center and buying process, describe what the marketing department actually does. What do salespeople actually do?

Activities

1. Interview someone you know who makes purchasing decisions as part of the job. The person may or may not be a professional purchasing agent as long as business purchasing decisions are a fairly regular part of their position. What are the key principles to making good

purchasing decisions at work? How do those principles influence people's purchases for their own personal consumption?

2. Locate three different types of websites that cater to markets discussed in this chapter. How do these differ from sites like eBay or Overstock.com? How are they similar? B2C models like Groupon and LivingSocial are being adopted by B2B companies. Examples include Bizy Deal; take a look at that site and identify the types of offerings that seem prevalent. What characteristics of the product or service would make such a model right for a B2B company?
3. Go to http://www.ism.ws/. What is the purpose of this site and the organization that created it? How does the ISM help its members with ethical dilemmas? Be specific, with specific examples from the site.
4. Many B2B marketers use NAICS to segment their market. Go to NAICS and click on the FAQs link to answer these questions. What is NAICS, and how is it used? How does NAICS handle market-based rather than production-based statistical classifications, and why is that distinction important?

4.8 Case Study: Knorr

Maybe you know someone with celiac disease. People with celiac disease have an autoimmune disorder that requires them to eat gluten-free foods. A growing number of people are diagnosed with the disease annually.

Knorr is a food brand that makes dried soup, sauces, and gravy mixes, many of which are naturally gluten free. Consequently, Knorr was in a good position to target its products toward people with celiac disease. You may have seen the brand at your local supermarket.

But it's not just individual consumers Knorr wanted to target with its gluten-free products. The brand also wanted to target one of its key business markets: Chefs and caterers. Knorr's research revealed that consumers who strive to be gluten-free have trouble finding caterers and chefs willing to produce gluten-free foods for events such as weddings and bar mitzvahs.

So, the brand's market research team set out to find out why. The team discovered chefs were worried they would accidentally contaminate what were supposed to be gluten-free foods with foods that contain gluten. Chefs also lacked tasty, gluten-free recipes.

To better meet this B2B market's needs, Knorr gave out thousands of gluten-free samples to chefs at various events and developed a gluten-free recipe guide with information about how to set up kitchens to safely prepare gluten-free foods. Knorr also teamed up with gluten-free expert Phil Vickery, a Michelin chef who conducted a dozen classes in the UK, where Knorr's parent company, Unilever, is based. The classes were live-streamed and recorded so chefs can refer to them later.

Knorr Case Study

Watch the highlights of Knorr's gluten-free masterclass with Phil Vickery.

View in the online reader

"As more and more people are diagnosed, and an increasing number of people choose to remove gluten from their diet, both chefs and [people with the disease] can benefit from providing more gluten-free dishes—and it can be easier than a lot of chefs think," Vickery says.

Today few campaigns would be complete without a social media campaign. So, during Coeliac UK Awareness Week, Knorr targeted chefs on as many social media networks as possible with information about the brand. Meanwhile, Unilever donated £2,000 to the Coeliac UK.

So, did the campaign work? Yes. Knorr got more press mentions and social media shares than it banked on. More people downloaded the recipe guide and videos than anticipated, and more product samples were disseminated than expected too. Better yet, Knorr has picked up sales and market share and is aiming to become the gluten-free B2B leader, a company spokesman says. Knorr also donated £2,000 to the Coeliac UK. And in 2020, the company gave more than $1 million worth of its products to help supply food pantries to support communities impacted by COVID-19.

The key takeaway? "Listen to your customers and your customers' customers to give them what they need—not what you want to give," advises Sean Callahan, an author and senior content marketing manager at LinkedIn.[16]

Case Study Questions

1. Do you think derived demand, fluctuating demand, or both were the driving force behind Knorr's gluten-free campaign?
2. Could Knorr have done more on social media to make the campaign a success? If so, what?

Endnotes

1. U.S. Bureau of Labor Statistics (2021), "Purchasing Managers, Buyers, and Purchasing Agents," *Occupational Outlook Handbook*, https://www.bls.gov/ooh/business-and-financial/purchasing-managers-buyers-and-purchasing-agents.htm.
2. Duena Blomstrom, "Nobody Gets Fired For Buying IBM. But They Should," *Forbes*, November 30, 2018, http://forbes.com.
3. Sina Shokoohyar and Elena Katok, "Incentivizing Suppliers Using Scorecards: A Behavioral Study," *Journal of the Operational Research Society*, February 2021,1–22.
4. (April 6, 2018), "The Seven Habits of Highly Effective Supply Chain Collaborators," *Supply Chain Quarterly*, http://www.supplychainquarterly.com/news/20180404-the-7-habits-of-highly-effective-supply-chain-collaborators/.
5. "Gartner Buyer Enablement Process Insights," (2019), http://gartner/com.
6. Gartner, "Gartner Says 80 percent of B2B Sales Interactions Between Suppliers and Buyers Will Occur in Digital Channels by 2025," (September 15, 2020), https://www.gartner.com.
7. "About Alibaba.com," (May 9, 2021), https://activities.alibaba.com/alibaba/following-about-alibaba.php?spm=a2700.8293689.0.0.500267afzvrlPv&tracelog=footer_alibaba.
8. "What Is Content Marketing?" Content Marketing Institute, http://contentmarketinginstitute.com/what-is-content-marketing/.
9. Tim Schoenberg, "Walmart Close to Resolving Bribery Probe for $300 Million," *Bloomberg* (May 9, 2017), https://www.bloomberg.com/news/articles/2017-05-09/wal-mart-said-close-to-resolving-bribery-probe-for-300-million.
10. Ben Miller, "Remnants of Colorado's White Wave Now Gone in Company Name," *Denver Business Journal*, (April 12, 2018), https://www.bizjournals.com/denver/news/2018/04/12/remnants-of-colorados-white-wave-now-gone-in.html.
11. Richard Water and Nikki Tait, "Intel Settles Antitrust AMD Suit for $1.2 Billion," (November 13, 2009), *Financial Times*, http://www.ft.com.
12. Tim Schoenberg (May 9, 2017), "Walmart Close to Resolving Bribery Probe for $300 Million," *Bloomberg*, https://www.bloomberg.com/news/articles/2017-05-09/wal-mart-said-close-to-resolving-bribery-probe-for-300-million.
13. "Apple Supplier Workers Describe Noxious Hazards at China Factory," (January 1, 2018) *Bloomberg*, https://www.bloomberg.com/news/articles/2018-01-16/workers-at-apple-supplier-catcher-describe-harsh-conditions.
14. Noel Kinder, "Our Carbon Footprint and Our Next Steps," (April 13, 2021), https://news.nike.com/news/our-carbon-footprint-and-our-next-steps.
15. Saabira Chaudhuri, "Carbon Labels Are Coming to Your Shampoo Bottle," (April 1, 2021); https://www.wsj.com/articles/carbon-labels-are-coming-to-your-shampoo-bottle-11617269401.
16. Isabelle Gustafson (May 27, 2020), "Knorr Provides Food Bank Employees with Lunches from Local Restaurants," *CStore Decisions*, https://cstoredecisions.com/2020/05/27/knorr-provides-food-bank-employees-with-lunches-from-local-restaurants/ (June 15, 2016) "Awards Case Study: Knorr Leverages Influencer Marketing to Boost Market Share," *B2B Marketing*, https://www.b2bmarketing.net/en/resources/b2b-case-studies/awards-case-study-knorr-leverages-influencer-marketing-boost-market-share; Sean Callahan (January 4, 2017), "Our Favorite B2B Marketing Campaigns," *LinkedIn Marketing Solutions Blog*, https://business.linkedin.com/marketing-solutions/blog/linkedin-b2b-marketing/2017/our-five-favorite-b2b-marketing-campaigns-of-2016; Daniel Woolfson (April 24, 2015), "Phil Vickery Teams Up with Knorr," *Morning Advertiser*, https://www.morningadvertiser.co.uk/Article/2015/04/24/Phil-Vickery-gluten-free-Knorr.

CHAPTER 5

Market Segmenting, Targeting, and Positioning

Suppose you have an idea for a great new offering you hope will become a hot seller. Before you quit your day job, you'll need to ask yourself, "Does my idea satisfy consumers' needs and add value to existing products?" "Who's going to buy my product?" and "Will there be enough of these people to make it worth my while?"

Certain people will be more interested in what you plan to offer than others. Not everyone needs homeowners' insurance, not everyone needs physical therapy services, and not every organization needs to purchase vertical lathes or CT scanners. Among those that do, some will buy a few, and a few will buy many. In other words, in terms of potential buyers, not all of them are "created equal." Some customers are more equal than others, however. A number of people might be interested in your product idea if it satisfies a need, adds value, is priced right, or if they are aware that your product exists.

People are alike in many ways, but also different. Companies try to group their customers together based on how they are alike. The groups are called segments.

Source: © Shutterstock, Inc.

Your goal is to figure out *which* people and organizations are interested in your product ideas. To do this you will need to divide or segment people and organizations into different groups of potential buyers with similar characteristics. This process is called **market segmentation** with the goal of finding groups big enough to be profitable and similar enough to want the same things. After all, your marketing budget is likely to be limited. You need to get the biggest bang for your buck by focusing on those people you truly have a shot at selling to, and tailoring your offering toward them.

market segmentation

The process of breaking down all consumers into groups of potential buyers with similar characteristics.

5.1 Targeted Marketing Versus Mass Marketing

Learning Objectives

1. Distinguish between targeted marketing and mass marketing and explain what led to the rise of each.
2. Describe how targeted marketing can benefit firms.
3. Explain why companies differentiate among their customers.

Kraft applies target marketing even for a simple product like Kraft Macaroni & Cheese.

Source: © Shutterstock, Inc.

targeted marketing

Differentiating some aspect of your marketing (the product, promotion, and/or price or place), based on different groups of customers.

mass marketing

Selling the same product to all consumers.

Targeted marketing, or *differentiated marketing*, means that you differentiate some aspect of your marketing (the product, promotion, price, or place), based on different groups of customers. Differentiated marketing is a newer phenomenon. **Mass marketing**, or undifferentiated marketing, came first. Mass marketing evolved along with mass production and involves selling the same product to everybody. You can think of mass marketing as a searchlight approach. A searchlight produces a broad beam of light to illuminate the large portions of the night sky. Like a searchlight, a mass marketing strategy attempts to appeal to the largest possible portion of a market with a specific product. A flashlight produces a narrower beam than a searchlight and is used to illuminate a smaller area, such as an area or a path within a large field. Like a flashlight, targeted marketing seeks to appeal to a specific segment of consumers within a market. Finally, a laser produces a pinpoint beam that can be used to produce a small dot on a wall.

Kraft Mac and Cheese was introduced in 1937, its appeal being low cost and good taste. For a long time, there was only one version of the product and Kraft promoted it with mass marketing tactics. Now, though, there are many different versions, such as microwavable single-servings, original flavor or thick and creamy, and other versions that appeal to different segments depending on such characteristics as when they like to eat it, if it is a family or a person eating alone, and so forth. These require more targeted marketing efforts.

Benefits of Segmenting and Targeting Markets

Breaking a market into segments can help you enlarge your customer base by giving you information with which to successfully adjust some component of your offering—the offering itself, its price, or the the way you service and market the product. More specifically, the process can help you do the following:

- Avoid head-on competition with other firms trying to capture the same customers. Walmart initially began in rural areas where Sears and other large retailers didn't have stores. Only when it got big enough to compete head-on did Walmart take on urban markets.
- Develop new offerings and expand profitable brands and products lines. Arby's and Popeyes have both grown considerably in the past few years with new offerings such as cheesesteak sandwiches (Arby's) and the spicy chicken sandwich (Popeyes).
- Remarket older, less-profitable products and brands. Ferguson, which makes plumbing products, moves older products from high-end plumbing distributors to Lowe's and Home Depot when newer designs come out.
- Identify early adopters, who are people who are inclined to adopt new products as soon as they hit the market. Rockler, which sells high-end woodworking tools, knows who likes to be the first with the latest shop gadget.
- Redistribute money and sales efforts to focus on your most profitable customers. PNC Bank regularly evaluates customer profitability for its treasury management services and alters sales efforts accordingly.
- Retain "at-risk" customers in danger of defecting to your competitors. T-Mobile is one of the best at recognizing who is likely to switch, and then making an offer to retain each customer.

The trend today is toward more precise, targeted marketing. One reason why is because most firms don't have the resources to market their products to everyone using all different mediums. Nor would such an effort be efficient, because no single product is right for each and every consumer. Instead, firms have to figure which groups of people are most likely to buy their products and focus their efforts on those customers.

Figuring out "who's who" in terms of your customers involves some detective work, though—often market research. A variety of tools and research techniques can be used to segment markets. Government agencies, such as the U.S. Census Bureau, collect and report vast amounts of population information and economic data that can reveal changing consumption trends. Technology is also making it easier for even small companies and entrepreneurs to gather information about potential customers. For example, the online game company GamePUMA.com originally believed its target market consisted of U.S. customers, but when the firm looked more closely at who was downloading games from its website, they were people from all over the globe. With the increased use of social media, companies are also able to get information about consumers' search behavior. Loyalty cards that consumers scan at many grocery and drugstores provide an incredible amount of information on consumers' buying behavior.

The great product idea you had? Consider tracking people's web browsing patterns and segmenting them into target groups. Even small businesses are able to do this cost-effectively because they don't need their own software and programs. For example, by simply signing up online for programs like Google Ads, you can access a plethora of data about what people are looking for on the web. You can locate potential customers by looking at blog sites and online discussion forums. If you have a website, you can download an application onto your iPhone that will give you up-to-the-minute information and statistics on your site's visitors.

Getting a read on potential target markets doesn't necessarily have to involve technology, though. Your own personal experience and talking to would-be buyers is an important part of the puzzle. Go where you think would-be buyers go—restaurants, malls, gyms, subways, grocery stores, daycare centers, and offices—and ask questions to find out what they do during the day, what they talk about, the products and services you see them using, and the quality of experiences they have using those products or services.

Segmenting and Targeting a Firm's Current Customers

Finding and attracting new customers is generally far more difficult than retaining your current customers. Think about how much time and energy you spend when you switch your business from one firm to another, even when you're buying something as simple as a haircut. If you aren't happy with your hairdresser and want to find a new one, you first have to talk to people with haircuts you like or read reviews of salons. Once you decide on a particular salon, you have to find it and explain to the new hairdresser how you want your hair cut and hope they get it right. Likewise, finding new customers, getting to know them, and figuring out what they really want is also a difficult process fraught with trial and error. That's why it's so important to get to know, form close relationships with, and focus your selling efforts on current customers.

Backroads, a California company focused on adventure-based travel increased its revenues by creating personalized marketing campaigns for people who had done business with the company in the past. Backroads looked at customers' past purchases, the seasons in which they took their trips, the levels of activity associated with them, and whether customers tended to vacation with children. Based on their findings, Backroads created three relevant trip suggestions for each customer and sent postcards and emails with links to customized web pages reminding each customer of the trips they had previously booked with Backroads and suggesting new ones. "In terms of past customers, it was like off-of-the-charts better [than past campaigns]," says Massimo Prioreschi, the vice president of Backroads' sales and marketing group.[1]

In addition to studying their buying patterns, firms also try to get a better understanding of their customers by surveying them, hiring marketing research firms to do so, utilizing loyalty programs, or using analytical tools to determine where they go online and what they buy. (A good source for finding marketing research companies is GreenBook.) For example, if you sign up to become a frequent flier with a certain airline, the airline will likely ask you a number of questions about your likes and dislikes. This information will then be entered into a customer relationship management (CRM) system, and you might be emailed special deals based on the routes you tend to fly. British Airways goes so far as to track the magazines its most elite fliers like to read so the publications are available to them on its planes.

Twitter is another way companies keep in touch with their customers and boost their revenues. Many chefs at high-end restaurants tweet their customers about the specials offered for the evening, and include pictures of ingredients and the final products. The tweets make diners feel like they have an inside track at the restaurants and that they are getting special attention from the chefs.

Likewise, Hansen's Cakes, a Beverly Hills, California, bakery, has about two thousand customers who visit its Facebook page. During her downtime at the bakery, employee Suzi Finer posts "cakes updates" and photos of the goodies she's working on to the site. Along with information about the cakes, Finer extends special offers to customers and mixes in any gossip about Hollywood celebrities she's spotted in the area. After Hansen's Cakes launched its Facebook page, the bakery's sales shot up 15–20 percent.[2] Finding ways to interact with customers that they enjoy—whether it's meeting or "tweeting" them, or putting on events and trade shows they want to attend—is the key to forming relationships with them.

Regardless of how well companies know their customers, it's important to remember that some customers are highly profitable, others aren't, and others actually end up costing your firm money to serve. Consequently, you will want to interact with some customers more than others. Believe it or not, some firms deliberately "untarget" unprofitable customers. Best Buy got a lot of attention (not all of it good) when it was discovered the electronics retailer had categorized its buyers into "personas," or types of buyers, and created customized sales approaches for each. For example, an upper-middle-class woman was referred to as a "Jill." A young urban man was referred to as a "Buzz." Pesky, bargain-hunting customers that Best Buy couldn't make much of a profit from were referred to as "devils" and taken off the company's mailing lists.[3]

The knife cuts both ways, though. Not all firms are equal in the minds of consumers, who will choose to do business with some companies rather than others. To consumers, market segmentation means: meet *my* needs—give me what *I* want.[4]

Steps companies take to target their best customers, form close, personal relationships with them, and give them what they want—a process called **one-to-one marketing**—are outlined in "Steps in One-to-One Marketing." In terms of our searchlight versus laser approach, you can think of one-to-one marketing as a laser approach. Like a laser, one-to-one marketing is used to create and appeal that targets one consumer.

Are you a "high maintenance" customer? Always trying to work a deal? If so, and you do business with Best Buy, the company may be aware of it.

Source: © Shutterstock, Inc.

one-to-one marketing

Forming close, personal relationships with customers and giving them exactly what they want.

One-to-one marketing is an idea proposed by Don Peppers and Martha Rogers in their 1994 book *The One to One Future*. The book described what life would be like after mass marketing. We would all be able to get exactly what we want from sellers, and our relationships with them would be collaborative, rather than adversarial. Twenty-five years later, are we there yet? Not quite, but it does seem to be the direction toward highly targeted marketing is heading.

Steps in One-to-One Marketing

1. **Establish short-term measures to evaluate your efforts.** Determine how you will measure your effort. Will you use higher customer satisfaction ratings, increased revenues earned per customer, number of products sold to customers, transaction costs, or another measure?
2. **Identify your customers.** Gather all the information you can about your current customers, including their buying patterns, likes, and dislikes. When conducting business with them, include an "opt in" question that allows you to legally gather and use their phone numbers and email addresses so you can remain in contact with them.

3. **Differentiate among your customers**. Determine who your best customers are in terms of what they spend and will spend in the future (their customer lifetime value), and how easy or difficult they are to serve. Identify and target customers who spend only small amounts with you but large amounts with your competitors.
4. **Interact with your customers, targeting your best ones**. Find ways and media in which to talk to customers about topics they're interested in and enjoy. Spend the bulk of your resources interacting with your best (high-value) customers. Minimize the time and money you spend on low-value customers with low growth potential.
5. **Customize your products and marketing messages**. Try to customize your marketing messages and products in order to give your customers exactly what they want—whether it's the product itself, its packaging, delivery, or the services associated with it.[5]

Key Takeaway

- Choosing select groups of people to sell to is called targeted marketing, or *differentiated marketing*. Mass marketing, or *undifferentiated marketing*, involves selling the same product to everyone. The trend today is toward more precise, targeted marketing. Finding and attracting new customers is generally far more difficult than retaining one's current customers, which is why organizations try to interact with and form relationships with their current customers. The goal of firms is to do as much business with their best customers as possible. Forming close, personal relationships with customers and giving them exactly what they want is a process called one-to-one marketing. It is the opposite of mass marketing.

Review Questions

1. Using the shotgun and rifle analogy, how do mass marketing, targeted marketing, and one-to-one marketing compare with one another?
2. How is technology making it easier for firms to target customers?
3. Outline the steps companies need to take to engage in one-to-one marketing with their customers.

5.2 How Markets Are Segmented

Learning Objectives

1. Understand and outline the ways in which markets are segmented.
2. Explain why marketers use some segmentation bases versus others.

Sellers can choose to pursue consumer markets, business-to-business (B2B) markets, or both. So, one obvious way to begin the segmentation process is to segment markets into these two types of groups.

segmentation bases

Criteria used to classify and divide buyers into different groups.

Different factors influence consumers to buy certain things. Many of the same factors can also be used to segment customers. A firm will often use multiple **segmentation bases**, or criteria, to classify buyers to get a fuller picture and create real value for them. Each variable adds a layer of information. Think of it as being similar to the way your professor builds up information on a PowerPoint slide to the point at which you are able to understand the material being presented.

There are all kinds of characteristics you can use to slice and dice a market. "Big-and-tall" stores cater to the segment of population that's larger sized. What about people with wide or narrow feet, or people with medical conditions, or certain hobbies? Next, we look primarily at the ways in which consumer markets can be segmented. Later in the chapter, we'll look at the ways in which B2B markets can be segmented.

Types of Segmentation Bases

Table 5.1 shows some of the different types of buyer characteristics used to segment markets. Notice that the characteristics fall into one of four segmentation categories: *behavioral, demographic, geographic,* or *psychographic*. We'll discuss each of these categories in a moment. For now, you can get a rough idea of what the categories consist of by looking at them in terms of how marketing professionals might answer the following questions:

- **Behavioral segmentation.** What benefits do customers want, and how do they use our product?
- **Demographic segmentation.** How do the ages, races, genders, and ethnic backgrounds of our customers affect what they buy?
- **Geographic segmentation.** Where are our customers located, and how can we reach them? What products do they buy based on their locations?
- **Psychographic segmentation.** What do our customers think about and value? How do they live their lives?

TABLE 5.1 Common Ways of Segmenting Buyers

By Behavior	By Demographics	By Geography	By Psychographics
• Benefits sought from the product • How often the product is used (usage rate) • Usage situation (daily use, holiday use, etc.) • Buyer's status and loyalty to product (nonuser, potential user, first-time user, regular user, heavy user)	• Age/generation • Income • Gender • Family life cycle • Ethnicity • Family size • Occupation • Education • Nationality • Religion • Social class	• Region (continent, country, state, neighborhood) • Size of city or town • Population density • Climate	• Activities • Interests • Opinions • Values • Attitudes • Lifestyles

Segmenting by Behavior

Behavioral segmentation divides people and organizations into groups according to how they behave with or act toward products. **Benefits segmentation**—segmenting buyers by the benefits they want from products—is very common. Take toothpaste, for example. Which benefit is most important to you when you buy a toothpaste: the toothpaste's price, ability to whiten your teeth, fight tooth decay, freshen your breath, or something else? Perhaps it's a combination of two or more benefits. If marketing professionals know what those benefits are, they can then tailor different toothpaste offerings to you (and other people like you). For example, Colgate 2-in-1 Toothpaste & Mouthwash, Whitening Icy Blast is aimed at people who want the benefits of both fresher breath and whiter teeth.

behavioral segmentation

Dividing people and organizations into groups according to how they behave with or act toward products.

benefits segmentation

Dividing the market into groups based on the benefits sought by consumers.

Vintage Colgate Ad

Watch the YouTube video to see a vintage Colgate toothpaste ad that describes the product's various benefits to consumers. (On-screen kissing was evidently too racy for the times.)

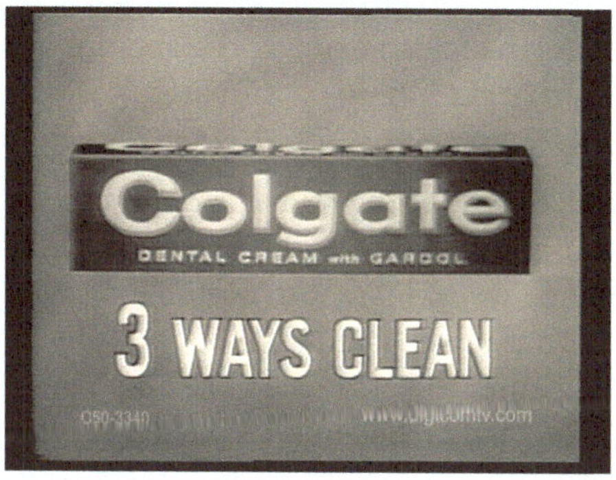

View in the online reader

Another way in which businesses segment buyers is by their usage rates—that is, how often, if ever, they use certain products. Harrah's, an entertainment and gaming company, gathers information about the people who gamble at its casinos. High rollers, or people who spend a lot of money, are considered "VIPs." VIPs get special treatment, including a personal "host" who looks after their needs during their casino visits. Companies are interested in frequent users because they want to reach other people like them. They are also keenly interested in nonusers and how they can be persuaded to use products.

The way in which people use products can also be a basis for segmentation. Avon Skin So Soft was originally a beauty product, but after Avon discovered that some people were using it as a mosquito repellant, the company began marketing it for that purpose. Eventually, Avon created a separate product called Skin So Soft Bug Guard, which competes with repellents like Off! Similarly, Glad, the company that makes plastic wrap and bags, found out customers were using its Press'n Seal wrap in ways the company could never have imagined. The personnel in Glad's marketing department subsequently launched a website that contained both the company's and consumers' use tips. Some of the ways in which people use the product are pretty unusual, as evidenced by the following comment posted on the site: "I have a hedgehog who likes to run on his wheel a lot. After quite a while of cleaning a gross wheel every morning, I got the tip to use 'Press'n Seal wrap' on his wheel, making clean up much easier! My hedgie can run all he wants, and I don't have to think about the cleanup. Now we're both GLAD!"

Was this customer who used Press'n Seal wrap to keep the hedgehog's wheel clean a lead user? That market segment isn't very big!

Source: © Shutterstock, Inc.

Although we doubt Glad will ever go to great lengths to segment the Press'n Seal market by hedgehog owners, the firm has certainly gathered a lot of good consumer insight about the product. (Incidentally, one rainy day, the author of this chapter made "rain boots" out of Press'n Seal for her dog. But when she later tried to tear them off of the dog's paws, he bit her. She is now thinking of trading him in for a hedgehog.)

customer's lifetime value (CLV)

The total monetary value of a customer over the customer's lifetime.

Value-based segmentation is another form of behavioral segmentation, and is based on a **customer's lifetime value**, or CLV. CLV is the total monetary value of a customer over the customer's lifetime. For example, if a student spends an average of $50 per month on clothing over five years while in college, that student is worth $600 per year or $3000 over their lifetime as a college student. Many firms will segment on CLV in some fashion, either on the basis of dollars spent with the firm or total dollars spent on the category. Back to the student example, if your store gets half of that student's spending, the CLV for you is $1500 but with a potential CLV of $3000.

Mathematically, CLV is expressed as:

$$CLV = \Sigma(R)_L$$

Or the sum of revenue over the lifetime of the customer. In the student example, we used a lifetime of five years, though the student will live much longer, because the purchasing habits of a college student are different than those of a young professional after graduation. More sophisticated methods of calculating CLV are based on gross margin, and account for the cost of acquiring the customer, the cost of maintaining that customer over the appropriate period, adjusted for the time value of money over the lifetime period.

Firms then divide their market into segments based on CLV. Cabela's, for example, divides their customers into five quintiles (20% of the total customer base in each quintile) based on CLV estimates and markets to each quintile differently. American Airlines, though, relies heavily on its loyalty program to determine how to market to customers based on CLV, as each level in the program is based on revenue. Those two examples illustrate how current customers are divided into value-based segments; companies will often then use other variables to identify potential customers who, if acquired, could become high value customers. For example, American Airlines may apply age, income, or other descriptors of high value customers to potential customers to then try to get those potential customers to switch to American.

Segmenting by Demographics

demographic segmentation

Segmenting buyers by personal characteristics such as their ages, incomes, ethnicity, and family sizes.

Segmenting buyers by personal characteristics such as age, income, ethnicity and nationality, education, occupation, religion, social class, and family size is called **demographic segmentation**. Demographics are commonly utilized to segment markets because demographic information is publicly available in databases around the world. You can obtain a great deal of demographic information on the website of the U.S. Census Bureau. Other government websites you can tap include FedStats and *The World Factbook*, which contains statistics about countries around the world. In addition to current statistics, the sites contain forecasts of demographic trends, such as whether some segments of the population are expected to grow or decline.

Age

At this point in your life, you are probably more likely to buy a car than a funeral plot. Marketing professionals know this. That's why they try to segment consumers by their ages. You're probably familiar with some of the age groups most commonly segmented (see Table 5.2) in the United States. Into which category do you fall?

TABLE 5.2 U.S. Generations and Characteristics

Generation	Also Known As	Birth Years	Characteristics
Seniors	"The Silent Generation," "Matures," "Veterans," and "Traditionalists"	1945 and prior	• Experienced very limited credit growing up • Tend to live within their means • Spend more on health care than any other age group • Internet usage rates increasing faster than any other group
Baby Boomers		1946–1964	• Second-largest generation in the United States • Grew up in prosperous times before the widespread use of credit • Account for 50 percent of U.S. consumer spending • Willing to use new technologies as they see fit
Generation X		1965–1979	• Comfortable but cautious about borrowing • Buying habits characterized by their life stages • Embrace technology and multitasking
Millennials	"Generation Y" and "Echo Boomers"	1980–2000	• Largest U.S. generation • Grew up with credit cards • Adept at multitasking; technology use is innate • Ignore media irrelevant to them
Generation Z	"iGen," "Pluralists"	2001–2012	• Very digitally attuned generation • Use social media to validate themselves and gain acceptance • Are practical, ambitious, and desire independence • Less willing to take risks
Generation Alpha	Like Gen Z, also called the "iGen"	2013–2025	• Growing up with wearable technology, virtual reality, and artificial intelligence • Children of millennials
Note: Not all demographers agree on the cutoff dates between the generations.			

Sources: Madison Edwards and Emily Herman (2020), "The 5 Active Generations and How to Market to Them" Green Buzz Agency; Michael T. Robinson (2021), "The Generations—Which Generation are You?" (careerplanner.com).

Millennials compose the largest generation. Millennials have come to embrace renting over owning products, even clothes. Le Tote is a company that rents everyday clothing, while Rent the Runway rents fancy evening gowns. Millennials are three times more likely to have rented a product online than non-millennials.[6]

Source: © Shutterstock, Inc.

The baby boomer generation is second to millennials in size; however, baby boomers are aging, and the size of the group will eventually decline. Still, they have significant buying power and, contrary to some beliefs, are pretty savvy when it comes to online shopping. They are also more interested in products that are sustainably sourced or made than you might expect, with 60 percent being willing to pay more for those types of products.[7]

By contrast, members of Generation Z have a lifetime of buying still ahead of them, which translates to a lot of potential customer lifetime value (CLV). CLV is the amount a customer will spend on a particular brand over his or her lifetime. Generation Z values their data privacy and while many do purchase products through social media, they actually enjoy shopping in a traditional store. Their personal value equation weights convenience over service, so they want easy check-out and fast delivery.[8]

Old Spice's resurgence was attributed to a brilliant advertising campaign but the work actually began years earlier by developing a broader product line aimed at a very specific—and younger—target market.

Source: © Shutterstock, Inc.

So which group or groups should your firm target? Some companies, like Harley Davidson, find themselves stuck in a generation that limits their ability to grow. Oldsmobile tried to convince younger buyers that it's "not your father's Oldsmobile" but they were unsuccessful and GM closed the division. Modern Bread was able to successfully rebrand itself to appeal to younger buyers. Through re-vamped packaging and socially aware campaigns like #belikebread "because bread doesn't discriminate," the brand enjoyed a rebirth.[9]

Old Spice was a dying brand of after-shave, with a reputation for being stodgy and purchased by the sort of men who weren't interested in being cool or in new products. To change, they rebuilt the product line with products aimed at younger men—body wash and deodorant—and made them better such as by eliminating the residue marks on shirts through new technology. Targeting tweeners who had yet to develop product loyalty, they focused on active teens, even delivering swag and free samples to skate parks and athletic events. The advertising campaign helped, no doubt, but the real resurgence was due to knowing their target market and creating the right value proposition. Now, it's the top brand, popular among millennials and Gen Z.[10]

Jeremy Herbert, Embark General

Source: Jeremy Hebert, used with permission.

Jeremy Herbert works for Embark General, an independent insurance agency that sells businesses insurance. "As a Marketing Coordinator who works with a team of people on how we can better reach our consumer, we usually start with the four common segmentations: geographic, demographic, psychographic, and behavioral. Segmentation better helps me assist how we need to come at the consumer, because everyone isn't the same." His company sells to businesses and to individual consumers. "We are oftentimes people's last hope at receiving car insurance. Most of our customers have hefty fines on tickets, etc. Sometimes we don't put as much emphasis on marketing too much because we know they need us." Even so, he's found that segmentation is very important. "We had a lot of different agents in different states, so a lot of our marketing *information* was the same, but the *content* was different. In some markets, we didn't use a lot of words because we began to realize a lot of our customer base didn't read or have a high school education. A lot of things had to be simple and straight to the point for them."

In a previous position with a restaurant, "Sometimes consumers would complain about our prices, after doing a small deep dive on where we were located, we realized the restaurant was in one of the poorest parts of the city. We had to tailor our prices to the people of the community. When we realized that the area we serviced was heavily family oriented, we would do events around that. It brought in the crowd and it invited us a community of people we didn't even think about servicing. I kept a chart of how much money we made daily and what were people buying the most of. Once we realized that certain items weren't selling, we began to offer 'build your own options.' A lot of our consumers liked that, but what it mainly helped us with was ingredients they liked and how we could continue to better serve them. We eventually made meals around them."

Other companies have introduced lower-cost brands targeting Generations X and Y, who have less spending power than boomers. Whole Foods opened 365, a spin-off chain of smaller, less-expensive stores to attract this demographic and other customers on tighter budgets. The Starwood hotel chain's W hotels, which feature contemporary designs and hip bars, are aimed at Generation Xers. And for backpacking millennial types (Generation Y?) a number of investors are opening designer youth hostels with vibrant bars, rooftop yoga classes, and private baths in the United States, which is a trend that has been growing Europe.

Online events such as the fashion shows broadcast over the web are also more likely to get the attention of younger consumers, as are text, email, and Twitter messages they can sign up to receive to get coupons, cash, and free merchandise. Advergames are also being used to appeal to the two demographic groups. **Advergames** are electronic games sellers create to promote a product or service. Would you like to play one now? Click on the following link and choose from an array of Disney games used to promote its *Cars* movie franchise.

advergames

Electronic games sellers create to promote a product or service.

Disney Cars Advergames

You can choose from an array of free games Disney uses to create stronger relationships with characters from the *Cars* movies.

Income

Millennials might appear to be a very attractive market when you consider they will be buying products for years to come and there are more millennials than any other demographic group. In fact, Gucci was the fastest growing luxury brand in 2019 and half of its sales are to millennials.[11] But would you change your mind if you knew that Gen X has the highest income per person and they spend more per person than any other generation? (Remember, though, it is the smallest generation.)[12] Baby boomers, however, are the largest in total spend, over $2.6 trillion/year.

Income is used as a segmentation variable because it indicates a group's buying power and may partially reflect their education levels, occupation, and social classes. Higher education levels usually result in higher-paying jobs and greater social status. The makers of upscale products such as Rolexes and Lamborghinis aim their products at high-income groups. Louis Vuitton, Christian Dior, and Prada are brands that have luxury suites with rooftop views, fine art, and tanning areas in some of their stores. High-income customers are given access to the suites to keep them shopping longer and buying more products.[13]

However, other firms aim their products specifically at lower-income consumers. The fastest-growing product in the financial services sector is prepaid debit cards, most of which are being bought and used by people who don't have bank accounts. Firms are finding that this group is a large, untapped pool of customers who tend to be more brand loyal than most. If you capture enough of them, you can earn a profit.[14] Based on the targeted market, businesses can determine the location and type of stores where they want to sell their products.

Sometimes income isn't always indicative of who will buy your product. Companies are aware that many consumers want to be in higher income groups and behave like they are already part of them. Mercedes Benz's less expensive line of "C" class vehicles is designed to appeal to these consumers.

Gender

Gender is a common basis for segmentation. While gender may be considered by many to be binary (male or female), biologically and psychologically, gender is more complicated. Brands are recognizing that gender can also be an expression (how one presents one's self) and an identity (how one feels). Because digital media can be so fine-tuned, slight variations in messaging can address these differences.

In addition to segmenting by gender, market researchers might couple gender with cohabitation status and other demographic characteristics. While slightly more women than men live alone, most adults cohabitate with someone, a fact that drives many household purchases.

Family Life Cycle

family life cycle

The stages families go through over time and how it affects people's buying behavior.

Family life cycle refers to the stages families go through over time and how it affects people's buying behavior. For example, if you have no children, your demand for pediatric services (medical care for children) is likely to be slim to none, but if you have children, your demand might be very high because children frequently get sick. You may be part of the target market not only for pediatric services but also for a host of other products, such as diapers, daycare, children's clothing, entertainment services, and educational products. A secondary segment of interested consumers might be grandparents, who are likely to spend less on day-to-day childcare items but more on special-occasion gifts for children. Many markets are segmented based on the special events in people's lives. Think about brides (and want-to-be brides) and all the products targeted at them, including websites and television shows such as *Say Yes to the Dress*, *My Fair Wedding*, *Platinum Weddings*, and *Bridezillas*.

Resorts also segment vacationers depending on where they are in their family life cycles. When you think of family vacations, you probably think of Disney resorts. Some vacation properties, such as Sandals, exclude children from some of their resorts. Perhaps they do so because some studies show that the market segment with greatest financial potential is married couples without children.

Keep in mind that although you might be able to isolate a segment in the marketplace, including one based on family life cycle, you can't make assumptions about what the people in it will want. Just like people's demographics change, so do their tastes. For example, over the past few decades U.S. families have been getting smaller. The same type of house that appeals to young couples also appeals to downsizing boomers.

Modest 2,000 sq. ft Craftsman-style homes are popular with millennials and boomers alike.

Source: Suzanne Tucker/Shutterstock.com

The trends toward larger cars and larger houses appear to be reversing. High housing prices, energy costs, and concern for the environment are leading people to demand smaller houses. To attract people wanting smaller homes, D. R. Horton, the nation's leading homebuilder, and other construction firms are now building smaller homes. But with teleworking growing in popularity, they're adding back dedicated office space in new homes, too.

Ethnicity

People's ethnic backgrounds have a big impact on what they buy. If you've visited a grocery store that caters to a different ethnic group than your own, you were probably surprised to see the types of products sold there. It's no secret that the United States is becoming—and will continue to become more diverse. Hispanic Americans are the largest and the fastest-growing minority in the United States, and they are very brand loyal. Companies are going to great lengths to court this group, but it takes more than just converting ads and packaging into Spanish. For example, recent consumer studies have shown that Hispanics of Cuban and Puerto Rican descent often act in opposite ways when compared to those of Mexican and other Hispanic descent.[15]

African Americans are the second-largest minority group in America with the second-highest buying power of any ethnic group in America. On a per capita basis, Asian Americans have more buying power, while Indigenous buying power is the fastest growing.

Table 5.3 contains information about the number of people in these groups and their buying power.

TABLE 5.3 Major U.S. Ethnic Segments and Their Spending

Group	Percentage of U.S. Population	Annual Spending Power
Hispanics	18.5	$1.5 trillion
African Americans	13.4	$1.3 trillion
Asian Americans	5.9	$1.0 trillion
Native Americans	1.3	$115 billion

Source: University of Georgia (2019), "Minority Markets Have $3.9 Trillion Buying Power," https://www..newswise.com/articles/minority-markets-have-3-9-trillion-buying-power; "US Census Bureau July 1 2019 Estimates" (web), United States Census Bureau.

As you can guess, even within various ethnic groups there are many differences in terms of the goods and services buyers choose. Consequently, painting each group with a broad brush would leave you with an incomplete picture of your buyers. For example, although the common ancestral language among the Hispanic segment is Spanish, Hispanics trace their lineages to different countries. Nearly 70 percent of Hispanics in the United States trace their lineage to Mexico; others trace theirs to Central America, South America, and the Caribbean.

All that Asians share is race. Chinese, Japanese, and Korean immigrants do not share the same language. Moreover, both the Asian and Hispanic market segments include new immigrants, people who immigrated to the United States years ago, and native-born Americans. So what language will you use to communicate your offerings to these people, and where?

Subsegmenting the markets could potentially help you. For example, Target Latino is a firm that specializes in marketing to the Hispanic population in the United States, and they segment that market based on the degree of acculturation into the broader U.S. culture. They note that Hispanics do not let go of their traditional customs or language. While they argue that European immigrants tried to assimilate by dropping their traditions and customs, you can still find signs in Czech, German, or Norwegian in rural towns and villages across the United States that were settled predominantly by people from one country. They divide the market into three groups: Unacculturated, who only speak Spanish, Semi-Acculturated, bilingual and can move easily from one culture to the other; and Fully Acculturated, proud of their traditions but with little Spanish vocabulary. While they argue that European immigrants tried to assimilate by dropping their traditions and customs, you can still find signs in Czech, German, or Norwegian in rural towns and villages across the United States that were settled predominantly by people from one country.

Segmenting by Geography

Suppose your great new product or service idea involves opening a local store. Before you open the store, you will probably want to do some research to determine which geographical areas have the best potential. For instance, if your business is a high-end restaurant, should it be located near the local college or country club? If you sell ski equipment, you probably will want to locate your shop somewhere in the vicinity of a mountain range where there is skiing. You might see a snowboard shop in the same area but probably not a surfboard shop. By contrast, a surfboard shop is likely to be located along the coast, but you probably would not find a snowboard shop on the beach.

During the COVID-19 pandemic, Hershey's realized that when the virus surged in an area, so did sales of the ingredients for s'mores—chocolate, graham crackers, and marshmallows. In fact, chocolate sales rose 40 to 50 percent in those areas, as more people stayed home and engaged in simple pleasures like making a fire in the backyard for cooking s'mores. Hershey CEO Michele Buck said local COVID-19 numbers influenced the company's marketing of the chocolate bars used in s'mores. "We were able to use the (COVID-19) case count trajectory as a foreshadow of where we should focus some of those efforts and build displays and put media in those markets," she noted.[16]

Geographic segmentation divides the market into areas based on location and explains why the check-out clerks at stores sometimes ask for your zip code, and why you get online ads for restaurants and stores in your area and not in other towns and cities. It's also why businesses print codes on coupons that correspond to zip codes. When the coupons are redeemed, the store can find out where its customers are located, or not located.

geographic segmentation

Segmenting buyers by where they are located.

Geocoding is a process that takes data such as this and plots it on a map. Geocoding can help businesses see where prospective customers might be clustered and target them with various ad campaigns, including direct mail. One of the most popular geocoding software programs is PRIZM. PRIZM, which is a product produced by the Nielsen Company, uses zip codes and demographic information to classify the American population into segments. The idea behind PRIZM is that "you are where you live." Combining both demographic and geographic information is referred to as **geodemographics** or neighborhood geography. The idea is that housing areas in different zip codes typically attract certain types of buyers with certain income levels.

geocoding

The process of plotting geographic marketing information takes on a map.

geodemographics

Combining both demographic and geographic information for marketing purposes.

To see how geodemographics work, visit Clarita's PRIZM product. Type in your zip code, and you will see **customer profiles** of the types of buyers who live in your area. Table 5.4 shows the profiles of buyers who can be found in the zip code 76137—the "Brite Lites, Li'l City" bunch, the "Up-and-Comers" set, and so forth. Click on the profiles on the site to see which one most resembles you.

customer profiles

The description of a type of customer based on market segmentation criteria.

TABLE 5.4 An Example of Geodemographic Segmentation for 76137 (Fort Worth, TX)

Number	Profile Name
30	*Pools and Patios: upper Midscale Younger Mostly with Kids*
14	*Kids and Cul-de-Sacs: Upper Middle-Age Family Mix*
25	*Up and Comers: Upper Midscale Younger Family Mix*
33	*Second City Startups: Upper Midscale Younger Mostly with Kids*
34	*Young and Influential: Upper Midscale Younger Mostly without Kids*

The tourism bureau for the state of Michigan was able to identify and target different customer profiles using PRIZM. Michigan's biggest travel segment is Chicagoans in certain zip codes consisting of upper-middle-class households with children. The bureau was also able to identify segments significantly different from the Chicago segment, including blue-collar adults in the Cleveland area who vacation without their children. The organization then created significantly different marketing campaigns to appeal to each group.

City size and **population density** (the number of people per square mile) are also used for segmentation purposes. Have you ever noticed that in rural towns, McDonald's restaurants are hard to find, but Dairy Queens (DQ) are usually easy to locate? McDonald's generally won't put a store in a town of fewer than five thousand people. However, this is prime turf for the "DQ"— because it doesn't have to compete with bigger franchises like McDonald's.

population density

The number of people per square mile.

In addition to figuring out where to locate stores and advertise to customers in that area, geographic segmentation helps firms tailor their products. If you find the same heavy winter coat you see at a Walmart in Montana at a Walmart in Florida, someone made a mistake! Because of the climate differences between the two places, the product mix in the two stores will be very different at different times of the year. Market researchers also look at migration patterns to evaluate opportunities. TexMex restaurants are more commonly found in the southwestern United States. However, northern states are now seeing more of them as more people of Hispanic descent move northward.

Segmenting by Psychographics

If your offering fulfills the needs of a specific demographic group, then the demographic can be an important basis for identifying groups of consumers interested in your product. What if your product crosses several market segments? For example, the group of potential consumers for cereal could be "almost" everyone, although groups of people may have different needs with regard to their cereal. Some consumers might be interested in the fiber, some consumers (especially children) may be interested in the prize that comes in the box, other consumers may be interested in the added vitamins, and still other consumers may be interested in the type of grains. Associating these specific needs with consumers in a particular demographic group could be difficult. Marketing professionals want to know *why* consumers behave the way they do, what is of high priority to them, or how they rank the importance of specific buying criteria. Think about some of your friends who seem a lot like you. Have you ever gone to their homes and been shocked by their lifestyles and how vastly different they are from yours? Why are their families so much different from yours?

psychographic segmentation

Segmenting people by their activities, interests, opinion, attitudes, values, and lifestyles.

Psychographic segmentation can help fill in some of the blanks. Psychographic information is frequently gathered via extensive surveys that ask people about their activities, interests, opinion, attitudes, values, and lifestyles. One of the most well-known psychographic surveys is VALS (which originally stood for "Values, Attitudes, and Lifestyles") and was developed by a company called SRI International in the late 1980s. SRI asked thousands of Americans the extent to which they agreed or disagreed with statements similar to the following: "My idea of fun at a national park would be to stay at an expensive lodge and dress up for dinner" and "I could stand to skin a dead animal."[17] Based on their responses to different statements, consumers were divided up into the following categories, each characterized by certain buying behaviors.

- **Innovators.** Innovators are successful, sophisticated, take-charge people with high self-esteem. Because they have such abundant resources, they exhibit all three primary motivations in varying degrees. They are change leaders and are the most receptive to new ideas and technologies. Innovators are very active consumers, and their purchases reflect cultivated tastes for upscale, niche products and services. Image is important to Innovators, not as evidence of status or power but as an expression of their taste, independence, and personality. Innovators are among the established and emerging leaders in business and government, yet they continue to seek challenges. Their lives are characterized by variety. Their possessions and recreation reflect a cultivated taste for the finer things in life.
- **Thinkers.** Thinkers are motivated by ideals. They are mature, satisfied, comfortable, and reflective people who value order, knowledge, and responsibility. They tend to be well educated and actively seek out information in the decision-making process. They are well informed about world and national events and are alert to opportunities to broaden their knowledge. Thinkers have a moderate respect for the status quo institutions of authority and social decorum but are open to consider new ideas. Although their incomes allow them many choices, Thinkers are conservative, practical consumers; they look for durability, functionality, and value in the products they buy.
- **Achievers.** Motivated by the desire for achievement, Achievers have goal-oriented lifestyles and a deep commitment to career and family. Their social lives reflect this focus and are structured around family, their place of worship, and work. Achievers live conventional lives, are politically conservative, and respect authority and the status quo. They value consensus, predictability, and stability over risk, intimacy, and self-discovery. With many wants and needs, Achievers are active in the consumer marketplace. Image is important to Achievers; they favor established, prestige products and services that demonstrate success to their peers. Because of their busy lives, they are often interested in a variety of time-saving devices.
- **Experiencers.** Experiencers are motivated by self-expression. As young, enthusiastic, and impulsive consumers, Experiencers quickly become enthusiastic about new possibilities but are equally quick to cool. They seek variety and excitement, savoring the new, the offbeat, and

the risky. Their energy finds an outlet in exercise, sports, outdoor recreation, and social activities. Experiencers are avid consumers and spend a comparatively high proportion of their income on fashion, entertainment, and socializing. Their purchases reflect the emphasis they place on looking good and having "cool" stuff.

- **Believers.** Like Thinkers, Believers are motivated by ideals. They are conservative, conventional people with concrete beliefs based on traditional, established codes: family, religion, community, and the nation. Many Believers express moral codes that are deeply rooted and literally interpreted. They follow established routines, organized in large part around home, family, community, and social or religious organizations to which they belong. As consumers, Believers are predictable; they choose familiar products and established brands. They favor American products and are generally loyal customers.
- **Strivers.** Strivers are trendy and fun loving. Because they are motivated by achievement, Strivers are concerned about the opinions and approval of others. Money defines success for Strivers, who don't have enough of it to meet their desires. They favor stylish products that emulate the purchases of people with greater material wealth. Many see themselves as having a job rather than a career, and a lack of skills and focus often prevents them from moving ahead. Strivers are active consumers because shopping is both a social activity and an opportunity to demonstrate to peers their ability to buy. As consumers, they are as impulsive as their financial circumstance will allow.
- **Makers.** Like Experiencers, Makers are motivated by self-expression. They express themselves and experience the world by working on it—building a house, raising children, fixing a car, or canning vegetables—and have enough skill and energy to carry out their projects successfully. Makers are practical people who have constructive skills and value self-sufficiency. They live within a traditional context of family, practical work, and physical recreation and have little interest in what lies outside that context. Makers are suspicious of new ideas and large institutions such as big business. They are respectful of government authority and organized labor but resentful of government intrusion on individual rights. They are unimpressed by material possessions other than those with a practical or functional purpose. Because they prefer value to luxury, they buy basic products.
- **Survivors.** Survivors live narrowly focused lives. With few resources with which to cope, they often believe that the world is changing too quickly. They are comfortable with the familiar and are primarily concerned with safety and security. Because they must focus on meeting needs rather than fulfilling desires, Survivors do not show a strong primary motivation. Survivors are cautious consumers. They represent a very modest market for most products and services. They are loyal to favorite brands, especially if they can purchase them at a discount.[18]

To find out which category you're in, take a VALS survey. VALS surveys have been adapted and used to study buying behavior in other countries, too. Note that both VALS and PRIZM group buyers are based on their values and lifestyles, but PRIZM also overlays the information with geographic data. As a result, you can gauge what the buying habits of people in certain zip codes are, which can be helpful if you are trying to figure out where to locate stores and retail outlets.

The segmenting techniques we've discussed so far in this section require gathering quantitative information and data. Quantitative information can be improved with *qualitative* information you gather by talking to your customers and getting to know them. (Recall that this is how Healthy Choice frozen dinners were created.) **Consumer insight** is what results when you use both types of information. You want to be able to answer the following questions:

consumer insight

An understanding of consumers that results when both quantitative and qualitative information are gathered about them.

- Am I looking at the consumers the way they see themselves?
- Am I looking at life from their point of view?

Best Buy asked store employees to develop insight about local consumer groups in order to create special programs and processes for them. Employees in one locale invited a group of retirees to their store to explain new TV technologies. The store sold $350,000 worth of equipment and televisions in just two hours' time. How much did it cost? The total cost included ninety-nine dollars in labor costs plus coffee and donuts.

Shelly Avery, Microsoft

Source: Shelly Avery, used with permission.

Shelly Avery, director of healthcare solutions for Microsoft, is working with pharmacies so they can adapt to lifestyle changes among their customers. These solutions generate better health and business results.

During the coronavirus pandemic, shopping moved online for many purchases but there are some purchases where you just need to talk with someone to make sure you get it right. Shelly Avery works for Microsoft and her clients include pharmacies. "Right now we are working on how pharmacies can have on-demand video calls with patients who have questions about their medications. So many people are avoiding going to the pharmacy these days and by making it easy more patients are able to get their questions answered. It's not just Google, it's talking to a live, educated person."

Segmentation in B2B Markets

Many of the same bases used to segment consumer markets are also used to segment B2B markets. For example, Goya Foods is a U.S. food company that sells different ethnic products to grocery stores, depending on the demographic groups the stores serve—Hispanic, Mexican, or Spanish. Likewise, B2B sellers often divide their customers by geographic areas and tailor their products to them accordingly. Segmenting by behavior is common as well. B2B sellers frequently divide their customers based on their product usage rates. Customers that order many goods and services from a seller often receive special deals and are served by salespeople who call on them in person. By contrast, smaller customers are more likely to have to rely on a firm's website, customer service people, and salespeople who call on them by telephone.

Researchers Matthew Harrison, Paul Hague, and Nick Hague have theorized that there are fewer behavioral and needs-based segments in B2B markets than in business-to-consumer (B2C) markets for two reasons: (1) business markets are made up of a few hundred customers whereas consumer markets can be made up of hundreds of thousands of customers, and (2) businesses aren't as fickle as consumers. Unlike consumers, they aren't concerned about their social standing or influenced by their families and peers. Instead, businesses are concerned solely with buying products that will ultimately increase their profits. According to Harrison, Hague, and Hague, the behavioral, or needs-based, segments in B2B markets include the following:

- **A price-focused segment,** which is composed of small companies that have low profit margins and regard the good or service being sold as not being strategically important to their operations.

- **A quality and brand-focused segment,** which is composed of firms that want the best possible products and are prepared to pay for them.
- **A service-focused segment,** which is composed of firms that demand high-quality products and have top-notch delivery and service requirements.
- **A partnership-focused segment,** which is composed of firms that seek trust and reliability on the part of their suppliers and see them as strategic partners.[19]

MRI Software first divides the market into two **vertical market segments**, vertical meaning that they are in the same business. The two businesses the company serves are commercial real estate companies and multi-family (apartment and condo) real estate companies. The company then breaks the market down by size of the company, both in terms of what they spend currently and what they could spend. The account exec then takes that information one step further, based on personal knowledge of the buyers, and groups them by how they like to buy (personality factors) and needs of the buyers. Each account executive then uses this information to alter the sales strategy for each account.

vertical market segment

In B2B marketing, a portion of an overall market that is engaged in the same business or profession.

Just as with consumer marketing, business marketing uses segmentation to make marketing more efficient. By crafting messages that are more relevant to each group in the market, marketing dollars aren't wasted on those who don't care about the message, whether it is targeting for digital messaging, selecting trade shows, or deciding whom to call on first and what to say.

Key Takeaway

- Segmentation bases are criteria used to classify buyers. The main types of buyer characteristics used to segment consumer markets are behavioral, demographic, geographic, and psychographic. Behavioral segmentation divides people and organizations into groups according to how they behave with or toward products. Segmenting buyers by personal characteristics such as a person's age, income, ethnicity, family size, and so forth is called demographic segmentation. Geographic segmentation involves segmenting buyers based on where they live. Psychographic segmentation seeks to differentiate buyers based on their activities, interests, opinions, attitudes, values, and lifestyles. Oftentimes a firm uses multiple bases to get a fuller picture of its customers and create value for them. Marketing professionals develop consumer insight when they gather both quantitative and qualitative information about their customers. Many of the same bases used to segment consumer markets are used to segment business-to-business (B2B) markets. However, there are generally fewer behavioral-based segments in B2B markets.

Review Questions

1. What buyer characteristics do companies look at when they segment markets?
2. Why do firms often use more than one segmentation base?
3. What two types of information do market researchers gather to develop consumer insight?

5.3 Selecting Target Markets and Target-Market Strategies

Learning Objectives

1. Describe the factors that make some markets more attractive targets than others.
2. Describe the different market-segmenting strategies companies pursue and why.
3. Outline the market-segmentation strategies used in global markets.

Selecting Target Markets

After you segment buyers and develop a measure of consumer insight about them, you can begin to see those that have more potential. That way you can focus your efforts, and your marketing budget, on people who have money to spend and want what you offer. An attractive market has the following characteristics:

- **It is sizeable (large) enough to be profitable given your operating cost.** India and China have about the same population but the market for cars in China is six times bigger because China has more people with enough money to buy cars.
- **It is growing.** The size of the middle class in countries other than the U.S. tripled over the past twenty years (the U.S. middle class declined), and that growth will continue. That's why Netflix, Starbucks, and others are focusing their growth efforts in other countries.
- **It is not already swamped by competitors, or you have found a way to stand out in a crowd.** IBM used to make PCs. However, after the marketplace became crowded with competitors, IBM sold the product line to a Chinese company called Lenovo.
- **Either it is accessible or you can find a way to reach it.** Accessibility, or the lack of it, could include geographic accessibility, political and legal barriers, technological barriers, or social barriers. For example, to overcome geographic barriers, the consumer products company Unilever has hired over 70,000 women in India and Pakistan to sell the company's products to rural consumers in 165,000 villages without stores. In Pakistan alone, this strategy reaches 4.5 million who were otherwise inaccessible.
- **The company has the resources to compete in it.** Elon Musk had the idea of building electric cars but to do so, he had to raise the money and he had to be wary of traditional car companies like GM and Mercedes. He also had to convince engineers that it was a good idea to join his company—and he did.
- **It "fits in" with your firm's mission and objectives.** Unilever produces all of its products in plants powered by renewable energy sources, as part of its commitment to sustainability. Its customers can count on ingredients that were also sourced sustainably.

Target Markets

Are women an attractive target market for yogurt sellers? The maker of this humorous YouTube video thinks so. (She seems to imply they are the only market.)

View in the online reader

Target-Market Strategies: Choosing the Number of Markets to Target

Kraft Mac and Cheese proved that mass marketing can work—at least for a while. Mass marketing is also efficient because you don't have to tailor any part of the offering for different groups of consumers, which is more work and costs more money. The problem is that buyers are not all alike. If a competitor comes along and offers these groups a product (or products) that better meet their needs, you will lose business.

Multisegment Marketing

Most firms tailor their offerings in one way or another to meet the needs of different segments of customers. Because these organizations don't have all their eggs in one basket, they are less vulnerable to competition. Marriott International is an example of a company that operates in multiple market segments. The company has different types of hotels and motels and permanent living facilities designed to meet the needs of different market segments. Marriott has invested in over thirty unique brands so consumers don't confuse the brand and the brand is not diluted. Some of the Marriott brands and their target markets are as follows:

- **Marriott Courtyard.** Targeted at over-the-road travelers.
- **Ritz-Carlton Hotels.** Targeted at luxury travelers.
- **Marriott Conference Centers.** Targeted at businesses hosting small- and midsized meetings.
- **Marriott ExecuStay.** Targeted at executives needing month-long accommodations.
- **Marriott Vacation Clubs.** Targeted at travelers seeking to buy timeshares.

multisegment marketing

Targeting multiple groups of consumers.

A **multisegment marketing** strategy can allow firms to respond to demographic changes and other trends in markets. For example, the growing number of people too old to travel have the option of moving into one of Marriott's "Senior Living Services" facilities, which cater to retirees who need certain types of care. A multisegment strategy can also help companies adjust to changing economic conditions by allowing customers to trade up or down among brands and products. Suppose you take a pay cut and can't afford to stay at Marriott's Ritz-Carlton hotels anymore. A room at a JW Marriott—the most luxurious of the Marriott-brand hotels but cheaper than the Ritz—is available to you. A multisegment strategy can also help companies deal with product life cycle issues. If one brand or product is "dying out," the company has others to compete.

Concentrated Marketing

concentrated marketing

Targeting a very select group of customers.

Some firms—especially smaller ones with limited resources—engage in concentrated marketing. **Concentrated marketing** involves targeting a very select group of customers. Concentrated marketing can be a risky strategy because companies really *do* have all their eggs in one basket. Boeing, for example, had to stop producing planes for two years while investigations examined why two jets crashed. Some of their suppliers, like Spirit Aerosystems which makes the fuselage, had to temporarily halt all operations because they couldn't afford the loss of that business.

niche marketing

Targeting an extremely select group of consumers.

Niche marketing involves targeting an even more select group of consumers. When engaging in niche marketing, a company's goal is often to be a big fish in a small pond instead of a small fish in a big pond.[20] For example, the harmonica market may not be very big but Hohner controls about 85 percent of it. They also make recorders, those plastic instruments that so many children learn to play, as well as accordions. None of these markets are large in comparison to other musical instruments like the guitar, but the company is approaching its 175th anniversary.

Sometimes, however, companies start out as niche marketers and then gain enough market share to grow bigger and expand their offerings. 511 began as a tactical gear provider to the FBI but has since grown to provide training gear for people involved in CrossFit, gear for hunting and camping, and the like. The CrossFit application was actually created by CrossFitters, then recognized and sold by the company. Similarly, Under Armour started out by making T-shirts that wicked away perspiration and selling them to pro sports teams. Today the company makes many different products that it sells to people all around the world.

A new trend related to niche marketing is to provide goods more oriented to a certain geographic area rather than goods aimed at the mass market. It's being done in an effort to attract the increasing number people who want to buy produce that is locally grown, shop at local boutiques, and so forth. To help regain some of its market share, Target has begun providing locally oriented collections of clothing, food, and household items tailored to different cities, such as Boston, Chicago, and San Francisco. In Boston, the retailer sells a marshmallow-and-peanut-butter spread popular among locals who use it to make sandwiches they call Fluffernutters.

Pamela Nefarkara, former VP of retail for Nike, says that geographic targeting is one way to appeal to minoritized communities. If a community has a higher proportion of Black people, for example, imagery used in a retail outlet could reflect that local community, as could each store's product mix. Further, geo-targeting digitally is also possible, again with locally-derived content and sensitivity to the make-up of the area.[21]

microtargeting

The process of gathering multiple sources of data available on people, everything from their tax and phone records to the catalogs they receive, so as to market to them.

Microtargeting, also called narrowcasting, involves gathering all kinds of data available on people—everything from their tax and phone records to the catalogs they receive and using that information to create highly personalized communications. One company that compiles information such as this is Acxiom. For a fee, Acxiom can provide you with a list of Latinx consumers who own two pets, drive an SUV, buy certain personal care products, subscribe to certain television cable channels, read specified magazines, and have income and education levels within a given range.

Clearly, there are privacy and ethical implications related to microtargeting. We will discuss more about how firms go about about gathering information of this kind and its implications when we discuss marketing research and intelligence in Chapter 10. Other ethical problems with targeting in general occur when firms prey on vulnerable consumers who may not be in the best position to make good decisions for themselves or spot deceptive advertising and marketing practices. Children, older adults, people with a mental disability, and those living in poverty are frequently taken advantage of by sellers that promise products that don't deliver or that aren't in their best interests. The providers of "pay day" loans—high-interest loans that cash-strapped consumers take out when they are trying to pay their bills before their paychecks come in—have often been criticized for the practices. Although the loans are legal, people who take them out are often desperate and end up in worse financial shape as a result.

Targeting Global Markets

Firms that compete in the global marketplace can use any combination of the segmenting strategies or none at all. A microcosm of the targeting strategies used in global markets is shown in Figure 5.1. If you're a seller of a metal like iron ore, you might sell the same product across the entire world via a metals broker. The broker would worry about communicating with customers around the world and devising different marketing campaigns for each of them.

FIGURE 5.1 Targeting Strategies Used in Global Markets

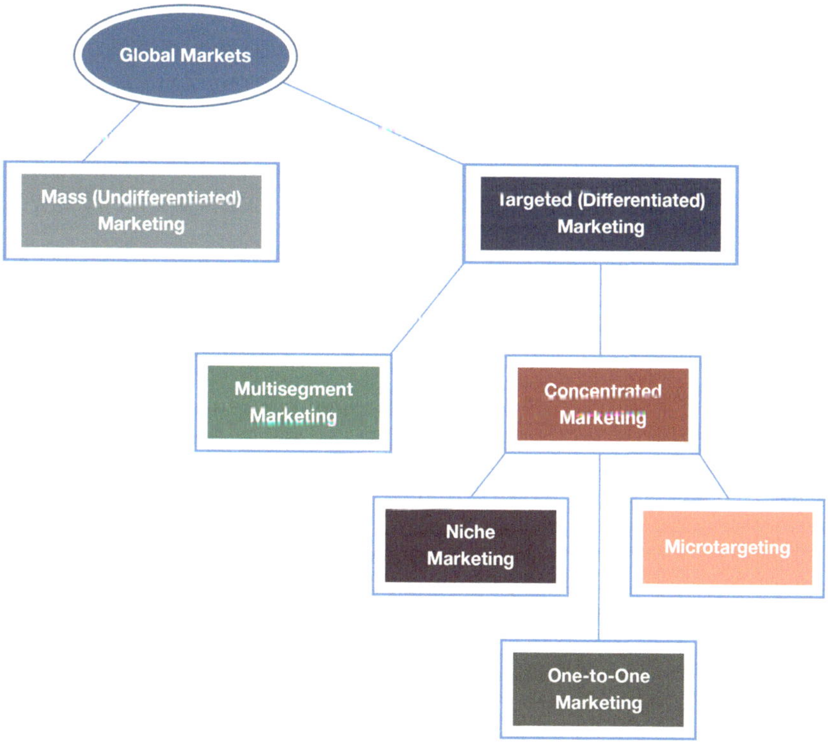

Most companies, however, tailor their offerings to some extent to meet the needs of different buyers around the world. For example, Mattel sells Barbie dolls all around the world—but not the same Barbie. Mattel has created thousands of different Barbie offerings designed to appeal to all kinds of people in different countries.

Pizza Hut has franchises around the world, but its products, packaging, and advertising are tailored to different markets. Squid is a popular topping in Asia, while vegetarian curry pizza is popular in India. Companies tailor products not only for different countries but also for different customers in different countries. For example, Unilever offers products specific to country markets, such as Sariwangi, a bagged tea offered in Indonesia; and Cif ecorefill is a home cleaning product specific to the UK where the interest in multi-use plastic bottles is higher than in other countries.

As mentioned earlier, sellers are increasingly targeting consumers in China, Russia, India, and Brazil because of their fast-growing middle classes. Take the cosmetics maker Avon. Avon's largest market is no longer the United States, but Brazil. Brazilians are extremely looks-conscious and increasingly able to afford cosmetic products as well as plastic surgery. General Motors (GM), the largest U.S. car company, has its largest market in China, and is the largest seller of new cars in China.

Other products are being developed abroad and then sold in the United States. Cosmetics are an example. They are increasingly being developed in Asia with ingredients used in Chinese medicine, such as bamboo grass and mushrooms. Moreover, such products are also targeted toward minority segments in the United States that are challenging the traditional notion of beauty.[22]

Other strategies for targeting markets abroad include acquiring (buying) foreign companies or companies with large market shares there. To tap the Indian market, Kraft bought the candy maker Cadbury, which controls about one-third of India's chocolate market. Likewise, to compete against Corona beer, the Dutch brewer Heineken has purchased Mexico's Femsa, which makes the beer brands Dos Equis, Tecate, and Sol.[23] However, some countries don't allow foreign firms to buy domestic firms. They can only form partnerships with them.

Still another strategy is to export products abroad or open your own sales outlets there. But regulatory and cultural barriers sometimes prevent foreign firms from "invading" a country and those companies who do open their own businesses, whether it be sales outlets and/or manufacturing facilities, run the risk of losing those if the government of that country gets into a trade war with the company's home country. If you plan to export to those foreign sales outlets and a trade war breaks out, you may find yourself priced out of the market by the country's tariffs.[24]

Key Takeaway

- A market worth targeting has the following characteristics: (1) It's sizeable enough to be profitable, given your operating costs; (2) it's growing; (3) it's not already swamped by competitors, or you have found a way to stand out in the crowd; (4) it's accessible, or you can find a way to reach it; (5) you have the resources to compete in it; and (6) it "fits in" with your firm's mission and objectives. Most firms tailor their offerings in one way or another to meet the needs of different segments of customers. A multisegment marketing strategy can allow a company to respond to demographic and other changes in markets, including economic fluctuations. Concentrated marketing involves targeting a very select group of customers. Niche marketing involves targeting an even more select group of consumers. Microtargeting, or *narrowcasting*, is an effort to "super target" consumers by gathering all kinds of data available on people—everything from their tax and phone records to the catalogs they receive. Firms that compete in the global marketplace can use any combination of these segmenting strategies or none at all. Sellers are increasingly targeting consumers in China, Russia, India, and Brazil because of their fast-growing middle classes. Firms are creating low-cost products to capture large markets in developing countries such as these and then selling the products in developed countries. However, firms are also finding it valuable to develop products abroad and sell them domestically. Other strategies for targeting markets abroad include acquiring foreign companies or forming partnerships with them and opening outlets abroad. Targeting customers abroad can sometimes be a risky strategy, depending on the economic and political conditions in a country.

Review Questions

1. What factors does a firm need to examine before deciding to target a market?
2. Which of the segmenting strategies discussed in this section is the broadest? Which is the narrowest?
3. Why might it be advantageous to create low-cost products for developing countries and then sell them in nations such as the United States? Do you see any disadvantages of doing so?

5.4 Positioning and Repositioning Offerings

Learning Objectives

1. Explain why positioning is an important element when it comes to targeting consumers.
2. Describe how a product can be positioned and mapped.
3. Explain what repositioning is designed to do.

Why should buyers purchase your offering versus another? If your product faces competition, you will need to think about how to "position" it in the marketplace relative to competing products. After all, you don't want the product to be just another "face in the crowd" in the minds of consumers. **Positioning** is how consumers perceive a product relative to the competition. Companies want to have a distinctive image and offering that stands out from the competition in the minds of consumers.

positioning

How consumers view a product relative to the the competition.

One way to position your product is to plot customer survey data on a perceptual map. A **perceptual map** is a two-dimensional graph that visually shows where your product stands, or should stand, relative to your competitors, based on criteria important to buyers. The criteria can involve any number of characteristics—price, quality, level of customer service associated with the product, and so on. An example of a perceptual map is shown in Figure 5.2. To avoid head-to-head competition with your competitors, you want to position your product somewhere on the map where your competitors aren't clustered.

perceptual map

A two-dimensional graph that visually shows where a product stands, or should stand, relative to its competitors.

FIGURE 5.2 An Example of a Perceptual Map

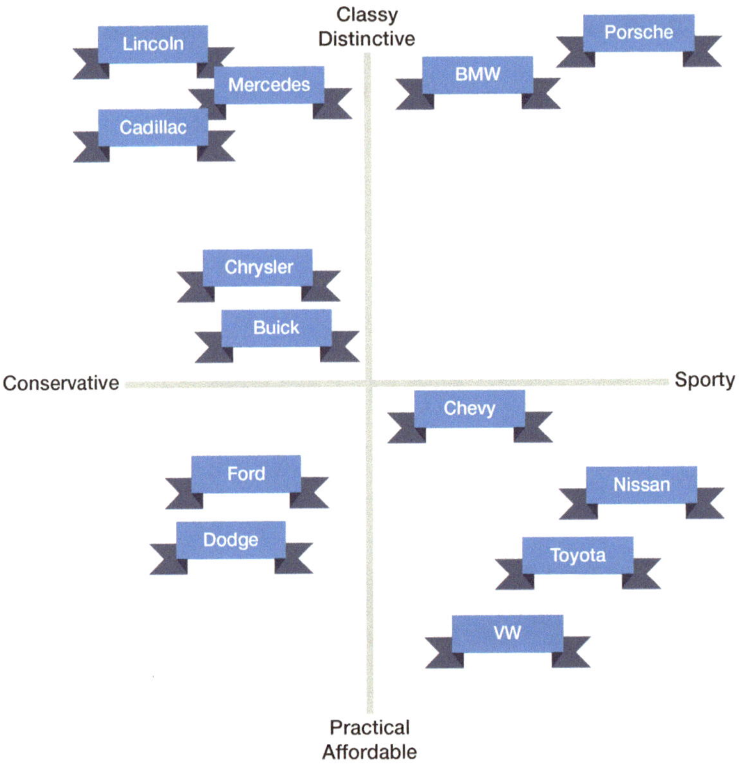

Source: Adapted from http://en.wikipedia.org/wiki/Perceptual_mapping.

tagline

A catchphrase designed to sum up the essence of a product.

Many companies use taglines in their advertising to try to position their products where they want them in the minds of consumers. A **tagline** is a catchphrase designed to sum up the essence of a product. Perhaps you have heard the hamburger chain Wendy's use the tagline, "It's better than fast food." The tagline is designed to set Wendy's apart from restaurants like McDonald's and Burger King—to plant the idea in consumers' heads that Wendy's offerings are less "fast foodish," given the bad rap fast food gets these days.

Of course, where you want to position your product and where you are actually able to will depend on what your firm's competitive advantage is based on. Simply adopting a tagline to try to position your product where you want it won't work if the tagline doesn't ring true or sound plausible to customers. What's better about your product? Is the actual product better, your company's image and reputation better, or the service you provide better? Are you able to offer the product at a better price or communicate its value more effectively with superior advertising and marketing campaigns? Surveying your customers about where your product falls relative to your competitors along each of these dimensions will help you better position it.

repositioning

The process of "moving" a product to a different place in the minds of consumers.

Sometimes firms find it advantageous to reposition their products—especially if they want the product to begin appealing to different market segments. **Repositioning** is an effort to "move" a product to a different place in the market and a different place in the minds of consumers. The i-house, a prefab house designed by Clayton Homes, a mobile home manufacturer, is an example. According to the magazine *Popular Mechanics*, the i-house "looks like a house you'd order from IKEA, sounds like something designed by Apple, and consists of amenities—solar panels, tankless water heaters, and rainwater collectors—that one would expect to come from an offbeat green company out of California selling to a high-end market."[25] Although the company no longer makes the i-house, it continues to look for ways to reposition its product by using more modern home designs and cutting-edge designs.[26]

Porsche's Panamera line of vehicles is a global model, but unlike Porsche's other cars, it's longer. Why? Because rich car buyers in China prefer to be driven by chauffeurs.[27] How do you think Porsche is trying to reposition itself for the future?

Key Takeaway

- If a product faces competition, its producer will need to think about how to "position" it in the marketplace relative to competing products. Positioning is how consumers view a product relative to the competition. A perceptual map is a two-dimensional graph that visually shows where a product stands, or should stand, relative to its competitors, based on criteria important to buyers. Sometimes firms find it advantageous to reposition their products. Repositioning is an effort to "move" a product to a different place in the minds of consumers.

Review Questions

1. Why do companies position products?
2. Explain what a tagline is designed to do.
3. Why might an organization reposition a product?

5.5 Discussion Questions and Activities

Discussion Questions

1. Think about some of your friends and what you have discovered by visiting their homes. Do they buy different things than you do? If so, why? How might a company distinguish you from them in terms of its targeting?
2. Is there ever a time when mass marketing is still appropriate in today's world? What are the pitfalls in microsegmenting?
3. Is it always harder to find new customers than it is to retain old ones, or does it depend on the business you're in?
4. Does one-to-one marketing have to be expensive? How can small organizations interact with their customers in a cost-effective way?
5. Are large companies better off using multisegment strategies and small companies better off using niche strategies? Why or why not?
6. Brands like Victoria's Secret, Gap, Old Navy, and others have struggled. What is it about marketing that they have difficulty with? Or is it just the natural order of things that brands rise and fall?
7. Do you think hotel companies have segmented the market too much and confused customers?

Activities

1. Visit American Civil Liberties Union to see a video they created in an effort to warn consumers about the information being collected about them. Do you think the video is far-fetched? Or

do you think consumers should be alarmed? In your opinion, do the potential benefits of marketers having your data exceed the potential downsides—or not?

2. Watch the video Positioning a Brand: Best Practices for Marketing Product Features With Humor, which illustrates the use of humor in several ads. As you watch, write down the product, who you think the target market is, and why.
3. Describe a product you like that you believe more people should use. As a marketer, how would you reposition the product to increase its use? The product doesn't have to be a brand, it could be something as simple as paper straws. Outline your strategy.
4. From the chapter, identify at least two markets that are growing and, using web resources, profile them as much as you can. What would you do differently if you were Starbucks targeting those markets? How would your ideas change if you were Dave's Bread?

5.6 Case Study: Cabela's and Bass Pro

Cabela's, founded in 1961 by the Cabela brothers in Sidney, Nebraska, is a national retailer of camping, fishing, hunting, hiking, boating, and other outdoor equipment, clothing, and gear. The chain was purchased by Bass Pro in 2017, an easy merger because the two retail chains were so similar in the markets served. Both companies began by building large destination stores, places that were fun for outdoors enthusiasts to go out of their way to visit. Stores included large aquariums with sports fish like bass, crappie, and the like, dozens of mounted animals like deer, bear, and antelope, an archery range, and in some cases, a gun range. Stores also house a demonstration fish tank for teaching fishing tips and demonstrating different lures with live fish.

Cabela's tried to reach more consumers with smaller stores, called Cabela's Outpost, 30,000 square feet as opposed to 200,000 to 250,000 square feet. These smaller stores were less successful, and the company decided to focus expansion on other areas of the business.

Bass Pro was founded ten year later, in 1971, in Springfield, Missouri, and the first store opened a year later. Like Cabela's stores are large, but Bass Pro's Outdoor World stores focus more on fishing and boating. Like Cabela's, they offer many classes to enhance the outdoors experience, and include topics like Dutch oven cooking. Bass Pro also has its own line of boats, due to the acquisition of White River Marine.

Cabela's business has been much more focused on hunting and gun sports. In fact, any time there is the potential for greater gun control, Cabela's gun sales increase. This reliance on gun sales has made Cabela's sales results look good at some times but sales are not as strong in other times.

There are still some markets in which Cabela's and Bass Pro each have stores. Online sales are big for both, too. In fact, loyal customers average fewer than three visits to a physical location in a given year, making most of their purchases online. Cabela's and Bass Pro also rely heavily on apparel sales, both sport-specific apparel (e.g. hunting vests, cold water gear for kayaking, etc.) and casual wear for everyday use.

Case Study Questions

1. Hunting is an outdoor sport that is declining in popularity as its primary customers are aging out, but that is the traditional core of Cabela's business. Boating sales exploded during the pandemic because it was a safe socially-distant activity. How can Cabela's attract new segments and what should those segments be? How can Cabela's leverage its success during the pandemic into a longer-term business by segmenting more carefully?
2. Visit the websites of both Cabela's and Bass Pro. Draw some conclusions about how they may serve different markets and provide evidence to support those conclusions. Is merging the two brands the answer? Why or why not?
3. Are there business markets that Cabela's could attract or partner with?

Endnotes

1. (July 9, 2009), "Lift Sales with Personalized, Multi-channel Messages: 6 Steps," http://www.marketingsherpa.com/article.php?ident=31299.
2. Jefferson Graham (April 1, 2009), "Cake Decorator Finds Twitter a Sweet Recipe for Success," *USA Today*, 5B.
3. Meg Marco (March 18, 2008), "LEAKS: Best Buy's Internal Customer Profiling Document," *The Consumerist*, http://consumerist.com/368894/leaks-best-buys-internal-customer-profiling-document.
4. "Market Segmentation," *The Market Segmentation Company*, http://www.marketsegmentation.co.uk/segmentation_tmsc.htm.
5. Curt Harler (December 2008), "Reaching the Unreachable," *Smart Business Cleveland*, 92; Don Peppers and Martha Rogers (May 1, 1999), "The Short Way to Long-Term Relationships," *Sales and Marketing Management*, 24; Don Peppers, Martha Rogers, and Bob Dorf (January–February 1999), "Is Your Company Ready for One-to-One Marketing?" *Harvard Business Review*, 151–60.
6. Alejandra Reyes-Vallarde (December 20, 2017), "As Millennials Embrace Renting over Owning — Even Clothes — Stores Are Taking Notice," *Los Angeles Times*, http://www.latimes.com/business/la-fi-retail-rentals-20171220-story.html.
7. Anonymous, (2021), "Baby Boomer Spending Habits in 2021," https://LexingtonLaw.com/blog/credit-cards/baby-boomer-spending-habits.html.
8. Anonymous, "Generation Z Spending Habits in 2021," https://Lexington-Law.com/blog/credit-cards/generation-z-spending-habits.html.
9. Sagrika Padha (2017), "4 Rebranding Stories We Can All Learn From," Marketing Maximus Magazine, https://pinklemonade.in/best-rebranding-stories.
10. Anonymous (2021), "Old Spice Demographics and Consumer Insights," https://snapshot.Numerator.com/brand/old-spice; Anonymous (2016), "How Old Spice Rebranded and Saved their Business," Marketing Gunslingers, https://marketinggunslingers.com/blog/old-spice.
11. Dominic-Madori (2020) "Retail is Courting Millennials," *Business Insider,* https://www.businessinsider.com/retail-courts-gen-z-spending-power-over-140-billion-2020.
12. Stefanie Horan (2020), "How Different Generations Spend Money," https://smartasset.com/checking-account/how-different-generations-spend-money-2020.
13. Christina Binkley (May 7, 2015), "Shop and Lounge Like a VIP," *Wall Street Journal*, D1.
14. Constantine von Hoffman (September 11, 2006), "For Some Marketers, Low Income Is Hot," *Brandweek*, http://cfsinnovation.com/content/some-marketers-low-income-hot.
15. Ericka Podesta McCoy (2021), "Multicultural Insights: The Importance of Granular Segmentation," Retail Touchpoints, https://retailtouchpoints.com/blog/multicultural-insights-the-importance-of-granular-segmentation.
16. Jenn Gidman (2021), "The Weird Correlation between S'mores and COVID," *Newser*, newser.com.
17. James H. Donnelly (2002), preface to *Marketing Management*, 9th ed., by J. Paul Peter, New York: McGraw-Hill Professional, 79.
18. "U.S. Framework and VALS™ Type," *Strategic Business Insights*, http://www.strategicbusinessinsights.com/vals/ustypes.shtml.
19. Matthew Harrison, Paul Hague, and Nick Hague, "Why Is Business-to-Business Marketing Special?" (whitepaper), *B2B International*, http://www.b2binternational.com/library/whitepapers/whitepapers04.php.
20. "Niche Marketing," BusinessDictionary.com, http://www.businessdictionary.com/definition/niche-marketing.
21. Darla Voronina (2018), "Geo-Targeting: Local PPC Strategy and Actionable Tips," https://www.semrush.com/blog/geo-targeting-local-ppc-strategy-actionable-tips/.
22. Hannah Baeh (2021), "On a Deeply Personally Level, Asian Americans Disrupting the Beauty Industry," https://www.cnn.com/style/article/asian-americans-beauty-industry-hyphenated/index.html.
23. Michael J. de la Merced and Chris V. Nicholson (January 11, 2010), "Heineken in Deal to Buy Big Mexican Brewer," *New York Times*, http://www.nytimes.com/2010/01/12/business/global/12beer.html.
24. Meg Luo (2018), "How Trade Wars Affect Corporate Performance," *US News & World Report*.
25. Ariel Schwartz (May 4, 2009), "Clayton Homes' i-house Combines Energy Efficiency and Modular Affordability," *Fast Company*, http://www.fastcompany.com/blog/ariel-schwartz/sustainability/clayton-homes-75k-energy-efficient-i-house.
26. (May 6, 2009), "Clayton 'i-house' Is Giant Leap from Trailer Park," *Knoxvillebiz.com*, http://www.knoxnews.com/news/2009/may/06/clayton-i-house-giant-leap-trailer-park/.
27. John Gapper (April 23, 2009), "Why Brands Now Rise in the East," *Financial Times*, 9.

CHAPTER 6

Product and Service Decisions

Why does anyone buy anything? For example, why buy an iPad or a Surface—and why choose one over the other?

No one buys a product or pays for a service just to have it. Even if someone buys an iPad just to look cool and not because of its features, the purchase was still made to accomplish a goal. In this chapter, we explore various types of offerings and the components of those offerings that are created to meet customers' goals.

6.1 What Comprises an Offering?

Learning Objectives

1. Distinguish between the three major components of an offering—product, price, and service.
2. Explain, from both a product-dominant and a service-dominant approach, the mix of components that compose different types of offerings.
3. Distinguish between technology platforms and product lines.

People buy things to solve needs and to meet goals. In the case of the iPad, the need may be to have better access to the web in order to access data or entertainment, to look cool, or both. Offerings are products and services designed to deliver value to customers—either to fulfill their needs, satisfy their "wants," or both. We discuss people's needs in other chapters. In this chapter, we discuss how marketing fills those needs through the creation and delivery of offerings.

Product, Price, and Service

Most offerings consist of a **product**, or a tangible good people can buy, sell, and own. If you search for storage capacity of iPad, you'll find that people have a lot of questions about how much memory to buy, what model will work for their situation, and the like. What they want to know is whether their needs will be met. **Features**, or physical characteristics of a product, determine what the product can do. For example, if reading books like this on your iPad is the primary way you use your iPad, you may have less storage need than someone who travels a lot and wants a large library of videos available. You won't be willing to pay more for the extra storage that the heavy video user will want if you only need half that much. When a feature satisfies a need or want, then there is a **benefit**. Features, then, matter differently to different consumers based on each individual's needs. Remember: The personal value equation is different for every customer because needs and tastes are different!

product

A tangible good that can be bought, sold, and owned.

features

A physical characteristic of a product.

benefit

The degree to which a feature satisfies a buyer's need or desire.

The price of these sweaters is one thing—total cost of ownership, though, depends on whether they can be dry cleaned or hand-washed only or machine washed.

Source: © Shutterstock, Inc.

price

The amount exchanged by the buyer to receive the value offered by the product or service.

total cost of ownership (TCO)

The total amount of time and money spent to acquire, use, and dispose of an offering.

service

An intangible component of an offering.

An offering also consists of a **price**, or the amount people pay to receive the offering's benefits. The price, though, is not the same as cost (remember the PVE contains cost, not price) . For example, many consumers think of a product's price as only the amount they paid; however, the true cost of owning an iPad, for example, is the cost of the device itself plus the cost of the apps, plus the internet service cost, and so forth. The **total cost of ownership (TCO)**, then, is the total amount someone pays to own, use, and eventually dispose of a product.

TCO is usually thought of as a concept businesses use to compare offerings. However, consumers also use the concept. For example, suppose you are comparing two sweaters, one that can be hand washed and one that must be dry cleaned. The hand-washable sweater will cost you less to own in dollars but may cost more to own in terms of your time and hassle. A smart consumer would take that into consideration. When we first introduced the personal value equation, we discussed hassle as the time and effort spent making a purchase. A TCO approach, though, would also include the time and effort related to owning the product—in this case, the time and effort to hand wash the sweater. One buyer may find that the hassle and time are worth it to save the money for dry cleaning, while another may prefer to spend money rather than time on taking care of the sweater.

A **service** is an action that provides a buyer with an intangible benefit. A haircut is a service. When you purchase a haircut, it's not something you can hold, give to another person, or resell. "Pure" services are offerings that are intangible, as they don't have any tangible characteristics associated with them. Skydiving is an example of a pure service. You are left with nothing after the jump but the memory of it (unless you buy a video of the event). Yes, a plane is required, and it is certainly tangible. But it isn't the product—the jump is. At times people use the term "product" to mean an offering that's either tangible or intangible. Banks, for example, often advertise specific types of loans, or financial "products," they offer consumers. Yet truly these products are financial services. The term "product" is frequently used to describe an offering of either type.

The intangibility of a service creates interesting challenges for marketers and buyers when they try to judge the relative merits of one service over another. Think for a moment about how you read and use reviews of a hotel, for example. Research shows that we tend to rely more on complaints than compliments, but that we judge complaints based on whether what is being said might apply to us or if it involved a random one-off event. For example, you might consider several complaints about a lack of cleanliness as more important than a complaint that a youth soccer team was there and made a lot of noise. How does the marketer promote quiet, clean rooms? Maybe with a photo like this one.

Hotels can promote clean, quiet rooms with images like this one, so that potential customers can assess the intangible qualities along with the tangible.

Source: © Shutterstock, Inc.

Services usually require the consumer to be physically present or involved. A haircut, a night in a hotel, or a flight from here to there all require the consumer to be physically present, and consumption of the service is not separate from the creation of the service. Unlike a physical product, which can be created and purchased off a shelf, a service often (but not always) involves the consumer in its creation.

Another challenge for many services providers is that services are perishable; they can't be stored. A night at a hotel, for example, can't be saved and sold later. If it isn't sold that day, it is lost forever. A barber isn't really paid for a haircut but for time and expertise (which is why you don't want to use the barber sporting the bad haircut—expertise matters). Services have difficult management and marketing challenges because of their intangibility.

Many tangible products have an intangible service component attached to them, however, and how different companies approach service can be very different. Apple, for example, has a fairly wide network of stores that can provide service help on an iPad; Microsoft added retail outlets to do the same for its Surface line of pad computers but the number is much smaller. Otherwise, a buyer has to rely on online service support through chat or a call center.

Customer experience (CX) involves every touchpoint a customer has with a brand or company, including promotions, visiting a website, ordering or scheduling offerings, and receiving products and services.

customer experience (CX)

Every touchpoint a customer has with a brand or company, including promotions, visiting a website, ordering or scheduling offerings, and receiving products and services.

The RATER Model

The service portion of any offering presents interesting challenges to marketers. Customers, especially in situations where there is co-creation, have difficulty in determining a personal value equation because judging the benefits of a service is so difficult to do. One model used to focus marketers' attention on key dimensions of services is the RATER model.

reliability
The ability of a service provider to deliver the same quality of service over time.

The first R stands for **reliability**, or the ability to deliver a specific level of quality over a number of trials. For example, airlines measure on-time departure, and you can find out how frequently a specific flight is on time for departure. Yet, most consumers would prefer that the plane arrive on time rather than depart on time. If you place greater value on arrival than departure, determining the carrier's reliability may be difficult. Reliability in many instances, though, is a function of good training. The better the training for personnel, the more likely they will deliver the same level of service every time, which is why hotels, restaurants, and other service providers develop scripts for their personnel to follow.

assurance
The degree to which a consumer can trust the service provider to live up to promises.

That's why the A stands for **assurance**, which really means the degree to which the consumer can trust the service provider to live up to promises. Marketers have to provide assurances of various kinds, such as guarantees or warranties which provide remedies if the service fails to live up to the promises. For example, if a flight is delayed due to mechanical issues with the plane, the airline has more responsibility for compensating passengers than when a delay is due to weather, something the airline has no control over. But assurances are not warranties. Warranties are remedies in the event of failure; assurance is a form of promotion that sets expectations for service quality.

tangibility
Tangible characteristics that signal an appropriate level of quality for the service being provided.

T stands for **tangibility**, or the tangibles that signal a level of quality consistent with the desired service outcomes. While a hotel provides a service, there are tangibles such as the shampoo that's provided, the appearance of furniture, and so forth from which you can draw inferences about the quality of the hotel. Higher-quality tangibles should signal a higher-quality service. For an accounting firm, the challenge is how to convince a customer that the service was worthwhile when the goal is to keep the client out of trouble with the IRS or SEC; success means that the client never actually experiences anything negative other than writing the check for taxes. Some firms, therefore, deliver materials to clients in nicely bound books or through a web or digital portal. This digital approach offers a tangible clue that the firm is up to date.

empathy
The degree to which a service provider can understand the wants and needs of a customer.

The E in the model stands for **empathy**, recognizing that services are typically delivered by individuals to individuals, and service providers need to be able to put themselves into the shoes of their customers to fully comprehend what is wanted and needed. Training is also important here, because personnel need to be able to ask questions and listen in order to understand those needs.

responsiveness
The ability of a service provider to respond to an individual consumer's interests and desires.

The final letter in the RATER model is for **responsiveness**, which reflects the service provider's ability to respond to consumers' interests and desires. Since most offerings have a service component, responsiveness often reflects post-purchase handling of complaints and problems.

In this discussion of the RATER model, we've focused on the service providers—those personnel who actually deliver the service. Marketing, though, has to be concerned with the development of the features of the service, how it is to be communicated, priced, and sold. For example, some business marketers create Service Level Agreements, or SLAs, which specify such things as how quickly a customer's request must be fulfilled or when service outputs have to be delivered. Dr. Debbie Qaqish, co-founder of The Pedowitz Group (a digital marketing agency), says her firm has specific SLAs negotiated with each client for each of the services that the company provides.

The Product-Dominant Approach to Marketing

From the traditional **product-dominant** perspective of business, marketers consider products, services, and prices as three separate and distinguishable characteristics. To some extent, they are. HP could, for example, add or strip out features from a piece of testing equipment and not change its service policies or the equipment's price. The product-dominant marketing perspective has its roots in the Industrial Revolution. During this era, businesspeople focused on the development of products that could be mass produced cheaply. In other words, firms became **product-oriented**, meaning that they believed the best way to capture market share was to create and manufacture better products at lower prices. A limitation, of course, is that the maker determined what was better, not the consumer. Marketing remained oriented that way until after World War II.

product-dominant

An approach to products and offerings that clearly separates the physical product from services and from price.

product-oriented

An approach to business that centers on capturing business by focusing on creating and manufacturing better products at lower prices.

The Service-Dominant Approach to Marketing

Who determines which products are better? Customers do, of course. Thus, taking a product-oriented approach can result in marketing professionals focusing too much on the product itself and not enough on the customer or service-related factors that customers want. Most customers will compare tangible products and the prices charged for them in conjunction with the services that come with them. In other words, the *complete* offering is the basis of comparison. So although a buyer will compare the price of product A to the price of product B, in the end, the prices are compared in conjunction with the other features and services of the products. The dominance of any one of these dimensions is a function of the buyer's needs.

The advantage of the **service-dominant** approach is that it integrates the product, price, and service dimensions of an offering. This integration helps marketers think more like their customers, which can help them add value to their firm's offerings. In addition to the product itself, marketers should consider what services it takes for the customer to acquire their offerings (e.g., the need to learn about the product from a sales clerk), to enjoy them, and to dispose of them (e.g., someone to move the product out of the house and haul it away), because each of these activities creates costs for their customers—either monetary costs or time and hassle costs.

Have you been to Five Guys? What's their core product? Their augmented product?

Source: © Shutterstock, Inc.

Critics of the service-dominant approach argue that the product-dominant approach also integrates services (though not price). The argument is that at the core of an offering is the product, such as an iPad, as illustrated in Figure 6.1. The physical product, in this case an iPad, is the **core product**. Surrounding it are services and accessories, called the **augmented product**, that support the core product. Together, these make up the complete product. One limitation of this approach has already been mentioned; price is left out. But for many "pure" products, this conceptualization can be helpful in bundling different augmentations for different markets. A core product is the central functional offering, but it may be augmented by various accessories or services, known as the augmented product.

service-dominant

An approach to offerings that integrates the physical product, attendant services, and price into the total offering.

core product

The physical component of an offering.

augmented product

Services and accessories that improve the core product's ability to deliver benefits.

FIGURE 6.1 Core and Augmented Products

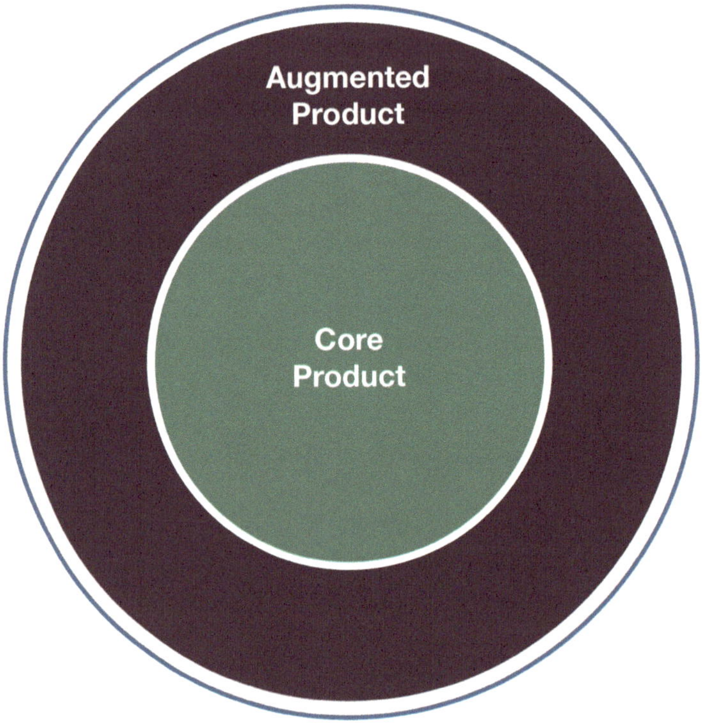

Today's empowered customers are now becoming more involved in the creation of benefits. Let's go back to that "pure" product, Campbell's Cream of Chicken Soup. The consumer may prepare that can as a bowl of soup, but it could also be used as an ingredient in making King Ranch Chicken. As far as the consumer is concerned, no benefit is experienced until the soup is eaten; thus, the consumer played a part in the creation of the final "product" when the soup was an ingredient in the King Ranch Chicken. Or suppose your school's cafeteria made King Ranch Chicken for you to consume; in that case you both ate a product and consumed a service.

Some people argue that focusing too much on the customer can lead to too little product development or poor product development. These people believe that customers often have difficulty seeing how an innovative new technology can create benefits for them. For example, few consumers were able to fully understand the potential of smart phones before they were introduced. In that instance, it was the vision of Steve Jobs of Apple and a few others that really drove the development of the smart phone. Researchers and entrepreneurs frequently make many discoveries and then products are created as a result of those discoveries. Another example is highway signs. A 3M engineer realized that the manmade crystals they were using on industrial sandpaper were able to refract light, just like any crystal. He flipped the crystals over so that the light was reflected in a more focused way. That's why you're able to see those super-bright highways signs.

The Sharing Economy

Uber and Lyft, the ride-sharing companies that are displacing taxicabs, and Vrbo, the room-sharing company that competes with traditional hotels, are perhaps the best-known examples of the sharing economy. The **sharing economy** is the use of information technology to allow owners of assets to increase utilization of their assets, whether for money or exchange of other goods or services (barter). You can see how this movement is based on service-dominant logic; that is, the realization that people want the benefits without the hassle or costs of ownership of assets like cars, washing machines, or even kitchens.

sharing economy

The use of information technology to allow owners of assets to increase utilization of those assets, whether for money or exchange of other goods or services (barter).

Note that companies like Rent the Runway, which allows people to rent expensive clothing for short periods, are not sharing economy companies. The difference is that Rent the Runway owns the clothes; Lyft does not own the cars. The similarity, though, is that these represent the growing trend of owning fewer things and renting as needed, a trend called *everything as a service*.

When business strategists talk about a company's go-to-market strategy or the firm's business model, think back to the sharing economy. If the benefit being sold is automobile transportation, there are several business models: selling cars, offering taxis, joining Uber or Lyft, or renting cars either on a transactional basis (such as Avis) or on a subscription basis (such as Zipcar). There's even the option of taking the bus or walking or renting a Lime scooter.

Product Levels and Product Lines

A product's **technology platform** is the core technology on which it is built. Take, for example, the iPad, which is based on cellular technology. In many cases, a new product is simply a different bundling of features and benefits based on the same basic technology. For example, Apple offers the iPad mini, based on the same technology.

This super bright metal stop sign is actually coated with manmade crystals, applied in a way that focuses the light for a brighter reflection—an idea a 3M engineer had for crystals originally created to make sandpaper.

Source: © Shutterstock, Inc.

In some instances, a new offering is based on a technology platform originally designed to solve different problems. Remember the bright road signs made with crystals originally designed for sandpaper? The crystal-making technology is an example of a technology platform, originally created to make industrial-grade sandpaper.

A technology platform isn't limited to tangible products. Knowledge can be a type of technology platform in a pure services environment. For example, the "bioesthetic" treatment model was developed to help people who experience TMJ, a jaw disorder that makes chewing painful. A dentist can be trained on the bioesthetic technology platform and then provide services based on it. There are, however, other ways to treat TMJ that involve other platforms, or bases of knowledge and procedures, such as surgery.

technology platform

The core, or basic, technology on which a product is built.

An important consideration for some companies is creating products that are unique or not easily copied. Without uniqueness, there is no reason for preference. Proprietary technology platforms can be one way that companies create unique offerings.

Few firms survive by selling only one product. Most firms sell several offerings designed to work together to satisfy a broad range of customers' needs and desires. A **product line** is a group of related offerings. Product lines are created to make marketing strategies more efficient. Campbell's condensed soups, for example, are basic soups sold in cans with red and white labels. But Campbell's Chunky is a ready-to-eat soup sold in cans that are labeled differently. Most consumers expect there to be differences between Campbell's red-label chicken soup and Chunky chicken soup, even though they are both made by the same company.

product line

A group of offerings that serve similar needs and are sold under the same name.

line depth

The number of variations in a single product line.

line extension

A new idea or offering that occurs when a company comes out with another model (related product or service) based on the same platform and brand as one of its other products.

line breadth

The number of different, or distinct, product lines offered by a company.

product mix

The entire assortment of products that a firm offers.

A product line can be broad, as in the case of Campbell's condensed soup line, which consists of several dozen different flavors. Or, a product line can be narrow, as in the case of Apple's iPad line, which consists of only a few different devices. How many offerings there are in a single product line—that is, whether the product line is broad or narrow—is called **line depth**. When new but similar products are added to the product line, it is called a **line extension**. Each new iPhone, for example, is a line extension. The Apple Watch, however, is a different product line, even though it relies on the same technology platform as an iPhone. Companies can also offer many different product lines. **Line breadth** (or width) is a function of how many different, or distinct, product lines a company has. For example, Campbell's has a Chunky soup line, condensed soup line, Kids' soup line, lower sodium soup line, and a number of non-soup lines like Pace Picante sauces, Prego Italian sauces, and crackers. The entire assortment of products that a firm offers is called the **product mix**.

As Figure 6.2 shows, there are four offering levels. Consider the iPad Mini. There is (1) the basic offering (the device itself); (2) the offering's technology platform (the cell technology used by the Mini); (3) the product line to which the Mini belongs (Apple's iPad line of pad computers); and (4) the product category to which the offering belongs (tablet computers as opposed to iPhones, for example).

FIGURE 6.2 Product Levels

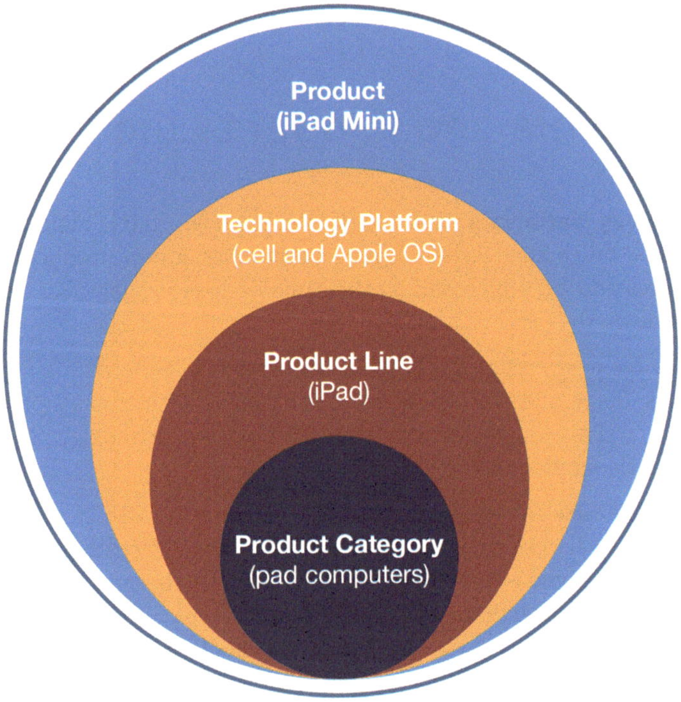

So how does a technology platform become a new product or service or line of new products and services? In another chapter, we take a closer look at how companies design and develop new offerings.

Key Takeaway

- Companies market offerings composed of a combination of tangible and intangible characteristics for certain prices. During the Industrial Revolution, firms focused primarily on products and not so much on customers. The service-dominant perspective to marketing integrates three different dimensions of an offering—not only the product but also its price and the services associated with it. This perspective helps marketers think more like their customers, which helps firms add value to their offerings. An offering is based on a technology platform, which can be used to create a product line. A product line is a group of similar offerings. A product line can be deep (many offerings of a similar type) and/or broad (offerings that are very different from one another and cover a wide range of customers' needs). The entire assortment of products that a company offers is called the product mix.

Review Questions

1. How do the product-dominant and service-dominant approaches to marketing differ?
2. Do "product-dominant" and "product-oriented" mean the same thing?
3. What is the difference between a technology platform and a product line?
4. The text describes the different business models for the automobile transportation market. What would drive consumers to select one specific model? How do terms like technology platform apply to the different models?
5. What is the difference between product depth and product breadth?

6.2 Types of Consumer Offerings

Learning Objectives

1. Define the various types of offerings marketed to individual consumers.
2. Explain why a single offering might be marketed differently to different types of consumers.

Products and services can be categorized in a number of ways. We will use these categories throughout the book because they are the most commonly referred to categories by marketers and because there are marketing implications for each. Consumer offerings fall into four general categories:

1. Convenience offerings
2. Shopping offerings
3. Specialty offerings
4. Unsought offerings

In this section, we will discuss each of these categories. Keep in mind that the categories are not a function of the characteristic of the offerings themselves. Rather, they are a function of how consumers want to purchase them, which can vary from consumer to consumer. What one consumer considers a shopping good might be a convenience good to another consumer.

Convenience Offerings

What products does your grocery store put by the checkout to appeal as impulse purchases? Who in this family is targeted?

Source: © Shutterstock, Inc.

convenience offering

Low-priced, frequently purchased products and services that require little shopping effort.

impulse offering

An offering that is purchased on impulse, without prior planning.

Convenience offerings are products and services consumers generally don't want to put much effort into shopping for because they see little difference between competing brands. For many consumers, bread is a convenience offering. A consumer might choose the store in which to buy the bread but be willing to buy whatever brand of bread the store has available. Marketing convenience items is often limited to simply trying to get the product in as many places as possible where a purchase could occur.

Closely related to convenience offerings are **impulse offerings**, or items purchased without any planning. The classic example is Life Savers, originally manufactured by the Life Savers Candy Company, beginning in 1913. The company encouraged retailers and restaurants to display the candy next to their cash registers and to always give customers a nickel back as part of their change so as to encourage them to buy one additional item—a roll of Life Savers, which just happened to cost a nickel!

Shopping Offerings

Wonder, Nature's Own, Dave's, or Home Pride? One consumer might not care, making these convenience goods; another might want only Dave's, making it a shopping good.

Source: © Shutterstock, Inc.

shopping offering

An offering for which the consumer will make an effort to compare various firms' offerings and select a brand.

A **shopping offering** is one for which the consumer will make an effort to compare and select a brand. Consumers believe there are differences between similar shopping offerings and want to find the right one or the best price. Buyers might visit multiple retail locations or spend a considerable amount of time visiting websites and reading reviews about the product, such as the reviews found in *Consumer Reports*. Remember, what might be a convenience offering to one buyer might be a shopping good to another.

Consumers often care about brand names when they're deciding on shopping goods. If a store is out of a particular brand, then another brand might not do. For example, if you prefer Crest Whitening Expressions toothpaste, and the store is out of it, you might put off buying the toothpaste until your next trip to the store. Or you might go to a different store or buy a small tube of some other toothpaste until you can get what you want. Note that even something as simple as toothpaste can become a shopping good for someone very interested in her dental health—perhaps after she's read online product reviews or consulted with her dentist. That's why companies like Procter & Gamble, the maker of Crest, work hard to influence not only consumers but also people like dentists, who influence the sale of their products.

Specialty Offerings

Specialty offerings are highly differentiated offerings, and the brands under which they are marketed are very different across companies, too. For example, exotic perfumes available only in exclusive outlets are considered specialty offerings. Specialty offerings are purchased less frequently than convenience offerings. Therefore, the profit margin on them tends to be greater.

Clive Christian perfumes cost hundreds of dollars and are considered specialty offerings. People will go to greater lengths to shop for these items and are willing to pay more for them.

Source: © Shutterstock, Inc.

Note that while marketers try to distinguish between specialty offerings, shopping offerings, and convenience offerings, it is the consumer who ultimately makes the decision. The restaurant market is clearly divided by offering types. Nobu, the high-end sushi restaurant, is clearly a specialty restaurant, while Long John Silver's is a convenience offering. Yet, for some loyal customers, they may prefer Captain D's and drive past a Long John Silver's to get there. Therefore, what might be a specialty offering to one consumer may be a convenience offering to another. The choice is the consumer's.

Marketing specialty goods requires building brand name recognition in the minds of consumers and educating them about your product's key differences. This is critical. For fashion goods, the only point of difference may be the logo on the product (for example, a Vineyard Vines versus a Polo label). Even so, marketers spend a great deal of money and effort to try to get consumers to perceive these products differently than their competitors'.

specialty offering

An offering that is highly differentiated from other offerings and is designed to satisfy a similar need or want.

Unsought Offerings

Unsought offerings are those that buyers do not generally want to have to shop for until they need them. Towing services and funeral services are generally considered unsought offerings. Marketing unsought items is difficult. Some organizations try to presell the offering, such as preneed sales in the funeral industry or towing insurance in the auto industry. Other companies, such as insurance companies, try to create a strong awareness among consumers so that when the need arises for these products, consumers think of their organizations first.

unsought offering

An offering consumers don't typically shop for until it is needed. Examples include funeral and towing services.

Key Takeaway

- Convenience offerings, shopping offerings, specialty offerings, and unsought offerings are the major types of consumer offerings. Convenience offerings often include life's necessities (bread, milk, fuel, and so forth), for which there is little difference across brands. Shopping goods do vary, and many consumers develop strong preferences for some brands versus others. Specialty goods are even more exclusive. Unsought goods are a challenge for marketers because customers do not want to have to shop for them until they need them.

Review Questions

1. What are the four types of consumer offerings? How do they differ from one another?
2. Is it possible for cemetery plots or caskets to be a shopping good or a specialty good? Or are they always unsought goods?

6.3 Types of Business-to-Business (B2B) Offerings

Learning Objectives

1. Define the various types of offerings marketed to businesses.
2. Identify some of the differences with regard to how the various types of business offerings are marketed.

Just like there are different types of consumer offerings, there are different types of business-to-business (B2B) offerings as well. But unlike consumer offerings, which are categorized by how consumers shop, B2B offerings are categorized by how they are used. The primary categories of B2B offerings are:

- capital equipment offerings
- raw materials offerings
- original equipment manufacturer (OEM) offerings
- maintenance, repair, and operations (MRO) offerings
- facilitating offerings

The grade of raw leather used to cover the sofa is purchased from suppliers as a commodity—that is, a certain grade that is the same across vendors, which compete on the basis of price and the availability of the product.

Source: © Shutterstock, Inc.

Capital Equipment Offerings

capital equipment offering

Tangible equipment business purchases that are depreciated.

Capital equipment is any equipment purchased and used for more than one year and depreciated over its useful life. Machinery used in a manufacturing facility, for example, would be considered capital equipment. Professionals who market capital equipment often have to direct their communications to many people within the firms to which they are selling, because the buying decisions related to the products can be rather complex and involve many departments. From a marketing standpoint, deciding who should get what messages and how to influence the sale can be very challenging.

Raw Materials Offerings

Raw materials offerings are materials firms offer other firms so they can make a product or provide a service. Raw materials are processed only to the point required to economically distribute them. Lumber is generally considered a raw material, as are iron, nickel, copper, and other ores. If iron is turned into sheets of steel, it is called a **manufactured material** because it has been processed into a finished good but is not a stand-alone product; it still has to be incorporated into something else to be usable. Both raw and manufactured materials are then used in the manufacture of other offerings.

Raw materials are often thought of as commodities, meaning that there is little difference among them. Consequently, the competition to sell them is based on price and availability. Natuzzi is an Italian company that makes leather furniture. The wood Natuzzi buys to make its sofas is a commodity. By contrast, the leather the company uses is graded, meaning each piece of leather is rated based on quality. To some extent, the leather is still a commodity, because once a firm decides to buy a certain grade of leather, every company's leather within that grade is virtually the same.

raw materials offering

Raw material products are materials firms offer other firms so they can make a product or provide a service. These offerings are processed only to the point required for economic handling and distribution.

manufactured material

A material that has been processed into a finished good but is not a stand-alone product; it still has to be incorporated into something else to be usable.

OEM Offerings or Components

An **original equipment manufacturer (OEM)** is a manufacturer or assembler of a final product. An OEM purchases raw materials, manufactured materials, and component parts and puts them together to make a final product. **OEM offerings or components**, like an on/off switch, are components, or parts, sold by one manufacturer to another that get built into a final product without further modification. If you look at that picture of the Natuzzi couch, you may notice that it sits on metal feet. The metal feet are probably made by a manufacturer other than Natuzzi, making the feet an OEM component. Dell's hard drives installed in computer kiosks, like the self-service kiosks in airports that print your boarding passes, are another example of OEM components.

original equipment manufacturer (OEM)

A company that assembles and manufactures a product into its final form.

OEM offerings or components

Products, or parts, sold by one manufacturer to another that get built into a final product without further modification.

MRO Offerings

Maintenance, repair, and operations (MRO) offerings refer to products and services used to keep a company functioning. Janitorial supplies are MRO offerings, as is hardware used to repair any part of a building or equipment. MRO items are often sold by distributors. However, you can buy many of the same products at a retail store. For example, you can buy nuts and bolts at a hardware store. A business buyer of nuts and bolts, however, will also need repair items that you don't, such as very strong solder used to weld metal. For convenience sake, the buyer would prefer to purchase multiple products from one vendor rather than driving all over town to buy them. So the distributor sends a salesperson to see the buyer. Most distributors of MRO items sell thousands of products, set up online purchasing websites for their customers, and provide a number of other services to make life easier for them.

maintenance, repair, and operations (MRO)

Offerings used to maintain, repair, and operate the physical assets of an organization.

Facilitating Offerings

Facilitating offerings include products and services that support a company's operations but are not part of the final product it sells. Marketing research services, banking and transportation services, copiers and computers, and other similar products and services fall into this category. Facilitating offerings might not be central to the buyer's business, at least not the way component parts and raw materials are. Yet to the person who is making the buying decision, these offerings can be very important. If you are a marketing manager who is selecting a vendor for marketing research or choosing an advertising agency, your choice could be critical to your own personal success. For this reason, many companies that supply facilitating offerings try to build strong relationships with their clients.

These janitorial products are examples of MRO items. Because most businesses buy MRO items in large quantities and because these firms also need products not available to the general public, they will generally buy these products from a distributor such as T&G Chemical rather than from a retailer.

Source: © Shutterstock, Inc.

facilitating offerings

Offerings that support an organization's ability to do business but do not go into the final product.

Key Takeaway

- Business buyers purchase various types of offerings to make their own offerings. Some of the types of products they use are raw materials, manufactured materials, and component parts and assemblies, all of which can become part of an offering. MRO (maintenance, repair, and operations) offerings are those that keep a company's depreciable assets in working order. Facilitating offerings are products and services a company purchases to support its operations but are not part of the firm's final product.

Review Questions

1. What types of offerings do businesses buy? How do the offerings differ in terms of how they are marketed?
2. As you learned early in the chapter, consumer offerings can belong to different categories depending on how the buyer wants to purchase them. Is the same true for business offerings?

6.4 Branding, Labeling, and Packaging

Learning Objectives

1. Understand the branding decisions firms make when they're developing new products.
2. Identify the various levels of packaging for new products.

What comes to mind when someone says Apple, Google, or Coke? According to BrandFinance, the Apple brand is the *strongest* brand in the world.[1] Not too long ago, Coca-Cola held the number one spot, but both Apple and Google have risen much faster. What is a "brand," and what do these studies mean when they report that one brand is the strongest or the best?

Branding

We have mentioned brands periodically throughout this book. But what is a brand? A **brand** is a name, picture, design, or symbol, or combination of those items, used by a seller to identify its offerings and to differentiate them from competitors' offerings. **Branding** is the set of activities designed to create a brand and position it in the minds of consumers.

Brands are important to companies because they represent authenticity and a promise of what the buyer is going to receive; in fact, marketers talk about this as the **brand promise**. If you are paying for a Vineyard Vines shirt, you want a Vineyard Vines shirt, not a knockoff or cheap imitation. Not all consumers always feel that way, however. Research shows that some consumers like to buy copies and take pleasure from fooling their friends.[2] Yet companies spend a great deal of money to protect their brands so that they can capitalize on the value.

A successful branding strategy is one that accomplishes what Coke and Apple have done—it creates consumer recognition of what the brand (signified by its name, picture, design, symbol, and so forth) means (again, the brand promise) and contributes to **brand equity** or the value of the brand. Consequently, when marketing professionals are considering whether a potential new offering fits a company's image, they are very concerned about whether the offering supports the organization's brand and position in the mind of the consumer. For this reason, many consider branding to be much more than how the product is packaged or labeled, and they are right. Characteristics of the offering, such as pricing and quality, have to support the brand's position. If Apple (the brand) stands for innovation, then products and services have to be innovative. But branding itself refers to strategies that are designed to create an image and position in the consumers' minds.

One challenge that international brands face is how brands translate from one country to another. Classic examples include KFC translating "Finger Lickin' Good" to "Eat Your Fingers Off." HSBC's slogan "Assume Nothing" came out as "Do Nothing" in some countries.[3]

Another challenge is the choice of color. While white may be associated with mourning death in Japan, it is associated with honesty and transparency in the U.S. Yellow is used to grab attention.[4] Have you noticed that Wendy's is moving away from yellow and red to just red? Red is associated with excitement but one criticism of the Wendy's move is that the stores are not as readily identifiable or easy to spot without the yellow.

A **brand name**, like Apple, is the spoken part of a brand's identity. A **brand mark** is the symbol, such as Coke's wave or Apple Computer's multicolor apple, associated with a brand. Brand names and brand marks are important to companies because consumers use them to make choices.

An important decision companies must make is under which brand a new offering will be marketed. For example, Black & Decker makes power tools for consumers under its Black & Decker brand, while tools for more serious do-it-yourselfers and professionals are manufactured under its DeWalt brand. If Black & Decker decided to add to its DeWalt line new products such as coolers, portable music systems, and other accessories construction professionals might find useful at a job site, the company would be creating a brand extension. A **brand extension** involves utilizing an existing brand name or brand mark for a new product category. Black & Decker has three choices: market these products under the Black & Decker brand, the DeWalt brand, or a new brand.

Why would Black & Decker add these accessories to the DeWalt line? If the company did, it would be because DeWalt already has a good reputation for high quality, long-lasting durability, and performance among construction professionals and because the company believes these professionals would be most likely to buy such products. These same professionals would trust the DeWalt brand to deliver. But if the company had developed a line of products that would sell to a different market or might be expected to deliver very different benefits to the same market, a new brand might be more effective.

For example, Procter & Gamble sells detergent for cleaning clothes and soap for cleaning dishes, yet doesn't have brands that are the same across those two applications. Both are versions

brand

A name, picture, design, or symbol, or combination of those elements, used by a seller to differentiate its offerings from competitors'.

branding

A set of activities designed to create a brand and position it in the minds of consumers.

brand promise

What the brand stands for; what value the company pledges the product carrying that brand will deliver.

brand equity

The value of the brand, including assets (or liabilities) such as brand loyalty, brand awareness, quality perceptions, and other factors associated with the brand all contribute to brand equity.

brand name

The spoken part of an identity used to describe of a brand.

brand mark

A symbol or logo used to identify a brand.

brand extension

The process of utilizing an existing brand name or brand mark for a new product category.

of soap. The company, though, believes that a key selling point is how each product is engineered for a specific job and the consumer needs a different brand for each job in order to trust the brand.

How a company like Black & Decker or Procter & Gamble goes about building this trust is the subject of later chapters. For now, let's consider whether it is better for a company to market a new product via a brand extension or create an entirely new brand for the product.

cannibalization

When a new product takes sales away from the same company's existing products.

One thing firms have to consider when they're branding a new offering is the degree of cannibalization that can occur across products. **Cannibalization** occurs when a firm's new offering eats into the sales of one of its older offerings. (Ideally, when you sell a new product, you hope that all of its sales come from your competitors' buyers or buyers that are new to the market.) A completely new offering, such as coolers and portable music systems, will not result in cannibalization for DeWalt power tools, whereas a line extension likely will. A brand extension will also result in some cannibalization if you sell similar products under another brand. For example, if Black & Decker already had an existing line of coolers and portable music systems when the DeWalt line of the same products was launched, the new DeWalt offerings might cannibalize some of the Black & Decker offerings.

Some marketers argue that cannibalization can be a good thing because it is a sign that a company is developing new and better offerings. These people believe that if you don't cannibalize your own line, then your competitors will.

Packaging Decisions

Another set of questions to consider involves the packaging on which a brand's marks and name will be prominently displayed. Sometimes the package itself is part of the brand. For example, the curves of Coca-Cola's Coke bottle is a registered trademark. If you decide to market your beverage in a similar-shaped bottle, Coca-Cola's attorneys will have grounds to sue you.

Sometimes the package itself is part of a licensed brand. Heineken created an intelligent bottle, called Ignite, that lit up when raised for a toast or when music is played to build recognition for its bottle and drive sales.

Source: © Shutterstock, Inc.

Packaging has to fulfill a number of important functions, including:

- communicating the brand and its benefits;
- protecting the product from damage and contamination during shipment, as well as damage and tampering once it's in retail outlets;
- preventing leakage of the contents; and
- presenting government-required warning and information labels.

Sometimes packaging can fulfill other functions, such as serving as part of an in-store display designed to promote the offering.

Primary packaging holds a single retail unit of a product. For example, a bottle of Coke, a bag of M&Ms, or a ream (five hundred sheets) of printer paper are all examples of primary packages. Primary packaging can be used to protect and promote products and get the attention of consumers. Primary packaging can also be used to demonstrate the proper use of an offering, provide instructions on how to assemble the product, or any other needed information. If warning or nutrition labels are required, they must be on the primary packaging. Primary packaging can be bundled together as well. Consumers can buy bottles of Coke sold in six-packs or cans of Coke in twelve-packs, for example.

primary packaging

Packaging designed to hold a single retail unit of a product.

Secondary packaging holds a single wholesale unit of a product. A case of M&M bags is an example, as are cartons of reams of paper. Secondary packaging is designed more for retailers than consumers. It does not have to carry warning or nutrition labels but is still likely to have brand marks and labels. Secondary packaging further protects the individual products during shipping. Sometimes, secondary packaging is also designed to be turned into a display for the product.

Tertiary packaging is packaging designed specifically for shipping and efficiently handling large quantities. When a Coca-Cola bottler ships cases of Cokes to a grocery store, they are stacked on pallets (wooden platforms) and then wrapped in plastic. Pallets can be easily moved by a forklift truck and can even be moved within the grocery store by a small forklift.

A product's packaging can benefit the customer beyond just protecting the offering while it's being shipped. No-spill caps, for example, can make it easier for you to use your laundry detergent or prevent spills when you're adding oil to your car's engine. And, as we have noted, secondary packaging (and also tertiary packaging) can serve as part of an in-store display, thereby adding value for your retailers.

Another set of packaging decisions concerns how to embed technology into packaging. **Smart packaging** is packaging with technology embedded that adds value to the consumer and/or the producer. There are three general categories of smart packaging.

Active packaging has reactive elements, based on mechanical or chemical elements, that can provide information. For example, Coors has a beer can that changes color when the beer reaches optimal drinking temperature.

Intelligent packaging has sensors and other computational technology embedded, and can include a display. One example is the Heineken Ignite bottle that lit up when raised for a toast or when music played.

Connected packaging has intelligent packaging technology hooked up with the internet in order to provide information, either to the consumer or to a producer or distributor. For example, a paper towel dispenser can send a signal to the housekeeping staff when it is running low. As another example, Johnnie Walker has embedded extremely thin electronic sensors in the label of the Blue Label bottle. These sensors can be used to identify where each bottle is in the supply chain, whether it has been opened, and even how much has been consumed. If sold at retail to a consumer, as soon as the sensor indicates that the bottle has been opened, a connected consumer could get drink recipes delivered to their smartphone.[5]

Another example of connected packaging is refillable containers that can determine when you're low on something like dishwasher detergent. Connected to your Alexa, these containers can then order refills for you and have them shipped to your door, combining reorders across different products to reduce shipping and packaging costs.

Key Takeaway

- A brand is a name, picture, design, or symbol, or combination of those items, used by a seller to identify its offerings and differentiate them from competitors' offerings. Branding is the set of activities designed to create a brand and position it relative to competing brands in the minds of consumers. An important decision companies must make is under which brand a new offering will be marketed. A brand extension involves utilizing an existing brand name or brand mark for a new product or category (line) of products. Cannibalization occurs when a company's new offering eats into the sales of one of its older offerings. It is something to be avoided in most cases, but it can also be a sign of progress because it means a company is developing new and better products. Packaging protects products from damage, contamination, leakage, and tampering, but it is also used to communicate the brand and its benefits, product warnings, and proper use.

secondary packaging

Packaging designed to hold a single wholesale unit of a product.

The man is wrapping these boxes to create tertiary packaging to be stacked on pallets and moved with a forklift. Each of the boxes, though, is an example of secondary packaging, containing a single wholesale unit of the product, such as 24 cans of bug spray or 12 boxes of dog food.

Source: © Shutterstock, Inc.

tertiary packaging

Packaging designed for shipping and efficiently handling large quantities of a product.

smart packaging

Packaging with technology embedded to add value to the consumer and/or producer.

active packaging

Smart packaging with reactive elements based on chemical or mechanical technology.

intelligent packaging

Smart packaging with sensors and other computational elements embbeded.

connected packaging

Smart packaging with intelligent technology hooked up with the internet in order to provide information, either to the consumer or to a producer or distributor.

Review Questions

1. How do brands help companies market their products?
2. What is the purpose of a brand extension?
3. When would you choose a brand extension over a new brand?
4. Name the basic types of packaging used in marketing.

6.5 Who Manages the Offering

Learning Objectives

1. Understand the people involved in creating and managing offerings.
2. Recognize the differences in organizing product marketing for consumer versus B2B companies.

Managing all of a company's offerings presents a number of challenges. Depending on the size of the company and the breadth of the company's offerings, several positions may be needed. In some companies, though, offerings are managed by the head of marketing.

brand manager

A person responsible for all business decisions regarding offerings within one brand. A brand manager is often charged with running his or her brand as if it is its own separate business.

product manager

Someone with business responsibility for a particular product or product line. Like brand managers, product managers must make decisions, such as which offerings to include, advertising selection, and others.

A brand manager is a position you will find in companies that have large numbers of brands, some of which might compete. For example, Procter & Gamble has several detergent brands. A **brand manager** is the person responsible for all business decisions regarding offerings within one brand, such as Tide detergent. By business decisions, we mean making decisions that affect profit and loss, which include such decisions as which offerings to include in the brand, how to position the brand in the market, pricing options, and so forth. Indeed, a brand manager is often charged with running the brand as if it were its own separate business.

A brand manager is much more likely to be found in consumer marketing companies. Typically, B2B companies do not have multiple brands so the position is not common in the B2B environment. What you often find in a B2B company is a **product manager**, someone with business responsibility for a particular product or product line. Like the brand manager, the product manager must make many business decisions, such as which offerings to include, advertising selection, and so on. Companies with brand managers include Microsoft, Procter & Gamble, SC Johnson, Kraft, Target, General Mills, and ConAgra Foods. Product managers are found at Teradata, IBM, Crown, Rockwell International, and many others.

The University of Georgia was the first to launch a graduate program in brand management, but the only major program now being taught in the United States is at the University of Wisconsin. The program is managed through the university's Center for Brand and Product Management. Most brand managers simply have an undergraduate degree in marketing, but it helps to have a strong background in either finance or accounting because of the profitability and volume decisions brand managers have to make. In the United Kingdom, a number of schools have undergraduate degree programs specializing in brand management, as does Seneca College in Toronto, Canada.

In some companies, a **category manager** has responsibility for business decisions within a broad grouping of offerings. For example, a category manager at SC Johnson may have all home cleaning products, which would mean that brands such as Pledge, Vanish, Drano, Fantastik, Windex, Scrubbing Bubbles, and Shout would be that person's responsibility. Each of those brands may be managed by a brand manager, who then reports directly to the category manager.

category manager

Someone responsible for managing a broad group of products that may belong to multiple manufacturers.

At the retail level, a category manager at each store is responsible for more than just one manufacturer's products. The home cleaning category manager would have responsibility for offerings from SC Johnson, as well as Procter & Gamble, Colgate-Palmolive, and many other producers.

Another option is to create a **market manager**, who is responsible for business decisions within a market. In this case, a market can be defined as a geographic market or region; a market segment, such as a type of business; or a channel of distribution. For example, SC Johnson could have regional insect control managers. Regional market managers would make sense for insect control because weather has an influence on which bugs are pests at any given time. A southern regional manager would want more inventory of the repellent Off! in March because it is already warm and the mosquitoes are already breeding and biting in the southern United States.

market manager

Someone responsible for managing efforts within a particular market, such as a geographic market or another grouping of customers into a market (e.g., a single industry or size).

In B2B markets, a market manager is more likely to be given responsibility for a particular market segment, such as all hospital health care professionals or doctor's offices. All customers such as these (retail, wholesale, and so forth) in a particular industry compose what's called a **vertical market**, and the managers of these markets are called **vertical market managers**. B2B companies organize in this way because

- buying needs and processes are likely to be similar within an industry;
- channels of communication are likely to be the same within an industry but different across industries.

vertical market

B2B customers that compose a particular industry, such as the health care industry.

vertical market managers

Marketing managers who oversee B2B products sold to a particular industry.

Because magazines, websites, and trade shows are organized to serve specific industries or even specific positions within industries, B2B marketers find vertical market structures (meaning each group serves a different industry) for marketing departments to be more efficient than organizing by geography.

Market managers sometimes report to brand managers or are a part of their firm's sales organizations and report to sales executives. Market managers are less likely to have as much flexibility in terms of pricing and product decisions and have no control over the communication content of marketing campaigns or marketing strategies. These managers are more likely to be tasked with implementing a product or brand manager's strategy and be responsible for their markets. Some companies have market managers but no brand managers. Instead, marketing vice presidents or other executives are responsible for the brands.

Key Takeaway

- Some companies bundle product and service management into the head of marketing but larger companies have special positions. Brand managers decide what products are to be marketed and how. Other important positions include category managers, market managers, and vertical market managers. Category managers are found in consumer markets, usually in retail. Market managers can be found in both consumer markets and B2B markets. However, vertical market managers are found only in B2B markets. Some companies have market managers but no brand managers. Instead, a vice president of marketing or other executive is responsible for the brands.

Review Questions

1. What is a brand manager?

2. How do brand managers differ from category managers?
3. What is a market manager?
4. Which type of manager has the most marketing responsibility?

6.6 Discussion Questions and Activities

Discussion Questions

1. You can choose to buy a can of soup online and pick it up or have it delivered, or you can go to the store and buy it. Are these options part of the intangible value of that soup? You can buy dehydrated soup (a powder in a pouch), concentrated soup (in a can), or whole soup (in a jar or can). Are there intangible benefits to the form of the soup, even if they each taste exactly the same?
2. What are the marketing implications for your company if buyers stop viewing your primary offering as a shopping good and begin considering it a convenience good? How would you respond to the change?
3. Can you market unsought goods? If so, how?
4. How does packaging add value for consumers and retailers? Review the section on active packaging—what do you think the coolest application would be if you had the chance to design the package of a product?
5. If consumers find the most value in the services of your offering rather than the tangible product, how will perishability, intangibility, variability, and inseparability influence your marketing? Be specific for each characteristic.
6. Choose two of the different marketing jobs or positions described in the book so far and compare and contrast the challenges associated with each. Which would you prefer and why?
7. Describe three decisions that would be made differently from a product-dominant approach when compared to a service-dominant approach. What is each decision, and how would it be different?
8. When would a product orientation be useful? Why?
9. Describe an example of a core product where there are many different augmented products and the augmented products are considered very different by the consumer or user.
10. The text says that branding is much more than labeling or packaging. Provide some examples where you believe the product did not live up to the brand. Using examples to illustrate how consistency works, discuss how the offering and the desired brand image have to be consistent.

Activities

1. Identify two brands for two different products that try persuade buyers to view the products being promoted as shopping items rather than convenience items. What is similar about the strategies employed in how they are promoted? Do you think the promotion plans are successful? Why or why not?

2. Identify a product for which packaging adds value and describe how that value is added for the consumer. Identify a second brand for which the organization uses primary packaging to distinguish the brand at the point of purchase, and describe how the package contributes to the branding. Do not use brands used as examples in the chapter. Finally, identify a pure service brand and describe how that service is "packaged."
3. Select two brands that serve the same market but are not discussed in the chapter. Using print advertising, screenshots from websites, and stills from commercials (use screenshots from streaming video), assemble supporting material that helps you describe what each brand stands for and how consumers view each brand. Is one brand better than the other? Why or why not?

6.7 Case Study: What's My Line?

Tre' Vandenberg was really frustrated. In his role as supervisor of plant equipment, he is responsible for ensuring that the equipment works in a safe fashion while also meeting production goals. Much of the equipment is antiquated, which is not really a problem because there are no current manufacturers of replacement equipment but the parts are easily machined when replacements are needed. But what is frustrating Tre' is the fact that modifications get made to the equipment and OSHA (the federal workplace safety agency) wants blueprints of the modifications, blueprints Tre' can't produce easily.

He shared his frustration with his friend, Keresha Brown, who is an artificial intelligence engineer, and she recognized that the problem can be solved with AI tools. The idea is to take a digital image of the piece that has been modified and apply AI to convert the image into a draft blueprint which can then be modified by an engineer in about 25 percent of the time that it would take to draft using traditional methods. She was able to secure grant funding from the government to create the initial test version that Tre' found works as planned

Tre' believes there is sufficient market demand as his company is not the only one to need it. They are pursuing venture capital to start a company, but every time they present to potential investors the question becomes "what's your actual product?" Are they selling a service that will take the images and convert to draft blueprints, or are they selling a full blueprinting service and delivering final complete blueprints, or do they just sell the software application and the training? One investor says that if this application requires a lot of change on the part of customers, they'd rather buy it as a full service.

Another question they get is will the market easily see the value? Or will potential buyers resist it because fewer engineers will be needed and people might lose their jobs?

Case Study Questions

1. Should Tre' and Keresha sell a product, a service, or some combination? What factors influence your choice?
2. Does the potential fear of losing one's job play into your decision on your answer to #1? If so, how would you sell or market your offering to minimize that response?
3. Why does the level of change required on the part of the customer matter? How does that impact how you market your offering?

Endnotes

1. "Global 500 2021," BrandFinance, brandirectory.com/rankings/global/table.
2. Kaushuk Samaddar and Preetha Menon (2020), "Non-deceptive Counterfeit Products: A Morphological Analysis and Future Research Agenda," *Journal of Strategic Marketing* DOI: 10.1080/0965254X.2020.1772348.
3. Beth Worthy (2018), "Hilarious and Lost In Translation: 6 Brand Slogans as Examples," gmrtranscription.com.
4. "The Psychology of Colors in Marketing," *Infographic from Entrepreneur and Fast Company,* https://i.pinimg.com/564x/8b/ae/c4/8baec49ec5f12421d26065b7b287caa5.jpg.
5. Amanda Williams (2021), "Smart Packaging Vs. Connected Packaging: What are the Differences?" https://www.jabil.com/blog/Smart-Packaging-v-Connected-Packaging.html.

CHAPTER 7

Developing and Managing Offerings

Having something that customers want to buy is important to any company. Most companies are started by people who get an idea about how to make something better. Hewlett-Packard, for example, began in 1939 in a garage (now a California Historic Landmark) when two young engineers, Bill Hewlett and Dave Packard, thought they had a better idea for designing and making a precision audio oscillator, which is an electronic device that tests sound. Their product was so much more precise than competitors' products that it was manufactured and sold around the world for over thirty years. In fact, it is probably one of the longest-selling electronic devices ever. It also sold for just $54, whereas competing products sold for over $200. Hewlett-Packard, now more commonly known as HP, has not been located in a little garage for many years. Yet the company's ability to grow by successfully designing and marketing new offerings continues.

Developing new offerings (products and services) is a constant process in most companies. In some instances, a company starts with a price and then develops products and services to fit that price. IKEA is an example of a company that does this. IKEA looks at the various prices consumers are willing to pay for home furnishings and then works backward to design products that match those prices (using a demand backward pricing strategy is discussed in the pricing chapter). In other situations, the goal is simply to develop a better product that adds value to existing products, and the price comes later. Hewlett-Packard's audio oscillator is an example of this type of product. When thinking about new service offerings, F33.ai, a consulting company, was created to help firms change their businesses dramatically by using disruptive technology and operationalizing artificial intelligence (AI).

Hewlett-Packard was founded in this California garage, which is now a national landmark.

Source: Twam [GFDL (http://www.gnu.org/copyleft/fdl.html) or CC-BY-SA-3.0 (http://creativecommons.org/licenses/by-sa/3.0/)], from Wikimedia Commons

Keep in mind that a "new" product need not be a never-before-seen innovation. It can also be a "new and improved" product, such as a better laundry detergent; a new flavor, color, or package; or an addition to a product or service line, such as Marriott adding the Courtyard by Marriott and the Fairfield Inn to its hotel lineup. Or, it can be a repositioned product or company. The clothing retailer Timberland is an example. The company is trying to reinvigorate its sales by adjusting its products and marketing to target more urban consumers rather than just hardcore outdoor enthusiasts.

What is new for one company may not be new to another. For example, one hotel may already have budget properties, but when a luxury hotel line adds a budget property, that property is considered a new offering for the company.

7.1 The New Offering Development Process

Learning Objectives

1. Identify an effective process for creating offerings and bringing them to market.
2. Understand the relative importance of each step in the new offering development process and the functions within each step.
3. Distinguish between the various forms of testing and analysis that take place before a new offering is brought to the market.

Most new offerings go through similar stages in their development process. Although the size of a company will affect how the different stages of their new product development process are conducted and whether products are test marketed before being introduced, the basic steps are generally the same. Figure 7.1 summarizes these steps.

FIGURE 7.1 The New Offering Development Process

Idea Generation

Product ideas can come from anywhere. Many companies, HP and Apple included, were launched in someone's garage after the founders got an idea for a product and then tried to make and sell it. Apple's Macintosh microcomputer was a low-cost knockoff of the Xerox Star, a software-equipped workstation. Apple's co-founder, Steve Jobs, saw the product demonstrated at a Xerox research center, and Xerox was an early investor in Apple.[1]

Hamilton Perkins, Hamilton Perkins Collection

Source: Hamilton Perkins, used with permission.

Hamilton Perkins got an idea for fashion bags made out of recycled plastic, specifically an outer shell made from recycled bottles and an inner lining made from vinyl billboards. One big market that he developed is the corporate market because a marketing manager saw his bags and thought her company could use them as gifts for clients. Now, Hamilton works with many companies to create custom bags that they use as gifts or awards. The lining for these bags comes from the customer's actual billboards or vinyl signs used at trade shows. "Our design process starts with identifying the recycled materials we will be working with and coordinating collection efforts to prepare for prototyping and sampling. We draw sketches and make computer aided designs to help us complete technical design patterns that our factories and artisans can follow for production. Once we agree on the finished product we will make samples and get a feel for how the products will perform and respond during everyday carry. We will get feedback on those interactions and iterate this process by style and collection." (His company is Hamilton Perkins Collection.)

Employees often come up with new product ideas, too. Motorola developed a prototype for a mobile phone that can be recharged by rubbing it on a smooth surface. A Motorola engineer came up with the idea while rollerblading. He wondered if a small generator could be created to capture and store the energy generated by rollerblade wheels. This idea, in turn, led to the development of a small roller ball (like you would find on an old-style computer mouse) built into the mobile phone. To power up the phone, you just give it a roll.

Ideas can also come from your customers. In fact, in business-to-business (B2B) markets, customers are probably the biggest source of new product ideas. Customers know what they need and want, which provides organizations an indication of market needs. Customers who are good at generating new product ideas or applications of products are called **lead users**. These people are often courted by manufacturers for this purpose. Lead users exist in consumer markets, too. Some companies like Gap create consumer panels that help them stay in touch with forward-thinking innovators, some of whom might also be influencers who blog or post and have large followings.

lead users

Potential customers who are innovative and develop new applications or new products for their own use without the aid of a supplier.

Customers are particularly important co-creators of offerings when they are consuming services. For example, if you provide your hairdresser with feedback while your hair is being cut, your input will alter the final style you receive. Similarly, a businessperson who provides her certified public accountant (CPA) with information and feedback about her firm will help the CPA develop better financial and tax plans for her business. Consumers' trends and preferences influence new product introductions as well as deletion of products. Coca-Cola Zero Sugar and Coca-Cola with coffee are examples of new products introduced in 2021.

Suppliers provide another source of ideas for new products. A supplier might develop a new product or technology that can be used to make yet another product, and then go to the makers of those products and suggest new versions of them. For example, McClancy Seasoning Co. makes spices that restaurants and food processing companies use in their food products. McClancy's research and development department works with companies such as Campbell's to help them develop new and better offerings.

Coca-Cola creates many new products based on consumer preferences and market trends around the globe.

Source: © Shutterstock, Inc.

Crowdsourcing is another way to come up with product ideas. **Crowdsourcing** is the process of obtaining product ideas, funding, and other contributions online from large numbers of people rather than just one's employees, customers, or suppliers. AppsCo is a crowdsourcing website where people can submit their ideas for web and mobile apps. If their ideas are chosen for development, they get cash prizes. Realizing that it's impossible for any organization to come up with all of the great ideas, General Electric now crowdsources ideas from entrepreneurs, innovators, and experts around the world to help it come up with new product ideas. **Crowdfunding** is the term used specifically for obtaining funding online for projects. Kickstarter and GoFundMe are examples of crowdfunding websites.

crowdsourcing

The process of obtaining product ideas, funding, and other contributions online from large numbers of people rather than just one's employees, customers, or suppliers.

crowdfunding

The process of obtaining funding online for projects.

Of course, companies also watch their competitors to see what they're doing. Some offerings are protected by patents or copyrights and can't be legally duplicated. The software that runs Apple's iPhone is an example. There are, however, different ways to achieve the same results as Apple has with its iPhone. Samsung, the world's largest producer of mobile phones, as well as LG, Motorola, and other companies provide similar functions but use the Android operating system developed by Google. The same is true for Nokia's phones, which use Microsoft's use Windows operating system.

Figure 7.2 shows some product ideas that came from each of the sources we have discussed—employees, customers, suppliers, and competitors. Innovations like the iPod, which radically changed how the music industry operates, are rare. However, many new ideas (and consequently new products/services) aren't actually new but rather are versions of products and services already available. A **line extension** occurs when a company comes out with another model (related product or service) based on the same platform and brand as one of its other products. For example, *Call of Duty WWII* and *Call of Duty Black Ops Cold War* were line extensions, part of the Call of Duty videogames.

line extension

A new idea or offering that occurs when a company comes out with another model (related product or service) based on the same platform and brand as one of its other products.

FIGURE 7.2 New Offering Ideas

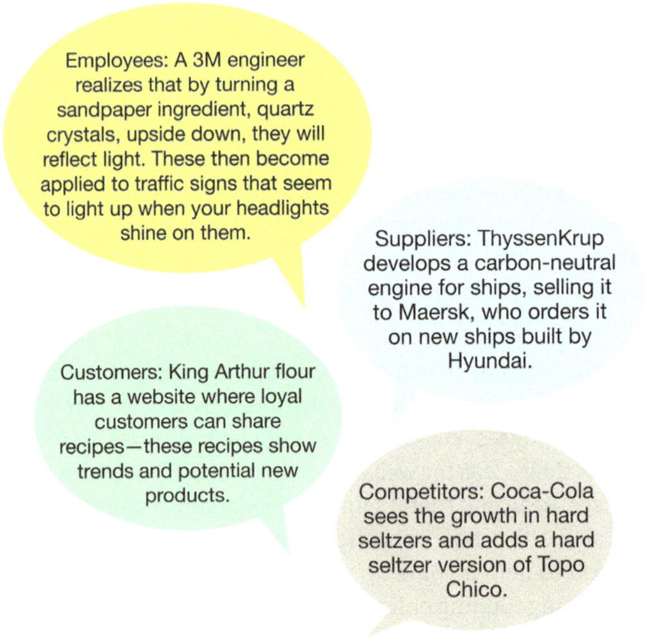

Keep in mind that idea generation is typically the least expensive step in the process of developing a new offering, whether you involve customers or not. As you move through the product development process, each step is usually more expensive than the last. Ideas for new offerings are relatively cheap and easy to generate; what is difficult and expensive is making them a reality.

Idea Screening

Not all new product ideas are good ones. Famous product blunders include Ford Motor Company's Edsel, Clear Pepsi, and Coca-Cola's New Coke. Less famous is Dell's cell phone for aging baby boomers. The phone's large size, large buttons, and large screen screamed, "I'm old and blind!", leading potential users to shun it in droves. Yes, even the big companies make big mistakes.

The purpose of idea screening is to try to avoid mistakes early in the development process. The sooner bad ideas are discarded, the less the investment made and lost. In the idea screening stage, the company tries to evaluate the new offering by answering these questions:

- Does the proposed offering add value for the customer? Does it satisfy a market need?
- Can the offering be made/ready within a stated time period to get it to market when needed?
- How many units of it will sell, and at what price?
- Can we manufacture and sell the product within budget and still make money?
- Do we need to provide the customer with after-sales service? If so, do we have the resources to do that?
- Does the offering fit our image and corporate strategy?

Some organizations conduct concept testing at this stage. **Concept testing** involves running the idea of the offering by potential consumers. The purpose is to get early consumer feedback before investing too much money in an offering that won't work. Some of the methods used to test concepts include **focus groups**, in which groups of eight to twelve consumers gather and react to the concept, and **depth interviews**, in which individuals are presented with the concept and can react to it individually. (Both are discussed in more detail in Chapter 10.) These methods can also be used later during the offering development process to test ideas, or for other purposes. Focus groups conducted virtually on the web and by phone actually helped to develop this textbook. Concepts may also be tested online by creating an image and having people representative of the target market provide feedback. Whether using focus groups, depth interviewing, or online methods, concepts must be evaluated by people representative of the target market or the feedback is not relevant.

Because screening considers the feasibility of actually making and servicing an offering, price and cost are important components. If the company cannot sell the product in sufficient quantities to generate a profit, the idea must be scrapped. Understanding the customer's personal value equation is an important consideration, too. If the value consumers receive from the product is less than the price the company charges for it, they will not buy it. In other words, the offering must be financially feasible to justify investing in it.

The Amazon Fire phone was a dismal failure, lasting only a year on the market. Amazon Fire TV, especially Amazon Fire TV Sticks for accessing streaming services on any TV, however, have been extremely successful.

Source: © Shutterstock, Inc.

concept testing

Presenting an idea for an offering (including possible marketing communication ideas) to consumers for their reaction early in the offering development process.

focus groups

A group of potential buyers brought together to discuss a marketing research topic with one another.

depth interviews

An exploratory research technique of engaging in detailed, one-on-one, question-and-answer sessions with potential buyers.

A good product doesn't just look right. It also works right, which is the idea behind process feasibility.

Source: © Shutterstock, Inc

process feasibility

The degree to which the manufacturing of a product or the delivery of a service can be done within the proper quality specifications on a repeatable basis; the degree to which an organization can actually make and service an offering.

financial feasibility

A new offering's ability to make money.

The offering must also have process feasibility. **Process feasibility** is the degree to which the company can actually make and service the product. Process feasibility affects **financial feasibility**. If the product's costs cannot be controlled when it's being made or serviced, the firm's financial goals won't be met. Process feasibility also affects customer satisfaction. For example, many manufacturers make great-looking faucets, yet one of your authors had to have the "guts" of one faucet replaced three times before it would work, only to find two other friends had the same experience with the same model. A product with a great-looking design is really only great if it works right.

The question of strategic fit, or whether an offering fits with an organization's mission, image, or strategy is a difficult one. The history of business is rife with examples of companies failing to develop winning new products only to see their competitors do so. For example, when the inventor Chester Carlson approached IBM executives with the idea of photocopying, the technology platform that later became the heart of Xerox, the executives turned Carlson down. They did not see the product fitting in with IBM's strategy and didn't fully consider the moneymaking potential of the product.

Companies will also spin out products that don't fit the core mission. Ario, for example, is a company that uses augmented reality technology to help build drawings for engineering. Developed by two engineers at Huntington Ingalls Industries (HII), the technology is used by HII but isn't a core part of their business, so the two were able to set up a business around the technology and apply it to other situations.

investment risk

The potential of losing one's money and time should a new offering fail.

opportunity risk

The potential loss of revenue a company risks when it chooses an alternative course of action such as launching a different offering.

Risks are also assessed at this point in the new product development process. There are two types of risks firms face. The first is **investment risk**, which is the possibility that the company will fail to earn the appropriate return on the money and effort (the investment) it puts into the new offering. The second is **opportunity risk**, or the risk that there is a better idea that gets ignored because the firm has invested in the idea at hand.

When a company is assessing fit, it is assessing its opportunity risk. When it is assessing feasibility (both financial and process), it is assessing its investment risk. Other risk-related questions include whether or not the offering can be developed on time and within budget. Assessing a product's feasibility continues throughout the entire new product development process.

Feature Specification

The next step involves narrowing down the product's features. Again, price enters the picture as the company considers which features are important to consumers at different price points. A premium (high-priced) offering is likely to be loaded with extra features. By contrast, a low-priced offering is likely to be a "bare-bones" product with few features.

quality function deployment (QFD)

A specific process for designing new offerings that begins by specifying a customer's requirements and then designing a product to meet those needs.

Quality function deployment (QFD) is a process whereby a company begins with the customer's desired benefits and then designs an offering that delivers those benefits. The benefits are linked to certain characteristics of the offering, which are then broken down into component part characteristics. From this list of component parts, the product is designed. Thus, the feature specifications process begins with a strong understanding of what consumers want and need.

HP has developed a number of computer printers using the QFD process. The QFD process has been particularly helpful when it comes to bundling the right features within HP's printer line because each printer model can be targeted to specific customer needs. Customers can then purchase the model that best suits their needs and doesn't have a bunch of features that don't add value for them.

Development

In the development stage, the actual offering is designed, specifications for it are written, and prototypes are developed. During this stage the firm also considers the offering's proposed strategy (promotion, distribution, pricing) and the product's manufacturing process. For example, when a restaurant is developing a new dish, it must not only taste good, but be made in a reasonable amount of time once it's ordered and prepared at a cost that earns the restaurant a profit. In terms of a manufacturer's offerings, using the same technology platform as another product (like Microsoft has done with Windows phones) can be very effective and cheaper. Using the same platform generally makes it easier for a company to train its technicians to service a new product.

Testing

During the testing stage, the offering is tested, first in the lab and then with real customers. Lab testing is also called **alpha testing**. Alpha testing ensures that the offering works like it's supposed to in a variety of different environments—that it meets its specifications, that is. For example, Kraft might launch a new food product that has to work in hot climates, cold climates, high humidity, dry climates, and high altitudes—all conditions that can change how well the product works.

alpha testing

The testing of a product in a laboratory setting.

The next step is beta testing. During **beta testing**, actual customers make sure the offering works under real-world conditions. Beta testing not only tests whether the offering works as advertised but also tests the offering's delivery mechanisms, service processes, and other aspects of marketing the product. This step can be an expensive. Depending on the product, some companies might find it better to simply launch the product and let the market respond to, or test, it once it is available for purchase.

beta testing

The testing of a product by a real customer in the customer's location.

In B2B settings, beta tests are usually conducted with lead users and preferred customers. The developer of the product needs a strong relationship with these customers because the product might still have bugs that need to be ironed out. If the relationship between the parties is "iffy," and the product or service needs a significant amount of changes, beta testing could damage the relationship between the two parties and hurt the developer of the product's sales.

Simultaneous to testing the offering's ability to meet its specs, the company is also developing and testing the marketing communication plan that will be used to launch the product. Many companies involve consumer panels or user communities, both for testing the offering and the communication plan. As we mentioned, JCPenney solicits the advice of a user community for its Ambrielle line of lingerie. The company frequently runs concepts by the group as well as sends actual prototypes to users to try on and report back to the company. Similarly, the data warehousing company Teradata has a "partner" organization that consists of a community of users who participate in the firm's product design and testing.

Some companies may conduct a **market test** in limited markets or nationwide. That is, companies test the complete launch of a product's marketing plan (and strategies) to ensure that the offering reaches buyers, gets positive feedback, and generates sales. For example, when one beverage maker tested the marketing plan for a new wine cooler, the firm first launched the product on the East Coast, where the beverage was promoted as a "Polynesian" drink; on the West Coast, the beverage was promoted as an "Australian" drink. The Polynesian version proved more popular, so in other new markets, that's how the beverage was advertised and packaged.

market test

When companies test the complete launch of a product's marketing plan (and strategies) to ensure that the offering reaches buyers, gets positive feedback, and generates sales.

Other companies may decide against a market test due to financial and competitive risks. Market tests are expensive, and small companies may prefer to use funds on promotion or distribution rather than a market test. Market tests also allow competitors to see ideas, which can be risky if a competitor is ready to enter the market.

Launch or Commercialization

rolling launch

Introducing a new offering across markets one by one in order to work out any challenges or problems related to marketing and supporting the offering.

Once an offering has been designed and tested, the company decides the best time to enter the market and make the product available to customers. Sometimes a company launches the offering to all of its markets at once. Other companies may use a **rolling launch** in which the offering is made available to certain markets first and then other markets later. A rolling launch might make sense if the company's service technicians need training. The company makes the offering available to one market after the first batch of its employees are prepared to service the product; then as new batches of employees are prepared to service the product, the company enters more markets.

A New Product Launch

A video to help consumers choose the right iPhone for their needs.

View in the online reader

Evaluation

Once an offering is launched, a firm's executives carefully monitor its progress. You have probably heard about the "box office" sales for new movies the first weekend following their release. The first weekend is a good predictor of how much money a movie will make overall. If the ticket sales for it are high during the first weekend, a studio's executives might decide to beef up the promotions for it. If the ticket sales for the movie are low, the studio might stop screening the movie in theaters altogether and instead release it via a streaming service such as Netflix or Amazon Prime. During the COVID-19 pandemic, these streaming services and other Video on Demand (VOD) providers became even more popular as people sought movies and even product information they could get at home. Similarly, many of the streaming services such as Netflix, Amazon Prime, and Disney Plus produced and streamed more of their own movies.[2]

For other types of offerings, important milestones might be the first ninety days after the product is launched, followed by a second period of ninety days, and so forth. However, be aware that firms are constantly in the process of evaluating their offerings and modifying them by either adding or subtracting the features and services associated with them, changing their prices, or how they are marketed. The length of time for milestones used to evaluate products may vary depending on the organization and other products or services being developed.

Key Takeaway

- Most companies put new offering ideas through a seven-step process, beginning with the idea generation stage. Ideas for new offerings can come from anywhere, including one's customers, employees, suppliers, large numbers of people on the internet, and one's competitors. The next step in the process is the idea screening stage, followed by the feature specifications, development, testing, and launching stages. After an offering is launched, it is evaluated. A company must balance an offering's investment risk (the risk associated with losing the time and money put into developing the offering) against the offering's opportunity risk (the risk associated with missing the opportunity to market the product and profit from it).

Review Questions

1. What are the seven steps in the offering development process? What are the key activities in each step?
2. Who are lead users?
3. How should a company evaluate new ideas? What are the criteria?
4. How does quality function deployment work?

7.2 Managing Products over the Course of the Product Life Cycle

Learning Objectives

1. Explain how organizations manage offerings after being introduced to the marketplace.
2. Explain how managing an offering may be different in international markets.
3. Explain the product life cycle and the objectives and strategies for each stage.

Thousands of new offerings, including convenience foods, health and beauty aids, electronics, automobiles, pharmaceutical products, hotels, restaurants, and so on, enter the marketplace each year. But what happens to them after they get there? Do they thrive, just survive, or fail? Once a product is created and introduced in the marketplace, the offering must be managed effectively. Only if managed well will the product's producer achieve its profit objectives and be able to sustain the offering in the marketplace. Since many offices now have open floor plans and areas for team collaboration, the newest product introduced by furniture manufacturer (AIS), Calibrate Community, provides many options for open plans with clear boundaries for personal space, defined team areas, and a sense of place and community.

The process of managing a product involves making many complex decisions, especially if the product is being introduced in global markets. Before introducing products in global markets, an organization must evaluate and understand factors in the external environment, including laws and regulations, the economy and stage of economic development, the competitors and substitutes, cultural values, and market needs. Companies also need expertise to successfully launch products in foreign markets.

Calibrate Community furniture for an open plan space.

Source: Courtesy of AIS Furniture

Given many possible constraints in international markets, companies might initially introduce a product in limited areas abroad. Other organizations, such as Coca-Cola, Apple, and McDonald's compete in markets worldwide. McDonald's, Burger King, and KFC have more restaurants in foreign markets than in the United States.[3]

A McDonald's restaurant in China.

Source: © Shutterstock, Inc.

Another difficult decision managing products involves product recalls. Delaying recalls may result in danger to consumers, but companies must determine if the problem is an isolated incident or something affecting multiple products. You may have heard about many food recalls, such as people getting sick from different types of lettuce. Automobiles and products for children such as toys with lead paint or small parts and many infant sleeping products, which can be a lot more dangerous, have also experienced safety recalls. For example, Fisher Price recalled Rock 'n Glide Soothers after four infants died. Boppy recalled over three million newborn loungers after eight infants died.[4]

Managers must also determine policies regarding returns and refunds, which both affect profits. Many customers have abused both return and refund policies, driving companies to change their strategies. Until recently, L.L. Bean allowed customers to return products at any time. However, people were abusing the policy by getting shoes from thrift shops or out of the trash. As a result, the new return policy is that customers have to return merchandise within one year of purchase. Decisions regarding recalls, returns, and refunds are typically made before a product is introduced, but problems can occur throughout a product's life cycle.

product life cycle (PLC)

The stages (introduction, growth, maturity, decline) that a product may go through over time.

The **product life cycle (PLC)** includes the stages a product/service goes through after development, from its introduction (launch or commercialization) to the end of the product. Just as children go through different phases in life (toddler, elementary school, adolescent, young adult), products and services also age and go through different stages. The PLC is a beneficial tool that helps marketers manage the stages of a product's acceptance and success in the marketplace, beginning with the offering's introduction, its growth in market share, maturity, and possible decline in market share.

Other tools such as the Boston Consulting Group matrix and the General Electric approach (see Chapter 2 Section 5 for discussion) may also be used to manage and make decisions about what to do with products. For example, when a market is no longer growing but the product is doing well (cash cow in the BCG approach), the company may decide to use the money from the cash cow to invest in other products rather than continuing to invest in the product in a no-growth market.

The product life cycle can vary for different products and different product categories. Figure 7.3 illustrates an example of the product life cycle, showing how a product can move through four stages. New computer products, mobile phones, and video games often have limited life cycles, whereas product categories such as diamonds and durable goods (kitchen appliances, for example) generally have longer life cycles.

FIGURE 7.3 The Product Life Cycle

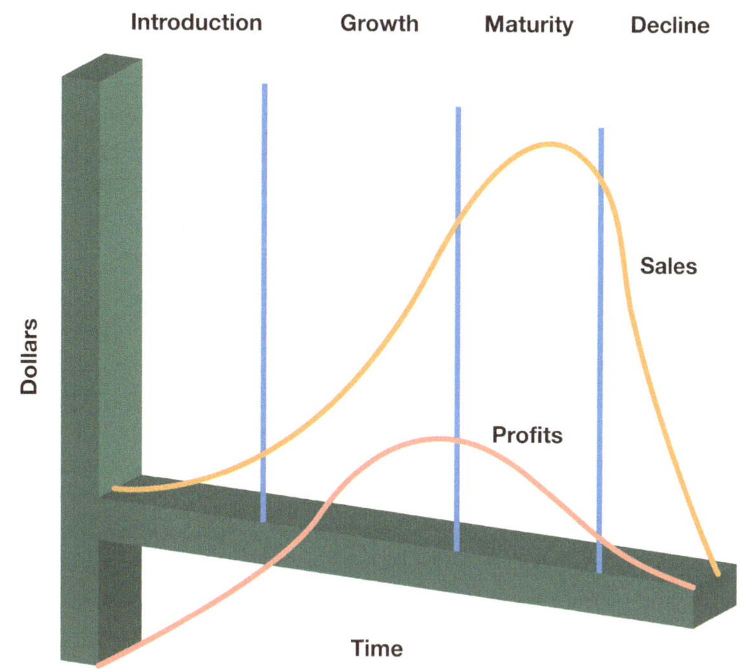

However, not all products go through all stages, and the length of a stage varies. Some products never experience market share growth and are withdrawn from the market. For example, Coca-Cola introduced Coca-Cola Energy in 2020 and announced it was being discontinued in 2021. By contrast, in the early 1980s, Diet Coke entered the growth stage soon after its introduction followed by the maturity stage, which lasted for decades, and remained there for many years. With soda consumption down and consumers buying fewer carbonated and artificially flavored drinks, sales of Diet Coke have declined. As a result of these changes in consumer preferences and buying habits, Coca-Cola plans to cut about 200 of its beverages and concentrate on those showing the most promise.[5] Other products, including frozen juice concentrate, powdered detergent, bar soap, and processed cheese slices face declining sales and could be taken off the market. Chewing gum and many types of candy are also being sold as companies try to strengthen their product offerings.

How a product is promoted, priced, distributed, or modified can vary throughout its life cycle. Let's now look at the various product life cycle stages and what characterizes each.

The sales of Diet Coke were steady for decades, but are declining as consumption of soda decreases.

Source: My100cans [Public domain], from Wikimedia Commons

The Introduction Stage

The first stage in a product's life cycle is the **introduction stage**. The introduction stage is the same as commercialization, or the last stage of the new product development process. Marketing costs are typically higher in this stage than in other stages. As an analogy, think about the amount of fuel a plane needs for takeoff relative to the amount it needs while in the air. Just as an airplane

introduction stage

The first stage of the product life cycle after a product is launched.

needs more fuel for takeoff, a new product or service needs more funds for introduction into the marketplace. Communication (promotion) is needed to generate awareness of the product and persuade consumers to try it, and placement alternatives and supply chains are needed to deliver the product to the customers. Profits are often low in the introductory stage due to the research and development costs and the marketing costs necessary to launch the product. In spring 2021, Reese's introduced their ultimate peanut butter lovers peanut butter cup with all peanut butter no chocolate (available for limited time). The product is a newer version of their traditional peanut butter cups, which were available for limited time in 2019 and 2020. Promotion for these products as well as all their new products is necessary to generate awareness.[6]

Peanut Butter Lovers Cup with Peanut Butter Shell Top; Ultimate Peanut Butter Lovers Cup has no chocolate—shell is all peanut butter.

Source: kiliweb photo and Open Food Facts

The length of the introductory stage varies for different products. However, by law in the United States, a company is only allowed to use the label "new" on a product's package for six months. An organization's objectives during the introductory stage often involve educating potential customers about its value and benefits, creating awareness, and getting potential customers to try the product or service. Getting products and services, particularly multinational brands, accepted in foreign markets can take even longer. Consequently, companies introducing products and services abroad generally must have the financial resources to make a long-term (longer than one year) commitment to their success.

The specific promotional strategies a company uses to launch an offering vary depending on the type of product or service and the number of competitors it faces in the market. Firms that manufacture products such as cereals, snacks, toothpastes, soap, and shampoos often use mass marketing techniques such as television commercials, internet campaigns, social media messages, and promotional programs such as coupons and sampling to reach consumers. For more technical or expensive products, such as investment and insurance products and home-security systems, companies often utilize professional selling, informational promotions, and in-store demonstrations so consumers can see how the products work. To sell to major wholesalers and retailers such as Walmart, Target, and grocery stores, manufacturers utilize professional selling. Many manufacturers use a combination of techniques to sell to all three groups: customers, retailers, and wholesalers.

Cheetos Mac' N Cheese in three flavors was introduced in 2020 and available at most retailers in fall 2021.

Source: © Shutterstock, Inc.

During the introduction stage, an organization must have distribution outlets (places where the product is sold or the service is available) and sufficient product quantities to meet demand. Cooperation throughout a company's supply chain can help ensure supply meets demand; however, some aspects may be out of the firm's control. For example, COVID-19 severely affected the supply chain with labor shortages, material shortages, and shipping delays. Retailers experienced shortages of cleaning and paper products where uncontrollable factors affected supply. Other companies introduced new products in limited outlets first, as Frito-Lay did when it introduced Cheetos Mac' N Cheese in Walmart and online in 2020 and with other retailers in fall 2021.[7] When supply is not a factor, companies must estimate demand or face shortages. You may remember eating Rice Krispies Treats, a very popular prepackaged product. When introduced, the product was so popular that Kellogg's could not keep up with its initial demand and ran ads apologizing to consumers for the problem.

Product pricing strategies in the introductory stage can vary depending on the type of product, competing products, the extra value the product provides consumers versus existing offerings, and the costs of developing and producing the product. Organizations want consumers to perceive that a new offering is better or more desirable than existing products. Two strategies that are widely used in the introductory stage are penetration pricing and skimming.

penetration pricing strategy

A strategy in which an organization offers a low initial price on a product so that it captures as much market share as possible.

A **penetration pricing strategy** involves using a low initial price to encourage many customers to try a product. The organization hopes to sell a high volume in order to generate substantial revenues. New varieties of cereals, fragrances of shampoo, scents of detergents, and snack foods are often introduced at low initial prices. Seldom does a company utilize a high price strategy with a product such as this. The low initial price of the product is often combined with advertising, coupons, samples, or other special incentives to increase awareness of the product and get consumers to try it.

A company uses a **skimming pricing strategy**, which involves setting a high initial price for a product, to more quickly recoup the investment related to its development and marketing. The skimming strategy attracts the top, or high end, of the market. Generally, this market consists of customers who are not as price sensitive or who are early adopters of products. Firms that produce expensive electronic products such as the Apple Watch, the Peloton bike, and ultra-high definition TVs charge high prices in the introductory stage. In conjunction with a skimming approach, the sellers of products such as these are also more likely to engage personal selling, ads, and television commercials, social media posts targeted to high-income and/or innovative customers, and placement of the product in a limited number of distribution outlets.

Peloton, a popular and highly regarded "aspirational" brand of exercise equipment, uses a price-skimming strategy.

Source: © Shutterstock, Inc.

skimming pricing strategy

A high initial price that companies set when introducing new products in order to get back money invested.

The Growth Stage

If sales rise and a product is accepted by the marketplace, it enters the growth stage of the product life cycle. The **growth stage** is characterized by increasing sales and profits. Companies typically begin to make a profit during the growth stage because more units are being sold and more revenue is generated. However, the high sales and profits attract competitors, who enter the market very quickly. For example, when Diet Coke experienced great success, Pepsi soon entered with Diet Pepsi. You'll notice that both Coca-Cola and Pepsi have similar competitive offerings in the beverage industry, including their own brands of bottled water, juice, and sports drinks.

growth stage

The stage of the life cycle in which sales increase and more competitors enter the market.

As additional customers begin to buy the product, manufacturers must ensure that the product remains available to customers or run the risk of them eventually buying competitors' offerings. When demand is higher than supply, the door opens for competitors to enter the market. This is typical in the growth stage. Consider what happened when Amana introduced the first microwave, which originally cost $500. As consumers in the United States and elsewhere saw and heard about the product, sales increased from forty thousand units to over a million units in only a few years. As a result of the high demand, many competitors entered the market, prices dropped, and microwaves entered the maturity stage.[8]

The first microwave on the market cost $500. Now you can buy one for as little as $50.

Source: © Shutterstock, Inc.

A company sometimes increases its promotional spending on a product a little later during its growth stage. Instead of encouraging consumers to try the product later on, which they may have already done, the promotions often focus on the specific benefits the product offers and its value relative to competitive offerings. In other words, although the company must still inform and educate customers about the product, it must counter the competition. Emphasizing the advantages of the product's brand name can help a company maintain its sales in the face of competition. Although different organizations produce appliances and electronics, having a highly recognized brand name such as Apple or Samsung strengthens a firm's advantage when competitors enter the market.

The number of distribution outlets (stores, dealers, online availability) utilized to sell the product can also increase during the growth stage as a company tries to reach as much of the marketplace as possible. Expanding a product's distribution and increasing its production to ensure its availability at different outlets usually results in a product's costs remaining high during the growth stage. The price of the product itself typically remains at about the same level during the growth stage, although some companies reduce their prices slightly to attract additional buyers and meet the competitors' prices. Companies hope that by increasing their sales, they also improve their profits.

The Maturity Stage

maturity stage

The stage of the product life cycle at which sales begin to level off and competitors have saturated the market.

After competitors enter the market and the number of potential new customers declines, the sales of a product typically begin to level off. This indicates that a product has entered the **maturity stage** of its life cycle. Intense competition causes profits to fall until only the strongest players remain.

Most consumer products and services are in the maturity stage of their life cycles; their buyers are repeat purchasers versus new customers. The maturity stage usually lasts longer than other stages. The sports drinks Gatorade and Powerade as well as many Reese's Peanut Butter Cups and M&Ms are in the maturity stage, but you'll notice new variations of the products. They have been around for a number of years, and their sales are steady.

Given the competitive environment in the maturity stage, many products are promoted heavily to consumers. The strategies used to promote the products often focus on the value and benefits that give the offering a competitive advantage. The promotions aimed at a company's distributors may also increase during the maturity stage.

Companies are also more likely to decrease the price of mature products to counter the competition. The problem with lowering prices is that it can result in "price wars" between companies and decrease all of their profits. To counter mobile phone pricing apps that allow shoppers to find identical products cheaper online and buy them, brick-and-mortar retailers like Target, Macy's, and others are signing agreements with top designers to make products no other company (online or otherwise) has.

Clearly companies are challenged to develop strategies to extend the maturity stage of their products so they remain competitive—and so are the marketing personnel who work for them. Usually these people's compensation levels are based on the sales of the products they manage, so they want to not just sustain them but grow them. How do they accomplish this? Many firms do so by modifying their target markets, offerings, or marketing strategies. Next, we look at each of these strategies.

To expand its declining target market (middle-aged men), Harley-Davidson is now courting women as well as minorities and millennials.

Source: © Shutterstock, Inc.

Modifying the target market helps a company attract different customers by seeking new users and going after different market segments. Financial institutions and automobile dealers realized that women have increased buying power and now market to them.

Finding new uses for a product in order to attract additional customers is another strategy. The maker of Pedialyte, a product that replaces nutrients and electrolytes when infants are ill, has found a new use for its product: curing hangovers. People discovered the product worked well for this purpose and began talking about it on social media. Abbott Laboratories, the maker of the product, subsequently launched a social media campaign aimed at adult users, and the sales of Pedialyte jumped dramatically upward.[9]

As we have indicated, many companies enter different geographic markets or international markets as a strategy to get new users. A product that might be in the mature stage in one country might be in the introductory stage in another market. Mobile phones were very popular in Asia before they were introduced in the United States. The sales of minivans have been declining in the United States but are increasing in China. Consequently, automobile manufacturers are expanding the number of minivans and the variety of them they offer in China.

Adam Massey, F33.ai

Source: Adam Massey, used with permission.

Adam Massey, chairman and CEO of F33.ai, a machine learning and cloud services company he founded in 2019, is a twenty-one-year enterprise software veteran. Adam's career spans large companies like Oracle, Interwoven, and Google, as well as several high-growth startups. He spent twelve years at Google Cloud where he originally joined to help launch the Google Workspace enterprise business and played a pivotal role in growing it to a market-leading, multi-billion dollar business. Along the way he played key leadership roles in both sales and alliances and built the Google Cloud channel and partner business from the ground up. Adam graduated from Clemson University in 1999 with a marketing degree.

Modifying the product, such as changing its packaging, size, flavors, colors, or quality, can also extend the product's maturity stage. Car manufacturers modify their vehicles slightly each year to offer new styles and new safety features and make more extensive modifications to them every three to five years. Kraft Foods extended the mature stage of different crackers such as Wheat Thins and Triscuits by creating different flavors. M&Ms, created in 1941, have remained a popular snack and have included new varieties and colors over the past sixty-one years with more new flavors, including M&Ms Crunchy Cookie available in 2022.[10]

Peanut butter and peanut M&Ms provide examples of how a company introduced new flavors to boost sales even while the original M&Ms remain popular. Similarly, Gucci, Prada, and other makers of designer handbags are finding that they have hit a wall in terms of the prices they charge for the bags and the number of them they can sell. So they are beginning to offer smaller bags for lower prices.

M&Ms Super Bowl Commercial, "Come Together"

Original and peanut M&Ms are two of the most popular snacks in America.

View in the online reader

But sometimes introducing new flavors or changing packages doesn't work. While many varieties of M&Ms appeal to consumers, Mars experienced several varieties including "carrot cake" M&Ms and "strawberried peanut butter" that were not popular at all.[11] A few years ago, PepsiCo redesigned the can for their flagship Pepsi brand, but consumers had mixed feelings about it.

Rebranding

This video promoting Pepsi-Cola's new design was well done, but it didn't convince consumers to buy more of the product.

View in the online reader

With more and more consumers buying staple goods and groceries online, the grocery industry has become extremely competitive, and some companies have gone out of business. To extend the mature stage and remain competitive, Lowes Foods targeted male shoppers with "beer dens" and "Sausage Works." Another chain, Hy-Vee, created a "reimagined" experience in 2021 high on technology including digital shelf pricing, television screens with digital marketing, and digital kiosks for consumers to order cakes and fresh foods. The stores also include many options for on-site fast dining as well as to-go meals.[12] Alfalfa's Market remodeled to make male customers feel more comfortable, making sure the exit could be seen, and stores were easy to navigate. COVID-19 created more challenges with many grocery stores having to temporarily discontinue their food bars, offer curbside pick-up, personal shopping and delivery, and/or utilize shopping/delivery services.

Cheetos Crunch Pop Mix

Consumers were encouraged to try Cheetos Crunch Pop Mix, which was advertised during the 2021 Super Bowl.

View in the online reader

When introducing products to international markets, firms must decide if the product can be **standardized** (kept the same) or how much, if any, **adaptation**, or changing, of the product to meet the needs of the local culture is necessary. Although it is much less expensive to standardize products and promotional strategies, cultural and environmental differences usually require some adaptation. In Asia, Burger King sells a squid burger. Because people of the Hindu faith in India don't eat beef, McDonald's sells Chicken Maharaja Macs instead of Big Macs there.

standardized

Keeping a product or service the same in all markets.

adaptation

The changes that an organization must make for a product or service to fit the local culture.

Product colors and packages as well as product names must often be changed because of cultural and legal differences. For example, in many Asian and European countries, Coca-Cola's diet drinks are called "light," not diet, due to legal restrictions on how the word diet can be used. GE makes smaller appliances such as washers and dryers for the Japanese market because houses tend to be smaller and don't have the room for larger models. Companies must also examine the external environment in foreign markets, since the regulations, competition, and economic conditions vary as well as the cultures.

In Europe, diet drinks are called "light," not diet. This Coca-Cola product is available in Germany.

Source: © Shutterstock, Inc.

Some companies modify the marketing strategy for one or more marketing variables of their products. For example, many coffee shops and fast food restaurants such as McDonald's offer specialty coffee and have been remodeled to include coffee bars, flat-screen televisions, and wi-fi access that competes with Starbucks. As a result, Starbucks' managers decided it was time to change the company's strategy. Over the years, Starbucks added lunch offerings at some of its stores, and a night menu with beer, wine, and small plates of food. Again, COVID-19 restrictions changed the way many restaurants operated, eliminating or limiting in-person dining, offering delivery or curbside pickup, changing the menu, adding kiosk menus, and enhancing cleanliness and social distancing when indoors.

The oldest operating McDonald's is this store in Downey, California. The store hasn't been remodeled since it opened in 1953.

Source: By Photo by Bryan Hong (Brybry26) - CC 2.5, https://commons.wikimedia.org/w/index.php?curid=1815290

The Decline Stage

decline stage

The stage of the life cycle at which sales drop and companies must decide whether to keep, modify, or drop a product.

When sales decrease and continue to drop to lower levels, the product has entered the **decline stage** of the product life cycle. In the decline stage, changes in consumer preferences, technological advances, and alternatives that satisfy the same need can lead to a decrease in demand for a product. How many of your fellow students do you think have used a typewriter or adding machine, or played an eight-track tape?

Some products decline slowly. Others go through a rapid level of decline. Many fads and fashions for young people tend to have very short life cycles and go "out of style" very quickly. (If you've ever asked your parents to borrow clothes for a "90's" party, you may be amused at how much the styles have changed.) Similarly, many students don't have landline phones or VCR players and cannot believe that some people still use the "outdated" devices. Some outdated devices, like payphones, disappear almost completely as they become obsolete.

Your parents or grandparents might still use a videocassette recorder (VCR) like this.

Source: © Shutterstock, Inc.

Companies must decide what strategies to take when their products enter the decline stage. To save money, some companies try to reduce their promotional expenditures on these products and the number of distribution outlets in which they are sold. They might implement price cuts to get customers to buy the product. Harvesting the product entails gradually reducing all costs spent on it, including investments made in the product and marketing costs. By reducing these costs, the company hopes that the profits from the product will increase until their inventory runs out. Harvesting often occurs with products like video game systems or cell phones which have a limited life cycle due to the introduction of new versions.

Another option for the company is divesting (dropping or deleting) the product from its offerings. The company might choose to sell the brand to another firm or simply reduce the price drastically in order to get rid of all remaining inventory. If a company decides to keep the product, it may make money if competing products drop out of the marketplace. Many companies decide the best strategy is to modify the product in the maturity stage to avoid having it enter the decline stage. As consumer trends change, some companies sell or spin off products that are in decline. Vanity Fair announced that it would spin off its Wrangler and Lee brand denims to focus on its more profitable brands such as North Face, Timberland, Vans, and JanSport.

Key Takeaway

- The product life cycle helps a company understand the stages (introduction, growth, maturity, and decline) a product or service may go through once it is launched in the marketplace. The number and length of stages can vary. When a product is launched or commercialized, it enters the introduction stage. Companies must try to generate awareness of the product and encourage consumers to try it. During the growth stage, companies must demonstrate the product's benefits and value to persuade customers to buy it versus competing products. Some products never experience growth. Most products are in the maturity stage. In the maturity stage, sales level off and the market typically has many competitors. Companies modify the target market, the offering, or the marketing mix in order to extend the maturity stage and keep a product from going into the decline stage. If a product goes into decline, a company must decide whether to keep the product, harvest and reduce the spending on it until all the inventory is sold, or divest the product.

Review Questions

1. Explain what a firm that sells a product with a limited life cycle (such as software) should do in each stage so there is not a lot of inventory left over when a newer version is introduced.
2. Explain why the marketing costs related to a product are typically higher during the introduction stage and why companies must generate awareness of the new product or service and encourage consumers to try it.
3. Explain why and when penetration and skimming pricing are used in the introduction stage.
4. What stage of the life cycle is a product in when the company cannot meet the demand for it and competitors begin to enter the market?
5. What different strategies do firms use to extend the life cycles of their products throughout the maturity stage?
6. How did Kraft extend the maturity stage of the product life cycle of Wheat Thins crackers?
7. Explain the difference between harvesting and divesting when a firm enters the decline stage.
8. Give an example of how the COVID-19 pandemic affected your favorite restaurant, store, barber/hair salon, and professional service providers such as a doctor or dentist.

7.3 Discussion Questions and Activities

Discussion Questions

1. Who owns an idea? If a customer comes up with an innovation involving your product, and your company thinks that innovation can be commercialized, who owns the new product?
2. Assume you come up with an idea for a new electronic product you think your fellow students would really like. How would you go through the product development process? How would you accomplish each step within that process?
3. Select a product you are familiar with and explain the stages of the product's life cycle and different ways in which a company can extend its mature stage.
4. Why, given the availability of good research practices, do so many new products fail?
5. What has been Apple's pricing strategy throughout its products' life cycles? If you made an Apple Watch copycat product, what would your price have to be in order to compete successfully?
6. What are the risks associated with beta testing? What criteria would you use to select customers when needing a beta test?
7. This textbook is an open-source text, meaning your professor can modify its contents. Further, it has multiple delivery modes. You can view it online or buy a color copy. What type of screening process do you think was used in developing this concept? How would that screening process differ from the screening process used to assess this specific book's potential? Describe what you think those two processes would look like. If you don't think the screening processes would differ, why?
8. You've got a really great idea for a new online business. But you need capital to get the business going, and when you ask investors for money, they want to know if you've done a market test and what the results were. Why are they asking for market test results? What are the risks associated with a market test? Are there other ways you can answer their real concerns without doing a market test?
9. What characteristics of a product would make it a good candidate for a phased launch? What would make the product a good candidate for a worldwide launch?
10. The product life cycle, the BCG matrix, and the GE approach have all been criticized for leading to early harvesting of older products and overinvesting in new products. Why did that happen when these tools were applied?
11. How do you think the COVID-19 pandemic will affect the design and introduction of new products, services, and businesses?

Activities

1. Take two existing offerings and combine them to create a new one. What type of offering is it? To whom would you sell it? What new benefits does the product offer, and how would you communicate them to potential buyers? What evidence could you generate to predict the likelihood of the new offering being successful?
2. Identify two new consumer products sold in a grocery store or by a mass merchandiser such as Walmart. Explain the strategies used to introduce each of the products and which strategy you feel will be most successful.

3. Identify three products that are sold in international markets and explain any differences in how the products have been changed to meet the needs of consumers in the international markets.
4. Provide an idea for a new service that you feel is needed as a result of the COVID-19 pandemic. Explain why it is needed and strategies necessary introduce service and make it successful.

7.4 Case Study: Gemelli Biotech Introduces Trio-Smart

The COVID-19 pandemic led to a nationwide lockdown in March 2020, limiting consumer access to many in-person services across sectors. Professional services such as labs for blood tests, in-person medical visits, and elective procedures were restricted in many markets. Gemelli Biotech's first offering, ibs-smart, a diagnostic blood test for IBS, required an in-person blood draw. As constraints on blood draw services became restrictive to Gemelli's growth, the company responded by reducing promotion for ibs-smart and accelerating the launch of their second product, trio-smart, a breath test that allowed for at-home sample collection.

Package showing Trio Smart, a breath test which allows at-home sample collection.

Source: Courtesy of Gemelli Biotech

Gemelli was able to launch trio-smart rapidly by adopting an iterative approach, going to market with a minimum viable product (MVP) and adding features over time. The diversification of their product portfolio allowed Gemelli to tell a more complete story about GI diagnostics and offer a complementary set of solutions. The company designed the ordering process for trio-smart to be virtual-first, allowing healthcare providers to place orders for their patients without in-office appointments. Similarly, Gemelli adapted their promotional efforts to include remote webinars and sponsorships of virtual trade shows. Key opinion leaders were included throughout the development process, providing Gemelli with insightful feedback and a powerful network of advocates.

Employing these strategies in a very challenging environment, Gemelli was able to successfully launch a new product and significantly accelerate the growth of their business.

Case Study Questions

1. While the COVID-19 pandemic accelerated the introduction of trio-smart, do you think consumers prefer the in-home convenience of testing rather than getting a blood test?
2. Gemelli adapted their promotional strategies for the introduction of trio-smart. As the product moves through the product life cycle, what changes should Gemelli make to their promotional strategies and ordering process?
3. As more and more people feel comfortable returning to doctors' offices and labs, what promotional strategies should Gemelli use to also increase demand of ibs-smart?

Endnotes

1. Lawrence M. Fisher (December 15, 1989), "Xerox Sues Apple Computer Over Macintosh Copyright," *New York Times*, http://www.nytimes.com/1989/12/15/business/company-news-xerox-sues-apple-computer-over-macintosh-copyright.html? pagewanted=1.
2. Morgan, Anaïs (2021), "The Complete Guide to VOD (and Why Your Business Needs to Be Using It," https://www.uscreen.tv/blog/what-is-vod/#why-is-vod-important, (July 7).
3. Dasckowski, Don (2020), "How American Fast Food Franchises Expanded Abroad," https://www.thebalancesmb.com/how-american-fast-food-franchises-expanded-abroad-1350955 (November 10).
4. Consumer Product Safety Commission (2021), https://www.cpsc.gov/Recalls/2021/The-Boppy-Company-Recalls-Over-3-Million-Original-Newborn-Loungers-Boppy-Preferred-Newborn-Loungers-and-Pottery-Barn-Kids-Boppy-Newborn-Loungers-After-8-Infant-Deaths-Suffocation-Risk, (September 23).
5. Prokop, Hannah (2021), "Coca-Cola Cuts Its Energy Drink," https://www.cspdailynews.com/beverages/coca-cola-cuts-its-energy-drink, (May 28).
6. O'Kane, Caitlin (2021), "Reese's is launching a new peanut butter cup—without chocolate," https://www.cbsnews.com/news/reeses-peanut-butter-cup-no-chocolate/, (March 3).
7. Hallinan, Bridget (2020), "Cheetos Now Makes Mac 'n Cheese—Here's How It Tastes," https://www.foodandwine.com/news/cheetos-mac-and-cheese-walmart-taste-test, (August 6).
8. "Microwave Oven," *Wikipedia,* http://en.wikipedia.org/wiki/Microwave_oven. Accessed January 20, 2010.
9. Andria Cheng (May 15, 2015), "Pedialyte Sales Grow into an Adult Market," *Wall Street Journal,* http://wsj.com; Kaitlyn Tiffany (2018), "How Pedialyte got Pedialit: Inside Pedialyte's journey from toddler flu remedy to hangover fix," https://www.vox.com/the-goods/2018/9/10/17819358/pedialyte-hangover-marketing-strategy-instagram-influencers.
10. Burginger, Lyndsay (2021), "Here's All the New M&M Flavors Coming Out This Year," https://www.wideopeneats.com/new-mm-flavors/ (September 9).
11. "M&Ms Grossest Flavors of All Time," (2013), https://affotd.com/2013/12/12/mms-grossest-flavors-of-all-time/, (December 13).
12. Redman, Russell (2021), "Hy-Vee opens 'reimagined' grocery store," https://www.supermarketnews.com/retail-financial/hy-vee-opens-reimagined-grocery-store, (September 17).

CHAPTER 8

How Marketing Channels Can Be Used to Create Value for Customers

Sometimes when you buy a good or service, it passes straight from the producer to you. But suppose every time you purchased something, you had to contact its maker? For some offerings, such as a haircut, this would work. But what about the products you purchase at the grocery store? You couldn't begin to contact and buy from all the makers of those products. It would be an incredibly inefficient way to do business.

Fortunately, companies partner with one another, alleviating you of this burden. For example, instead of Procter & Gamble selling individual toothbrushes to consumers, it sells many of them to a drugstore close to you, which then sells them to you and other people.

The specific avenue a seller uses to make a finished good or service available to you for purchase—for example, whether you are able to buy it directly from the seller, at a store, online, from a salesperson, and so on—is referred to as the product's **marketing channel** (or *distribution channel*). All of the people and organizations that buy, resell, and promote the product "downstream" as it makes its way to you are part of the marketing channel. This chapter focuses on downstream channels. In the next chapter, we look not only "downstream" but also "upstream" at the people and organizations that supply the materials and services and that allow products to be made in the first place.

marketing channel

The group of organizations involved in selling and promoting goods from the time they are produced until they reach end users.

8.1 Marketing Channels and Channel Partners

Learning Objectives

1. Explain why marketing channel decisions can result in the success or failure of products.
2. Understand how supply chains differ from marketing channels.
3. Describe the different types of organizations that work together as channel partners and what each does.

Today, marketing channel decisions are as important as the decisions companies make about the features and prices of products. Consumers have become more demanding. They are used to getting what they want. If you can't get your product to them when, where, and how they want it, they will simply buy a competing product. In other words, *how* companies sell has become as important as *what* they sell.

channel members

The firms a company partners with to actively promote and sell a product as it travels through its marketing channel to users.

intermediaries

Third parties that facilitate the supply and sale of products from manufacturers to users.

The firms a company partners with to actively promote and sell a product as it travels through its marketing channel to users are referred to by the firm as its **channel members** (or partners). Companies strive to choose not only the best marketing channels but also the best channel partners. A strong channel partner like Walmart can promote and sell the heck out of a product that might not otherwise turn a profit for its producer. In turn, Walmart wants to work with strong channel partners it can depend on to continuously provide it with great products that fly off the shelves. By contrast, a weak channel partner can be a liability.

The simplest marketing channel consists of just two parties—a producer and a consumer. Your haircut is a good example. When you get a haircut, it travels straight from your hairdresser to you. No one else owns, handles, or remarkets the haircut to you before you get it. However, many other products and services pass through multiple sales organizations before they get to you. These organizations are called **intermediaries** (or *middlemen* or *resellers*).

Companies partner with intermediaries not because they necessarily want to (ideally they could sell their products straight to users) but because the intermediaries can help them sell the products better than they could working alone. In other words, the intermediaries have some sort of capabilities the producer needs: contact with many customers or the right customers, marketing expertise, e-commerce, shipping capabilities, and the ability to lend the producer credit are among the types of help a firm can get by utilizing a channel partner.

Intermediaries also create efficiencies by streamlining the number of transactions an organization must make, each of which takes time and costs money to conduct. As Figure 8.1 shows, by selling the tractors it makes through local farm machinery dealers, the farm machinery manufacturer John Deere can streamline the number of transactions it makes from eight to just two.

FIGURE 8.1 Using Intermediaries to Streamline the Number of Sales Transactions

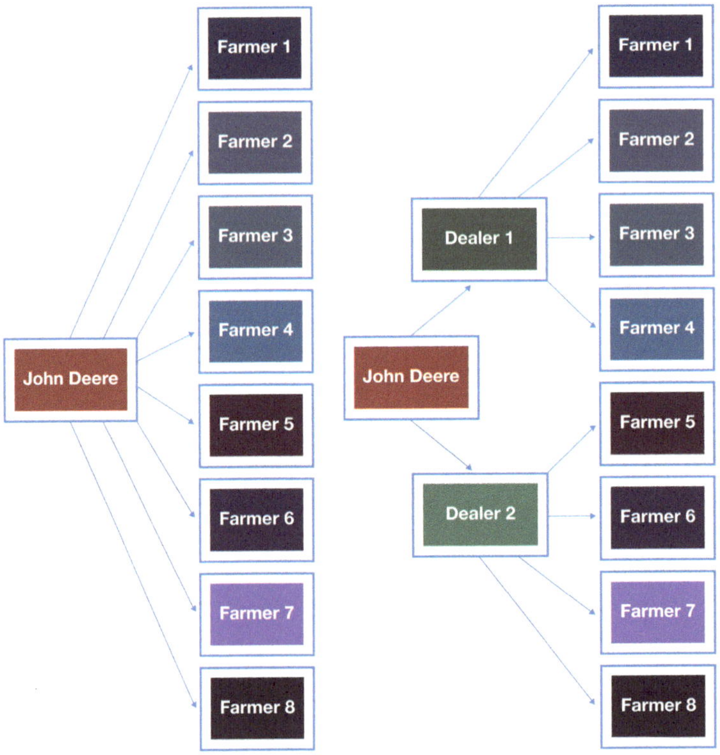

The marketing environment is always changing, so what was a great channel or channel partner yesterday might not be a great channel partner today. Changes in technology, production techniques, and your customer's needs mean you have to continually reevaluate your marketing channels and the channel partners you ally yourself with. Moreover, when you create a new product, you can't assume the channels that were used in the past for similar products are the best ones.[1] A different channel or channel partner might be better.

A classic example is Microsoft's digital encyclopedia, Encarta, which was first sold on CD and via an online subscription in the early 1990s. Encarta nearly destroyed Encyclopedia Britannica, a firm that had dominated the print encyclopedia business for literally centuries. Ironically, Microsoft had actually tried to partner with Encyclopedia Britannica to use its encyclopedia information to make Encarta, but was turned down.

Digital downloads gave way to streaming services like Spotify as the major marketing channel for recording artists.

Source: © Shutterstock, Inc.

Today, Encarta no longer exists. It's been put out of business by the free online encyclopedia, Wikipedia. Likewise, digital downloads and CDs used to be the major marketing channels for recording artists. Today, if you want to make money as a recording artist, your record label will need to partner with a streaming music service like Spotify, Apple Music, or Tidal. And believe it or not, sales of vinyl records are now growing exponentially.[2] The point is that products and their marketing channels are constantly evolving. Consequently, you and your company have to be ready to evolve, too.

Marketing Channels Versus Supply Chains

In the past few decades, organizations have begun taking a more holistic look at their marketing channels. Instead of looking at only the firms that sell and promote their products, they have begun looking at *all* the organizations that figure into any part of the process of producing, promoting, and delivering an offering to its user. All these organizations are considered part of the offering's **supply chain**.

supply chain

All the organizations that participate in the production, promotion, and delivery of a product or service from the producer to the end consumer.

The supply chain includes producers of the raw materials that go into a product. If it's a food product, the supply chain extends back through the distributors all the way to the farmers who grew the ingredients and the companies from which the farmers purchased the seeds, fertilizer, or animals. A product's supply chain also includes transportation companies such as railroads that help physically move the product, and companies that build websites for other companies. If a software maker hires a company in India to help it write a computer program, the Indian company is part of the partner's supply chain. These types of firms aren't considered channel partners because it's not their job to actively sell the products being produced. Nonetheless, they all contribute to a product's success or failure.

Firms are constantly monitoring their supply chains and tinkering with them so they are as efficient as possible. This process is called **supply chain management**, and we will discuss it in detail in Chapter 9. Supply chain management is challenging. If done well, it's practically an art.

supply chain management

The process of managing and refining supply chains so as to make them as efficient as possible.

Types of Channel Partners

Let's now look at the basic types of channel partners. To help you understand the various types of channel partners, we will go over the most common types of intermediaries. The two types you hear about most frequently are wholesalers and retailers. Keep in mind, however, that the categories we discuss in this section are just that—categories. In recent years, the lines between wholesalers, retailers, and producers have begun to blur considerably. Microsoft started out as a producer of goods, but later opened up its own retail stores like Apple has done, only to close them again and sell all of its products online.[3] As you will learn later in the chapter, Walmart, Amazon, and other large retailers now produce their own store brands and sell them to other retailers. Similarly, many producers have outsourced their manufacturing, and although they still call themselves manufacturers, they act more like wholesalers.

Wherever organizations see an opportunity, they are beginning to take it, regardless of their positions in marketing channels. The ride-sharing service Uber is another example of how a company's channel partners can become its competitors. A few years ago Uber began partnering with a company called Breeze, which leases cars by the week to people who want to become Uber drivers. Later, Uber decided to take on this task directly. The company was signing up 500,000 drivers a month and probably figured leasing the cars itself would be a good a source of revenue.

Wholesalers

wholesalers

Businesses that purchase products in large quantities, can store the products, can break the pallets down into cases or units, and can deliver the desired quantity of a product to distributors, retailers, and/or consumers.

Wholesalers obtain large quantities of products from producers, store them, and break them down into cases and other smaller units more convenient for retailers to buy, a process called "breaking bulk." Wholesalers get their name from the fact that they resell goods "whole" to other companies without transforming the goods. For example, if you are trying to stock a small electronics store, you probably don't want to purchase a truckload of iPhones. Instead, you probably want to buy a smaller assortment of iPhones as well as other merchandise. Via wholesalers, you can get the assortment of products you want in the quantities you want. Some wholesalers carry a wide range of different products. Others carry narrow ranges of products.

Most wholesalers "take title" to goods—that is, the wholesalers buy and own them—until they are purchased by other sellers. Wholesalers such as these assume a great deal of risk on the part of companies further down the marketing channel as a result. For example, if the iPhones you plan to purchase are stolen or damaged during shipment, or become outdated because a new model has been released, the wholesaler suffers the loss—not you. Electronics products, in particular, become obsolete very quickly. Think about the cell phone you owned just a few years ago. Would you want to have to use it today?

There are many types of wholesalers. The three basic types of wholesalers are merchant wholesalers, brokers, and manufacturers' agents, each of which we discuss next.

Merchant Wholesalers

merchant wholesalers

Wholesalers that take title to the goods.

distributors

Businesses that purchase large quantities of products, can store products, can sell products, can deliver desired quantities of products, and can offer services. Distributors generally take title to products and employ a sales force to actively market their products.

Merchant wholesalers are wholesalers that take title to goods. They are also sometimes referred to as **distributors**, *dealers*, or *jobbers*. Merchant wholesalers include both full-service wholesalers and limited-service wholesalers. Full-service wholesalers perform a broad range of services, such as stocking inventories, operating warehouses, supplying credit to buyers, employing salespeople to assist the companies that buy their products, and delivering goods to them. Maurice Sporting Goods is a large North American full-service wholesaler of hunting and fishing equipment. The firm's services include helping its retail customers figure out which products to stock, how to price them, and how to display them.

Limited-service wholesalers offer fewer services to their customers but charge lower prices. These wholesalers might not offer delivery services, extend their customers credit, or have sales forces that actively call on sellers. *Cash-and-carry wholesalers* are an example. Small retailers often buy from cash-and-carry wholesalers to keep their prices as low as big retailers that get large discounts due to the huge volumes of goods they buy.

Drop shippers are another type of limited-service wholesaler. Although drop shippers take title to goods, they don't actually take possession of them or handle them, sometimes because they deal with goods that are large or bulky. Instead, drop shippers earn a commission by finding sellers and passing their orders along to producers, which then ship them directly to the sellers. E-commerce has greatly facilitated drop shipping. You have probably purchased an item on eBay or Amazon that involved a drop shipper. The seller relayed the order to a drop shipper, who passed it along to the manufacturer, who then shipped the item straight to you.

Mail-order or *web wholesalers* sell their products to industrial and institutional customers using catalogs or websites instead of sales forces, and then ship the products to buyers. *Truck jobbers* (or *truck wholesalers*) actually store products, which are often highly perishable (e.g., fresh fish), on their trucks. The trucks make the rounds to businesses, which inspect and select the products they want straight off of the trucks.

Rack jobbers sell specialty products, such as books, hosiery, and magazines that they display on their own racks in stores. Rack jobbers retain the title to the goods while the merchandise is in the stores for sale. Periodically, rack jobbers count what's been sold off the racks and then bill the stores for those items.

Brokers and Affiliates

Brokers, or *agents*, don't purchase or take title to the products they sell. Their role is limited to negotiating sales contracts for producers. Clothing, furniture, food, and commodities such as lumber and steel are often sold by brokers. They are generally paid a commission for what they sell and are assigned to different geographical territories by the producers with whom they work. Because they have excellent industry contacts, brokers and agents are "go-to" resources for both consumers and companies trying to buy and sell products.

brokers

Representatives of one or more manufacturers who sell products on their behalf to consumers, wholesalers, and distributors but do not take title to them.

The most common form of agents and brokers consumers encounter are in real estate. Real estate agents work for brokers, who act as sort of a head agent and market the company's services while making sure that all legal requirements are met.

Real estate brokers and agents with excellent contacts are able to quickly match up buyers and sellers.

Source: © Shutterstock, Inc.

An **affiliate** is a person or organization that uses its website to market a different company's products, usually via online ads, and is paid a commission for each product sold. In other words, affiliates drive online traffic to other websites so as to sell products and then get paid for doing so. For example, when you book an airline flight on Expedia, you may be offered a deal from Avis, Hertz, or another rental car company. If you go ahead and rent a car, the rental car company pays Expedia a commission. If you don't, Expedia gets no commission. Like brokers and agents, affiliates don't take title to goods. They simply connect sellers with buyers who are likely to be interested in their products.

An affiliate marketing channel can be set up anywhere people congregate online—on blogs, search engines, news websites, social media websites, and YouTube. Discount sites such as Groupon and comparison shopping sites such as Compare.com also serve as affiliates to sellers. Sellers like to sign up affiliates that attract a lot of online visitors who fit their target markets because doing so extends the marketing reach of the sellers instantly.

affiliate

A person or organization that uses its website to market and sell another company's product for a commission.

Manufacturers' Sales Offices or Branches

Manufacturers' sales offices or branches are selling units that work directly for manufacturers and are found in business-to-business settings. For example, Konica Minolta Business Solutions (KMBS) has a system of sales branches that sells commercial scanners, printers, cloud computing solutions, and other office services to businesses. As a consumer, it would be rare for you to interact directly with a manufacturer's sales office.

manufacturers' sales offices or branches

Selling units that work directly for manufacturers. A type of factory outlet store.

Retailers

retailers

Businesses that purchase products from manufacturers, wholesalers, agents, or distributors and then sell them to consumers.

supermarkets

Self-service retailers that provide a full range of food products to consumers as well as some household products.

drugstores

Stores that specialize in selling over-the-counter medication, prescriptions, and health and beauty products and offer services such as photo developing.

convenience stores

Miniature supermarkets that stock a limited assortment of products. Many of them sell gasoline and are open twenty-four hours a day.

specialty stores

Stores that sell a certain type of product.

category killer

A firm that sells a high volume of a product in a particular category.

department stores

Stores that carry a wide variety of household and personal types of merchandise such as clothing and jewelry.

superstores

Large department stores that carry a broad array of general merchandise as well as groceries. Superstores are also referred to as *hypermarkets* and *supercenters*.

Retailers buy products from wholesalers, agents, or distributors and then sell them to consumers. Retailers vary by the types of products they sell, their sizes, the prices they charge, the level of service they provide consumers, and the convenience or speed they offer.

Supermarkets, or grocery stores, are self-service retailers that provide a full range of food products to consumers, as well as some household products. Supermarkets can be high, medium, or low range in terms of the prices they charge and the service and variety of products they offer. Whole Foods and Central Market are grocers that offer a wide variety of products, generally at higher prices. Midrange supermarkets include stores like Albertsons and Kroger. Aldi and Food 4 Less are examples of supermarkets with a limited selection of products and service but low prices. **Drugstores** specialize in selling over-the-counter medications, prescriptions, and health and beauty products and offer services such as photo developing.

Convenience stores are miniature supermarkets. Many of them sell gasoline and are open twenty-four hours a day. Often they are located on corners, making it easy and fast for consumers to get in and out. Some of these stores contain fast food franchises like Church's Chicken and Jack in the Box. Consumers pay for the convenience in the form of higher markups on products. In Europe, as well as in rural parts of the United States, you'll find convenience stores that offer fresh meat and produce.

Specialty stores sell a certain type of product, but they usually carry a deep line of it. Zales, which sells jewelry, and Williams-Sonoma, which sells an array of kitchen and cooking-related products, are examples of specialty stores. The personnel who work in specialty stores are usually knowledgeable and often provide customers with high levels of service. Specialty stores vary by size. Many are small. Others are giant specialty stores called category killers. A **category killer** sells a high volume of a particular type of product and, in doing so, dominates the competition, or "category." Petco and PetSmart are category killers in the retail pet products market. Home Depot is a category killer in the home improvement market.

Department stores carry a wide variety of household and personal merchandise such as clothing and jewelry. Many are chain stores. The prices department stores charge range widely, as does the level of service shoppers receive. Neiman Marcus, Saks Fifth Avenue, and Nordstrom sell expensive products and offer extensive personal service to customers. The prices department stores such as JCPenney, Kohl's, and Macy's charge are midrange, as is the level of service shoppers receive. Walmart, Kmart, and Target are discount department stores with cheaper goods and limited amounts of customer service.

Superstores are oversized department stores that carry a broad array of general merchandise as well as groceries. Banks, hair and nail salons, and restaurants such as Starbucks are often located within these stores for the convenience of shoppers. You have probably shopped at a SuperTarget or a huge Walmart with offerings such as these. Superstores are also referred to as *hypermarkets* and *supercenters*.

Warehouse clubs are supercenters that sell products at a discount. They require people who shop with them to become members by paying an annual fee. Costco and Sam's Club are warehouse clubs. **Off-price retailers** are stores that sell a variety of discount merchandise that consists of seconds, overruns, and the previous season's stock other stores have liquidated. Big Lots, Ross Dress for Less, and dollar stores are off-price retailers.

Outlet stores are discount retailers that operate under the brand name of a single manufacturer. They sell a variety of merchandise that may consist of seconds, overruns, and the previous season's stock, as well as first-run merchandise. Often located in rural areas but also along interstate highways, these stores have lower overhead than similar stores in big cities due to their lower rents.

Online retailers can fit into any of the previous categories; indeed, most traditional stores also have an online version. You can buy from JCPenney.com, Walmart.com, BigLots.com, and so forth. Other online stores, like Wayfair.com, Overstock.com, and Amazon.com operate only on the web.

Used retailers are retailers that sell used products. Online versions, like eBay and Craigslist, sell everything from used airplanes to clothing. Traditional stores with a physical presence that sell used products include Half-Priced Books and clothing consignment or furniture stores like Amelia's Attic. Consignment stores do not take title to the products but only retail them for the seller.

Pop-up stores are small temporary stores. They can be kiosks or temporarily occupy unused retail spaces. Sometimes the stores are used to create excitement and "buzz" for a retailer that then drives customers to their regular stores. More commonly, though, pop-up stores are used for seasonal sales, such as a costume store before Halloween or the Hillshire Farms sausage and cheese shops you see at the mall just before Christmas.

Not all retailing goes on in stores. **Nonstore retailing**—retailing not conducted in stores—has always existed and continues to take new forms. P&G, the huge consumer-products maker of everything from Pampers to Crest toothpaste, works with many wholesalers and retailers. However, after losing market share to direct online sellers like the Dollar Shave Club, P&G started Gillette on Demand to do the same. The service allows customers to order razor refills not only on the web but also by text message.

Online sales, selling on social media, party selling, telemarketing, and selling to consumers via catalogs, vending machines, TV, and livestreamed events are also examples of nonstore retailing. Livestreams allow viewers to chat with hosts, ask them questions, and even buy products via text messages. The popularity of livestreaming events on Amazon, Facebook, and Instagram grew exponentially during the pandemic because people were stuck at home. The Tommy Hilfiger brand livestreamed a show in China that attracted 14 million viewers and sold 300 hoodies in two minutes. Small sellers are using livestreams, too.[4]

warehouse clubs

Supercenters that sell products at a discount to people who pay an annual membership fee to join them.

off-price retailers

Stores that sell a variety of discount merchandise that consists of seconds, overruns, and the previous season's stock other stores have liquidated.

outlet stores

Stores that sell a variety of merchandise that may consist of seconds, overruns, and the previous season's stock, as well as first-run merchandise, all from one manufacturer.

online retailers

Companies that sell products directly to consumers via the web.

used retailers

Stores that sell products that have already been used.

pop-up stores

Small temporary stores designed to generate "buzz" for a retailer and drive customers to its regular stores.

Live-streaming shopping events like this one took off during the pandemic.

Source: © Shutterstock, Inc.

nonstore retailing

Retailing not conducted in stores.

Key Takeaway

- How a product moves from raw material to finished good to the consumer is a marketing channel, also called a distribution channel. Marketing channel decisions are as important as the decisions companies make about the features and prices of products. Channel partners are firms that actively promote and sell a product as it travels through its channel to its user. Companies try to choose the best channels and channel partners to help them sell products because doing so can give them a competitive advantage.

Review Questions

1. Why are marketing channel decisions as important as pricing and product feature decisions?
2. What are the benefits of looking at all of the organizations that contribute to the production of a product versus just the organizations that sell them?

3. Why do channel partners rely on each other to sell their products and services?
4. How do companies add value to products via their marketing channels?
5. Explain how marketing channels have evolved and are continuing to evolve.

8.2 Typical Marketing Channels

Learning Objectives

1. Describe the basic types of channels in business-to-consumer (B2C) and business-to-business (B2B) markets.
2. Explain the advantages and challenges companies face when using multiple channels and alternate channels.
3. Explain the pros and cons of disintermediation.
4. List the channels firms can use to enter foreign markets.

FIGURE 8.2 Typical Channels in Business-to-Consumer (B2C) Markets

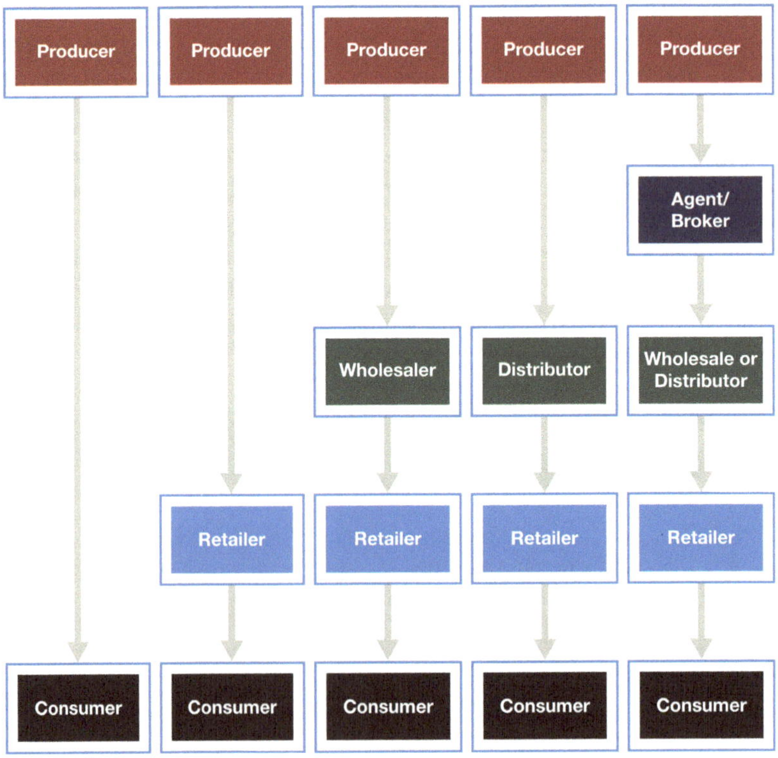

Figure 8.2 shows the typical channels in business-to-consumer (B2C) markets. As we explained, the shortest marketing channel consists of just two parties—a producer and a consumer. A channel such as this is a **direct channel**. By contrast, a channel that includes one or more intermediaries—say, a wholesaler, distributor, or broker or agent—is an **indirect channel**. In an indirect channel, the product passes through one or more intermediaries. That doesn't mean the producer will do no marketing directly to consumers. For example, Levi's runs ads on TV designed to appeal directly to consumers. However, the seller also has to focus its selling efforts on intermediaries because they can help with the selling effort. Not everyone wants to buy jeans directly online from Levi's.

direct channel

A marketing channel that consists of a producer and a consumer.

indirect channel

A marketing channel that consists of a producer, a consumer, and one or more intermediaries.

FIGURE 8.3 Typical Channels in Business-to-Business (B2B) Markets

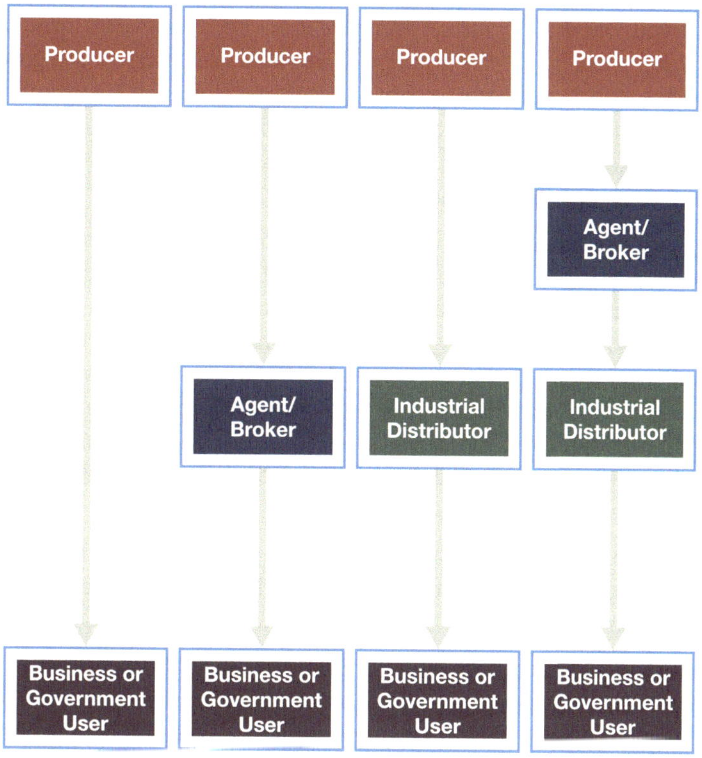

Figure 8.3 shows the marketing channels common in business-to-business (B2B) markets. Notice how the channels resemble those in B2C markets, except that the products are sold to businesses and governments instead of consumers like you. The **industrial distributors** shown in Figure 8.3 are firms that supply products that businesses or government departments and agencies use but don't resell. Grainger Industrial Supply, which sells tens of thousands of products, is one of the world's largest industrial distributors. More than 3 million businesses worldwide buy the company's products, which range from padlocks to painkillers.

Name the product your company needs, and you can probably buy it from Grainger Industrial Supply.

Source: © Shutterstock, Inc.

industrial distributors

Intermediary firms that sell products that businesses or government departments and agencies use but don't resell.

Disintermediation

disintermediation

A situation that occurs when intermediaries are cut out of marketing channels.

You might be tempted to think middlemen, or intermediaries, are bad. If you can cut them out of the deal—a process marketing professionals call **disintermediation**—products can be sold more cheaply, can't they? Large retailers, including Target and Walmart, sometimes bypass middlemen. Instead, they buy their products directly from manufacturers and then store and distribute them to their own retail outlets.

However, sometimes cutting out the middleman is desirable, but not always. A wholesaler with buying power and excellent warehousing capabilities might be able to store and deliver a product to a seller more cheaply than its producer could acting alone. Walmart doesn't need a wholesaler's buying power, but your local In-n-Out convenience store does. Likewise, hiring a distributor will cost a producer money. However, if the distributor can help the producer sell greater quantities of a product, it can increase the producer's profits. Moreover, when you cut out the middlemen you work with, you have to perform the functions they once did. Maybe it's storing the product or dealing with hundreds of retailers. More than one producer has ditched its intermediaries only to rehire them later because of the hassles involved.

Nonetheless, disintermediation isn't likely to stop. The internet facilitates a certain amount of disintermediation by making it easier for consumers and businesses to contact one another without going through any middlemen. Today, most people book trips online without going through travel agents. People also shop for homes online rather than using real estate agents. To remain in business, intermediaries need to find new ways to add value to products—which is exactly what they are doing. For example, although there are fewer travel agents than there were in the past, there are many more travel-related internet sites—Expedia, Tripadvisor, and Priceline, to name just a few—that book people's trips by serving as affiliates to airlines, hotels, and other providers of travel and leisure services.

However, for some products, disintermediation via the internet doesn't work so well. Insurance is an example. You can buy it online directly from companies, but many people want to buy through an agent they can talk to for advice.

Dell originally sold its computers only straight to customers. Today it sells them through many different channels.

Source: © Shutterstock, Inc.

Sometimes it's simply impossible to cut out middlemen. Do sales representatives for Coca-Cola want to take the time and trouble to personally sell people individual cans of Coke? No. They are no more capable of selling individual Cokes to people than Santa is capable of delivering toys to children around the globe. In contrast, Dell Computer made its mark by selling computers straight to users. (Michael Dell, the company's founder, originally sold computers to buyers by telephone out of his college dorm room.) But now Dell sells its products through retailers such as Best Buy as well. Dell found that to compete effectively, its products needed to be placed in stores alongside Hewlett-Packard, Apple, and other computer brands.[5]

Multiple Channels and Alternate Channels

Marketing channels can get a lot more complex than the channels shown in Figure 8.2 and Figure 8.3. Look at the channels in Figure 8.4. Notice how in some situations, a wholesaler will sell to brokers, who then sell to retailers and consumers. In other situations, a wholesaler will sell straight to retailers or straight to consumers. Manufacturers also sell straight to consumers, and, as we explained, sell straight to large retailers like Target.

FIGURE 8.4 Alternate Channel Arrangements

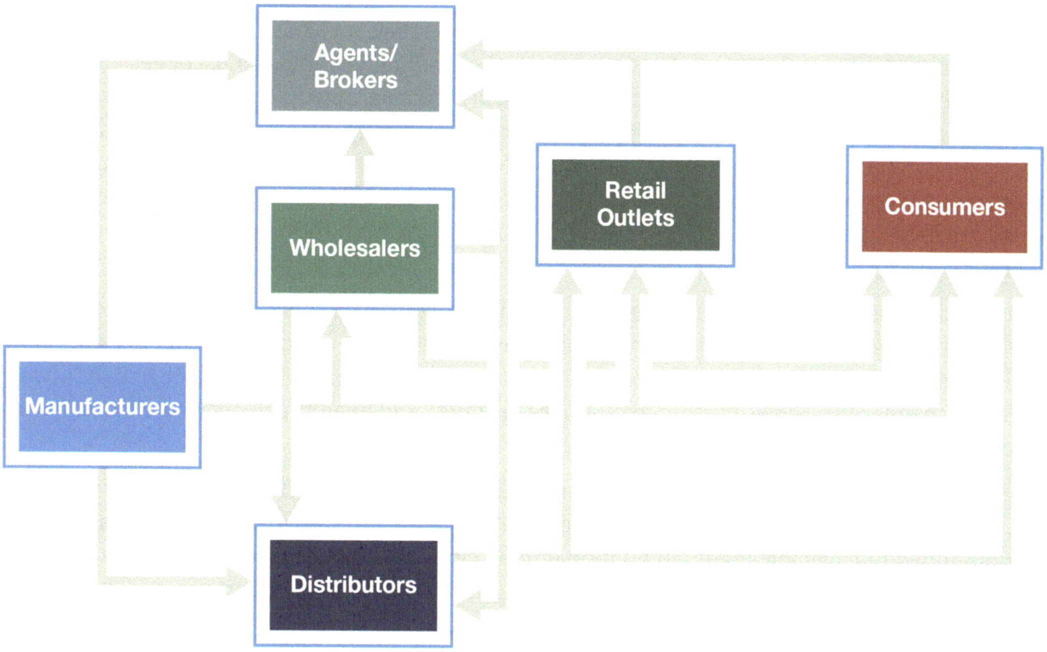

The point is that firms can and do utilize multiple channels. Take Levi's, for example. You can buy a pair of Levi's from a retailer such as Kohl's, or directly from Levi's on its website or at one of the outlet stores it owns around the country. You can also buy a pair of Levi's from a seller who scours retail stores for bargains and then resells the products on eBay and Amazon for a profit. DWNY LLC, based in Ocean, New Jersey, makes millions of dollars annually by dispatching teams of professional shoppers to find bargains. DWNY then resells them on Amazon and other sites.

The key is understanding the different target markets for your product and designing the best channel to meet the needs of customers in each. There are even people who will be more likely purchase your products if they don't have to shop for them at all. That's the idea behind Wantable. Wantable is a try-before-you-buy online retailer. Personal stylists put together custom outfits online and ship them to customers. No shopping required.

Amazon broadened its clothing sales with its Amazon Prime Wardrobe program. Customers pick out clothes online and have them shipped to their homes. If the customers like the clothes, they keep them. If not, they can easily return them.

Source: © Shutterstock, Inc.

Similarly, it used to be that if you wanted to buy the latest designer clothing, you almost always went to a store like Neiman Marcus. But that has changed as well. Moda Operandi is one of a number of startup companies that are attempting to make luxury shopping more convenient for younger, tech-savvy customers. Moda Operandi conducts its fashion and trunk shows online. Customers put down a 50 percent deposit on the designer clothing they want to buy online, and receive it as soon as the new fashions are actually manufactured.[6]

Perhaps there is a group of customers interested in your products, but they demand deep discounts and are willing to wait for the products. For these people, Wish might be more their speed. Wish is an app that enables people to buy super-inexpensive, unbranded clothing and other products, often from China. The goods are then shipped directly to the customer from China via the least-expensive, and very slowest, method possible.

In addition to its other channels, QVC also sells products via text. Customers can sign up to get alerts about products for sale and buy them on their mobile phones.

Source: © Shutterstock, Inc.

Many people regularly interact with companies via numerous channels before making buying decisions. Using multiple channels can be effective. More than one study has shown that the more marketing channels your customers utilize, the more loyal they are likely to be to your products. As a result, companies work hard to try to integrate their selling channels so users get a consistent experience. For example, QVC's TV channel, website, mobile app, Facebook page, and Twitter account, all have the same look and feel. When companies fully integrate all of their systems so they can communicate with one another and offer the consumer a seamless experience, this is referred to as *omnichannel experience*. However, if you see a product on TV, research it online, but go to the store and can't find it, that's not a good experience, even though the seller used multiple channels to engage you.

Disney does a good job helping customers achieve an omnichannel experience. The company's My Disney Experience tool allows people to plan their trips from start to finish. A mobile app allows visitors to locate attractions and view the estimated wait time for each. Disney's MagicBands (wearable wristbands) also allows visitors to purchase products and open the doors to their hotel rooms without having to dig into their wallets or purses.

A company can also use a marketing channel to set itself apart from the crowd. Jones Soda Co. initially placed its own funky-looking soda coolers in skate and surf shops, tattoo and piercing parlors, individual fashion stores, and national retail clothing and music stores. The company then began an up-and-down-the-street "attack," placing its products in convenience and food stores. Later the company was able to sell its drinks to bigger companies like Starbucks, Barnes & Noble, Safeway, Target, and 7-Eleven stores and more recently to club stores like Costco and Sam's.[7]

strategic channel alliances

An agreement formed by two or more firms to deliver their products via a channel. The products and organizations can be similar or different.

Some companies find ways to increase their sales by forming **strategic channel alliances** with one another. For example, although stand-alone circuses have become a thing of the past (the Ringling Brothers Circus shut down after nearly a century in business), they are finding new places to do business—by forming alliances with state fairs. It's a trend that's expected to continue because the two family-oriented attractions are a good fit for one another and tend to boost each other's revenues.[8] Harley-Davidson has a strategic channel alliance with Best Western. Harley Davidson customers can sign up to receive points and other discounts by staying at Best Western hotels and motels.

International Marketing Channels

Many consumer and business market opportunities in the United States are well developed and growing only slowly. However, opportunities for growth abound in other countries. Nowadays, Coca-Cola earns most of its income abroad, not in the United States. Mexico, China, and Brazil, are the company's largest foreign markets. Most recently, the beverage maker has been focusing on India.[9]

The question is, how do companies enter these markets? Via what marketing channels? Some developing countries lack good intermediary systems. In these countries, firms are on their own in terms of selling and distributing products downstream to users. Other countries have elaborate marketing channels that must be navigated. Consider Japan, for example. Japan has an extensive, complicated system of intermediaries, each of which demands a cut of a company's profits. Carrefour, a global chain of hypermarkets, tried to expand there but eventually left the country because its marketing channel system was so complicated. Walmart managed to develop a fledgling presence in Japan after acquiring the Japanese supermarket operator Seiyu, which it later ended up selling due to its lackluster performance.[10]

As you learned in Chapter 2 and Chapter 5, acquiring part or all of a foreign company is a common strategy for companies. It is referred to as making a direct foreign investment. However, you also have learned that some nations don't allow foreign companies to do business within their borders or buy local companies. The Chinese government blocked Coca-Cola from buying Huiyuan

Juice, that country's largest beverage maker. Corruption and unstable governments also make it difficult to do business in some countries. Similarly, the banana company Chiquita found itself in the bad position of having to pay off rebels in Colombia to prevent them from seizing the banana plantations of one of Chiquita's subsidiaries.

One of the easier ways of utilizing intermediaries to expand abroad is by creating a joint venture. You first learned about joint ventures in Chapter 2. A joint venture is an entity created when two parties agree to share their profits, losses, and control with one another in an economic activity they jointly undertake. The German automaker Volkswagen struggled to penetrate Asian markets, so it signed an agreement with Suzuki, a Japanese company, in an effort to challenge Toyota's dominance in Asia.

Do joint ventures work? Some do, but many fail, particularly when they involve companies from different countries. However, in some countries, such as China and India, it is the only way foreign companies are allowed to do business there.

An even easier way to enter foreign markets is to simply export your products. Microsoft didn't do well with its Zune MP3 player in the United States, so the company subsequently redesigned the product and launched it in other countries. Companies can sell their products directly to other firms abroad, or they can hire intermediaries such as brokers and agents that specialize in international exporting to help them find potential buyers for their products.

McDonald's has a franchise in the Louvre. How about a little art viewing with your Big Mac?

Source: © Shutterstock, Inc.

Recall that many companies, particularly those in the United States, have expanded their operations via franchising. Franchising grants an independent operator the right to use a company's business model, name, techniques, and trademarks for a fee. McDonald's is the classic example of a franchise. Unlike Walmart, McDonald's has had no trouble making headway in Japan. It has done so by selling thousands of franchises there. In fact, Japan is McDonald's second-largest market after the United States. The company also has thousands of franchises in Europe and other countries. There is even a McDonald's franchise in the Louvre, the prestigious museum in Paris that houses the *Mona Lisa*. Licensing is similar to franchising. For a fee, a firm can buy the right to use another firm's manufacturing processes, trade secrets, patents, and trademarks for a certain period of time.

Key Takeaway

- A direct marketing channel consists of just two parties—a producer and a consumer. By contrast, a channel that includes one or more intermediaries (wholesaler, distributor, or broker or agent) is an indirect channel. Firms often utilize multiple channels to reach more customers and increase their effectiveness. Some companies find ways to increase their sales by forming strategic channel alliances with one another. Other companies look for ways to cut out the middlemen from channels, a process known as disintermediation. Direct foreign investment, joint ventures, exporting, franchising, and licensing are some of the channels by which firms attempt to enter foreign markets.

Review Questions

1. Why are direct marketing channels possible for some products and not others?
2. Explain the value middlemen can add to products.
3. Name some companies that have multiple marketing channels for their products. What are those channels?
4. How do marketing channels differ around the world? Why is it sometimes hard for firms to penetrate foreign markets?

8.3 Functions Performed by Channel Partners

Learning Objectives

1. Describe the activities performed in channels.
2. Explain which organizations perform which functions.

Different organizations in a marketing channel are responsible for different value-adding activities. The following are some of the most common functions channel members perform. However, keep in mind that "who does what" can vary, depending on what the channel members actually agree to in their contracts with one another.

Disseminating Marketing Communications and Promoting Brands

push strategy

A strategy in which businesses are the target of promotions so products get "pushed" through their marketing channels and sold to consumers.

Somehow wholesalers, distributors, retailers, and consumers need to be informed—via marketing communications—that an offering exists and that there's a good reason to buy it. Sometimes, a push strategy is used to help marketing channels accomplish this. A **push strategy** is one in which a manufacturer convinces wholesalers, distributors, or retailers to sell its products. Consumers are informed via advertising and other promotions that the product is available for sale, but the main focus is to sell to intermediaries.

The problem with a push strategy is that it is less likely to focus on the needs of the actual users of the products. Coca-Cola used a push strategy for years before realizing that instead of focusing on moving beverages through a retailer's back door and into their warehouse, it needed to help them sell to shoppers through the retailer's front door. College textbook publishers are in a similar position today. Traditionally, they have concentrated their selling efforts on professors and bookstore managers. (Has a textbook company ever asked you what you want out of a textbook?)

FIGURE 8.5 A Push Versus a Pull Strategy

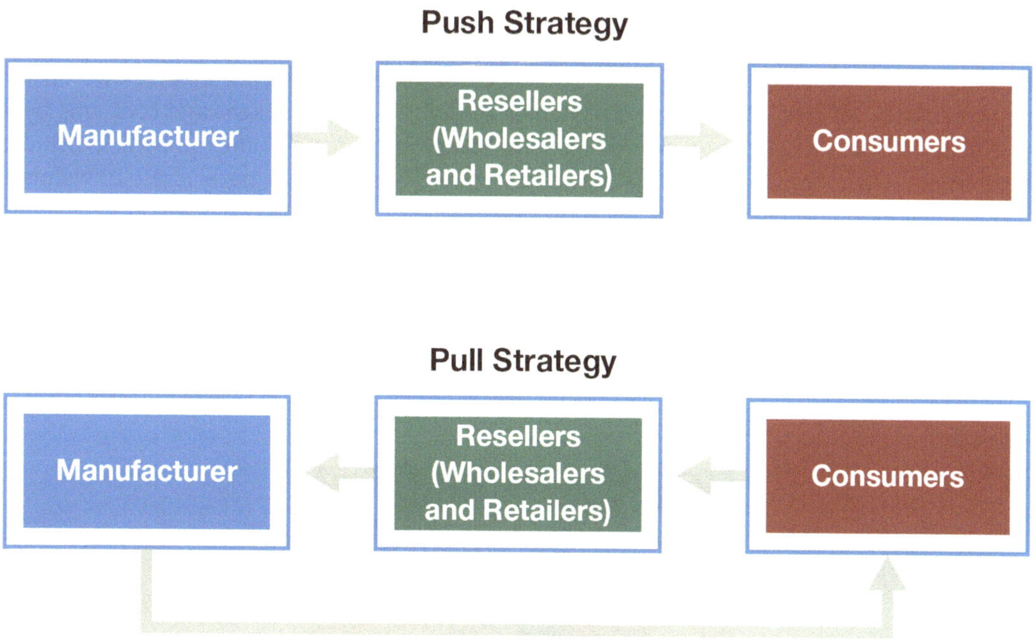

Like Coca-Cola, textbook publishers are rethinking their sales and marketing channel strategies. That's what entrepreneurs Jeff Shelstad and Eric Frank did when they launched FlatWorld, the publisher of this textbook. One of FlatWorld's strategies is to deliver its products via marketing channels that are more cost-effective.[11]

By contrast, a **pull strategy** focuses on creating demand for a product among consumers so that businesses agree to sell the product. A good example of an industry that utilizes both pull and push strategies is the pharmaceutical industry. Pharmaceutical companies promote their drugs to pharmacies and doctors, but they also run ads designed to persuade individual consumers to ask their physicians about drugs that might benefit them.

pull strategy

A strategy in which consumers are targeted with sales promotions such as coupons, contests, games, rebates, mail-in offers.

In many cases, two or more organizations in a channel jointly promote a product to retailers, purchasing agents, and consumers and work out which organization is responsible for what type of communication to whom. For example, the ads from Target, Walmart, and other retailers that run in Sunday newspapers are often a joint effort between the manufacturers and the retailers that sell the products. The actual forms and styles of communication will be discussed more in the promotions and sales section of the book.

Sorting and Regrouping Products

As we explained, many businesses don't want to receive huge quantities of a product. One of the functions of wholesalers and distributors is to break down large quantities of products into smaller units and provide an assortment of different products to businesses.

For example, cranberry farmers have large crops to sell. You don't want to buy large amounts of cranberries, make your own juice or cranberry sauce, or dry them into craisins for salads. So the farmers sell their produce to a co-op, which sorts the berries by size; large ones become craisins while others are destined to become either juice or sauce, depending on their liquid content. Those are then sold to the juice and sauce producers.

Storing and Managing Inventory

If a channel member has run out of a product when a customer wants to buy it, the result is often a lost sale. That's why most channel members stock, or "carry," reserve inventory. However, storing products is not free. Warehouses cost money to build or rent and heat and cool; employees have to be paid to stock shelves, pick products, ship them, and so forth. Some companies, including Walmart, put their suppliers in charge of their inventory. The suppliers have access to Walmart's inventory levels and ship products when and where the retailer's stores need them.

Warehouse Robots

Increasingly, warehouses use robots to pluck inventory from shelves, as this video shows. But like employees, robots cost money, too.

View in the online reader

Storing and managing inventory is not just a function provided for retailers, though. Storage also involves storing commodities like grain prior to processing. Gigantic grain elevators store corn, wheat, and other grains until processors, like Oroweat, need them. You can buy fresh bread in a grocery store every day because the wheat was stored first at a grain elevator until it was needed.

Distributing Products

Walmart doesn't just own its own warehouses. It also owns its own fleet of semi-trucks.

Source: © Shutterstock, Inc.

Physical goods that travel within a channel need to be moved from one member to another and sometimes back again. Some large wholesalers, distributors, and retailers own their own fleets of trucks for this purpose. In other cases, they hire third-party transportation providers—trucking companies, railroads, and so forth—to move their products.

Being able to track merchandise like you can track a FedEx package is extremely important to channel partners. They want to know where their products are at all times and what shape they are in. Losing inventory or having it damaged or spoiled can wreak havoc on a company's profits. So can not getting products on time or being able to get them at all when your competitors can.

Assuming Ownership Risk and Extending Credit

If products *are* damaged during transit, one of the first questions asked is who owned the product at the time. In other words, who suffers the loss? Generally, no one channel member assumes all of the ownership risk in a channel. Instead, it is distributed among channel members depending on the contracts they have with one another and their free on board provisions. A **free on board (FOB)** provision designates who is responsible for what shipping costs and who owns the title to the goods and when.

free on board (FOB)

A contract term that designates which party is responsible for a product's shipping costs and owns the title to the goods and when.

However, the type of product, the demand for it, marketing conditions, and the clout of the various organizations in its marketing channel can affect the contract terms channel members are willing to agree to. Some companies try to wait as long as possible to take ownership of products so they don't have to store them. During an economic downturn, channel members often try to hold as little inventory as possible because it reduces their costs, and if it doesn't sell right away it can become obsolete.

During the COVID-19 pandemic, many sellers closed stores to save on costs and pare down their inventories. The chocolate maker Godiva is an example. It closed all of its stores in the United States and Canada and began selling its products online and through other retailers. The strategy may have worked for Godiva. However, it won't always solve a seller's problems because shoppers don't automatically move online. In other words, shrinking the number of your stores to grow doesn't always work.[12]

Godiva chocolates altered its marketing and sales channels during the COVID-19 pandemic.

Source: © Shutterstock, Inc.

Extending credit is another function of channel partners. It's customary in many industries to give one's supply chain partners a certain number of days to pay, and if needed by offering them long-term financing. Providing your supply chain partners with funds for promotional purposes is a growing strategy as well. A **market development fund**, which is also sometimes called a *co-op fund*, is a fund a manufacturer or brand offers its channel partners to help create awareness and promote the brand in a new market or in a new way. Generally, the more successful a channel partner is selling a brand, the more funds it will get from the manufacturer, or producer.

market development fund

A fund a manufacturer or brand offers its channel partners to help create awareness and promote the brand in a new market or in a new way.

Sharing Marketing and Other Information

Each of the channel members has information about the demand for products, trends, inventory levels, and what the competition is doing. The information is valuable and can be doubly valuable if channel partners trust one another and share it. More information can help each firm in the marketing channel perform its functions better and overcome competitive obstacles. For example, Amazon has tried to make headway selling clothing and shoes online in Europe. However, the company is being outdone by Zalando SE, an online seller founded a decade later than Amazon. Why? Because Zalando allows brands like Adidas and Tommy Hilfiger to access data from the site to figure out what people are buying, whereas Amazon does not.[13]

That said, confidentiality is a huge issue among supply chain partners because they share so much information with one another, such as sales and inventory data. For example, a salesperson who sells Tide laundry detergent for P&G will have a good idea of how many units of Tide Walmart and Target are selling. However, it would be unethical for the salesperson to share Walmart's numbers with Target or Target's numbers with Walmart. Many business buyers require their channel partners to sign nondisclosure agreements as part of purchasing contracts. A **nondisclosure agreement (NDA)** is a contract that specifies what information is proprietary, or owned by a partner, and how, if at all, the partner can use that information.

nondisclosure agreement (NDA)

A contract that specifies information that is proprietary, or owned by a channel partner, and how, if at all, the other partners can use that information.

Key Takeaway

- Different organizations in a marketing channel are responsible for different value-adding activities. These activities include disseminating marketing communications and promoting brands, sorting and regrouping products, storing and managing inventory, distributing products, assuming the risks of products, and sharing information.

Review Questions

1. Explain the difference between a pull and a push strategy when it comes to marketing communications.
2. Why is taking ownership of products an important marketing channel function?
3. Which firms manage inventory in marketing channels?

8.4 Marketing Channel Strategies

Learning Objectives

1. Describe the factors that affect a firm's channel decisions.
2. Explain how intensive, exclusive, and selective distribution differ from one another.
3. Explain why some products are better suited to some distribution strategies than others.

Channel Selection Factors

Selecting the best marketing channel is critical because it can mean the success or failure of your product. One of the reasons the internet has been so successful as a marketing channel is because it's available nearly anywhere.

Airports aren't everywhere. But because fewer people are going to shopping malls, higher-priced brands have expanded their marketing reach by selling everything from electronics to purses and perfumes in airports at duty-free shops. Essentially, major international airports from Dubai to London are being turned into giant shopping malls with gates.[14]

Duty-Free Shopping

At 23,000 sq. ft, this duty-free shop at Sydney International Airport is one of the largest in the world.

View in the online reader

What channel selection factors should you look at as a seller? Should you sell your product on the internet, at malls, or airports? And what channel partners should you work with? Next, let's look at questions such as these.

Type of Customer

The internet isn't necessarily the best channel for every product. For example, do you want to closely examine the fruits and vegetables you buy to make sure they are ripe enough or not overripe? Then online grocery shopping might not be for you. You also can't smell perfume online. Clearly, how your customers want to buy products will have an impact on the channel you select. In fact, it should be your prime consideration.

First of all, are you selling to a consumer or a business customer? Generally, these two groups want to be sold to differently. Most consumers are willing to go to a grocery or convenience store to purchase toilet paper. The manager of a hospital trying to replenish its supplies would not. The hospital manager would be buying a lot more toilet paper than an individual consumer and would expect to be called upon by a distributor, but perhaps only semiregularly. Thereafter, the manager might want the toilet paper delivered on a regular basis and the cost billed to the hospital via automatic systems. Likewise, when businesses buy expensive products such as machinery and computers or products that have to be customized, the firms generally expect to be sold to personally by salespeople and receive special payment terms.

Type of Product

The type of product you're selling will also affect your marketing channel choices. Perishable products often have to be sold through shorter marketing channels than products with longer shelf lives. For example, a yellowfin tuna bound for the sushi market will likely be flown overnight to its destination and handled by few intermediaries. By contrast, canned tuna can be shipped by "slow boat" and handled by more intermediaries.

Valuable and fragile products also tend to have shorter marketing channels. Automakers generally sell their cars straight to car dealers (retailers) and rental-car companies rather than through wholesalers first. The makers of corporate jets often sell them straight to corporations, which demand they be customized to certain specifications.

Channel Partner Capabilities

Your ability versus the ability of other types of organizations that operate in marketing channels can affect your channel choices as well. If you are a massage therapist, you deliver your product straight to your client. If you produce downloadable products like digital books or recordings, you can sell your products straight to customers on the internet. Hypnotic World, a UK producer of self-hypnosis recordings, is such a company. If you want to stop smoking or lose weight, you can pay for and download a recording to help you.

But suppose you've created a great new personal gadget—something that's tangible, or physical. You've managed to sell it via a few channels—say, on TV (via QVC or HSN perhaps) and on the web. Now you want to get the product into retail stores like Target and Walmart. If you can get the product into these stores, you can increase your sales exponentially. In this case, you might want to contract with an intermediary—perhaps an agent or a distributor that will convince the corporate buyers of those stores to carry your product.

The Business Environment and Technology

After partnering with UberEats for its food delivery, Footprints Cafe in Brooklyn, New York, got swamped with orders.

Source: © Shutterstock, Inc.

The general business environment, such as the economy, can also affect the marketing channels chosen for products. For example, think about what happens when the value of the U.S. dollar declines relative to the currencies of other countries. When the dollar falls, products imported from other countries cost more to buy relative to products produced and sold in the United States. For example, products made in China become less attractive because they have gotten more expensive. As a result, some companies then look closer to home for their products and channel partners.

Technological changes affect marketing channels, too, of course. The internet vastly changed how products are bought and sold. For one, an internet sales channel gives companies more control over how their products are sold and at what prices than if the companies leave the job to another channel partner such as a retailer. Plus, a company selling on the internet has a digital footprint, or record, of what shoppers look at, or click on, at its site. As a result, it can recommend products they appear to be interested in and target them with special offers and prices.[15]

The development of mobile phone apps has also had a big impact on sales and marketing channels. Footprints Cafe in Brooklyn, New York, is an example of what a good channel partner and app can do for a business. For years, Footprints' owner, Bob Gordon, handled the home delivery of the cafe's meals himself. But then Gordon decided to partner with UberEats, Uber's food delivery service. Orders started pouring in. Uber Eats' app and marketing reach allowed the restaurant to gain more new customers than ever before, without spending money for ads on Facebook and Groupon as the restaurant had done before, Gordon says.[16]

The Olive Garden has a different strategy. Even during the pandemic, the restaurant chain refused to partner with third-party mobile app delivery services, deeming them too expensive. Given its size, and channel power, Olive Garden has been able to successfully pursue that strategy. A small restaurant like Footprints Cafe might not have been able to do so.[17]

Competing Products' Marketing Channels

How your competitors sell their products can also affect your marketing channels. As we explained, Dell sells computers to firms like Best Buy instead of just to consumers. P&G sells Gillette razors online to compete with the Dollar Shave Club.

As you have learned, you don't always have to choose the channels your competitors rely on. Moreover, the channels that create the most value change over time. In the late 1990s, Netflix turned the video rental business on its head by coming up with a new marketing channel to deliver movies to home viewers, beginning with direct mail and then moving to internet delivery.

To stay competitive and allow people to watch the shows they want to see when they want to watch them, broadcast and cable channels such as HBO, Disney, and ESPN began streaming their shows on Netflix and other streaming services like Hulu and Sling TV. Thereafter, the networks began their own streaming services, such as HBO MAX and Disney+, for example. Meanwhile, Amazon has begun airing live NFL games on Amazon Prime. Netflix and other streaming services now produce their own original shows exclusively available on just their channels, at least initially.

Did you miss an episode of *Ted Lasso*? If so, you can only watch it online only at Apple TV+, at least for now.

Source: © Shutterstock, Inc.

CTV ads

Highly targeted ads delivered via streaming devices and services.

Chelsea Sumrow, American Home Shield

Source: Chelsea Sumrow, used with permission

Chelsea Sumrow understands the importance of capitalizing on new channels as well. Sumrow is the vice president of marketing and brand management at American Home Shield, which sells home warranties to new home buyers. Because houses are selling so fast and for such high prices, selling home warranties through buyers' realtors presents a challenge.

Sumrow and her colleagues devised a strategy to "blow up" the old rules (a process she describes as "fun"). They did so by successfully targeting homebuyers following a home sale with connected TV (CTV) ads. **CTV ads** are ads delivered via streaming devices and services such as Hulu, Netflix, and Apple+. Reaching streaming audiences is important because so many consumers are "cutting the cord" and no longer watching regular TV. CTV ads can also be highly targeted. For example, different people in the same household will be targeted with different ads, depending on the types of shows they stream.

Factors That Affect a Product's Intensity of Distribution

intensive distribution

A strategy of selling a product in as many outlets as possible.

Firms that choose an **intensive distribution** strategy try to sell their products in as many outlets as possible. Intensive distribution strategies are often used for convenience offerings—products customers purchase on the spot without much shopping around. Soft drinks and newspapers are an example. You see them sold in many different places. Redbox, which rents DVDs out of vending machines near restaurants, drugstores, and grocery stores, has made headway using an intensive distribution strategy.

Inventive Vending Machines

The array of vending machines around the world is surprising. Cannabis cookies anyone?

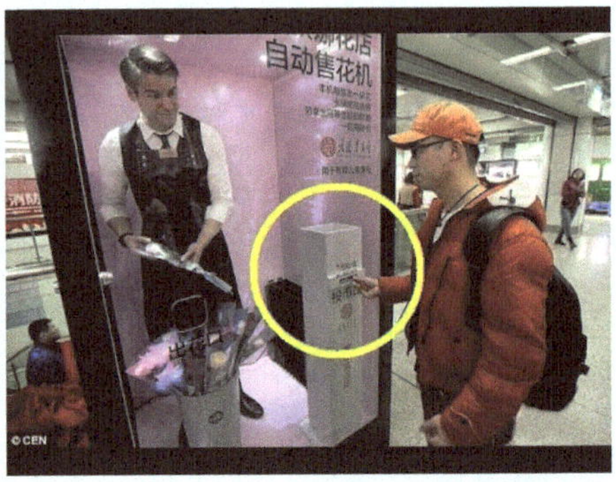

View in the online reader

selective distribution

A strategy of selling products at specific outlets and/or locations.

By contrast, **selective distribution** involves selling products at select outlets in specific locations. For instance, Sony TVs can be purchased at a number of outlets, such as Best Buy, Target, or Walmart, but the same models are generally not sold at all of those outlets. The lowest-priced Sony TVs are at Walmart; the better Sony models are more expensive and found in stores like Best Buy or specialty electronics stores. By selling different models with different features and price points at different outlets, a manufacturer can appeal to different target markets.

exclusive distribution

A strategy of selling products through one or a few retailers in a specific location.

Exclusive distribution involves selling products through one or very few outlets. Most students often think exclusive means high priced, but that's not always the case. Exclusive simply means limiting distribution to only one outlet in any area. Doing so can be a strategic decision based on applying the scarcity principle to create demand. For example, supermodel and actress Sofia Vergara's line of furniture is sold exclusively at the furniture company Rooms To Go. HGTV stars Joanna and Chip Gaines have a line of products sold exclusively at Target. Retailers team up with brands such as these in order to create a sense of quality based on scarcity that will not only apply to the brand but to the store.

Shows on network TV are distributed exclusively as well. In this instance, the choice isn't so much about applying the scarcity principle as it is about controlling risk. A company that produces a TV series will sign an exclusive deal with a network like ABC, CBS, or Showtime, and the series will initially appear only on that network. Later, reruns of the shows are often distributed selectively to other networks and streaming services. That initial exclusive run, however, is intended to protect the network's investment by giving the network the sole right to broadcast the show.

Joanna and Chip Gaines' Hearth & Hand collection is sold exclusively at Target stores.

Source: melissamn/Shutterstock.com

To control the image of their products and the prices at which they are sold, the makers of upscale products often prefer to distribute their products exclusively as well. Expensive perfumes and designer purses are examples. Distributing a product exclusively to a limited number of organizations under strict terms can help prevent a company's brand from deteriorating or losing value. For this reason, as we explained in Chapter 3, some companies have refused to sell their products on Amazon. Exclusive distribution can also prevent products from being sold cheaply in gray markets. A **gray market** is a market in which a producer hasn't authorized its products to be sold. The choice to distribute intensively, selectively, or exclusively is a strategic decision based on many factors, such as the nature of the brand, the types and number of competitors, and the availability of retail choices.

gray market

A market in which a producer hasn't authorized its products to be sold.

Key Takeaway

- Selecting the best marketing channel is critical because it can mean the success or failure of your product. The type of customer you're selling to will have an impact on the channel you select. In fact, this should be your prime consideration. The type of product, your organization's capabilities versus those of other channel members, the way competing products are marketed, and changes in the business environment and technology can also affect your marketing channel decisions. Various factors affect a company's decisions about the intensity of a product's distribution. An intensive distribution strategy involves selling a product in as many outlets as possible. Selective distribution involves selling a product at select outlets in specific locations. Exclusive distribution involves selling a product through one or very few outlets.

Review Questions

1. Why are good channel decisions critical to a product's success?
2. What factors affect channel-selection decisions?
3. Which kinds of products are more likely to be distributed using exclusive marketing strategies?

8.5 Channel Dynamics

Learning Objectives

1. Explain what channel power is and the types of firms that wield it.
2. Describe the types of conflicts that can occur in marketing channels.
3. Describe the ways in which channel members achieve cooperation with one another.

Channel Power

channel power

The ability to influence a channel partner's goals and efforts.

channel leaders

A strong channel member that wields channel power.

Strong channel partners often wield what's called **channel power** and are referred to as **channel leaders**, or *channel captains*. In the past, big manufacturers like P&G and Dell were often channel captains. Today, big retailers like Amazon, Walmart, Costco, and Target are commanding more channel power. They have millions of customers and are bombarded with products wholesalers and manufacturers want them to sell. As a result, these retailers increasingly are able to call the shots. Category killers like Home Depot and Petco are in a similar position.

Consumers like you are gaining marketing channel power, too. Regardless of what one manufacturer produces or what a local retailer has available, you can use the internet to find whatever product you want at the best price available and have it delivered when, where, and how you want.

Channel Conflict

channel conflict

A dispute among channel members.

A dispute among channel members is called a **channel conflict**. Channel conflicts are common. Part of the reason for this is that each channel member has its own goals, which are unlike those of any other channel member. The relationship among them is not unlike the relationship between you and your boss (assuming you have a job). Both of you want to serve your organization's customers well. However, your goals are different. Your boss might want you to work on the weekend, but you might not want to because you need to study for a Monday test.

All channel members want to have low inventory levels but immediate access to more products. Who should bear the cost of holding the inventory? What if consumers don't purchase the products? Can they be returned to other channel members, or is the organization in possession of the products responsible for disposing of them? Channel members try to spell out details such as these in their contracts with one another.

But no matter how "airtight" their contracts are, there will still be points of contention among channel members. Channel members are constantly asking their partners, "What have you done (or not done) for me lately?" Wholesalers and retailers frequently lament that the manufacturers they work with aren't doing more to promote their products—for example, distributing coupons for them, running Facebook and TV ads, and so forth—so the products will move off store shelves more quickly. Meanwhile, manufacturers want to know why wholesalers aren't selling their products faster and why retailers are placing them at the bottom of shelves where they are hard to see. Apple opened its own retail stores around the country, in part because it didn't like how its products were being displayed and sold in other companies' stores.

Dr. Thunder is Walmart's store-brand equivalent of Dr. Pepper.

Source: © Shutterstock, Inc.

Channel conflicts can also occur when manufacturers sell their own products online. When they do, wholesalers and retailers often feel like they are competing for the same customers when they shouldn't have to. Likewise, manufacturers often feel slighted when retailers dedicate more shelf space to their own store brands. **Store brands** are products retailers produce themselves or pay manufacturers to produce for them. Dr. Thunder is Walmart's store-brand equivalent of Dr. Pepper.

store brands

Products retailers produce themselves or pay manufacturers to produce for them.

A retailer doesn't have to promote its brands to get them on its own shelves like a "regular" manufacturer would or pay to place the products high on its own website when a customer does an online search. Consequently, store brands are often priced more cheaply. Moreover, some retailers sell their store brands to other retailers, creating competition for manufacturers.

Vertical Versus Horizontal Conflict

The conflicts we've described so far are examples of vertical conflict. A **vertical conflict** is conflict that occurs between two different types of members in a channel—say, a manufacturer, an agent, a wholesaler, or a retailer. By contrast, a **horizontal conflict** is conflict that occurs between organizations of the same type—say, two manufacturers that each want a powerful wholesaler to carry only its products.

vertical conflict

Conflict that occurs between two different types of members of the channel.

horizontal conflict

Conflict that occurs between organizations of the same type.

Horizontal conflict can be healthy because it's competition driven. But it can create problems, too. A number of years ago, Walmart experienced a horizontal conflict among its phone suppliers. The suppliers were engaging in a price war and cutting the prices to all the retail stores they sold to. However, Walmart wasn't selling any additional phones due to the price cuts. It was just selling them for less and making less of a profit on each one.[18]

Dumping can also lead to horizontal conflict. **Dumping** is the practice of selling for a period of time a large quantity of goods in another country at a price too low to be economically justifiable. The goal of dumping is to drive your competitors out of a market and then raise your price. Typically, dumping is made possible by government subsidies that allow a company to lower its prices relative to international competitors that have to operate without government subsidies. Global economic agreements prohibit dumping and specify penalties when it occurs. However, the process can take very long to resolve. And by the time it is resolved, a competitor may have already been driven out of business.

dumping

Selling a large quantity of goods in another country at artificially low prices to drive your competitors out of business.

Channel leaders like Amazon, Walmart, and Home Depot usually have a great deal of say when it comes to how channel conflicts are handled, which is to say that they usually get what they want. But even the most powerful channel leaders strive for cooperation. A manufacturer with channel power still needs good retailers to sell its products; a retailer with channel power still needs good suppliers from which to buy products. One member of a channel can't squeeze all the profits out of the other channel members and still hope to function well. Moreover, because each of the channel partners is responsible for promoting a product through its channel, to some extent they are all in the same boat. Each one of them has a vested interest in promoting the product, and the success or failure of any one of them can affect that of the others.

Flash back to Walmart and how it managed to solve the conflict among its phone suppliers: Because the different brands of phones were so similar, Walmart decided it could consolidate and use fewer suppliers. It then divided its phone products into market segments—inexpensive phones with basic functions, midpriced phones with more features, and high-priced phones with many features. The suppliers chosen were asked to provide products for one of the three segments. This gave Walmart's customers the variety they sought. And because the suppliers selected were able to sell more phones and compete for different types of customers, they stopped undercutting each other's prices.

Achieving Channel Cooperation Ethically

What if your company is not Amazon, Walmart, or a channel member with a great deal of power? How do you build relationships with channel partners and get them to cooperate with you? One way is by emphasizing the benefits of working with your firm. For example, if you are a seller whose product and brand name are in demand, you want to point out how being one of a retailer's "authorized sellers" can boost store traffic and revenues.

Oftentimes companies produce data, informational materials, and case studies showing their partners how they can help boost their sales volumes and profits. Channel partners also want to feel assured that the products coming through the pipeline are genuine and not knockoffs and that there will be a steady supply of them. Your goal is to show your channel partners that you understand issues such as these and help them generate business.

In some instances, Walmart has had trouble attracting manufacturers because it demanded to buy their products at ultra-low prices. At one point the Campbell Soup Company had trouble negotiating a deal with Walmart because Campbell's felt like it was getting squeezed over promotional pricing and shelf space. (Imagine not being able to buy Campbell's soup at Walmart.) All of the people and organizations in a marketing channel want to make a profit. But if you squeeze too much profit out of your channel partners, they will want to do business with someone else rather than you.

Boar's Head creates in-store displays like the banner shown here to help its channel partners sell its products. This one appeared in a Kroger.

Source: Photo courtesy of Amy Ray

Producing marketing and promotional materials their channel partners can use for sales purposes can also facilitate cooperation among companies. In-store displays, brochures, banners, photos for websites, and advertisements the partners can customize with their own logos and company information are examples. Look at the banner in the photo on this page. Although it looks like it was made by the grocery store displaying it, it wasn't. It was produced by Boar's Head, a meat supplier, for the grocer Kroger and other grocers.

Educating your channel members' sales representatives is an extremely important part of facilitating cooperation, especially when you're launching a new product. The reps need to be provided with training and marketing materials in advance of the launch so their activities are coordinated with yours. Microsoft is a company that does a good job of training its partners. Before launching new operating systems, Microsoft provides thousands of its partners with sales and technical training.

In addition, companies run sales contests to encourage their channel partners' sales forces to sell what they have to offer. Offering your channel partners certain monetary incentives, such as market development funds and discounts for selling your product, can help, too.

What shouldn't you do when it comes to your channel partners? Take them for granted, says John Addison, the author of the book *Revenue Rocket: New Strategies for Selling with Partners*. Addison suggests creating a dialogue with them via one-on-one discussions and surveys and developing "partner advisory councils" to better understand their needs.

You also don't want to "stuff the channel," says Addison. Stuffing the channel occurs when, in order to meet its sales numbers, a company offers its channel partners deep discounts and unlimited returns to buy a lot of a product. The problem is that such a strategy can lead to a buildup of inventory that gets steeply discounted and dumped on the market and sometimes on gray markets. This can affect people's perceptions of the product and its brand name. And what happens to any unsold inventory? It gets returned back up the channel in the next accounting period, taking a toll on the "stuffer's" sales numbers.

Lastly, you don't want to risk breaking the law or engage in unfair business practices when dealing with your channel partners. We have already discussed confidentiality issues and dumping. Another issue channel partners sometimes encounter relates to resale price maintenance agreements. A **resale price maintenance agreement** is an agreement whereby a producer of a product restricts the price a retailer can charge for it. The producers of upscale products often want retailers to sign resale price maintenance agreements because they don't want the retailers to deeply discount their products. Doing so would "cheapen" their brands, the producers believe. Producers also contend that resale price maintenance agreements prevent price wars from breaking out among their retailers, which can lead to the deterioration of prices for all of a channel's members.

resale price maintenance agreement

An agreement whereby a producer of a product restricts the price a retailer can charge for it.

Both large companies and small retail outlets have found themselves in court as a result of price maintenance agreements. Although the U.S. Supreme Court hasn't ruled that all price maintenance agreements are illegal, some states have outlawed them on the grounds that they stifle competition. In some countries, such as the United Kingdom, they are banned altogether. The safest bet for a manufacturer is to provide a "suggested retail price" to its channel partners.

Channel Integration: Vertical and Horizontal Marketing Systems

Another way to foster cooperation in a channel is to establish a vertical marketing system. In a **vertical marketing system**, channel members formally agree to closely cooperate with one another. A vertical marketing system can also be created by one channel member taking over the functions of another member; this is a form of disintermediation known as **vertical integration**.

vertical marketing system

A system in which channel members located at different levels within a channel formally agree to cooperate with one another.

vertical integration

A strategy of disintermediation, or growth through acquisition or development of operations, or that eliminates middlemen in the channel.

P&G has traditionally been a manufacturer of household products, not a retailer of them. But the company's long-term strategy is to compete in every personal-care channel, including salons, where the men's business is underdeveloped. Consequently, P&G purchased The Art of Shaving, a seller of pricey men's shaving products located in upscale shopping malls. P&G also runs retail boutiques around the globe that sell its prestigious SK-II skincare -line.[19]

forward integration

A form of vertical integration where the company adds downstream operations, either by acquisition or by growth; the opposite of backward integration.

backward integration

A form of vertical integration where the company integrating channel operations moves upstream, toward manufacturing.

conventional marketing system

A marketing system in which the channel members have no affiliation with one another.

horizontal marketing system

A system in which two companies at the same channel level agree to cooperate with one another to sell their products.

horizontal integration

Adding to operations at the same level in the distribution channel, usually through the acquisition of competitors.

Vertical integration can be **forward**, or downstream, as in the case of P&G just described. **Backward integration** occurs when a company moves upstream in the supply chain—that is, toward the beginning. An example occurred when Walmart bought McLane, a grocery warehousing and distribution company. As much as physical facilities, Walmart also wanted McLane's operating knowledge in order to improve its own logistics.

Franchises are another type of vertical marketing system. They are used not only to lessen channel conflicts but also to penetrate markets. Recall that a franchise gives a person or group the right to market a company's goods or services within a certain territory or location. McDonald's sells meat, bread, ice cream, and other products to its franchises, along with the right to own and operate the stores. And each of the owners of the stores signs a contract with McDonald's agreeing to do business in a certain way.

By contrast, in a **conventional marketing system** the channel members have no affiliation with one another. All the members operate independently. If the sale or the purchase of a product seems like a good deal at the time, an organization pursues it. But there is no expectation among the channel members that they *have* to work with one another in the future.

A **horizontal marketing system** is one in which two companies at the same channel level—say, two manufacturers, two wholesalers, or two retailers—agree to cooperate with one another to sell their products or to make the most of their marketing opportunities. The arrangement is sometimes called **horizontal integration**. Via Technologies, a computer chip manufacturer that competes with Intel, teamed up with a number of Chinese companies with no PC-manufacturing experience to produce inexpensive tablet computers.[20] The more computers the PC makers sold, the more computer chips Via Technologies sold.

Key Takeaway

- Channel partners that wield channel power are referred to as channel leaders. A dispute among channel members is called a channel conflict. A vertical conflict is one that occurs between two different types of members in a channel. By contrast, a horizontal conflict is one that occurs between organizations of the same type. Channel leaders are often in the best position to resolve channel conflicts. Vertical and horizontal marketing systems can help foster channel cooperation, as can creating marketing programs to help a channel's members all generate greater revenues and profits.

Review Questions

1. What gives some organizations more channel power than others?
2. Why do channel conflicts occur?
3. Which organization(s) has the most power to resolve channel conflicts?
4. How can setting up vertical and horizontal marketing systems prevent channel conflicts?

8.6 Discussion Questions and Activities

Discussion Questions

1. What's the ideal number of marketing channels a firm should have?
2. Is a pull strategy superior in all markets?
3. Is selling power the only source of channel power? From what other sources could an organization derive channel power?
4. The chapter listed a number of scenarios that can cause channel conflicts. What other factors can you think of that might cause channel conflicts?
5. What are some reasons for backward integration? For forward integration? Does such integration always benefit the consumer?
6. Direct-to-consumer advertising for pharmaceuticals is a pull strategy, designed to get consumers to ask their doctors to prescribe certain medications. What are the pros and cons of this practice? Are these always pros and cons to pull strategies? What might the pros and cons be for push strategies involving pharmaceuticals?
7. What are some brands that you think use selective or exclusive channels? How does channel choice, in those instances, influence consumer perceptions of value? In what situations might selective or exclusive channels add real value?
8. Of the channel functions described in the chapter, which is the most important and why? The least important? Why?
9. How does disintermediation benefit the consumer? How might it harm the consumer? Can you think of any revolutionary businesses created in the past few years due to disintermediation? Be sure to describe one not mentioned already in the chapter.

Activities

1. Think of some products you currently use. Are there any you would like to buy via different marketing channels? Do you think the products could be successfully marketed this way?
2. Describe a time in which you did business with a company and received conflicting information from its different channels (for example, a store's website versus a visit to the store). How did it affect your buying experience? Have you done business with the company since?
3. Break into groups and make a list of four to five different types of products. Decide which channels should be used to distribute each product. Present your findings to your class and see if they agree with you.
4. Make a list of products you believe failed because of poor marketing channel choices.

8.7 Case Study: Primark

Primark has a strong following in the UK and is trying to become as popular in the U.S. market.

Source: © Shutterstock, Inc.

Can a clothes retailer that doesn't sell online succeed? That's what people are questioning when it comes to Primark. Primark is a Dublin-based clothing retailer of trendy, super-low-priced clothing.

Primark has more than 400 stores in fourteen countries worldwide. The retailer has developed a cult-like following in Europe and is trying to do the same in the United States. Primark entered the U.S. market a few years ago. The company opened up nine stores but then scaled back a number of them due to lower sales than expected. It is now expanding in the United States again.

Why were Primark's sales low in the United States initially? For one, people weren't yet familiar with the brand. Primark's stores are also huge and mostly located in malls, which in the United States are seeing less customer "traffic" than trendy downtown areas are.

In addition, Primark doesn't sell online. The free shipping and returns customers demand don't fit in with the company's low-priced, high-volume sales model. Customers can look at products online and see their prices but they can't buy them there. That hurt the company during the global COVID-19 pandemic, and Primark's sales dropped sharply.

Not being able to do business with a company via multiple marketing channels is a major strategic liability, some retailing analysts contend. However, Primark hasn't ruled out a channel that allows customers to buy clothes online and pick up their orders in stores.

Primark is still fine-tuning its economics and marketing channels in the United States, says a company spokesperson. Once that's accomplished, the retailer hopes to give its American competitors like H&M and Forever 21 a run for their money like it has done in Europe.[21]

Case Study Questions

1. Should Primark change its marketing channels for the United States? Why or why not?
2. When and where does it not make sense for a brand to sell in as many channels as possible? Does what the competition is doing matter?
3. Some analysts say that demographic shifts have taken a toll on the middle class, and low-cost retailers like Primark and dollar stores now have an edge. Do you agree?

Endnotes

1. Robert J. Bowman, (August 5, 2021), "100 Great Supply Chain Partners: It Takes a Team to Win," *SupplyChain Brain,* https://www.supplychainbrain.com/articles/33501-great-supply-chain-partners-of-2021-it-takes-a-team-to-win.
2. Ed Christman (July 17, 2021), "Streams Up 11 Percent, Vinyl Sales Double in First Half," *Billboard,* 20.
3. Warren Shouldberg (July 1, 2020), "Microsoft Closing Its Stores For One Reason: They Are Bad," *Forbes,* https://www.forbes.com/sites/warrenshoulberg/2020/07/01/microsoft-closing-its-stores-for-one-reason-they-are-bad/?sh=57f944ac4eec.
4. Suzanne Kapner (October 11, 2020), "Levi's, Hilfiger Push a New Kind of Online Shopping," *Wall Street Journal,* https://www.wsj.com/articles/levis-hilfiger-push-a-new-kind-of-online-shopping-it-looks-a-lot-like-qvc-11602424800; Dima Shvets (August 12, 2021), "Integrating 'Shopatainment' Into Your Marketing Strategy," *Forbes,* https://www.forbes.com/sites/forbesbusinesscouncil/2021/08/12/integrating-shopatainment-into-your-marketing-strategy/?sh=60723e674482.
5. John Moore (May 7, 2021), "Dell Channel Partners Adopt Ecosystems, Industry Focus," *Tech Target,* https://searchitchannel.techtarget.com/news/252500415/Dell-channel-partners-adopt-ecosystems-industry-focus.
6. Lizette Chapman (February 18, 2015), "Moda Operandi Brings High End to Digital," *Wall Street Journal,* B5B.
7. Christopher Doering (April 26, 2021), "Once a Trendy Beverage, Jones Soda Fights to Convince Skeptics It Can Win Again," *Food Dive,* https://www.fooddive.com/news/once-a-trendy-beverage-jones-soda-fights-to-convince-skeptics-it-can-win/598051/.
8. Charles Passy (September 28, 2017), "Signs of Life for Circus Industry—at the State Fair," *Wall Street Journal,* https://www.wsj.com/articles/signs-of-life-for-circus-industryat-the-state-fair-1506607200.
9. IANS (September 09, 2021), "Using Local Ingredients To Be Industry's Core Focus: Coca-Cola India," *Brand Equity.com,* https://brandequity.economictimes.indiatimes.com/news/business-of-brands/using-local-ingredients-to-be-industrys-core-focus-coca-cola-india/86065743.
10. Yo Tanaka (November 21, 2020), "How Walmart Flopped in Japan, and Elsewhere Overseas," https://asia.nikkei.com/Spotlight/Comment/How-Walmart-flopped-in-Japan-and-elsewhere-overseas.
11. Julian Mitchell (October 24, 2017), "FlatWorld: The Publishing Platform Rewriting The Rules of Textbook Economics," *Forbes,* https://www.forbes.com/sites/julianmitchell/2017/10/04/flatworld- the-publishing-platform looking-to-rewrite-the-rules-of-textbookeconomics/?sh=5a485fca44ca.
12. Suzanne Kapner (November 16, 2020), "Closing Stores Doesn't Always Pay Off," *Wall Street Journal,* B3.
13. Jeannette Neumann and Laura Stevens (April 30, 2018), "Amazon Is Taking Over the World? Not in Europe," *Wall Street Journal,* https://www.wsj.com/articles/in-europe-amazon-com-remains-out-of-fashion-1525080604.
14. Scott McCarney (March 15, 2018), "U.S. Airports Play Catchup in Duty Free Shopping," *Wall Street Journal,* A-13.
15. Mark Jaction (September 16, 2021), "Many SMEs Are stepping Up Their Digital Presence after the Blockade," *Texas News Today,* https://texasnewstoday.com/many-smes-are-stepping-up-their-digital-presence-after-the-blockade/462795/.
16. Mike Isaac (September 23, 2017), "One Surprise Standout for Uber: Food Delivery," *New York Times,* https://www.nytimes.com/2017/09/23/technology/ubereats-food-delivery.html.
17. Mike Isaac (September 23, 2017), "One Surprise Standout for Uber: Food Delivery," *New York Times,* https://www.nytimes.com/2017/09/23/technology/ubereats-food-delivery.html.
18. Michael Hitt, Stewart Black, and Lyman Porter (2011), *Management,* 3rd ed., Upper Saddle River, NJ: Prentice Hall.
19. Staff (January 8, 2019), "SK-II Debuts on Global Stage of Innovation at CES 2019 with the Future X Smart Store," *PR Newswire,* https://www.prnewswire.com/news-releases/sk-ii-debuts-on-global-stage-of-innovation-at-ces-2019-with-the-future-x-smart-store-300774889.html.
20. Kathrin Hill (May 18, 2009), "Via to Help New PC Makers Enter the Netbook Market," *Financial Times,* 16.
21. George Anderson (September 9, 2021), "Primark Picking up Pace of U.S. Expansion after Being Slowed by the Pandemic," *Retailwire,* https://www.retailwire.com/discussion/primark-picking-up-pace-of-u-s-expansion-after-being-slowed-by-the-pandemic/ Saabira Chaudhuri (December 24, 2017), "Fast-Fashion Chain Primark Is Slow Off the Mark in U.S." *Wall Street Journal,* https://www.wsj.com/articles/fast-fashion-chain-primark-is-slow-off-the-mark-in-u-s-1514128384; Mary Hanbury (July 22, 2018), "This Cheap European Clothing Chain Is Coming for H&M and Forever 21 in America," *Business Insider,* https://www.businessinsider.com/hm-competitor-primark-opens-store-in-brooklyn-photos-2018-7; Andrea Felsted (April 27, 2018), "Primark Hearts America," *Bloomberg,* https://www.bloomberg.com/news/articles/2018-04-17/primark-hearts-america.

CHAPTER 9

Using Supply Chains to Create Value for Customers

Suppose you have developed a great new product such as a video game *and* managed to get it sold in every marketing channel you can. So, that's the end of the story, right? Not quite. Sooner rather than later, in addition to focusing on the firms "downstream" that sell your product, you will also look "upstream" at your suppliers and "sideways" at potential firms to partner with.

As we explained in Chapter 8, your product's supply chain includes not only the downstream companies that actively sell the product but also all the other organizations that have an impact on it before, during, and after it's produced. Those companies include the providers of the raw materials your firm uses to produce it, the transportation company that physically moves it, and the firm that helped build the web pages to promote it. If you hired a programmer in India to help write computer code for the game, the Indian programmer is also part of the product's supply chain. If you hired a company to process copies of the game returned by customers, that company is part of the supply chain as well. Large organizations with many products can have literally thousands of supply chain partners. Service organizations also need supplies to operate, so they have supply chains, too.

As you learned at the end of the last chapter, the process of designing, monitoring, and altering supply chains to make them as efficient as possible is called **supply chain management**. The term *supply chain management* was first coined by an American industry consultant in the early 1980s, but it's an old idea. Part of Henry Ford's strategy in the early 1900s was to extract as much efficiency (and money) as he could by taking ownership of the supply chains for his automobiles. Ford owned the foundries that converted raw iron ore to steel for his cars. He also owned the plantations from which rubber was extracted to produce his automobiles' tires, and the ships on which the materials and finished products were transported.[1]

supply chain management

The process of designing, monitoring, and altering supply chains to make them as efficient as possible.

Many companies still take a narrow view of their supply chains; they look at supply chains mainly in terms of the costs they can save. Cost reduction is definitely an important part of supply chain management. After all, if your competitors can produce their products at a lower cost, they could put you out of business.

Rather than pushing products onto customers, Zara pulls customers into its stores by creating value for them.

Source: © Shutterstock, Inc.

Keep in mind, however, that a firm can produce and deliver a product so cheaply that no one will buy it because it's shoddy. That's why smart companies view their supply chains as an integral part of their marketing plans. In other words, these companies also look at the ways their supply chains can create value for customers to give their firms a competitive edge.

Today, the term **value chain** is sometimes used interchangeably with the term *supply chain*. The idea behind the value chain is that your supply chain partners should do more for you than perform just basic functions; each one should help you create more value for customers as the product travels along the chain—preferably more value than your competitors' supply chain partners can add to their products.

value chain

A term that is sometimes used interchangeably with the term supply chain. The idea behind the value chain is that your supply chain partners should do more for you than perform just basic functions.

Zara, a trendy but inexpensive clothing chain headquartered in Spain, is a good example of a company that has managed to create value for its customers with smart supply chain design and execution. To get the hottest fashions in the hands of customers sooner, Zara began working more closely with its supply-chain partners and internal design teams. Its highly automated inventory system allows it to quickly figure out what is selling and what's not and deliver cutting-edge fashion in a matter of days. In addition, Zara has partnered with a company that creates 3D software. The software allows shoppers to use their mobile phones to click on tags in stores to see models wearing the outfits they are interested in buying. All of these activities are designed to create more value for customers than Zara's competitors can.[2]

9.1 Sourcing and Procurement

Learning Objectives

1. Explain why sourcing and procurement activities are an important part of supply chain management.
2. Describe the reasons why outsourcing and offshoring occur.
3. Explain some of the drawbacks companies face when they outsource their activities.

sourcing

The process of evaluating and hiring individual businesses to supply goods and services to your organization.

procurement

The process of purchasing goods and services for your organization.

outsource

Hiring an organization to do a task your firm previously performed.

freight forwarders

An organization whose duties include consolidating small loads of freight, negotiating rates for their shipment, and booking space for them on transportation vehicles and in warehouses.

third-party logistics (3PLs) firms

Firms to which other companies outsource their entire order processing and shipping departments.

Sourcing is the process of evaluating and hiring individual businesses to supply goods and services to your business. **Procurement** is the process of actually purchasing those goods and services. Sourcing and procurement have become a bigger part of a supply manager's job in recent years, in part because businesses keep becoming more specialized. Just like Ford's workers became more efficient by performing specialized tasks, so too have companies.

Ford Motor Company no longer produces its own tires for its cars. It buys them from tire producers like Michelin and Goodyear. It's still possible to "own" your supply chain, though. The diamond company De Beers owns its own mines, distributorships, and retail diamond stores. The problem is that it's very costly to own multiple types of companies and difficult to run them all well, too.

Firms look up and down their supply chains and outside them to see which companies can add the most value to their products at the least cost. If a firm can find a company that can add more value than it can to a task or business function, it will often **outsource** the task to that company. After all, why do something yourself if someone else can do it better or more cost-effectively?

Rather than their own fleets of trucks, ships, and airplanes, most companies outsource at least some of their transportation tasks to shippers such as Roadway and FedEx. Other companies hire freight forwarders to help them. You can think of **freight forwarders** as travel agents for freight.[3] Their duties include negotiating rates for shipments and booking space for them on transportation vehicles and in warehouses. A freight forwarder also combines small loads from various shippers into larger loads that can be shipped more economically. However, it doesn't own its own transportation equipment or warehouses.

Other companies go a step further and outsource their entire order processing and shipping departments to **third-party logistics (3PLs) firms**. FedEx Supply Chain and UPS Supply Chain Solutions (which are divisions of FedEx and UPS, respectively) are examples of 3PLs. A 3PL is one-stop shipping solution for a company that wants to focus on other aspects of its business. Firms that receive and ship products internationally often hire 3PLs so they don't have to deal with the headaches of transporting products abroad and completing import and export paperwork for them.

The Growth of Outsourcing and Offshoring

Beginning in the 1990s, companies began to outsource a lot of other activities besides transportation. Their goal was twofold: (1) to lower their costs, and (2) to focus on the activities they do best.

You might be surprised by the functions firms outsource. In fact, many "producers" of products no longer produce them at all but outsource their production instead.

Most clothing companies, including Nike, design products but don't make them. Instead, the companies send their designs to firms in nations with low labor costs, and those companies manufacture the products. The Crest SpinBrush (toothbrush) wasn't designed by Procter & Gamble, the maker of Crest. A small company called Church & Dwight Co. developed the technology. P&G purchased the right to market and sell the product under the Crest brand before later selling it to Arm & Hammer, which makes baking soda-based consumer products.

Likewise, many large pharmaceutical companies no longer develop all of their drugs. The companies outsource the task to smaller drug developers, which in recent years have had better track records developing best-selling pharmaceuticals. And it's not only big companies that are outsourcing. A recent survey of small businesses found that 80 percent of them plan to outsource various functions. Many of the businesses are doing so to improve their operational efficiency and access the knowledge of experts to help their organizations grow.[4]

Outsourcing work to companies abroad is called **offshoring**. The functions commonly either outsourced or offshored range widely. They include the following.

offshoring

Outsourcing functions abroad.

- Product development
- Business process operations (accounting, HR, etc.)
- Warehousing and transportation
- Supply-chain planning
- Purchasing and procurement
- Manufacturing
- Returns and customer service

Pros and Cons of Outsourcing and Offshoring

A company faces a number of tradeoffs when it outsources or offshores an activity. The loss of control—particularly when it comes to product quality and safety—is one of them. Just ask Lumber Liquidators: in 2016, the U.S. company had to pull all of its Chinese-made laminate flooring from its stores' shelves when it was revealed that the flooring contained formaldehyde, which is a carcinogen. Lumber Liquidators' stock price subsequently plummeted, customers sued the company in droves in 2015, and it was investigated by the U.S. Consumer Product Safety Commission and paid $33 million in fines when the lawsuit was settled in 2019.[5] But Lumber Liquidator isn't the only company to experience problems. In one global survey, more than one-fifth of the companies that outsource functions said they have experienced "frequent" and "serious" quality problems.

The U.S. Consumer Product Safety Commission randomly inspects products, but there is no way the commission's personnel can begin to test them all. To protect their customers, many companies either test their suppliers' products themselves or contract with independent labs to do so. For example, if you sell a product to Walmart, you need to be prepared to send it to such a lab to ensure it meets certain requirements.[6] Companies also do onsite audits, or checks, of their suppliers. Other companies station employees with their suppliers on a permanent basis to be sure that the quality of the products the suppliers are producing is acceptable.

The loss of control of their technology is another outsourcing risk companies face. Some countries are better about protecting patented technologies and designs than others, and some supply chain partners are more trustworthy than others. How can you be sure your supply chain partner won't steal your technology? Oftentimes you can't. A number of years ago, General Motors began working with a Chinese firm to produce a car called the Spark for the Chinese market. But before GM could even get the automobile plant up and running, the U.S. automaker alleged that the design of the car had been stolen, sold to another company, and knockoffs of the vehicle were being driven around China's streets.[7]

Even before the Apple Watch Series 7 was announced, Chinese copycats had already started selling cheaper lookalike watches.

Source: © Shutterstock, Inc.

social responsibility

The idea that companies should manage their businesses not just to earn profits but to advance the well-being of society.

environmental sustainability

The idea that firms should engage in business practices that have the least impact on the environment so that it is sustained for future generations.

Another aspect of outsourcing relates to the social responsibility and environmental sustainability companies exhibit in terms of how they manage their supply chains. **Social responsibility** is the idea that companies should manage their businesses not just to earn profits but to advance the well-being of society. **Environmental sustainability** is the idea that firms should engage in business practices that have the least impact on the environment so that it's sustained for future generations. That can be a problem when a firm outsources work to low-wage countries, where environmental laws are often lax.

In particular, consumers are becoming increasingly alarmed about the impact of the climate crisis. Surveys show that environmental sustainability, social responsibility, and climate are becoming more important to consumers and the firms that serve them. One survey found that 77 percent of Americans are concerned about the environmental impact of what they buy; 76 percent of Americans say they would switch from their preferred brands to other brands if they offset carbon emissions.[8]

Increasingly, adroit companies are seeing the upside of voluntarily producing more sustainable products with fewer greenhouse gas emissions and disposing of them in ethical ways, regardless of where the products are produced. The reasons for doing so include the following:

- To achieve regulatory compliance
- To fulfill the customer's requirements
- To improve the company's image
- To increase the customer's confidence
- To differentiate the firm from its competitors

Walmart and Target rate their suppliers based on the environmental costs of producing their products. Walmart has an online shopping portal on Walmart.com that helps customers identify and purchase products from suppliers that are leaders in sustainability.[9] The outdoor clothing company Patagonia takes both social responsibility and environmental sustainability seriously. Patagonia tries to design, source, produce, and recycle its products so they cause the least environmental damage possible. The company will even repair the products you buy from it.

Likewise, Starbucks and other companies have joined the Fair Trade movement. Members of the Fair Trade movement pay farmers and producers in developing countries higher prices for utilizing sustainable practices. The prices consumers pay for products with fair-trade labels are often higher, but one study showed that consumers expect them to be, and that sales actually increased when the prices of such products went up.[10]

To be certified as Fair Trade producers, famers have to improve the soil and water quality, manage pests, avoid using harmful chemicals, manage waste, reduce their greenhouse gas emissions, and protect biodiversity.

Source: © Shutterstock, Inc.

Another drawback of outsourcing is the time it takes for products to make their way to the United States and into the hands of consumers. The time it takes is a big issue because it affects how responsive a company is to its customers. Retailers don't like to wait for products. Waiting might mean their customers will shop elsewhere if they can't find what they want. As we explained in Chapter 8, for this reason and others, some companies are outsourcing their activities closer to home.

Nearshoring occurs when a company moves some of its functions from a country that is further away to one that is closer to where it is headquartered. For example, in 2020, the United States imposed stiff tariffs on certain products made in China. To avoid having to pay the tariffs, some U.S. firms operating there nearshored their operations to Mexico.

nearshoring

When a company moves some of its functions from a country that is further away to one that is closer to where it is headquartered.

When firms can't resolve their supplier problems, they find other suppliers to work with or they move the activities back in-house, which is a process called **insourcing**. Insourcing can actually help set your company apart these days. The credit card company Discover doesn't outsource its customer service to companies abroad. Perhaps that helps explain why one survey ranked Discover number one in customer loyalty.

insourcing

When firms move activities, such as logistics, in-house.

Matching a Company's Sourcing Strategies with the Needs of Its Customers

Your customer should ultimately be the focus of any insourcing and outsourcing decision you make. After all, unless the product gets recycled, the customer is the last link in the supply chain. Not all customers have the same product and service requirements, though. It might be acceptable for a company that sells PCs to individual consumers to outsource its tech support, perhaps to a firm in India that can perform the function at lower cost. However, a company that buys an expensive, customized computer network is probably going to want to deal directly with the maker of the product if the network goes down—not personnel from another company in another country.

Many of Patagonia's customers are outdoor enthusiasts willing to pay $300 or more for a jacket made from recycled plastic bottles. A customer at Walmart might not be.

Source: © Shutterstock, Inc.

Similarly, if you're producing an expensive car for Ferrari-type buyers, purchasing bargain-basement-priced parts from a low-cost supplier could leave your customers dissatisfied—especially if the parts fail and their cars break down. Conversely, if you're designing a low-end automobile, top-of-the-line parts could make it too expensive for low-end buyers.

Key Takeaway

- Sourcing is the process of evaluating and hiring other businesses to supply goods and services to your business. Procurement is the process of actually purchasing those goods and services. Sourcing and procurement have become a bigger part of a supply-chain manager's job in recent years, in part because businesses keep becoming more specialized. Companies outsource activities to lower their costs and to focus on the activities they do best. Companies face numerous tradeoffs when they outsource activities, which can include a loss of control and product-quality and safety and environmental problems. Nearshoring occurs when a company moves some of its functions from a country that is further away to one that is closer to where it is headquartered. Insourcing occurs when firms move their activities back in-house, which is a process called insourcing. Customers should be the focus of any insourcing and outsourcing decisions companies make.

Review Questions

1. What are some of the supply chain functions firms outsource and offshore?
2. Describe the pros and cons of different procurement and sourcing activities.
3. How does outsourcing differ from offshoring?
4. Under what circumstances might a company be better off either nearshoring or insourcing an activity?

9.2 Demand Planning and Inventory Control

Learning Objectives

1. Explain why demand planning adds value to products.
2. Describe the role inventory control plays when it comes to marketing products.
3. List the reasons why firms collaborate with one another for the purposes of inventory control and demand planning.

Demand Planning

Imagine you are a marketing manager who has done everything in your power to help develop and promote a product—and it's selling well. But now your company is running short of the product because the demand forecasts for it were too low. (This is the scenario Nintendo faced when it initially released its Switch gaming console.) Not only is the product shortage going to adversely affect the profitably of your company, but it's going to adversely affect you too. Why? Because you, as a marketing manager, probably earn either a bonus or commission from the products you work to promote, depending on how well they sell. And, of course, you can't sell what you don't have.

demand planning

The process of estimating how much of a good or service customers will buy from you.

As you can probably tell, the best marketing decisions and supplier selections aren't enough if your company's demand forecasts are wrong. **Demand planning** is the process of estimating how much of a good or service customers will buy from you. If you're a producer of a product, this will affect not only the amount of goods and services you have to produce but also the materials you must purchase to make them.

During the pandemic the Hershey Company used COVID-19 case counts to find out where people were staying home and therefore more likely to be snacking on its products. The company then routed more of its products to those locales.

Source: © Shutterstock, Inc.

Demand planning also affects your **production scheduling**, or the management of the resources, events, and processes needed to create an offering. For example, if demand is heavy, you might need your staff members to work overtime. Closely related to demand forecasting are lead times. A product's **lead time** is the amount of time it takes for a customer to receive a good or service once it's been ordered. Lead times also have to be taken into account when a company is forecasting demand.

production scheduling

The management of the resources, events, and processes needed to create an offering.

lead time

The amount of time it takes for a customer to receive a good or service once it's been ordered.

Sourcing decisions—deciding which suppliers to use—are generally made periodically. *Forecasting decisions* must be made more frequently—sometimes daily. One way for you to predict the demand for your product is to look at your company's past sales. This is what most companies do. But they don't stop there. Why? Because changes in many factors—the availability of materials to produce a product and their prices, global competition, tariffs, oil prices (which affect shipping costs), and even the weather—can change the picture. Consequently, firms should always have contingency plans in place.

For example, after President Trump enacted tariffs on foreign steel and aluminum in 2018, companies in many industries had to alter their forecasting decisions (as well their sourcing decisions) rapidly.[11] Recessions can have an impact too. If you base your production, sales, and marketing forecasts on the data gathered during a recession, chances are your forecasts will be wildly wrong once the economy recovers. Or consider what happens if a product is recalled. If your firm is part of the supply chain for it, you will need to quickly change your forecasts.

The promotions you run will also affect demand for your products. To promote Kentucky Grilled Chicken's addition to its lineup, KFC gave away coupons online for free orders of the chicken. Twenty-four hours after uploading the coupons, the company nearly ran out of the product and had to turn many unhappy customers away. Other customers were given "rain checks" (certificates) they could use to get free grilled chicken later.

KFC's Kentucky Grilled Chicken was finger-lickin' good—if you could get it. The chain nearly ran out of the birds following an online promotion.

Source: © Shutterstock, Inc.

In addition to looking at the sales histories of their firms, supply chain managers also consult with marketing managers and sales executives when they are generating demand forecasts. Sales and marketing personnel know what promotions are being planned because they work closely with customers and know what their needs are and if those needs are changing.

Firms also look to their supply chain partners to help with their demand planning. **Collaborative planning, forecasting, and replenishment (CPFR)** is a practice whereby supply chain partners share information and coordinate their operations. Walmart has developed a web-based CPFR system called Retail Link. Retailers can log into Retail Link to see how well their products are selling at various Walmart stores, how soon more products need to be shipped to the company and where, how any promotions being run are affecting the profitability of their products, and so forth. Many firms involve their suppliers before even producing a product so they can suggest design changes, material choices, and production recommendations.

collaborative planning, forecasting, and replenishment (CPFR)

A practice whereby supply chain partners share information and coordinate their operations.

Not all firms are wild about sharing every piece of information they can with their supply chain partners though. Some retailers view their sales information as an asset—something they can sell to information companies like Information Resources, Inc., which provides competitive data to firms that are willing to pay for it.[12]

The Tata Nano was priced at just $2,900 when it was introduced to the market. To make a safe, reliable car at such a low cost, Tata Motors, an Indian company, collaborated on the car's design with its suppliers. Eliminating one of the car's two windshield wipers was one result.

Source: © Shutterstock, Inc.

However, the trend is clearly toward more shared information, or what businesspeople refer to as **supply chain visibility**. After all, it makes sense that a supplier will not only be more reliable but also be in a better position to add value to your products if it knows what your sales, operations, and marketing plans are—and what your customers want. By sharing more than just basic transaction information, companies can see how well operations are proceeding, how products are flowing through the chain, how well the partners are performing and cooperating with one another, and the extent to which value is being built in to products for customers.

Demand-planning software and systems can also be used to create more accurate demand forecasts. **Demand-planning software** compiles data from a variety of sources to better predict a firm's demand—for example, from a firm's sales history, point-of-sale data, warehouses, suppliers, promotion information, and economic and competitive trends. To further ensure a company's demand forecasts are as up to date as possible, some systems allow sales and marketing personnel to input purchasing information into their mobile devices after consulting with their customers.

supply chain visibility

A situation in which supply chain partners share information with one another so they can see how well the chain is working.

demand-planning software

Software that amalgamates data from a variety of sources to better predict a firm's demand.

inventory control

The process of ensuring your firm has an adequate amount of products and a wide enough assortment of them to meet your customers' needs.

stockout

A situation that occurs when a firm runs out of a product a customer wants to buy.

Inventory Control

Demand forecasting is part of a company's overall inventory control activities. **Inventory control** is the process of ensuring your firm has an adequate supply of products and a wide enough assortment of them to meet your customers' needs. In Japan, 7-Eleven is a company that's extremely in tune to demand forecasting. The company's point-of-sale systems at its checkout counters monitor what is selling well and when, and stores are restocked with those items immediately—sometimes via motorcycle deliveries that zip in and out of traffic along Japan's crowded streets.

One of the goals of inventory management is to avoid stockouts. A **stockout** occurs when you run out of a product a customer wants to buy. Stockouts usually result in lost sales, because customers will simply look elsewhere to buy the product. When the 9/11 attack on the World Trade Center occurred, many Americans rushed to stores to buy batteries, flashlights, American flags, canned goods, and other products for fear that a much bigger attack was coming.

Many retailers sold out of items and could not replenish them for several days, partly because their inventory tracking systems only counted up what was needed at the end of the day. Walmart, on the other hand, took count of what was needed every five minutes. Before the end of the day on 9/11, Walmart had purchased enough American flags to meet demand. Other retailers were out of flags and out of luck—there were no more to be had because Walmart had bought them all from suppliers.

To help avoid stockouts, most companies keep a certain amount of safety stock on hand. **Safety stock** is backup inventory that serves as a buffer in case the demand for a product surges or the supply of it drops off for some reason. Maintaining too much inventory, though, ties up money that could be spent other ways—perhaps on marketing promotions. Inventory also has to be insured, and in some cases, taxes must be paid on it. Products in inventory can also become obsolete, deteriorate, spoil, or "shrink." **Shrinkage** is a term used to describe a reduction or loss in inventory due to shoplifting, employee theft, paperwork errors, or supplier fraud.

safety stock

Backup inventory that serves as a buffer in case the demand for a product surges or the supply of it drops off for some reason.

shrinkage

A term used to describe a reduction or loss in inventory due to shoplifting, employee theft, paperwork errors, and supplier fraud.

Just-in-Time Inventory Systems

To lower the amount of inventory and still maintain the stock they need to satisfy their customers, organizations like Walmart and others increasingly use **just-in-time inventory systems**. Firms with just-in-time inventory systems keep very little inventory on hand. Instead, the firms contract with their suppliers to ship inventory as they need it and even sometimes manage their inventory for them—a practice called **vendor-managed inventory (VMI)**.

Dell is an example of a company that utilizes a just-in-time inventory system that's vendor managed. Dell carries very few component parts. Instead, its suppliers carry them. They are located in small warehouses near Dell's assembly plants worldwide and provide Dell with parts "just-in-time" for them to be assembled. Dell uses algorithms and artificial intelligence to predict the volume of orders for various products and parts, and then alerts its suppliers so they are able to provide them on time.[13]

Dell's inventory and production system also allows customers to get their computers built exactly to their specifications, a production process called **mass customization**. This helps keep Dell's inventory levels low. Instead of a huge inventory of expensive, already-assembled computers consumers may or may not buy, Dell simply has the parts on hand, so that the computers can be configured or reconfigured should consumers' preferences change. Because mass customization lets buyers "have it their way," it also adds value to products, for which many customers are willing to pay extra.

just-in-time inventory systems

A system in which a firm keeps very little inventory on hand. Instead, its suppliers ship it inventory as needed.

vendor-managed inventory (VMI)

The practice of having your suppliers monitor your inventory levels.

mass customization

Mass producing goods customized to the specifications of individual consumers.

Product Tracking

Being able to track products as they move through the supply chain is vital for companies. You are familiar with bar codes, which have been used to track inventory since the 1970s. You have probably watched a checkout person scan a barcode off of a product identical to the one you wanted to buy—perhaps a pack of gum—because the barcode on your product was missing or wouldn't scan.

A radio frequency tag is similar to a barcode, only better, because the number on it is truly unique. A **radio-frequency identification (RFID) tag** is an electronic tag that emits radio signals that can record and track a shipment as it comes in and out of a facility. If you have unlocked your car door remotely, microchipped your dog, or waved a tollway tag at a checkpoint, you have used RFID technology. See Figure 9.1 to get an idea of how radio-frequency technology works.

radio-frequency identification (RFID) tag

An electronic tag that emits radio signals to track a product.

Unlike barcodes, RFID tags make it possible to distinguish between two identical products. The codes contain information about when the product was manufactured, where it shipped from, and where it is going to. Being able to tell the difference between "seemingly" identical products can help companies monitor their expiration dates if the products are recalled for quality or safety reasons. The technology can also be used to combat "fake" products, or knockoffs, in the marketplace.

FIGURE 9.1 How RFID Technology Works

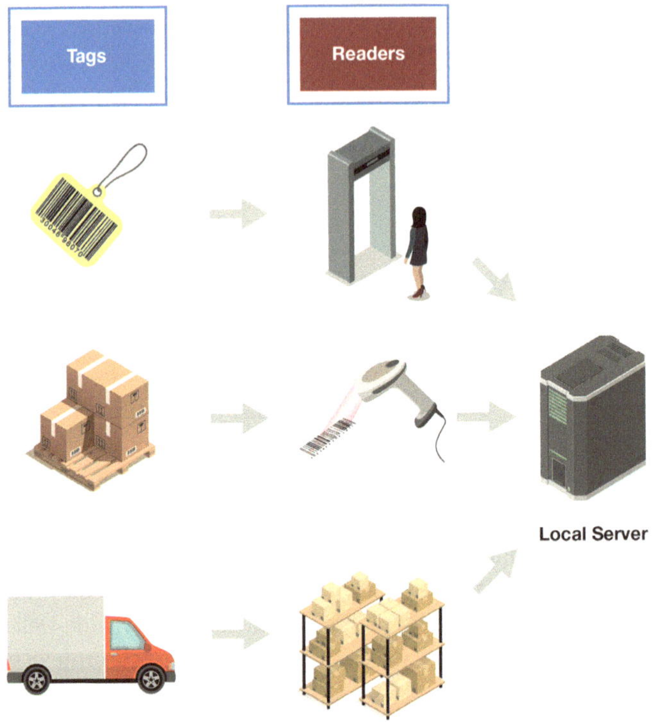

From a supply-chain and marketing standpoint, RFID technology can benefit both companies and consumers. Zara found that after installing the technology, not only was it able to allow shoppers to click on the tags to see models wearing outfits, the company was also able to keep much better track of its stock and the buying trends of its customers at each of its stores and replenish its clothing racks more quickly. "It's helping us in everything we do in stores," says Zara's chief executive Pablo Isla about RFID technology.[14]

Zara's customers benefit because they don't go to a store and see stockouts or have to sift through older fashions. In addition, the technology doesn't require cashiers to scan barcodes item by item. Instead, an electronic product reader can automatically tally up the entire contents of a shopping cart. As a customer, wouldn't that add value to your shopping experience?

blockchain

A digital ledger that provides a secure way of making and recording transactions that are recorded chronologically and publicly within computer networks on the Cloud and can't be changed.

Blockchain is the newest supply chain tracking system firms are trying to implement. **Blockchain** is a digital ledger that provides a secure way of making and recording transactions that are recorded chronologically and publicly within computer networks on the Cloud and can't be changed. It is the technology behind bitcoins, for one to ensure that a bitcoin can't be copied. Blockchain is not yet being used widely in supply chains. Nonetheless, companies are experimenting with it to track everything from coffee and mobile phones, to turkeys.

IBM has created a blockchain system to verify the authenticity of jewelry—from where it is mined to how it is mined. Was it done in a sustainable way, and were workers not exploited? Research has shown that consumers are willing to pay more for products when they can verify details such as these.[15]

Is the jewelry you want to buy real? An IBM blockchain system may be able to ensure it is.

Source: © Shutterstock, Inc.

RFID tags like the one shown on the collar of this shirt help Zara track products.

Source: © Shutterstock, Inc.

Key Takeaway

- The best marketing decisions and supplier selections aren't enough if your company's demand forecasts are wrong. Demand forecasting is the process of estimating how much of a good or service a customer will buy from you. If you're a producer of a product, this will affect not only the amount of goods and services you have to produce but also the materials you must purchase to make them. Demand forecasting is part of a company's overall inventory control activities. Inventory control is the process of ensuring your firm has an adequate amount of products and a wide enough assortment of them to meet your customers' needs. One of the goals of inventory control is to avoid stockouts without keeping too much of a product on hand. A growing number of companies are using RFID and blockchain technology to better manage their inventories, gather more information on the products their customers are demanding, and provide those products to them when and where they want to purchase them.

Review Questions

1. Why are demand forecasts made more frequently than sourcing decisions?
2. How can just-in-time and vendor-managed inventories add value to products for customers?
3. Why and how do companies track products?

9.3 Warehousing and Transportation

Learning Objectives

1. Understand the role warehouses and distribution centers play in the supply chain.
2. Outline the transportation modes firms have to choose from and the advantages and disadvantages of each.

Warehousing

At times, the demand and supply for products can be unusually high. At other times, it can be unusually low. That's why companies generally maintain a certain amount of safety stock, oftentimes in warehouses. As a business owner, it would be great if you didn't have excess inventory you had to store in a warehouse. In an ideal world, materials or products would arrive at your facility just in time for you to assemble or sell them. Unfortunately, we don't live in an ideal world.

Toys are a good example. Most toy makers work year-round to be sure they have enough toys available for sale during the holidays. However, retailers don't want to buy huge numbers of toys in July. They want to wait until November and December to buy large amounts of them. Consequently, toy makers warehouse them until that time. Likewise, during the holiday season, retailers don't want to run out of toys, so they maintain a certain amount of safety stock in their warehouses.

Some firms store products until their prices increase. Speculators, including investment banks and hedge funds, have been known to buy and hold oil if they think its price is going to rise. In 2020, Saudi Arabia and Russia got into an oil price war and the price of crude dropped. So what did the Saudis do? They hired oil tankers to warehouse the extra oil at sea until buyers could be found for it.[16]

Ships like this oil tanker sometimes serve as warehouses.

Source: © Shutterstock, Inc.

distribution center

A warehouse or storage facility where the emphasis is on processing and moving goods on to wholesalers, retailers, or consumers rather than to storage.

A **distribution center** is a warehouse or storage facility where goods are sorted and then distributed to wholesalers, retailers, or consumers. A few years ago, companies were moving toward large, centralized warehouses to keep costs down.

Today, however, the trend has shifted back to smaller warehouses. Using smaller warehouses is a change that's being driven by customer considerations rather than costs. The long lead times that result when companies transport products from Asia, the Middle East, and South America are forcing international manufacturers and retailers to shorten delivery times to consumers.

Half of the clothing Zara sells worldwide is made near the company's headquarters but is delivered to stores in small batches twice a week by truck or plane.[17] Warehousing products regionally, closer to consumers, can also help a company tailor its product selection to better match the needs of customers in different regions.

One of the newer trends in warehousing is *on-demand warehousing,* which is the process of matching businesses that need to store inventory on a temporary basis with warehouses that have excess space. The Port Authority of New York and New Jersey developed a database that enables companies to pinpoint vacant space for short-term use, especially during seasonal spikes or periods of disruption like the pandemic.[18] Often apps are used for this purpose. UPS's Ware2Go tool helps shippers find on-demand warehousing. STORD and Flexe are competing tools.

How Warehouses and Distribution Centers Function

SKU (stock-keeping unit)

A label used to distinguish a product that is unique because of some characteristic, such as manufacturer, size, color, or model.

So how do you begin to find a product or pallet of products in a warehouse or distribution center the size of a dozen or more football fields? To begin with, each type of product that is unique because of some characteristic—say, because of its manufacturer, size, color, or model—must be stored and accounted for separately from other items. To help distinguish it, its manufacturer gives it its own identification number, called a **SKU (stock-keeping unit).** The photo of a box being scanned on this page shows an example of a SKU that appears on a box of products. When the product enters the warehouse, it is scanned and given an "address," or location, in the warehouse where it is stored until it is plucked from its shelf and shipped.

Stock-keeping units like the one being scanned here track products and information about them.

Source: © Shutterstock, Inc.

Warehouses and distribution centers are also becoming increasingly automated. **Electronic data interchange (EDI)** is an electronic format companies use to exchange business documents from computer to computer rather than via paper or email. EDI is faster and makes for greater visibility among supply chain partners because they can all check the status of orders electronically. And, as you learned in Chapter 8, some warehouses use robots to picks products from shelves.

electronic data interchange (EDI)

An electronic format companies use to exchange business documents from computer to computer rather than via paper or email.

Phantom Auto has developed forklifts that can be operated remotely with video and audio. The forklift operators can be located anywhere, which in a tight labor market is an advantage, and they can switch between different locations depending on demand.[19]

No, It's Not a Video Game

Watch this forklift being operated remotely by a worker.

View in the online reader

At other warehouses, employees use voice-enabled headsets to pick products. Via the headsets, the workers communicate with a computer that tells them where to go and what to grab off of shelves. As a result, the employees are able to pick products faster and more accurately than they could by looking at a sheet of paper or computer screen.

Cross-docking is a way to get products to customers faster as well. Products that are cross-docked spend little or no time in warehouses. As Figure 9.2 shows, a product being cross-docked will be delivered via truck to a dock at a warehouse where it is unloaded and put straight onto other trucks bound for retail outlets.

FIGURE 9.2 How Cross-Docking Works

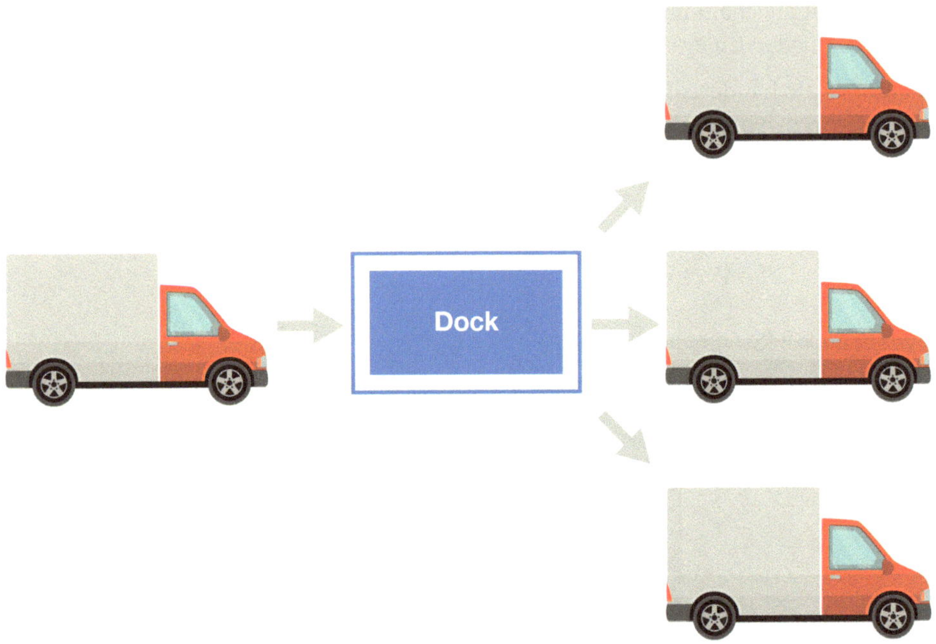

However, during the COVID-19 pandemic, goods were so scarce that some producers skipped warehousing products altogether and instead delivered products straight to stores. Doing so also reduced the the costs associated with warehouses and distribution centers.[20]

The warehousing and distribution processes we have described are just a few aspects of *very* complicated operations. For example, it's pretty amazing to think about how the 1.5-million plus packages Amazon ships every day from its distribution centers ultimately end up in the right customer's hands. After all, how many times have you had to look really hard to find something you put in your own closet or garage? Processing orders—order fulfillment—is a key part of the job in supply chains. Why? Because delivering what was promised, when it was promised, and the way it was promised are key drivers of customer satisfaction.

Transportation

Not all goods and services need to be physically transported. When you get a massage, oil change, or a manicure, the services pass straight from the provider to you. Other products are transported electronically. Downloads of songs, software, movies, and books are an example. So are broadcast, cable, and satellite television programs and psychic readings delivered via Zoom.

logistics

The physical flow of materials in the supply chain.

Other products, of course, have to be physically shipped. **Logistics** refers to the physical flow of materials in the supply chain. You might be surprised by some of the physical distribution methods that companies use. For example, in some countries where the road systems are poorly developed or nonexistent, Coca-Cola delivers syrup to its bottlers via camelback. More commonly, though, products that need to be transported physically to get to customers are moved via air, rail, truck, water, and pipeline.

Delivery Logistics

How products are delivered around the world might surprise you.

View in the online reader

Trucks

More products are shipped by truck than by another means. Trucks can go anywhere there are roads, including straight to customers' stores and homes. By contrast, planes, trains, and ships are more limited as to where they can go. Shipping by truck is also fast relative to other modes (except for air transportation). However, it's also fairly expensive. Some goods—especially those that are heavy or bulky—would require so many trucks and drivers it would be economically unfeasible to use them over long distances. Coal is a good example of such a product. It would take four to five hundred trucks and drivers to haul the amount of freight that one coal train can. The amount of CO_2 emitted by trucks is also high relative to some of the other transportation modes, so it's not the greenest solution.

Water

International trade could scarcely be conducted without cargo shipping. Cargo ships transport "loose" cargo such as grain, coal, ore, petroleum, and other mined products. But they also transport consumer products—everything from televisions to toys. Consumer goods are often shipped in intermodal containers. **Intermodal containers** are metal boxes. The largest containers are 53 feet long and a little under 10 feet tall. The biggest cargo ships are huge and carry as many 15,000 containers, which are loaded on and off the ships by giant cranes. By contrast, the maximum a train can carry is around 250 containers stacked on top of each other.

The good news about shipping via waterway is that it is inexpensive. The bad news is that it's very slow. In addition, many markets aren't accessible by water, so another method of transportation has to be utilized as well.

Cargo ships like this one can transport thousands of intermodal containers.

Source: © Shutterstock, Inc.

intermodal containers

Metal boxes used to ship consumer goods.

Air

Air freight is the fastest way to ship goods. However, it can easily cost ten times as much to ship a product by air as by sea.[21] High-dollar goods and a small fraction of perishable goods are shipped via air. Freshly cut flowers and fresh seafood bound for sushi markets are examples. Keeping perishable products at the right temperature and humidity levels as they sit on runways and planes can be a challenge. These products often have to be shipped in special types of containers with coolants. Freight forwarders are often hired to arrange the packing for perishables traveling by air and to ensure they don't deteriorate while they are in transit.

Railroads

Railroads carry many of the same products as cargo ships—only over land. A significant percentage of intermodal containers offloaded from ships end up on railcars bound for inland destinations. The containers then are trucked shorter distances to distribution centers, warehouses, and stores. Businesses that need to ship heavy, bulky goods often try to locate their facilities next to railroads. Lumber mills are an example.

In terms of speed and cost, shipping by rail falls somewhere between truck and water transportation. It's not as slow and inexpensive as moving goods by water. However, it's not as fast as shipping them by truck. Nor is it as expensive. So, when the price of fuel rises, shippers that use trucks often look at other transportation alternatives such as rail.

Grace Kung, BNSF Railway

Source: Photo courtesy of Amy Ray

Grace Kung, a marketing and sales professional with BNSF Railway, knows how to create value for customers when it comes to supply chains. Kung is responsible for ensuring that thousands of pieces of sophisticated military equipment get shipped each year as part of the nation's "speed of war" initiative. The equipment has to get to the right places at the right times. Frequently that means finding new staging and shipping areas BNSF has never utilized. And it all has to be done in the nick of time so National Guard personnel are present to load and unload the equipment when the trains arrive. "It's a very competitive business," says Kung. "If we don't capture the business, a competing railroad will."

Is marketing a good career? Yes, says Grace Kung. "It's all about understanding customers' challenges from their perspective and then meeting their needs," she says.

Pipelines

Pipelines are generally used to transport oil, natural gas, and chemicals. Two-thirds of petroleum products are transported by pipeline, including heating oil, diesel, jet fuel, and kerosene. Pipelines are costly to build, but once they are constructed, they can transport products cheaply. For example, for about one dollar you can transport a barrel of petroleum products via pipeline from Houston to New York. The oil will move three to eight miles per hour and arrive in two to three weeks, depending on the size of the pipe, its pressure, and the density of the liquid.[22]

Like other products, products shipped via pipelines often have to be moved using two different transportation modes. Once your petroleum has made it to New York, to get it to a refinery, you will probably need to move it by rail or truck. The material in pipelines can also be stolen like other products being transported can. In Mexico, for example, drug gangs have tapped into pipelines in remote areas and stolen billions of pesos in oil.[23]

Transportation Tradeoffs and Logistics Trends

Companies face different tradeoffs when choosing transportation methods. Which is most important? Speed? Cost? Frequency of delivery? The flexibility to respond to different market conditions? Again, it depends on your customers. The transportation modes should be based on what they want and are willing to pay for. Which modes also depend to some extent on the nature of the product you're selling and the best way for you to minimize your transportation costs. It's probably not cost-effective or even possible for a lumber producer to ship loads of lumber overnight. Nor would most buyers of lumber want to pay the extra costs of having it shipped that way.

Goya Foods faces many transportation tradeoffs, not due to the nature of its product so much as due to the wide variety of customers it serves in the United States and Mexico. For example, Goya sells more than 1,600 canned food products. Because the types of beans people prefer often depends on their cultures—whether they are of Cuban, Mexican, or Puerto Rican descent, and so forth—the company sells thirty-eight varieties of beans alone.

Almost daily, Goya's truck drivers deliver products to tens of thousands of food stores. Delivering daily is more costly than dropping off jumbo shipments once a week and letting stores warehouse goods. However, it allows Goya to offer stores a greater variety and ensure that products match each store's demographics. "Pink beans might sell in New York City but not sell as well in Texas or California," says the company's CEO.[24]

Clearly, logistics decisions and systems are complex and getting more so. Instacart and Shipt have mobile app systems that allow people like you to pick up and deliver packages to consumers and get paid for it. For the past couple of years, a company called Antwork has been delivering fast food in China via drones. Likewise, Starship Technologies has built a six-wheel robot that's been delivering groceries in Great Britain since 2018. Meanwhile, in Miami, Austin, and Washington, DC, Walmart is testing self-driving delivery cars.[25]

Delivery Robots

Ex-Google employees created the Nuro, a driverless delivery vehicle that has been approved to operate in California.

View in the online reader

Online sellers are also working with shippers like FedEx, UPS, and DHL to implement *click-and-collect systems:* Consumers buy products online, and they are then are shipped to drugstores, convenience stores, and dedicated shipping outlets like UPS stores. Customers then pick up, or collect, the packages on their way home from work or school. Dropping off multiple packages in one location is faster, less expensive, and cuts down on re-delivery costs when customers aren't home to get packages that must be signed for. The method also cuts down on the number of packages stolen from people's doorsteps.

Click and collect is also becoming a more popular delivery method utilized by brick-and-mortar retail stores—especially by consumers who want to order online, pick up the same day, and not have to pay shipping costs. Dedicated collection points in stores allow buyers to pick up the products quickly, as do groups of lockers—some of which are temperature-controlled.[26] Home Depot and Walmart both have locker systems in a number of their stores. Click-and-collect systems also help to build foot traffic in stores; while picking up a package, a customer might buy something else.

UPS Delivers

This video shows how UPS uses lockers to deliver packages to customers.

View in the online reader

As you can probably tell, just as products, customers, and firms change over time, so will logistics systems change to better meet their needs.

Key Takeaway

- Some firms store products until their prices increase. A distribution center is a warehouse or storage facility where the emphasis is on processing and moving goods on to other parts of the supply chain. Warehousing products regionally can help a company tailor its product selection to better match the needs of customers in different regions. Logistics refers to the physical flow of materials in the supply chain. Not all goods and services need to be physically transported. Some are directly given to customers or sent to them electronically. Products that need to be transported physically to get to customers are moved via, air, rail, truck, water, and pipelines. The transportation modes a firm uses should be based on what its customers want and are willing to pay for, as well as be cost-effective for the firm.

Review Questions

1. How do warehouses and distribution centers differ?

2. What is cross-docking and why might a company choose to cross-dock a product?
3. What kinds of products can be delivered electronically? What kinds need to be physically transported?
4. What are some of the most recent transportation and logistical trends?

9.4 Track and Trace Systems and Reverse Logistics

Learning Objectives

1. Understand why being able to trace products is important to organizations and their customers.
2. Explain what reverse logistics is and why firms utilize it.

Shippers are highly anxious when their products are in transit because the merchandise is valuable and because it is exposed to more risks when it's traveling across the country than when it's sitting in a warehouse or store. Shippers want to know where the goods are, when they will arrive, and what kind of shape they are in. After all, they can end up in the wrong place, be damaged, or be stolen.

Captain Phillips

In 2009, Somali pirates hijacked the container ship the Maersk Alabama and held its crew and 17,000 metric tons of freight hostage. The incident was later dramatized in the blockbuster film *Captain Phillips*, starring Tom Hanks.

View in the online reader

Track and Trace Systems

track and trace systems

Systems that electronically record the paths shipments take.

In recent years, **track and trace systems** that electronically record the paths shipments take have become almost as important to businesses as shipping costs themselves. Being able to help trace products helps a company anticipate events that could disrupt the supply chain, including order shipping mistakes, bad weather, and accidents, so they can be averted.

Today most product shipments can be traced at least to some extent with GPS, bluetooth wireless signals, and other types of technology. GPS devices are sometimes placed on containers, railcars, and trucks to track the movement of expensive shipments. Tracing individual products is harder, though. Produce is a product that's hard to trace. You have probably noticed that some types of produce have barcodes on them but many other types of produce don't. Products that are combined to make other products are also hard to trace. Although more firms are beginning to use systems that utilize electronic product codes and RFID tags, many other firms still aren't.

California uses a track-and-trace system to ensure cannabis isn't crossing state lines or going into the black market. The system also makes it easy to recall a product if there is something wrong with a particular batch.

Source: © Shutterstock, Inc.

Being able to trace products is important not only to businesses but also to consumers. Consumers are more interested than ever in knowing where their products come from—particularly when there is a product-contamination problem. Products containing salmonella-infested peanuts and tomatoes, and contaminated milk and ice cream have sickened and caused the deaths of consumers and their pets across the globe. Even if the source of the contaminated product is known, consumers often can't tell exactly where the products originated from, so they stop buying them altogether. This can be devastating for companies up and down the supply chain.

Companies are working to develop systems that may one day make it possible to trace all products, including animals, people, and components no matter where they are. The concept and technology being developed to accomplish this is called the Internet of Things (IoT). IoT refers to all of the devices that via sensors can now be connected to the web and tracked as a result.

Internet of Things

This video explains how the Internet of Things (IoT) works.

View in the online reader

A Norwegian company called TraceTracker helped make IoT a reality. Using *blockchain* technology (see Section 6 to learn more about blockchain), you can trace products, verify their origins, and provide businesses with global supply chain analytics in the process. The goal is to be able to identify and track each batch of every product that is merged together in the global food chain, from raw ingredients to products on supermarket shelves.

Meanwhile, handheld RFID tag readers and mobile apps allow consumers to track the origin and other information about the products they are considering buying. A customer at Big Red's, a seafood wholesaler and retailer in the Boston area, can scan a QR (quick response) code with a mobile phone and instantly get information on where a fish was caught and even the boat that caught it. (The following graphic explains how QR codes work.)[27]

How QR codes work.

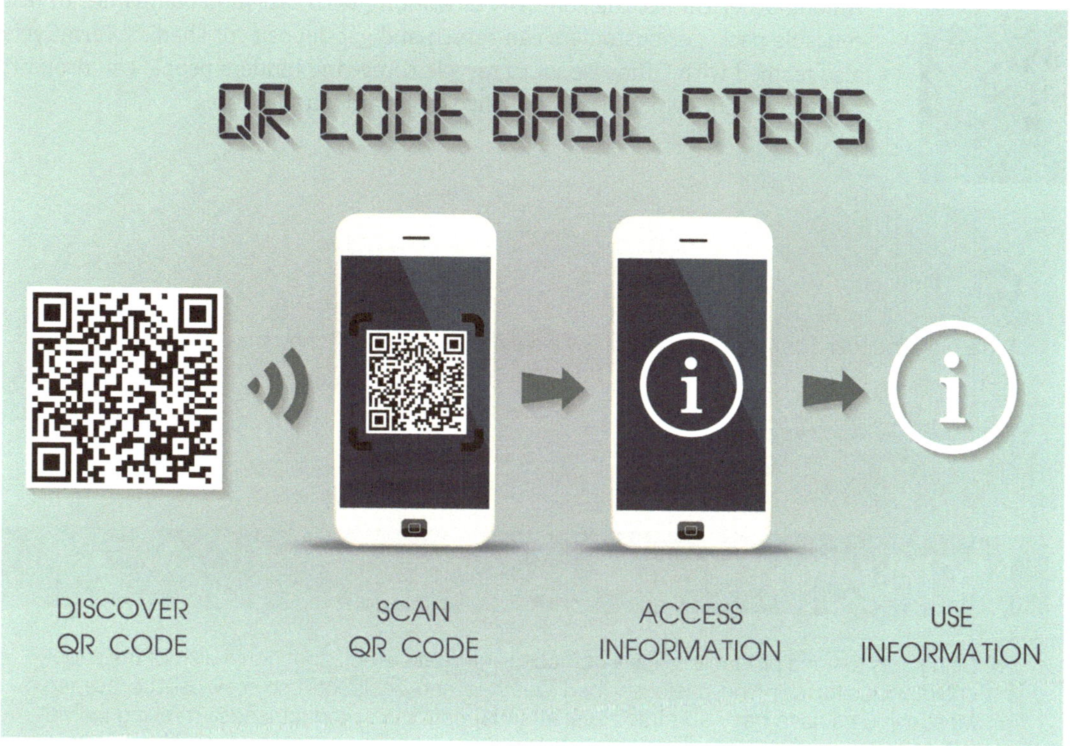

Source: © Shutterstock, Inc.

Reverse Logistics

So what happens if products end up broken or unusable as they travel through their supply chains? And what do companies do with scrap materials and other "junk" produced, such as packaging? Increasingly, firms now run products and materials such as these backward through the supply chain to extract value from them. The process is known as **reverse logistics**.

reverse logistics

Running broken, defective, and scrap products backward through the supply chain so as to extract value from them.

Patagonia developed a reverse logistics systems for environmental reasons. After garments made by Patagonia are worn out, consumers can mail them to the company or return them to a Patagonia store. Patagonia then recycles them into usable fibers that are later made into new garments. The company has also convinced other clothing makers to do the same, even though it can add to the cost of products.

The first product collected and recycled by Patagonia was, believe it or not, its polyester-spandex underwear because it has no buttons or zippers that have to be removed.

Source: © Shutterstock, Inc.

Most companies set up reverse logistics systems to "turn trash into cash." Pittsburgh-based Genco is firm that specializes in reverse logistics. Companies like Best Buy and Target hire Genco to find buyers for defective or broken products. One study found companies can recover up to 0.3 percent of their annual sales this way, which for Best Buy would amount to $100 million a year.[28]

TerraCycle is a company dedicated to extracting value from waste and using it to create new products—a process that's being called "upcycling." In addition to selling fertilizer in used (but relabeled) plastic bottles, TerraCycle makes backpacks and pencil cases out of the metallic juice pouches used in drink boxes. Among other things, the company is working with fast-food companies to test reusable packages customers can return and get deposit for them.[29] TerraCycle also teamed with Office Depot to recycle three-ring binders people can drop off at Office Depot, which also helps drive foot traffic to the stores.[30]

Recycling

TerraCycle founder Tom Szaky explains how his company makes money while saving the planet, too.

View in the online reader

Key Takeaways

- Being able to trace products helps a company anticipate events that could disrupt the supply chain, including shipping mistakes, bad weather, and accidents, so they can be averted. Most shippers have track and trace systems that can track product loads. Tracking individual products, especially after they are combined to make other products, is more difficult.
- Consumers are more interested than ever in knowing where their products come from—particularly when there is a contamination problem with an offering. Reverse logistics is the process of running damaged and defective products and scrap materials backward through the supply chain to extract value from them. Companies are increasingly employing reverse logistics not only to save money but for environmental reasons.

Review Questions

1. Why is being able to track products important to companies? Why is it important to consumers? How can it add value to products?
2. What place does reverse logistics have in a company's supply chain?

9.5 Discussion Questions and Activities

Discussion Questions

1. Why do marketing professionals care about and participate in supply chain decisions?
2. What criteria do you think companies look at when evaluating the performance of their supply chain partners? Make a list of them.
3. Is the electronic delivery of products always better? To what extent does it depend on the customer?
4. Discuss the supply chain for education at your college. What elements does it consist of? What aspects of its delivery could be improved upon? What sort of alternate sourcing and delivery methods might be used? Can education be warehoused? How?

Activities

1. Research the distribution system for Coca-Cola. What elements of Coca-Cola's supply chain were you unaware of?
2. Get into groups of four. Then choose a product and outline the supply chain for it. If you need to, use the web to research the product. Then discuss with your group how you believe the supply chain could be used to create additional value for customers. Present your findings to your class.

9.6 Case Study: Can Blockchain Improve the Supply Chain for Web Ads?

As you learned in this chapter, blockchain is a digital ledger that provides a secure way of making and recording transactions chronologically and publicly that can't be changed within computer networks on the Cloud. People are attempting to use blockchain to track everything in the supply chain from bitcoin to jewelry and turkeys. Watch the following short video to get an idea of how blockchain works.

Understanding Blockchain

Blockchain technology described in two minutes.

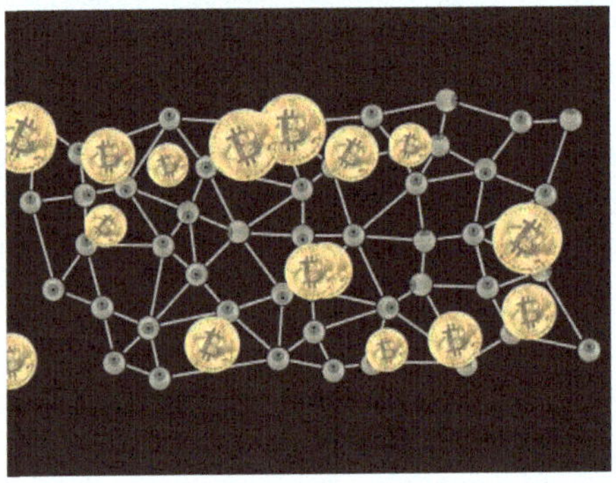

View in the online reader

What about internet ads? Can blockchain be used to track them? Who keeps track of all those ads popping up everywhere? And who keeps track of the number of people who click on them, which, as you will learn in Chapter 12, is how companies like Google make money.

The task is more complicated than you might think. The sheer volume of online ads purchased is huge. Companies worldwide spend about $223 billion annually on them. Hundreds of thousands of ads are purchased every second via online auctions. The company that bids the highest for a prime ad spot wins.

However, humans don't usually bid on the ads: multiple computers do the bidding, making tallying the ads even tougher to monitor. An advertiser can try to manually audit the number of ads it bought across all networks, but it can be difficult to do.

Worse yet, "bots"—computer robots—are being programmed to generate false clicks made to look like human clicks. Companies pay for ads based on the number of people who click on and/or view them, so bots drive up the costs of advertising on the web. So are advertisers really getting their money's worth when it comes to their web-ad spending, or are they being defrauded? Many of them are concerned.

The supply chain for web ads is also more complicated than you might think. For example, a company might buy an ad on Google, but usually there are a number of intermediaries that take a cut of what the company pays for the ad: the company's media, or ad agency, which created the ad and initiated its launch on the web; an ad trading desk, which brokers the trades much like trading desks on stock exchanges do; and so forth. Consequently, if the volume of ads people see and click on are wrong—say, 9,000 versus 10,000—the revenues of many organizations are affected.

Can blockchain solve some of these problems? IBM, Anheuser-Busch, and Nestlé are among the many companies that think so, and they are working with tech firms to try to implement blockchain and other verification methods to prevent the fraud. The effort appears to be working. A recent study found that online ad fraud is down or has shifted to platforms where it's more difficult to detect.[31]

Case Study Questions

1. If computers are used to buy ads, why do you think getting accurate counts of them displayed and clicked on is hard to count?
2. What other types of products do you think could benefit from being tracked and using blockchain technology?

Endnotes

1. Gregory R. Piche, *The Four Trials of Henry Ford* (Chirp Books: Cambrige, MA: 2020).
2. Pamela Danzinger (April 23, 2018), "Why Zara Succeeds: It Focuses On Pulling People In, Not Pushing Product Out," *Forbes*, https://www.forbes.com/sites/pamdanziger/2018/04/23/zaras-difference-pull-people-in-not-push-product-out/#38ba606a23cb.
3. Karen E. Thuermer (September 2021), *Logistics Management,* 58.
4. Staff (January 20, 2021), "Eighty Percent of Small Businesses Plan to Outsource in 2021, Citing the Ability to Save Time, Grow Their Business, and Work with Expert," *PR Newswire,* https://www.prnewswire.com/news-releases/80-of-small-businesses-plan-to-outsource-in-2021-citing-the-ability-to-save-time-grow-their-business-and-work-with-experts-301212311.html.
5. Chelsey Dulaney (May 8, 2015), "Firm Halts Sales of Chinese Flooring," *Wall Street Journal*, B6.
6. Walmart Corporation (n.d.), *U.S. Product and Quality Compliance Manual,* https://corporate.walmart.com/media-library/document/u-s-product-quality-and-compliance-manual/_proxyDocument?id=00000170-5a64-da20-a3f3-7bf53fd40000.
7. Bureau of International Information Programs, U.S. Department of State (January 13, 2005), "China Pressed to Forcefully Attack Intellectual Property Theft," America.gov, http://www.america.gov/st/washfile-english/2005/January/20050113180002asesuark0.9782831.html#ixzz0Mada2mLk.
8. Staff (March 22, 2021), "GreenPrint Survey Finds Consumers Want to Buy Eco-Friendly Products, but Don't Know How to Identify Them," *Business Wire,* https://www.businesswire.com/news/home/20210322005061/en/GreenPrint-Survey-Finds-Consumers-Want-to-Buy-Eco-Friendly-Products-but-Donât-Know-How-to-Identify-Them.
9. Andrew Winston (February, 24, 2015), "Can Walmart Get Us to Buy Sustainable Products?" *Harvard Business Review,* https://hbr.org.
10. Sarah Morlock, (September 8, 2021), "It's Time to Make the Switch to Organic Coffee: Here's Why," *Yahoo Lifestyle,* https://www.yahoo.com/lifestyle/time-switch-organic-coffee-why-130023511.html.
11. Steve Banker (March 2, 2018), "Trump's Tariffs, Trade Wars And The Supply Chain," *Forbes,* https://www.forbes.com/sites/stevebanker/2018/03/02/trumps-tariffs-trade-wars-and-the-supply-chain/#4cd286d6729a.
12. Donald J. Bowersox and David J. Closs (2000), "Ten Mega-Trends That Will Revolutionize Supply Chain Logistics," *Journal of Business Logistics 21*(2), 11.
13. Steve McDowell (September 7, 2021), "Dell Technologies Brings AI To The Edge," *Forbes,* https://www.forbes.com/sites/moorinsights/2021/09/07/dell-technologies-brings-ai-to-the-edge/?sh=60dd2924c19e.
14. Christopher Bjork (June 10, 2015), "Euro Buoys Zara's Parent; A 'Cracking Start' to 2015," *Wall Street Journal,* http://wsj.com.
15. Ron Miller (April 26, 2018), "IBM introduces a Blockchain to Verify the Jewelry Supply Chain," https://techcrunch.com/2018/04/26/ibm-introduces-trustchain-a-blockchain-to-verify-the-jewelry-supply-chain/.
16. Summer Said and Benoit Faucon (April 2, 2020), "Extra Saudi Oil Sails to Nowhere," *Wall Street Journal,* B11.
17. Christopher Bjork (June 10, 2015), "Euro Buoys Zara's Parent: A 'Cracking Start' to 2015," *Wall Street Journal,* http://wsj.com.
18. Staff (March 2, 2021) "Four Modern Warehouse Trends to Watch in 2021," Easyship, https://www.easyship.com/blog/modern-warehouse-trends.
19. Jennifer Smith (March 25, 2021), "Robots Take on Warehouse Tasks," *Wall Street Journal,* B1.
20. Annie Gasparro, Jennifer Smith, and Jaewon Kang (March 24, 2020), "Grocers Revamp Inventory Strategies," *Wall Street Journal,* B4.
21. James F. Thompson, C. F. H. Bishop, and Patrick E. Brecht, "Air Transport of Perishable Products," Division of Agriculture and Natural Resources, University of California, Publication 2168 (Oakland: ANR Communication Services): 1.
22. (April 15, 2005), "Oil Pipelines: Small Price, Big Value," *In the Pipe*, http://www.enewsbuilder.net/aopl/e_article000391720.cfm.
23. Staff (December 4, 2020), "Petroleum Theft Continues to Plague Pemex as Pipelines Remain a Target," *Mexico News Daily,* https://mexiconewsdaily.com/news/petroleum-theft-continues-to-plague-pemex-as-pipelines-remain-a-target/.
24. Hernando Ramírez-Santos (September 17, 2021), "Goya Foods: Heading Towards Global Expansion," *Abasto,* https://abasto.com/en/news/goya-foods-heading-towards-global-expansion/.
25. Christopher Mims (April 25, 2020), "The Scramble for Delivery Robots Is On and Startups Can Barely Keep Up," *Wall Street Journal,* https://www.wsj.com/articles/the-scramble-for-delivery-robots-is-on-and-startups-can-barely-keep-up-11587787199.
26. Robbie Whelan (May 19, 2015), "Lockers: The Newest Trend in Logistics," *Wall Street Journal,* B5.
27. (August 25, 2015), "Most Manufacturers Are Using the Internet of Things to Improve Operations," *Supply Chain Quarterly,* http://www.supplychainquarterly.com.
28. (July 24, 2008), "Reverse Logistics: From Trash to Cash," *BusinessWeek*, http://www.businessweek.com/magazine/content/08_31/b4094046657076.htm.
29. Katie Deighton (September 23, 2020), "Returnable Fast-Food Cups Tested," *Wall Street Journal*, B3.
30. Stacie Sherman and Elise Young (November 27, 2017), "This Guy Makes Money Off Your Cigarette Butts and Flip-Flops," *Bloomberg*, https://www.bloomberg.com/news/features/2017-11-27/terracycle-makes-money-off-your-recycled-cigarette-butts-and-flip-flops.
31. Sources: Kaya Ismail (September 7, 2021), "How Blockchain Is Changing Advertising," *CMS Wire*, https://www.cmswire.com/digital-marketing/how-blockchain-is-changing-advertising/; Patience Haggin (May 1, 2019 "Online Ad Fraud Is Down, Study Finds," *Wall Street Journal,* https://www.wsj.com/articles/online-ad-fraud-is-down-study-findsor-at-least-its-harder-to-detect-11556715600; Lara O'Reilly (July 12, 2018), "Big Advertisers Embrace Blockchain to Root Out Digital Spending Waste," *Wall Street Journal,* https://www.wsj.com/articles/big-advertisers-embrace-blockchain-to-root-out-digital-spending-waste-1531396800; Steve Olenski (February 26, 2018), "Why Digital Advertising Needs A Blockchain Solution," *Forbes*, https://www.forbes.com/sites/steveolenski/2018/02/16/why-digital-advertising-needs-a-blockchain-solution/#24dfb76f1f71; (March 23, 2017), "List of Advertisers to Leave Google over YouTube Backlash," *Financial Times,* https://www.ft.com/content/5fbf4a36-0fc7-11e7-a88c-50ba212dce4d.

CHAPTER 10

Gathering and Using Information: Marketing Research and Market Intelligence

Once you have come up with a great idea for an offering, how will you know if people will want to buy it? If they *are* willing to buy it, what will they want to pay? Will they be willing to pay enough so that you can earn a profit from the product? Wouldn't it be great if you had a crystal ball that would give you the answers to these questions? After all, you don't want to quit your day job to develop a product that's going to be a flop.

In a sense, you do have such a crystal ball. It's called marketing research. **Marketing research** is the process of collecting, analyzing, and reporting marketing information that can be used to answer questions or solve problems to improve a company's bottom line. Marketing research includes a wide range of activities. (By contrast, **market research** is a narrower activity. It is the process of researching a specific market to determine its size and trends.)

marketing research

The process of collecting, analyzing, and reporting marketing information that can be used to improve a company's bottom line.

market research

The process of researching a specific market to determine its size and trends.

Although marketing research isn't foolproof, it can take some of the guesswork out of decision making. Back to your great product idea: what, for example, should you name your product? Naming a product might sound like a minor decision, but it's not. Just ask the bug spray maker OUT International. A number of years ago, the company came up with what it thought was a really cute name for bug spray that would appeal to children. The product was called "Hey! There's a Monster in My Room!" OUT International hoped children would go wild exterminating bugs in their rooms like the characters in the movie *Ghostbusters* do evil spirits. The problem was that the name of the product itself scared kids. They wanted nothing to do with it.[1]

Marketing research can help you:

- develop product ideas and designs
- determine if there is demand for your product so you know whether or not to produce it
- identify market segments for your product
- make pricing decisions
- evaluate packaging types
- evaluate in-store promotions
- measure the satisfaction of your customers
- measure the satisfaction of your channel partners
- evaluate the effectiveness of your website and social media campaigns
- test the effectiveness of ads and their placement
- make marketing channel decisions

Google Glasses were taken off the market because researchers hadn't nailed down the problems the glasses were actually solving for wearers (plus they looked pretty funky). But that hasn't dissuaded Ray-Ban, Facebook, Snapshot, and other companies from trying to develop more functional smart glasses that can be voice controlled.

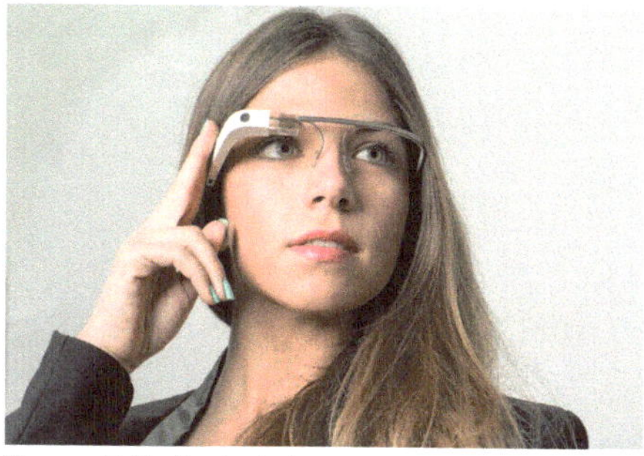

Source: © Shutterstock, Inc.

market intelligence

Information gathered on a regular, ongoing basis to enable a firm's decision makers to stay in touch with what's happening in the marketplace.

Closely related to marketing research is market intelligence, which is often referred to as *competitive intelligence*. Whereas marketing research involves solving a specific marketing problem at a specific point in time, **market intelligence** involves gathering information on a regular, ongoing basis about what's happening in the marketplace. For example, if you own a convenience store, part of your daily market intelligence gathering would include checking around to see what competing stores are charging for gasoline and to see what types of products are being sold and advertised by your competitors.

If you're a small business owner, and you're talking to your customers and suppliers about new product ideas, you're engaging in market intelligence. If you go so far as to survey your customers with a questionnaire about a new type of service you're considering offering, you are engaging in marketing research. In big companies, marketing departments are often responsible for gathering market intelligence. But they are by no means the only group to do so. We'll discuss more about who in an organization does which activities in a moment.

A little marketing research might have helped: In 1966, the Beatles' record company released hundreds of thousands of copies of this album. Do you think it was well received? No! Many people would not even pick the album up, let alone buy it. The company quickly realized it had made a mistake, recalled the albums, and pasted a different cover over the top. But some of the albums accidentally didn't get the paste-over. If you can find one, it could be worth thousands of dollars.

Source: Wikipedia, https://en.wikipedia.org/wiki/File:The_Beatles_-_Butcher_Cover.jpg

10.1 Marketing Information Systems and the Rise of Big Data

Learning Objectives

1. Explain what big data is and describe the components of a marketing information system.
2. Explain the situations in which marketing research should be used versus market intelligence.
3. Describe the limitations of market intelligence and its ethical boundaries.
4. Explain when marketing research should and should not be used.

A great deal of marketing information is being gathered all the time by companies as they engage in their daily operations. Any type of contact a company has with its customers is what marketing professionals call a **touchpoint**. When a purchase is made and recorded, this is a touchpoint, and the marketing information related to it should be captured. When a sales representative records the shipping preferences of a customer in a firm's customer relationship management (CRM) system, this is also marketing information that should be collected.

touchpoint

Any type of contact a company has with its customers.

That said, truly understanding customers involves not just collecting quantitative data (numbers) related to people but qualitative data, such as comments about what they think. When a firm gets a customer complaint on its website or one one of its social media sites, this too is information that should be put to use. All of this data, as well as other types of data from sources outside the firm, can be used to generate consumer insight.

However, CRM systems mostly collect a company's transactional information—lists of customers, what they bought, their shipping addresses, and so on. By contrast, in larger companies, qualitative data, such as the websites visited by customers, their email responses, audio recordings of customer-service interactions with them, and their social media comments, are likely to be stored in a company's customer data platform.[2] A **customer data platform (CDP)** is populated with information gathered both internally and externally to create a "profile" or fuller picture of an individual customer. The company can then make better use of the information to do marketing research, more accurately target customers, and conduct effective ad campaigns geared toward them, among other things. Today, the trend is toward CDP systems versus CRM systems.

customer data platform (CDP)

An IT system populated with information gathered both internally and externally to create a "profile" or fuller picture of an individual customer.

Because of the internet and other technology, companies are able to gather massive amounts of both qualitative and quantitative data, both internally and externally, like they have never been able to before. **Big data** is a buzzword people are using to refer to the massive amounts of online and offline data being gathered today. It consists of anonymous data about people who may or may not be customers, rather than a firm's customers. A company might store this information in a data management platform (DMP). A DMP is used to target groups of consumers automatically with online advertisements, a topic we'll discuss more in Chapter 12.

big data

The massive amounts of data being gathered by internet and computer systems today.

Like it or not, a huge amount of big data is for sale about people, including not only their purchases, marital statuses, and credit ratings, but what they eat, if they exercise, which brands they like and don't like, how they spend their time, and what they think about certain topics.

Increasingly, this information is being gathered by internet-connected devices that automatically upload data to the web. Your mobile phone and fitness tracker are examples. Do you want socks that pair with your Bluetooth device and provide you with information about the pace of your morning jog? What about yoga pants that offer you feedback on your poses? Both now exist.[3] They are part of the Internet of Things we discussed in Chapter 9.

Likewise, eventually you may own a "smart" refrigerator that uploads via cameras information about the groceries you do and do not have in your refrigerator. A mobile app may allow you to ask your refrigerator questions, such as "how much milk do I have?" and it will tell you. And recall the MagicBands Disney gives customers who visit its theme parks? The RFID-enabled wrist bands not only allow customers to electronically pay for the meals and souvenirs they buy at the parks, but also automatically upload information about the activities visitors like to do and how much time they spend doing them.

Do you want "big data" to know what's in your refrigerator? What if it can get you discounts on the food you buy?

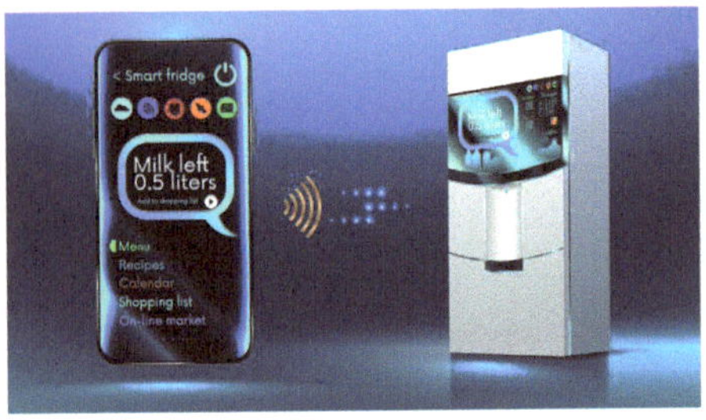

Source: © Shutterstock, Inc.

Does all of this data gathering sound sinister? When asked, people often say they don't like data being gathered on them, but the fact is that, to some extent, they do. Shoppers on Amazon like that the company knows what they ordered last, and the information is recorded in case they have a problem. Likewise, you probably appreciate that when you search the web for insurance or other products, many of the offers that show up are ones you're actually interested in, rather than ads for products you don't want. If you walk by your favorite restaurant and get a mobile ad that offers you a discount, that is also a good thing. And if your grocery store targets you with a coupon for milk, which it learned you need via big data? Great! You get the milk for less than you would otherwise.

To be sure, big data is giving firms valuable insight about people, how to engage them so they become customers, and ensure they remain loyal ones. However, as you probably know, it's become the subject of a lot of controversy, too. We will talk more about the privacy aspects of big data later in the chapter.

Ideally, a marketing information system should include not only transactional data, data about individual customers, and big data, it should include the following:

- a system for recording internally and externally generated data and reports
- analytics functions to help managers with their marketing decision making
- a system for collecting market intelligence on an ongoing basis
- a system for conducting and recording marketing research

Internally Generated Data and Reports

clickstream data

Data generated about the number of people who visit a website and its various pages, how much time they spend on each, what they "like" and don't like, and what they buy or don't buy.

As we explained, an organization generates and records a lot of information as part of its daily business operations, including sales and accounting data, and data on inventory levels, backorders, customer returns, and complaints. Firms are also constantly gathering information related to their websites, such as clickstream data. **Clickstream data** is data generated about the number of people who visit a website and its various pages, how much time they spend on each, what they "like" and don't like, and what they buy or don't buy. Companies also buy clickstream data from external sources, which we will talk about later in this chapter.

Companies use clickstream data in all kinds of ways. They use it to monitor the total number of visitors a site gets, to see which areas of the site people aren't visiting and explore why, and to automatically offer visitors products and promotions based on their browsing patterns. A number of years ago, Netflix awarded a million-dollar prize to a group of scientists to plow through web data generated by millions of Netflix users to develop algorithms to improve the company's predictions of what shows people will like to watch.

Today, Netflix uses a plethora of information to provide viewers with what they want. The information includes where viewers are located, what shows they click on or don't, the devices they use and when and where they use them, as well as comments from Facebook, Twitter, and other social media sites. The goal is to develop individualized viewing suggestions for Netflix's customers.

Netflix got so confident that it could predict what viewers want that it now successfully develops its own shows. *Stranger Things, House of Cards,* and *Bridgerton* are examples. Doing so was a move TV industry experts thought was very risky for Netflix but that has paid off for the company. Ninety-three percent of Netflix's original shows have gotten renewed for a second season. Contrast that with broadcast channels, which cancel after one season about two-thirds of the new shows they bet on.[4]

Most companies make a certain amount of internal data available to their employees, managers, vendors, and trusted partners. The trick is integrating all the information you collect so it can be used by as many people as possible in your organization to make good decisions. Unfortunately, in many organizations, information isn't always shared very well among departments. Even within departments, it can be a problem. It's not uncommon for one group in a marketing department to research a problem related to a brand, uncover certain findings that would be useful to other brand managers, but never communicate the findings.

Big companies with multiple products, business units, and databases purchased and installed in different places and at different times often have such vast amounts of information that they can't put it all on an intranet. Nor can all of the information be put it into a customer data platform (CDP) because the data may not be directly marketing related. For example, the information may be more closely related to areas such as the company's production, distribution, or accounting functions. Consequently, getting hold of the right information can be hard for a marketer to find. The information could be right under your nose and you might not know it.

data warehousing

A location for combining and storing data.

dashboards

A display of information used by managers to make decisions easier; often dynamic in the sense that a manager can click on the display to probe deeper into the numbers and get more detail.

Mike Ray, BNSF Railway

Source: Photo courtesy of Amy Ray

Mike Ray is an expert at data mining—hunting down information for decision makers at BNSF Railway. (And no, he doesn't wear a hard hat to mine the data. He does need to wear one while he is in a BNSF railyard though.) Ray works for BNSF Railway and is one of BNSF's "go-to" employees when it comes to gathering marketing data. Ray, a manager with BNSF's Marketing and Economic Development group, knows how to access different databases and write computer programs to extract the right information from the right places at BNSF, a process known as data mining.

Combining data into one location is called **data warehousing**, and it makes Ray's analysis easier. He then captures the information and displays it in **dashboards**, computer screens that make the data easily understood so that managers can detect marketing trends. A dashboard might display a piece of information, such as the number of railcars of freight sold in West Virginia. A marketing manager can then click on the number and get more detail about whether a particular marketing campaign had an effect on the freight volumes.

Analytics and Artificial Intelligence (AI)

analytics software

Software that utilizes a firm's data, regression models, linear programming, and other statistical methods to help managers who are not computer experts make decisions.

Data is no good unless you have a way to analyze it. **Analytics software** and apps allows managers who are not computer experts to gather the information, including information not generated by regular reports, and make sense of it. The software incorporates algorithms, regression models, forecasting, linear programming, simulations, and other statistical methods. Oracle Corporation's Crystal Ball is one brand of analytical software.

Cabela's—a camping, hunting, fishing, and hiking retailer—has managed to refine its marketing efforts considerably using analytics software developed by the software maker SAS. The software helps Cabela analyze sales transactions, market research, and demographic data associated with its large database of customers. Cabela's then combines the information with web browsing data to gain a better understanding of its customers' marketing channel preferences and to make other marketing decisions.

Cabela's' analytics software has helped the outdoor sporting retailer reach the right customers via the right marketing channels.

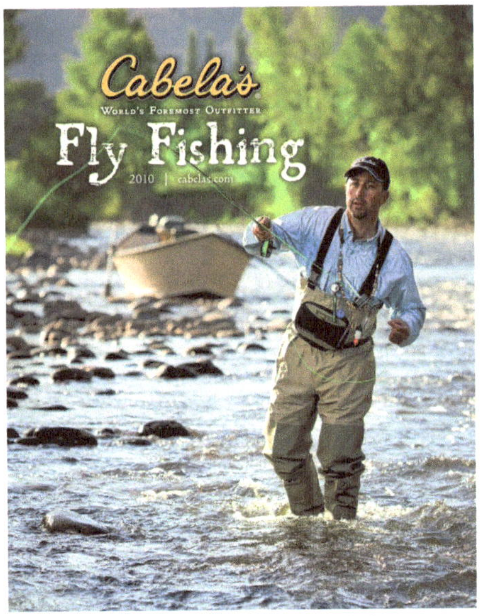

Source: © Cabela's Inc., used with permission.

Being able to answer "what if" types of questions is a burgeoning area of marketing called predictive analytics. **Predictive analytics** is an advanced branch of analytics that utilizes sophisticated techniques such as data mining, statistics, experiments, and machine learning to detect patterns and develop models used to predict future outcomes. For example, "If we spend ten percent more of our advertising on mobile-phone ads instead of Facebook ads, what effect will it have on sales?"

The retailer Target uses predictive analytics to try to understand what its individual customers want and influence their buying habits. Target has actually used predictive analytics to successfully determine whether its customers are pregnant, often before they have told their families they are. Why would Target care if someone is pregnant? Because people with new babies on the way spend a lot of money buying diapers, car seats, baby clothes, and many other items for babies. And how does Target know the women are pregnant? By noting whether they have purchased products such as unscented lotions, vitamins with certain ingredients, washcloths, and cotton balls.[5] Target is then able to capture these people's business by offering them deals on baby products before its competitors do.

Companies also increasingly hire outside firms to analyze their data for them. For example, in the past, clothing retailers have largely relied on gut instinct to figure out what, where, and how products would sell. "You'd put your ideas in play and then wait and see if you were right," says Brian Beitler, the chief marketing officer for Qurate Retail Group. If the products didn't sell, they would then have to be marked down drastically. Now many retailers, including Lane Bryant, the GAP, and other companies, rely on the information generated by companies such as Applied Predictive Technologies (APT) rather than rely on professional buyers who think certain fashions are "hot" (or not). The statisticians at APT crunch the data collected from stores to determine what types of products should be sold in different parts of the country, where products should best be displayed in stores, and how much of a discount products should or should not be sold at.

predictive analytics

An advanced branch of analytics that utilizes sophisticated techniques such as data mining, statistics, experiments, and machine learning, to detect patterns and develop models used to predict future outcomes.

Although statistics have long been used by retailers in the past, they are collecting so much more data now from their loyalty programs, big data, and other sources, that it's often more efficient to have outside experts who use cutting-edge techniques to analyze the data and provide recommendations to managers based on it.[6] Not all companies rely on outside firms to crunch their numbers, though. Kroger, the nation's leading supermarket company, has elaborate labs it uses to conduct much of its own research, and is recruiting data scientists from around the world to help with the task. For example, Kroger uses more than 850 algorithms to personalize the coupons it sends to 12 million of its customers. Have they gone a diet? Had children? Retired? Kroger offers them the right coupons, and customers redeem them in far greater numbers than the customers of other companies. "We know our customers better than anyone," says one Kroger executive.[7]

The online home-goods seller Wayfair has found that by utilizing AI and algorithms, the time it takes its customers to find what they need and add the items to their carts has been cut in half.

Source: © Shutterstock, Inc.

Keep in mind that companies don't just outsource data crunching. Companies both large and small are able to outsource any and all of the activities we discuss in this chapter to outside marketing research firms—and they do. And often they can get the information back quickly, in part thanks to big data, which has sped up the marketing-research process tremendously. Zappi and Dynata are two marketing research companies that promise to get decision makers answers to their marketing questions in a matter of hours at a low cost.

Artificial intelligence also has the potential to speed up marketing-research processes. **Artificial intelligence (AI)** is the ability of machines and computers to do things commonly associated with intelligent beings, such as the ability to reason, discover meaning, generalize, or learn from past experiences. For example, if you spell your friend's name wrong in a text, and your phone corrects it based on the way you have spelled it in the past, you are seeing AI at work. Digital assistants on mobile phones such as Siri (on iPhones) and Cortana (on Windows phones) and Alexa, Amazon's virtual assistant, also illustrate how AI is being used.

artificial intelligence (AI)

The ability of machines and computers to do things commonly associated with intelligent beings, such as the ability to reason, discover meaning, generalize, or learn from past experience.

In terms of marketing research, AI is proving to be enormously helpful. Companies are awash with big data; what they need is some way to make better sense of it. AI can quickly analyze video, audio, and text messages gathered and formulate follow-up questions for consumers who are being interviewed, among other tasks. The information is allowing companies to figure out which customers are most receptive to their sales and marketing efforts and which ones aren't and why. Another crucial area is the "search" function on e-commerce sites. AI is being used in conjunction with computer algorithms to help potential customers find what they are looking for, even if they aren't quite sure what it is they want initially.[8]

Market Intelligence

A good internal reporting system can tell a manager what happened inside her firm. But what about what's going on *outside* the firm? What is the business environment like? Are credit-lending terms loose or tight, and how will they affect what you and your customers are or are not able to buy? How will rising fuel prices and alternate energy sources affect your firm and your products? Do changes like these present business obstacles or opportunities? Moreover, what are your competitors up to? Statistics on a spreadsheet cannot tell you this. Consequently, not gathering market intelligence leaves a company vulnerable.

Gathering market intelligence involves a number of activities, including scanning the internet, publications, and economic data produced by the government to find out about trends and what the competition is doing. In big companies, personnel in a firm's marketing department are primarily responsible for their firm's market intelligence and making sure it gets conveyed to decision makers. Let's now examine some of the sources of information you can look at to gather market intelligence.

Search Engines, Corporate Websites, and Social Media

An obvious way to gain market intelligence is by examining your competitors' websites, following them on their social-media sites, and doing basic internet searches. Suppose you run a small business. If you want to find out what the press is writing about your company, your competitors, or any other topic you're interested in, you can sign up to receive free alerts via a service such as Google Alerts.

Suppose you want to monitor what people are saying about you or your company on blogs, the comment areas of websites, and social networks such as Facebook and Twitter. You can do that by searching each site or by utilizing a social-media monitoring tool such as SocialMention or Crimson Hexagon (now Brandwatch). All the good (and bad) things people have remarked about the company or topic turn up. Doing so is also a great way to uncover your competitors' shortcomings.

Social Media Listening

This video shows how the guitar-maker Fender used a social-media listening tool to reach female guitar players and better target them.

View in the online reader

sentiment analysis

A method of examining content in blogs, tweets, and other online media such as Facebook posts to determine what people are thinking at any given time.

Social-media monitoring firms such as these can also provide your company with a sentiment analysis. A **sentiment analysis** is a method of examining the content in blogs, tweets, and other online media (other than news media) such as Facebook posts and making sense of it. For example, does the word "suck" often appear in conjunction with your brands or company? If so, you likely have a problem.

A sentiment analysis is often done to determine how the market is reacting to new products that have been launched. The Centers for Disease Control & Prevention (CDC) has used sentiment analysis to track the progress of viruses; as people post or tweet how sick they are, the CDC can determine where the the viruses are increasing or decreasing. AI is also being used for sentiment analysis purposes. IBM's Watson Sentiment Analysis product is one such tool.

Structured data is concrete information that fits neatly into a spreadsheet—information such as what a consumer spent, what product(s) the person purchased, at what store, and so on. In other words, structured data is information that is easily quantifiable, can be manipulated, and is reportable. In contrast, *unstructured data*, such as information that's gleaned from people's comments and photos on the web, Facebook, and Twitter, is not as easily analyzed and reported. Nonetheless, companies that specialize in collecting big data are finding better and better ways to gather and make sense of unstructured data.

Publications

The Economist, *Wall Street Journal*, *Forbes*, *Fortune*, the *McKinsey* reports, the *Financial Times* and their associated websites are good general business publications to read to learn about general business trends. Other publications provide information about marketplace trends and activities in specific industries. *Consumer Goods Technology* provides consumer information packaged-goods firms want to know. *Progressive Grocer* provides information about issues important to grocery stores. *InformationWeek* provides information relevant to people and businesses working in the area of technology. *World Trade* provides information about issues relevant to organizations shipping and receiving goods from other countries. As a marketing professional, you don't want to overlook publications specific to your industry.

Trade Shows and Associations

Trade shows are another way companies learn about what their competitors are doing. (If you are a marketing professional working a trade show for your company, you will want to visit all of your competitors' booths and see what they have to offer relative to what your company has to offer.) And, of course, every field has a trade association that collects and disseminates information about trends, breakthroughs, new technology, new processes, and challenges in that particular industry. The American Marketing Association, Food Marketing Institute, Outdoor Industry Association, Semiconductor Industry Association, Trade Promotion Management Association, and Travel Industry Association provide their member companies with a wealth of information and often deliver daily news updates on industry happenings.

Salespeople

A company's salespeople provide a vital source of market intelligence. Suppose one of your custom, high-dollar products (say, an expensive piece of equipment) is selling poorly. Will you initially look to newspapers and magazines to figure out why? Will you consult a trade association? Probably not. You will first want to talk to your firm's salespeople to get their "take" on the problem. Salespeople are the eyes and ears of their organizations. Perhaps more than anyone else, salespeople know how products are faring in the marketplace, what the competition is doing, and what customers are looking for.

Whether it's a CRM or a CDP, a system for recording this information is crucial. Some companies circulate lists so their employees have a better idea of the market intelligence they might be looking for. Textbook publishers are an example. They let their sales representatives know the types of books they want to publish and encourage their representatives to look for good potential textbook authors among the professors to whom they sell.

Suppliers and Industry Experts

Your suppliers can provide you with a wealth of information. Good suppliers know which companies are moving a lot of inventory, and oftentimes they have an idea why. In many instances they will tell you, if the information you're looking for is general enough so they don't have to divulge any information that's confidential or that would be unethical to reveal—which is an issue we'll talk more about later in the book. Befriending an expert in your industry, along with business journalists and writers and influential bloggers can be helpful, too. Often these people are "in the know" because they get invited to review products.

Customers

Lastly, when it comes to market intelligence don't neglect observing how customers are behaving. They can provide many clues, some of which you will be challenged to respond to. For example, as we mentioned in Chapter 3, during the economic downturn that accompanied the COVID-19 pandemic, many wholesalers and retailers noticed consumers began buying smaller amounts of goods—just what they needed to get by during the week. Seeing this trend, and realizing that they couldn't pass along higher costs to customers, a number of consumer-goods manufacturers "shrank" their products slightly rather than raise prices. You perhaps noticed that some of the products you buy got smaller—but not cheaper.

Marketing Research

Marketing research is what a company has to resort to if it can't answer a question by using any of the types of information we have discussed so far—market intelligence, internal company data, big data, analytics, and so forth. As we have explained, marketing research has generally been used in the past to answer specific questions. The name you should give your new product is an example. Unless your company has previously done some specific research on product names—what consumers think of them, good or bad—you're probably not going to find the answer to that question in your internal company data.

agile marketing

Using data and analytics to continuously identify promising opportunities or solutions and conduct tests quickly.

Although internal data and big data are often generated on a regular basis, in the past, marketing research was often not ongoing but done on an as-needed or project basis. If an organization decided that it needed to conduct marketing research, it would either conduct marketing research itself or hire a marketing research firm to do it. Today, however, *agile marketing* is becoming more the norm. **Agile marketing** is the practice of using data and analytics to continuously identify promising opportunities or solutions and conduct market tests quickly. A high-functioning agile marketing organization can run hundreds of campaigns simultaneously and test multiple new ideas every week.[9] Why is this important? Because often the company that can pivot and be the "first to market" with a product wins.

Nonetheless, marketing research can be expensive. You therefore have to weigh the costs of the research against the benefits. What questions will the research answer, and will knowing the answers result in the firm earning or saving more money than the research costs?

Marketing research can also take time. If a quick decision is needed to solve a pressing problem, it might not be possible to do the research. Lastly, sometimes the answer to the problem is obvious, so there is no point in conducting the research. For example, if one of your competitors comes up with a new offering and consumers are clamoring to get it, you certainly don't need to undertake a research study to see if such a product would survive in the marketplace.

Alex J. Caffarini, the founder of Analysights, a marketing analytics consulting firm, believes there are a number of other reasons companies mistakenly do marketing research. Caffarini's explanations (shown in parentheses) about why a company's executives sometimes make bad decisions are somewhat humorous. Read through them:

- *"We've always done this research."* (The research has taken on a life of its own; this particular project has continued for years and nobody has questioned whether it was still relevant.)
- *"Everyone's doing this research."* (The company's competitors are doing it, so managers and marketing professionals are afraid they will lose a competitive advantage if their firm does not; yet no one asks what value the research is creating.)
- *"The findings are nice to know."* (Great—spend a lot of money to create a wealth of useless information. If the information is nice to know, but you can't do anything with it, you're wasting money.)

- *"If our strategy fails, having done the research will show that we made our best educated guess."* (They're covering their butts. If things go wrong, they can blame the findings, or the researcher.)
- *"We need to study the problem thoroughly before we decide on a course of action."* (They're afraid of making a tough decision. Conducting marketing research is a good way to delay the inevitable. In the meantime, the problem gets bigger, or the window of opportunity closes.)
- *"The research will show that our latest ad campaign was effective."* (They're using marketing research to justify past decisions. Rarely should marketing research be done after the fact.)[10]

Is Marketing Research Always Correct?

To be sure, marketing research can help companies avoid making mistakes. Take Tim Hortons, a popular coffee chain in Canada that has been expanding in the United States and internationally. Hortons tried opening some drive-through kiosks in Ireland, but the service was a flop. Why? Because cars in Ireland don't have cup holders. Would marketing research have helped? Probably. So would a little bit of market intelligence. It would have been easy for an observer to see that trying to drive a car and hold a cup of hot coffee at the same time is difficult.

That said, we don't want to leave you with the idea that marketing research is infallible. As we indicated at the beginning of the chapter, the process isn't foolproof. In fact, marketing research efforts have rejected a lot of good ideas. The idea for telephone answering machines was initially rejected following marketing research. So was the hit sitcom *Seinfeld*, which some TV critics consider to be the best sitcom of all time. Even big companies, like Coca-Cola, have made marketing research mistakes that have led to huge flops. In the next section, we'll discuss the steps related to conducting marketing research. As you will learn, many things can go wrong along the way that can affect the results of research and the conclusions drawn from it.

Key Takeaway

- Many marketing problems and opportunities can be solved by gathering information from a company's daily operations and analyzing it. Analytics software and applications allow managers who are not computer experts to gather this information, including information not generated by regular reports, make sense of it, and base their decisions on it. Companies also increasingly hire outside firms to analyze their data for them. Predictive analytics is an advanced branch of analytics that utilizes sophisticated techniques to predict future outcomes. Agile marketing involves using data and analytics to continuously identify promising opportunities or solutions and conduct tests quickly. Market intelligence involves gathering information on a regular, ongoing basis to stay in touch with what's happening in the marketplace. Marketing research is what a company has to resort to if it can't answer a question by using market intelligence, internal company data, or analytical software. Marketing research is not infallible, however.

Review Questions

1. Describe the components of a marketing information system and how it can be used in conjunction with big data, predictive analytics, and artificial intelligence.
2. What activities are part of market intelligence gathering?
3. How does the time frame for conducting marketing intelligence differ from the time frame in which marketing research data is gathered?

10.2 Steps in the Marketing Research Process

Learning Objective

1. Describe the basic steps in the marketing research process and the purpose of each step.

The basic steps used to conduct marketing research are shown in Figure 10.1. Next, we discuss each step.

FIGURE 10.1 Steps in the Marketing Research Process

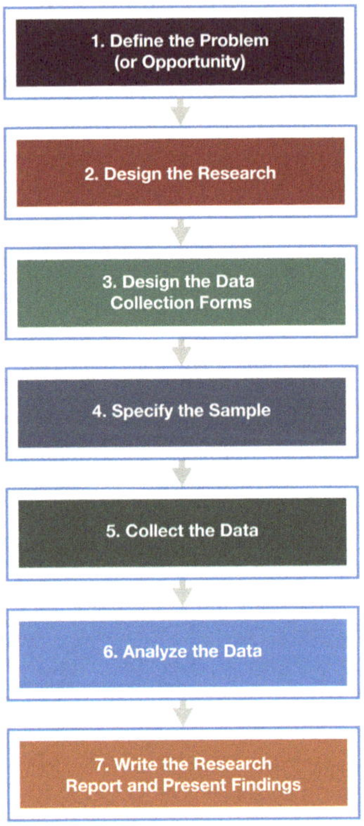

Step 1: Define the Problem (or Opportunity)

There's a saying in marketing research that a problem half defined is a problem half solved. Defining the "problem" of the research sounds simple, doesn't it? Suppose your product is tutoring other students. You have been tutoring for a while, and people have begun to realize you're darned good at it. Then suddenly your business drops off. Or it explodes, and you can't cope with the number of students you're being asked to help. If the business has exploded, should you try to expand your services? Perhaps you should subcontract with some other people who are good at tutoring. You would refer students to be tutored, and the tutors would give you a cut of their pay for each student you referred.

Both of these scenarios—either too little business or too much — would be a problem for you, wouldn't they? They are problems insofar as they cause you headaches. But are they really *the* problem? Or are they the symptoms of something bigger? For example, maybe your business has dropped off because your school is experiencing financial trouble and has lowered the number of scholarships given to incoming freshmen. Consequently, there are fewer total students on campus who need your services.

Conversely, if you're swamped with people who want you to tutor them, perhaps your school admitted more students than usual, so there are a greater number of them who need your services. Alternately, perhaps you ran an ad in your school's online college newsletter, and that led to the influx of students wanting you to tutor them.

Businesses are in the same boat you are as a tutor. They take a look at symptoms and try to drill down to the potential causes. If you approach a marketing research company with either scenario—either too much or too little business—the firm will seek more information from you such as the following:

- In what semester(s) did your tutoring revenues fall (or rise)?
- In what subject areas did your tutoring revenues fall (or rise)?
- In what sales channels did revenues fall (or rise): Were there fewer (or more) referrals from professors or other students? Did the ad you ran result in fewer (or more) referrals this month than in the past months?
- Among what demographic groups did your revenues fall (or rise)—women or men, people with certain majors, or first-, second-, third-, or fourth-year students?

The key is to look at all potential causes so as to narrow the parameters of the study to the information you actually need to make a good decision about how to fix your business if revenues have dropped or whether or not to expand it if your revenues have increased.

The next task for the researcher is to put into writing the research objective. The **research objective** is the goal(s) the research is supposed to accomplish. The marketing research objective for your tutoring business might read as follows:

research objective

The goal(s) marketing research is supposed to accomplish.

To survey college professors who teach 100- and 200-level math courses to determine why the number of students referred for tutoring dropped in the second semester.

This is admittedly a simple example designed to help you understand the basic concept. If you take a marketing research course, you will learn that research objectives get a lot more complicated than this. The following is an example:

"To gather information from a sample representative of the U.S. population among those who are very likely to purchase an automobile within the next six months, which assesses preferences (measured on a 1–5 scale ranging from 'very likely to buy' to 'not likely at all to buy') for the diesel model at three different price levels. Such data would serve as input into a forecasting model that would forecast unit sales, by geographic regions of the country, for each combination of the model's different prices and fuel configurations."[11]

Now do you understand why defining the problem is complicated and half the battle? Many a marketing research effort was doomed from the start because the problem was improperly defined. Coke's ill-fated decision to change the formula of Coca-Cola in 1985 is a classic case. Coke spent four years researching "the problem": Pepsi had been creeping up on Coke in terms of market share over the years as well as running a successful promotional campaign called the "Pepsi Challenge." The Pepsi Challenge encouraged consumers to do a blind taste test to see if they agreed that Pepsi was better.

In fact, people seemed to like the taste of Pepsi better in blind taste tests. So, the formula for Coke was changed. But the outcry among the public about the change was so great that the new-Coke formula didn't last long—a matter of months—before the old formula was reinstated. Some marketing experts believe Coke incorrectly defined the problem as "How can we beat Pepsi in taste tests?" instead of, "How can we gain market share against Pepsi?"[12]

Change Can Be Humorous

This humorous video shows how Pepsi tried to capitalize on the New Coke blunder.

View in the online reader

Step 2: Design the Research

research design

An outline that specifies the research data to be gathered, from whom, how, and when the data will be analyzed once it has been obtained.

primary data

Data collected using hands-on tools such as interviews or surveys to answer a question for a specific research project.

secondary data

Data already collected by your firm or another organization for purposes other than the marketing research project at hand.

The next step in the marketing research process is to do a research design. The **research design** is your "plan of attack." It outlines what data you are going to gather and from whom, how, and when you will collect the data, and how you will analyze it once it's been obtained. Let's look at the data you're going to gather first.

There are two basic types of data you can gather. The first is primary data. **Primary data** is information you collect yourself, using hands-on tools such as interviews, surveys, or experiments specifically for the research project you're conducting. **Secondary data** is data that has already been collected by someone else, or data you have already collected for another purpose. Collecting primary data is more time consuming, work intensive, and expensive than collecting secondary data. Consequently, you should always try to collect secondary data first to solve your research problem, if you can. A great deal of research on a wide variety of topics already exists. If this research contains the answer to your question, there is no need for you to replicate it. Why reinvent the wheel?

Sources of Secondary Data

Your company's internal records are a source of secondary data. So are any data you collect as part of your marketing intelligence gathering efforts. Government agencies are secondary sources as well because they collect and report information on demographics, economic and employment data, health information, and balance-of-trade statistics, among a lot of other information. The U.S. Census Bureau collects census data every ten years to gather information about who lives where. Basic demographic information about the sexes, ages, races, and types of housing in which people live in each U.S. state, metropolitan area, and rural area is gathered so that population shifts can be tracked for various purposes. The main purpose is to determine the number of legislators each state should have in the U.S. House of Representatives. For the U.S. government, this is primary data. For marketing managers, it is an important source of secondary data. The World Bank and the United Nations are two international organizations that collect a great deal of information. Their websites contain many free research studies and data related to global markets.

Your firm can also purchase syndicated research. **Syndicated research** is primary data marketing research firms collect on a regular basis and sell to other companies that may have an interest in it. J.D. Power is a provider of syndicated research. The company conducts independent, unbiased surveys of customer satisfaction, product quality, and buyer behavior for various industries. The company is best known for its research in the automobile sector.

syndicated research

Primary data marketing research firms collect on a regular basis and sell to other companies.

One of the best-known sellers of syndicated research is Nielsen, which produces, among other things, the Nielsen ratings. The Nielsen ratings measure the size of TV, streaming video, and video-gaming audiences. A competitor of Nielsen is IRI (Information Resources, Inc.). IRI also sells **scanner-based research**. Scanner-based research is information collected by scanners at checkout stands in stores. Each week IRI collects information on the millions of purchases made at stores. These companies then compile the information and sell it to firms in various industries that subscribe to their services.

scanner-based research

Information collected by scanners at checkout stands in stores.

By contrast, MarketResearch.com is an example of a marketing research aggregator. A **marketing research aggregator** is a marketing research company that doesn't conduct its own research and sell it. Instead, it buys research reports from other marketing research companies and then sells those reports in their entirety or in pieces to other firms. MarketResearch's website features a huge number of studies in every category imaginable that you can buy for relatively small amounts of money.

marketing research aggregator

A marketing research company that doesn't conduct its own research but instead buys it from other marketing research companies and then sells the reports in their entirety or in pieces to other firms.

Market research aggregators buy research reports from other marketing research companies and then resell them in part or in whole to other companies so they don't have to gather primary data.

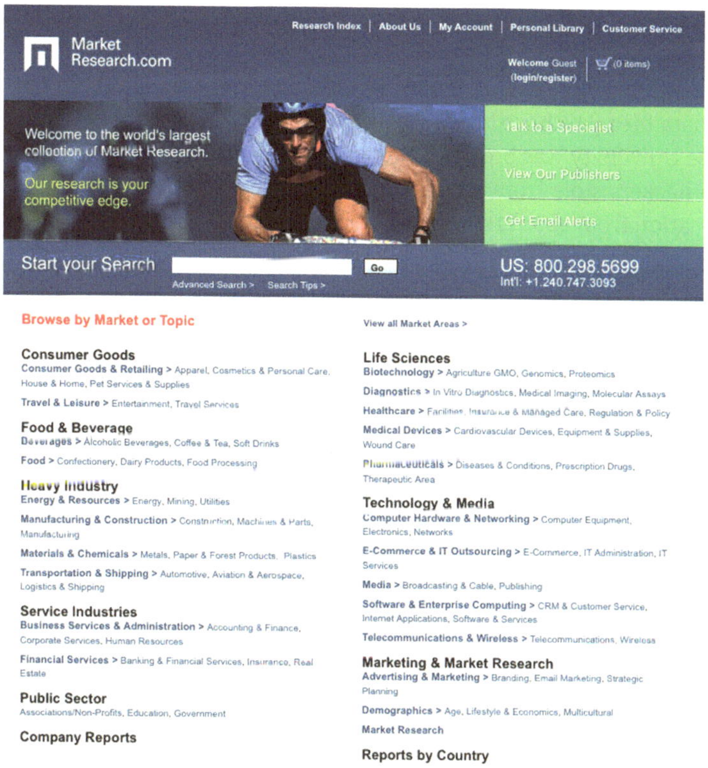

Source: http://www.marketresearch.com

data brokers

Companies that gather both online and offline information about consumers, create detailed profiles of them, and sell them to other firms.

Data brokers gather both online and offline secondary data about consumers, create detailed profiles of them, and then sell the information to other firms. The information can come from many sources: public records, cookies (files websites place on a person's computer to remember the person's preferences), information sold to them by credit card companies, Facebook and Google, location information based on our mobile phone apps, loyalty program information they purchase from retailers, and even information gleaned from obituaries in newspapers. It's not uncommon for a data broker to collect a thousand pieces of information on a single individual. Axicom, CoreLogic, and Epsilon are some of the largest data broker companies.

Data Brokers

Watch this short video to get a better idea about the type of information data brokers gather on you, where they get it, and what they do with it.

View in the online reader

Consumers are concerned about the information gathered about them though. One reason why is because data breaches have become common. In 2021, information about nearly 10,000 students at Syracuse University was breached after a college employee's email password was stolen.[13] A few years ago hackers stole from the credit-reporting agency Equifax social security numbers and other information from about 146 million Americans.

location-based ads

Ads targeted toward consumers based on their locations, which are identified by the mobile devices they use.

As a result, Verizon and Sprint are among the companies that have clamped down on the data they provide to data brokers, including information about where mobile phone users are located at any given moment. This may make it harder for firms to send you **location-based ads.**

Social media presents a problem as well. During the 2016 election between Hillary Rodham Clinton and Donald Trump, a company worked around Facebook's privacy controls to get personal data on Facebook users and their friends. The company then targeted people with quizzes that covertly indicated their voting preferences and aimed campaign ads at them. And by taking the quizzes, the Facebook users inadvertently allowed the company to get personal data on all of their friends. More recently, after facing backlash and a $650 million legal settlement that it had violated a state law, Facebook's parent company, Meta, decided to delete one billion facial profiles it had had collected from users who had opted into its facial recognition program.[14]

chief privacy officer (CPO)

A top-level executive responsible for developing policies to ensure his or her firm is collecting information legally and accurately, and that it's not being misused.

To avoid backlash from consumers, a number of data brokers as well as other companies now have chief privacy officers. A **chief privacy officer (CPO)** is a top-level executive responsible for developing policies to ensure his or her firm is collecting information legally, collecting information accurately, and not misusing that information.

Table 10.1 recaps the sources of primary data versus secondary data we've discussed in this chapter.

TABLE 10.1 Examples of Primary Data Sources versus Secondary Data Sources

Primary Data Sources	Secondary Data Sources
Interviews	Census data
Surveys	Websites
Experiments	Publications
Field observations	Trade associations
	Syndicated research
	Aggregated research
	Data brokers

Gauging the Quality of Secondary Data

When you are gathering secondary information, it's always good to be a little skeptical of it. Sometimes studies are commissioned to produce the result a client wants to hear—or wants the public to hear. For example, throughout much of the twentieth century, numerous studies found that smoking was good for people's health. The problem was that the studies were commissioned by the tobacco industry.

Web research can also pose certain hazards. Suppose you are researching competing products online. There are many biased sites that try to mislead people with data that is favorable to the products they are trying to sell. Unscrupulous sellers also create bogus ratings for products and give them "likes" on Facebook and other social media sites. Or they outsource the task to *click farms*. Click farms hire low-wage workers, often in other countries, to create fake ratings and generate likes and followers on social media sites.

And as you have learned, advertisers try to use the information people post on social media sites. The problem is that information can be hard to interpret. Suppose someone posts a photo without labeling what it is? How can advertisers use the information? To try to fill in the gaps, Facebook's employees try to label the posts so they make more sense to advertisers.[15] But there is some guesswork involved in the process. Another problem is that what people on social media *say* they do or like often doesn't jive with what they actually say or do offline.[16]

Gauging the Credibility of Secondary Data: Questions to Ask

- Who gathered this information?
- For what purpose?
- What does the person or organization that gathered the information have to gain by doing so?
- Was the information gathered and reported in a systematic manner?
- Is the source of the information accepted as an authority by other experts in the field?
- Does the information provide objective evidence to support the position presented?

Types of Research Design

Now let's look specifically at the types of research designs that are utilized. By understanding different types of research designs, a researcher can solve a client's problems more quickly and efficiently without jumping through more hoops than necessary. Research designs fall into one of the following three categories:

1. Exploratory research design
2. Descriptive research design
3. Causal research design (experiments)

exploratory research design

A less-structured type of research design used to initially investigate a marketing research project that hasn't yet been defined well enough for an in-depth study to be conducted.

qualitative research

Any form of research that results in data that is not quantitative and often seeks to answer questions such as why consumers do something, rather than how much or how often they do it.

An **exploratory research design** is useful when you are initially investigating a problem but you haven't defined it well enough to do an in-depth study of it. Perhaps via your regular market intelligence, you have spotted what appears to be a new opportunity in the marketplace. You would then do exploratory research to investigate it further and "get your feet wet," as the saying goes. Exploratory research is less structured than other types of research, and secondary data is often utilized.

One form of exploratory research is qualitative research. **Qualitative research** is any form of research that includes gathering data that is not quantitative. Doing so often involves exploring questions such as *why* as much as *what* or *how much*. Depth interviews and focus group interviews, discussed next, are examples of qualitative research.

A depth interview—engaging in detailed, one-on-one, question-and-answer sessions with potential buyers—is an exploratory research technique. However, unlike surveys, the people being interviewed aren't asked a series of standard questions. Instead, the interviewer is armed with some general topics and asks questions that are open ended, meaning that they allow an interviewee to elaborate. "How did you feel about the product after you purchased it?" is an example of a question that might be asked in a depth interview.

A depth interview also allows a researcher to ask logical follow-up questions such as, "Can you tell me what you mean when you say you felt uncomfortable using the service?" or "Can you give me some examples?" to help dig further and shed additional light on the research problem. Depth interviews can be conducted in person, via phone, or a platform such as Zoom. The interviewers either takes notes or record the interviews. Depth interviews are, however, expensive to conduct. Sometimes they are reserved for interviews with executives or industry experts.

Focus groups and case studies are often utilized for exploratory research as well. A focus group is a group of potential buyers who are brought together to discuss a marketing research topic with one another. A moderator is used to focus the discussion, the sessions are recorded, and the main points of consensus are later summarized by the market researcher. Textbook publishers often gather groups of professors at educational conferences to participate in focus groups, but they can also be conducted online.

The Basic Steps of Conducting a Focus Group

1. Establish the objectives of the focus group. What is its purpose?
2. Identify the people who will participate in the focus group. What makes them qualified to participate? How many of them will you need, and what they will be paid?
3. Obtain contact information for the participants, and send out invitations.
4. Develop a list of questions.
5. Choose a facilitator.
6. Choose a location or technology in which to hold the focus group and how it will be recorded.
7. Conduct the focus group. If the focus group is not conducted electronically, provide name tags for the participants, pens and notepads, any materials the participants need to see, and refreshments. Record participants' responses.
8. Summarize the notes from the focus group and write a report for management.

A **case study** looks at how another company solved the problem that's being researched. Sometimes multiple cases, or companies, are used in a study. Case studies have a mixed reputation though. Some researchers believe it's hard to generalize, or apply, the results of a case study to other companies. Nonetheless, collecting information about companies that encountered the same problems your firm is facing can give you a certain amount of insight about what direction you should take.

case study

A study that looks at how another company, or companies, solved a problem being researched.

Two other types of qualitative data used for exploratory research are ethnographies and projective techniques. In an **ethnography**, researchers interview, observe, and often record people while they work, live, shop, and play. Campbell's Soup Company has used ethnography techniques to figure out how to make its products more attractive to millennials.[17] Likewise, The Walt Disney Company has used ethnographers to uncover what boys aged six to fourteen like. It's an attractive market segment for Disney but one the company has struggled with. The ethnographers visit the homes of boys, observe the things they have in their rooms to get a sense of their hobbies, and accompany them and their mothers when they shop to see where they go, what the boys are interested in, and what they ultimately buy.[18]

ethnography

A type of study whereby marketing researchers interview, observe, and often videotape people while they work, live, shop, and play.

Digital ethnographies are also becoming more common. A **digital ethnography** is an ethnography conducted by following an online community with the members' permission. There are pros and cons to the approach: One pro is that doing so is easier, less expensive, and less intrusive than following people around physically. Again, one con is that it's hard to replace the in-depth insights that can be obtained by *seeing* how people actually behave rather than how they *say* they behave online.[19]

digital ethnograph

An ethnography that is conducted by following an online community with the members' permission.

Projective techniques are used to reveal information research respondents might not share by being asked directly. Asking a person to complete sentences such as the following is one technique:

People who buy Louis Vuitton handbags __________.

(Will they reply with "are cool," "are affluent," or "are snobs," for example?)

KFC's grilled chicken is ______.

projective techniques

An exploratory research technique used to reveal information research respondents might not reveal by being asked directly.

Or, the person might be asked to finish a story that presents a certain scenario. Word associations are also used to discern people's underlying attitudes toward goods and services. Using a word-association technique, a market researcher asks a person to say or write the first word that comes to his or her mind in response to another word. If the initial word is "fast food," what word does the person associate with it? Is it "McDonald's?" If many people reply that way, and you're conducting research for Burger King, that could indicate Burger King has a problem.

Completing cartoons is yet another type of projective technique. It's similar to asking a person to finish a sentence or story, only with the pictures. People are asked to look at a cartoon such as the one shown in Figure 10.2. One of the characters in the picture will have made a statement, and the person is asked to fill in the empty cartoon "bubble" with how they think the second character will respond.

FIGURE 10.2 Example of a Cartoon-Completion Projective Technique

Source: © Shutterstock, Inc.

In some cases, your research might end with exploratory research. Perhaps you have discovered your organization lacks the resources needed to produce the product your company is considering selling. In other cases, you might decide you need more in-depth, quantitative research, such as descriptive research or causal research, which are discussed next. Most marketing research professionals advise using both types of research. On the one hand, the qualitative-type research used in exploratory research is often considered too "lightweight." (The top-rated TV sitcom *Seinfeld*, which aired on NBC from 1989–1998, is one of many products initially rejected by focus groups.) However, relying solely on quantitative information often results in market research that lacks ideas.

Focus Groups

How useful are focus groups really? Watch the video for a funny caveman's spoof on them.

View in the online reader

Descriptive Research

Anything that can be observed and counted falls into the category of descriptive research design. A study using a **descriptive research design** involves gathering hard numbers, often via surveys, to describe or measure a phenomenon to answer the questions of *who, what, where, when,* and *how.* "On a scale of 1–5, how satisfied were you with your service?" is a question that illustrates the information a descriptive research design is supposed to capture.

descriptive research design

A study that involves gathering hard numbers, often via surveys, to describe or measure a phenomenon to answer the questions of *who*, *what*, *where*, *when*, and *how*.

Physiological measurements also fall into the category of descriptive design. **Physiological measurements** measure people's involuntary physical responses to marketing stimuli, such as an advertisement, to see what they think about products versus what they say about them. The 2016 U.S. presidential election underscored the need to more correctly gauge how people feel versus what they say after pollsters and data experts incorrectly predicted Hillary Clinton would trounce Donald Trump. Were voters telling the truth about their preferences when surveyed? Likewise, are consumers telling the truth about products and services they are asked about?

physiological measurements

Measurements that record people's involuntary physical responses to marketing stimuli, such as an advertisement.

In an earlier chapter, we explained that researchers even scan the brains of consumers. Eye tracking is another cutting-edge type of physiological measurement. It involves recording the movements of a person's eyes when they look at some sort of stimulus, such as an ad or web page. The Walt Disney Company has a research facility in Austin, Texas, that it uses to take physical measurements of viewers when they see Disney programs and advertisements. The facility measures three types of responses: people's heart rates, skin changes, and eye movements (eye tracking).

This woman is wearing headgear for an eye-tracking study.

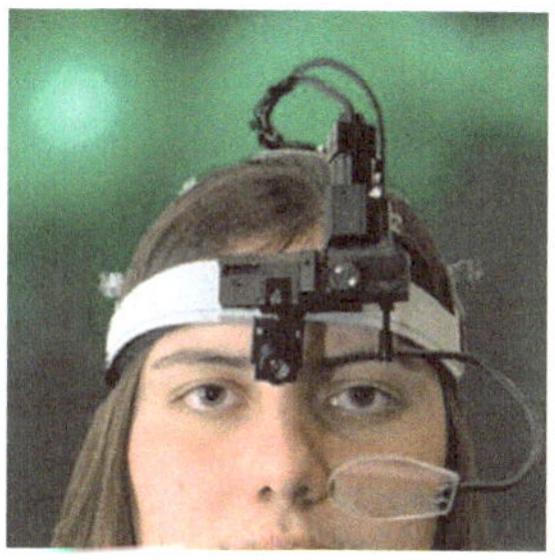

Source: Joabro17 at English Wikipedia, Public domain, via Wikimedia Commons

A strictly descriptive research design instrument—a survey, for example—can tell you how satisfied your customers are. It can't, however, tell you why. Nor can an eye-tracking study tell you *why* people's eyes tend to dwell on certain types of ads—only that they do. Artificial intelligence can't tell you why a consumer might be excited (or unexcited) by a product either. To answer "why" questions, an exploratory research design or causal research design is needed.

Causal Research

Causal research design examines cause-and-effect relationships. Using a causal research design allows researchers to answer "what if" types of questions. In other words, if a firm changes *X* (say, a product's price, design, placement, or advertising), what will happen to *Y* (say, sales or customer loyalty)? To conduct causal research, the researcher designs an experiment that "controls," or holds constant, all of a product's marketing elements except for one. (Or, by using advanced research techniques, a few elements can be studied at the same time). The one variable is changed, and the effect is then measured. For example, the lighting or music in the "store" might be changed, or the shopper might be offered one promotion on a product and then a different promotion later. Sometimes the experiments are conducted in a laboratory using a simulated setting designed to replicate the conditions buyers would experience. Virtual reality headsets are also being used to replicate store, or buying, conditions.

causal research design

A type of research design that examines cause-and-effect relationships to allow researchers to answer "what if" types of questions.

Why is being able to control the setting so important? Let's say you are an American flag manufacturer and you are working with Walmart to conduct an experiment to see where in its stores American flags should be placed to increase their sales. Next, an attack on American soil occurs. In the days afterward, flag sales skyrocket—people buy flags no matter where they are displayed. Obviously the attack would skew the experiment's data.

Beverage makers often test products in certain markets to gauge how they will they sell in other markets.

Source: © Shutterstock, Inc.

field experiment

A marketing research experiment conducted in a natural setting such as a store versus a simulated setting in a laboratory or on a computer.

test market

The place an experiment is conducted or the demographic group of people an experiment is administered to.

An experiment conducted in a natural setting such as a store is referred to as a **field experiment**. Companies sometimes do field experiments either because it is more convenient or because they want to see if buyers will behave the same way in the "real world" as they do in a laboratory, on a computer, or in another type of simulated setting. The place the experiment is conducted or the demographic group of people the experiment is administered to is considered the **test market**.

Before a large company rolls out a product or service to the entire marketplace, it will often place the offering in a test market to see how well it will be received. Amazon is opening brick-and-mortar retail stores in select locations to see how they perform. Says Professor Terry Esper of Ohio University: "The reality is that consumers really do prefer to go to stores, especially for certain product categories."[20] Electronic items and clothing, which people want to try on, are examples.

Many companies use experiments to test all of their marketing communications. For example, the online discount retailer Overstock carefully tests all of its marketing offers and tracks the results of each one. (Recall our discussions earlier in the book about A/B testing.) One study the company conducted looked at twenty-six different variables related to offers it emailed to several thousand customers.

Step 3: Design the Data-Collection Forms

If the behavior of buyers is being formally observed, and a number of different researchers are conducting observations, the data obviously need to be recorded via a standardized data-collection format. Otherwise, the data collected will not be comparable. The items collected could include a shopper's sex; their approximate age; whether the person seemed hurried, moderately hurried, or unhurried; and whether or not they read the label on products, used coupons, and so forth.

The same is true when it comes to surveying people with questionnaires. Surveying people is one of the most commonly used techniques to collect quantitative data. Surveys are popular because they can be easily administered to large numbers of people fairly quickly. However, to produce the best results, the questions need to be carefully designed.

Questionnaire Design

Most questionnaires follow a similar format: They begin with an introduction describing what the study is for, followed by instructions for completing the questionnaire and, if necessary, returning it to the market researcher. The first few questions that appear on the questionnaire are usually basic, warm-up type questions the respondent can readily answer, such as the respondent's age, level of education, place of residence, and so forth. The warm-up questions are then followed by a logical progression of more detailed, in-depth questions that get to the heart of the question being researched. Lastly, the questionnaire wraps up with a statement that thanks the respondent for participating in the survey and explains when and how they will be compensated for participating.

How the questions themselves are worded is extremely important. It's human nature for respondents to want to provide the "correct" answers to the person administering the survey, so as to seem agreeable. In other words, people will try to tell you what you want to hear on a survey. Consequently, care needs to be taken that the survey questions are written in an unbiased, neutral way. In other words, they shouldn't lead a person taking the questionnaire to answer a question one way or another by virtue of the way they are worded. The following is an example of a leading question.

Don't you agree that teachers should be paid more?

The questions also need to be clear and unambiguous. Consider the following question:

Which brand of toothpaste do you use?

The question sounds clear enough, but is it really? What if the respondent recently switched brands? What if she uses Crest at home, but while away from home or traveling, she uses Colgate's Wisp disposable mini tooth-brush product? How will the respondent answer the question? Rewording the question so it's more specific will help make the question clearer. For example:

Which brand of toothpaste have you used at home in the past six months? If you have used more than one brand, please list each of them.

Sensitive questions have to be asked carefully. For example, asking a respondent, "Do you consider yourself a light, moderate, or heavy drinker?" can be tricky. Few people want to admit to being heavy drinkers. You can "soften" the question by including a range of answers, as the following example shows:

How many alcoholic beverages do you consume in a week?

__0–5 alcoholic beverages

__5–10 alcoholic beverages

__10–15 alcoholic beverages

Many people don't like to answer questions about their income levels. Asking them to specify income ranges rather than divulge their actual incomes can help.

Other research question "don'ts" include using jargon and acronyms that could confuse people. "How often do you IM?" [instant message] is an example. Also, don't muddy the waters by asking two questions in the same question, something researchers refer to as a **double-barreled question**. "Do you think parents should spend more time with their children and/or their teachers?" is an example of a double-barreled question.

double-barreled question

A survey question that is potentially confusing because it asks two questions in the same question.

Open-ended questions, or questions that ask respondents to elaborate, can be included. However, they are harder to tabulate than **closed-ended questions**, or questions that limit a respondent's answers. Multiple-choice and yes-and-no questions are examples of closed-ended questions.

open-ended questions

Questions that ask respondents to elaborate upon, or explain, their answers.

closed-ended questions

Questions that limit a respondent's answers. Multiple-choice and yes-and-no questions are examples of closed-ended questions.

Testing the Questionnaire

You have probably heard the phrase "garbage in, garbage out." If the questions are bad, the information gathered will be bad, too. One way to make sure you don't end up with garbage is to test the questionnaire before sending it out to find out if there are any problems with it. Is there enough space for people to elaborate on open-ended questions? Is the typeface readable?

To test the questionnaire, marketing research professionals first administer it to a number of respondents face to face. This gives the respondents the chance to ask the researcher about questions or instructions that are unclear or don't make sense to them. The researcher then administers the questionnaire to a small subset of respondents in the actual way the survey is going to be disseminated, whether it's delivered in person, via phone, by mail, or online.

Getting people to participate and complete questionnaires can be difficult. If the questionnaire is too long or hard to read, many people won't complete it. Eliminate any questions that aren't necessary or that are ambiguous (can be misinterpreted). Including some sort of monetary incentive for completing the survey will increase the number of completed questionnaires.

Step 4: Specify the Sample

sample

A subset of potential buyers that is representative of your entire target market, or population being studied.

population

The entire target market being studied.

sampling error

Any type of marketing research mistake that results because a sample was utilized.

sampling frame

The list from which a research sample is drawn. The sampling frame won't perfectly match the population.

probability sample

A research sample in which each would-be participant has a known and equal chance of being selected.

nonprobability sample

A research sample that's not drawn in a systematic way.

convenience sample

Type of nonprobability sample that's drawn because it's readily available and convenient to do so.

Once you have created your questionnaire or other marketing study, how do you figure out who should participate in it? Obviously, you can't survey or observe all potential buyers in the marketplace. Instead, you must choose a sample. A **sample** is a subset of potential buyers that is representative of your entire target market, or **population** being studied. Sometimes market researchers refer to the population as the *universe* to reflect the fact that it includes the entire target market, whether it consists of a million people, a hundred thousand, a few hundred, or a dozen. "All unmarried people over the age of eighteen who purchased a Dyson V15 Detect vacuum cleaner in the United States during 2021" is an example of a population that has been defined.

Obviously, the population has to be defined correctly. Otherwise, you will be studying the wrong group of people. Not defining the population correctly can result in flawed research, or sampling error. A **sampling error** is any type of marketing research mistake that results because a sample was utilized. For example, although internet surveys are fast and less expensive to conduct, they are sometimes criticized because the people who take these surveys don't really represent the overall population. On average, internet survey takers tend to be somewhat more educated and tech savvy. Consequently, if they solely constitute your population, even if you screen them for certain criteria, the data you collect could end up being skewed.

The next step is to put together the **sampling frame**, which is the list from which the sample is drawn. The sampling frame can be put together using a directory, customer list, or membership roster. Keep in mind that the sampling frame won't *perfectly* match the population. Some people will be included on the list who shouldn't be. Other people who should be included will be inadvertently omitted. It's no different than if you were to conduct a survey of, say, 25 percent of your friends, using friends' names you have in your cell phone. Most of your friends' names are likely to be programmed into your phone, but not all of them. As a result, a certain degree of sampling error always occurs.

There are two main categories of samples in terms of how they are drawn: probability samples and nonprobability samples. A **probability sample** is one in which each would-be participant has a known and equal chance of being selected. The chance is known because the total number of people in the sampling frame is known. For example, if every other person from the sampling frame were chosen, each person would have a 50 percent chance of being selected.

A **nonprobability sample** is any type of sample that's not drawn in a systematic way, so the chances of each would-be participant being selected can't be known. A **convenience sample** is one type of nonprobability sample. It is a sample a researcher draws because it's readily available and convenient to do so. Surveying people on the street as they pass by is an example of a convenience sample. The question is, are these people representative of the target market?

For example, suppose a grocery store needed to quickly conduct some research on shoppers to get ready for an upcoming promotion. Now suppose that the researcher assigned to the project showed up between the hours of 10 a.m. and 12 p.m. on a weekday and surveyed as many shoppers as possible. The problem is that the shoppers wouldn't be representative of the store's entire target market.

For example, what about commuters who stop at the store before and after work? Their views wouldn't be represented. Neither would people who work the night shift or shop at odd hours. As a result, there would be a lot of room for sampling error in this study. For this reason, studies that use nonprobability samples aren't considered as accurate as studies that use probability samples. Nonprobability samples are more often used in exploratory research.

Lastly, the size of the sample has an effect on the amount of sampling error. Larger samples generally produce more accurate results. The larger your sample is, the more data you will have, which will give you a more complete picture of what you're studying. However, the more people surveyed or studied, the more costly the research becomes. Statistics can be used to determine a sample's optimal size. If you take a marketing research or statistics class, you will learn more about how to determine the optimal size.

Of course, if you hire a marketing research company, much of this work will be taken care of for you. Many marketing research companies, like ResearchNow, maintain panels of prescreened people they draw upon for samples. In addition, the marketing research firm will be responsible for collecting the data or contracting with a company that specializes in data collection. Data collection is discussed next.

Step 5: Collect the Data

As we have explained, primary marketing research data can be gathered in a number of ways. Surveys, taking physical measurements, and observing people are just three of the ways we discussed. If you're observing customers as part of gathering the data, keep in mind that if shoppers are aware of the fact, it can have an effect on their behavior. For example, if a customer shopping for feminine hygiene products in a supermarket aisle realizes she is being watched, she could become embarrassed and leave the aisle, which would adversely affect your data.

To get around problems such as these, some companies set up cameras or two-way mirrors to observe customers. Organizations also hire mystery shoppers to work around the problem. A **mystery shopper** is someone who is paid to shop at a firm's establishment or one of its competitors to observe the level of service, cleanliness of the facility, and so forth, and report his or her findings to the researcher.

mystery shopper

A person who is paid to shop at a firm's establishment or one of its competitors to observe the level of service, cleanliness of the facility, and so forth, and report his or her findings to the firm.

Survey data can be collected in many different ways and combinations of ways. The following are the basic methods used:

- face-to-face (can be computer aided)
- phone (can be computer aided or completely automated)
- text message (SMS) or multimedia message (MMS)
- mail and hand delivery
- email and the web

A face-to-face survey is, of course, administered by a person. In years past, it was common for researchers in the United States to knock on people's doors to gather survey data. However, door-to-door interviews are less common today, partly because people are afraid of crime and are reluctant to give information to strangers. Nonetheless, "beating the streets" is still a legitimate way questionnaire data is collected. Face-to-face surveys are also commonly used in developing countries to collect information from people who cannot read or lack phones and computers.

A plus of face-to-face surveys is that they allow researchers to ask lengthier, more complex questions because the people being surveyed can see and read the questionnaires. The same is true when a computer is utilized. For example, the researcher might ask the respondent to look at a list of six or seven retail stores on a computer tablet and rank the stores from best to worst. The same question wouldn't work so well over the phone because the person couldn't see the list. The question would have to be rewritten. Another drawback with phone surveys is that people often screen such calls using caller ID and and voicemail.

Probably the biggest drawback of both surveys conducted face-to-face and administered over the phone by a person is that they are labor intensive and therefore costly. How many times have you been asked to be surveyed by another person? Mailing out questionnaires is costly too, and the response rates can be rather low.

By contrast, gathering survey data collected by a computer, either via phone or on the internet, or via text and multimedia messages can be very cost-effective. SurveyMonkey is a platform that allows you to create online questionnaires and email them to people for free or at a low cost in dozens of languages. It also has prescreened consumer panels and focus groups you can utilize, data analysis tools, and tools to create graphics to put in your final research report.

Google Surveys, Trumpia.com, PollEverywhere.com, and SMS-Track.com allow companies to send surveys via text messages (SMS) and multimedia messages (MMS) to people's mobile phones. Multimedia messages also allow companies to show survey takers images, such as photos of products and their packaging, advertisements, and videos. Survey takers can also be enlisted based on their locations, such as when they walk into your store or a competitor's store. Or, they can be recruited as mystery shoppers to take pictures or videos of various marketing situations.

Surveys such as these are also fast, which is a major plus. Instead of taking weeks to collect the information, it can be collected in matter of days or even hours. You can also reach a broader geographic group than you could if you had to personally interview people.

Another plus for internet and automated surveys is that there is less room for human error. For instance, there's no risk that the interviewer will ask a question wrong or use a tone of voice that could mislead the respondents. If the questions are sensitive, respondents are also likely to feel more comfortable entering their answers electronically on computers or phones than divulging the information to another person face-to-face or over the phone. For example, a study conducted by Frederick Conrad of the University of Michigan and Michael F. Schober of the New School for Social Research, found that people who responded to text-message surveys about sensitive topics such as sex, drug use, and religion were more likely to provide accurate and honest data than when the surveys were conducted by voice.

However, like mail surveys, internet and phone surveys are easy to ignore. In addition, the 1991 Telephone Consumer Protection Act prohibits firms from sending automatic unsolicited survey calls to people on their mobile phones, unless they have opted to receive the calls by signing up for, say, Google Surveys. Instead, the calls must be placed by an actual person, which makes collecting information via mobile phones more expensive and time consuming.

Lastly, before the data collection process begins, human surveyors and observers need to be trained to look for the same things, ask questions the same way, and so forth. If the surveyors are using rankings or rating scales, they need to be "on the same page," as to what constitutes a high ranking or a low ranking. As an analogy, you have probably had some teachers grade your college papers harder than others. The goal of the training is to avoid a wide disparity between how different observers and interviewers record the data.

For example, if an observation form asks the observers to describe whether a shopper's behavior is hurried, moderately hurried, or unhurried, they should be given an idea of what defines each rating. Does it depend on how much time the person spends in the store or in the individual aisles? How fast they walk? In other words, the criteria and ratings need to be spelled out.

Collecting International Marketing Research Data

Gathering marketing research data in foreign countries poses special challenges. However, that doesn't stop firms from doing so. Although marketing research companies are located all across the globe, most of the largest ones are headquartered in the United States. That said, it's not uncommon for these firms to earn more of their revenues abroad than they do in the United States. There's a reason for this: many U.S. markets are saturated in terms of the amount that they can grow.

Coke is an example. As you learned earlier in the book, most of the Coca-Cola Company's revenues are earned in markets abroad. To be sure, the United States is still a huge market when it comes to the revenues marketing research firms generate by conducting research in the country. Still, emerging countries with growing middle classes—countries such as China and India—are hot new markets companies want to research and tap.

What kind of challenges do firms face when trying to conduct marketing research abroad? As we explained, face-to-face surveys are commonly used in developing countries to collect information from people who cannot read or lack phones and computers. By contrast, in some countries, including many Asian countries, it's considered taboo or rude to try to gather information from strangers either face-to-face or over the phone. In many Muslim countries, women are forbidden to talk to strangers.

And how do you figure out whom to survey in foreign countries? That in itself is a problem. In the United States, researchers often ask if they can talk to the heads of households to conduct marketing research. But in countries in which domestic servants or employees are common, the heads of households aren't necessarily the principal shoppers; their domestic employees are.[21]

Translating surveys is also an issue. Hiring someone who is bilingual to translate a survey into another language can be a disaster if the person isn't a native speaker of the language to which the survey is being translated.

One way companies try to deal with translation problems is by using back translation. When **back translation** is used, a native speaker translates the survey into the foreign language and then translates it back again to the original language to determine if there were gaps in meaning—that is, to see if any information became distorted or lost in translation. And it's not just the language that's an issue. If the research involves any visual images, they, too, could be a point of confusion. Certain colors, shapes, and symbols can have negative connotations in other countries. For example, the color white represents purity in many Western cultures, but in China, it is the color of death and mourning.

back translation

A process whereby a native speaker translates a research instrument such as a survey into a foreign language and then back again to the original language to determine if there are gaps in meaning.

Also, look back at the cartoon-completion exercise in Figure 10.2. What would women in Muslim countries who aren't allowed to converse with male sellers think of it? Chances are, the cartoon wouldn't provide you with the information you're seeking if Muslim women in some countries were asked to complete it.

One way marketing research companies are dealing with the complexities of global research is by merging with or acquiring marketing research companies abroad. Nielsen is the largest marketing research company in the world. The firm operates in more than a hundred countries and employs more than forty thousand people. Many of its expansions have been the result of acquisitions and mergers.

Step 6: Analyze the Data

Once all the data collected, the researchers begin the **data cleaning**, which is the process of removing data that have accidentally been duplicated (entered twice into the computer) or correcting data that have obviously been recorded wrong. Microsoft Excel or another statistical program is then used to tabulate, or calculate, the basic results of the research, such as the total number of participants and how collectively they answered various questions. The programs can also be used to calculate averages, such as the average age of respondents, their average satisfaction, and so forth. The same can done for percentages, and other values you learned about, or will learn about, in a statistics course, such as the standard deviation, mean, and median for each question.

data cleaning

The process of removing research data that have accidentally been duplicated (entered twice into the computer) or correcting data that have obviously been recorded wrong.

The information generated by the programs can be used to draw conclusions, such as what *all* customers might like or not like about an offering based on what the sample group liked or did not like. The information can also be used to spot differences among groups of people. For example, the research might show that people in one area of the country like the product better than people in another area. Trends to predict what might happen in the future can also be spotted.

If there are any open-ended questions respondents have elaborated upon—for example, "Explain why you like the current brand you use better than any other brand"—the answers to each will appear together, one on top of another, so researchers can compare and summarize the information. As we have explained, qualitative information such as this can give you a fuller picture of the results of the research.

Part of analyzing the data is to see if it seems sound. Does the way in which the research was conducted seem sound? Was the sample size large enough? Are the conclusions that become apparent from it reasonable?

valid (study)

A study that actually tests what it was designed to test and not something else.

reliable (study)

A study that, when repeated, produces the same or nearly the same result.

The two most commonly used criteria used to test the soundness of a study are (1) validity and (2) reliability. A study is **valid** if it actually tested what it was designed to test. For example, did the experiment test what it was designed to test? Did it reflect what could really happen in the real world? If not, the research isn't valid. If you were to repeat the study and get the same results (or nearly the same results), the research is said to be **reliable**. If you get a drastically different result if you repeat the study, it's not reliable. The data collected, or at least some it, can also be compared to, or reconciled with, similar data from other sources, either gathered by your firm or by another organization, to see if the information seems on target.

Step 7: Write the Research Report and Present Its Findings

If you end up becoming a marketing professional and conducting a research study after you graduate, hopefully you will do a great job putting the study together. You will have defined the problem correctly, chosen the right sample, collected the data accurately, analyzed it, and your findings will be sound. At that point, you will be required to write the research report and perhaps present it to an audience of decision makers. You will do so via a written report and, in most cases, a slide or PowerPoint presentation based on your written report.

The six basic elements of a research report are as follows:

margin of error

A measure of the possible inaccuracy of the data reported in a survey.

1. **Title Page.** The title page explains what the report is about, when it was conducted and by whom, and who requested it.
2. **Table of Contents.** The table of contents outlines the major parts of the report, as well as any graphs and charts, and the page numbers on which they can be found.
3. **Executive Summary.** The executive summary summarizes all the details in the report in a very quick way. Many people who receive the report—both executives and nonexecutives—won't have time to read the entire report. Instead, they will rely on the executive summary to quickly get an idea of the study's results and what to do about them.
4. **Methodology and Limitations.** The methodology section of the report explains the technical details of how the research was designed and conducted. The section explains, for example, how the data were collected and by whom, the size of the sample, how it was chosen, and whom or what it consisted of (e.g., the number of women versus men or children versus adults). The section also includes information about the statistical techniques used to analyze the data. Every study has errors—sampling errors, interviewer errors, and so forth. The methodology section should explain these details so decision makers can consider their overall impact. The **margin of error** is the overall tendency of the study to be off kilter—that is, how far it could have gone wrong in either direction. Think about how newscasters present presidential poll information before an election. They say something to this effect: "This candidate is ahead 48 to 44 percent, plus or minus 2 percent." That "plus or minus" is the margin of error. The larger the margin of error is, the less likely the results of the study are accurate. The margin of error needs to be included in the methodology section.

5. **Findings.** The findings section is a longer, fleshed-out version of the executive summary that goes into more detail about the statistics uncovered by the research that bolster the study's findings. If you have related research or secondary data on hand that back up the findings, it can be included to help show the study did what it was designed to do.
6. **Recommendations.** The recommendations section should outline the course of action you think should be taken based on the findings of the research and the purpose of the project. For example, if you conducted a global market research study to identify new locations for stores, make a recommendation for the locations.[22]

Key Takeaway

- Step 1 in the marketing research process is to define the problem. Businesses take a look at what they believe are symptoms and try to drill down to the potential causes so as to precisely define the problem. The next task for the researcher is to put into writing the research objective, or goal, the research is supposed to accomplish. Step 2 in the process is to design the research. The research design is the "plan of attack." It outlines what data you are going to gather, from whom, how, and when, and how you're going to analyze it once it has been obtained. Step 3 is to design the data-collection forms, which need to be standardized so the information gathered on each is comparable. Surveys are a popular way to gather data because they can be easily administered to large numbers of people fairly quickly. However, to produce the best results, survey questionnaires need to be carefully designed and pretested before they are used. Step 4 is drawing the sample, or a subset of potential buyers who are representative of your *entire* target market. If the sample is not correctly selected, the research will be flawed. Step 5 is to actually collect the data, whether it's collected by a person face to face, over the phone, or with the help of tablets or the internet. The data-collection process is often different in other countries. Step 6 is to analyze the data collected for any obvious errors, tabulate the data, and then draw conclusions from it based on the results. The last step in the process, Step 7, is writing the research report and presenting the findings to decision makers.

Review Questions

1. Explain why it's important to carefully define the problem or opportunity a marketing research study is designed to investigate.
2. How does primary data differ from secondary data? What are the sources of each?
3. Describe the different types of problems that can occur when marketing research professionals develop questions for surveys, especially those conducted online.
4. How does a probability sample differ from a nonprobability sample?
5. What makes a marketing research study valid? What makes a marketing research study reliable?
6. What sections should be included in a marketing research report? What is each section designed to do?

10.3 Discussion Questions and Activities

Discussion Questions

1. Are small business owners at a disadvantage if they lack the marketing research resources large companies have? Why or why not?
2. What drawbacks do you see associated with conducting surveys online? Are privacy issues greater with online surveys than with other forms of administering surveys, such as phone, face-to-face, or mail?
3. Why do you think so many marketing research companies are conglomerating—that is, merging with or acquiring one another? Is it solely to conduct global marketing research?
4. Suppose you need to conduct research on consumer acceptance for a new product. Describe the process you would use. How would your project change if the product solved an embarrassing problem? What would your challenges be in that situation?
5. Given the way people tweet about customer service, why do companies still use mystery shoppers? Why not simply follow tweet volume and content to see if service is good?
6. You are working for an organization that provides clean water technology to communities in Africa. They've never worked in Malawi but want to and need to understand how consumers source water, how they prepare it (sterilize or clean it), and how they use it. You know that a study was done on water sources, water preparation, and water uses in Kenya. What type of research would the Kenya study be considered and how would you go about validating its findings for Malawi (a different country in Africa)? How would your answer change if your organization was considering a community in a remote area of Nicaragua? (By the way, this question is based on a real situation involving Living Water International, a student project at Baylor University and funded by 3M that examined Somotillo, Nicaragua, and a study done in Kenya by Boston University's School of Public Health.)
7. Your CEO is personally involved in developing a new product that is really cool, but you have your doubts about whether it really delivers any additional benefits over what is already available. When you pitch the idea of a marketing research study to test consumer response, she says, "Are you kidding? Why waste the money and time, as well as let our competitors know what we've got? Let's get this to market!" But the market launch will cost $3 million, and your company's profits last year were only $5 million. How would you respond? How would your answer differ if the launch only cost $300,000?
8. The chapter mentions using salespeople and channel partners as sources of information. Describe how you would go about this and if or why salesperson/channel partner input is important when trying to make the following decisions:
   a. when trying to design the booth for use at trade shows
   b. when trying to decide which features to add or subtract from a product
   c. making pricing decisions
9. Describe how you would use projective techniques to help your university understand how prospective students make schooling decisions. Be specific when describing how you would use the technique, providing examples of questions.
10. In *Freakonomics*, Steven Levitt describes a study of public housing residents that began with the question, "How does it feel to be poor and black?" He says that's a bad question to start a survey with. Why? (There are multiple reasons.)
11. You sell manufacturing equipment for a Chinese company that imports the equipment into your country. You want to do a research project on potential brand names for a new product line, and have to choose among the following sampling ideas or projects. For each one, identify what type of study and sample you have, discuss the pros and cons, and then at the end, make a decision.

a. Stopping 200 people at a trade show and showing potential brand names to them to get their reaction.
b. Hosting a breakfast or lunch at a trade show to get three groups of ten people to provide feedback to the names and logos.
c. Send an email to your customers with a link to a URL that has the various names, and let them vote.

Activities

1. In this activity, you will conduct a survey using either Zoomerang.com or SurveyMonkey.com. Divide into groups of four people. Each group should do the following:
   a. Choose a food service establishment on or near your campus. Then create a ten-question survey designed to gauge how satisfied customers are with the establishment's food and service.
   b. Decide how you will deliver the questionnaire you've created. Choose a sampling frame, or list of people from which you will draw your sample.
   c. Administer the survey. After you have collected the results, analyze them and write a research report with the sections outlined in the chapter.
   d. Contact the owner or manager of the establishment and present him or her with the findings. If your research is helpful to the manager, who knows? It might earn you a free meal or at least some money-off coupons.
2. Would you like to own an electric car? Team up into small groups of three or four people. As a team, use secondary data to research the viability of selling electric cars profitably. Utilize some of the sources mentioned in the chapter. Try to determine the population of electric car buyers. Lastly, write a research report based on your findings. Each group should present its findings to the class. Do the findings differ from group to group? If so, why?

10.4 Case Study: Keaty Real Estate

Jim Keaty, the owner of Keaty Real Estate in LaFayette, Louisiana, is always looking for better ways to sell property. Keaty says the biggest challenge he and his agents have is converting *leads* (people his agents contact)—that is, getting them to say "yes" to either buy or sell real estate with the company.

But despite today's hot real estate market, more leads aren't always necessarily better. Quality leads are. In other words, you want to find the "hot" leads—people who are definitely thinking about selling or buying homes, not just kind of thinking about it. Otherwise, you will waste a lot of time on leads that won't pay off.[23]

This is definitely true when you're trying to find people who are willing to sell their property. Sure, you can make a lot of phone calls to people you know or are acquainted with. You can contact local homebuilders, who will usually pay agents for selling their homes. You can knock on the doors of people who are listing their properties "for sale by owner" and use social media to hunt down sellers. And agents do.

But that's time consuming. The hot leads dry up quickly, too, because many homeowners agree to sign with the first real estate agent who contacts them. Or, they contract with online brokers like Opendoor.com, which maybe won't offer the buyer or seller the most personal service or best price but can close deals quickly.[24]

That's where big data is helping. Keaty works with LeadsToday.com, a small data broker that specializes in real estate. LeadsToday tracks people's life events like job changes, pregnancies, divorces, and children heading to college—clues that could indicate homeowners are genuinely considering buying or selling their houses. LeadsToday provides leads to realtors who then use the information to precisely target potential customers with online ads and other types of ads as well as contact buyers and sellers directly to talk to them about their specific housing situations.

Does targeting potential real estate customers this way sound creepy? "That's how it goes," says a homeseller who learned that he was targeted with a LeadsToday ad that led him to a good real estate agent.[25] The practice has worked out for Keaty, too. It has made a huge difference in the success of his business, he says.

Case Study Questions

1. Is using big data to help sell real estate any different than using it to sell other products? Why or why not?
2. Think of a small company you, your friends, or your parents have worked for. Could it use big data to better market its products? If so, how?
3. Is it really possible for small companies to compete with big companies with more data? If so, how? Does it depend on the type of business?

Endnotes

1. Gael F. Cooper (August 12, 2021), "14 Products that Flopped Big Time," *MoneyTalkNews*, https://www.moneytalksnews.com/slideshows/14-products-that-flopped-big-time/ ; Seth Stern (July 2, 2002), "The Museum of Food Failures," *Christian Science Monitor*, http://www.csmonitor.com/2002/0702/p18s03-hfks.html.
2. Barry Levine (November 1, 2016), "MarTech Landscape: What is a Customer Data Platform?" *MarchTech Today*, https://martechtoday.com/martech-landscape-customer-data-platform-192126.
3. Lucy Danziger (October 5, 2017), "The New Workout Secret: Clothing Sensors That Up Your Game," *Wall Street Journal*, https://www.wsj.com/articles/when-your-gym-shorts-tell-you-to-work-out-harder-1507215619.
4. Tim Appelo, (September 1, 2021), "The Surprising Secrets Behind How Netflix Recommends Shows You Watch," *AARP*, https://www.aarp.org/entertainment/television/info-2021/how-netflix-recommendations-work.html.
5. Kasereka Henrys (April 19, 2021), "Role of Predictive Analytics in Business," *SSRN*, https://ssrn.com/abstract=3829621 or http://dx.doi.org/10.2139/ssrn.3829621.
6. Christina Binkley (April 30, 2015), "How Fashion Retailers Know Exactly What You Want," *Wall Street Journal*, D3.
7. Heather Haddon (October 16, 2017), "Grocers Imagine the Store of the Future," *Wall Street Journal*, R8.
8. Angus Loten (November 4, 2020), "In Search of Better Online Reccomondations," *Wall Street Journal*, R2.
9. David Edelman, Jason Heller, and Steven Spittaels (November 9, 2016), "Agile Marketing: A Step-by-Step Guide," McKinsey and Company, https://www.mckinsey.com/business-functions/marketing-and-sales/our-insights/agile-marketing-a-step-by-step-guide.
10. Alex J. Caffarini, "Ten Costly Marketing Mistakes and How to Avoid Them," Analysights, LLC.
11. Alvin Burns and Ronald Bush (2010), *Marketing Research*, 6th ed. Upper Saddle River, NJ: Prentice Hall, 85.
12. Alvin Burns and Ronald Bush (2010), *Marketing Research*, 6th ed. Upper Saddle River, NJ: Prentice Hall, 87–88.
13. Michael Sessa (February 10, 2021), "SU Data Breach Exposes Nearly 10,000 Names, Social Security Numbers," *The Daily Orange*, http://dailyorange.com/2021/02/names-social-security-numbers-of-syracuse-university-students-exposed-in-data-breach/.
14. Staff (November 2, 2021), "Facebook to Delete Users' Facial Recognition Data after Privacy Complaints," *NPR*, https://www.npr.org/2021/11/02/1051504165/facebook-delete-facial-recognition-data-privacy
15. Eric Posner, and Glen Weyl (April 21–22, 2018), "Want Our Personal Data? Pay For It," *Wall Street Journal*, C3.
16. "It Still Pays to Listen to Customers" (May 24, 2001), *Wall Street Journal*, R4.
17. Aaron Back (September 9, 2020), "Campbell Needs to Strike While Soup Is Still Hot," *Wall Street Journal*, https://www.wsj.com/articles/campbell-needs-to-strike-while-soup-is-still-hot-11607530885.
18. Brook Barnes (April 15, 2009), "Disney Expert Uses Science to Draw Boy Viewers," *New York Times*, http://www.nytimes.com.
19. Liam Kay (March 26, 2021) "Key Lessons from MRS Digital Ethnography Summit," *ResearchLive*, https://www.research-live.com/article/news/tuning-in-key-lessons-from-mrs-digital-ethnography-summit/id/5081802.
20. Mark Arehart (September 7, 2021), "Amazon Rumored to be Considering Ohio as Test Market for New Retail Space," *WKSU*, https://www.wksu.org/economy/2021-09-06/amazon-rumored-to-be-considering-ohio-as-test-market-for-new-retail-space.
21. Naresh Malhotra, *Marketing Research: An Applied Approach*, 6th ed. Upper Saddle River, NJ: Prentice Hall, 764.
22. Sherrie Mersdorf (August 24, 2009), "How to Organize Your Next Survey Report," *Cvent*, http://survey.cvent.com/blog/cvent-survey/0/0/how-to-organize-your-next-survey-report.
23. "369: Defying Real Estate Struggles with Jim Keaty," *Pat Hiban's Real Estate Rockstar Radio*, https://hibandigital.com/jimkeaty3/.
24. Patrick Clark (August 11, 2021), "Opendoor Shares Surge as Zillow Rival Boosts Home Purchases," *Bloomberg*, https://www.bloomberg.com/news/articles/2021-08-11/opendoor-doubles-home-purchases-enticing-owners-in-hot-market.
25. Stefanos Chen, "How Real Estate Uses Big Data to Track Clients," *Wall Street Journal*, http://www.wsj.com/articles/how-real-estate-uses-big-data-to-track-clients-1431615728.

CHAPTER 11

Integrated Marketing Communications and Traditional Media Marketing

Communication helps businesses grow and prosper, creates relationships, strengthens the effectiveness of organizations, and allows people to learn about one another. Technology such as the internet, mobile phones, and social media affects the way we communicate and is changing the media landscape and the type of messaging strategy organizations use.

Do you feel lost without your cell phone? Are you more likely to respond to text messages than phone calls? Do you use the print publications (magazines, newspapers, references) at the library, or do you find all your references online? Do your parents and grandparents prefer different communication methods than you? Think about how you get information and then think about how organizations can communicate with you and other target markets about their products, services, or causes. As we utilize new sources of information, the media and message strategies used by businesses must also change. However, organizations still want consumers to get consistent messages, regardless of how they receive the information.

11.1 Integrated Marketing Communications (IMC)

Learning Objectives

1. Understand the meaning of integrated marketing communications (IMC).
2. Understand why organizations may change their promotional strategies to reach different audiences.

Once companies have developed products and services, they must communicate the value and benefits of the offerings to current and potential customers in both business-to-business (B2B) and business-to-consumer (B2C) markets. **Integrated marketing communications (IMC)** is an approach designed to deliver a consistent message to a target market using different types of media such as TV, radio, magazines, the internet, mobile phones, professional selling, and social media. In other words, the different communications should all reinforce one another.

integrated marketing communications (IMC)

An approach designed to deliver a consistent message to a target market using different types of media.

Popeyes Creates and Introduces New Chicken Sandwich

View in the online reader

KFC Introduces New Chicken Sandwich

View in the online reader

Bojangles Introduces New Chicken Sandwich

View in the online reader

Chick-fil-A Original Chicken Sandwich

View in the online reader

Delivering consistent information about a brand or an organization helps establish it in the minds of consumers and potential customers across target markets. When Popeyes introduced their chicken sandwich in August 2019, followed by Chick-fil-A's promotion claiming their sandwich was the original, the "chicken sandwich war" appeared to begin. Popeyes' chicken sandwich became an instant success, leading to an increase in sales of almost 40 percent in one quarter. Other restaurants who served chicken wanted to join in the success and began creating their own versions of the chicken sandwich. Ironically, almost every sandwich introduced had fried chicken on a buttered bun with two pickles, same as Chick-fil-A's original sandwich. The chicken sandwich wars continued throughout the pandemic and 2021.[1] Let's look at some of the commercials aired by different restaurant chains. Notice both Popeyes commercials show how the chicken sandwich is made with butter and pickles, the price, and the tag line, "Love That Chicken From Popeyes," sharing a consistent message regardless who watches it. As you watch the Popeyes', KFC's, and Bojangles' commercials, notice the chicken is fried and served on a buttered bun with two pickles for every competitor, which is the sandwich created by Chick-fil-A in 1964.

Changes in communication technology and instant access to information through the internet and digital marketing, including social media, explain one of the reasons why integrated marketing communications have become so important. Consumers are also changing. With immediate access to so many sources of information, consumers collect more product information on their own. Consequently, marketers must organize and assemble available information to build a consistent brand message and make it relevant. Making a message relevant is important because consumers are constantly bombarded by advertising, so they ignore much of it. The goal of IMC is to coordinate the messages to build the brand and develop strong customer relationships while also helping customers satisfy their needs.

United Parcel Service (UPS) has long had a reputation for their package delivery service. During the COVID-19 pandemic with many businesses closed, employees working remotely, and people isolating and shopping from home, more and more customers depended on online orders and delivery services such as UPS. Shipping medical supplies and equipment became critical for doctors and medical responders to treat patients. Not only did medical staff begin seeing thank you notes across the nation, but UPS also received thank you notes. The thank you notes medical professionals, grocery stores, service providers, and delivery services such as UPS received, provided the idea behind the UPS campaign, #Thanks for Delivering." What began as a social media campaign to express gratitude to everyone (not only UPS drivers) risking their safety for others quickly became a message of gratitude which spread across communities and was shown on television, news channels, in neighborhoods (sidewalks, front steps, etc.), throughout communities, and across social media platforms. The positive publicity enhanced UPS's image and the consistent message of gratitude across media illustrates IMC.[2]

UPS #Thanks for Delivering

UPS video shows customers' appreciation for delivering during the COVID-19 pandemic.

View in the online reader

Changing Media

More consumers and business professionals are seeking information and connecting with other people and businesses using their computers, phones, and tablets. The work and social environments are changing, with more people having virtual offices, texting on their cell phones, and/or communicating through social media sites such as Facebook, LinkedIn, Snapchat, Instagram, TikTok, and Twitter. As the media landscape changes, the money that organizations spend on different types of advertising is changing as well. In 2020, worldwide spending on digital ads—search ads, social media ads, and video ads—was $378 billion or 58.2 percent of total spent on media ads. Ad spending on all traditional media including television declined, with radio, newspapers, and magazines experiencing the biggest drops. Ad spending (not including political ads) in the United States reflected similar patterns with digital media accounting for approximately 51 percent, television accounting for 43 percent, and other media accounting for only six percent of the total $214.6 billion spent on media ads.[3]

Many people feel lost without their cell phones. They are a major source of information for consumers and a medium for advertisers.

Source: © Shutterstock, Inc.

Most college students are part of Gen Z driving the change toward new communication technologies. Millennials, aged 26–41, also influenced adoption of communication technologies. You might opt to get promotions via **mobile marketing**—say, from stores on your cell phone as you walk by them or via a mobile gaming device that allows you to connect to the web.

mobile marketing

Marketing media that is available in different places such as cell phones or on forms of transportation.

Traditional media (such as magazines, newspapers, and television) as well as **out-of-home advertising**, such as billboards and movable promotions, compete with media such as the internet, social media, texting, mobile phones, and information people post about products on blogs and YouTube. You might have noticed that the tray tables on airplanes sometimes have ads on them. This is an example of out-of-home advertising. You have probably also seen ads on the insides of subway cars, in trains and buses, and even in bathroom stalls. These, too, are examples of out-of-home advertising.

out-of-home advertising

Billboards and movable promotions that are displayed in a broad range of public spaces, including tray tables on airplanes, the insides of subways, trains, buses, and even in bathroom stalls.

The inside walls of many subways provide an opportunity for advertisers to reach commuters with their messages.

Source: © Shutterstock, Inc.

Key Takeaway

- Integrated marketing communications (IMC) is an approach designed to deliver one consistent message to a target market using different types of media. As the media landscape changes, marketers are changing the type of promotions they use in order to reach their target markets. For example, less money is being budgeted for traditional media such as TV, print, and radio ads, and more money is budgeted for online, social media, and mobile ads.

Review Questions

1. Explain the concept of integrated marketing communications.
2. How is the media used by organizations changing? What age group is driving the change?
3. What factors are causing the media landscape to change?
4. What are some different types of digital media? Which types are most popular with college students?

11.2 The Promotion (Communication) Mix

Learning Objectives

1. Understand the different components of the promotion (communication) mix and why organizations have to consider all those components when designing an IMC program.
2. Outline the differences between the types of communication that target many people simultaneously versus the types of communication that target individuals.

Although the money that organizations spend promoting their offerings is likely to get distributed among different media channels, a company still wants to send its customers and potential consumers a consistent message. The different types of marketing communications an organization uses comprise its **promotion or communication mix**, which consists of advertising, sales promotions, direct marketing, public relations and publicity, sponsorships (of events and experiences), digital, and professional selling. Digital marketing including online, social media, and mobile marketing is discussed in Chapter 12 while professional selling is discussed briefly in this chapter and in more detail in Chapter 13.

promotion or communication mix

Communication tools that may include advertising, sales promotions, public relations and publicity, digital marketing, professional selling, and direct marketing.

Advertising involves paying to disseminate a message that identifies a brand (product or service) or an organization being promoted to many people at one time. The typical media that organizations utilize for advertising include digital marketing, which is rapidly increasing in use, television, magazines, newspapers, direct mail, and radio. Digital marketing including the internet, mobile devices, and social media platforms are discussed in Chapter 12.

advertising

A message that is paid for and sent to large groups of the population at one time with an identified organization or brand (product or service) being promoted.

Consumer sales promotions consist of short-term incentives such as coupons, contests, games, rebates, free samples, and mail-in offers that supplement the advertising and sales efforts. Sales promotions include promotions that are not part of another component of the communication mix and are often developed to get customers and potential customers to take action quickly, make larger purchases, and/or make repeat purchases.

consumer sales promotions

Promotional activities (coupons, contests, rebates, mail-in offers) companies do in addition to advertising, public relations, and professional selling in order to help sell a product.

In business-to-business marketing, sales promotions are typically called **trade promotions** because they are aimed at channel members who conduct business or trade with consumers. Trade promotions include trade shows and special incentives given to retailers to market particular products and services, such as extra money, in-store displays, and prizes.

trade promotions

Business-to-business marketing sales promotions such as trade shows, sponsorships, and event marketing.

Direct marketing involves the delivery of personalized and often interactive promotional materials to individual consumers via channels such as mail, catalogs, internet, email, telephone, and direct-response advertising. Direct-response advertising is advertising that urges consumers to "act now" by providing them with a direct way to contact the advertiser, such as by calling a toll-free ordering number, mailing in a business reply card, or clicking on an online ad. By targeting consumers individually, organizations hope to get them to take action.

direct marketing

Delivering personalized promotional materials directly to individual consumers. Materials may be delivered via mail, catalogs, internet, email, telephone, or in person.

digital marketing

An umbrella term for marketing products interactively using newer media and usually, but not always, the internet.

professional selling

An interactive, personal, paid promotional approach between a buyer and a seller.

Digital marketing is an umbrella term for marketing products interactively using newer media and the internet. Digital marketing, which is discussed in detail in the next chapter, includes search engine, e-commerce, mobile, video, and social media marketing.

Professional selling is an interactive, paid approach to marketing that involves a buyer and a seller. The interaction between the two parties can occur in person, by telephone, or via another technology. Whatever medium is used, developing a relationship with the buyer is usually something the seller desires.

When you interview for internships or full-time positions and try to convince potential employers to hire you, you are engaging in professional selling. The interview is very similar to a buyer-seller situation (dyad). Both the buyer and seller have objectives they hope to achieve. Business-to-business marketers generally utilize professional selling more often than most business-to-consumer marketers. If you have ever attended a Pampered Chef party or purchased something from an Amway or Mary Kay representative, you've been exposed to professional selling whether the purchase was made through the representative in person or online.

Pampered Chef and Tastefully Simple have built their businesses primarily on the professional selling skills of their consultants. Professional selling is used more in business-to-business markets than in business-to-consumer markets.

Source: © Shutterstock, Inc.

Public relations (PR) involves communication designed to help improve and promote an organization's image and products. PR is often perceived as more neutral and objective than other forms of promotion because much of the information is tailored to sound as if it has been created by an organization independent of the seller. Public relations materials include press releases, publicity, and news conferences. While other techniques such as product placement, social media posts, and sponsorships, especially of events and experiences, tend to generate a lot of PR, the growth of expenditures and importance of sponsorships are so critical for so many companies that it is often considered a separate component in the communication mix. Many companies have internal PR departments or hire PR firms to find and create public relations opportunities for them. As such, PR is part of a company's promotion budget and their integrated marketing communications.

public relations (PR)

The process of creating a positive image for a company, an offering, or a person via publicity.

sponsorships

The financial or other support for events, venues, or experiences that provide the opportunity to target specific groups and enhance a company's image.

Sponsorships typically refer to financial support for events, venues, or experiences and provide the opportunity to target specific groups. Sponsorships enhance a company's image and usually generate public relations. Festivals have become popular social trends, especially among millennials who may be indifferent to traditional advertising. More companies, including T-Mobile, Grubhub, Bud Light Seltzer, and Bumble are finding it worthwhile to sponsor music, film, and other types of festivals such Lollapalooza, Coachella, and Bonnaroo. By providing entertaining experiences, companies activate their brands at festivals where millennials (as well as people from other generations) wander around for an entire weekend. The sponsors set up air-conditioned tents with flashy displays and amenities such as cell-charging stations, freebie beverages, and sample products to lure in potential customers when they need a little downtime from the festivals' events.[4]

Key Takeaway

- Although the money organizations spend promoting their offerings is likely to get distributed among different media channels, a company still wants to send its customers and potential consumers a consistent message. The promotion (communication) mix is composed of advertising, professional selling, public relations, sponsorships (of events and experiences), sales promotions, direct marketing, professional selling, and digital marketing such as online, social media, and mobile marketing.

Review Questions

1. Define each component of the promotion (communication) mix.
2. Why has sponsoring events such as music festivals become such a key component of the promotion mix?
3. How do you think the promotion mix is changing for many businesses?

11.3 Factors Influencing the Promotion Mix, Communication Process, and Message Problems

Learning Objectives

1. Understand that different factors can affect the promotion mix.
2. Understand the communication process.
3. Understand different types of message problems.

Factors Influencing the Promotion Mix

A marketing manager from one company might decide to focus on social media, whereas a marketing manager from another company might decide to focus her company's efforts on television commercials. Why do companies select different types of media for what may be perceived as similar messages? As Figure 11.1 shows, a number of factors affect the choice of promotion mix elements.

FIGURE 11.1 Factors That Influence Selection of Promotion Mix

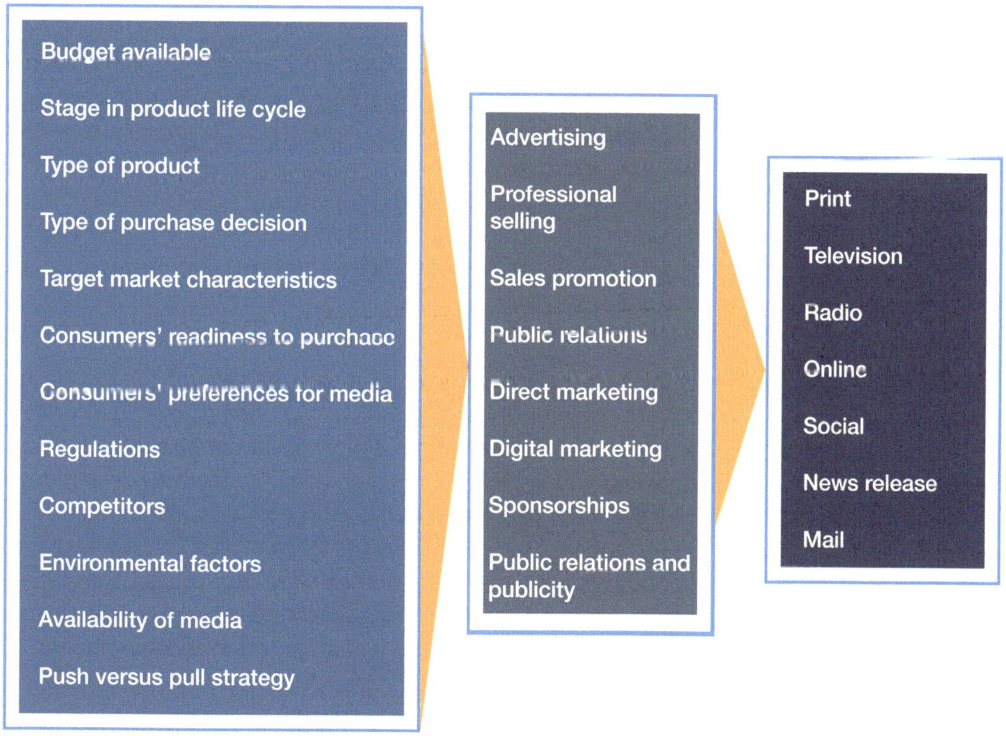

reach

The number of people exposed to a message.

frequency

How often people are exposed to a message.

Budget Available. For many companies, the budget available to market a product determines what elements of the promotion mix are utilized. The budget affects a promotion's **reach** (number of people exposed to the message) and **frequency** (how often people are exposed). For example, many smaller companies lack the money to create and run commercials on top-rated television shows or during the Super Bowl and must rely on less-expensive methods such as social media, which is also faster to implement. However, both large and small companies want to get the biggest bang for their advertising buck by maximizing their reach. As a result, firms keep track of what they are spending on different types of media, attempt to measure its impact, and then adjust their spending based on that information.

Stage in the product life cycle. The stage in the product life cycle also affects the type and amount of promotion used. Consumers and businesses won't buy a product if they do not know about it. Consequently, products in the introductory stages typically need a lot more promotional dollars to create awareness in the marketplace. More communication is needed in the beginning of the product life cycle to build awareness and trial.

Type of product and *type of purchase decision*. Different products also require different types of promotion. Very technical products and very expensive products (high involvement) often need to be sold by professional salespeople so the customer understands how the product operates and its different features. By contrast, a fifteen- or thirty-second TV or radio ad is more likely to be used to sell convenience goods and familiar products people purchase routinely. Customers don't need to learn how to use these products or spend a lot of time buying them, so the ads are designed to help consumers keep the products in mind.

Target market characteristics and *consumers' readiness to purchase*. In order to select the best methods to reach different target markets, organizations need to know what types of media different targets use, how often they make purchases, where they make purchases, and what their readiness to purchase is as well as characteristics such as age, gender, and lifestyle. Some people are early adopters and want to try new things as soon as they are available, and other groups wait until products have been on the market for a while. Some consumers might not have the money to purchase different products, although they will need the product later. For example, most college freshmen are not ready to purchase new cars on their own.

Consumers' preferences for various media. As you have learned, different types of consumers prefer different types of media. College-aged students often prefer digital marketing, especially social media as well as online, cell phone, and mobile marketing more than older consumers. Media preferences have been researched extensively by academics, marketing research companies, and companies to find out how consumers want to be reached. While many brands in the consumer packaged goods (CPG) industry have typically utilized television commercials to promote their brands, the pandemic transformed the way many companies did advertising. To increase sales, many CPG brands moved to digital ads during the pandemic, increasing digital ad spending by over 5 percent.[5]

Regulations and *environmental factors*. Regulations can affect the type of promotion used. For example, laws in the United States prohibit tobacco products from being advertised on television. In some Asian countries, controversial products such as alcohol cannot be advertised during Golden (prime) time on television when young children are more likely to see the advertisements. The strength of the economy can have an impact as well. In a weak economy, some organizations use more sales promotions such as coupons to get consumers into their stores. The risk is that consumers may begin to expect coupons and not want to buy items unless they can get a discount on them. When costs for materials and transportation rose during the pandemic and continued to rise with inflation, many companies increased prices and eliminated discounts as well as coupons.

Competitors. On one hand, companies keep a close eye on the promotion mixes of their competitors to see what combinations of media they are using and how effective the mixes are with consumers. If a company achieves a great deal of success using a certain type or combination of media, you can bet other companies will follow suit. You saw this with this "chicken sandwich war" discussed earlier in the chapter. Other companies also introduced new chicken sandwiches with television commercials and social media posts. On the other hand, it's not uncommon for firms to choose different promotional mixes than their competitors to differentiate themselves. However, with the growth of digital many competitors as well as substitute products are turning to digital and trying to connect with customers.

Availability of media. Organizations must also plan their promotions based on availability of media. The top-rated television shows and Super Bowl ad slots, for example, often sell out quickly. Magazines tend to have a longer lead time, so companies must plan far in advance for some magazines. By contrast, radio, social media, and online media may be immediate, but companies have to be careful to follow recommended guidelines and regulations.

Uncontrollable events can affect a company's promotions, too. For example, when a disaster such as a hurricane occurs, TV stations often cut advertisements to make way for continuous news coverage. If there is a crisis or disaster and your company is in the middle of a promotion being advertised on TV, you will likely have to scramble to reach consumers via another medium. The pandemic led many brands to switch advertising funds to digital marketing strategies.

Push versus pull strategy. Recall that we discussed push and pull strategies in Chapter 8 when we discussed marketing channels. Which strategy a firm chooses depends on whether a firm is running promotions that target consumers (pull) or a firm's intermediaries (push), such as its wholesalers and retailers. Most companies use a combination of both.

The Communication Process

perceptual process

The way in which people select the information they are exposed to, pay attention to it, interpret it, and retain it.

Do you stream shows or record movies so you can watch them when you want without television commercials? Do you even watch regular television? Have you ever watched someone use the remote to skip the commercials or zap (change channels) to look at different shows? Think about which shows you choose to watch, which social media platforms you utilize, and what other types of media you use. The **perceptual process** is how a person decides what to pay attention to and how to interpret and remember different things, including information in advertising. By selecting a show, a movie, a social media platform, or even an elective class in school, you're choosing what you're exposed to and what gets your attention. However, your selection does not ensure you'll pay attention, remember, or correctly interpret what you see or hear.

Think about what else you are doing when you watch a show or movie, study, or perhaps use your computer during class. Imagine you're ready to watch a movie with friends. The volume is turned up so you can hear all the messages as well as the movie. If you're talking to your friends before the movie begins, do you hear or pay attention to the commercials prior to the movie? Do you remember which products were advertised? If you're with a friend and hear someone else say your name, do you pay more attention to the person talking about you than to your friend?

With so many different types of distractions and technology as well as recording devices, imagine how difficult it is for an advertiser to get you to pay attention, much less remember its message. Do you remember the terms you memorized for a test a day later? Do you know your friends' phone numbers and email addresses, or do you just find their names on your contact list? To increase people's retention of their marketing messages, advertisers often repeat them multiple times in different places, in different posts, across social media platforms and often on traditional media such as television. However, marketers must be careful that consumers don't get so tired of the message that their consumers react negatively to it and the product.

encodes

Senders must translate or convert benefits and value of a product or service into a message for the message channel selected.

decodes

Receivers interpret messages.

Figure 11.2 illustrates how messages are sent and received. The source (or sender) **encodes**, or translates, a message so that it's appropriate for the message channel—say, for a print advertisement, TV commercial, or store display—and shows the benefits and value of the offering. The receiver (customer or consumer) then **decodes**, or interprets, the message. For effective communication to occur, the receiver must interpret the message as the sender intended.

Message Problems

You're ready to go home on a Friday afternoon and you hear someone mention an upcoming event on Saturday. However, you did not listen to all the details and assume the event is the next day, not the following Saturday. Since you already made other plans for the next day, you don't even consider showing up the following Saturday. Has this ever happened to you? Have you missed an event because you didn't interpret a message correctly? The same thing can happen with marketing messages. If you do not hear a message correctly or misinterpret it, you might think a product or service provides different benefits or is easier or harder to use than it really is.

interference

Any distractions or noise that senders and receivers face during the transmission of a message.

Interference, or noise, can distort marketing messages. Factors such as poor reception, poor image, problems with a server or technology, or a low battery can interfere with your getting messages. Interference includes any distractions receivers and senders face during the transmission of a message. This is a particular problem today for marketers because increasingly consumers are multitasking. They don't just sit and watch a show. Instead, they are likely to be on online and possibly texting their friends at the same time. As a result, marketing messages can be misinterpreted.

The same thing may happen if you're studying for an exam while you're talking to a friend or watching a show. The conversation or show interferes with remembering what you're reading. If a friend tells you a story, then you tell another friend, and that person tells someone else, will the message be the same after it is relayed to multiple people? If you miss class and borrow someone else's notes, do you understand what they mean? Not only must advertisers try to present consistent messages, they must also try to ensure that you interpret the message as they intended.

feedback

Means of telling sellers you saw their information and wanted to try their product.

Purchasing a product provides the sender with **feedback**, which often tells the seller that you saw information and wanted to try the product. If you use any coupons or promotions when you buy a product, the advertiser knows which vehicle you used to get the information. Market research and warranty registration also provide feedback.

We tend to purchase products and remember information that has some relevance to our personal situation or beliefs. If you have no need for a product or service, you might not pay attention to or remember the messages used to market it. Advertisers also want you to remember their brands so that you'll think of their goods and services when you need to make a purchase.

FIGURE 11.2 The Communication Process

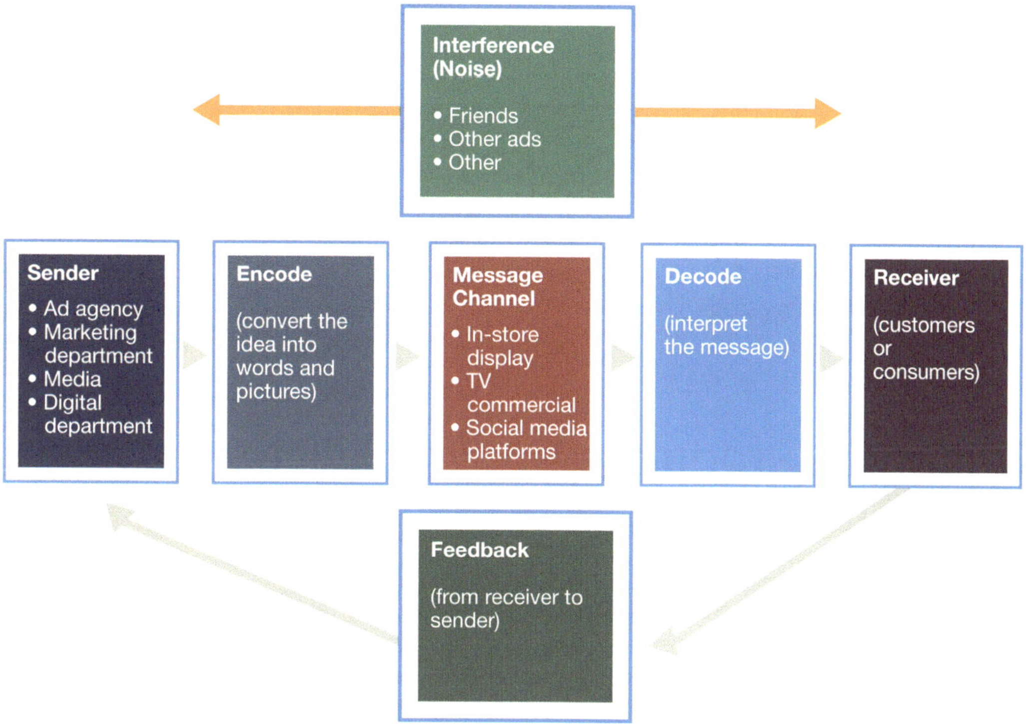

Key Takeaway

- Many factors, such as a firm's marketing budget, the type of product, regulations, target customers, and competitors, influence what composes the promotion mix. Depending on what medium is used, marketers use the communication process to encode or translate ideas into messages that can be correctly interpreted (decoded) by buyers. However, marketers must determine how to get consumers' attention and avoid as much interference and noise as possible. Perceptual processes include how a person decides what to pay attention to and how to interpret and remember different things.

Review Questions

1. Explain the communication process and factors that can interfere with interpretation of messages.
2. What is the perceptual process and how does it relate to promotion?
3. What is the difference between encoding and decoding a message?
4. How does being on social media or online interfere with your getting messages during movies?
5. What factors get you to pay attention to promotions?
6. What media do you use most frequently? What promotions do you remember?

11.4 Message Strategies

Learning Objectives

1. Understand what a unique selling proposition is and how it is used.
2. Understand different types of promotion objectives.
3. Identify different message strategies.

Utilizing a Product's Unique Selling Proposition (USP)

unique selling proposition (USP)

A specific product benefit consumers will remember.

When organizations want to communicate value, they must determine what message strategies work best for them. Smart organizations determine a product's **unique selling proposition (USP)**, or a specific benefit that consumers will remember. Robinhood's "Investing for Everyone" is a good example of a unique selling proposition. Likewise, Nike's global slogan "Just Do It" has been used for over six decades. It helps consumers think of all the things that they, like professional athletes, are capable of doing, not only when they use Nike's wide variety of sporting products, but also in life.

Nike "Just Do It" commercial

Nike products encourage athletes to excel in sports and in life.

View in the online reader

When deciding on a message strategy, organizations must consider the audience, the objectives of the promotion, the media, and the budget, as well as the USP and the product. Knowing your audience and who you are trying to reach is critical. Nike and Coca-Cola have been extremely successful in adapting their promotions to different international markets. Both companies have very popular global brands.

The food maker Kraft's global brands are also very successful, and Kraft's promotions are consistent across media. The company uses the visuals from its commercials as pictures in its print ads in both English and Spanish versions. But although sometimes the same promotions work in different cultures (countries), others must be adapted for different international audiences—similar to the way products may be adapted for international markets. Companies must be careful of how words translate, how actions are interpreted, how actors (or models) look, and what different colors in ads may mean.

The more advertisers know about the consumers (or businesses) exposed to the message, the better. Commercials for golf products shown during golf tournaments focus specifically on golfers. Many times commercials that appeal to one target market may not appeal to other markets. Not so with Progressive's Insurance Commercials, which focus on young people not becoming their parents when buying and insuring their first home! The commercials, introduced during the pandemic, provided a bright spot while many commercials focused on the uncertainty people faced.

Progressive Insurance Commercial with Dr. Rick Appeals to All Generations

The humorous commercials appeal to young people as well as their parents.

View in the online reader

The Organization's Promotion Objectives

Advertisers must also examine their promotion objectives. What are they trying to accomplish with their promotions? Are they trying to build awareness for a new product, wanting to get people to take action immediately, or interested in having people remember their brand in the future? Building **primary demand**, or demand for a product category, such as orange juice, might be one objective, but a company also wants to build **selective demand**, or demand for its specific brand(s), such as Tropicana orange juice. Some of the other types of objectives firms try to achieve with promotions include:

- differentiating a product from competing products
- educating consumers
- creating awareness
- repositioning a product
- improving store traffic and sales volumes
- capturing a greater share of the market with a product
- retaining customers and building brand loyalty
- creating "buzz" for a product
- strengthening the image of a company or brand

primary demand

Demand for a product category (e.g., orange juice) versus a product brand (e.g., Tropicana).

selective demand

Demand for a specific brand (Tropicana orange juice).

AIDA model

A model designed to get the attention, interest, desire, and action of consumers.

To achieve their promotion objectives, many firms use the **AIDA model**, which stands for *attention, interest, desire,* and *action*. First, companies focus on getting the attention of consumers by making them aware of a product or service, which is especially important for new offerings. If consumers or businesses are not aware of a product or service, they won't buy it. Once consumers or businesses are aware of products or services, organizations try to increase consumers' interest in them and persuade consumers that their brands are best (i.e., create desire for the products). Ultimately, companies want consumers to take action or purchase their products or services.

Message Characteristics

Coke Zero

In 2009, Coke used the same approach as it did with its 1980 award-winning Mean Joe Greene commercial. But this time the product being advertised was Coke Zero, which was replaced in 2021 with Coca-Cola Sugar Free.

View in the online reader

Organizations must also determine what type of appeal to use and how to structure their messages. Some common advertising appeals are humorous, emotional, fear-inducing, rational (informative), and environmentally conscious. Appeals that stress how fun a product is or how it will improve a person's health, financial situation, social status, or looks are also common. If you were asked to name your favorite commercial, would it be one with a humorous appeal? Many people like commercials that use humor because they are typically entertaining and memorable. Humor sells, but firms must be careful that the brand is remembered. Some commercials are very entertaining, but consumers cannot remember the brand or product.

Each year, some of the most talked-about commercials take place during the Super Bowl. Many people watch the game just to see the commercials. Watch the following YouTube videos to see one of the top ten Super Bowl commercials of all time and how later commercials relied on a similar approach. Notice how many of them use a humorous appeal. Do you think some are more effective than others? In other words, will viewers actually buy the product(s)?

Pepsi's Humor

View in the online reader

Companies must also be careful when using fear appeals so consumers don't get too alarmed or frightened. Reebok had to discontinue a TV commercial because it upset so many people. The ad showed a bungee jumper diving off a bridge, followed by a shot of just his shoes hanging from the bridge by the bungee cord. That ad provoked people because it implied the jumper had fallen to his death.

Firms also decide whether to use strategies such as an open-ended or closed-ended message; a one-sided or two-sided message; or slogans, characters, or jingles. An **open-ended message** allows the consumer to draw his or her own conclusion, such as a commercial for perfume or cologne. A **closed-ended message** draws a logical conclusion.

open-ended message

A promotional message that allows the consumer to draw his or her own conclusions.

closed-ended message

A promotional message that draws a logical conclusion.

Most messages are one sided, stressing only the positive aspects of a product, similar to what you include on your résumé. However, two-sided messages are often used as well. They are common in content marketing. Recall that when firms utilize content marketing they are trying to educate consumers about the pros and cons of a product and then persuade them that the pros outweigh the cons. Two-sided messages are often used when a product is complex and needs explaining or when required by law such as pharmaceutical products. Two-sided advertising can also be used for products that are routinely purchased. For a number of years, Heinz ran ads with the tagline "still the slowest ketchup in town." The point of the ad was that even though Heinz ketchup is really slow coming out of the bottle, it is thick and rich and therefore worth the wait. Consumers are likely to view a two-sided message positively because it makes it appear that the seller has been honest about both the positive and negative aspects of the product.

The order of presentation also affects how well consumers remember a brand. If you forgot about a twenty-five page term paper that you had to write before the next day of class, which sections of the paper would you try to make the strongest? Would it be the beginning, the end, or the middle of the paper? Many students argue that either the beginning or the end is most important, hoping that the instructor does not read the entire paper carefully. The same strategy is true for commercials and advertisements. The beginning and the end of the message should be strong and include the brand name. That way, if consumers hear or read only part of the message, they will hopefully remember the brand name.

Companies often use characters or mascots and/or jingles or slogans to get the attention of consumers and help them remember their brands. When you think of Campbell's soup, do you think "Mm, mm good"? Campbell's began using the slogan with radio ads in 1931 and later made it a registered trademark. Apparently, "Mm, mm good" still resonates with consumers as Campbell's still uses it in television commercials.

B-O-L-O-G-N-A

This commercial first aired in the 1973. It was so cute that many consumers still can't forget the song—or the Oscar Mayer brand.

View in the online reader

Other classic characters (mascots) or symbols you may be familiar with include the Jolly Green Giant, the Pillsbury Doughboy, and Oscar Mayer's Wienermobile. The Wienermobile first hit the road in 1936 and is a fully integrated part of the company's marketing communications plan. You can follow the Wienermobile on Twitter and Instagram and buy Wienermobile-related gear and toys on Oscar Mayer's website. You can also download a driving game app that provides updates on the exact location of the vehicle at any point in time. Oscar Mayer also has an app that lets you add the Wienermobile to any photo you take. (Anybody want to create a selfie with the Wienermobile?)

"The best thing about Wienermobile sightings is that, unlike Sasquatch, the Wienermobile is real," say the folks at Oscar Mayer.

Source: © Shutterstock, Inc.

How successful are advertisers in making sure consumers know their brands? Try the brand quiz and see how many brand icons you know.

For nearly a century the Jolly Green Giant helped people remember General Mills' product lineup.

Source: © Shutterstock, Inc.

But although many of the characters and jingles have stayed the same for decades, companies have to be prepared to change not only their mascots, jingles, and messaging strategies, but their products and other elements of the marketing and promotion mix as the consumers they target change. The Jolly Green Giant is an example. For ninety years the mascot helped General Mills sell the company's canned and frozen products. But recently General Mills sold the giant and its Green Giant product lineup to another company. Why? Because many shoppers favor fresh food rather than canned and frozen food.

Likewise, Campbell's Soup has changed its products, packaging, and messaging to attract millennials and people who want fresher, less-processed foods. The company also rolled out an ad campaign called "Real Real Life," which is designed to appeal to the growing number of nontraditional families in the United States—families that often have a lot of spending power.

Campbell's Inclusivity

This commercial targets nontraditional families and represents a new messaging strategy for Campbell's Soup.

View in the online reader

Key Takeaway

- Organizations must determine promotion objectives, or what they want to accomplish with their promotions. For example, if a company has a new brand, it may want to generate awareness or attention. Later, the company may focus on persuading customers to buy its brand. Each brand needs a unique selling proposition (USP), or specific benefit consumers will remember. To achieve their promotion objectives, many firms use the AIDA (attention, interest, desire, and action) model. Organizations must also determine what type of appeal to use and how to structure their messages. Some of the common advertising appeals are humorous, emotional, fear, rational (informative), and environmentally conscious. Appeals that stress how fun a product is or how it will improve a person's health, financial situation, social status, or looks are also common. Using characters or mascots and/or jingles or slogans is another way to get the attention of consumers and help them remember brands.

Review Questions

1. Identify the different promotion objectives companies may use.
2. What are some of the message strategies organizations use?
3. What is the difference between an open-ended and a closed-ended message?

11.5 The Promotion Budget

Learning Objectives

1. Understand different ways in which promotion budgets can be set.
2. Understand how the budget can be allocated among different media.

percent-of-sales method

A budgeting technique based on a set percentage of current or projected sales.

affordable method

A budgeting technique whereby companies spend what they think they can afford promoting a product.

competitive parity

A budgeting method whereby companies make sure their promotion budgets are comparable to their competitors'.

objective and task method

A budget based on a company's promotion objectives and the costs of the activities and tasks necessary to accomplish those objectives.

The promotion budget is a critical factor when it comes to deciding which message strategies to pursue. Several methods can be used to determine the promotion budget. The simplest method typically involves using a **percentage of last year's sales** or the projected sales for the next year. This method does not take into account any changes in the market or unexpected circumstances. However, many firms use this method because it is simple and straightforward.

Small businesses often use the **affordable method**, or what they think they can afford. Unfortunately, things often cost more than anticipated, and the business may not have enough money. Many small businesses think they're going to have money for promotions, but they run out and cannot spend as much on the promotions as they had hoped. Such a situation may have happened to you when you planned a weekend trip based on what you thought you could afford, and you did not have enough money. As a result, you had to modify your plans and not do everything you planned.

Other companies may decide to use **competitive parity**—that is, they try to keep their promotional spending comparable to the competitors' spending level. This method is designed to keep a brand in the minds of consumers. During a recession, some firms feel like they must spend as much—if not more—than their competitors to get customers to buy from them. Other companies are forced to cut back on their spending or pursue more targeted promotions. When Kmart was in bankruptcy, the firm cut back on its expenditures yet kept its advertising inserts (freestanding inserts, or FSI) in Sunday newspapers to try and remain competitive with other businesses using inserts. However, their strategy did not work. With the chicken sandwich wars, most competitors ran television commercials and many are still shown.

A more ideal approach is the **objective and task method**, whereby marketing managers first determine what they want to accomplish (objectives) with their communication. Then they determine what activities—commercials, sales promotions, digital, and so on—are necessary to accomplish the objectives. Finally, they conduct research to figure out how much the activities, or tasks, cost in order to develop a budget.

Part of the budgeting process includes deciding how much money to allocate to different media. As you have learned, spending changes are occurring as the media landscape continues to change. Figure 11.3 shows what percentage of advertising spending worldwide was allocated to different types of media in 2020, according to information reported by Statista. Spending on digital, social media, and mobile marketing, which are included in the internet category of the chart, are by far growing the fastest.

FIGURE 11.3 Global Ad Spending on Different Types of Media, 2021

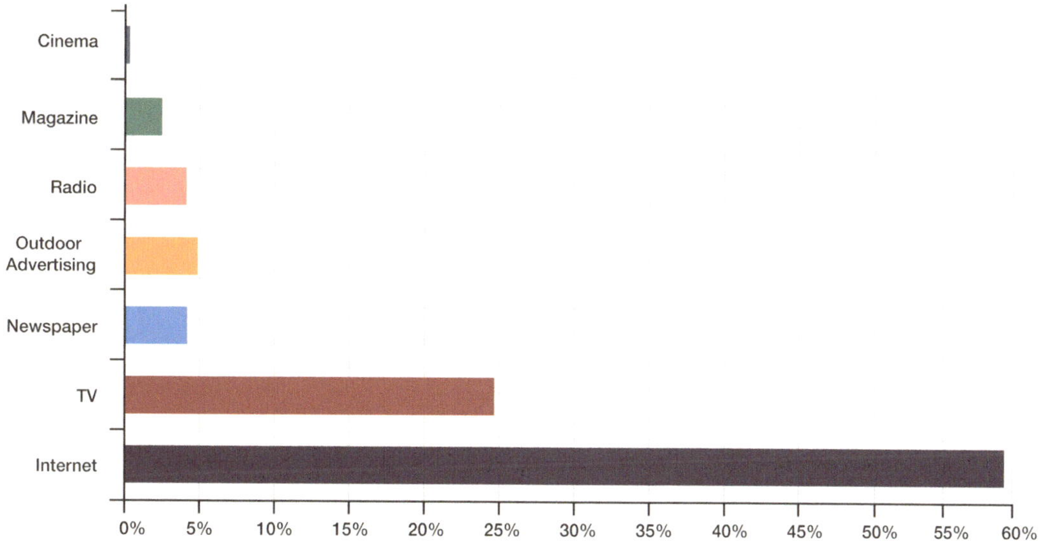

Source: Adapted from Guttmann, A. (2022), "Distribution of Advertising Spending Worldwide in 2021, by Medium," https://www.statista.com/statistics/376260/global-ad-spend-distribution-by-medium/ (February 17).

Another factor firms consider when choosing among media is the cost per contact. The **cost per contact** is what it costs a firm to reach one receiver of a marketing message. Recall that we talked about how many cents it costs an advertiser to reach each viewer of a Super Bowl commercial. In practice, marketing professionals measure contact costs in terms of one thousand people contacted rather one person contacted.

Thanks to social media and digital marketing, the cost per contact of an ad can sometimes be much lower than what a firm originally calculates. Dollar Shave Club (DSC) went from a start-up to a strong competitor, thanks to video. Their first video generated almost five million views in three months and resulted in over 12,000 orders in 48 hours. Now owned by Unilever, who bought DSC for $1 billion in 2016, DSC has advertised during the Super Bowl as well as many popular sports shows. Their commercials tend to be humorous, attracting and retaining a loyal customer base.[6]

A different type of "mobile" marketing: The Stubb's BBQ trailer travels around the country promoting the company's brand name and product. (This is actually an example of out-of-home advertising.)

Source: Photo courtesy of Stubb's Legendary Kitchen

cost per contact

The cost to reach one receiver of a marketing message.

Dollar Shave Club (DSC) Commercial

Dollar Shave Club's humorous commercials appeals to their growing customer base.

View in the online reader

Key Takeaway

- Companies can determine how much to spend on their promotions using several different methods. The percent of sales method, in which companies use a set percentage of sales for their promotion, is often the easiest method to use. Small companies often focus on what they think they can afford, whereas other organizations may try to keep their promotional spending relatively equal to their competitors' spending. The objective and task approach takes a firm's objectives into consideration and the costs of the tasks necessary to accomplish those objectives in order to determine a promotion budget. Part of the budgeting process includes deciding how much money to allocate to different media. Another factor firms consider when choosing among media is the cost per contact, or receiver, of a message. In practice, marketing professionals put this measure in terms of the cost per one thousand people contacted.

Review Questions

1. Explain four different ways to set a product's promotion budget.
2. Why are digital and mobile marketing growing so fast?

11.6 Advertising and Direct Marketing

Learning Objectives

1. Understand the difference between media and vehicles.
2. Explain the similarities and differences between advertising and direct marketing.
3. Understand the benefits of direct marketing and what types of direct marketing organizations often utilize.

Advertising

medium

The general types of communication (e.g., television or radio) available for advertisers.

Advertising is paid promotion with an identified sponsor that reaches many people at one time and can be repeated many times. One of the biggest issues an organization must address is which **medium** or media provides the biggest bang for the buck, given a product's characteristics and target market. For example, a thirty-second ad aired during Super Bowl LV cost $5.5 million, resulting in $545 million of ad revenues. Because only 96.4 million people, the smallest audience since 2007, watched the game, the cost per ad was approximately 5.7 cents per viewer.[7] Do high-priced commercials such as these pay off in terms of sales, when you consider the fact that they reach so many people? Many advertising professionals believe many of the commercials don't, yet they probably do create brand awareness or a public relations type of effect since many people tune in and then talk about Super Bowl commercials, while many other commercials go viral.

Whether it's a commercial on the Super Bowl or an ad in another medium, each has different advantages and disadvantages. For example, mobile phones provide access to people on the go, although the reception people get varies in different markets. Radios, magazines, and newspapers are also portable. People tend to own more than one radio, but there are so many radio stations in each market that it may be difficult to reach all of your target customers. People are also doing other activities, such as driving or studying, while listening to the radio. And lacking visuals, radio must rely solely on audio to get people's attention.

Of course, television does allow for visuals. Like with radio, many people multitask while watching television. Others record shows and skip commercials, change channels during commercials, or leave the room. In an effort to get people's attention, for years advertisers increased the volume of television commercials. While the Federal Trade Commission passed a regulation effective in 2010 that prohibits advertisers from changing the volume levels of TV commercials, many consumers still notice that some commercials are louder than the regular shows.

The first issue of *Sports Illustrated* was published August 16, 1954. Today, the companies that advertise in *Sports Illustrated* can do so not only in the magazine but also on the publication's website.

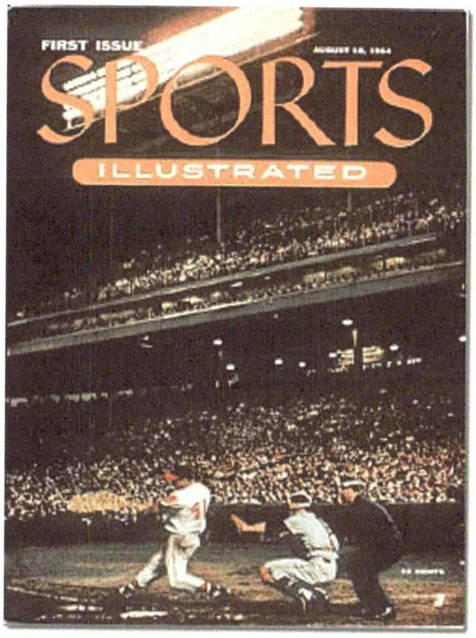

Source: By Source, Fair use, https://en.wikipedia.org/w/index.php?curid=22655745

People save magazines for a long time, but advertisers must plan in advance to run their ads in certain issues. Because of the internet, both magazines and newspapers are suffering in terms of readership and advertising dollars. Many major newspapers, such as papers in Seattle and Chicago, have gone out of business. Other newspapers are free online but still make printed copies available, such as the *Wall Street Journal* and *USA Today*. The fact that local retailers get cheaper rates for advertising in local newspapers may encourage both local businesses and consumers to support newspapers in some markets.

Within each different medium, an organization might select a different vehicle. A **vehicle** is the specific means within a medium to reach a selected target market. For example, if a company wants to develop television commercials to reach teenagers, it might select a TV show like *NCIS or FBI* as the best vehicle. If an organization wants to use magazines to reach males interested in sports, it might use *Sports Illustrated* or the publication's website, SI.com, where readers can get up-to-date information about sporting events and scores.[8]

vehicle

The specific means, such as a particular magazine or a specific television show, within a medium to reach a selected target market.

With so many things competing for consumers' attention, advertisers continue to seek creative ways to get their names and messages in front of consumers. Working with Amazon, advertisers use a creative approach by designing specially designed boxes to promote events and products. The first bright yellow box shipped by Amazon promoted the movie, *Minions*. The boxes generated awareness of the movie (and related goods) and included the date the movie would be available. To celebrate the thirty-fifth anniversary of Super Mario, Amazon worked with Nintendo to create bright red boxes with Super Mario and Luigi. Think of how many people get packages from Amazon and the number of people who would see the bright yellow or red boxes.[9]

Business-to-business companies may also use brochures to supplement their promotions. Sales representatives often share brochures with both current and potential customers. Brochures are also popular at trade shows and conventions (see discussion of Trade Promotions in Section 8). See an example of a trade promotion below.

The cover of a Calibrate Community brochure.

Source: Courtesy of AIS, Inc.

Direct Marketing

Recall that catalogs and brochures mailed to people are examples of direct marketing. Direct marketing allows organizations to target a specific set of customers, test different marketing strategies before rolling them out to all targeted consumers, and then readily measure how well the campaign worked by looking at its return on investment (ROI). For example, a firm may test a brochure by sending it to people in a specific target market, such as current customers in a geographic area. If the response is good, the firm will then send the brochure to all its current customers as well as potential customers. If the response is good, the firm will then send the brochure to its entire target market. The effect of direct marketing is also easily measurable. If you know how many brochures you sent, and how many people responded by buying the item advertised in the brochure, it's easy to figure out whether the campaign paid off or not. However, consumers often ignore attempts to reach them via direct marketing.

telemarketing

A form of direct marketing that involves contacting people by phone.

Telemarketing involves direct marketing by phone. You may have just sat down for dinner when the phone rings with a local charity calling to raise money. The calls always seem to come at dinner or at other inconvenient times. Although expensive, telemarketing can be extremely effective for charitable organizations and different service firms and retailers. However, because some consumers have negative perceptions of telemarketers, many organizations do not use them. The National Do Not Call Registry, which was established in 2008, prohibits for-profit organizations from calling phone numbers registered with the Federal Trade Commission, subject to certain exceptions. For example, a call from an organization that you have established a business relationship with is legal. A call from an organization that you have never heard of or have never done business with is not legal, but enforcement has become difficult. Organizations also call cell numbers and obtain phone numbers that look familiar to people they are calling. Wireless carriers have taken actions to reduce spam calls.

As you have learned, direct response advertising includes an offer and a call to action. You may be watching television when an interesting product is shown. The announcer says, "Call now and receive a bonus package." The advertiser wants consumers to call to purchase the product or to get more information. The internet is a less-expensive direct response medium for direct marketing, and, as you will learn in Chapter 12, a highly profitable one. All of the marketing emails you get urging you to buy products now are an example of direct response advertising conducted over the internet. Direct response advertising can be measured whereas other methods may not be so easy to measure.

Matt Mitcho—Gemelli Biotech

Source: Gemelli Biotech, used with permission.

Matt Mitcho, CEO and Founder of Gemelli Bio, has over twenty years of experience in the pharmaceutical industry. He has launched and grown three billion-dollar brands, won numerous awards for innovative marketing initiatives, and built and led highly engaged teams committed to success but grounded in ethical decision making. He strongly believes that great work and great brands are born when culture, sound strategy, and timely execution meet. Focusing on these three pillars has led to incredible success. Matt received his MBA from Kenan-Flagler Business School at the University of North Carolina and his BS degree in public affairs from Indiana University.

Key Takeaway

- Advertising is paid communication that has an identified sponsor and reaches many people at one time. Once companies decide on different media (e.g., magazines or television), they must also select specific vehicles (e.g., *Sports Illustrated* or the Super Bowl). Direct marketing allows organizations to target specific individuals and use personalized direct response advertising. Telemarketing, the internet, direct mail, and catalogs are examples of direct marketing methods.

Review Questions

1. Why do you think so many organizations rely on advertising to communicate with customers and potential customers?
2. What is the difference between a medium and a vehicle? Give examples of each.
3. Why is direct marketing successful even though some consumers may not like it?

11.7 Public Relations, Sponsorships, and Product Placements

Learning Objectives

1. Understand the concept of public relations and why organizations allocate part of their promotional budgets to it.
2. Understand what the different types of public relations tools are.
3. Explain how sponsorships work.
4. Explain what a product placement is.

Public Relations

You just finished reading a great magazine story about a local restaurant even though you know the company has experienced several lawsuits and many customer complaints. The story makes the restaurant sound like a great corporate citizen and the best place to eat in town. Sometimes a company gets "free" publicity such as news stories or reviews about its products and services in the mass media, even though the organization has no control over the content of the stories and might not even know about their publication. How did a restaurant with so many complaints manage to get such a great story written about it? How did it get good coverage when it might not be deserved? Perhaps the restaurant used part of its promotion budget to pay for public relations efforts to generate positive stories and positive publicity.

Public relations (PR) includes information that an organization wants its public (customers, employees, stakeholders, general public) to know. PR involves creating a positive image for a company, an offering, or a person via publicity. PR has become more important in recent years because there are now so many media outlets people pay attention to, including YouTube, social networking platforms, and blogs. It's pretty easy for anyone to say anything about a company in a public forum and for the information to spread fast. Indeed, publicity is a double-edged sword; it can result in negative news, such as a poor review of a movie, restaurant, or car, or positive news.

Good public relations efforts result in positive news by helping a firm create rapport with its customers, promote what it has to offer, and supplement its sales efforts. PR puts a positive spin on news stories. Companies also use PR to promote products and to supplement their sales efforts.

Many organizations that engage in public relations have in-house PR departments, media relations groups, or investor relations groups. Other organizations sometimes hire external PR firms or advertising agencies to find and create public relations opportunities for them. PR specialists must build relationships with people at different media outlets to help get their stories placed. Universities, hospitals, government organizations, and charitable organizations often hire PR people to help disseminate positive information about their services and to increase interest in what they do. As such, PR is part of a company's promotion budget and their integrated marketing communications.

PR specialists also help political campaign managers generate positive information in the press. PR specialists can handle crisis communication and put a positive view on situations when something bad happens to an organization or person. In foreign markets, PR agencies may help ensure product concepts are understood correctly. Getting all PR stories placed in desired media is not guaranteed. A lot of time and effort is spent getting to know people who can help publish or announce the information to the public. Organizations work hard to get favorable news stories, so while publicity sounds free, building relationships with journalists does cost money.

Companies use a variety of tools for their public relations purposes, including annual reports, brochures, newspapers, and magazines for both employees and the public; websites to show good things they're doing; speeches; blogs; videos; and podcasts. Some of the most commonly used PR tools include press releases and news conferences.

Tonya Harrell is the director of marketing for IntellecTechs, an information technology firm in Virginia Beach, Virginia, and one of America's fastest growing private companies. Harrell engages in a wide variety of PR activities in her role: She promotes the company to the community by working closely with the firm's media designer to produce sales materials, social media, and advertising. Writing press releases, planning the logistics and media coverage for events, promoting them, and serving as a spokesperson for the company are also part of her duties.

Tonya Harrell—IntellecTechs

Source: Photo courtesy of Tonya Harrell

As the director of marketing for IntellecTechs, Tonya Harrell tries to align the business's values and core beliefs with its marketing plan. "As I search for marketing opportunities, I look for something of value, whether it's delivering on my company's return on investment or supporting our community initiatives," Harrell says.

"Last year I worked with a local organization to assist with planning a Veterans Day memorial service," says Harrell. "Our company provided support in obtaining speakers for the event, military personnel to provide ceremonial services, promoted the event to the local news agencies, coordinated with local news agencies for on-air time to promote it, and worked as a liaison with a local business to assist with sponsoring food and beverage for the event."

Press Releases

Part of a company's public relations efforts includes putting a positive spin on news stories. A press release is a news story written by an organization to promote a product, organization, or person. Consider how much better a story or a product recommendation is likely to be perceived when the receiver thinks the content is from an objective third party rather than an organization writing about itself. Public relations personnel frequently prepare press releases in hopes that the news media will pick them up and disseminate the information to the public. However, there is no guarantee that the media will use a press release. Some of the PR opportunities that companies may seek to highlight in their press releases include charity events, awards, new products, company reports, and things they are doing to improve the environment or local community.

Read the following two examples of press releases. The first story focuses on recognition AIS received from the *Boston Business Journal* for the third year in a row, acknowledging AIS as one of the most charitable organizations in the state of Massachusetts. The second press release and picture provide an example of how a company like Stubb's BBQ teams up with Mobile Loaves & Fishes, a charity that helps feed the hungry, to help feed unhoused and people living in poverty, and restock food banks around the country. The story enhances the already positive image of both organizations.

AIS Press Release

AIS Named One of the Most Charitable Companies in Massachusetts by *Boston Business Journal*

Leominster, MA—August 16, 2021—AIS, a leading manufacturer of commercial office furniture and seating, has been named by the Boston Business Journal as an honoree of the publication's 2021 Corporate Citizenship Awards, a recognition of the region's top corporate charitable contributors.

The Business Journal annually publishes this list to showcase companies that promote and prioritize giving back to their communities—a feat that is even more important during times of turmoil and crisis, such as those experienced over the past year. This year, ninety-eight companies qualified for the distinction by reporting at least $100,000 in cash contributions to Massachusetts-based charities in 2020. The honorees include companies from such industry sectors as financial and professional services, health care, technology, retail, manufacturing, and professional sports.

AIS's stewardship extended throughout Massachusetts and beyond, with the company giving back more than $3.5 million in cash, in-kind and service contributions locally and across the country.

Among its most notable charitable efforts over the past year, AIS donated and delivered 600,000 high-quality face masks to over 500 organizations in Massachusetts and thirty additional states through the company's Sew the Masks program.

AIS began making high-quality facemasks when the COVID-19 pandemic intensified in the spring of 2020. That May, after seeing the demand for masks would continue, AIS established a nationwide Sew the Masks initiative based on Rosie the Riveter, the World War II icon. The company activated internal production lines and nearly 1,000 volunteer "Rosies" in forty-five states to create masks at their home sewing machines.

In partnership with the United Way of North Central Massachusetts and a number of sponsors, the Sew the Masks program provided masks to first responders, frontline workers, food banks and local schools as well as Election Day 2020 poll workers and city officials in nearly 270 cities and towns in Massachusetts and 80 precincts in Washington, DC.

"AIS is honored to be a recipient of the Boston Business Journal Corporate Citizenship Award for the third year in a row, alongside many extraordinary companies in the Boston area. I am so proud of and thankful for our employees, partners and the Rosies in Massachusetts and across the country who helped to make a difference in the Sew the Masks program to fight the spread of COVID-19," AIS CEO Bruce Platzman said.

Philanthropy is part of AIS's DNA, and Platzman in particular is passionate about giving back to the community. Some of the nonprofit organizations that AIS has supported include Make-A-Wish® Massachusetts and Rhode Island, United Way of North Central Massachusetts, the cities of Leominster and Fitchburg, Catie's Closet, the American Red Cross, Designs for Dignity, Worcester Animal Rescue League, Base Hoopz, Partners in Literacy, and the Montachusett Interfaith Hospitality Network. Platzman currently serves on the board of directors of Make-A-Wish® Massachusetts and Rhode Island and the North Central Massachusetts Chamber of Commerce.

AIS has also partnered with Seven Hills ASPiRE!, a program for people with intellectual and developmental disabilities, autism and brain injury to develop the skills necessary to pursue interests in employment. Additionally, the company teams up with local high schools and universities for a "day in the life" of manufacturing opportunities and provides tours and mentoring to these up-and-coming students.

For several years in a row, AIS has participated in the United Way Combat Hunger initiative. Typically held in December, AIS team members pack more than 20,000 meals for North Central Massachusetts families in need.

About a decade ago, the rapidly growing AIS was being wooed by other states and even Mexico to relocate operations. Platzman and the company's board of directors chose to remain in Massachusetts and located headquarters and manufacturing operations in Leominster where AIS now employs more than 800.

Knowing the pandemic has taken its toll on the businesses and people in the northeast, AIS is now driving the ReNEW England initiative. Grounded in the multiplier-effect principle and reinforcing the premise that buying locally and regionally can accelerate the rebound of the region's economy, Platzman is sharing his company's dedication to sourcing as much materials as possible from neighbors while encouraging other businesses in New England to do the same.

"I've spent my entire life in Massachusetts," Platzman said. "I love our great state and the people who live here. When everyone commits to supporting each other through meaningful employment and business opportunities and worthy charitable efforts, our local communities will benefit and the overall economic health of the area will improve more rapidly."

AIS will be honored at the Business Journal's 16th Annual Corporate Citizenship Awards virtual ceremony on Sept. 9.

"During a time filled with unprecedented events and change, it's incredible to think that so many companies still gave so generously to charities in Massachusetts," said Boston Business Journal Market President and Publisher Carolyn Jones. "The philanthropic companies prioritize the welfare of our communities, and we are excited to be able to honor them."[10]

Stubb's Press Release

Stubb's Teams Up with Mobile Loaves & Fishes to Launch "Feed the World Tour"

Tuesday, May 26, 5 p.m. @ Wooldridge Park

AUSTIN—Stubb's Legendary Kitchen will kick off its twelve-city "Feed the World Tour" this Tuesday, May 26 at 5 p.m. in Wooldridge Square Park, 9th and Guadalupe Streets, by serving chopped beef sandwiches with famous Stubb's barbecue sauce to homeless and working poor people from one of Mobile Loaves & Fishes' special catering trucks, which serve people in six cities every day.

Source: Photo courtesy of Stubb's Legendary Kitchen

Kurt Koegler, president of Stubb's Legendary Kitchen, will join Alan Graham, Mobile Loaves' founder/president, and volunteers from the company and MLF volunteers to serve the sandwiches and distribute Stubb's T-shirts. The Austin-based company chose Mobile Loaves as its partner to kick off the "Feed the World Tour," which is named for the stated mission of Texas Bar-B-Q legend, C.B. "Stubb" Stubblefield, who said: "I was born hungry. I want to feed the world."

> After leaving Austin, the tour will swing through the Southeast, up the East Coast and into Washington, D.C. where the Stubb's team will compete at the annual BBQ Battle on Pennsylvania Avenue. In each city, Stubb's Legendary Kitchen and company president Koegler will barbecue for the homeless and help restock depleted food banks.
>
> "Stubb was a cook but more than that, a lover of people. The values that guided his life still guide the company that bears his name. Stubb's life truly is in every bottle of sauce and marinade we make. All of us at Stubb's are thrilled to be working with Mobile Loaves and bringing all of Stubb's Love and Happiness to those who all too often need it most" said Koegler.
>
> "The economy has placed greater demand on organizations like Mobile Loaves and local food banks, so we couldn't think of a better time to show our support," Koegler said. "Stubb's greatest joy was feeding the people who came from all around for a taste of his famous barbecue, and it is an honor for us to fulfill his mission with our Feed the World Tour."
>
> "We're honored to be selected as Stubb's charity partner for the kick-off of this awesome tour," Graham said. "As someone who once was poor and hungry, C.B. 'Stubb' Stubblefield is smiling in heaven to know that his creation is helping feed brothers and sisters on the street here in Austin and around the country. We look forward to connecting Stubb's with people on the streets here and in the other cities we serve."[11]

crisis communication

The process of countering the negative effects a company experiences when it receives extremely bad publicity.

Press releases and other PR activities can also be used for damage control purposes. **Crisis communication** is the process of countering the negative effects a company experiences when it receives extremely bad publicity. Domino's Pizza was forced to engage in damage control after two of its employees created a video doing disgusting things to pizzas and then posting it to YouTube. If the publicity is particularly bad, as it was for Domino's, a company might hold a press conference or prepare a speech for the top executive to give. For example, the president of Domino's spoke on video to try to control the damage to Domino's business and posted the video on YouTube. When KFC ran out of chicken and had to close about 700 restaurants, being transparent and turning to Twitter helped the company get rid of rumors.[12]

Online Reputation Management

online reputation management (ORM)

The process of monitoring what's being said about your company on the internet in an effort to influence people's perceptions about the firm.

Online reputation management (ORM) is the process of monitoring what's being said about your company on the internet in an effort to influence people's perceptions about the firm. ORM is an important part of PR because, as you know, negative information and images about a company can spread like wildfire online. Negative information online is also hard to combat because companies usually don't control the social networks and websites the information appears on.

Sometimes the information posted is false. Chinese companies actually pay people to go online and disparage their competitors' products. At one point, KFC had to refute a rumor that its Chinese restaurants were cooking up chickens that each had eight legs.[13]

Sometimes, however, the negative information is true. Some goods and services are truly bad and get rated as much on social media. UPS had to go into crisis communication mode after someone posted a video online of an employee recklessly tossing packages around rather than handling them carefully.[14] The effort included putting out press releases and calling a news conference.

PR personnel routinely dispute false information and bogus reviews and get them removed from third-party websites they don't control, such as Yelp, Trivago, and Amazon. Of course, a firm can simply delete negative comments on its own websites that it controls. But doing so can be problematic. Why? Because people whose posts get deleted usually post their messages over and over again online as well as complain on other social networks and websites that their posts are being deleted. It's better to immediately acknowledge a customer's complaint and resolve it before the negative information spreads.

Dell Computer created a new department called the Social Media Command Center after customers complained publicly online about being trapped in "Dell Hell" when they tried to get good customer service from the computer maker. An army of Dell employees at the command center use sophisticated technology to determine what's being said about Dell online and how exactly to help customers solve their problems.

Online reputation doesn't always have to involve salvaging your company's reputation, though. It can also be used to enhance your reputation. What Daniel McCawley, the owner of the Atomic Grill eatery in Morgantown, West Virginia, did to promote his restaurant on social media is an example of online reputation management at its finest. McCawley was monitoring what customers were saying about the restaurant on Urbanspoon when he noticed an online comment to the effect that the waitstaff at the restaurant ought to "show more skin."

The remark upset McCawley, who is the father of young girls and has five sisters. So, he announced on the restaurant's Facebook page that the Atomic Grill would be running a temporary promotion in which *a lot* of skin would be shown: potato skins, that is. He also posted a photo of an order of them and noted that the profits from the "Show Our Skin" campaign would be donated to the West Virginia Foundation for Rape Information Services.

There's more than one way to "skin" a problem that develops on social media.

Source: © Shutterstock, Inc.

It didn't take long for the "Show Our Skin" campaign to spread like wildfire on social media as well as get the attention of media outlets nationwide. As a result of McCawley's creative thinking, hundreds of people who had never been to the restaurant before showed up to buy potato skins and exhibit (pardon the pun) their support for the foundation.

Lastly, although it's a widespread practice that is hard to combat, it's not a good idea to try to improve your reputation by paying people to provide fake "likes" online. According to the U.S. Federal Trade Commission, an advertiser buying fake "likes" is very different from an advertiser offering incentives for "likes" from actual consumers. If "likes" are from nonexistent people or people who have no experience using the product or service, they are clearly deceptive, and both the purchaser and the seller of the fake "likes" could face legal action.

Sponsorships

Many of you have heard of the Staples Center, where the Los Angeles Lakers (NBA), Los Angeles Clippers (NBA), Los Angeles Kings (NHL), and Los Angeles Sparks (WNBA) have played sports since the arena opened. But imagine how many more people have heard about the Staples Center which hosts over 250 events a year, with some of the more famous events including the Grammy Awards, concerts (BTS, Kane Brown, Beyoncé, Taylor Swift, Garth Brooks, Bruce Springsteen), and Michael Jackson's public memorial in July 2009. All the news stories talking about tickets and information about the memorial provided "free" publicity and a great return on its sponsorship for the office supplies store, Staples, for which the center is named. Staples paid $116 million in 1999 for naming rights of the center for twenty years and became permanent in late 2009, making them the first lifetime corporate sponsor for a venue in a primary market. In 2021, the Lakers extended their agreement through 2041 to continue playing in the Staples Center.[15]

The Staples Center in Los Angeles is an example of a venue sponsorship.

Source: © Shutterstock, Inc.

A sponsorship involves paying a fee to have your name associated with different things, such as the following:

- a particular venue (Mercedes Benz Field, the Staples Center, AT&T's Performing Arts Center)
- a superstar's apparel (football star Tom Brady with sweatshirt from Brady, his own apparel line; golfer Jordan Spieth wearing Under Armour clothing)
- an event (Macy's Thanksgiving Day Parade, the Chick-fil-A Peach Bowl)
- a cause (Bank of America's support of the Special Olympics, the Ronald McDonald House)
- Higher Learning Commission educational workshops, information session
- a NASCAR vehicle (such as the cars with FedEx or Lowe's on hood of cars)

Mars, Inc., the maker of M&Ms, is one of the many companies that sponsor NASCAR racing teams.

Source: © Shutterstock, Inc.

Even though sponsorships are expensive, they are growing in popularity as corporations seek ways to strengthen their corporate image, increase their brand awareness, differentiate their products, and reach their target markets. Worldwide, corporations spend tens of billions of dollars annually on sponsorships. Over two-thirds of the sponsorships in North America are for sports, followed by entertainment and performing arts and causes, such as the Susan G. Komen Race for the Cure.[16]

Cause-related marketing, such as sponsoring the Susan G. Komen Race for the Cure, is one of the fastest-growing types of sponsorships. It occurs when a company supports a nonprofit organization in some way. Bank of America is one of the corporate sponsors of the Special Olympics, and American Airlines raises money for breast cancer research with an annual celebrity golf and tennis tournament. Cause-related marketing can have a positive PR impact by strengthening the affinity people have for a company that does it.

cause-related marketing

When a company supports a nonprofit organization in some way in order to generate positive public relations.

Special Olympics Competitor

Bank of America generates positive PR as one of the corporate sponsors for Special Olympics.

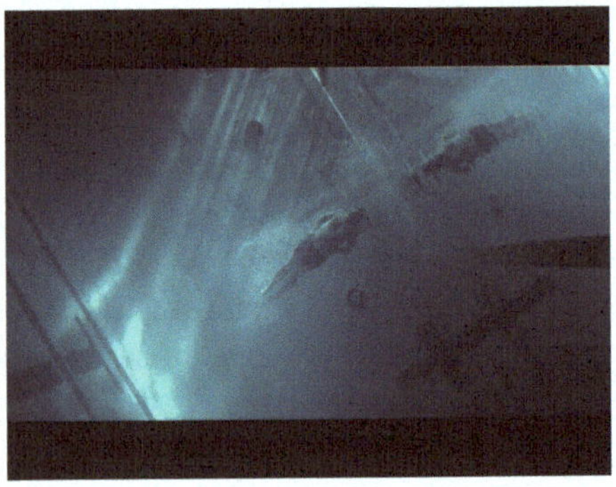

View in the online reader

Product Placements

product placement

Getting a company's product included as part of a television show, movie, video game, special event, or book.

Getting a company's product included as part of a television show, movie, video game, special event, or book is called a **product placement**. With over $23 billion (globally) to be spent on product placement 2021, the trend continues to increase. As more consumers subscribe to streaming services, watch prerecorded shows and videos, and skip ads at beginning of videos as well as commercials throughout television shows, product placement has become more popular.[17]

Classic examples of streaming go back many years, but two extremely successful placements included Reese's Pieces and Heineken. Way back in 1982, Hershey's paid $1 million to have Reese's Pieces featured in the movie *E.T. the Extra-Terrestrial*. Heineken paid $45,000,000 for James Bond to take a quick sip of its beer rather than a martini in the movie *Skyfall*.[18] For years, Coca-Cola paid to have cups of Coke placed on the judges' table on the show *American Idol*.

Product placements are designed to generate exposure, brand awareness, and interest in a product. Although most product placements appear in television shows and movies, they also appear in online videos, computer games, and books.

Typically, a company pays a fee for a product placement. So, technically, a product placement is a type of advertising. However, like public relations and sponsorships, it's a subtle type of advertisement rather than an overt sales pitch.

Sometimes a company pays nothing if the product is needed for a show in some way or as part of the plot. The final episode of the AMC series *Mad Men* ended with a 1971 Coke ad featuring the song "I'd Like to Buy the World a Coke." The Coca-Cola Company didn't pay for the ad but did give the show permission to use it.[19]

Mad Men: Scene from the Final Episode

The Coca-Cola Company paid nothing when the AMC series *Mad Men* showed this ad at the end of the show's final episode.

View in the online reader

Key Takeaway

- Public relations (PR) are the activities organizations engage in to create a positive image for a company, product, service, or a person. A press release, which is a commonly used PR tool, is designed to generate publicity, but there is no guarantee journalists will use it in the stories they write. Online reputation management (ORM) is an important part of PR because negative information and images about a company can spread like wildfire online. Sponsorships are designed to increase brand awareness, improve a company's image, and reach target markets. Product placements are designed to generate exposure, brand awareness, and interest in a product.

Review Questions

1. Why are public relations efforts funded by firms?
2. Who does the public relations for a firm?
3. Why is it critical for firms to engage in online reputation management?
4. Why are sponsorships becoming more popular?

11.8 Sales Promotions

Learning Objectives

1. Describe the different types of sales promotions companies use to get customers to buy their products.
2. Understand the different types of sales promotions companies use with their business customers.
3. Understand why sales promotions have become such an integral part of an organization's promotion mix.
4. Differentiate between push and pull strategies.

flash sale

A sale that offers a deep discount on a product (or products) for a limited number of hours.

Sales promotions are activities that supplement a company's advertising, public relations, and professional selling efforts. They create incentives for customers to buy products more quickly and make larger purchases. Sales promotions are often temporary. Sometimes they are *very* temporary. A **flash sale** is a sale that offers a deep discount on a product (or products) for only a number of hours. Zulily is an online website that specializes in flash sales. "Deals of the day" and airline tickets that are discounted for only a short amount of time are also examples of flash sales. Most flash sales are aimed at consumers rather than B2B buyers. Let's look at some of the other types of consumer sales promotions firms use.

Consumer Sales Promotions

sample

A small amount of a product given to consumers to try for free.

Samples, coupons, premiums, contests, and rebates are consumer sales promotions. Do you like free samples? Most people do. A free **sample** allows consumers to try a small amount of a product in the hope that they will purchase it. The strategy encourages trial and builds awareness of a product. You have probably purchased a product that included a small free sample with it—for example, a small amount of conditioner packaged with your shampoo. Perhaps you went to a store that provided free samples of different food items. Although sampling is an expensive strategy, it is usually very effective for food products. People try the product, and the person providing the sample tells them about the product and mentions any special prices for it.

coupons

Provide an immediate price reduction off an item that is reimbursed to the retailer by the manufacturer.

In many retail grocery stores, coupons are given to consumers with the samples. **Coupons** provide an immediate price reduction off an item. The amount of the coupon is later reimbursed to the retailer by the manufacturer. The retailer also gets a handling fee for accepting coupons. When the economy is weak, more consumers cut out coupons and look for special bargains such as double coupons and buy-one-get-one-free (BOGO) coupons. They may also buy more store brands.

Consumers frequently download digital coupons from stores' websites or other online sources. Some consumers also cut coupons from the inserts in newspapers or magazines. Other consumers find them on their cell phones. Over 80 percent of diapers are purchased with coupons. Procter & Gamble recently announced that they would reduce the amount of coupons as they move to higher prices on Pampers. In India and some other countries, most of the coupons used are digital. Paper coupons are more common in the United States, but are losing popularity as newspaper sales decline.

Point-of-purchase displays are in-store shelves where products are prominently displayed along with materials to market them. Often point-of-purchase displays are located near checkout stands or at the ends of aisles. The goal of the displays is to get consumers to buy a brand or product immediately. Some point-of-purchase displays include coupon machines placed next to the products.

point-of-purchase displays

Shelves in stores where products are prominently displayed along with materials to market them.

Other sales promotions include incentives such as free items, free shipping, and sweepstakes. For example, some online merchants such as Zappos offer free shipping and free return shipping to encourage consumers to shop online. Some firms have found that the response they get to their online sales promotions is better than the response they get to traditional sales promotions.

Another very popular sales promotion for consumers is a premium. A **premium** is something you get either for free or for a small shipping and handling charge with your proof of purchase (sales receipt or part of package). Remember wanting your favorite cereal because there was a toy in the box? The toy is an example of a premium. Sometimes you might have to mail in a certain number of proofs of purchase to get a premium. The purpose of a premium is to motivate you to buy a product multiple times. What many people don't realize is that when they pay the shipping and handling charges, they may also be paying for the premium.

premiums

Something consumers get for free or for a small handling charge with proof of purchase.

Contests are sales promotions people enter or participate in to have a chance to win a prize. The Publishers Clearing House Sweepstakes and the Monopoly Game at McDonald's are both examples of contests. The organization that conducts the sweepstakes or contest hopes you will not only enter its contest but buy some magazines (or more food) when you do.

contests

Sales promotions that people enter or participate in order to win a prize.

Events are another sales promotion tool. Check out the following video about the surprise event the Fanta brand held to promote its soft drinks. **Product demonstrations** are also used in conjunction with sales promotions. Do you need a shave? Periodically stores in the Art of Shaving chain will walk customers through the perfect shave. "When [customers] can see that shaving brush in action, the rich warm lather, the aftershave balm . . . it lends to the interactive experience," says Cari White, a regional director for the Art of Shaving.[20]

product demonstrations

A demonstration designed to show customers how a product works and answer any questions they might have.

Events and product demonstrations are examples of experiential marketing. **Experiential marketing** is marketing that that allows customers to physically interact with a brand using as many of their senses as possible (touch, smell, taste, and so on). More brick-and-mortar stores are utilizing experiential marketing to better compete with online sellers. You can't get a shave online, after all.

experiential marketing

Marketing that allows customers to physically interact with a brand using as many of their senses as possible.

Experiential Marketing

Watch this video to see an example of experiential marketing conducted by the Fanta soft drinks brand.

View in the online reader

loyalty programs

Sales promotions designed to get repeat business.

Loyalty programs are sales promotions designed to get repeat business. Loyalty programs include things such as frequent-flier programs, hotel programs, and shopping cards for grocery stores, drugstores, and restaurants. Sometimes point systems are used in conjunction with loyalty programs. After you accumulate so many miles or points, an organization might provide you with a special incentive such as a free flight, free hotel room, or free sandwich. Many loyalty programs, especially hotels and airlines, have partners to give consumers more ways to accumulate and use miles and points.

rebates

Promotions whereby part of the purchase price of an offering is refunded to a customer after the customer completes a form and sends in the proof of purchase (sales receipt).

Rebates are popular with both consumers and the manufacturers that provide them. When you get a rebate, you are refunded part (or all) of the purchase price of a product after completing a form and sending it to the manufacturer with your proof of purchase. The trick is completing the paperwork on time. Although different types of sales promotions work best for different organizations, rebates are very profitable for companies because many consumers forget or wait too long to send in their rebate forms. Consequently, they do not get any money back. Rebates sound great to consumers until they forget to send in their forms.

Trade Promotions

trade promotions

Sales promotions aimed at businesses.

In business-to-business (B2B) marketing, sales promotions are typically called trade promotions because they are targeted to channel members who conduct business or "trade" with consumers. **Trade promotions** include trade shows, conventions, event marketing, trade allowances, training, and special incentives given to retailers to market particular products and services, such as extra money, in-store displays, and prizes.

trade show

An event in which firms in a particular industry display and demonstrate their offerings to other organizations they hope will buy them.

Trade shows are one of the most common types of sales promotions in B2B markets. A **trade show** is an event in which firms in a particular industry display and demonstrate their offerings to other organizations they hope will buy them. There are typically many different trade shows in which one organization can participate. Using displays, brochures, and other materials, representatives at trade shows can identify potential customers (prospects), inform customers about new and existing products, and show them products and materials. Representatives can also get feedback from prospects about their company's products and materials and perhaps about competitors.

Companies also gather competitive information at trade shows because they can see the products other firms are exhibiting and how they are selling them. The photo that follows is an example of a trade show display that showcases the products produced by the Korean electronics firm LG. Trade shows can be very successful, although the companies that participate in them need to follow up on the leads generated at the shows. Companies sometimes use webinars to showcase their products when their business customers can't attend trade shows.

An LG electronics display at a trade show.

Source: © Shutterstock, Inc.

Conventions, conferences, or meetings with groups of professionals also provide a way for sellers to show potential customers different products. For example, a medical convention might be a good opportunity to display a new medical product or type of medical device. Sales representatives and managers often attend conventions to market their products. An example of the booth with information on Gemelli Biotech's products ibs-smart and trio-smart is shown below.

conventions

Meetings of groups of professionals that provide a way for sellers to show potential customers different products.

Gemelli Biotech's Booth showcasing ibs-smart and trio-smart.

Source: Used with permission of Gemelli Biotech

sales contests

Contests designed to motivate salespeople to increase their sales of particular products.

trade allowances

Allowances (including money) that firms provide their channel partners to motivate them to promote certain products.

advertising allowance

An allowance (money) a manufacturer provides to retailers to advertise its products in local newspapers.

training

Assistance an organization offers its channel partner's salespeople to help them understand how the organization's products work and how consumers can be enticed to buy them.

Sales contests, which are often held by manufacturers or vendors, provide incentives for salespeople to increase their sales. Often, the contests focus on selling higher-profit or slow-moving products. The sales representative with the most sales of the product wins a prize such as a free vacation, company recognition, or cash.

Trade allowances give channel partners—for example, a manufacturer's wholesalers, distributors, retailers, and so forth—different incentives to push a product. One type of trade allowance is an **advertising allowance** (money) to advertise a seller's products in local newspapers. An advertising allowance benefits both the manufacturer and the retailer. Typically, the retailer can get a lower rate than manufacturers on advertising in local outlets, saving the manufacturer money. The retailer benefits by getting an allowance from the manufacturer.

Another sales promotion that manufacturers, such as those in the tool or high-tech industries, offer businesses is **training** to help their salespeople understand how the manufacturers' products work and how consumers can be enticed to buy them. Many manufacturers also provide product demonstrations to show a channel partner's customers how products work and answer any questions they might have. Demonstrations of new video game systems and computers are extremely popular and successful in generating sales.

Free merchandise, such as a tool, television, or other product produced by the manufacturer, can also be used to get retailers to sell products to consumers. In other words, a manufacturer of televisions might offer the manager of a retail electronics store a television to push its products. If a certain number of televisions are sold, the manager gets the television. Have you ever been to an electronics store or a furniture store and felt like the salesperson was pushing one particular television or one particular mattress? Perhaps the salesperson was getting **push money**, or a cash incentive from the manufacturer to *push* a particular item. The push to sell the item might be because there is a large amount of inventory of it, it is being replaced by a new model, or the product is not selling well. Table 11.1 recaps the different types of sales promotions designed for both consumers and businesses.

Intuitive Surgical is the maker of the da Vinci robot, a new type of technology used to make surgeries easy to perform and less invasive. Intuitive Surgical often demonstrates the robot at surgical conventions.

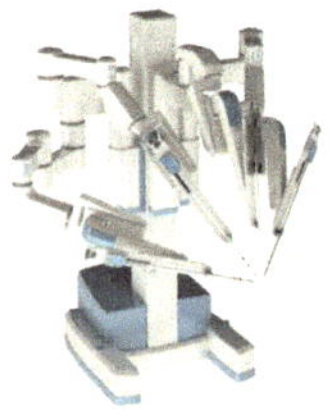

Source: © Shutterstock, Inc.

TABLE 11.1 Examples of Sales Promotions

Consumer Sales Promotions	Business-to-Business Sales Promotions
Coupons	Trade shows and conventions
Sweepstakes or contests	Sales contests
Premiums	Trade and advertising allowances
Rebates	Product demonstrations
Samples	Training
Loyalty programs	Free merchandise
Point-of-purchase displays	Push money

free merchandise

A product or service a seller offers retailers to get them to push it toward consumers.

push money

A cash incentive a manufacturer provides its channel partners to sell particular items.

Push Versus Pull Strategies

Businesses must also decide whether to use a push strategy or a pull strategy. Recall that a push strategy involves promoting a product to businesses (middlemen), such as wholesalers and retailers, who then *push* the product through the channel promoting it to final consumers. Manufacturers may set up displays in retail outlets for new products or provide incentives such as price discounts to the retailer so the retailer can promote or push the product to consumers.

Companies use a pull strategy when they target final consumers with promotions. In other words, a company promotes its products and services to final consumers to *pull* consumers into the stores or get the consumers asking for the product. If a manufacturer sends coupons to consumers or places them in newspapers, it hopes the consumers will take the coupons to stores and buy the product. Their pull, or desire, for the product causes wholesalers and retailers to buy it to try to meet the demand. Many manufacturers use both a push strategy and a pull strategy, promoting their products and services to both final consumers and their trade partners (e.g., retailers and wholesalers).

Key Takeaway

- Companies use sales promotions to get customers to take action (make purchases) quickly. Sales promotions increase the awareness of products, help introduce new products, and often create interest in the organizations that run the promotions. Coupons, contests, samples, and premiums are among the types of sales promotions aimed at consumers. Trade promotions, or promotions aimed at businesses, include trade shows, sales contests, trade allowances, and push money.

Review Questions

1. What are the objectives of sales promotions?
2. What is a trade promotion?
3. Identify and provide an example of three sales promotion tools targeted at consumers.
4. Identify and provide an example of three sales promotion tools targeted at businesses.
5. Explain the difference between a push strategy and a pull strategy.

11.9 Discussion Questions and Activities

Discussion Questions

1. Provide an example of how an organization, such as your university, uses different media to present a consistent message using integrated marketing communications (IMC). Who is their target, what is their message, and what media should they use?
2. In your opinion, what are the advantages and disadvantages of advertising on the radio, in magazines, on television, through direct marketing, and on the internet?
3. Explain the different types of public relations tools that a company can use to generate interest in its products.
4. What types of sponsorships are becoming more popular, and why?
5. Give an example of an organization's promotional strategy and how it gets consumers to select it, pay attention to it, and retain it as intended.
6. Give an example of the unique selling proposition for one of your favorite brands. What is your unique selling proposition?
7. Think about and provide examples of two different message strategies you've seen in commercials in the last year. Why do you think they were or were not effective?
8. As the manufacturer of small appliances, explain how you might plan to use both a push strategy and pull strategy.
9. What type of sales promotions do you feel are most effective for college students?

Activities

1. Identify your three favorite and least favorite commercials and explain why you like or don't like each one. Notice whether there are similarities in your preferences. In other words, are your favorite commercials humorous? Are your least favorite commercials annoying?
2. Write a press release about special activities your college or university is doing to help the environment or community.
3. Identify your favorite television show and explain what product placements you think would be successful. Would you change your recommended product placements if you were making recommendations for shows that appealed more to parents or grandparents?
4. Create a message strategy for a cover letter to go with your résumé.
5. Outline three message strategies that you feel would get consumers' attention in television commercials and in print ads.
6. Create a sales promotion you think will attract a lot of students to your favorite fast food restaurant.
7. You are applying for a job in an advertising agency. Write an ad about yourself, explaining your unique selling proposition and why they should hire you.
8. Watch television at three different times (late night, midday, and prime time). What types of commercials were shown at each time? Did you notice a difference in quality, products/services advertised, or creativity? Why do you think there was a variance?
9. What media do you think would be most (and least) effective for college students? Why?

11.10 Case Study: Credit Cards for Students and Recent Graduates

College students, especially seniors, are a primary target market for credit cards. Major credit card companies know that students as well as new graduates need to establish credit and have a means of making major purchases while they are in school and when they move to new cities. As such, many credit card companies purchase mailing lists or have "affinity agreements" with universities in exchange for students' contact information. These agreements may involve putting college and university names and logos on the cards. Regardless, credit cards issued to students and recent grads are generally very profitable for the issuer and also for the school.

Students typically receive multiple credit card offers. Some students have reported getting over sixty credit card offers within a month. What's troublesome is that students often don't have credit, yet they can obtain multiple credit cards, possibly leading to even higher student debt. Due to security issues, most credit card offers use traditional media such as direct mail and telemarketing.

Given that college students typically utilize digital marketing, especially social media, rather than any kind of traditional media, it is somewhat surprising how many students and recent graduates sign up for new credit cards. Sometimes it's free miles, discounts on gasoline, or even money back on purchases that entice people to sign up for a credit card. Credit card companies have to decide on promotions and special deals to incentivize students to sign up for their cards.

Case Study Questions

1. Why is direct mail effective for credit card solicitations?
2. What other traditional media do you think credit card companies utilize?
3. What benefits should credit card companies promote and what media should they use to get students' attention?

Endnotes

1. Cobe, Patricia (2021), "A Brief History of the Chicken Sandwich Wars," https://www.restaurantbusinessonline.com/food/brief-history-chicken-sandwich-wars (January 7).
2. The Martin Agency (2020), "The Martin Agency and UPS Launch #ThanksForDelivering," https://www.interpublic.com/case-study/the-martin-agency-and-ups-launch-thanksfordelivering/, (April 13); Scott, David Meerman (2020), "#ThanksForDelivering: How Businesses Can Support Essential Workers," https://www.davidmeermanscott.com/blog/-how-businesses-support-essential-workers, (May 12).
3. Vranica, Suzanne (2020), "Google, Facebook and Amazon Gain as Coronavirus Reshapes Ad Spending," https://www.wsj.com/articles/google-facebook-and-amazon-gain-as-coronavirus-reshapes-ad-spending-11606831201?mod=searchresults_pos8&page=1, (December 1); Cramer-Flood, Ethan (2021) "Worldwide Digital Ad Spending 2021," https://www.emarketer.com/content/worldwide-digital-ad-spending-2021 (April 29).
4. Riegler, Jared (2021), "LOLLAPALOOZA SPONSORSHIP RECAP 2021," https://sponsorunited.com/lollapalooza-sponsorship-recap-2021/, (August 3); Directo-Meston, Danielle (2021), "Updated: Here's Your Guide to the Best Upcoming Music Festivals and Latest Safety Rules," https://www.hollywoodreporter.com/shop/best-music-festivals-2021-1234995260/ (August 31).
5. Goetzen, Nina (2020), "The consumer packaged goods industry will grow digital spend by 5.2 percent this year as the pandemic drives search marketing," https://www.businessinsider.com/consumer-packaged-goods-industry-grows-digital-spend-this-year-2020-9, (September 24).
6. Mansour, Iris and Max Rice (2020) "How Dollar Shave Club used video to grow to a $1 billion exit," https://jilt.com/blog/dollar-shave-club-video/, (January 24).
7. Steinberg, Brian (2021), "NBC Seeks Record $6 Million for Super Bowl Commercials (EXCLUSIVE)," https://variety.com/2021/tv/news/super-bowl-commercials-price-record-1234998593/ (June 16).
8. Sports Illustrated (2020), "2021 Media Kit,"https://images.saymedia-content.com/.image/cs_srgb/MTc3MTkyNzg3MTY5NTE5MzUz/2021_si_media-kit_maven_113020.pdf, (November 30).
9. Eng, Heather (2021), "When a box becomes a billboard: Amazon's on-box advertising," https://advertising.amazon.com/blog/on-box-advertising (June 24).
10. https://www.ais-inc.com/about/news-events/ais-named-one-of-the-most-charitable-companies-in-massachusetts-by-boston-business-journal.
11. Mobile Loaves & Fishes Blog (May 22, 2009), "Stubb's Teams Up With MLF to Launch 'Feed The World' Tour!" http://mobileloavesandfishes.typepad.com/weblog/2009/05/stubbs-teams-up-with-mlf-to-launch-feed-the-world-tour-homeless.html.
12. Influential Agency (2019), "6 examples of crisis communication and what you can learn," https://www.thisisinfluential.com/blog/pr/6-examples-of-crisis-communication-and-what-you-can-learn/, (February 11).
13. Laurie Burkett (June 2, 2015), "KFC: Eight-Legged Chickens Is a Lie," *Wall Street Journal*, B3.
14. Jon Humbert, "UPS driver caught on camera kicking, throwing packages," *KOMO News*, http://komonews.com/news/local/ups-driver-caught-on-camera-kicking-throwing-packages.
15. Los Angeles Daily News (2019), "20 of Staples Center's biggest music moments to celebrate the L.A. arena's 20th anniversary," https://www.dailynews.com/2019/10/11/20-of-staples-centers-biggest-music-moments-to-celebrate-the-l-a-arenas-20th-anniversary (October 11); Leiweke, Tim (2009), "Staples gets lifetime naming rights for Staples Center," https://www.bizjournals.com/losangeles/stories/2009/10/19/daily5.html (October 19); Arent Fox (2021), "STAPLES Center Arena Lease Through 2041," https://www.arentfox.com/perspectives/press-releases/arent-fox-advises-la-lakers-extension-staples-center-arena-lease.
16. Event Architecture (2018), "IS AN EVENT SPONSORSHIP WORTH THE COST?" https://www.event-architecture.com/blog/2018/9/5/is-an-event-sponsorship-worth-the-cost, (September 5).
17. Fossen, Beth L. (2021), "Some product placement resonates with TV viewers more. Here's the trick." https://www.popsci.com/technology/product-placement-tv-psychology/,(September 8).
18. (April 2, 2016), "Product Placement in Movies: 5 Blatantly Obvious Examples," *New York Film Academy*, http://nyfa.edu.
19. Suzanne Vranica and Amol Sharma (May 18, 2015), "'Mad Men' Dream a Dream for Coke," *Wall Street Journal*, http://wsj.com.
20. Joyce Smith (December 8, 2012), "You Can't Try This at Home: Stores Strike Back," *Kansas City Star*, http://www.kansascity.com.

CHAPTER 12

Digital Marketing

As we indicated in Chapter 11, digital marketing has become an important part of firms' integrated marketing communications strategies. But what exactly is digital marketing? **Digital marketing** is an umbrella term for marketing products interactively using newer media and usually, but not always, the internet. Sending a text message to reach customers is an example of digital marketing because consumers can reply back to the message instantly.

digital marketing

An umbrella term for marketing products interactively using newer media and usually, but not always, the internet.

Although they might include a phone number to call or a website to go to, traditional media, such as TV, radio, and print and billboard ads, for example, don't allow consumers to respond to marketing messages instantly with a click or two. Consequently, they aren't considered forms of digital marketing. Digital marketing and the term *online marketing* are sometimes used interchangeably, but technically, online marketing refers to marketing that happens solely via the internet.

Digital marketing has drastically changed how companies are advertising and engaging with their customers, particularly millennials and Generation Z. "Digital has changed our industry completely," says Maurice Lévy, the chief executive officer of the Publicis Groupe, a major global ad agency. "If you don't change you are out of the picture."[1]

Fashion designer Rebecca Taylor questioned whether her customers were really seeing much of her products at fashion shows. So after fifteen straight years of exhibiting her designs on the runway, she decided to alter her promotion mix. Instead of participating in fashion shows, Taylor invested the half-million dollars she annually spends to create online shows and email campaigns and engage on social networks such as Instagram, Facebook, and Pinterest.[2] Taylor's digital show caught on and other designers took notice and followed her lead. "Digital Fashion Week" is now an annual event in New York City.

Established companies like Rebecca Taylor aren't the only ones using digital marketing, though. Small firms, such as startups, are finding that digital marketing is a good a way to level the playing field with larger competitors, for one because it is generally much less expensive than regular advertising. Any business can create a Facebook page, open a Twitter account, or post a video to YouTube for free and get exposure to potential customers. And if the message is especially compelling and goes **viral**, the company will get a lot more exposure to customers. (Recall we discussed viral marketing in Chapter 11.) Compare that to buying a thirty-second Super Bowl ad, which in 2022 cost $7 million.

viral

When a message spreads rapidly (like a computer virus).

Leticia Sedberry, Artist

Source: Leticia Sedberry, used with permission

Leticia Sedberry, a modern artist in Colleyville, Texas, has found that she sells more art using digital media than hanging it in galleries. Sedberry has a website, runs ads on Facebook, and is active on Instagram. "I make it a point to spend a few hours every week on digital marketing," she says. "I can really see an uptick in sales when I do."

12.1 Email Marketing and Search Engine Marketing

Learning Objectives

1. Explain why email marketing is so effective.
2. Define search engine marketing.
3. Describe how search engine optimization (SEO) works.

Email Marketing

As you learned in Chapter 11, email marketing is a type of direct marketing. Email marketing is highly cost-effective. Estimates vary, but some studies have found that every one dollar spent on email marketing yields a return of anywhere from twenty to forty dollars. Email marketing is also easy to administer, can be personalized, and can be highly targeted. That's why every time you buy a product at a store the checkout clerk politely asks you for your email address. The effectiveness of email as a marketing tool is also why websites request your email address. Often they do so by offering people something in return for doing so, such as a discount on a product or access to a free newsletter. Once people have signed up, they are referred to as *subscribers*.

Part of the reason why email marketing is so effective is because it's easy to miss seeing or to ignore other types of digital ads on social media and elsewhere. However, most people check their email messages daily. The emails can't be completely ignored because people have to at least read their subject lines to see whether they want to read them.

To increase the odds of emails being opened, marketing professionals try to craft short but engaging email subject lines. This can be done in any number of ways. The following are examples of subject line alternatives and strategies based on an ad campaign run by Tropical Travelers, a Pennsylvania-based travel agency:

TABLE 12.1 Strategies for Crafting Engaging Email Subject Lines

Strategy	Subject Line Example
Ask a question	Destination wedding . . . want rock star treatment?
Personalize the email	Hey Andrea: Want rock star treatment at your destination wedding?
Appeal to scarcity	Want rock star treatment at your destination wedding? Book by 12/31
Make a list	Top 10 ways to get rock star treatment at your destination wedding

Using symbols such as emojis and animated objects (called GIFS) in subject lines can also attract attention. However, marketers run the risk that email recipients will find them annoying or too cutesy and delete the emails. Using overly sales-like language like "FREE" and "Act now!" can also result in an email being immediately deleted.

The body of the email should be eye-catching and explain the benefits of the product or service (how will it make the receiver's life better?). The body should also ask the receiver to take action. What action does the sender want the receiver to take, exactly? Become a subscriber? Buy a product? To ensure emails are well received, companies often draft multiple versions of messages and initially test them to see which are most likely to get opened and acted upon.

Savvy marketers don't solely focus on selling products to their customers with every email they send, though. Instead, they strive to nurture long-term, mutually beneficial relationships with their customers. Pampered Chef is an example. The company, which sells cooking-related products, doesn't just send emails designed to solicit sales. It also frequently sends its customers recipes and ideas for hosting parties.

Routine or transactional emails can also help a company establish and maintain relationships with customers and improve email response rates. Examples include emails welcoming new subscribers and emails letting buyers know what the status of their orders and any returns are. Asking buyers to provide feedback or rate products are other examples.

The downside of email marketing is that people can get annoyed by emails, and spam is common. The laws related to spam vary by state and by country. U.S. law requires firms to give consumers the choice to "opt out" or "unsubscribe" to unsolicited emails. Blasting customers nonstop with emails can also land your company on an email "blacklist" such as SpamCop.net. Blacklists are sites that monitor "rogue" email senders and notify members of the digital marketing community to block them.

Pampered Chef provides emails to recipients that show how to use the company's products.

Source: PamperedChef.com

Search Engine Marketing (SEM)

search engine marketing (SEM)

Marketing designed to get internet traffic to a firm's website by making it more visible in search engine results.

search engine optimization (SEO)

Making a website more visible so that it shows up nearer to the top of the list in search-engine rankings.

pay-per-click ads

An internet ad a company doesn't pay anything for unless someone actually clicks on it.

Search engine marketing (SEM), or *search marketing*, for short, is designed to get internet traffic to a firm's website by making it more visible in search engine results. Making a site more visible so that it shows up at the top, or closer to the top, of the rankings is called **search engine optimization (SEO)**. The algorithms of search engines are constantly being adjusted so the most sought-after information and advertisements that generate the most revenue get top rankings. For example, if your website takes too long to load, it will get pushed down in a search engine's rankings. The same thing will happen if people click on your website and leave it right away, say, because your content isn't appealing or the site is poorly designed and hard to navigate. If you look at online job ads for marketing professionals, you will notice that many require applicants to have SEM and SEO experience, and experience with Google Analytics, which we'll discuss later in the chapter.

Search engine marketing can be either unpaid or paid. Adjusting the content on your website so that it shows up higher in the rankings, say, by including or changing certain keywords on your website or by improving your content, is an example of unpaid search engine marketing. In contrast, banner ads and the clickable ads you see next to the results when you type in a keyword on a search engine such as Google or Bing (or on a search engine on a social media site) are examples of search engine marketing companies have paid for. Ads such as these are referred to as **pay-per-click ads**. When a company runs a pay-per-click ad, it doesn't pay anything for the ad unless someone actually clicks on it. Google is the biggest seller of pay-per-click advertising, and it is the largest source of revenue for the company.

Pay-per-click ads are easy to set up. Anyone can build one by using a product such as Google's AdWords or Facebook's Power Editor. With a few clicks, you can design the ad, specify the URL you want potential customers to end up on once they click on the ad, and research and list the keywords you think they are mostly like to use when looking for information or products you are selling. You then specify which search engines or types of pages you want the ad to appear on and whether it should appear locally, nationally, or internationally. Finally, you make a bid to try to get the ad ranked as high as you can on the search engine's results. If yours is the highest bid, you get the highest ranking. If it's the second-highest bid, you get the second ranking, and so on.

Google AdWords Tutorial

To learn exactly how to create a pay-per-click ad on Google, watch this in-depth tutorial video.

View in the online reader

As you can probably tell, getting outspent by one's competitors can be an issue when a company is trying to generate sales with pay-per-click ads. Many people online don't scroll down very far to look at all of the results a search engine pulls up but instead choose the first one or two. And, of course, if a lot of people click on a company's listing or ad, but ultimately don't buy much, the firm won't see much of a return on its investment from the ad. A competitor can also drive up your advertising costs by repeatedly clicking on your pay-per-click ads.

Search engine results can be manipulated as well. For example, it's not uncommon for unscrupulous companies (particularly in China) to hire people to click on ads as well as create glowing phony reviews on e-commerce sites. Why? Because sellers and products with a lot of sales and good ratings get bumped up in search engine results, which results in even better sales. One study found that a one-star bump up in ratings for a hotel led to 25 percent more bookings.[3] However, fake clicks and ratings will ultimately undermine a seller's efforts after people catch on to the scam. For this reason, Amazon has been trying to crack down on fake ratings on its e-commerce site.[4]

The good news with pay-per-click ads is that if an ad isn't working (generating clicks), a company can take it down at any time and make changes to it. In fact, most major companies run numerous versions of pay-per-click ads initially when they are launching a new campaign. The companies then evaluate the ads to figure out which are working best, and where. Those that are working well are retained. Those that aren't are taken down.

Another upside of pay-per-click ads is that companies can easily retarget customers with them. After clicking on an ad, many people won't initially buy a product. They might have to think about it some or do more research. **Retargeting** allows companies to show these people the same ads or similar ads after they leave the landing pages they have been routed to. You are familiar with this practice. It's why after you leave an e-commerce website, you keep seeing ads related to the product(s) you looked at, even when you switch devices, browsers, and websites.

retargeting

Technology that display the same ads or similar ads after a person leaves the landing pages they have been routed to, even when they switch devices, browsers, and websites.

However, Google and Apple are among the major companies that now give people the option to *not* to be tracked with ads automatically. The companies have also made it more difficult for organizations (other than themselves) to gather information about an individual person (rather than just broad categories of people) without that person's permission.[5] That's why you have probably clicked on a website and gotten a message such as the following asking you to allow "cookies":

This website uses cookies. We use cookies to personalize content and ads, to provide social media features, and to analyze our traffic. We also share information about your use of our site with our social media, advertising, and analytics partners who may combine it with other information that you've provided to them or that they've collected from your use of their services.

A cookie is a small data files that get exchanged with a server when you get on a website. The cookie matches you with your browsing history so you see ads and content geared toward what you're interested in.

Key Takeaway

- Email marketing is a type of direct marketing. It's highly cost-effective, easy to administer, can be personalized, and targeted because the offers are often based on information a seller has about consumers' past purchases. Search engine marketing (SEM), or search marketing for short, is designed to get internet traffic to a firm's website by making it more visible in search engine results. Making a site more visible so that it shows up at the top, or closer to the top, of the rankings is called search engine optimization (SEO). Adjusting the content on your website so that it is shows up higher in the rankings, say by including or changing certain keywords on your website, is an example of unpaid search engine marketing. Banner ads and the clickable ads you see next to the results when you type in a keyword on a search engine such as Google or on social networks are examples of search engine marketing that companies have paid for. When a company runs a pay-per-click ad, it doesn't pay anything for the ad unless someone actually clicks on it. If the ad isn't generating clicks, a company can easily take it down it and revise it. Customers may then be retargeted with ads if they don't initially purchase a product.

Review Questions

1. What makes email marketing so cost-effective?
2. What is the difference between unpaid search engine marketing and paid search engine marketing?
3. What are some of the plusses and minuses of pay-per-click ads for companies?

12.2 E-Commerce Marketing and M-Commerce (Mobile) Marketing

Learning Objectives

1. Describe e-commerce marketing and what firms can do to enhance the effectiveness of their e-commerce strategies.
2. Describe m-commerce and the types of advertising it supports.
3. Explain why mobile marketing is a key part of firms' integrated marketing communications.

E-Commerce Marketing

We first discussed e-commerce in Chapter 4. Using an e-commerce site to market and sell products is an important part of integrated marketing communications strategy. To compete with online sellers, brick-and-mortar stores like Walmart and Target need e-commerce sites. And, of course, some companies sell products no other way except on their e-commerce sites.

It's not enough to attract customers with pay-per-click ads and other types of marketing to your e-commerce site if you can't make a conversion. A **conversion** occurs when a person on an e-commerce site takes action and moves from being a browser on the site to being a buyer. A conversion isn't likely to occur if customers can't easily find what they are looking for on the web page they initially get routed to, which is called the **landing page**. If the landing page is slow to load, or if potential customers don't see the product they saw in the online ad they viewed, they could get confused and leave the landing page.

Need an e-commerce site to sell your artwork or other products? Shopify and BigCommerce are two popular platforms individuals and firms use to build their sites.

Source: Published with permission from artist Leticia Sedberry, lwsart.com.

conversion

When a person on an e-commerce site takes action and moves from being a browser on the site to being a buyer.

landing page

A web page that appears after a person clicks on a search engine result or an online ad.

Ideally, a landing page should mirror the ad in terms of its design and the copy and descriptions used. That's why, for example, Target always includes the red target symbol in its ads as well as all of its landing pages and homepage. Table 12.2 shows the other different elements a landing page can have.

TABLE 12.2 Landing Page Elements

product name
photo of product
video of product
product ratings
product reviews
add to cart/buy button
quantity selection
customization options
shipping choices
favorites button
follow button
social media links/buttons

However, including too many details and images on a landing page can make it difficult for people to find what they are looking for and can result in lost sales. The goal of the landing page should be to direct, or move, customers toward what you want them to do on the page.

One way companies refine or optimize their websites as well as apps, ads, emails, and the other marketing messages is by conducting A/B testing. (Recall that we first discussed alpha and beta (A/B) testing in conjunction with product development in Chapter 7.) eBags, an online luggage retailer, used A/B testing to determine what effect adding stars or ratings to its site would have on its sales. To do so, the company made two versions of its site accessible for a period of time to two small groups of test customers. One group saw the version of the site with the stars (option A), and the other group saw the version of the site without the stars (option B). eBags discovered that by adding the stars, sales increased by 8 percent.[6] A/B testing works best when only one element is being changed—such as stars or no stars or whether the buy button is located in one area on the page or another, for example. For this reason A/B testing is also often referred to as *split testing*.

A/B testing is useful when trying to decide a single element to change.

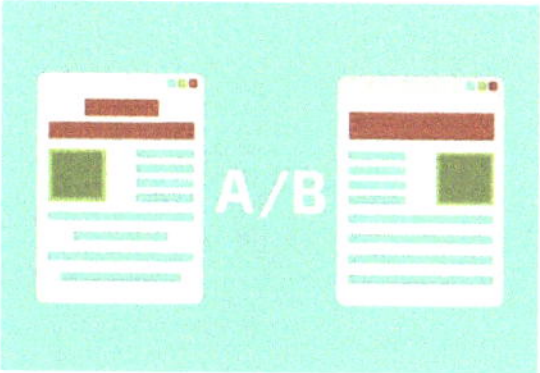

Source: © Shutterstock, Inc.

multivariate testing

A test in which multiple variables, or elements, are tested to see which combination of them works best.

As its name implies, **multivariate testing** involves testing multiple variables instead of just one or two to see which combination of them works best. For instance, consumers would look at a number of different website designs with different elements, and how the consumers responded to them would be recorded. As you can imagine, multivariate testing takes longer and generally requires the use of analytics software, such as Google Analytics.

An e-commerce site's design isn't everything, though. If buyers are worried that their credit card and personal information may be compromised when they purchase a product online, converting them is going to be a tough job. A growing list of companies have had to deal with e-commerce security breaches caused by hackers. Texas, California, Maine, and Washington are among the states that require companies to notify people that their personal information has been breached, and some states publish the names of the companies online.[7] According to a study by KPMG, 19 percent of consumers would completely stop shopping at a retailer after a breach, and 33 percent would take a break from shopping there for an extended period.[8]

M-Commerce (Mobile) Marketing

M-commerce

Transactions that take place on mobile devices.

M-commerce refers to transactions that take place on mobile devices. M-commerce and the advertising related to it are exploding. U.S. consumers alone are spending more time on their mobile phones than ever. About half of the respondents in one survey said they spend 5–6 hours per day on their phones.[9] Facebook's mobile advertising revenues comprise most of its ad revenues for its parent company, Meta Platforms. In some industries, such as the travel industry, mobile ads cost more than desktop ads. Moreover, Google has found that people who click on mobile search ads make more actual store visits. This is making mobile ads more attractive to advertisers.

Because m-commerce is skyrocketing, many companies take a "mobile-first" approach to designing their e-commerce sites and digital advertising campaigns. In other words, the companies are designing them to work first and foremost on mobile devices. Taking a mobile-first approach also pays off because when it comes to search-engine rankings, search engines such as Google bump up the rankings for sites that are easy to view and use on mobile devices.

Text messages (SMS), multimedia messages (MMS), and search ads are commonly used mobile marketing techniques. The cosmetics maker Avon created an "instant messaging brochure" that allows its sales reps to create and send a customer a personalized shopping cart via WhatsApp or Facebook Messenger. On its launch day the platform received more than a half million visits from consumers across twelve countries.[10] Advergames (seeChapter 5) are also becoming more popular.

Banner ads—the rectangular ads that appear on your mobile phone—are inexpensive and annoy people, surveys say, but they are widely used in m-commerce as well. So are popup and video ads you have to click out of. You probably get more video ads on your phone than you do on your computer.

Moreover, mobile phones are a handy shopping tool consumers can use on the go, which allows companies to target them with information wherever they may be. Target posts signs in its stores encouraging customers to send text messages to certain numbers to get coupons. Companies also put quick response (QR) codes like the one in the photo on this page on products and displays, and other promotional materials. Consumers can scan the codes with their mobile phones to get more information about a product, online reviews about it, and discounts. In addition, the QR code will often indicate whether the product is in stock at a store.

Mobile phones also make proximity, or location-based marketing, possible. Pilgrim SDK, a spinoff of Foursquare, works on that principle. For example, the social network Snapchat—which allows people to post pictures and videos that disappear after ten seconds—teamed up with McDonald's to run deals that appeared on people's mobile phones when they were near McDonald's restaurants. One study found that 57 percent of consumers are more likely to engage with location-based advertising, which is growing rapidly.[11]

QR codes allow consumers to scan promotional materials and products for more information about them as well as get discounts on them.

Source: © Shutterstock, Inc.

Because they can increase a firm's sales markedly, developing apps for mobile phones has become a critical part of firms' integrated marketing strategies. For some firms, not only are their mobile apps part of their integrated marketing strategies, but their sales models revolve entirely around the apps. What would Uber be without an app?

Apps are becoming increasingly sophisticated, with features such as augmented reality, and photo- and voice-search capabilities. IKEA has an app that utilizes **augmented reality**, which allows a digital image to be superimposed, or incorporated, into a person's real world. Augmented reality is the technology that makes the pokémon show up in the game Pokémon GO. IKEA has developed an app called IKEA Place that utilizes augmented reality. People use the app and the cameras on their phones to superimpose IKEA products in their rooms. That way, shoppers can see if the products look right before buying them.

augmented reality

Technology whereby a digital image can be superimposed, or incorporated, into a person's real-world view.

Likewise, Pinterest now has an app feature called Lens, which is essentially a visual search engine. Lens allows people to use their mobile phones to take pictures of things they see and like and then find similar items on Pinterest. Target has teamed up with Pinterest to utilize its Lens technology in its app. People can take pictures of items and find similar products at Target. Target and other beauty brands are also using the Lens app to allow shoppers to virtually try on different types of makeup.[12]

Apps that utilize voice assistants like Alexa and Siri have also become popular mobile tools. Also called **chatbots,** they are computer programs that utilize artificial intelligence to comprehend what people say and conduct human-like conservations with them. Amazon, Domino's, and Starbucks are among the many companies that either experimented with or utilized chatbots. However, customers can get frustrated if they try to ask the bots complex questions, which often the bots can't answer. "In my opinion, [chatbots] are not necessarily a replacement for human interaction because the answers are going to be canned," says Evelyn McMullen, a research manager for Nucleus Research Manager.[13]

chatbots

Computer programs that comprehend and conduct human-like conservations.

Other apps allow consumers to experience virtual reality. **Virtual reality (VR)** is the use of computer-generated images to immerse people in a digital environment, often with the use of a head-mounted display and in some instances with their mobile phones. VR is being used for many different purposes in addition to games—for sports, to train medical, military, and aviation personnel, and you guessed it—to market products. Volvo and Lexus have used VR to offer test drives of their vehicles to potential buyers who might not otherwise step foot into their showrooms. Marriott has used the technology to send potential customers on "virtual trips" to its hotels in London and Hawaii. The British retailer Topshop used VR in conjunction with a live-streamed fashion show. People who experienced it felt like they were sitting in the front row near the models and celebrities at the event. Read the case study at the end of this chapter to see how the *New York Times* utilized VR and mobile phones to promote the publication and expand its readership.

Google Cardboard is an inexpensive VR viewing device. You slip your phone into it, and with the help of an app, you can have a VR experience.

Source: © Shutterstock, Inc.

One of the downsides of using VR and augmented reality for marketing purposes is that developing the apps can be expensive. That said, their use is likely to rise as marketers look for new ways to engage consumers with rich experiences.

virtual reality (VR)

The use of computer-generated images to immerse people in a digital environment, often with the use of a head-mounted display.

Key Takeaway

- Using an e-commerce site to market and sell products is an important part of integrated marketing communications strategy. One way companies refine, or optimize their websites as well as apps, ads, emails, and the other marketing messages is by conducting A/B testing and multivariate testing. M-commerce refers to transactions that take place on mobile devices. Because m-commerce is increasing rapidly and is likely to continue to do so, more companies are taking a "mobile-first" approach to designing their e-commerce sites and digital advertising campaigns. Search ads and banner ads are commonly used mobile marketing techniques. So are videos and advergames. Mobile shopping apps, which are becoming increasingly sophisticated, are critical to a digital marketing strategy. Chatbots are computer programs that utilize artificial intelligence to comprehend what people say and conduct human-like conservations with them, largely for voice ordering and simple customer service requests. The use of chatbots and augmented reality and virtual reality are on the rise as well.

Review Questions

1. What obstacles can prevent an e-commerce conversion from taking place?
2. How can developing an app help a company sell goods and services?
3. What advantage does taking a mobile-first approach to designing a firm's e-commerce sites and digital advertising campaigns offer?
4. For what other marketing purposes do you think chatbots and augmented reality could be used?

12.3 Social Media Marketing

Learning Objectives

1. Describe the ways in which companies are using social media marketing.
2. Outline some of the challenges related to social media marketing.
3. Explain what some of the best practices are for using social media to market products.

social media marketing (SMM)

The process of using social networking websites to engage potential customers and market and sell products to them.

Social media marketing (SMM) is the process of using social networking websites to engage potential customers and market and sell products to them by posting information that's valuable to people. Keep in mind that this is different than simply posting pay-per-click ads on social media sites.

Social networks can be roughly categorized into the categories shown in Table 12.3.

TABLE 12.3 Types of Social Networks and Examples

Type of Social Network	Examples
General purpose networks	Facebook
Blogs	WordPress, Blogger
Microblogs	Twitter, Tumblr
Social news sites	Digg, Reddit
Review sites	Yelp, TripAdvisor
Photo-sharing networks	Instagram, Pinterest, Snapchat
Video-sharing networks	YouTube, TikTok, Vimeo

According to the Pew Research Center, in 2021, the top five social networks were as follows:

1. YouTube 81%
2. Facebook 69%
3. Instagram 40%
4. Pinterest 31%
5. Snapchat 25%

Although it's a less traditional type of social network, more Americans regularly get on YouTube than any other platform. However, that is changing. As the Coronavirus pandemic raged, TikTok began attracting the most visitors, even outnumbering the visitors to Google. Nonetheless, it is Facebook that gets the lion's share of spending from advertisers. Why? Because with 3 billion users, the revenue it generates for advertisers by far dwarfs the revenue other social media sites deliver.

That said, each social network has its own features and distinct "personality," and appeals to different types of users. For example:

- Women are far more likely than men to use Pinterest.
- Latinos use WhatsApp far more than other demographic groups in the United States.
- LinkedIn users are more likely to be college educated and have high incomes.
- Whereas 65 percent of adults ages 18–29 say they use Snapchat, just 2 percent of those 65 and older do.[14]

As a result, some networks are better suited to some demographic groups than others. So each network requires different marketing techniques.

Social Media Marketing Challenges

As we have noted, social media is complex and rapidly changing. New social networks spring up frequently. Every time one does, marketing professionals have to try to figure out how it works, what type of advertising and promotion it lends itself to, and what the financial return of using it might be. We'll talk about financial returns later in the chapter. Next, let's look at some of the other challenges social media presents for marketing professionals

Lack of Control

Originally, social networks weren't designed to be advertising venues. They were designed to give people a way to congregate, share information, and entertain themselves online. But wherever people congregate, advertisers will soon follow. The fact that social networks were created for users and are largely controlled by users rather than advertisers has upended traditional marketing and shifted the balance of power.

In the past, advertising was largely a one-way type of communication. This allowed firms to tightly control the messages they sent about their products. But with social media, messages are being sent by everyone in all different directions. This has given consumers more influence about what is said about companies and products, both good and bad.

Noisy Channels

Because so many people contribute comments and information on social networks, figuring out how to be "heard" on them is a challenge. Some marketing professionals compare the process to shouting from a mountaintop and hoping someone will shout back. Shouting is not the best possible strategy to use on social media, though.

As we indicated in Chapter 4, just as it's rude to barge into a party and loudly start talking about yourself, companies that want to achieve success generally can't barge onto social networks and bombard people with overtly commercial ads, products, and deals. Instead, companies have to make themselves want to be heard by offering people information they value and want to hear about or that makes life more fun and more meaningful to them.

One millennial commenting about the use of social media for advertising purposes put it this way: "Entertain me, make me happy, capture my attention, speak to my conscious, and then leave me the heck alone!" Translation: On social networks, a soft-sell type of approach to marketing usually is more effective. Facebook is aware of this. Even though Facebook wants to sell ads, in order to ensure that its users are seeing information they truly value, the network blocks News Feed posts it deems overly commercial and spam-like. And when it comes to online ad auctions, Facebook sells spots to the highest bidder; however, Facebook also runs ads produced by companies that get outbid for the top spots on the platform but whose content is more relevant to Facebook's viewers.[15]

Timing Issues

Tweriod and Twitonomy are online products that can be used to determine the best time to send tweets and how many of them to send as well as how often your competitors are doing so.

Source: © Shutterstock, Inc.

People on different social networks demand different amounts of interactions. Consequently, companies have to determine how often to post information and develop schedules based on their specific audiences. (The same is true for sending emails.) Bloggers often post at regular intervals daily. They know if they don't, visitors looking for new posts are less likely to return to the blogs. Twitter users expect to be responded to very quickly. American Airlines responds to more than 6,000 tweets a day. If a company on Twitter isn't responsive or delays responding, it can face a torrential backlash from users.

However, people can feel as if they are being spammed when a company posts too often. Starbucks is on Facebook, Instagram, LinkedIn, Twitter, and YouTube, but the company posts sparingly and about things it believes its customers will truly be interested in. MeetEdgar is an online tool that can help marketers figure out how often to post, the best times to do it, and how to schedule automated postings on different networks.

Posting in response to current events or holidays is a common strategy companies use. However, doing so can backfire if a company appears to be taking advantage of the situation simply to sell its products. For example, after the Supreme Court ruled that same-sex marriage was guaranteed by the Constitution, Seth MacFarlane, who wrote and directed the movie *Ted 2*, was widely derided for sending the following tweet, which had absolutely nothing to do with the movie:

Celebrate the legalization of same-sex marriage by going to see Ted 2 *as he fights for HIS rights!*

Similarly, American Apparel got backlash for the following tweet, which appeared to try to capitalize on Hurricane Sandy, which devastated the East Coast:

In case you're bored during the storm. 20% off everything for the next 36 hours. Just enter SandySale at checkout.

Regardless of the timing, marketers should never post messages that are unnecessarily negative or mean-spirited. Not only can it result in backlash for a company, it can get a person fired.

Social Media Marketing Strategies

As we have indicated, some marketing techniques work better on social networks than others. Next let's look at some of these techniques.

Using Visuals

Most marketing professionals agree that using more images and fewer words works better on social media. Not only is a picture worth a thousand words, images are also more engaging than blocks of text. Using sharp, eye-catching images is important for all social media sites, but especially sites like YouTube, Pinterest, and Instagram. The TLC show *Cake Boss* makes the most of images on social media. Each cake and baking directions the show's host Buddy Valastro posts on YouTube and Instagram can't help but make even a non-baker want to tune into the show.

Cake Boss

A YouTube video with great visuals like this one might want to make you want to tune into *Cake Boss.*

View in the online reader

Using Humor and Fun When Appropriate

On a social network such as LinkedIn, maintaining a formal demeanor is important. On other networks, companies get a better response by showing some personality and being a bit more casual. Duluth Trading, an outdoor work-and-leisure retailer, has worked hard to keep its social media, TV, and other ads, like the following for men's underwear, fun.

Duluth Trading Co.

What average underwear feels like.

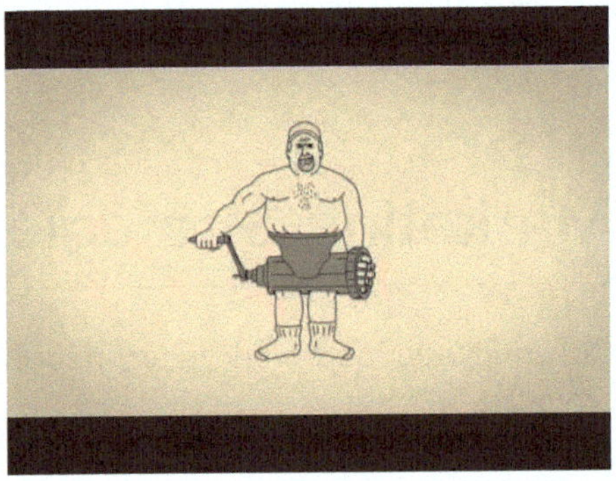

View in the online reader

Researching insurance products is generally boring, but Progressive Insurance, Aflac, and other companies have made it more fun to learn about their products by using fictional characters on social media to pitch them. Flo, Progressive Insurance's perky spokesperson, has her own Facebook page where she regularly offers useful insurance tips to the nearly 5 million or so people who have "liked." The Aflac duck has a pretty good gig on Facebook, too, where he performs wacky stunts, offers product advice, and has about 800,000 likes.

Squatty Potty

WARNING: You can't show this on TV. Advertising the Squatty Potty, a product featured on the TV show *Shark Tank,* was tricky because going to the bathroom is a topic that's "borderline gross," says Squatty Potty's CEO. So the company hired a marketing firm to create this funny (but off-color) ad. It's been shared millions of times on social media and helped fuel the product's sales.

View in the online reader

Games and contests can engage people and make fans of them on social media sites. Dunkin' Donuts and Taco Bell are among many companies that encourage their customers to take selfies with their products and that hold selfie contests via social media. One widely shared Taco Bell selfie featured a skydiver biting into a burrito while free-falling. Selfies are examples of user-generated content. **User-generated content (UGC)** is content such as photos, blogs, videos, podcasts, and other types of material individuals create, often free of charge, to share with other people.

user-generated content (UGC)

Content such as photos, blogs, videos, podcasts, and other types of material individuals create, usually free of charge, to share with other people.

Striving for Authenticity

An ongoing challenge companies face when using social media is appearing authentic. In other words, firms don't want to come across like they are just trying to hawk products, like American Apparel did with the email it sent prior to Hurricane Sandy. Instead, companies want to reinforce the idea that they are legitimate participants on social networks and deserve to be part of people's lives.

Burberry, Coach, Tiffany, and other companies are hiring professional photographers to take pictures that look more like the photos actual people take on their mobile phones—pictures the firms believe are more likely to get shared on social media sites. Roxanne Rohmann hates ads online and on TV. But recently she "liked" a promotional photo on Facebook posted by the Michael Kors brand. "I don't feel like they're trying to sell something," Rohmann said about the photo, which looked like it was shot with a mobile phone.

Advertisements such as this that don't look like ads but instead blend into the content around them are called **native ads**. Native ads don't just appear just online. They can appear in print, on TV, and elsewhere. Some people complain that native ads are trickery because many people can't tell if they are looking at an ad. However, some advertising experts believe native ads have a bright future because they are subtle. Viewers don't feel like they are being interrupted by them like they are with regular commercials and ads.[16]

native ads

Advertisements that don't look like ads but instead blend into the content around them.

DotDash is another example of a company that strives to be subtle. DotDash is an internet company that owns various online magazines and question-and-answer sites, such as Investopedia. Instead of relying heavily on pay-per-click ads, DotDash posts lists of "best product" evaluations and links to buy them. (Perhaps you have clicked on a list like this one and bought something as a result.) Lists such as these that don't seem "ad-like" and are highly effective.

As Chapter 3 explained, another way to achieve authenticity is to partner with "influencers" on social media—that is, celebrities and other people who already have large numbers of followers online. The influencers then talk about or feature products rather than a company doing it. Sometimes influencers earn hundred of thousands of dollars for doing so. For example, influencers with more than a 1,000 followers on YouTube and a certain number of views can sign up with YouTube to run ads on their channels so as to earn money. For every 1,000 ad views, advertisers pay a certain rate to YouTube. YouTube takes 45 percent of the revenue, and the influencer gets the rest.[17]

You might be familiar with the funny YouTube star Lisa Koshy. Koshy is an authentic, self-made influencer whose wacky antics have earned her tens of millions of subscribers and followers on YouTube, Twitter, Instagram, and Snapchat. Many of these people are millennials or members of Generation Z. They use multiple networks and streaming services and watch far less TV than other demographic groups. As consumers, they can be hard to reach. Nike, Calvin Klein, AMC Theaters, and Procter & Gamble have lined up to pay Koshy to work their products into her skits so as to reach this demographic.[18]

This Lisa Koshy Video is "Sponsored" (by Nike)

View in the online reader

It should be noted that recently, some companies have stopped partnering with influencers because it turns out that some of them create phony accounts to inflate their follower numbers so as to earn more money from advertisers. Conversions—what is actually sold as a result of an influencer—can also be difficult to gauge. And, of course, many people (including you, perhaps), don't like companies mucking up the social media sites they like with product mentions, ads, and "sponsored" posts.[19]

Making Messages Meaningful

Making advertising meaningful is particularly important to Gen Z and millennials, who tend to be altruistic. A Brookings Institution study found that an overwhelming number of millennials say they are more likely to buy products from companies involved in social causes. Attributes they want reflected in their purchases and the companies they financially support include kindness, empathy, and social responsibility. Ben & Jerry's scores high with this demographic as a result of the social-justice stances the company has taken. Starbucks' efforts to improve the environment and fight climate change appeal to these consumers as well.[20]

The Eileen Fisher clothing brand used social media to enhance its reputation as a socially conscious clothing brand by participating in a film called *True Cost*. The film documents how the fast-fashion trend, which is often referred to as cheap chic, is adversely affecting the environment and garment and poor workers in other countries. The company promoted the film on social media and elsewhere.

True Cost Trailer

A film exploring the effects of "fast fashion."

View in the online reader

Providing information that is meaningful is one of the reasons why companies have turned to content marketing such as this. Recall that content marketing is the process of creating and distributing relevant and valuable content to attract, acquire, and engage a clearly defined and understood target audience—with the objective of driving profitable customer action.[21] Product tutorials on YouTube and elsewhere that explain how to use products are examples of content marketing. Done right, content marketing is authentic and effective.

Optimizing Across Sites

Once a business has created content its potential customers are interested in for one site, say, Facebook, they often edit or rework the copy and graphics so that it can be used on other social media sites. For example, a company might use just the headline from a Facebook post and a photo and put the material on Twitter. That's what Starbucks did to help explain why the company decided to stop using plastic straws in its drinks. This is a cost-effective way for a company to reach more people and optimize its exposure across sites.

Starbucks used a short post with a photo on Twitter to help explain why the company stopped using plastic straws.

Source: https://twitter.com/starbucks/status/1020394531185758209?lang=en

Including links to other social media sites, which are called *plugins*, is essential because they make it easier for people to share a company's content on other sites. You are familiar with plugins. They are the colorful buttons you see on one site that link you to another. Share and like buttons also make it easier to share a company's content and improve the chances the firm's content will get looked at.

Is it possible for a company to be on too many social media sites? The answer is yes. There are hundreds if not thousands of them. No firm can be on all of them. Instead, a company must choose those most suited for its brand and that provide the best financial return. Also, if a company is on a social media site, someone within the company needs to monitor what's being said about it, which takes time and money.

Firms use plugins like these on their social media sites to reach more people and gain followers.

Source: © Shutterstock, Inc.

community managers

People firms hire to help them implement and manage their social media campaigns.

Community managers are people companies hire to help them implement and manage their social media campaigns. Among other things, community managers are responsible for listening to what's being said about a firm. As you have learned, Google Alerts is one tool that can be used for monitoring. You enter keywords, such as your company's name, its key officers, and competitors, and when they appear online, you are electronically notified and sent a link to the content. As we explained in Chapter 11, "social listening" is important, because negative information online is also hard to combat. Why? Because companies usually don't control the social networks and websites the information appears on. Community managers are also responsible for getting content created for social media sites, scheduling posts, assisting customers who ask for help who have posted messages, as well as thanking customers for providing good posts and reviews.

Key Takeaway

- Social media marketing is the process of using social networking websites to engage potential customers and market and sell products to them. Facebook is the social network with the most users worldwide. It is also the social network most companies use because it generates the most revenue for them. Each network appeals to different types of users and requires slightly different marketing techniques. The challenges of using social media include the fact that companies can't directly control what's being said about them on social networks, it can be difficult to be "heard" due to the number of people posting messages on the networks, and timing messages can pose problems. Some of the best practices for using social media include using visuals and presenting positive and meaningful messages that are authentic and fun when appropriate, and optimizing a company's content across sites. Community managers are people firms hire to help them implement and manage their social media content and campaigns.

Review Questions

1. Why is social media marketing becoming a more important part of integrated marketing communications?
2. Why do different social networks require different marketing techniques?
3. What obstacles do firms face when using social networks to market their products?
4. What techniques can firms use to ensure their messages on social media will be received well?

12.4 Measuring the Effectiveness of Digital Marketing

Learning Objectives

1. Explain how analytical tools help firms improve their digital marketing efforts.
2. Describe some of the metrics marketers study when analyzing their firm's digital marketing efforts.

Was your last social media marketing campaign effective? Did the sales of your products increase? And how about those pay-per-click ads? How much money did you spend on them compared to the revenues they generated? Digital marketing allows you to answer questions such as these using various metrics and online tools. One of the positive aspects of digital marketing is that the results are easier to measure because digital media is interactive. People either respond with a click or they don't. In contrast, if you see a product in a TV ad and later buy it, it's harder for the company that ran the ad to tell if you bought the product because of the ad or for another reason.

Marketing professionals look at and study far more digital marketing metrics than we are able to go into in this textbook. However, Table 12.4 will give you an idea of some of the metrics that are commonly used.

TABLE 12.4 A Sample of Digital Marketing Metrics and Their Explanations

Metric	Explanation
Bounce rate	The percentage of visitors who leave a site after viewing only one page on a website.
Buzz	The number of trending topics, blog mentions, likes, forwards, and retweets generated.
Click-through rate	The percentage of people who click on ad to get to a landing page.
Conversions	The number of sales or sales leads generated.
Cost per conversion	The amount paid per conversion.
Cost per click	The amount paid per click on an ad.
Email open rate	The number of emails opened divided by the total number of email messages sent.
Engagement rate	The number of fans, views, likes, shares, comments, and check-ins generated.
Page views	The total number of pages visitors looked at on a website.
Reach	A measure of the number of unique visitors to a website, page and video views, and the time visitors spend on the site.
Shopping cart abandon rate	A rate that refers to how frequently visitors begin the checkout process but then stop before a purchase is made.
Time on page	The average amount of time visitors spend on a particular page on a website.
Time on site	The average amount of time visitors spend on all pages on a website.
Traffic by channel	The number of people who arrived at the website via searches, links from other websites, and social media sites.
Visitors	The number of actual people who visit a website.
Visits	The total number of times a website was visited.
New visitors	The total number of new visitors to a website in a given time period.
Return visitors	The total number who returned to the website in a given period.

Google Analytics is the most widely used digital analytics tool, and it's free. All a marketer needs to do is go to the site, create an account, and then enter the URL for his or her firm's website, mobile site, blog, YouTube channel, or other social media site to see a huge array of statistics related to it. The statistics include, among other things, the countries and websites visitors are coming from, how long on average they stay on the site(s), how many times they visit, what they click on, and the number of conversions that occur as a result. It can also tell you what pages they spend the most time on, what pages are performing poorly (not being visited often), and the devices visitors are using.

Other more sophisticated metrics include:

- Scroll tracking. Scroll tracking indicates how far down a page users scroll, and it can be set up to indicate whether or not people made it to certain points. For example, did they scroll far enough down to see the buy button? Did they read through your entire email? If they didn't, you can tell at which point they quit and make adjustments.
- Heat maps. A heat map is a visual that shows where people are dwelling on your website either visually or by clicking on the site. Red areas indicate that an area is "hot" and are navigated to frequently, whereas blue areas indicate that an area is "cold" and not getting much attention.

Google Analytics

To see the types of statistics Google Analytics tracks, and how to install it to check the statistics on your site, check out this YouTube video.

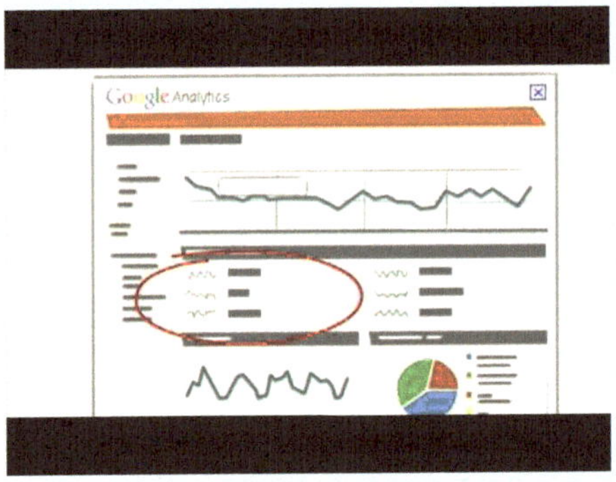

View in the online reader

According to Glassdoor.com, on average, digital marketing analysts in the United States earn about $63,000 per year.

Source: © Shutterstock.com

bounce rate

The rate at which people leave a page immediately after clicking on it.

Google isn't the only company with analytical tools, though. Most social media sites provide free analytical tools to their users along with tutorials that explain how to use them. HootSuite, Crowdbooster, Simply Measured, and Tracx are online products you can purchase to analyze statistics on the social networks you use. Most of these companies offer free versions of their products, but the pay versions provide more robust information.

The ability to examine statistics to see what's working and what isn't allows a company to make informed decisions about how to modify its digital marketing campaigns (as well as other types of marketing campaigns) and continue to improve them over time. For example, if a company is utilizing content marketing, but not converting very many visitors, it may need to add some sort of "call to action" at the end of the content or offer a discount to persuade consumers to actually make a purchase.

If a company's visits are particularly low on one social network versus the others it uses, this signals that the firm may need to do more work to beef up its engagement on that network or utilize other networks more. A high **bounce rate** , the rate at which people leave a page immediately after clicking on it could indicate that the link to the page being visited is broken and needs to be fixed. If a lot of people are using their mobile devices to get to the site, perhaps the company needs a mobile version of it.

Anastasia Helton, ID Agent

Source: Anastasia Heltom

Does information discussed in this chapter intrigue you? Do you like analyzing numbers and doing detective work based on what they reveal? If so, a career utilizing digital marketing and other marketing tools might be a good career for you. It has been for Anastasia Helton. Helton is the senior director of product marketing at ID Agent, a cybersecurity company.

"It's not easy—you have to know your products through and through and be well-informed about the marketplace trends and your competition," Helton says about the marketing work she does. "I need to stay on top of what's going on in my industry, what our competitors are up to, and what customers and analysts are saying about us. So I subscribe to and read several cybersecurity industry newsletters, competitor blogs, analyst reports, and Reddit forums where our and our competitors' products are discussed."

"I also enjoy making plans and then executing them (or overseeing their execution)," Helton says. "I am talking about new product releases here. A lot goes into releasing a new software product or a new feature to the market. There are so many things to consider and tasks to accomplish, both internally and externally, for a launch to be successful. I get to manage this process and get a cross-functional team together for each launch to see to the different aspects of the launch, like pricing and packaging, new marketing materials creation, external and internal announcements, website updates, sales and support teams training, marketing campaigns to support the launch and many, many more. Sometimes it feels overwhelming just how many different activities must take place to prepare for a launch. But after everything is completed successfully and the product is selling and bringing in new revenue for the company, it's very satisfying to know that you played an important part in it."

Key Takeaway

- One of the positive aspects of digital marketing is that the results are easier to measure because digital media is interactive. People either respond with a click or they don't. Marketing professionals look at and study a wide array of digital marketing metrics. Google Analytics is the most widely used digital analytics tool, but most social media sites provide free analytical tools to their users, and online products can be purchased for this purpose. The ability to examine statistics to see what's working and what isn't allows a company to make informed decisions about how to modify its digital marketing campaigns (as well as other types of marketing campaigns) and continue to improve them over time.

Review Questions

1. Why are the results of digital marketing easy to measure?
2. What types of digital marketing statistics do marketing professionals analyze?
3. What do marketers do with the marketing statistics they collect?

12.5 Discussion Questions and Activities

Discussion Questions

1. What are the different ways in which a company can improve its search engine rankings?
2. What types of e-commerce sites are most successful? What factors make them a success?
3. What are pros and cons of using social media to market products?
4. Discuss the ways in which a company can use data to refine its digital marketing campaigns.

Activities

1. Examine the subject lines of ten emails you received recently from firms. Rank the subject lines from first to worst based on how effective you believe they are.
2. Think of a mobile app you might create. What would its purpose be, and how would you market it?
3. Go to the Coca-Cola Company's corporate websites on Facebook, Instagram, Pinterest, and LinkedIn. How does the firm's content differ from site to site?
4. You've been asked to create a new social media networking site. What would you name the site, and what would you suggest to make it better than existing sites?

12.6 Video Case Study: *The New York Times*

NYT VR: Transforming the Storytelling Experience

The *New York Times* VR app grew out of the shared vision of the *Times'* newsroom, its advertising department, and brand partners to realize virtual reality as a mainstream form of storytelling.

View in the online reader

Case Study Questions

1. Like many newspapers, *The New York Times* has struggled to attract younger viewers and retain subscribers. What other types of technologies could help older brands like the *Times* connect with new customers?
2. In 2021, the *Times* experienced a sharp increase in the number of digital subscribers it has along with increases in its digital ad revenues. Why do you think this might have occurred?

Endnotes

1. Jack Marshall and Suzanne Vranica (June 26, 2015), "In Cannes, Advertisers Try on Digital," *Wall Street Journal,* http://wsj.com.
2. Staff (September 28, 2021), "Wunderkind Integrates with Salesforce Marketing Cloud to Help eCommerce Brands Scale Personalized Experiences at Every Step of the Customer Lifecycle," *PR Newswire,* https://www.prnewswire.com/news-releases/wunderkind-integrates-with-salesforce-marketing-cloud-to-help-ecommerce-brands-scale-personalized-experiences-at-every-step-of-the-customer-lifecycle-301371002.html; Christina Binkley (April 9, 2015), "Can a Fashion Gamble, Skipping the Runway, Pay Off?" *Wall Street Journal,* D3.
3. Jo Craven McGinty (November 18, 2016), "For Hotels, Online Reviews Really Matter to the Bottom Line," *Wall Street Journal,* https://www.wsj.com/articles/for-hotels-online-reviews-really-matter-to-the-bottom-line-1479477602.
4. Staff (August 18, 2021), "Amazon Hits Chinese Sellers with Crackdowns on Fake Reviews," *Bloomberg,* https://www.bloomberg.com/news/articles/2021-08-18/amazon-amzn-cracks-down-on-fake-reviews-hitting-chinese-retailers.
5. Sara Morrison (March 3, 2021), "Google Is Done with Cookies, but that Doesn't Mean It's Done Tracking You," *Vox,* https://www.vox.com/recode/2021/3/3/22311460/google-cookie-ban-search-ads-tracking.
6. Pierre DeBois (October 4, 2021), "How to Get Started With A/B Testing," *CMS Wire,* https://www.cmswire.com/digital-marketing/how-to-get-started-with-ab-testing/; Stu Woo (December 23, 2011), "Retailers Tweak Sites to Spur Sales," *Wall Street Journal,* B7.
7. Staff (June 15, 2021), "Texas Amends Law Requiring State AG to publicly post data breach notifications," *Reuters,* https://www.reuters.com/legal/legalindustry/texas-amends-law-requiring-state-ag-publicly-post-data-breach-notifications-2021-06-15/.
8. Dennis Green and Mary Hanbury (July 20, 2018), "If You Shopped at These 15 Stores in the Last Year, Your Data Might Have Been Stolen," *Business Insider,* https://businessinsider.com/data-breaches-2018-4.
9. Staff (July 7, 2021), "Average Time Spent Daily on a Smartphone in the United States 2021," https://www.statista.com/statistics/1224510/time-spent-per-day-on-smartphone-us/.
10. Becky Bargh (July 2, 2018), "Avon Launches 'Instant Messaging Brochure' for Personalized Shopping," *Cosmetics Business,* https://www.cosmeticsbusiness.com/news/article_page/Avon_launches_instant_messaging_brochure_for_personalised_shopping/144556.
11. Staff (July 19, 2021), "Global Location Based Advertising (LBA) Market to Reach US$523.3 Billion by the Year 2027," GlobeNewsWire, https://www.globenewswire.com/news-release/2021/07/19/2264666/0/en/Global-Location-Based-Advertising-LBA-Market-to-Reach-US-523-3-Billion-by-the-Year-2027.html.
12. Sarah Perez (January 22, 2021), "Pinterest Launches an AR-Powered Try-On Experience for Eyeshadow," *TechCrunch,* https://techcrunch.com/2021/01/22/pinterest-launches-an-ar-powered-try-on-experience-for-eyeshadow/.
13. Maria Korolov (October 4, 2021), "What Is a Chatbot? Simulating Human Conversation for Service," CIO,https://www.cio.com/article/3635168/what-is-a-chatbot-simulating-human-conversation-for-service.html.
14. Brokke Auxier and Monica Anderson (April 7, 2021), "Social Media Use in 2021," https://www.pewresearch.org/internet/2021/04/07/social-media-use-in-2021/.
15. Laura Forman (November 3, 2021), "Meta Delivers for Its Advertisers," *Wall Street Journal,* B14.
16. Robert Williams (July 14, 2021) "Native Advertising Has Key Role in Future of Ad-Supported TV," *BeetTV,* https://www.beet.tv/2021/07/native-advertising-has-key-role-in-future-of-ad-supported-tv-triplelifts-michael-shields.html.
17. Amanda Perelli (October 15, 2021), "How Much Money YouTubers with 1 Million Subscribers Make," https://www.yahoo.com/news/much-money-youtubers-1-million-124853437.html.
18. Amanda N'Duka (December 2020) "'Liza on Demand' Star Liza Koshy Inks Overall Deal With Westbrook Inc.," *Deadline,* https://deadline.com/2020/12/liza-on-demand-liza-koshy-overall-deal-westbrook-inc-1234656259/; John Jurgensen (November 26, 2017), "A Self-Made Star Shows One Way to Crack the Code," *Wall Street Journal,* https://www.wsj.com/articles/a-self-made-star-shows-one-way-to-crack-the-gen-z-code-1511719567.
19. Lauren Cochrane (February 6, 2021), "Perfect Storm: Have the Influencers Selling a Dream Lost Their Allure?" *The Guardian,* https://www.theguardian.com/media/2021/feb/06/perfect-storm-have-the-influencers-selling-a-dream-lost-their-allure.
20. Jeff Fromm (September 30, 2020), "On Ben And Jerry's, Gen-Z, And Social Justice," *Forbes,* https://www.google.com/search?q=social+justice+and+appeal+to+millennials&oq=social+justice+and+appeal+to+millennials&aqs=chrome..69i57.8602j0j9&sourceid=chrome&ie=UTF-8.
21. Joe Pulizzi (June 6, 2012), "Six Useful Content Marketing Definitions," *Content Marketing Institute,* http://contentmarketinginstitute.com/2012/06/content-marketing-definition/.

CHAPTER 13

Professional Selling

The clock in Ted Schulte's home office was striking 11:00 p.m. His family had gone to bed an hour ago. Yet Schulte, an account representative who sells pacemakers for Boston Scientific, was on the phone talking to one of his clients, a cardiologist. The cardiologist was performing surgery at 7:00 a.m. the next day. His patient had a number of health problems that caused the doctor to question which pacemaker would best suit her needs. The cardiologist's questions had to be answered immediately so the right materials and tools would be available for the procedure. The best expert on the matter was not another physician in this case—it was Schulte.

When you visit your physician, you want to think that training and education have completely prepared your physician for dealing with whatever condition sent you there. The reality is, however, that salespeople play a major role in the continuing education of doctors, surgeons, and all health care professionals. Salespeople bring information on clinical studies, answer questions, and perform other educational tasks for the physicians they visit. Similarly, the house or apartment you live in may have been designed by an architect, but that architect learns about new materials and design elements from salespeople, each of whom is an expert in a particular product category. Yes, salespeople have to sell, but they also play an important role in educating customers about new solutions to their problems.

Salespeople play an important role in our economy. They are vital to customers and companies alike—responsible for achieving a company's revenue goals while solving customers' problems. In this chapter, we explore the role professional selling plays in terms of a company's marketing strategy. We also look at the factors that enhance a firm's success when it markets and sells its products through salespeople.

13.1 The Role Professional Salespeople Play

Learning Objectives

1. Recognize the role professional selling plays in society and in firms' marketing strategies.
2. Identify the different types of sales positions.

You've created a great product, you've priced it right, and you've set a wonderful marketing communication strategy in motion. Now you can just sit back and watch the sales roll in, right? Probably not. Unless your company is able to sell the product entirely over the internet, you probably have a lot more work to do. For example, if you want consumers to also be able to buy the product in a retail store, someone will first have to convince the retailer to carry the product.

"Nothing happens until someone sells something," is an old saying in business. Without sales revenue, a company cannot exist and salespeople are often the ones that make the sales. However, salespeople are expensive. Often they are the most expensive element in a company's marketing strategy. As a result, they have to generate enough business justify a firm's investment in them.

What Salespeople Do

Salespeople act on behalf of their companies by doing the following:

- create value for their firms' customers
- manage relationships, both with customers and inside the company
- relay customer and market information back to their organizations

Salespeople work with customer to create value by ensuring that customer needs are fully identified. Based on the identified needs, salespeople offer solutions with the right offerings, bringing their expertise to bear on the customer's problems, challenges, or opportunities.

Salespeople don't meet customer needs on their own. They work with departments like finance or customer credit, shipping, manufacturing, and service so that those departments can provide the right solutions for customer issues in a profitable fashion. Salespeople are also representatives of these areas, making sure that the customer has an accurate picture of what can be done.

In addition to acting on behalf of their firms, sales representatives also act on behalf of their customers. Whenever a salesperson goes back to her company with a customer's request, be it for quicker delivery, a change in a product feature, or a negotiated price, she is voicing the customer's needs. Her goal is to help the buyer purchase what serves his or her needs the best. Like Ted Schulte, the salesperson is the expert but, in this case, an expert representing the customer's needs back to the company. When the company responds to those needs, the salesperson has played a role in creating value.

From society's perspective, selling is wonderful when professional salespeople act on behalf of both buyers and sellers. While the balance of value may swing to the company in some instances and to the customer in others, on the whole, salespeople play an important role in society.

Yet, sometimes salespeople find balancing the needs of both company and customer difficult because these expectations may conflict. Not all needs can be fully satisfied, and salespeople can't give away products or services. Customers sometimes have unfair expectations.

Sometimes, though, salespeople face suspicion and doubt from customers. In fact, many people think all salespeople are unethical in part because certain types of salespeople have earned poor reputations that have tarnished the entire profession. As a result, some business students avoid sales despite the very high earnings potential and personal growth opportunities. You might be surprised to learn, however, that one study found that salespeople are less likely to exaggerate in order to get what they want than are politicians, preachers, and professors. Another study looked at how business students responded to ethical dilemmas versus how professional salespeople responded. What did the study find? That salespeople were more likely to respond ethically than the business students were.

In general, salespeople handle these conflicting expectations well. Society benefits because salespeople help buyers make more informed decisions and help their companies succeed, which, in turn, creates jobs for people and products they can use. Most salespeople also truly believe in the effectiveness of their company's offerings. Schulte, for example, is convinced that the pacemakers he sells are the best there are. When this belief is coupled with a genuine concern for the welfare of the customer—a concern that most salespeople share—society can't lose.

Many marketing majors begin their career in sales. While a growing number of universities are offering a major in sales, the demand for professional salespeople often outstrips supply, creating opportunities for marketing majors. Sales is a great place to start a career not only because the earnings can be at the top of any business major but because sales is the only place to really learn what is happening in the market.

Creating Value

Consider the following situations:

- At the beginning of the chapter, we described a real-life situation—a cardiac surgeon with a high-risk patient is wondering what to do. The physician calls Ted Schulte at Boston Scientific to get his input on how to handle the situation. Schulte recommends the appropriate pacemaker and offers to drive one hundred miles early in the morning in order to be in surgery with the doctor to answer any questions that might arise during the surgery.
- A banker works with a mortgage company client to resolve a fraud issue involving a real estate transaction. That banker, really a salesperson who manages the relationship with clients, develops a software solution that prevents that type of fraud and starts a company now selling over $10 million a year.
- Sanderson Farms, a chicken processor, wants to build a new plant in central Texas, between Austin, Dallas, and Houston. The chambers of commerce for several towns in the area vie for the project. The chamber representative from Waco, though, locates an enterprise zone that reduces the company's taxes for a period of time, and then works with a local banker to get the company better financing. In addition, the rep gets a local technical college involved so Sanderson will have enough trained employees. These factors create a unique package that sells the company on setting up shop in Waco.

All these are true stories of how salespeople create value by understanding the needs of their customers and then creating solutions to meet those needs. Salespeople can adapt the offering, such as in the Sanderson Farms example, or they can adapt how they present the offering so that it is easier for the client to understand and make the right decision.

Adapting a message or product on the fly isn't something that can be easily accomplished with other types of marketing communication. Granted, some websites are designed to adapt the information and products they display by applying artificial intelligence. But unless the site has a "chat with a representative" feature, there is no real dialogue occurring (and even then, that chat representative could be automated and not human). The ability to engage in dialogue helps salespeople better understand their customers and their needs and then create valuable solutions for them.

Note also that creating value means making sales. Salespeople sell—that's the bulk of the value they deliver to their employers. There are other ways in which they deliver value, but it is how much they sell that determines most of the value they deliver to their companies.

Salespeople aren't appropriate channels for companies in all situations, however. Some purchases don't require the salesperson's expertise. Or the need to sell at a very low cost may make retail stores or online selling more attractive. But in situations requiring adaptation of the product or the message, customer education, and other value-adding activities, salespeople can be the best channel to reach customers.

Managing Relationships

Because their time is limited, sales representatives have to decide which accounts they have the best shot at winning and which are the most lucrative. Once a salesperson has decided to pursue an account, a strategy is devised and implemented, and if a sale happens, the salesperson is also responsible for ensuring that the offering is implemented properly and to the customer's satisfaction.

Salespeople prefer building relationships with customers who can buy more than once. In order to earn the right for future business, salespeople have to ensure that the company satisfies the customer's requirements. Sometimes, that means building relationships across the company so that adaptations are correctly made to the offering, that the financial terms are properly conducted, and that shipments are correct and on time.

We've already emphasized the notion of "customers for life" in this book. Salespeople recognize that business is not about making friends, but about making and retaining customers. Although buyers tend to purchase products from salespeople they like, being liked is not enough. Salespeople have to ensure that they close the deal with the customer. They also have to recognize that the goal is not to just close one deal, but as many deals as possible in the future; we'll discuss strategies for managing different types of customer relationships later in this chapter.

Gathering Information

boundary spanners

People who work both inside and outside their organizations. Salespeople are boundary spanners.

Salespeople are **boundary spanners**, in that they operate outside the boundaries of the firm and in the field. As such, they are the first to learn about what competitors are doing. An important function for them, then, is to report back to headquarters about their competitors' new offerings and strategies.

Similarly, salespeople interact directly with customers and, in so doing, gather a great deal of useful information about their needs. The salespeople then pass the information along to their firms, which use it to create new offerings, adjust their current offerings, and reformulate their marketing tactics. The trick is getting the information to the right decision makers in firms. Many companies use customer relationship management (CRM) software like Salesforce to provide a mechanism for salespeople to enter customer data and others to retrieve it. A company's marketing department, for example, can then use that data to pinpoint segments of customers with which to communicate directly. In addition to using the data to improve and create marketing strategies, the information can help marketing decision makers understand who makes buying decisions, resulting in such decisions as targeting trade shows where potential buyers are likely to be. In other words, marketing managers don't have to ask salespeople directly what customers want; they can pull that information from a customer database.

Aplicor is a computer software program that enables salespeople to capture and track information on their accounts. This information can then be used by marketing managers to design better marketing strategies and offerings. The system also helps salespeople manage their accounts better because they have access to more customer information.

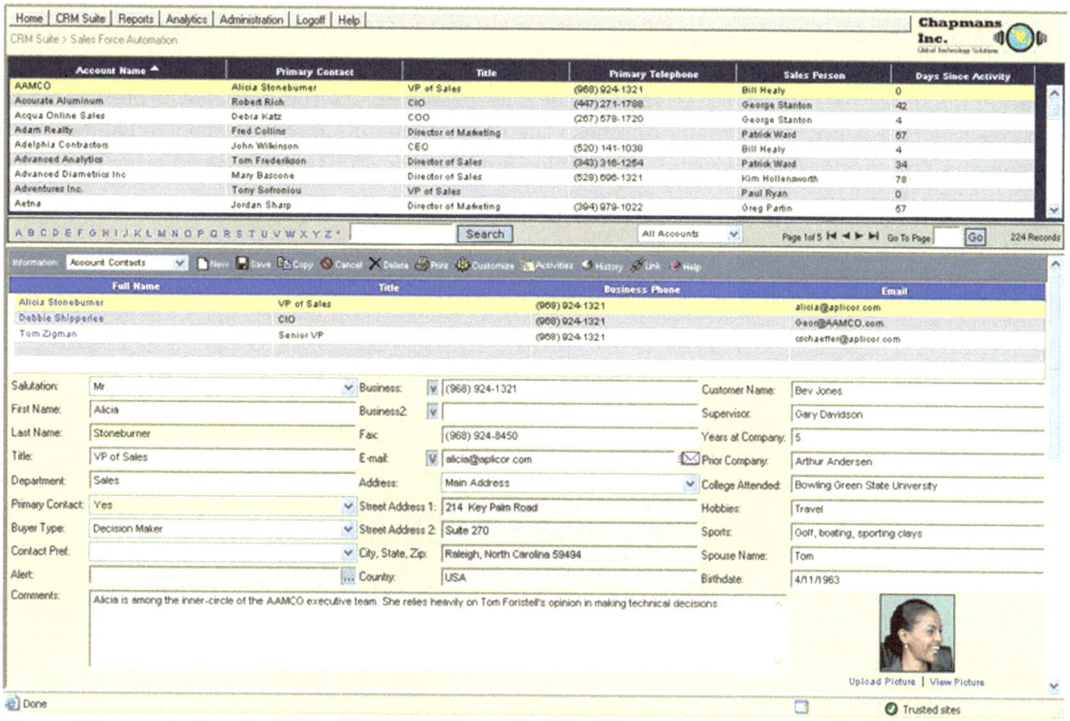

Source: Aplicor, used with permission

Types of Sales Positions

There are different ways to organize salespeople. They can be categorized by the customers they work with, such as whether those customers are consumers, other businesses, or government institutions. Another way to categorize salespeople is by the size of their customers. Most professional sales positions involve selling to other businesses, but many also sell to consumers like you. For the purposes of this book, we will categorize salespeople by their activities. Using activities as a basis, there are four basic types of salespeople: missionary salespeople, trade salespeople, prospectors, and account managers. In some discussions, you'll hear that there are three types: **order getters**, **order takers**, and **sales support**. The four we describe in the following are all types of order getters; that is, they actively seek to make sales by calling on customers. We'll also discuss order takers and sales support after we discuss the four types of order getters.

order getters

A salesperson who actively solicits purchases from customers.

order takers

A salesperson whose primary responsibility is fielding requests from customers who either come into the company's location (store or distributorship) or call or contact a contact center.

sales support

A staff that helps salespeople by pricing and by preparing proposals and other pre-sale and post-sale activities.

Missionary Salespeople

missionary salesperson

A salesperson who calls on people who make decisions about products but don't actually buy them.

A **missionary salesperson** calls on people who make decisions about products but don't actually buy them, and while they call on individuals, the relationship is business-to-business. For example, a pharmaceutical representative might call on a physician to provide the doctor with clinical information about a medication's effectiveness. The salesperson hopes the doctor will prescribe the drug. Patients, not doctors, actually purchase the medication. Similarly, salespeople call on your professors urging them to use certain textbooks. But you, the student, choose whether or not to actually buy the books.

Mary Gros, Teradata

Source: Mary Gros, used with permission

Missionary salespeople who call on doctors or professors work to convince them to prescribe or require the product, but there are some who work with market influencers whose prescription may come in the form of a recommendation in an article, blog post, etc. Mary Gros works for Teradata, a company that develops data warehousing solutions. She works with consultants, bloggers and journalists, and even professors—individuals who are influencers in data warehousing. Part of her job is organizing conferences such as the Teradata Influencer Summit that bring these thought leaders together, not only to learn about Teradata's solutions but also to stay on top of their field. "I really enjoy bringing people together," she says, "especially when I can track it to impact such as a new customer or a customer who has added to their Teradata applications."

Mary Gros holds a type of missionary sales position. She helps connect professors and other influencers with Teradata people and customers so that they will write, teach, and consult about Teradata products and services.

Trade Salespeople

A **trade salesperson** is someone who calls on retailers and helps them display, advertise, and sell products to consumers. Eddy Patterson is a trade salesperson. Patterson calls on major supermarket chains like HEB for Stubb's BBQ, a company that makes barbecue sauces, rubs, marinades, and other barbecuing products. Patterson makes suggestions about how Stubb's products should be priced and where they should be placed in store so they will sell faster. Patterson also works with his clients' advertising departments to create effective ads and fliers featuring Stubb's products.

Trade salespeople like Eddy Patterson for Stubb's help retailers promote and sell products to consumers.

Source: Photo courtesy of Stubb's Legendary Kitchen

Prospectors

A **prospector** is a salesperson whose primary function is to find prospects, or potential customers. The potential customers have a need, but for any number of reasons, they are not actively looking for products to meet those needs—perhaps because they lack information about where to look for them or simply haven't had the time to do so. Prospectors often knock on a lot of doors and make a lot of phone calls, which is called *cold calling* because they do not know the potential accounts and are therefore talking to them "cold." Their primary job is to sell, but the activity that drives their success is prospecting. Many salespeople who sell to consumers would be considered prospectors, including salespeople such as insurance or financial services salespeople, or cosmetic salespeople such as those working for Avon or Mary Kay.

trade salesperson

Someone who calls on retailers and provides them assistance with merchandising and selling products to consumers.

prospector

A salesperson whose primary responsibility is prospecting, or finding potential customers. The salesperson might be responsible for closing the sales or simply turning the prospects over to someone else to close.

Michelle Kaserman, Tom James Company

Source: Michelle Kaserman, used with permission

Michelle Kaserman has been selling custom tailored clothing to busy professionals in their office or home for fifteen years. She loves the flexibility of her job, not only being able to work around raising children but also being able to decide on whom to call. While she has a strong client base, she also likes "calling on new prospects, unlimited earning potential, working around my personal/family's schedule, personal relationships with clients who become friends, getting to pick who I work with (sell to) are just a few things that come to mind."

In some B2B situations, the prospector finds a prospect and then turns it over to another salesperson to close the deal. Or the prospector may take the prospect all the way through the sales process and close the sale.

Account Managers

Brenda Lipscomb (in the red dress), as an account exec selling medical solutions such as IV infusion systems to hospitals and other providers that offer infusion-related services, loves the fact that she and her company can make a positive impact in patients' health.

Source: Brenda Lipscomb, used with permission

Account managers are responsible for ongoing business with a customer who uses a product. A new customer may be found by a prospector and then turned over to an account manager, or new accounts may be so rare that the account manager is directly responsible for identifying and closing them. For example, if you sold beds to hospitals, new hospital organizations are rare. A new hospital may be built, but chances are good that it is replacing an existing hospital or is part of an existing hospital chain, so the account would already have coverage.

But that's entirely the market that Brenda Lipscomb serves, selling IV infusion systems. What drives her is the impact of her products on the lives of patients. "There are two main reasons why I love what I do," Brenda says. "Focusing on the end user of our product is what drives my need to provide a solution. That is what matters. If you keep the end user authentically in mind, you will always be successful in sales! The other is my competitive nature, I hate to lose."

Among other activities, account managers also try to identify lead users (people or organizations likely to use new, cutting-edge products) and build relationships with them. (Recall that we discussed lead users in Chapter 6.) Lead users are in a good position to help improve a company's offerings or develop new ones. Account managers work closely with these lead users and build relationships across both their companies so that the two organizations can innovate together.

account manager

A salesperson responsible for ongoing business with a customer who uses a product. Satisfying long-term customers and persuading them to reorder products are important activities for account managers.

Other Types of Sales Positions

Earlier, we stated that there are also order takers and sales support. These other types of salespeople do not actively solicit business. Order takers, though, do close sales while sales support do not. Order takers include retail sales clerks and salespeople for distributors of products, like plumbing supplies or electrical products, who sell to plumbers and electricians. Other order takers may work in a call center, taking customer sales calls over the phone or internet when customers initiate contact. Such salespeople carry sales quotas and are expected to hit those sales numbers.

Sales support work with salespeople to help make a sale and to take care of the customer after the sale. At Dynata, a marketing research company headquartered in Dallas, sales support help salespeople price projects and prepare bids. At Oracle, an information systems provider, sales support assist by engineering solutions and, like at Dynata, pricing offerings and preparing proposals. At Dynata, the sales support staff also helps deliver the project, whereas at Oracle, another team takes over when the sale is made.

Key Takeaway

- Salespeople act as representatives for other people, including employees who work in other parts of their companies. Salespeople create value for their customers, manage relationships, and gather information for their firms. There are four types of salespeople: missionary salespeople, trade salespeople, prospectors, and account managers. Order takers and sales support also engage in sales activities.

Review Questions

1. Salespeople play three primary roles. What are they?
2. Salespeople create value in what two ways?
3. How does each type of salesperson create value?

13.2 Customer Relationships and Selling Strategies

Learning Objectives

1. Understand the types of selling relationships that firms seek.
2. Be able to select the selling strategy needed to achieve the desired customer relationship.

Customer Relationships

Some buyers and sellers are more interested than others in building strong relationships with each other. Generally speaking, however, all marketers are interested in developing stronger relationships with large customers, whether they become functional relationships or partnerships. Why? Because serving one large customer can often be more profitable than serving several smaller customers, even when the large customer receives quantity discounts. Serving many small customers—calling on them, processing all their orders, and dealing with any complaints—is time consuming and costs money. The delivery process provides perhaps the most obvious example. Delivering a large load to one customer can be accomplished in just one trip. By contrast, delivering smaller loads to numerous customers will require many stops on the trip, therefore taking a lot longer and costing more. Sometimes, having fewer but larger customers can be more profitable than having more but small customers. One metric that some marketers pay attention to is called **cost to serve** and is how much it costs to take care of a customer. Stronger relationships are highly desirable with high sales volume but low cost-to-serve customers.

cost to serve

All costs incurred because of one customer, including delivery, technical service, special adaptations made to products, billing costs, and any other costs incurred; cost to serve varies by customer.

Marketers also want stronger relationships with customers who are innovative, such as lead users. Similarly, marketers seek out customers with status or who are recognized by others for having expertise. For example, Holt Caterpillar is a Caterpillar construction equipment dealer in Texas and is recognized among Caterpillar dealers for its innovativeness. Customers such as Holt influence others (recall that we discussed these opinion leaders in Chapter 3). When Holt buys or tries something new and it works, other Cat dealers are quick to follow. If you were selling products and services that Caterpillar dealers might want, you would do well to start with Holt.

Salespeople are also tasked with maintaining relationships with market influencers who are not their customers. As mentioned earlier, Mary Gros at Teradata works with professors and with consultants so they know all about Teradata's data warehousing solutions. Professors who teach data warehousing influence future decision makers, whereas consultants and market analysts influence today's decision makers. Thus, Gros needs to maintain relationships with both groups.

Types of Sales Relationships

Think about the relationships you have with your friends and family. Most relationships operate along a continuum of intimacy or trust. The more you trust a certain friend or family member, the more you share intimate information with the person, and the stronger your relationship is. The relationships between salespeople and customers are similar to those you have, which range from acquaintance to best friend (see Figure 13.1).

FIGURE 13.1 The Relationship Continuum

As this figure depicts, business relationships range from transactional, or one-time purchases, to strategic partnerships that are often likened to a marriage. Somewhere in between are functional and affiliative relationships that may look like friendships.

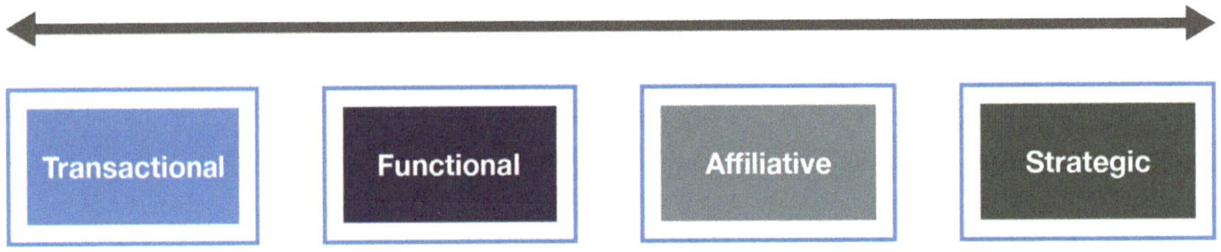

transactional relationships

Purchases that are made with little likelihood of any repeat purchase.

functional relationships

A limited but ongoing relationship that can develop when a buyer continues to purchase a product out of habit, as long as needs are met.

affiliative selling relationships

Relationships between buyer and seller based on friendship and trust, generally occurring when a buyer relies on a salesperson for expertise.

strategic partnership

A relationship in which both the buyer and seller commit time and money to expanding the "pie" for both parties, based on trust and mutual commitment.

At one end of the spectrum are **transactional relationships**; each sale is a separate exchange, and the two parties have little or no interest in maintaining an ongoing relationship. For example, when you fill up your car with gas, you might not care if it's gas from Exxon, Shell, or another company. You just want the best price. If one of these companies went out of business, you would simply do business with another.

Functional relationships are limited, ongoing relationships that develop when a buyer continues to purchase a product from a seller out of habit, as long as her needs are met. If there's a gas station near your house that has good prices, you might frequently fill up there, so you don't have to shop around. If this gas station goes out of business, you will be more likely to feel inconvenienced. MRO (maintenance, repair, and operations) items, such as such as nuts and bolts used to repair manufacturing equipment, are often sold on the basis of functional relationships. There are small price, quality, and services differences associated with the products. By sticking with the product that works, the buyer reduces his costs.

Affiliative selling relationships are more likely to occur when the buyer needs a significant amount of expertise from the seller, and trust is an issue. Ted Schulte, the pacemaker salesperson, describes one segment of his market as affiliative; the people in this segment trust Schulte's judgment because they rely on him to help them make good decisions on behalf of patients. They know that Schulte wouldn't do anything to jeopardize that relationship.

A **strategic partnership** is one in which both the buyer and seller commit time and money to expand "the pie" for both parties. This level of commitment is often likened to a marriage. For example, ThyssenKrup manufactures the engines that Hyundai uses in building cargo ships. Maersk was the first to order these, buying eight. ThyssenKrup and Hyundai work together to advance the state of engine technology because it gives them both an edge. Every time Hyundai sells a ship, ThyssenKrup sells one or more engines. A more carbon-neutral engine enables companies like Maersk to meet global sustainability objectives, which means more sales for ThyssenKrup as well as Hyundai. As a result, the engineers and other personnel from both companies work very closely in an ongoing relationship.

Going back to the value equation, in a transactional relationship, the buyer calculates the value gained after every transaction. As the relationship strengthens, value calculations become less transaction oriented and are made less frequently. There will be times when either the buyer or the seller engages in actions that are not related directly to the sale but that make the relationship stronger. For example, a ThyssenKrup engineer may spend time with Hyundai engineers simply educating them on a new technology. No specific sale may be influenced, but the relationship is made stronger by delivering more value.

Note that these types of relationships are not a process—not every relationship starts at the transactional level and moves through functional and affiliative to strategic. Nor is it the goal to make every relationship a strategic partnership. From the seller's perspective, the motivation to relate is a function of an account's size, innovation, status, and total lifetime value.

Maersk ordered eight Hyundai ships with new ThyssenKrup green methanol engines that are carbon neutral. All three companies are working together for greater fuel efficiency and sustainability.

Source: © Shutterstock, Inc.

Selling Strategies

A salesperson's selling strategies will differ, depending on the type of relationship the buyer and seller either have or want to move toward. There are essentially four selling strategies: script-based selling, needs-satisfaction selling, consultative selling, and strategic partnering.

Script-Based Selling

Salespeople memorize and deliver sales pitches verbatim when they utilize a **script-based selling** strategy. Script-based selling is also called *canned selling*. The term "canned" comes from the fact that the sales pitch is standardized, or "straight out of a can." Back in the late 1880s, companies began to use professional salespeople to distribute their products. Companies like National Cash Register (NCR) realized that some salespeople were far more effective than others, so they brought those salespeople into the head office and had them give their sales pitches. A stenographer wrote each pitch down, and then NCR's sales executives combined the pitches into one effective script. In 1894, the company started one of the world's first sales schools, which taught people to sell using the types of scripts developed by NCR.

script-based selling

A form of selling in which the salesperson memorizes a sales pitch and delivers it verbatim to each prospective customer.

Script-based selling works well when the needs of customers don't vary much. Even when customers do vary, a script can provide a salesperson with a polished and professional description of how an offering meets each of their needs. The salesperson will ask the customer a few questions to uncover his or her need, and then provide the details that meet it as spelled out in the script. Scripts also ensure that the salesperson includes all the important details about a product.

Script-based selling is associated with inside salespeople, but the truth is most salespeople devise effective ways of describing products and services and use these scripts over and over.

Source: © Shutterstock, Inc.

Needs-Satisfaction Selling

The process of asking questions to identify a buyer's problems and needs and then tailoring a sales pitch to satisfy those needs is called **needs-satisfaction selling**. This form of selling works best if the needs of customers vary, but the products being offered are fairly standard. The salesperson asks questions to understand the needs then presents a solution. The method was popularized by Neil Rackham, who developed the SPIN selling approach. SPIN stands for situation questions, problem questions, implications, and needs-payoff, four types of questions that are designed to fully understand how a problem is creating a need. For example, you might wander onto a car lot with a set of needs for a new vehicle. Someone else might purchase the same vehicle, but for an entirely different set of reasons. Perhaps this person is more interested in the miles per gallon, or how big a trailer the vehicle can tow, whereas you are more interested in the vehicle's style and the amount of legroom and headroom it has. The effective salesperson would ask you a few questions, determine what your needs are, and then offer you the right vehicle, emphasizing those points that

needs-satisfaction selling

The process of asking questions to identify a potential buyer's needs and then tailoring the sales pitch to satisfy those needs.

meet your needs best. The vehicle's miles per gallon and towing capacity wouldn't be mentioned in a conversation with you because your needs are about style and room.

Consultative Selling

consultative selling

A selling strategy in which a salesperson uses special expertise to create a somewhat customized solution to a buyer's problem.

To many students, needs-satisfaction selling and consultative selling seem the same. The key difference between the two is the degree to which a customized solution can be created. With **consultative selling**, the seller uses special expertise to solve a complex problem in order to create a somewhat customized solution. For example, Ideal Impact is a company that creates customized solutions to make church buildings more energy efficient. Ideal Impact salespeople work with their customers over the course of a year or longer, as well as with engineers and other technical experts, to produce a solution.

Some companies, such as Grocery Supply Company (GSC), do annual account reviews with their largest customers and some customers, such as John Deere, do annual reviews with all of their major vendors. These reviews are meant not only to obtain feedback on how GSC is doing, but also learn about the customer's plans for the future and co-create solutions for reaching those goals. Similarly, Deere and other large companies initiate annual account reviews with their suppliers for the same purpose. Part of that review includes scoring the vendor on such aspects as on-time delivery, accurate billing, and other performance measures, but the review also includes sharing of strategy for the coming year. The need to leverage the seller's expertise is recognized by these companies and brought into play through such reviews and other methods.

Strategic-Partner Selling

strategic-partner selling

A situation in which a buyer and seller jointly invest resources and share their expertise to create solutions designed to grow one another's businesses.

When the quality of the relationship between the buyer and seller moves toward a strategic partnership, the selling strategy gets more involved than even consultative selling. In **strategic-partner selling**, both parties invest resources and share their expertise with each other to create solutions that jointly grow one another's businesses. Schulte, for example, positions himself as a strategic partner to the cardiologists he works with. He tries to become a trusted partner in the patient care process.

In some instances, the account reviews mentioned above can lead to the development of strategic partnering. Amplex is a manufacturer of cell phones for companies that put their brand on the phone; TracFone is one of their customers. Amplex's COO, Mika Jaaskelainen, meets with TracFone quarterly. He then shares the general results of the meeting with all Amplex employees, as well as any specific issues TracFone has. When a company engages in a strategic partnership strategy, it takes company-wide commitment to the partnership. If the logistics manager isn't committed, for example, and fails to meet a goal, then the entire relationship can be questioned by the buyer.

Choosing the Right Sales Strategy for the Relationship Type and Selling Stage

The sales strategy types and relationship types we discussed don't always perfectly match up as we have described them. Different strategies might be more appropriate at different times. For example, although script-based selling is generally used in transactional sales relationships, it can be used in other types of sales relationships as well, such as affiliative-selling relationships. An affiliative-sales position may still, for example, require demonstrating new products, a task for which a script is useful. Likewise, the same questioning techniques used in needs-satisfaction selling might be used in relationships characterized by consultative selling and strategic-partner selling.

So when is each method most appropriate? Again, it depends on how the buyer wants to buy and what information the buyer needs to make a good decision.

The typical sales process involves several stages, beginning with the preapproach and ending with customer service. In between are other stages, such as the needs-identification stage (where you would ask SPIN questions), presentation stage, and closing stage (see Figure 13.2).

The preapproach is the planning stage. During this stage, a salesperson may use LinkedIn to find the right person to call and to learn about that person. In addition, a Google search may be performed to find the latest news on the company, while a search of financial databases, such as Standard & Poor's, can provide additional news and information. A salesperson may also search internal data to determine if the potential buyer has any history with the company. Note that such extensive precall planning doesn't always happen; sometimes a salesperson is literally just driving by, sees a potential customer, and decides to stop in, but in today's information age, a lot of precall planning can be accomplished through judicious use of web-based resources.

In the approach, the salesperson attempts to capture enough of the prospective customer's attention and interest to continue the sales call. If it is a first-time call, introductions are needed. A benefit that could apply to just about any customer may also be offered to show that the time will be worthwhile. In this stage, the salesperson is attempting to convince the buyer to spend time exploring the possibility of a purchase.

FIGURE 13.2 The Typical Sales Process

A typical sales process starts with the preapproach and moves through several stages to the close. Good salespeople continue with making sure the customer gets the product, uses it right, and is happy with it.

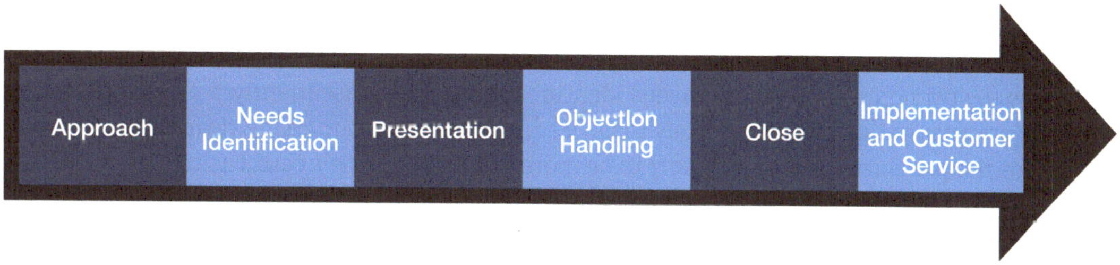

With the buyer's permission, the salesperson then moves into a needs identification section. In complex situations, many questions are asked, perhaps over several sales calls. These questions will follow the SPIN outline or something similar. Highly complex situations may require that questions be asked of many people in the buying organization. In simpler situations, needs may not vary across customers, so a canned presentation is more likely. Then, instead of identifying needs, needs are simply listed as solutions are described.

A presentation is then made that shows how the offering satisfies the needs identified earlier. One approach to presenting solutions uses statements called FEBAs. FEBA stands for feature, evidence, benefit, and agreement. The salesperson says something like, "This system has advanced gaming video chips [Feature], the only ones that Gaming News gave five stars [Evidence]. All your friends will want to play with you at your apartment because you'll have the best gaming system [Benefit]. Isn't that the type of video you'd like for your system [Agreement]?"

Note that the benefit was tied to something the customer said was important. A benefit only exists when something is satisfying a need. Some customers might want their friends coming over to play; others may want the high quality video to simply have the best game experience whether their friends are there or not; while still others may not care whether the video quality is all that high. For this latter group, the advanced chips are of no benefit.

objection

A statement by a buyer of concern about an offer or salesperson.

Objections are concerns or reasons not to continue that are raised by the buyer, and can occur at any time. A prospect may object in the approach, saying there isn't enough time available for a sales call or nothing is needed right now. Or, during the presentation, a buyer may not like a particular feature. For example, the buyer might find that the automatic zoom leads the camera to focus on the wrong object. Salespeople should probe to find out if the objection represents a misunderstanding or a hidden need. Further explanation may resolve the buyer's concern, or there may need to be a trade off; yes, a better zoom is available but it may be out of the buyer's price range, for example.

close

A request for a commitment or decision from the buyer.

When all the objections are resolved to the buyer's satisfaction, the salesperson should ask for the sale. Asking for the sale is called the **close**, or a request for a decision or commitment from the buyer. In complex selling situations that require many sales calls, the close may be a request for the next meeting or some other action. When the close involves an actual sale, the next step is to deliver the goods and make sure the customer is happy.

There are different types of closes. Some of these include:

- Direct request: "Would you like to order now?"
- Minor point: "Would you prefer red or blue?" or "Would you like to view a demonstration on Monday or Tuesday?"
- Summary: "You said you liked the color and the style. Is there anything else you'd like to consider before we complete the paperwork?"

When done properly, closing is a natural part of the process and a natural part of the conversation. But if pushed inappropriately, buyers can feel manipulated or trapped and may not buy even if the decision would be a good one.

The sales process used to sell products is generally the same regardless of the selling strategy used. However, the stage being emphasized will affect the strategy selected in the first place. For example, if the problem is a new one that requires a customized solution, the salesperson and buyer are likely to spend more time in the needs identification stage. Consequently, a needs-satisfaction strategy or consultation strategy is likely to be used. Conversely, if it's already clear what the client's needs are, the presentation stage is likely to be more important. In this case, the salesperson might use a script-based selling strategy, which focuses on presenting a product's benefits rather than questioning the customer.

Key Takeaway

- Some buyers and sellers are more interested in building strong relationships with one another than others. The four types of relationships between buyers and sellers are transactional, functional, affiliative, and strategic. The four basic sales strategies salespeople use are script-based selling, needs-satisfaction selling, consultative selling, and strategic-partner selling. Different strategies can be used in different types of relationships. For example, the same questioning techniques used in needs-satisfaction selling might be used in relationships characterized by consultative selling and strategic-partner selling. The sales process used to sell products is generally the same regardless of the selling strategy used. However, the strategy chosen will depend on the stage the seller is focusing on. For example, if the problem is a new one that requires a customized solution, the salesperson and buyer are likely to spend more time in the needs-identification stage. Consequently, a needs-satisfaction strategy or consultation strategy is likely to be used.

Review Questions

1. Do customer relationships begin as transactional and move toward strategic partnerships? Is a strategic partnership always the salesperson's goal?
2. How does each sales strategy vary?
3. Which step of the sales process is most important, and why? How would the steps of the sales process vary for each type of sales position?

13.3 Sales Metrics (Measures)

Learning Objectives

1. Describe the sales cycle.
2. Understand the selling metrics that salespeople use.
3. Understand the selling metrics that sales managers and executives use.

The Sales Cycle

A key component in the effectiveness of salespeople is the sales cycle. The **sales cycle**—how long it takes to close a sale—can be measured in steps, in days, or in months. As Figure 13.3 shows, the sales cycle is depicted as a **funnel** because not all the people and firms a salesperson talks to will become buyers. In fact, most of them won't. The cycle is shaped like a funnel because there are more leads than suspects, more suspects than prospects, and more prospects than customers as some people say "No" along the way.

The cycle starts with a **lead**, which is often nothing more than contact information of someone who might be interested in the salesperson's product. Sometimes, companies will categorize leads as hot, warm, or cold, based on how interested the potential buyer seems to be. For example, if the lead was first met at a trade show, the lead might be scored as hot if a decision was going to be made soon, in the next thirty days, for example. A cold lead might be someone who just picked up some literature and didn't hang around to watch a demonstration. To follow up on the lead, the salesperson might phone or drop by to see the person identified in the lead. This stage of the sales process is called the **approach**. (Recall that prior to the approach the salesperson may engage in preapproach planning and research.) During the approach, the salesperson introduces himself or herself and his or her company to the buyer. If the buyer shows interest, the salesperson then moves to the next step in the sales process.

sales cycle

The amount of time or number of steps it takes to make a sale; also called the sales pipeline or funnel.

funnel

The amount of time or number of steps it takes to make a sale; also called the sales cycle or pipeline.

lead

The contact information for someone who might be interested in a salesperson's product.

approach

The first step in the sales process. The salesperson introduces himself or herself and the company to the buyer and determines if the buyer has any interest in purchasing the firm's products.

FIGURE 13.3 The Sales Cycle
The sales cycle starts with leads, some of whom become suspects. Some suspects become prospects, and some prospects become customers.

A **suspect** is a person or organization that has an interest in an offering, but it is too early to tell what or if they are going to buy. They've agreed to meet with the salesperson and will possibly listen to the sales script or participate in a needs-identification process. During the needs-identification stage, the salesperson is trying to qualify the account as a prospect. **Qualifying** a prospect is a process of asking questions to determine whether the buyer is likely to become a customer. A **prospect** is someone with the **b**udget, **a**uthority, **n**eed, and **t**ime frame (**BANT**) to make a purchase. In other words, the person has the money to make the purchase and the authority to do so; the person also needs the type of product the salesperson is selling and is going to buy such a product soon.

suspect

A person or organization that has an interest in an offering but hasn't indicated if they are going to purchase.

qualifying

A process of asking questions to determine whether a buyer is likely to become a customer.

prospect

Someone who has the budget, authority, need for, and time to purchase a product.

BANT

An acronym for the characteristics of a qualified prospect. A BANT has the budget, authority, need for, and timeframe to purchase a product.

Once the purchase has been made, the sales cycle is complete. If the relationship between the company and the buyer is one that will be ongoing, the buyer is considered one of the salesperson's "accounts." Note that the buyer made a decision each step of the way in the cycle, thereby moving further down the funnel. She decided to consider what the salesperson was selling and became a suspect. She then decided to buy something and became a prospect. Lastly, she decided to buy the salesperson's product and became a customer.

Optvo salespeople are meeting with potential customers at a trade show in Cologne, Germany. A good show will result in a high number of leads, suspects, and prospects. In some markets, most sales for the year are made at the show.

Source: © Shutterstock, Inc.

Metrics Used by Salespeople

As you know, the key metric, or measure, salespeople are evaluated on are the revenues they generate. Sometimes the average revenue generated per customer and the average revenue generated per sales call are measured to determine if a salesperson is pursuing customers that are the most lucrative or using their time effectively. How many prospects and suspects a salesperson has in the **pipeline** are two other measures. The more potential buyers there are in the pipeline, the more revenue a salesperson is likely to generate.

pipeline

The amount of time or number of steps it takes to make a sale; also called the sales cycle or funnel.

Conversion ratios are an extremely important metric. **Conversion ratios** measure how good a salesperson is at moving customers from one stage in the selling cycle to the next. For example, how many leads did the salesperson convert to suspects? A 10:1 ratio means it took ten leads for the salesperson to get one suspect who agreed to move to the next step. A salesperson with a 5:1 ratio only needs to pursue five leads to get a suspect. If the representative can make only ten sales calls in a day, then the salesperson with the 5:1 ratio will have produced two suspects versus just one suspect for the other salesperson. As a result, the second rep will have more suspects in the pipeline at the end of the day. Similarly, how many suspects did the salesperson convert to prospects and finally to customers? If all the other conversion ratios (suspect-to-prospect ratio and prospect-to-customer ratio) are the same for the two salespeople, then the rep with the 5:1 ratio will close twice as many sales as the one with a 10:1 ratio.

conversion ratios

The rate at which a salesperson moves, or converts, potential customers from one stage of the sales cycle to the next.

Salespeople can track their conversion ratios to identify which stages of the sales cycle they need to focus on in order to improve their performance. For example, the sales representative with the 10:1 ratio can study what the rep with the 5:1 ratio is doing in order to try to improve his efficiency and sales levels. His conversion ratios also tell him how many sales calls he has to make each day or week to generate a sale and how many calls must be made on leads, suspects, and prospects to convert them.

How many sales calls of each type a representative has to make in a certain period of time are **activity goals**. As Figure 13.4 illustrates, activities and conversions drive sales. More calls translate into more conversions, and more conversions translate into more sales. You can think of it as sort of a domino effect.

activity goals

The number and type of sales calls a representative is expected to make in a certain period of time.

A **win-loss analysis** is an "after the battle" review of how well a salesperson performed given the opportunities she faced. Each sales opportunity after the customer has bought something (or decided to buy nothing) is examined to determine what went wrong and what went right. (Keep in mind that to some extent, all salespeople think back through their sales call to determine what they could have said or done differently and what they should say or do again in the future.) When several professionals are involved in the selling process, a win-loss analysis can be particularly effective because it helps the sales team work together more effectively in the future. Like a team watching a film after a football game, each member of the sales team can review the process for the purpose of improvement. When the results are fed to managers, the analysis can help a company develop better products. A marketing manager who listens carefully to what salespeople say during a win-loss analysis can develop better advertising and marketing campaigns. Communicating the same message to the entire market can help shorten the sales cycle for all a company's sales representatives.

win-loss analysis

The process of reviewing each sales cycle after it is completed to identify key factors that accounted for the win or the loss of a sale.

bonus

Pay based on overall sales performance; it may be based on how well an individual salesperson does, how the team does, or how the company performs.

commission

Pay based on a single sale.

Another important metric used by many salespeople is how much money they will make. Most salespeople are paid some form of incentive pay, such as a bonus or commission, which is determined by how much they sell. A **bonus** is paid at the end of a period of time based on the total amount sold, while a **commission** is typically thought of as a payment for each sale. For example, commission may be paid as a percentage, such as 10 percent of the sales price, or may be paid as a dollar per sale, such as one hundred dollars for every unit sold. A bonus plan can be based on how well the company, the individual salesperson, or the salesperson's team does. For example, a salesperson may get a bonus if one hundred units are sold. Some salespeople are paid only on the basis of commission, but most are paid a salary plus a commission or a bonus.

Commissions are more common when sales cycles are short and selling strategies tend to be more transactional than relationship oriented. Perhaps one exception is financial services. Many financial services salespeople are paid a commission but expected to also build a long-lasting relationship with clients. Some salespeople are paid only salary. As might be expected, these salespeople sell very expensive products that have a very long sales cycle. If they were only paid on commission, they would starve before the sale was made. They may get a bonus to provide some incentive, or if they receive a commission, it may be a small part of their overall compensation.

FIGURE 13.4 How Activities and Conversions Drive Sales

Activities, or sales calls of various types, drive conversions, which then drive sales.

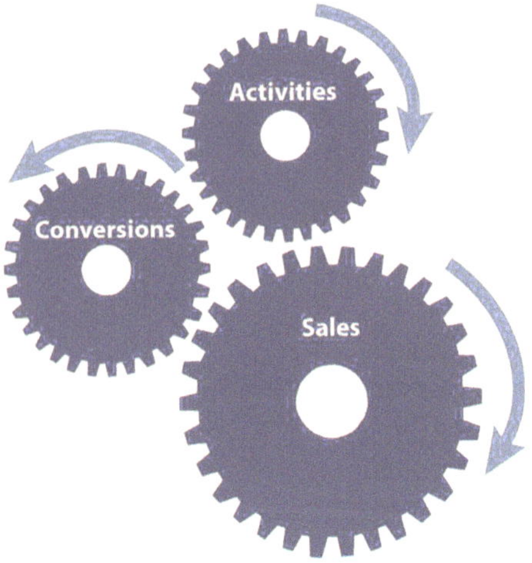

Metrics Used by Sales Managers

The sales manager is interested in all the same metrics as the salesperson, plus others. The metrics we discussed earlier can be used by the sales manager to evaluate salespeople, promote them, or pinpoint areas in which they need more training. Sales managers also use sales cycle metrics to make broader decisions. Perhaps everyone needs training in a particular stage of the sales process, or perhaps the leads generated by marketing are not effective, and new marketing ideas are warranted. Sales cycle metrics at the aggregate level can be very useful for making effective managerial decisions.

Sales managers also look at other measures such as *market share*, or how much of the market is buying from the firm versus its competitors; sales by product or by customer type; and sales per salesperson. Sales by product or by product line, especially viewed over time, can provide the sales executive with insight into whether a product should be divested or needs more investment. If the sales for the product line are declining but the product's market share is holding firm, then the entire market is shrinking. A shrinking market can mean the firm needs to look for new markets or develop new offerings.

sales quotas

The minimum level of sales performance for an individual salesperson.

Time is yet another element that sales managers look at. If the firm's sales are declining, is the company in a seasonal slump it will come out of, or does the firm have a serious, ongoing problem? Sales executives are also constantly concerned about what the firm's sales are doing relative to what was forecast for them. Forecasts turn into **sales quotas**, or minimum levels of sales performance for each salesperson. In addition, forecasts turn into orders for raw materials and component parts, inventory levels, and other expenditures of money. If the forecast is way off, then money is lost, either because the company ran out of products or because too much was spent to build up inventories that didn't sell.

In Table 13.1and Table 13.2, you can see a sample of data a sales manager may review. As you can see, most of the sales teams are performing near quota. But what about the Midwest? Selling 7 percent more is a good thing, but an astute manager would want to know why sales were short by over $200,000. Inventory can be balanced against the Southeast's shortfall, but that adds cost to ship from the plant to Atlanta, then to Chicago. Accurate forecasts would have put that product in the Midwest's Chicago warehouse to start with.

TABLE 13.1 An Example of the Sales Data Sales Managers Utilize

Tables such as this provide information that managers use to evaluate regional sales performance against expected sales, or quota.

Analysis by U.S. Region

Region	Quota	Actual	Difference	Performance
Northeast	$4,167,000	$4,147,400	-$19,600	99.5%
Southeast	$3,588,250	$3,425,100	-$163,150	95%
Midwest	$3,472,500	$3,698,875	$226,375	107%
Northwest	$5,093,000	$5,209,880	$116,880	102%
Southwest	$5,112,750	$5,120,250	$7,500	100%
Western	$4,861,500	$4,948,920	$87,420	102%
Total	$26,295,000	$26,550,425	$255,425	101%

TABLE 13.2 An Example of the Sales Data Sales Managers Utilize

Tables such as this provide information that managers use to evaluate individual sales performance against expected sales, or quota.

Analysis by Salesperson (Southwest Region)

Salesperson	Quota	Actual	Difference	Performance
Becky (Atlanta: South)	$868,000	$851,000	-$17,000	98%
Juan (South Florida)	$804,000	$810,000	+$6,000	101%
Jerry (Carolinas)	$592,000	$416,000	-$176,000	70%
Mack (Alabama/Miss.)	$370,000	$372,000	+$2,000	103%
Earl (Atlanta: North)	$609,000	$631,000	+$22,000	104%
Dave (Tennessee)	$345,000	$345,000	$0	100%
Total	$3,588,000	$3,425,000	-$163,000	95%

Similarly, a manager would be concerned about Jerry's lack of sales. That one salesperson accounts for the entire region's shortfall against quota. Was the shortfall due to Jerry's inability to sell, or did something happen in the territory? For example, if a hurricane came ashore in the Carolinas or if Jerry had a health problem arise, the manager's concern would be different than if Jerry lost a major account or had a history of failing to reach quota.

Sales executives don't just focus on sales, though. They also focus on costs. Why? Because many sales executives are held accountable not only for their firms' sales levels but also for profit levels. Money has to be spent to sell products, of course: If the firm spends too little, the sales force will be unable to perform effectively. If the budget to attend trade shows is cut, for example, the quantity and quality of leads salespeople get could fall—and so could their sales. But if the firm spends too much on trade shows, the cost per lead generated increases with no real improvement in the sales force's productivity. Perhaps the "additional" leads are duplicates or take too much time to follow up on.

Customer satisfaction is another important metric. Salespeople and their bosses want satisfied customers. Dissatisfied customers not only stop buying a company's products, they often tell their friends and family members about their bad purchasing experiences. Sometimes they go so far as to write blogs or bad product reviews on websites such as G2.com. Some research studies have shown that average customer satisfaction scores are less important than the number of complaints a company gets. Perhaps it's because of the negative word-of-mouth that unhappy customers generate.

In addition to tracking complaints, companies measure customer satisfaction levels through surveys. An average score of 3 on a scale of 1 to 5 could mean two things. The score could mean that everyone is, on average, happy and therefore gave the company a rating of 3.0. Or the score could mean that half of the customers are wildly enthusiastic and gave the company a 5 while the other half are bitterly disappointed and rated the company a 1. If the latter is the case, then half of the company's customers are telling their friends about their negative experience and discouraging many others from buying. Sometimes companies hire firms like TeleSight, an organization capable of tracking satisfaction scores for an entire industry. Using a service like this, the sales executive can not only track the company's customer satisfaction scores but also see how they compare with the scores of the industry overall.

Key Takeaways

- The sales cycle is a basic unit of measurement indicating how long it takes to close a sale. Salespeople examine their performance at each stage of the sales cycle in order to identify specific areas for improvement. A salesperson who shortens the cycle is able to generate more revenue with the same amount of effort. Salespeople also track their conversion ratios to identify which stages of the sales cycle they need to work on.
- Sales executives track the same metrics as individual salespeople but at the aggregate level. If many salespeople are struggling with one stage of the sales cycle, for example, then additional training or marketing may be needed, or a new strategy is necessary. Sales executives also look at their firm's sales relative to their forecasts in order to spot possible trends. A firm's sales trends affect many of the other decisions the company's executives have to make, including manufacturing and output decisions. Sales managers also have to manage their company's selling costs. Sales managers are often responsible for a firm's sales and its profit levels.

Review Questions

1. How might the sales cycle vary across the types of sales positions? How do salespeople use the sales cycle to manage their performance?
2. What is the relationship between conversion ratios and activity goals? How do salespeople use this information? How do sales executives use the information?
3. What metrics do sales executives use that salespeople are less concerned with?

13.4 Ethics in Sales and Sales Management

Learning Objectives

1. Compare and contrast common ethical challenges facing salespeople and sales managers.
2. Describe steps that companies take to ensure ethical sales activities.

When faced with an opportunity to exaggerate in job interviews, who would exaggerate more: professors, politicians, preachers, or salespeople? As mentioned at the start of this chapter, in one study, salespeople were less likely to engage in exaggeration of their skills and abilities than were professors, politicians, and preachers. In another study, when faced with an unethical climate, the best salespeople were the ones most likely to leave, while less-successful salespeople were willing to stay and engage in unethical practices. These studies surprise many people, but only those people who aren't in sales. Most salespeople are scrupulously ethical and, like Ted Schulte mentioned at the start of the chapter or Brenda Lipscomb profiled earlier, they are in sales because they really enjoy working to help people solve problems.

Common Ethical Issues for Salespeople

What are the most common ethical issues facing salespeople? Many of the most common situations you could face as a salesperson involve issues such as the following:

- a customer asking for information about one of their competitors, who happens to be one of your customers
- deciding how much to spend on holiday season gifts for your customers
- a buyer asking for something special, which you could easily provide but aren't supposed to give away
- deciding to play golf on a nice day, since no one knows if you are actually at work or not

Let's examine each of the issues. In the first issue, a customer owns the information about their business. The salesperson may know that information, such as how many cases of the product they purchase or who their customers are, but that salesperson does not have the right to share that information with the customer's competitor; that information belongs to the customer. In many instances, a buyer may ask the seller to sign a nondisclosure agreement (a contract that says they can't share that information with anyone, also called an NDA) because in order to serve the buyer, the seller will gain access to important private information about that buyer. But even if there is no nondisclosure agreement, courts are likely to agree with the buyer that the seller has an obligation to protect the buyer's information.

In the second issue, the concern is whether the gift is so extravagant that it is considered a bribe. In some companies, such as IBM and Walmart, buyers are not allowed to accept so much as a free cup of coffee from a seller. These companies do not allow their buyers to receive promotional items such as a pen or coffee cup with the seller's logo on it because they want every vendor to have free access to sales opportunities and earn the business on their merits, not their freebies. Many buyers would question the motives of a salesperson giving too large a gift. Most salespeople agree that lavish entertainment and gifts are becoming less important in business because decision makers know these add to the costs of doing business and they'd rather get a better price than be entertained.

Gift giving is viewed differently in different cultures, both national cultures and corporate cultures. The examples of Walmart and IBM reflect corporate cultures but in some countries, gift-giving may be considered normal. Companies in the United States, however, have to abide by the Foreign Corrupt Practices Act which essentially extends U.S. law on bribery to any U.S. company operating in any country. So even if bribery is expected or legal elsewhere, a U.S. company's salesperson cannot follow those local customs legally.

Lavish gifts may be nice, but many buyers will wonder if the salesperson giving the gift is trying to buy their business.

Source: © Shutterstock, Inc.

The third issue is tough for salespeople because there are two factors involved: a possible violation of company policy and providing an unfair advantage to one customer. For example, when a customer has to wait for a shipment, it seems reasonable to be provided a free sample or a trial unit to tide them over. But the company may feel otherwise. Customers may not know that their special request could get the salesperson in trouble, and the request may be reasonable, but against company policy. In that instance, the salesperson should not follow through on the request, though it might make sense to see if the policy can be changed. The second factor, though, is a bit more difficult because the request can be unfair to other customers, and may cause legal problems. As long as the special request can be provided to anyone who asks for it, no law is broken. What if the special request is for a discount? Pricing discrimination laws could come into play if such a discount is not made available to all who ask. What if the request isn't illegal, but other customers find out and get upset that they weren't offered the same benefit? Then the salesperson may get a reputation for being untrustworthy.

In the final issue, the question is whether the salesperson is cheating the company out of time and effort. Some argue that a salesperson who is paid straight commission (paid by the sale) is not stealing anything from the company, but others argue that even in that instance, the company is being deprived of possible sales that would be gained if the salesperson was working.

misrepresentation

Claiming a product does something that it does not do.

These are not the only issues that salespeople face. In the United States, two basic principles of business are that everyone should have an equal opportunity to earn business, and the customer remains free to make a choice. Manipulation, a form of unethical sales behavior, unfairly reduces or eliminates a buyer's ability or opportunity to make a choice. Persuasion, on the other hand, may influence a buyer's decision, but the decision remains the buyer's. Manipulation can include **misrepresentation**, or claiming a product does something it doesn't, but it can also include withholding important information, using hard-sell tactics, and other unfair sales tactics.

However, as mentioned earlier, salespeople tend to be ethical people. The use of manipulative sales tactics is actually pretty rare.

Company Safeguards

Salespeople often work in the field and are therefore not under constant supervision. Even inside salespeople may be able to get away with less than ethical behavior, as no supervisor can watch or hear everything. So how do companies manage ethical practices?

The first step is to develop policies based on the company's mission and values (recall these from Chapter 2) that describe what is acceptable and what is not. Good ethical policies not only list or describe appropriate and inappropriate behaviors, they also describe the underlying principles. Not all ethical dilemmas can be listed in a policy, so by detailing the principles and values that make up the reasoning behind the policies, salespeople and sales managers will be more prepared to respond appropriately.

Codes of ethics, or ethics policies, can be pretty detailed. Shell's ethics policy, for example, is a book over twenty pages long! Not only do these cover how salespeople (and other company representatives) should interact with customers, they also detail how employees should treat each other and how the company's vendors should be treated. (To see an example of a brief code of ethics for salespeople, visit Sales and Marketing Executives International's website.)

A good second step is to train all salespeople and sales managers on the policy. One reason for such training is to secure greater support and application of the policy, but another reason is that, should a salesperson engage in an unethical or illegal activity, the company is protected. The Federal Sentencing Guidelines (FSG) were first developed in 1987 and then updated in 2007, and specify what happens to companies when employees commit breaches of ethics. Companies that have solid policies, easily available documentation on policies and procedures, and training for all employees on those policies can rightfully claim under the FSG that any unethical employee was acting against company policies and on his or her own, should anyone file charges against the company. Solid policies and employee training can then be used as a defense against such charges, and the company would not be held liable.

Yet training alone is insufficient. The company must also enforce the policy and have procedures in place that make enforcement possible. For example, a company should have a mechanism for reporting unethical activity in a way that protects the person making the report. Many companies have anonymous message boxes that enable an employee to report unethical activity. One similar and common practice is to have an ethics office charged with investigating any complaints. The FSG require that companies also have internal auditing procedures to ensure that misconduct can be detected.

Note that these codes of ethics, the FSG, and the policies and procedures affect all employees. These were not created just because of salespeople. Marketers have faced ethics challenges in how claims are made in advertising, while supply chain managers have encountered dilemmas in dealing ethically with vendors. Managers, in any area of the firm, encounter challenges regarding equal opportunity and creating an appropriately professional work environment.

Challenges Facing Sales Managers

Sales managers face the same challenges in managing salespeople that all managers face. These include ensuring that hiring, compensation, motivation, and other management practices are not discriminatory; that sexual harassment does not exist in the workplace; and that employees are treated with dignity and respect.

Other challenges may arise, though. For example, salespeople have to be in front of customers when customers are available. Earlier, we discussed how the number of calls made can impact a salesperson's success. So should a sales manager schedule all training sessions on weekends, when buyers are at home and not available for sales calls? Does the answer to that question change if the salesperson is paid a salary or a commission?

Recently, one sales manager reported a customer who said he did not want Muslims calling on him. Another sales manager said when she and her salesperson (another woman) sat down with a buyer (a male), the buyer had pornography on his computer monitor. Do those sales managers assign new salespeople to the accounts? Or do they "fire" the customer? If the customer was to be fired, the salesperson would lose commission. Yet in both instances, the managers said they fired the customer, an action that both salespeople were happy with, and they were reassured that the loss of the sale wouldn't be held against them. The loss of the commission was worth it.

Should a sales manager schedule training outside of normal business hours so salespeople don't lose time for selling? Does the answer depend on how those salespeople are paid?

Source: © Shutterstock, Inc.

In sales, several laws apply that also apply in other areas of marketing but are more prominent in sales. For example, the Uniform Commercial Code (UCC) determines when a sale is a sale. Typically, a sale is a sale when the product is delivered and accepted by the buyer. In most instances, the customer can cancel the order with no penalty unless accepted. Sales managers have to be aware of such laws in order to avoid creating policies that can be illegal.

Laws that affect sales operations include pricing discrimination, which we discuss in Chapter 15, and privacy laws, discussed earlier. In addition, laws regarding hiring practices, workplace safety, and others can affect sales managers. If global sales situations arise, the Federal Corrupt Practices Act—which prohibits bribery and other practices that might be culturally acceptable elsewhere but that are illegal in the United States—comes into play.

For these reasons, sales managers should develop close working relationships with the human resources department. These professionals, along with the legal department, are charged with staying abreast of legal changes that influence management practice.

Key Takeaways

- Salespeople are, for the most part, caring, ethical professionals. They do face unique ethical challenges because of their job, including how to handle unethical requests from customers and making sure that they know and follow all company policies for interacting with customers. American salespeople have the added constraint that what's illegal in the United States is illegal for them in other countries because of the Foreign Corrupt Practices Act, even if the behavior in question is acceptable to those countries' laws and practices.
- Sales managers have all the usual management concerns, such as fair hiring practices. According to the Federal Sentencing Guidelines, managers also have to develop policies and practices that codify ethical behaviors, train salespeople on the ethics policies, and ensure that the policies are followed. In addition, sales managers have to be aware of laws such as the Universal Commercial Code and others that govern sales transactions.

Review Questions

1. Do salespeople deserve the bad image or negative stereotype? Why or why not?
2. Do ethics get in the way of success in sales? Why or why not?
3. What safeguards do companies enact to ensure ethical behavior among salespeople and sales managers?

13.5 Aligning Sales and Marketing

Learning Objectives

1. Identify the ways in which the marketing function supports the sales function.
2. Describe how the sales group of a company can support its marketing efforts.

Marketing supports sales efforts in many ways, from generating leads to making sure customers are using products properly and obtaining the results they desire. Salespeople need good marketing to support their efforts. Unfortunately, in too many situations, sales and marketing operate independently.

If an engineer at a potential customer company shows an interest, the salesperson may label that engineer as a suspect. At this point, a mild level of interest is beginning to grow, and the salesperson can interact with the engineer to determine if that person truly has a need, can make a purchase, and plans to do so soon. If that engineer or company truly has a need and meets those criteria, the account moves from suspect to prospect. At that point, the salesperson will want to prove that the product meets the needs and budget, and close the sale. When that happens, the account becomes a customer.

In each of these stages, marketing can support the salesperson—or not. The degree to which marketing and sales work together varies from company to company.

Traditionally, sales and marketing are like oil and water—the departments don't mix well. Salespeople are typically among the highest paid employees in an organization. At Pak-Sher, for example, the highest paid five employees include three salespeople. Marketing personnel may make significantly less and, as a result, jealousy can occur.

Another factor that hurts the relationship between sales and marketing is performance. Salespeople tend to discount the value of activities that create strong brands but don't generate leads. Further, in antiquated systems, salespeople often receive poor quality leads or are given the leads well after the customers have made a purchase. In these situations, salespeople tend to consider all marketing as a waste because they don't see what they want in terms of performance.

The challenge, of course, is how to get the two groups to work together, because when marketing and sales are aligned, sales productivity will increase. In some organizations, such as Xerox, all marketing managers start out as salespeople. In this type of organization, there is no *us versus them* because the typical career progression includes time in marketing for all sales managers and vice versa. Other companies, such as Cardinal Health, aren't structured that way, so managers have to learn to work together. One place to start aligning sales and marketing is to understand what marketing does for sales.

What Marketing Does for Sales

A firm's sales and marketing groups can work well together. We'll focus first on how marketing helps salespeople.

Marketing Shortens the Sales Cycle

A company's marketing activities include creating advertising and promotional campaigns, participating in trade shows, and preparing collateral. **Collateral** is printed or digital material salespeople use to support their message. It can consist of brochures, position papers, case studies, clinical studies, market studies, and other documents.

collateral

Printed or digital material, such as brochures, position papers, case studies, clinical studies, market studies, or other documents created by marketing professionals.

Clint Corley, enterprise account executive with the software company KaiNexus, says he works closely with marketing so that "the collateral is relevant to our customers. Since the sales group has the most interactions with our market, it is our job to provide feedback around topics of discussion, pain points, and problems that our customers are trying to solve so we can generate content relative to those topics. Ultimately, that content drives website traffic, creates interest and generates sales leads." He notes that they work together to have good material throughout the sales cycle. "Our marketing group does an incredible job of ensuring we have collateral for specific customer use cases, objections, and value identification for every stage in the sales pipeline."

Collateral can be used in **content marketing**, a marketing strategy that is used to generate interest by providing relevant and useful information. Many companies try to position themselves as **thought leaders**, on the premise that if the brand is known for innovation and knowledge, consumers will be more likely to want to do business with them. Recall Mary Gros and her role with Teradata—she works with thought leaders so that they will work with Teradata, helping to build a brand for the company in thought leadership. When she is successful, salespeople find it easier to sell more quickly.

content marketing

A marketing strategy that relies on producing useful and relevant information (content) to generate interest in a company's offerings.

thought leaders

Brands that are viewed as the more innovative and knowledgeable companies, used as a marketing strategy, often in conjunction with content marketing, to generate brand preference.

Salespeople also use collateral to support their claims. Although a pharmaceutical rep selling a drug might claim it works faster than competing medications, a clinical study would carry more weight. If such a study existed, the drug maker's marketing department would prepare a brochure to give to doctors that highlights those findings. Salespeople use collateral to persuade customers that their solution is the best available, thus shortening the sales cycle.

lead management

The process of identifying and qualifying leads in order to capture new business.

closed-loop lead management systems

Information systems that track sales leads from the point at which the marketer identifies them to the point at which they are closed.

Marketing professionals also support salespeople by providing them with lead management. **Lead management** is the process of identifying and qualifying leads in order to grow new business. **Closed-loop lead management systems** are information systems that are able to track leads all the way from the point at which the marketer identifies them to when they are closed. Figure 13.5 illustrates the process and shows how marketing groups use the information to evaluate which of their activities are earning their companies the biggest bang for their buck.

FIGURE 13.5 How a Closed-Loop Management System Works

A closed-loop lead management system can result in better investment decisions for marketing managers because they can learn what marketing actions shorten sales cycles and create more sales.

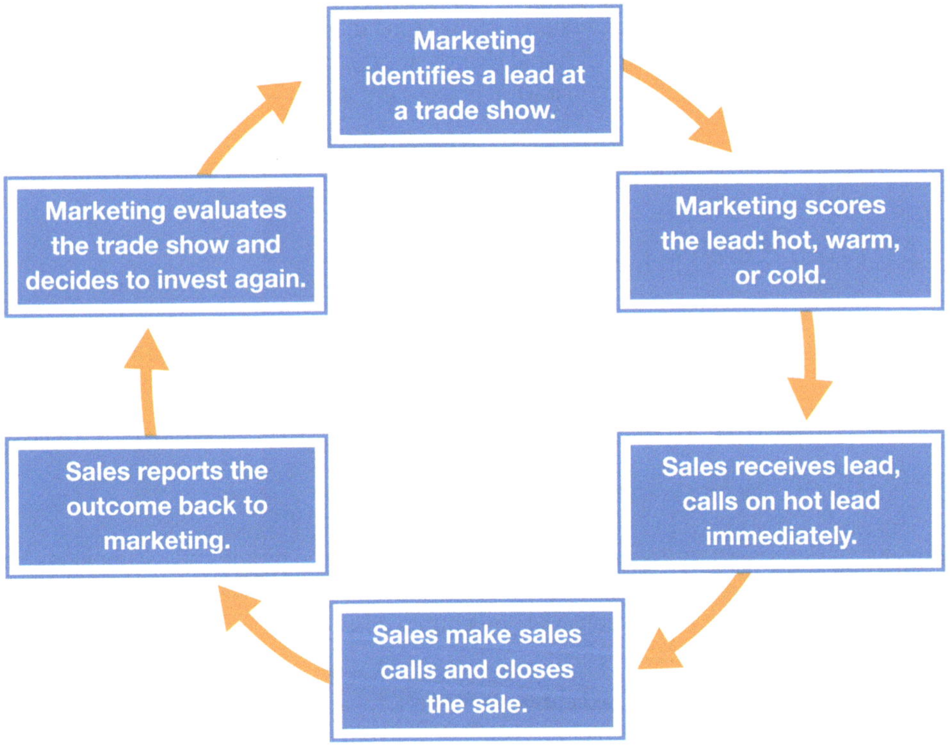

Unfortunately, many companies lack such a system. In many cases, marketing personnel identify leads, turn them over to sales representatives, and that's the last they hear of them. Was the lead a good one, and did it ultimately lead to a purchase? Was the trade show that produced the lead worth the money spent attending it? These companies don't know. Closing the loop (meaning closing the feedback loop to marketing) gives marketing personnel insight into what works and what doesn't.

What's surprising is that, after spending several hundred thousand dollars on a trade show, by some estimates, only about one-third of companies follow up on the leads. As noted earlier, some salespeople may not receive leads quickly, with the result that many have already purchased competitors' offerings before the salesperson can call. After that happens a few times, a salesperson is likely to give up and not call any leads. Whatever the cause, a lack of lead follow-up wastes millions of marketing dollars.

Marketing Improves Conversion Ratios by Scoring Leads

Marketing groups also help their firms' salespeople improve their conversion ratios by scoring the leads they send them. **Lead scoring** is a process by which marketing personnel rate the leads to indicate whether a lead is hot (ready to buy now), warm (going to buy soon), or cold (interested but with no immediate plans to buy). As you can imagine, someone who has had a conversation at a trade show with a company representative; seen a demonstration; and answered questions about her budget, authority, need, and time, is close to being a prospect already. The more hot leads you put into the sales cycle, the more conversions to prospects and customers you can expect.

lead scoring
The process of rating leads based on the readiness of potential buyers to purchase products.

Lead scoring is not just a function of asking questions, however. Sage, the software company, scores leads based on behaviors by the potential customer. A potential customer who visits the company's website, downloads a case study about how a Sage product solved certain problems for a customer, and then clicks a link on a follow-up email to watch an online demo of the offering has shown a significant amount of interest in the product. True, the lead has not answered questions concerning BANT. The buyer's behavior, though, indicates a strong interest—a much stronger interest than someone who clicked a link in an email and only watched a portion of the demo. Sage, based on data showing when prospects are likely to respond positively to a sales call, will score each lead on those behaviors and when the time is right, a salesperson will call.

When should marketing pass a lead on to sales? The answer depends on the sales cycle and where that person is in the process. For example, if there was an in-depth discussion of needs at a trade show, the person might be scored as a suspect and passed immediately on to sales. But if the person just wanted to get some information, then there may be additional marketing messages sent and depending on the person's response, the contact information and history would be passed along to a salesperson when the account is ready for a sales call. Closed-loop lead management systems provide marketing managers with the information they need to know when to pass the account along to sales versus when more marketing conversations are effective.

Improving conversions is not just a matter of finding more hot leads, however. Marketing personnel can improve salespeople's conversions by providing materials that help buyers make good decisions. Advertising, a company's website, activities at trade shows, and collateral can all help, and in the process, improve a sales force's conversion ratios. To be sure, some educated buyers, once they have more information about a product, will realize they don't need or want it and will go no further. But this is better than their buying the product and becoming angry when it fails to meet their expectations.

What Sales Does for Marketing

Without the help of their firms' salespeople, marketers would be at a serious disadvantage. Salespeople talk to customers every day. They are the "eyes and ears" of their companies. More than anyone else in an organization, they know what customers want.

Salespeople Communicate Market Feedback

Salespeople are responsible for voicing their customers' ideas and concerns to other members of the organization. After all, if marketing managers are going to create collateral to educate them, they need to know what they need and want in the way of information. That knowledge comes from salespeople. How the information is conveyed, though, varies from situation to situation and company to company.

Accenture, the management consulting firm, engages in projects with clients that cost hundreds of thousands of dollars, if not millions. After each sale is concluded, the account management team reviews the process in excruciating detail, win or lose. Questions such as "Did we have the right information to give to the client at the right time?" or "Were our offerings aligned with their needs?" are answered. After the review, executives decide whether the company needs to produce additional marketing material to support the offering, create new offerings, or follow up on any other ideas generated by the review.

By contrast, KMBS salespeople sell copiers and printers that range from $5,000 to $150,000. A KMBS sale generally isn't as large as an Accenture sale, but KMBS has many more sales going on at any given time than Accenture does. The sheer volume of sales at KMBS makes it harder for salespeople to get the information related to those sales to the company's decision makers. For that reason, KMBS uses CRM software to track all its prospects and their key buying criteria. If the sale is lost, the reasons for it can be entered into the software, as well as information about the competing product the buyer purchased. At both KMBS and Accenture, marketing personnel then use this win/loss analysis to improve each company's marketing and sales efforts.

Astute marketing professionals, however, do not rely totally on CRM software to understand what makes markets tick. As we have explained, they also spend time with real customers and with salespeople. Andrea Wharton, a marketing executive with Alcatel, is responsible for her company's presence at trade shows. Wharton spends a great deal of time talking to salespeople in order to find out what messages are effective, and she uses that information to create Alcatel's exhibit booths for trade shows. She then works in the booth at the shows so she can talk directly with customers and get their reactions firsthand.

Changing the offering can be the outcome of what occurs when salespeople convey information provided by their customers. Perhaps customers are asking for additional product features, faster delivery, or better packing to reduce the number of damaged products shipped.

Durcon, a manufacturer of impervious countertops like the kind used in scientific laboratories, had a salesperson who happened to have a friend in the construction business. During the course of a conversation, she realized that her friend was looking for impermeable countertops for use in bars. Her friend wanted countertops that looked really cool but provided an added layer of safety in a food use situation. The salesperson took that information back to her company, and a new product line was born.

Managing the collaboration in new product design is often the function of salespeople when products are customized. One form of customization occurs when a supplier creates an assembly or product that fits in another company's product. For example, John Deere manufactures tractors in plants located in Iowa, Brazil, France, Germany, and India. Companies that make parts like carburetors or belts and hoses design those specifically for Deere, a process that involves the account executive.

This elegant sushi bar is actually part of a trade show booth used by Durcon, a manufacturer of impermeable countertops. The product was created because a salesperson learned that a bar owner was looking for impermeable countertops but the ones used in laboratories were ugly.

Source: Durcon, Inc., used with permission

Salespeople Monitor the Competition

Salespeople also track the actions of their competitors and what customers buy, and enter the information into their firms' CRM systems. When marketing managers examine the marketing and sales efforts of their competitors, they are looking for their weak spots and strengths. The weak spots can be capitalized on, whereas the strengths need to be minimized.

More specifically, marketing managers need to know which companies are the strongest competitors based on the percentage of deals they win. Knowing this information can help a firm analyze its own competitive strengths and weaknesses and develop better marketing messages, sales strategies, offerings, or a combination of the three. Marketing managers also want to know which competitors the sales force most frequently finds itself competing against. If prospects consider the same competitor's product time and time again relative to your product, then the competitor's marketing and sales efforts are very similar to yours. In this case, you might need to develop some counter tactics your salespeople can use to eliminate the product from the prospect's consideration set. Those tactics could include focusing on certain features only your product has or helping your buyers feel secure in the purchase by pointing out how long you've been in business.

Key Takeaways

- Marketing personnel support a firm's sales force by shortening the sales cycle and improving conversions. The sales cycle is shortened whenever a marketing activity or marketing communication either eliminates a prospect's need to take a step in the sales cycle or speeds up the stages in the cycle. Marketing managers also create printed and digital materials called collateral designed to help persuade buyers.

- Lead management and lead scoring are two other ways in which marketing professionals help their firm's salespeople. If a closed-loop lead management is used, marketing managers can determine what tactics and messages works best and make sound marketing investments.
- In turn, salespeople support marketing personnel by communicating their customers' needs and ideas back to them. Salespeople are also the first to spot the actions of competing firms, including which companies and products are the strongest competitors. The marketing department then uses the information to create better marketing messages, sales strategies, offerings, or a combination of the three.

Review Questions

1. What marketing activities support salespeople, and how does that support help them? Be specific.
2. What do salespeople do to support marketing managers? Be specific.
3. What is a closed-loop lead management, and what are its benefits to salespeople?

13.6 Outsourcing the Sales Function

Learning Objectives

1. Identify the primary types of outsourcing salespeople.
2. Characterize the strengths and weaknesses of outsourcing sales groups.

Some companies outsource certain sales functions. They do so because it is more efficient to hire a sales force that represents multiple products lines to a single set of customers. In this section, we'll introduce several types of outsourced salespeople, as well as the reasons for and challenges associated with outsourcing various sales activities.

Types of Outsourced Salespeople

A company can outsource part or all of the sales cycle. When a company hires a call center to make phone calls and set up appointments, it is outsourcing only the lead-to-suspect conversion portion of the sales cycle. In other words, every appointment the center sets up would be with a suspect. The suspect-to-prospect and prospect-to-customer conversions could then be the responsibility of either the outsourcer or another type of sales organization it hires for that purpose.

independent agents
Independent salespeople a company hires to sell its products. Independent agents set their own hours, determine their own activities, and for the most part, manage themselves.

Independent agents are salespeople who are not employees of the company. They set their own hours, determine their own activities, and for the most part, manage themselves. Typically, they are paid on a straight commission basis—that is, based only on the revenues they generate for the company. Independent agents often sell competing products from competing companies. Financial services, including insurance for competing companies, are often sold by independent agents. In other industries, agents are less likely to sell for competing companies. From the buyer's point of view, an independent agent representing multiple products lines should mean the buyer is in a better position to find the best offering with the least amount of hassle.

A **manufacturer's representative** is an agent that sells a manufacturer's product. Typically, they don't sell competing products; rather, they sell complementary products—products that the same buyer wants to purchase. For example, an agent who sells bathroom faucets for one manufacturer might sell bathroom towel rods and mirrors for another manufacturer. When a company hires a manufacturer's rep, it does so because the rep is already selling to the desired market. The company is trying to "buy" access to the market by hiring a sales force that has already sold products to customers desired by the company. Buyers are more willing to see the rep because of the broad array of products they offer.

Independent insurance agents like Don Tolly can sell insurance for competing products.

Source: © Shutterstock, Inc.

manufacturer's representative

A type of independent agent who represents manufacturers. Typically, the person represents noncompeting manufacturers that sell complementary products.

We discussed distributors in Chapter 8. Distributors often have salespeople who complete the entire sales cycle. Recall that distributors receive and manage inventory. However, they may or may not take title to the inventory before reselling it. Industrial distributors often employ both field salespeople, who call on customers where they are located, and inside salespeople, who may sell products by phone or by email at the distributors' locations as well as handle customers who come to those locations. Distributors are like manufacturers' representatives in that they can sell offerings from multiple manufacturers. Some distributors are exclusive, meaning they sell the products of only one manufacturer.

Advantages and Disadvantages of Outsourcing

Outsourcing some of its sales efforts can provide a producer with several advantages. We've already mentioned a few, such as gaining access to more buyers because the organizations and people to which the company has outsourced sell a broader array of products to the right customers. Having a broad array to choose from is more desirable from a buyer's perspective. Moreover, outsourced salespeople have existing relationships with the buyers that can be leveraged. Thus, entering new markets, such as new product markets or new countries, via distributors, independent agents, or manufacturer's representatives can increase the speed at which the company's offerings penetrate a market. These people and organizations also possess key market information and understand competitors and their strategies—information marketers can leverage.

In terms of a company's costs, outsourcing can be less expensive. The company that outsources the work doesn't bear the responsibility and expense of training the salespeople, except to inform them about the company's products. In addition, because the salespeople often work on a straight commission basis, the company only pays them when they sell its products.

The disadvantages of outsourcing can be boiled down to one word: control. Distributors, manufacturer's representatives, and agents are independent. They can decide what to sell and when to sell it. Unlike an employee who can be required to offer your product, they can choose to offer a customer a competing product or simply a different product than the one you sell. Nor can you force them to make sales calls. If it is a beautiful day and the golf course beckons, you may find your rep somewhere on the links.

To deal with control issues, companies often create incentive programs to motivate independent agents and manufacturer's representatives. Attractive commissions are more likely to get your product mentioned on every call. So are spiffs. **Spiffs** (a term that began as an acronym for *special promotion incentive funds*) are short-term bonus payments companies use to encourage salespeople to sell certain products. Also keep in mind that salespeople want to pitch products that are easy to sell and have short sales cycles. Why? Because they get rewarded for making sales. To the extent you can shorten a product's sales cycle and increase their conversions, you will gain their attention, time, and effort.

spiffs

A word that originally meant "special promotion incentive funds" and now is used for any short-term bonus payments companies use to encourage salespeople to sell certain products.

In addition to creating incentives for independent salespeople, a company will usually employ a sales manager to work with them. The sales manager's job is about selling as much as it is about managing, though. The manager has to constantly sell the agents on selling the company's offerings, and provide them with product information and tips that help them do so.

Finally, just as they listen to their own sales forces, good marketing professionals pay attention to what the independent salespeople and organizations they work with are saying. Not only can marketing managers create better strategies by doing so, they will create strategies that get used. In other words, the salespeople will be more likely to support those strategies with their own efforts because they believe in them.

Key Takeaways

- Outsourcing the sales function can be done through distributors, independent agents, and manufacturers' representatives, as well as other types of sales organizations. The entire sales cycle can be outsourced or only parts of it. Outsourcing can cost less and requires less investment than a company-employed sales force. Moreover, independent agents, distributors, and manufacturers' representatives often have established relationships that make it easier for a company to enter and penetrate new markets.
- Outsourcing the sales function(s) means that a company will lose some control over its sales activities. To counteract that loss of control, companies try to devise attractive compensation schemes, as well as effective marketing strategies for the independent sales organizations and people with whom they work. Companies also hire sales managers to manage the relationships with the outsourced sales staff.

Review Questions

1. Which parts of the sales cycle can be outsourced, and to whom?
2. When does outsourcing make the most sense? The least sense? Why?
3. What can marketers do to make outsourced sales functions more likely to succeed?

13.7 Discussion Questions and Activities

Discussion Questions

1. As a customer, would it be important for you to know how your salesperson was paid? Why or why not?
2. Under what conditions should the salesperson be responsible for handling customer complaints?
3. How would the roles of the salesperson differ in a product-dominant organization versus a service-dominant setting? Look at the types of sales roles in the chapter—do you think some are more or less likely to be in a product dominant setting? Or in a service setting?
4. Assume you sell plumbing supplies via a distributor that sells to retailers and industrial customers.

   a. What can you, as the manufacturer's sales representative, do to shorten the distributor's sales cycle? To improve its conversions?
   b. Assume you are the distributor and you have five salespeople working for you. Two call on plumbing companies and large construction companies at job sites, whereas the other three work as salespeople in your warehouse to handle walk-in customers. What can you do with marketing to shorten the sales cycle of each group? How might your efforts affect the performance of each group differently?
5. Assume you invented a new technology that makes designing and engineering new products a lot cheaper to do. When you talk to manufacturers, though, they are skeptical because the new method is so radically different from any technology they have ever used before.
   a. What do you think the sales cycle for the technology would look like? What would the most important step of the sales cycle be? Why?
   b. What type of sales force would you utilize, and why?
   c. What marketing activities could help you shorten the sales cycle, and how?
6. In many organizations, marketing and sales do not get along very well. Describe what you would expect to be the results in an organization such as this. If you were hired by one of those organizations as the Chief Marketing Officer, how would you go about fixing this? What would your answer be if you were placed in charge of the sales force?
7. Based on this chapter, what are three questions you would want to ask in a job interview if you were interviewing for an entry-level position?
8. Salespeople can't lie but customers can—for example, customers don't have to tell the truth about how much they have to spend but salespeople have to tell the truth about price. Why is that?

Activities

1. Contact a salesperson and ask if you can spend a half-day observing sales calls. Whether you are able to observe or not, ask these questions: What are the segments within that salesperson's territory? How do they make decisions, and what are the key sales activities?
2. Pair up for a role-play. One of you is trying to recruit new members into a student organization, so the other plays the prospective member. Then flip roles. One of you is trying to persuade the other to go on a leadership retreat for a weekend. When you are the one being persuaded, don't make it easy. Think about why you would or would not be persuaded, then make the other work to figure it out.
3. Find job postings for entry level sales positions in three different industries. These should be jobs that you could apply for as a new college graduate. What are commonalities across the positions, and what are differences? Determine what type they are, using the terminology from the chapter.

13.8 Case Study: Turner

Turner Inc., a company comprised of five business units and headquartered in Chesapeake, was founded when Frank Turner returned from World War II and bought a truck to begin trucking goods from the Port of Norfolk to cities like Pittsburgh. Since then, the family-owned business has grown to the following units:

- Turner Packing & Crating (operating under the name American Packing and Crating): A company that was acquired last summer, they do specialized crating and packaging for items that are shipped internationally and do not fit into containers, either because they weigh too much or are too big. Prior to the acquisition Turner utilized this company to service existing Turner customers, and many American Packing and Crating customers are potential customers for the other Turner services. This unit has its own integrated sales group that has not been assimilated by Turner since the acquisition.
- Turner Logistics: A Freight Brokerage Company. This unit takes calls from customers who need their shipping containerized for export, or need their containers shipped from a port to a distribution center, or need to ship less than a container. As such, they also handle much of the sales for Turner Transportation and Turner Distribution.
- Turner Distribution: Seven distribution centers totaling two million square feet are available to companies to store goods.
- Turner Air Freight (under the name Superior Air Freight): A freight-forwarding and freight brokerage. Historically this unit has operated independently from the others.
- Turner Transportation: A trucking company, it has its own customers who only buy Turner Transportation services, as well as customers who use other division services.

The company has begun to re-organize from a product/service approach (as listed above) to a vertical market approach. From the beginning, the company never had anyone who called on customers; they only have customer service personnel who take calls when customers call them, take orders, and recommend other divisions' services when appropriate. As far as marketing goes, they have a website, and they participate in a few trade shows.

Devon Turner has now taken over the company. The great-grandchild of the founder, Devon wants to aggressively grow the company, to include more active marketing and hiring a sales team that will drum up new business and grow sales with existing accounts. They are also moving from inbound only and customer-service personnel to more growth-oriented, outward-facing salespeople. That's why the company is re-organizing around vertical markets (meaning customers of the same industry) instead of by division. Devon believes this structure will create expertise in the particular problems of an industry that will help the salespeople better serve those customers while growing sales for all of the divisions within each customer. So instead of a customer using Turner for transportation and another company for warehousing, the goal is to capture all of a customer's logistics and supply chain management needs.

Turner operates based on a set of values and with the following vision and mission.

Vision: To be a leader and trusted partner in providing the highest quality supply chain solutions with an aggressive pursuit of generational growth.

Mission: Deliver customer-focused logistics services by promoting a family atmosphere with a can-do attitude that prioritizes the well-being of employees and the communities they live in while maintaining profitability that drives continued growth.

Values:

- *Integrity*—Do what is right and be honest always. Thinking ethically and with a safety mindset for every decision, no matter how big or small, sets the foundation for all activities at Turner. Handling adversity with integrity is especially important and this is when deep trust is established between ourselves and with our customers.
- *Family*—Turner is a family of employees, customers, vendors and friends. We respect one another, we hold each other accountable, we look out for each other, and we grow together. Strong personal relationships create a quality work environment that fosters both employee well-being and the highest quality service for our customers.
- *Drive*—Hard work is how we get things done, but simply working hard is not enough. We take pride in individual initiative to constantly seek out creative ways to satisfy customers and solve problems. Our relentless pursuit of efficiency with time, miles, dollars, equipment, and everything in between is what defines us as true logistics professionals.

Case Study Questions

1. So far, Turner has had neither a marketing department nor a sales force. Sales have been handled by customer service personnel who take calls as they come in. Marketing consists of a website (built by a technology company) and not much else. Which should come first, marketing or sales, and why?
2. What would marketing do for the new vertical market approach? What would its role be, and what would you consider success for marketing?
3. What type of sales position would they need? Justify your choice. How should they be compensated and how should their performance be measured? Does the company's goals and values affect your answer? Why or why not?
4. If they were short on capital and wanted to outsource sales, could they? Should they?

CHAPTER 14

Customer Satisfaction, Loyalty, and Empowerment

The marketing concept, described in Chapter 1, reminds us that the customer should be at the center of a firm's activities and that the company that thrives is the one that serves customers' needs better than the competition. Yet often it is the customer who is most adept at serving the customer's needs. Allowing consumers to take control of the marketing activities aimed at them is what **customer empowerment** is about. Today, technology makes it possible for the customer to do exactly that. But why is it important to empower customers?

customer empowerment

Providing tools that enable customers to take control or influence marketing.

The key is that consumers want an experience specific to satisfying their needs. Empowering them actually doesn't hurt the marketer—it actually increases the marketer's ability to satisfy needs more effectively which increases the firm's success. Repeated studies of CMOs show that the factors that empower customers are central to marketing success.[1]

Research shows that customer empowerment is a function of three things: creating feedback channels that are easy and widely available, asking for and encouraging feedback about products, and enabling customers to participate in the design of offerings. Previously, we discussed how customers can participate in the design of offerings. In this chapter, we focus on those ubiquitous feedback channels, as well as strategies to solicit and encourage feedback.

14.1 Customer Communities

Learning Objectives

1. Understand strategies involving online and personal forms of influencer marketing.
2. Relate influencer marketing to other forms of social communities and marketing strategies.

If you are about to buy a new personal watercraft like a Jet Ski®, Sea Doo®, or WaveRunner®, where do you go to learn about which one is best? Like many buyers, you probably turn to the internet and search for product review sites. In fact, not only will sites like PersonalWatercraft.com tell you which one is best, but which one is best under what conditions and how to take care of it, and most of the material has been posted by other consumers.

The point is that consumers talk. They talk to each other, and they post their thoughts and opinions online. **Word of mouth**, or the passing of information and opinions, has a powerful influence on purchasing decisions. You rely on word of mouth when you register for classes. For example, you ask other students about which professors are best and how hard their classes are. If you have no one to ask, you can look at online sites such as ratemyprofessors.com.

word of mouth

The passing of information and opinions verbally.

buzz

Word of mouth that includes blogs, articles, and other forms of promotion.

Buzz refers to the volume or amount of word of mouth going on in a market, whether positive or negative or both. However, in addition to traditional word of mouth, buzz includes blogs, articles, social media posts posts, tweets, and other communications about an offering.

When you see that a topic is trending on your favorite social media site, you are looking at a measure of buzz. Buzz, though, happens whether you want it or not, as Peloton found out when they aired a commercial that many consider sexist as the premise of the ad was that a woman needed to tone up and lose weight in order to make her husband happy. The commercial was criticized and lampooned so much that the stock plummeted. The buzz turned around during the COVID-19 pandemic as consumers found home exercise one way to escape. While the company tried to influence buzz in both instances, external factors and influencers were the ones in charge.

Exceptionally good and bad service generates word of mouth. In addition to the reviews that get posted, don't you tell friends about a great experience? Or complain on a social media site when it all goes bad? For that reason, customer service is one area that some companies invest in to create positive word of mouth. Drury Hotels is one such company, and they've won JD Power Customer Satisfaction awards for more than fifteen years in a row. Some companies, though, consider customer service to be a marketing channel to the point that they train their customer service representatives to identify sales opportunities and pitch products. Dell, some airlines, banks, and others have been soundly criticized for taking this approach because customers felt that all they got was a sales pitch instead of a solution to their problem. Other companies consider customer service to be a marketing channel only to the extent that it generates positive word of mouth—do a great job with tough customers and encourage a positive review on a website. This latter perspective recognizes that when customers want service, they don't want to be sold. It also recognizes that empowered customers can help market a product.

Drury Inn has won JD Power Customer Satisfaction Awards sixteen years in a row because of their hyper focus on good service.

Source: © Shutterstock, Inc.

Influencer Marketing

A marketing strategy being used increasingly often is **influencer marketing**, or targeting people known to influence others so that they will use their influence in the marketer's favor. You know influencers—those people on Facebook, Pinterest, and other social media channels that post regularly, bring new products to your attention, and share hacks. Most of those, though, are paid influencers. Recall Mary Gros's story in the previous chapter—she is engaged with influencers, some of whom might be paid industry analysts but some, like professors, are just people whom others turn to for expertise. Further, many influencers are the lead users we discussed in the chapter on designing offerings.

influencer marketing

Targeting individuals known to influence others so they will use their influence in the marketer's favor.

Those social media influencers, though, are often compensated and they are rewarded more for how many people they can influence or reach than if they are lead users or early adopters. In fact, research indicates that younger consumers, particularly females ages 14–19, recognize the potential bias of compensated influencers and are less likely to rely on them than do millennials.[2]

In fact, influencers are different from **brand advocates**, consumers who just love a brand and recommend it whenever possible. Paid influencers are measured by how big their following is, while brand advocates are measured by how often they recommend the product. Paid influencers are motivated by how much they get compensated, while brand advocates are motivated by a desire to help their friends and acquaintances enjoy the product. So it is no wonder that consumers are six times more likely to trust an advocate over an influencer.[3]

brand advocates

consumers who are passionate about a brand, recommend it whenever possible, and not compensated for their influence.

Part of customer empowerment is listening to customers, and an important element in influencer marketing is to empower potential influencers. If you spend some time on Procter & Gamble's (P&G) Crest toothpaste website, you might be given a chance to complete a survey. (Someone who is very interested in dental care is more likely to take the survey.) The survey asks if you talk about dental care products, if you research such products, and if you influence others. These questions and questions like them are used to identify influencers. P&G then provides influencers with product samples and opportunities to participate in market research. The idea is that new offerings should be co-created with influencers because they are more likely to be both lead users and early adopters of new offerings, and influence other people's decisions to buy them.

One strategy companies adopt is to create a user group that will help each other enjoy offerings more, recommend the company to friends, and other forms of positive influence. A **community**, in the marketing sense, is a social group that centers its attention on a particular brand or product category. Another term for a community is a **social network**. Companies try to use social network technology to create a place for the members of a community to gather. That's why King Arthur Flour, for example, created a Facebook site where customers can learn about baking, share baking tips, and watch baking shows. While the goal is ultimately to sell more flour, the company is also trying to create a stronger social network. They were very successful, so much so that they became a model for how to build an online business, yet all they do is sell flour!

community

A form of a social group that centers its attention around a particular brand or product category.

social network

A community or social group that centers its attention on a particular brand or product category.

King Arthur Flour just sells flour—but they built a strong online baking community and their flour sells at a 25 percent premium over other brands!

Source: © Shutterstock, Inc.

A stronger social network means that the company has more relationships, or ties, with more consumers, and that the ties are are strong. Think about your friends and your own personal social network; you have good friends, friends, and acquaintances. You'll share more personal information and want to spend more time with good friends than you will with acquaintances. The same is true with brands. You'll share more information and spend more time with brands you trust. For the brand, the goal is to have as many 'good friends' as possible in the market you wish to serve.

Ross Gordon started a Facebook community he called Bass Fishing Favorites in 2010. The intention was to create a community site where bass anglers could share tips and ideas, post pictures of monster bass, and tell stories of the one that got away. The site became so popular that he quit his day job in 2012 and began Catch, a company that now offers a monthly subscription box of lures and other bass-catching products, as well as serves as an e-commerce site to sell other items. In 2020, the number of people angling for bass increased by over 10 percent, leading Catch to create the Bassmobile, a full-sized trailer that serves as a classroom to accelerate these new anglers' bass-catching mastery. Catch is taking the Bassmobile on the road so that anglers all over the United States can learn more about bass fishing.[4]

But there are key members of a social network, those that influence the behavior of others. Some do it professionally, as already mentioned. Others do it naturally, either because of their position in the community (a pastor, for example) or because they are just well liked by a lot of people. And others become influencers because of their intrinsic interest and expertise on a topic; people reach out to these experts (who may or may not be brand advocates) for advice when faced with purchases decisions. Those are the influencers that companies want to attract to their influencer panels.

Organizing and Managing Influencer Panels

Table 14.1 lists the different characteristics used to qualify members of an influencer panel. In addition to these variables, the company also wants to collect demographic and psychographic information, either directly from the influencer or through a company like Prizm (mentioned in Chapter 5). Thus, when the company test markets communications or offerings with the group, it can gain a better understanding of how well those efforts will work with different groups of consumers.

TABLE 14.1 Characteristics Used to Qualify the Members of Influencer Panels

Characteristic	Definition
Active Influencer	Willing to tell others, but more important, others listen and act on the influencer's opinion.
Interested	Has a greater intrinsic interest in the product category than the average user.
Heavy User	Actually uses or consumes the offering regularly, preferably more than the average user.
Loyal	Sticks to one brand when it works. Note, however, that this category could include someone who isn't loyal because the right offering meeting his or her needs hasn't yet been created.
Lead User	Willing to try new products and offer feedback. In some instances, modify an offering to suit their own needs; you want lead users to suggest the modifications so you can see how and why they do so.

An influencer panel does not necessarily become a community. If the communication that occurs is only between the marketer and the individual members of the panel, no community forms. The members must communicate with one another for a community to exist. As an example of a social networking strategy that doesn't rely on building a community, Procter & Gamble (P&G) looks for bloggers who write on subjects of importance to moms. P&G then offers these bloggers samples of new Pampers products before these products reach the market, research reports on Pampers, and other things that might find a way into blogs. The goal is to influence the bloggers who already influence women; as already noted, though, many are compensated for mentioning brands and therefore less trusted by consumers. This strategy, though, does not require that P&G create a community through a website or other activity (although P&G does create influencer panels through other techniques).

Research has repeatedly examined the value of social media influencers such as bloggers compared to loyal customers and friends. The question that the study tried to answer was whether it was better to spend marketing dollars providing samples of a new product to loyal customers or to influencers. The answer? Loyal customers actually have greater value when a new product is being launched because they influence people like themselves, people who are likely to become loyal customers. In fact, no matter what generation your customer is in, personal referrals outweigh influencers.[5] The best communities are those that include loyal customers *and* influencers on social media.

As a marketing professional, how do you find influencers? The answer is that they have to be actively recruited. As you learned earlier in the chapter, P&G surveys people looking at its websites. If you answer the survey questions in a way that shows you meet the criteria listed in Table 14.1, you might be asked to join a P&G panel. Another method is to ask a customer whose complaint you have just resolved to take a survey, then invite him or her to join the panel, if qualified. After all, someone who has taken the time to complain might also be motivated to participate on a panel. Still another recruiting method is to send random surveys to households to identify people who would be good panel participants.

Once you create an influencer panel, you have to activate it. After all, influencers do not want to be singled out only to be ignored. However, marketing professionals should be able to answer the following three questions before they activate a panel:

1. **What do we want from the influencer panel?** Usually, companies want feedback on new offerings and new marketing communications, as well as active word-of-mouth promotions. Panelists need to know when you are merely testing a new offering versus introducing it to the marketplace. You don't want word of mouth about a new product that isn't yet ready to be sold.

2. **How much are the panel members willing to do?** Companies want to keep their panelists actively engaged, which requires asking how often they want to participate on the panel, as well as giving them the right to "opt out" of a particular activity if they must. In some instances, you may put out a general call for help, such as posting a notice on an online bulletin board that you need volunteers to test a product. Or you might just simply send influencers product samples, ask them to try them, and respond to a questionnaire. In addition, the processes by which they engage have to be easy for them to complete. For example, asking a lot of information up front makes the sign-up process more difficult. If all you need is an email address, just ask for the email address. Any additional information can be gathered later.
3. **What's in it for the panel members?** What do they get out of participating? They of course get to try free, new products that might improve their lives—or will one day improve their lives if a company heeds their advice. For many influencers, the product category is one that was already important to them. The chance to try a product before anyone else does and provide feedback to a manufacturer who has singled them out for their opinion might be all these people want.

Social Networking Sites and Other Social Media

As we have indicated, communities spring up naturally. Online, social networking sites like Facebook and LinkedIn are used to create communities. For example, when a marketer creates a Facebook page for an offering such as a movie, a community forms around the movie. A community around a movie might not be as enduring as Bass Fishing Favorites or NikePlus groups, but it serves its purpose—at least until the movie is old news and newer movies come out and get attention. When you become a "fan" of something like a movie, you are part of the buzz. Of course, some movies become franchises for multiple sequels and co-promoted product lines and events, with deeply committed communities such as Star Wars and the Avengers.

viral marketing

The attempts by marketers to encourage fast-spreading positive word of mouth, primarily through digital media.

One result of social networking is **viral marketing**, or the spread of a company's message (like a computer virus) through the community. Most viral internet sensations are accidental; for example, when a hurricane hit Houston, Mack McIngvale put a message on his company's Facebook page that simply said, "If you are stranded, let us know and we will come get you." He then had company trucks, which ride very high off the ground, rescue people stranded by the floods that accompanied the storm. Most of those people were taken to one of his furniture stores, where they stayed until floodwaters receded. This act of public service went viral, though Mack and his team did nothing to promote it. As a friend of Mack's, one of your authors has been asked if he did it as a publicity stunt. The answer is no. The drivers were volunteering; many came in even though they were off and no one asked them to do so. Mack did have a sale after the hurricane to sell the furniture used during the storm by those who stayed at the store.

Keep in mind that communities are not places, they are social networks. Snapchat, Twitter, What'sApp, and Instagram are places, not social networks. Communities may form and use those places to create a social network but the network is comprised of the people.

Fans of the Avengers series of movies and graphic novels will dress like characters in the series, meet at conventions like Comic-Con, and talk in Facebook groups, just like any other community!

Source: © Shutterstock, Inc.

A key aspect of viral marketing is user generated content (UGC), those videos that average people create and post on YouTube or TikTok. When these are interesting or funny, they can go viral, such as the one posted by Jaden Hamilton on TikTok where he, an employee at a local Target, claimed to be holding a Walmart shopping cart hostage. Brands as varied as Tinder, Trojan, and Burlington Coat Factory commented, tweeted, and re-posted it, contributing to the video's spread. **Organic spread**, or sharing by ordinary people and not brands or paid influencers, is viewed as more trustworthy and likely to lead to sales.[6]

Communities are also not just a consumer phenomenon. In the B2B world, communities can be formalized into users' groups, which are like clubs for people who use a company's products and services. For example, the customers of Teradata, Mary Gros's company, have formed a users group. Annually, the group holds a conference where members talk about how they use Teradata's products. For example, one of your authors has presented to a Teradata conference about Cabela's use of Teradata offerings to strengthen their Deer Nation community.

organic spread

Reposting of social media content by ordinary people, not companies or paid influencers.

Key Takeaway

- Word of mouth is a powerful form of influence. Customer communities form around social networks, which marketers can use to both promote offerings and gather market information. Companies create influencer panels that provide insight into effective offerings and provide word of mouth.

Review Questions

1. Is an influencer panel the same as a community?
2. If a company doesn't create an influencer panel, are there still influencers? If so, who are they influencing, and how?
3. What internet tools, other than influencer panels, create or support word of mouth?

14.2 Loyalty Management

Learning Objectives

1. Understand the value of customer loyalty.
2. Distinguish attitudinal loyalty from behavioral loyalty.
3. Describe the components of a successful loyalty program.

It's 8:00 p.m. and you're starving. You open the refrigerator and find a leftover chicken breast, half an onion, and some ketchup. But what can you do with these ingredients? You could search online for recipes that contain them, or you could post a question about what to do with them at a website like Kraft.com.

Companies like Kraft build websites such as Kraft.com to create the types of communities we discussed earlier. If you posted your question at Kraft.com, you might have an experience like one woman did—in 24 hours, 853 people viewed the question, and she had twenty-two answers to choose from. Another question had 3,341 viewers over ten days. Why has Kraft's web marketing team worked so hard to create an environment in which people can do this?

One important reason is loyalty. Kraft wants loyal customers—customers who buy Kraft products instead of other brands at every opportunity, who recommend its products to their friends, and are willing to pay a little more to get Kraft quality. Early research on loyalty showed that loyal customers were less expensive to market to, more willing to pay a premium for a particular brand, more willing to try new products under the brand name, more likely to recommend the brand to their friends, and more willing to overlook a problem related to the brand.[7] That said, more recent research shows that the benefits that come from loyal customers are not automatic and that it takes careful management for those benefits to be sustained.[8]

behavioral loyalty

The degree to which a customer habitually buys a product and does not respond to competitors' offerings.

attitudinal loyalty

The degree to which a customer prefers or likes a brand.

Loyalty has two dimensions. One dimension of loyalty is **behavioral loyalty**, meaning that the customer buys the product regularly and does not respond to competitors' offerings. The second dimension is **attitudinal loyalty**, which is the degree to which the customer prefers or likes the brand, or the emotional attachment one has for the brand.

Behavioral Loyalty

Most marketers would be happy with behavioral loyalty because it does, after all, result in sales. Yet behavioral loyalty doesn't mean that the customer is immune to your competitors' offerings. Nor does it mean the customer is willing to pay more for your brand. For example, a businessperson might regularly book trips on American Airlines because it flies to the one or two destinations the traveler has to visit regularly. But a lower price on another airline or one scheduled at a more convenient time might persuade the flier to switch to another carrier.

Habitual purchases are a form of behavioral loyalty. Comparison shopping takes time and effort (hassle in the value equation), so buyers are often willing to forgo looking for substitute products. Habitual purchases are commonly made for low-involvement offerings. You might regularly purchase a Coke at a drive-through restaurant near your house rather than take the time, energy, and gasoline to look for a Coke that's cheaper. In this instance, you are displaying behavioral loyalty to the restaurant simply because it is convenient.

Marketers engage in many activities to both encourage and discourage behavioral loyalty. Loyalty programs, such as an airline offering travelers frequent-flier miles, can encourage behavioral loyalty. But coupons and other special price promotions can break behavioral loyalty patterns and can be useful when companies try to get customers behaviorally loyal to a competitor to switch to their brand. We'll discuss loyalty programs in more detail later in this chapter.

Attitudinal Loyalty

As we explained, attitudinal loyalty refers to how much someone likes a brand and is willing to act on that preference. Keep in mind, however, that a person's *willingness* to act on a preference doesn't necessarily mean she will purchase your product: If you sell Ferraris, and she is unemployed, she might be unable to afford one.

Cause-related marketing, which we discussed in Chapter 12, can foster attitudinal loyalty among a company's community of customers. Companies that engage in **cause-related marketing** choose causes that are important to the customer communities in which they operate. American Airlines sponsors the Susan G. Komen Foundation, an organization that is working to cure breast cancer. KitchenAid sponsors Cook for the Cure, which also benefits the foundation. Both companies support breast cancer awareness because the cause is important to their female customers.

cause-related marketing

When a company supports a nonprofit organization in some way in order to generate positive public relations.

Note, however, that cause-related marketing should be sincere. You can probably quickly tell when a person or organization is insincere. So can your customers. Sincerity also breeds trust. For example, when Eunice Azzani volunteered for the San Francisco AIDS Foundation, she did so because the cause was important to her and Korn/Ferry International, the executive search firm for which she is a managing director. While working for the cause, Azzani met executives with Mervyn's, Wells Fargo, and other major corporations, who later engaged her company to conduct executive searches. They knew they could trust her to do high-quality work and that she was sincere about her place in the community.[9]

Starbucks "Every Name's a Story" Commercial (UK)

This commercial, which won an award in the UK, was created by Starbucks to support transgender rights.

View in the online reader

Of course, there are many other methods of building attitudinal loyalty. As we mentioned, advertising can create feelings for a brand, as can sponsoring a sports team or cultural event. In the next section, we discuss loyalty programs, one way that companies try to manage both affective and behavioral dimensions of loyalty.

Loyalty Programs

Loyalty programs are marketing efforts that reward a person or organization for frequent purchases and the consumption of offerings. For example, Lone Star Park's Star Player Rewards program awards members points for each dollar they spend at the track. The more points they earn, the better the prize is for which they can redeem their points.

loyalty programs

Marketing efforts that reward the frequent purchase and consumption of an offering.

Lone Star Park is a horseracing track in Grand Prairie, Texas. The park rewards frequent attendees through its Star Player Rewards program, which tracks members' purchases and bets. Members can also compete in special contests and participate in special events, such as being able to meet famous jockeys.

Source: © Shutterstock, Inc.

The data a firm collects from a loyalty program can be very useful in terms of designing and improving the company's offerings. When members initially sign up for a loyalty program, they provide a great deal of demographic information to the organization. Their behavior can then be tracked as well. For example, Lone Star Park can determine who sits in what section of the track by what tickets members purchase, as well as where they purchase their refreshments or place their bets. The track can also determine members' preferences for food and drink products or services such as betting clerks and betting machines. When the track has nonracing events, such as a concert, the events can be promoted to Star Players based on their prior selections. Depending on how the members respond, additional offers can be made or not made to them.

cross-promotion marketing

A method in which two or more groups act together to reach potential customers.

Lone Star Park might also team up to create an offering with American Airlines. For example, the track and the airline could compare customer lists and determine which Star Players members are also members of American's AAdvantage frequent-flier program. These individuals could then be offered discounts on trips to Louisville, Kentucky, where the Kentucky Derby is held. Such an offer is called **cross-promotion marketing**. A cross-promotion can be used to introduce new marketing members to a community; in this case, Lone Star Park is introducing American to the horseracing community. The cross-promotion creates credibility for the new member, just as you are more likely to accept a recommendation from a friend.

The Positive Effects of Loyalty Programs

When loyalty programs work, they result in one or more of the four effects of loyalty: the blocker effect, the spreader effect, the accelerator effect, and the longevity effect. We'll start by describing the longevity effect.

FIGURE 14.1 The Positive Effects of Loyalty Programs

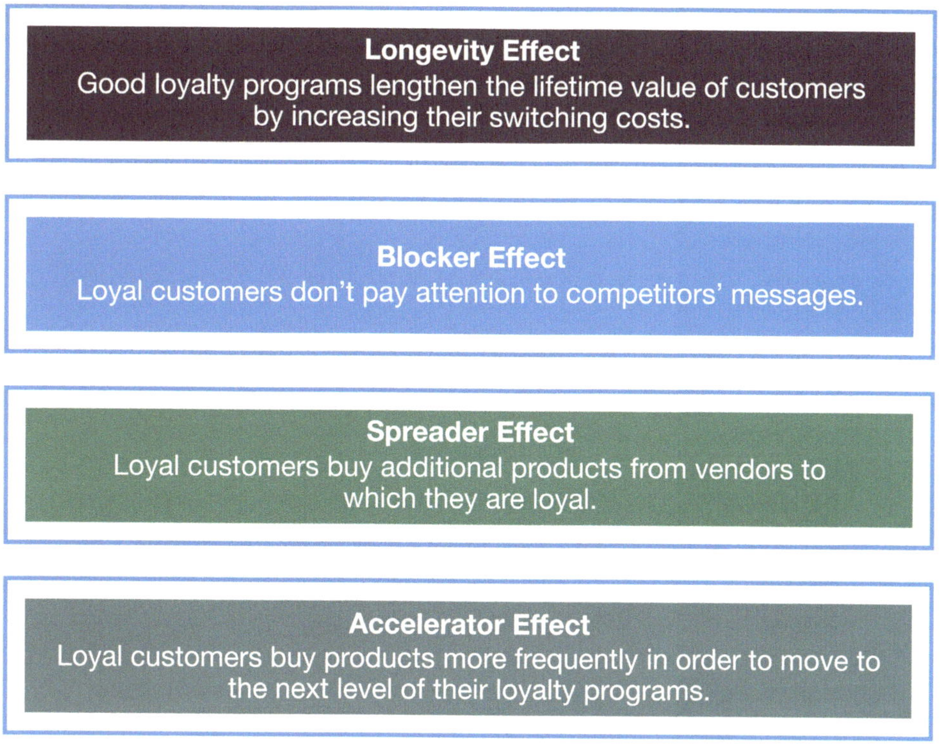

The Longevity Effect

The **longevity effect** is lengthening the lifetime value of a customer. We discussed customer lifetime value (CLV) in earlier chapters. One result of a good loyalty program is that your buyers remain your customers for longer. Because a loyalty company has better information about its customers, it can create offerings that are more valuable to them and keep them coming back. Consider a loyalty program aimed at customers as they progress through their life stages. A grocery store might send diaper coupons to the mother of a new baby and then, five years later, send the mother coupons for items she can put in her child's school lunches.

longevity effect
The process of lengthening a customer's lifetime value over time.

Loyalty programs also affect the longevity of customers by increasing their switching costs. **Switching costs** are the costs associated with moving to a new supplier. For example, if you are a member of a frequent-flier program, you might put up with some inconveniences rather than switching to another airline. So if you are a member of Southwest Airlines' Rapid Rewards program, you might continue to fly Southwest even though it cancelled one of your flights, made you sit on a plane on the ground for two hours, and caused you to miss an important meeting. Rather than starting over with American Airlines, you might be inclined to continue to book your flights on Southwest so you can take a free trip sooner.

switching costs
The costs associated with moving to a new supplier of an offering.

The Blocker Effect

blocker effect

A loyalty program that results in members blocking out marketing communications from competitors.

deal-prone

Willing to succumb to a special offer or lower price.

The blocker effect is related to switching costs. The **blocker effect** works this way: The personal value equation of a loyalty program member is enhanced because they don't need to spend any time and effort shopping around. And because there is no shopping around, there is no need for the member to be perceptive to competitors' marketing communications. In other words, the member of the program "blocks" them out. Furthermore, the member is less **deal-prone**, or willing to succumb to a special offer or lower price from a competitor.

This looks like a great sale, likely to appeal to a deal-prone buyer, but the blocker effect would prevent a buyer who is loyal elsewhere from taking advantage of the low prices.

Source: © Shutterstock, Inc.

The blocker effect can be a function of switching costs—the costs of shopping around as well as the hassles of having to start a new program over. However, the effect can also be a function of *relevance*. Because the loyalty marketer has both information on who the buyer is and data on what the buyer has already responded to, more relevant communications can be created and aimed at the buyer. In addition, because belonging to the program has value, any communication related to the program is already more relevant to the buyer.

The Spreader Effect

spreader effect

A loyalty program that results in buyers being more likely to try related products offered by a marketer.

The **spreader effect** refers to the fact that members of a loyalty program are more likely to try related products offered by the marketer. For example, an American Airlines AAdvantage member who also joins the company's Admiral's Club airport lounge creates additional revenue for the airline, as does the member's purchase of a family vacation through American's Vacation services.

The spreader effect becomes even more pronounced when a cross-promotion is added to the mix. Earlier we mentioned Lone Star Park might team with American to offer a trip package to the Kentucky Derby. Another example is Citibank offering you AAdvantage miles if you get a Citibank

Visa card through American's AAdvantage program. Cross-promotions such as these encourage loyalty program members to try even more products from more producers.

The Accelerator Effect

When rats running in a maze get closer to the cheese, they speed up. Companies that offer tiered programs—loyalty programs that offer better benefits as the customer reaches higher point levels—do so because consumers speed up, or accelerate, purchases when they are about to reach a higher award level in a loyalty program; this is called the **accelerator effect** of a loyalty program. In American's AAdvantage program, for example, a member gets "Platinum" status after flying sixty flights or sixty thousand miles. Platinum members get special awards, like more frequent upgrades to first class, boarding ahead of everyone else, not having to pay for the second piece of luggage and other fees, and double mileage toward free flights. Someone who has fifty flights and just needs ten more to become Platinum will start to fly American more frequently until the Platinum level is reached. Then, American hopes that the other effects (blocker, spreader, etc.) will occur.

accelerator effect

The effect of a loyalty program that, as a consumer approaches the next level of benefits, the rate of consumer's purchases increases.

Companies can capitalize on the accelerator effect by making it easy for members to track their progress and notifying them when they are close to reaching subsequent levels. American helps its AAdvantage fliers track their progress by sending them monthly updates on their levels and by making the information readily available on the same app that you can book flights. Couple such a notification with a special offer, and a company is likely to see even greater acceleration. The accelerator effect can also be used with promotions that create short-term, loyal behavior. Pepsi created a promotion with Amazon in which purchasers could accumulate points toward free music downloads. The promotion, launched with a Justin Timberlake Super Bowl ad, was a knockoff of Coca-Cola's MyCokeRewards.com. Although they weren't formal loyalty programs, both promotions led to an accelerator effect as customers got close to the award levels they needed to redeem prizes.

Criteria for Successful Loyalty Programs

Just having a loyalty program is no guarantee of success, though. Eight studies of more than a dozen grocery store loyalty programs in the United States and Europe showed that five programs had no impact on the loyalty of customers, two increased sales but not profits, two had mixed results, and five had positive results.[10] There are, however, several characteristics of loyalty programs that can make them effective, each of which is discussed next.

Good Performance by a Company

The first characteristic of an effective loyalty program is performance. No loyalty program can overcome a company's poor performance. Even the most loyal buyer can put up with subpar performance for only so long.

Responsiveness by a Company

Responsiveness is how well a company can take customer information (such as complaints) and alter what they do to satisfy the customer. Loyal customers are more willing to complete surveys and participate in market research, but they expect companies to use the information wisely. For example, when customers complain, they expect their problems to be fixed and the company to use the information so that the same problems don't recur. Likewise, the members of influencer panels expect to be listened to. If you ignore their input, you are likely to alienate them, causing them to switch brands.

A company's responsiveness—or lack thereof—also becomes evident to buyers when they spot a better offer. Precisely at that moment, they realize that the company that created the better offer was more responsive and worked harder to meet their needs.

Shared Identity Among Participants

Loyal customers are like sports fans—they wear their "team's" colors. That's why loyalty programs have names that sound prestigious, like Continental's "Elite Pass" program or American's "Executive Platinum" program. Loyal customers also want to be recognized for their loyalty. Hampton Inn, which is part of the Hilton family of hotels, is one company that could do a better of job of recognizing its customers—literally. One of the authors stays regularly at the same Hampton Inn, only to be greeted every time on arrival with the question, "Is this your first stay with us?" The author is not only a regular guest at that hotel but a member of Hilton Honors, the hotel's loyalty program. But apparently the Hampton Inn's reservation system doesn't provide that information to its front desk clerks. If you fail to recognize customers who are loyal, you are essentially telling them that their business isn't that important to you.

Clear Benefits

What are the benefits of being loyal? A loyalty program should make those benefits clear. For example, Southwest Airlines boards by numbers, and Rapid Rewards members get to board first. Travelers who are not Rapid Rewards members can easily see the special treatment members receive. If the elements of scarcity and status can be created by a loyalty program, the benefits of belonging to it will be obvious to customers.

Community Development

Finally, marketers who can put loyal customers together with other loyal customers are likely to build a community around the common experience of consumption. At Lone Star Park, common consumption is obvious—people are actually together. Building a community in which people don't actually consume goods and services together can be a bit more difficult, but recall that Kraft has done so with its online presence. Members of Kraft.com still share their experiences, recipes, questions, and answers, thereby creating a sense of "we're in this together." Some of the postings might be related directly to Kraft products, whereas others might only be indirectly related. Nonetheless, they all provide Kraft with insight into what its customers are thinking. Meanwhile, its customers become more loyal as they participate on the website.

Keep in mind that a loyalty program isn't necessary to create loyalty. Lexus doesn't have a formal loyalty program. Yet studies show that Lexus owners are the most loyal luxury car buyers. Over half of all Lexus owners buy another Lexus. (The brand's slogan is "Once a Lexus buyer, always a Lexus buyer.") By contrast, Mercedes-Benz has a loyalty program, but only 40 percent of its buyers purchase another Mercedes.

A company can also offer its customers loyalty benefits that are not a part of a formal loyalty program. For example, Mercedes-Benz gives loyal buyers an opportunity to suggest new features via a contest, for which there is no prize other than the recognition the winner gets because his idea was selected. And like many other car manufacturers, Mercedes offers owners special trade-in deals. The challenge with loyalty promotions that lie outside loyalty programs is collecting the information marketers need to target customers.

Panera Bread offers an interesting alternative to the traditional loyalty program. The company has a points card but instead of tiers, they offer random rewards. Customers are randomly given thank you gifts (such as a free dessert), in addition to the points benefits. Of course, there is an algorithm behind the "random" rewards, but their belief is that a thank you is a more powerful way to generate loyalty than to create tiers. The point here is that you don't need a loyalty program to say thank you to important customers.

Key Takeaway

- Customer loyalty is both behavioral and attitudinal. Habitual purchases are a form of behavioral loyalty. Cause-related marketing can foster attitudinal loyalty among a company's community of customers, as can loyalty programs. Loyalty programs can have four positive effects: They can increase the longevity, or lifetime value, of customers; block competitors' marketing efforts; encourage customers to buy related offerings; and accelerate their purchases. Loyalty programs don't automatically create loyalty among customers, though. Loyalty is created when a company performs well, responds to its customers, identifies its loyal customers, makes the benefits of its loyalty program transparent (obvious), and the firm builds a community among its customers.

Review Questions

1. What are the benefits of having loyal customers? Why or how do those benefits occur?
2. What is the difference between loyalty and loyalty programs?
3. How can you create loyalty without having a loyalty program?

14.3 Customer Satisfaction

Learning Objectives

1. Understand satisfaction and satisfaction strategies.
2. Design a customer satisfaction measurement system.
3. Describe complaint management strategies.

Customer Satisfaction Defined

What comes to mind when you hear someone say, "A satisfied customer"? Perhaps it is an image of someone smiling with the pride of knowing he got a good deal. Or perhaps it is the childlike look of happiness someone exhibits after purchasing a new pair of shoes that are just the right color. Whatever your picture of a satisfied customer is, **customer satisfaction** is typically defined as the feeling that a person experiences when an offering meets his or her expectations. When an offering meets the customer's expectations, the customer is satisfied.

customer satisfaction

The feeling that results when an offering meets a consumer's expectations.

Improving customer satisfaction is a goal sought by many businesses. In fact, some companies evaluate their salespeople based on how well they satisfy their customers; in other words, not only must the salespeople hit their sales targets, they have to do so in ways that satisfy customers. SAP is one company that pays its salespeople bonuses if they meet their customer satisfaction goals.

Customer satisfaction scores have been relatively stable for the past few years, as illustrated in Table 14.2. You might think that if increasing the satisfaction of customers were, indeed, the goal of businesses, the scores should show a steady increase. Why don't they? Maybe it's because just satisfying your customers is a *minimal* level of performance. Clearly customer satisfaction is important. However, it isn't always good predictor of a customer's future purchases or brand loyalty. For example, one study of customer satisfaction examined car buyers. Although the buyers rated their satisfaction levels with their purchases 90 percent or higher, only 40 percent of them purchased the same brand of car the next time around. That's because needs change between purchases (recall the impact of life cycles on purchases as just one reason why) for long-term products like cars. Alternatively, for hotels, satisfaction plays a big role in predicting loyalty and future purchases.[11]

TABLE 14.2 Industry-Average Customer Satisfaction Scores, 2000, 2010, and 2020

For some categories, such as cars, customer satisfaction scores are relatively stable, while appliances appear to have declined and computers improved but are now stable.

	2000	2010	2020
Appliances	85	81	79
Computers	72	78	78
Electronics	83	85	80
Cars	80	83	78

Source: Data from American Customer Satisfaction Index, Data from: American Customer Satisfaction Index, http://www.theacsi.org

Keep in mind, though, that satisfaction scores are a function of what the customer expected as well as what the company delivered. So the flat or even declining scores in Table 14.2 may reflect rising customer expectations as well as improved products. In other words, the better offerings get, the more it takes to satisfy consumers.

There is also a downside to continuously spending more to satisfy your customers. Recent research shows that firms that do so can experience higher sales revenues. However, after the additional spending costs are factored in, the net profits that result are sometimes marginal or even negative. Nonetheless, satisfaction is not unimportant. A company's performance on key factors is critical both in terms of the loyalty and satisfaction it generates among its customers.[12]

Customer Satisfaction Strategies

So what or how much should you do to improve the satisfaction of your customer? If customer satisfaction can be defined as the feeling a person experiences when an offering meets his or her expectations, then there are two critical ways to improve customer satisfaction. The first is to establish appropriate expectations in the minds of customers. The second is to deliver on those expectations.

We know that dissatisfied customers are likely to tell many more friends about their negative experiences than satisfied customers are about good experiences. Why? Because there's more drama in unmet expectations. A story about met expectations—telling a friend about a night out that was average, for example—is boring. Jan Carlzon, a former Scandinavian Airlines executive, was famous for promoting the concept of "delighted" customers. Carlzon's idea was that delighting customers by exceeding their expectations should result in both repeat business and positive word of mouth for a firm because customer delight was worth talking about. Of course, this model assumes that the consumer cares about the extra service, which may or may not be the case.

Establishing appropriate expectations in the minds of customers is a function of the prepurchase communications the seller has with them. If you set the expectations too low, people won't buy your offering. But if you set the expectations too high, you run the risk that your buyers will be dissatisfied. A common saying in business is "underpromise and overdeliver." In other words, set consumers' expectations a bit low, and then exceed those expectations in order to create delighted customers who are enthusiastic about your product. A seller hopes that enthusiastic customers will tell their friends about the seller's offering, spreading lots of positive word of mouth about it.

In some instances, though, marketers have to change negative experiences to positive expectations. Bruce Williams, who owns his own marketing agency, worked to make Virginia Beach a welcoming venue for a late-summer event aimed for the Black market. In 1989, a riot at a Black college event at the beach began a downward slide to the point that in 2013, Black people were avoiding Virginia Beach all year long. Bruce, along with city tourism officials, sponsors, and other partners, was able to create Africana Virginia Beach Weekend Featuring the Funkfest Beach Party, a two-day event just prior to Labor Day. Through social media and traditional channels, Bruce promoted the event successfully. In 2018, the event drew over 20,000 attendees, filling hotel rooms that now have to be booked a year in advance. The event is now the largest in Virginia Beach each year and has changed the perception of the city among African Americans.

Marketing was key to bringing visitors back to Virginia Beach Africana Weekend and the Funk Fest Beach Party by resetting positive expectations.

Source: Bruce Williams & Associates, used with permission

One customer satisfaction strategy that grew out of Carlzon's idea of delighting customers is to empower customer-facing personnel. Customer-facing personnel are employees who meet and interact with customers. In a hotel, this might include desk clerks, housekeepers, bellmen, and other staff. Empowering these employees to drop what they're doing in order to do something special for a customer, for example, can certainly delight customers. In some organizations, employees are even given a budget for such activities.

Ritz-Carlton employees each have an annual budget that can be spent on customer service activities, such as paying for dry cleaning if a customer spilled red wine on a dress in the hotel's restaurant. Sewell Cadillac is famous for how its employees serve its customers. An employee will even pick up a customer up on a Sunday if a Sewell-purchased car breaks down. Other dealers might delegate such a service to another company, but at Sewell, the same salesperson who sold the car might be the person who handles such a task. To Sewell, customer service is too important to trust to another company—a company that perhaps won't feel the same sense of urgency to keep car buyers as satisfied as Sewell does.

Companies like Ritz-Carlton also monitor Twitter and other social media so that any problems can be identified in real time. For example, one newlywed tweeted that the view outside her window of another wall was no way to spend a honeymoon. A Ritz-Carlton employee caught the tweet and employees at the hotel responded with a room upgrade. Bruce Williams also monitors Twitter to ensure that Funkfest delivers on customer expectations.

Empowerment is more than simply a budget and a job description—frontline employees also need customer skills. Companies like Ritz-Carlton and Sewell spend a great deal of time and effort to ensure that employees with customer contact responsibilities are trained and prepared to handle small and large challenges with equal aplomb.

Another customer satisfaction strategy involves offering customers warranties and guarantees. Warranties serve as an agreement that the product will perform as promised or some form of restitution will be made to the customer. Customers who are risk-averse find warranties reassuring.

One form of dissatisfaction is **postpurchase dissonance**, which we described in Chapter 3. Recall that it is also called *buyer's remorse*. Postpurchase dissonance is more likely to occur when an expensive product is purchased, the buyer purchases it infrequently and has little experience with it, and there is a perception that it is a high-risk purchase. Many marketers address postpurchase dissonance by providing their customers with reassuring communications.

postpurchase dissonance
A situation in which consumers rethink their decisions after purchasing products and wonder if they made the best decision.

Measuring Customer Satisfaction

To measure customer satisfaction, you need to able to understanding what creates it. Just asking customers, "Are you satisfied?" won't tell you much. Yet many companies often measure the satisfaction of their customers on the basis of only a few questions: "How satisfied were you today?" "Would you recommend us to your friends?" and "Do you intend to visit us again?"

In fact, the Net Promoter Score (NPS) is a very common[13] measure of satisfaction and comprises the single question, "Would you recommend us to your friends?" Then, the number of customers who said "No" is subtracted from the number who said "Yes" to derive the NPS. In spite of this measure being the most widely used metric for satisfaction, research indicates it is a poor measure of intentions to repurchase.[14] And of those who do use it, only one in five has examined whether the willingness to recommend is a good predictor of loyalty or customer lifetime value.[15]

Effective customer satisfaction measures have several components. The two general components are the customer's expectations and whether the organization performed well enough to meet them. A third component is the degree of satisfaction.

To figure out if a customer's expectations were met and they are delighted, more detail is usually required. Companies might break the offering into major components and ask how satisfied customers were with each. For example, a restaurant might ask the following:

- Were you greeted promptly by a host? By your server at your table?
- Was your order taken promptly?
- How long did you wait for your food?
- Was the food served at the appropriate temperature?

These questions assume that each aspect of the service is equally important to the customer. However, some surveys ask customers to rate how important they are. Other surveys simply "weight," or score, questions so that aspects that are known to be more important to customers have a greater impact on the overall satisfaction score. For example, a restaurant might find that prompt service, good taste, and large portions are the only three factors that usually determine customers' overall satisfaction. In that case, the survey can be shortened considerably. At the same time, however, space should be left on the survey so customers can add any additional information that could yield important insight. This information can be used to find out if there are customer service problems that a firm wasn't aware of or if the preferences of consumers in general are changing.

Bruce Williams used such surveys to address declining attendance at the Norfolk Waterfront Jazz Festival. Festival organizers didn't think a jazz-only lineup would sell, but it was supposed to be a jazz festival! The mismatch between the audience and the performance lineup led to serious problems with ticket sales. Bruce used satisfaction measures to drive the point home that patrons wanted only jazz. Once management realized the problem, Bruce then targeted media to tout a jazz-only event, and the attendance went from less than 4,000 to over 10,000. In addition, NPS measures were over 90 percent.

Norfolk Waterfront Jazz Festival customer satisfaction surveys were important to identifying problems in the offering. When fixed, customer satisfaction scores improved, and attendance more than doubled.

Source: Bruce Williams, used with permission

You will still find customer satisfaction survey cards that just ask, "How satisfied were you today?" "Would you recommend us to your friends?" and "Do you intend to visit us again?" The information obtained from these surveys can still be useful if it's paired with a more comprehensive measurement program. For instance, a sample of customers could be given the opportunity to provide more detailed information via another survey, and the two surveys could be compared. Such a comparison can help the company pinpoint aspects that need improvement. In addition, the company has given every customer an opportunity to provide input, which is an important part of any empowerment strategy.

Complaint Management Strategies

When buyers want to complain about products or companies, they have many ways to do so. They can complain to the companies they're upset with, tell their friends, or broadcast their concerns on the internet. People who use every internet site possible to bash a company are called *verbal terrorists*. The term was coined by Paul Greenberg, a marketing analyst who authored the wildly popular book *CRM at the Speed of Light*.

Studies also show that if a company can resolve a customer's complaint well, then the customer's attitude toward the company is improved, possibly even beyond the level of his or her original satisfaction. Some experts have argued, perhaps jokingly, that if this is the case, a good strategy might be to make customers mad and then do a good job of resolving their problems. Research shows, however, that companies are vulnerable; if a customer tweets about a bad experience, a competitor can respond and steal the customer. Practically speaking, the best practice is to perform at or beyond customer expectations so fewer complaints will be received in the first place.

Customers will complain, though, no matter how hard firms try to meet or exceed their expectations. Many times, those complaints will go on Yelp or some other review site. Proactive marketers monitor such sites to identify poor customer perceptions. Attic Birds, an online retailer specializing in vintage products, had a customer who received a piece of glassware that broke in shipment. While the company responded and the customer was ultimately satisfied, she didn't delete or update her online complaint. Online complaints can live a long time in cyberspace, even when the complaint is in the form of a suggestion and simply reflects an opportunity to improve the experience.

When a complaint is made, the process for responding to it is as important as the outcome. And consumers judge companies as much for whether their response processes seem fair as whether they got what they wanted. For that reason, some companies create customer service departments with specially trained personnel who can react to complaints. Other companies invest heavily in preparing all customer-facing personnel to respond to complaints. In addition, artificial intelligence systems like SAP's Ariba Customer Support system can apply AI to prompt the customer for additional information and accelerate their search to the right answer. Jens Trotzky, head of Artificial Intelligence Technology for Customer Solution Support & Innovation at SAP, says that they're also using AI to identify and resolve potential problems before they arise.[16]

Still other companies outsource their customer service. When the service is technical, marketers sometimes outsource the resolution of complaints to companies that specialize in providing technical service. Computer help lines are an example. Technical-support companies often service the computer help lines of multiple manufacturers. A company that outsources its service nonetheless has to make sure that customer complaints are handled as diligently as possible. Otherwise, customers will be left with a poor impression.

Handling the Complaint Process

A good customer-complaint–handling process involves the steps listed below. Note that one step is to acknowledge the customer's feelings. A customer who is angry or upset due to a failure does not want to be patronized or have his or her problems taken lightly. The situation is important to the customer and should be important to the person listening and responding to the complaint.

- Listen carefully to the complaint.
- Acknowledge the customer's feelings.
- Determine the root cause of the problem.
- Offer a solution.
- Gain agreement on the solution and communicate the process of resolution.
- Follow up, if appropriate.
- Record the complaint and resolution.

Note that the complaint-resolution process involves communicating that process and gaining agreement on a solution, even if the customer sometimes might not like the outcome. They still need to know what to expect.

Finally, the complaint process includes recording the complaint. We stated earlier that a firm's best strategy is to perform at or beyond the customer's expectations to minimize the number of complaints it receives in the first place. Analyzing your company's complaints can help you identify weak points in a service process or design flaws in a product, as well as potential miscommunications that are raising customer' expectations unreasonably. To conduct this analysis, however, you need a complete record of the complaints made.

A complaint record should reflect the main reason an offering failed so that patterns can be observed and rectified to prevent more complaints. Typically, the failure can be attributed to one (or more) of the following four gaps:[17]

1. The **communication gap**. Overstating the offering's performance level, thereby creating unrealistic expectations on the part of customers.
2. The **knowledge gap**. Not understanding the customer's expectations or needs, which then leads a company to create a product that disappoints the customer.
3. The **standards gap**. Setting performance standards that are too low despite what is known about the customer's requirements.
4. The **delivery gap**. Failing to meet the performance standards established for an offering.

You can attribute the complaints your company receives to one of the four gaps and then use the information to figure out what must be done to fix the problem, assuming you have one. If the problem is overstating the performance, then perhaps your firm's marketing promotions materials should be reviewed. If it appears that the offering is simply not meeting the needs of your customers, then more work should be done to identify exactly what they are. If your firm is aware of the needs of its customers but there is a gap between their requirements and the standards set for your firm's performance, then standards should be reviewed. Finally, your company's processes should be examined to ensure that standards are being met.

Keep in mind that the complaint-handling process itself is subject to complaints. As we mentioned, customers want a process that's fair, even if the outcome isn't what they hoped for. Consequently, monitoring your firm's customer satisfaction levels also means you must monitor how satisfied customers are with how their complaints were handled.

communication gap

A gap that occurs when a marketer overstates the performance level of a product, thereby creating unrealistic expectations on the part of consumers.

knowledge gap

A firm's failure to understand a customer's expectations or needs, which then leads it to create an offering that disappoints the customer.

standards gap

A gap that results when a marketer sets performance standards for a product that are too low, in spite of what is known about the customer's requirements.

delivery gap

A gap that results when a product fails to meet its performance standards.

Key Takeaway

- Measuring customer satisfaction is an important element of customer empowerment. But satisfaction alone is a minimal level of acceptable performance. It means that the customer's expectations were met. Getting positive word of mouth requires exceeding those expectations. To minimize the number of complaints a company needs an effective process of both handling complaints and understanding their causes, so any problems can be corrected. Because the complaint process itself is subject to complaints, monitoring your firm's customer satisfaction levels also means you must monitor how satisfied customers are with your company's complaint-handling system.

Review Questions

1. Should a company be happy or concerned if most customers are satisfied?
2. Why have customer satisfaction scores remained relatively steady over the past few years?
3. What are the desired outcomes, from a marketer's perspective, of a complaint-management process?
4. How would marketing management use customer satisfaction survey results?

14.4 Ethics, Laws, and Customer Empowerment

Learning Objectives

1. Apply general ethical principles and concepts to online marketing.
2. Explain the laws that regulate online and other types of marketing.

You are about to graduate and move to another city to start a new job. Your employer is paying for your moving expenses, so you go online to see what people have to say about the different moving companies. One company has particularly good reviews, so you hire it. Yet what actually happens is vastly different—and a complete disaster. Little surprise, then, when you later discover that the company actually paid people to post those positive reviews!

Unfortunately, such an experience has happened so often that the Federal Trade Commission (FTC) created rules regarding endorsements and whether companies need to announce their sponsorship of messages.

sugging

Any form of selling under another guise or under a phony front.

Once upon a time, before the days of the internet, any form of selling under another guise or a phony front was called **sugging** (a word created from the first letters of *selling under the guise*, or SUG). The term was primarily applied to a practice in which a salesperson would pretend to be doing marketing research by interviewing a consumer, and then turn the consumer's answers into a sales pitch. More recently, some companies have hired young, good-looking, outgoing men and women to hang out in bars and surreptitiously promote a particular brand of alcohol or cigarettes; in this case, they were pretending to be just a regular consumer. Sugging seems to be a good term to apply to fake reviews, as well.

Truly, in no other marketplace should the term *caveat emptor* apply as strongly as it does on the internet. Caveat emptor means "let the buyer beware," or "it's your own fault if you buy it and it doesn't work!" Product reviews can be posted by anyone—even by a company or its competitors. So how do you know which ones to trust? Oftentimes you don't. Yet many of us do trust them under certain conditions. There have to be a lot of reviews so that we can be confident they're from real people, and we also look at the negative reviews to see what the problem was. For example, you might overlook one or two negative complaints about poor or rude service at a hotel but you won't overlook reviews that say that it was dirty. We also tend to look at when the reviews were posted—if all of the negative ones are old, then we probably aren't too worried.[18]

Would you stay here? Studies show that a few bad reviews won't deter a consumer but recent reviews that complain about core features like cleanliness in a hotel do lead consumers to avoid a company.

Source: © Shutterstock, Inc.

While sugging isn't illegal, it isn't fair. Not only is the content potentially misrepresented, but the source certainly is. As you already know, a marketer cannot make promises about an offering's capabilities unless those capabilities are true. Sugging is similar—it involves misrepresenting or lying about the source of the information in an effort to gain an unfair advantage.

The consequences of being caught while sugging can be high. Even if the information posted was actually an accurate depiction of the offering's capabilities and benefits, consumers will be less likely to believe it—or any other of the company's marketing communications, for that matter. The loss of trust makes building any kind of lasting relationship with a buyer extremely difficult to do.

Legal Requirements

So far, there are no regulations regarding sugging, although that may change if the FTC decides a crackdown is needed. There are, however, regulations affecting how one uses email to sell.

Specifically, the **CAN-SPAM Act** prohibits the use of email, faxes, and other technology to randomly push a message to a potential consumer. **Spam** is a term for unwanted commercial email similar to junk mail. Using email and other forms of technology to sell is legal if the seller and the buyer have a preexisting relationship or if the buyer has given his or her permission.

CAN-SPAM Act

A law that prohibits the use of email, fax, and other technology to randomly send messages to potential consumers.

Permission marketing is a term that was created to suggest that marketers should always ask for permission to sell or to offer buyers marketing messages. The idea was that when permission is granted, the buyer is willing to listen. Now, however, anything "free" online requires that you sign up and give "permission," not just to get the freebie but also all kinds of future spam and annoying messages. You might also inadvertently give a seller permission to sell your name and contact information. When you sign up for contests or agree to the seller's privacy statement when you order something online, you may have given them permission to resell your contact information to one of their "partners."

spam

Any unwanted commercial email similar to junk mail.

Immediately following a conversation, the Amazon Web Services salesperson will enter information about the visitor into a lead management software system so that the appropriate follow up will happen after the trade show.

Source: © Shutterstock, Inc.

In the B2B world, when attendees sign up for a trade show, they often give the show's exhibitors permission to send them emails and other information. A challenge for the marketer, though, is to get the email through the attendee's spam filter, even though the attendee gave permission.

Privacy Laws

privacy laws

Laws that limit the amount and type of information a company can collect about a consumer and also specify how that information can be used or shared.

Gramm-Leach-Bliley Act

A legal act that requires certain institutions to provide written notice of their privacy policies.

privacy policies

Statements about how a company will use and protect a consumer's private data.

U.S. **privacy laws** apply to both internet marketing and other forms of commerce. The laws limit the amount and type of information a company can collect about a consumer and also specify how that information can be used or shared. In the EU, the types of data a company can collect are fewer, and the sharing of information is far more restricted, particularly since the adoption of the General Data Protection Regulation (GDPR). For example, a company cannot share information about customers in one division with another division. For this reason, many U.S. companies are having to adopt practices in conformity with the GDPR. (Sending out unsolicited emails to potential buyers is also restricted in Europe.)

The **Gramm-Leach-Bliley Act** of 1999 requires financial institutions to provide written notice of their privacy policies. **Privacy policies** are statements regarding how a company will use and protect a consumer's private data. The law was broadened in 2003 to apply to a wider array of companies and consumer information.

The FTC requires a company to follow its policy or face severe penalties, even if the company is not required by the Gramm-Leach-Bliley Act to have a privacy policy. If you own a bookstore and you have a privacy policy, even though the law doesn't require you to have one, you have to follow the FTC's rules. And if you decide to change your privacy policy (for example, you decide to sell your customer list to Amazon), you have to notify your customers of the new policy.

For an example of a privacy policy, take a look at Amazon's.

What kind of data do companies want on you? They want to know where you live so they can apply data about your neighborhood to know you better and create marketing messages more likely to persuade you to buy something. They want to know how much you make to see if you can afford a higher-priced product. They want to know about the other things you buy, because that will likely affect what you buy in the future. If you own a boat, for example, you're more likely to buy fishing gear in the future. If you buy fishing gear, you're more likely to buy Performance Fishing Gear (clothes) from Columbia, and so on. The more they know, the more they can create offers tailored to fit your lifestyle and entice you to buy.

Some organizations also have data, such as your social security number, that criminals could use to steal your identity. For example, think about how much information your university has on you. They not only have your social security number, but they may also have your financial information (through financial aid), your health information (through the campus health center), and your vehicle information (through parking fees). Protecting that information so you aren't harmed is a huge responsibility for the university.

Privacy policies and privacy laws apply to both business customers and individual consumers. As we explained in Chapter 8, many business buyers require vendors to sign nondisclosure agreements (NDAs) that specify what information is proprietary, or owned by the customer, and how, if at all, the seller can use that information. NDAs are not an online tool specifically but are often used in the normal course of business.

What about the offering itself? When you buy something online, you don't get to see it first, so how do you know it is what the seller says it is, and what can you do if it isn't? The **Uniform Commercial Code (UCC)** (first mentioned in Chapter 13) is a group of laws that govern commercial practices in the United States. The UCC defines many aspects of sales, such as when a sale actually takes place and what warranties buyers can expect. Other laws also govern the transaction but in general, you have a period of time in which you can legally return the product unless specified otherwise prior to the sale. The UCC also provides additional rights such as warranties and other promises.

Uniform Commercial Code (UCC)

A group of laws that govern commercial practices in the United States.

Warranties and Promises

A **warranty** is a promise by the seller that an offering will perform as the seller said it would. The UCC makes a distinction between two types of warranties. The first is an **expressed warranty**, which is an oral or written statement by the seller regarding how the product should perform and the remedies available to the consumer in the event the offering fails.

warranty

A promise or assurance by a seller that an offering will perform as the seller represented it would.

expressed warranty

An oral or written statement by the seller regarding how a product should perform and the remedies available to the consumer in the event of its failure.

A warranty is a promise that the product will work and offers remedies, such as free service, if the product needs it within a specific period of time following the purchase.

Source: © Shutterstock, Inc.

implied warranty

An obligation for a seller to provide an offering of at least average quality, beyond any written statements.

An **implied warranty** is an obligation for the seller to provide an offering of at least average quality, beyond any written statements. For example, when you buy a new car, there is an implied warranty that it will run as promised after you drive it off the lot. You also have the right to expect average quality for any characteristic of a product that you buy online, except for those characteristics specifically described in the online material. If you were able to inspect the product before you bought it, such as looking at it in a store, the implied warranty only applies to those aspects you couldn't inspect or observe in the store.

Where the law gets tricky is when it comes to other forms of writing. Marketing messages, whether written in a brochure or advertisement or stated by a salesperson, are considered implied warranties. Any written statement about what the offering does has to be true, or it violates the UCC's definition of an implied warranty (and is therefore punishable by law).

Keep in mind that a salesperson can create an implied warranty in an email or during an online chat session if they make a promise. Even if the salesperson says something that contradicts a company's written material elsewhere, the consumer has the right to believe what the salesperson says. As such, the salesperson's promise is legally binding.

Protecting Your Company

bot

Short for robot; a kind of program that performs automatic functions online.

As a marketer, you have an obligation to protect your company from consumers who might not have honest intentions. For example, have you noticed how you sometimes have to reproduce a strange-looking set of letters or words before you are allowed to make a purchase when buying something online? That simple step prevents automatic ordering by bots. A **bot**, which is short for *robot*, is a kind of program that performs automatic functions online. One of those functions could be to purchase products, such as tickets to a highly desirable sporting event, that the buyer can then resell at a higher price. Or a bot could be used to obtain many units of a freebie that someone can then resell. Bots can be used for many illicit purposes; a good marketer anticipates their uses and creates barriers to prevent being taken advantage of.

A legal tool to help protect your company is the Digital Millennium Copyright Act. This act is designed to prevent copyrighted material from being pirated online. While prominent cases involve downloading music, your marketing information is also included. When you find a good way to market your offerings online, a competitor can't just steal your communications and insert their name. You are protected by this act.

phishing

Soliciting personal information to steal an identity and use it to generate cash fraudulently.

What is very difficult to protect against is **phishing**, or soliciting personal information to steal an identity and use it to generate cash fraudulently. However, you may find it reassuring to your customers to remind them of your privacy policies and your customer contact practices. For example, a bank may remind its customers that it will never ask for a social security number by email. Making sure your customer contact policies protect your customers can also help protect them against phishing from someone pretending to be you or your company.

Key Takeaway

- Sugging is selling under any phony type of front. It includes posting fake reviews about products online. Sugging damages a seller's trust among buyers and should never be done. U.S. laws govern how products can be marketed, both those that are sold electronically and through more traditional channels. Companies must have permission before they can send you spam, and they have to tell you how they will gather and use your personal information. Warranties—expressed and implied—are binding no matter how companies deliver them. Good marketers anticipate less-than-honest activities by individuals and take steps to prevent them. Bots are online robots that some people use to take advantage of marketers.

Review Questions

1. What damage is done by sugging? If the customer buys your product, was the sugging OK? How does sugging differ online versus in person?
2. What does the CAN-SPAM Act do?
3. When do you mind a company having a lot of information on you, and when is it OK? Are there advantages to you as a consumer when a company knows a lot about you? Are there disadvantages? What safeguards are there for consumers?
4. How can a bot hurt a marketer?

14.5 Discussion Questions and Activities

Discussion Questions

1. Many companies have suffered because of things their founder or CEO said or did, while others have made large and public contributions to support social initiatives. Do you pay much attention to how companies act? Which companies stands out to you and why?
2. When successfully building loyalty and community, trust seems to be the biggest factor. How can a company build trust? Should consumers trust companies? Why or why not? Do you think some consumers are just more prone to being loyal to companies and other consumers are not? Why or why not?
3. Assume you've built an online company selling shoes that you have made especially for your brand. How would your company demonstrate responsiveness? How would you design a feedback system so that your company could be responsive? How would a feedback system vary if your company sold to shoe retailers instead of directly to consumers?
4. Compare and contrast influencer panels and crowdsourcing. If consumers know that professional influencers are paid by the brands they recommend, why do consumers continue to follow those influencers, read their blogs, and so forth? And if consumers are less likely to trust professional influencers, why do companies still use them?
5. You've noticed a pattern in tweets complaining about service. Do you offer something for free? What if those complaints are made on review sites—how do you communicate that you identified the problem and those complaints are no longer relevant?
6. Facebook got into trouble over giving out too much information on its users. DNA test companies, like 23andMe, are also facing privacy concerns, and Europe's stringent privacy regulations are affecting any company operating globally. Do you worry about your data and how it is used? How do you feel about your data being used by marketers? Does it improve offerings or make you more susceptible to buying things you really don't need?
7. Think about websites you visit regularly. Are any likely to be a community site? Is the site managed by a company that sells products to the community?
8. Discuss the tension marketers might feel when describing their product. Do they underpromise and overdeliver? Or do they promise the moon to get sales?
9. Describe a situation where you had a legitimate complaint about a company's offering. How did the company handle it? Was it handled well? What were the company's consequences of the situation?
10. Customer empowerment is a relatively recent phenomenon. Give some examples of your own consumer activity in which you experienced empowerment. Contrast that with situations

where you wished you had more power to experience the offering differently. What is the relationship of co-creation of value with empowerment?

11. Have you clicked on an ad on Facebook? Do you 'like' companies, movies, or offerings in social media? What has happened when you liked something? Discuss whether you think some consumers are more prone to like offerings than others and why.

Activities

1. Go online to the M&Ms website and evaluate it. You will have to go through more than just the main landing page—click on the current contests and other pages to get all the data you need. What does the company do to build loyalty? To build community? Are there opportunities for feedback? Does the company partner with other organizations to leverage the loyalty those other companies enjoy with their customers? If so, what is M&Ms doing? Overall, what do you think is most effective about the site? What is the least effective?
2. Many schools are trying to build loyalty programs that strengthen alumni ties. Assess and critique any loyalty program your school has (take a look at athletics first, as that's usually where they start). Then redesign it. Be explicit in describing how your program will create the four effects of a loyalty program.

14.6 Case Study: Quicker Car Rental

Frank had had enough. As a QuickStart member of Quicker Car Rental, he was used to being able to skip the line at the counter and go directly to his car. But this time, he had to wait in line for forty-five minutes to get a car at the Atlanta airport because his name wasn't on the board for QuickStart service.

After each rental, Quicker sends a survey to the renter. When Frank got his, he blasted the company. He noted that while his wait was forty-five minutes, he saw two more people go up to the board, not see their names, and get in the line that had grown significantly. Those two, he was sure, had to wait for an hour or more.

On the Net Promoter Score question, he answered with a 1, which means would not refer a friend under any cirumstances. In the comments, he detailed his reasoning. And he put his email in for possible follow-up.

The manager of the Atlanta airport location received a copy of the survey and sent an email to Frank that said, "I'm sorry you had this experience. We always post the QuickStart members' names so they can go directly to their car and save the hassle of waiting in the line. Let me know the next time you come to Atlanta and I'll make sure you are taken care of."

Frank switched to another car company the next time he went to Atlanta, in spite of the fact that he had been a loyal Quicker Car Rental customer for over ten years. But while reserving a car some months later, he realized that even though he had logged into the QuickStart portal to make his reservation, that didn't mean that he would be automatically placed on the QuickStart board. What probably happened was that he forgot to enter his QuickStart number when making the reservation. He wondered if he should give them another try. Nah. . . .

Case Study Questions

1. Why did Frank switch? Rewrite the email in such a way that Frank would stay.
2. Evaluate the situation and make some recommendations. (Hint: There are at least three service failures here.)
3. If Frank had fumed on Twitter while still in line, what should Quicker do? What could they really do?
4. The only benefit of being a QuickStart member is avoiding the line—there are no levels, no other rewards. If you were the Director for Customer Loyalty at Quicker Car Rental, how would you design a low-cost to you, high-value to the customer loyalty program?

Endnotes

1. Some of the studies include Girish Ramani & V. Kumar (2008), "Interaction Orientation and Firm Performance," *Journal of Marketing* 72(1), 27–41; Oguz Ali Acar and Stefani Punatoni (2016), "Customer Empowerment in the Digital Age," *Journal of Advertising Research* 56(1), 4–8; "New study reveals valuable benchmarking insights for marketing leaders," CMO Study: Valuable Benchmarking Insights for Leaders | Deloitte US.
2. Michelle King (2018), "Three Things You Need to Know about Marketing to Gen Z Women," *Forbes*, https://www.forbes.com/sites/michelleking/2018/07/10/a-new-report-reveals-three-things-you-need-to-know-about-marketing-to-gen-z-women/?sh=4a8ce79a6cc1.
3. Lauren Stewart (2016), "Five Ways to Approach Customer Mishaps and Come Out on Top," Smart Insights.
4. Tara Weiss (2021), "Amid Rough Waters, an Ecommerce Company Hooked Aspiring Anglers With Community and Content," *Adweek*, Ecommerce Company Hooks New Anglers With Community, Content (adweek.com).
5. Lizzie Lee (2019), "Are Friends and Family the New Power Influencers?," Mention Me, Are friends & family the new power influencers? (mention-me.com).
6. Emmy Liederman (2021), "Average People Now Run the Influencer Economy, and Brands Must Embrace User-Generated Content," *Adweek*, Are Average Joes Disrupting the Influencer Economy? (adweek.com).
7. Fred Reicheld and Thomas Teal (2001), *The Loyalty Effect: The Hidden Force Behind Growth, Profits and Lasting Value*, Boston: Harvard Business Press.
8. Tarun Kushwaha and Venkatesh Shanker (July 2013), "Are Multi-Channel Customers Really More Valuable? The Moderating Role of Product Characteristics," *Journal of Marketing 77*, 67–85.
9. Steven Van Yoder, "Cause-Related Marketing," http://www.streetdirectory.com/travel_guide/5529/marketing/cause_related_marketing.html.
10. John F. Tanner, Jr., "Putting the R Back into CRM," presented at CRM World, August 18, 2021.
11. Nazari, Narges, Azmawani Abd Rahman, Yuhanis BA Aziz, and Haslinda Hashim (2020) "The Effects of Customer Satisfaction on the Performance of Small and Medium-Sized Hotels" *Tourism and Hospitality Management 26(1)*, 69–96.
12. Gustavo Souki and Cid G. Filho (2008), "Perceived Quality, Satisfaction and Customer Loyalty: An Empirical Study in the Mobile Phones Sector in Brazil," *International Journal of Internet and Enterprise Management* 5(4), 298–314.
13. Fred Reichheld (December 2003), "The One Number You Need to Grow," *Harvard Business Review,* https://hbr.org/2003/12/the-one-number-you-need-to-grow/ar/1.
14. Kai Kristensen and Jacob Eskildsen (2008), "Is the NPS a Trustworthy Performance Measure?" *TQM Journal 26*(2), 202–14.
15. Lerzan Aksoy (2013), "How do you measure what you can't define? The current state of loyalty measurement and management," *Journal of Service Management 24*(4), 356–81, 793C.
16. Sophia Stoltze (2021), "Three Questions about AI Answered," https://blogs.one.int.sap/sapnews_en/2021/08/three-questions-about-ai-answered/.
17. Michael Levy Barton Weitz, and Dhruv Grewal (2019), *Retailing Management*, 10th ed., Burr Ridge, IL: McGraw-Hill.
18. Yuping Liu-Thompkins (2019), "Customer Loyalty Explained," Pub Science Series, presented Nov. 19, 2019.

CHAPTER 15

Price, the Only Revenue Generator

Many people will stand in line or even camp out for something free, even if it takes hours. Although the practice was cancelled during the COVID-19 pandemic, when a new Chick-fil-A opens, they typically offer the first one hundred customers a free meal every week for a year. So how do sellers make any money if they always offer goods and services on sale or for a special deal? Many sellers give customers something for free hoping they'll buy other products, but a careful balance is needed to make sure a profit is made. Are free products a good pricing strategy?

In previous chapters, we looked at the offering (products and services), communication (promotion), and place (the other marketing mix variables), all of which cost firms money. Price is the only marketing mix variable or part of the offering that generates revenue. Buyers often relate the price to value. They must feel they are getting value for the price paid. Pricing decisions are extremely important as organizations compete for "share of wallet," or customers' resources. So how do organizations decide how to price their goods and services?

Some of shoppers' favorite four-letter words include FREE, SALE, and BOGO (Buy One Get One Free).

Source: © Shutterstock, Inc.

15.1 The Pricing Framework and a Firm's Pricing Objectives

Learning Objectives

1. Understand the factors in the pricing framework.
2. Explain different pricing objectives organizations may select.

Prices can be easily changed and easily matched by competitors. Consequently, the product's price alone might not provide a company with a sustainable competitive advantage. Nonetheless, prices can attract consumers to different retailers/sellers and businesses to different suppliers.

Organizations must remember that the prices they charge should be consistent with their offerings, promotions, and distribution strategies. In other words, it wouldn't make sense for an organization to promote a high-end, prestige product, make it available in only a limited number of stores, and then sell it for an extremely low price. The price, product, promotion (communication), and placement (distribution) of a good or service should convey a consistent image. If you've ever watched episodes of *The Price Is Right*, which celebrated its fiftieth anniversary in 2021, you may wonder how people guess prices of the products. Watch the video clip below to see some of the price guessing on *The Price Is Right*.

Price is Right Contestants Get Close to Actual Price

Contestants guess price of prizes.

View in the online reader

The Pricing Framework

pricing objectives

What an organization wants to accomplish with its pricing.

Before pricing a product, an organization must determine its **pricing objectives**. In other words, what does the company want to accomplish with its pricing? Companies must also estimate demand for the product or service, determine the costs, and analyze all factors (e.g., competition, regulations, and economy) affecting price decisions. Then, to convey a consistent image, the organization should choose the most appropriate pricing strategy and determine policies and conditions regarding price adjustments. The basic steps in the pricing framework are shown in Figure 15.1.

FIGURE 15.1 The Pricing Framework

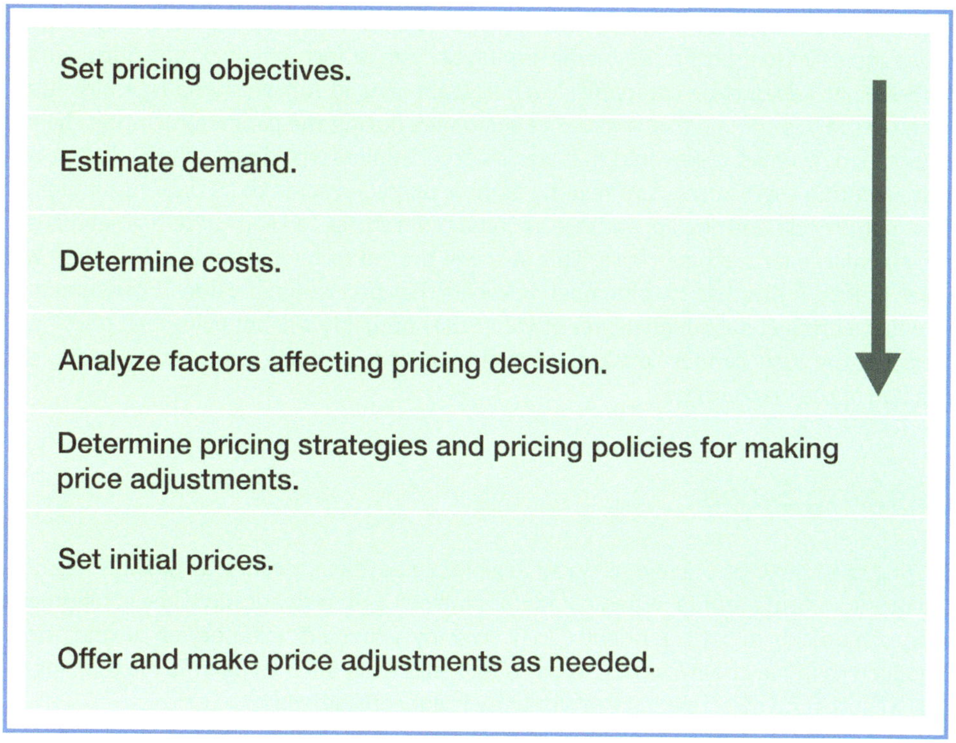

A Firm's Pricing Objectives

Different firms want to accomplish different things with their pricing strategies. For example, one firm may want to capture market share, another may be solely focused on a targeted rate of return (ROI), another may focus on maximizing its profits, and another may want to be perceived as having prestigious products. Other pricing objectives companies may set include profit-oriented objectives, sales-oriented objectives, and status quo objectives.

Earning a Targeted Return on Investment (ROI)

ROI, or return on investment, is the amount of profit an organization hopes to make given the amount of assets, or money, it has tied up in a product. ROI is a common pricing objective for many firms. Companies typically set a certain percentage, such as 10 percent, for ROI in a product's first year following its launch. For example, if a company has $100,000 invested in a product and is expecting a 10 percent ROI, it would want the product's profit to be $10,000.

Maximizing Profits

Many companies set their prices to increase their revenues as much as possible relative to their costs. However, large revenues do not necessarily translate into higher profits. To maximize its profits, a company must also focus on cutting costs or implementing programs to encourage customer loyalty.

In weak economic markets, many companies manage to cut costs and increase their profits, even though their sales/revenues are lower. How do they do this? Norfolk Southern reduced costs with more efficient operations and lower fuel and material costs. Although revenues were down, Norfolk Southern managed to increase profits during the COVID-19 pandemic.[1] Other companies such as Coca-Cola eliminated products and reduced personnel costs during COVID-19. Dell has also cut jobs to increase their profits. Reducing employee costs unfortunately occurs during many economic recessions. Meanwhile, companies such as Walmart and Amazon, who typically offer lower prices and deliver, continued to attract more customers during the pandemic. During the last economic recession, Walmart discovered that wealthier consumers who didn't usually shop at Walmart began frequenting their stores. As a result, Walmart upgraded some of its offerings and improved the checkout process and the appearance of some of its stores to keep these high-end customers happy and enlarge its customer base. This strategy proved to be profitable and helped Walmart maximize profits. A firm has to remember, however, that prices signal value. If consumers do not perceive that a product has a high degree of value, they probably will not pay a high price for it. Furthermore, cutting costs cannot be a long-term strategy if a company wants to maintain its image and position in the marketplace.

Maximizing Sales

Maximizing sales involves pricing products to generate as much revenue as possible, regardless of what it does to a firm's profits. When companies are struggling financially, they sometimes try to generate cash quickly to pay their debts. They do so by selling off inventory or cutting prices temporarily. Such cash may be necessary to pay short-term bills, such as payroll. Maximizing sales is typically a short-term objective since profitability is not considered.

Maximizing Market Share

Some organizations try to set their prices in a way that allows them to capture a larger share of the sales in their industries. Capturing more market share doesn't necessarily mean a firm will earn higher profits, though. Nonetheless, many companies believe capturing a maximum amount of market share is necessary for their survival. In other words, they believe if they remain a small competitor they will fail. Firms in the cellular phone industry are an example. The race to be the biggest cell phone provider has hurt companies like Motorola, the maker of the world's first cell phone. While Motorola's market share in the United States went up the first half of 2021, their market share is typically relatively low, especially compared to Samsung and Apple.

Maintaining the Status Quo

status quo

An objective a firm sets to maintain its current prices and/or its competitors' prices.

Sometimes a firm's objective may be to maintain the **status quo** or simply meet, or equal, its competitors' prices or keep its current prices. Airline companies are a good example. Have you ever noticed that when one airline raises or lowers its prices, the others all do the same? If consumers don't accept an airline's increased prices (and extra fees) such as the charge for checking in with a representative at the airport rather than checking in online, other airlines may decide not to implement the extra charge and the airline charging the fee may drop it. Similarly, when one airline eliminated change fees during the COVID-19 pandemic, other carriers also eliminated change fees. Companies, of course, monitor their competitors' prices closely when they adopt a status quo pricing objective.

Key Takeaway

- Price is the only marketing variable that generates money for a company. All the other variables (product, communication, distribution) cost organizations money. A product's price is the easiest marketing variable to change and also the easiest to copy. Before pricing a product, an organization must determine its pricing objective(s). A company can choose from pricing objectives such as maximizing profits, maximizing sales, capturing market share, achieving a target return on investment (ROI) from a product, and maintaining the status quo in terms of the price of a product relative to competing products.

Review Questions

1. What are the steps in the pricing framework?
2. In addition to profit-oriented objectives, what other types of pricing objectives do firms utilize?
3. How can companies cut costs to increase profits during economic recessions?

15.2 Factors That Affect Pricing Decisions

Learning Objectives

1. Understand the factors that affect a firm's pricing decisions.
2. Understand why companies must conduct research before setting prices in international markets.
3. Learn how to calculate the breakeven point.

Having a pricing objective isn't enough. A firm also has to look at a myriad of other factors before setting its prices. Those factors include the customers whose needs the offering is designed to meet; demand; the external environment—such as the competition, the economy, and government regulations; product aspects such as cost, nature of offering, and stage of life cycle; transportation and storage charges; and promotion expenses. If a company plans to sell its products or services in international markets, research on the factors for each market must be analyzed before setting prices. Organizations must understand buyers, competitors, the economic conditions, and political regulations in other markets before they can compete successfully. Next we look at each of the factors and what they entail.

Customers

How will buyers respond? Three important factors include whether the buyers perceive the product offer's value, the number of buyers (size of the market), and their sensitivity to price changes. Will customers buy the product, given its price, or will they believe the value is not equal to the cost and choose an alternative or decide they can do without the product or service? Equally important is how much buyers are willing to pay for the offering. Figuring out how consumers may respond to prices involves judgment as well as research.

price elasticity

The amount of sensitivity to price changes, which affects the demand for a product.

Price elasticity, or people's sensitivity to price changes, affects the demand for products. Think about a pair of sweatpants with an elastic waist. You can stretch an elastic waistband like the one in sweatpants, but it's much more difficult to stretch the waistband of a pair of dress slacks. Elasticity refers to the amount of stretch or change. For example, the waistband of sweatpants may stretch if you pull on it. Similarly, the demand for a product may change if the price changes. Imagine the price of a twelve-pack of sodas increasing to $6.50 a pack. People are likely to buy a lot more soda when on sale at buy two, get one free (or $13.00 for three, 12-packs) than they are at $6.50 per twelve-pack. Conversely, the waistband on a pair of dress slacks remains the same (doesn't change) whether you pull on it or not. Likewise, demand for some products won't change even if the price changes. The formula for calculating the price elasticity of demand is as follows.

$$\text{Price elasticity} = \text{percentage change in quantity demanded} \div \text{percentage change in price}$$

price elastic

Consumers are very sensitive to price changes and buy more at low prices and less at high prices.

price inelastic

Buyers are not sensitive to price changes and demand is relatively unchanged.

When consumers are very sensitive to the price change of a product—that is, they buy more of it at low prices and less of it at high prices—the demand for it is **price elastic**. Durable goods such as TVs, stereos, and freezers are more price elastic than necessities. People are generally more likely to buy them when their prices drop and less likely to buy them when their prices rise. By contrast, when the demand for a product stays relatively the same and buyers are not sensitive to changes in its price, the demand is **price inelastic**. Demand for essential products such as many basic food and first-aid products is not as affected by price changes as demand for many nonessential goods.

The number of competing products and substitutes available affects the elasticity of demand. Whether a person considers a product a necessity or a luxury and the percentage of a person's budget allocated to different products and services also affect price elasticity. Some products, such as cigarettes, tend to be relatively price inelastic since most smokers keep purchasing them regardless of price increases and the fact that other people see cigarettes as unnecessary. Service provider, such as utility companies in markets in which they have a monopoly (only one provider), face more inelastic demand since no substitutes are available.

Competitors

How competitors price and sell their products will have a tremendous effect on a firm's pricing decisions. If you want to buy a certain pair of shoes, but the price is 30 percent less at one store than another, what would you do? Because companies want to establish and maintain loyal customers, they will often match their competitors' prices. Some retailers, such as Home Depot, will give you an extra discount if you find the same product for less somewhere else. Similarly, if one company offers you free shipping, you might discover other companies will, too. With so many products sold online, consumers can compare the prices of many merchants before making a purchase decision.

The availability of substitute products affects a company's pricing decisions as well. If you can find a similar pair of shoes selling for 50 percent less at a third store, would you buy them? There's a good chance you might. Recall from the five forces model discussed in Chapter 2 that merchants must look at substitutes and potential entrants as well as direct competitors.

The Economy and Government Laws and Regulations

The economy also has a tremendous effect on pricing decisions. In Chapter 2 we noted that factors in the economic environment include interest rates and unemployment levels. When the economy is weak and many people are unemployed, companies often lower their prices. During times of market disruptions or unusual situations, such as the COVID-19 pandemic, supply and labor shortages as well as shipping delays can affect prices as well as demand. In international markets, currency exchange rates also affect pricing decisions.

Federal and state regulations affect pricing decisions. Regulations are designed to protect consumers, promote competition, and encourage ethical and fair behavior by businesses. For example, the **Robinson-Patman Act** limits a seller's ability to charge different customers different prices for the same products. The intent of the act is to protect small businesses from larger businesses that try to extract special discounts and deals for themselves in order to eliminate their competitors. However, cost differences, market conditions, and competitive pricing by other suppliers can justify price differences in some situations. In other words, the practice isn't illegal under all circumstances. You have probably noticed that restaurants offer senior citizens and children discounted menus. The movies also charge different people different prices based on their ages and charge different amounts based on the time of day, with matinees usually less expensive than evening shows. These price differences are legal as long as they are offered to everyone in the age group or everyone attending the matinee. We will discuss more about price differences later in the chapter.

Robinson-Patman Act

A U.S. act that limits price discrimination (charging different customers different prices for the same product and quantities of it purchased).

Price fixing, which occurs when firms get together and agree to charge the same prices, is illegal. Usually, price fixing involves setting high prices so consumers must pay a high price regardless of where they purchase a good or service. Video game systems, LCD (liquid crystal display) manufacturers, auction houses, and airlines are examples of offerings where price fixing existed in the past. When a company is charged with price fixing, it is usually ordered to take some type of action to reach a settlement with buyers.

price fixing

When firms get together and agree to charge the same prices.

Price fixing isn't uncommon. Nintendo and its distributors in the European Union were charged with price fixing and increasing the prices of hardware and software. Sharp, LG, and Chunghwa collaborated and fixed the prices of the LCDs used in computers, cell phones, and other electronics. Virgin Atlantic Airways and British Airways were also involved in price fixing for their flights. Sotheby's and Christie's, two large auction houses, used price fixing to set their commissions.

One of the most famous price-fixing schemes in history involved Robert Crandall, the CEO of American Airlines in the early 1990s. Crandall called Howard Putnam, the CEO of (former) Braniff Airlines, since the two airlines were fierce competitors in the Dallas market. Unfortunately for Crandall, Putnam taped the conversation and turned it over to the U.S. Department of Justice. Their conversation went like this:

Crandall: "I think it's dumb—to pound—each other and neither one of us making a [expletive] dime."

Putnam: "Well . . ."

Crandall: "I have a suggestion for you. Raise your—fares twenty percent. I'll raise mine the next morning."

Putnam: "Robert, we—"

Crandall: "You'll make more money and I will, too."

Putnam: "We can't talk about pricing."

Crandall: "Oh, [expletive] Howard. We can talk about any [expletive] thing we want to talk about."[2]

unfair trade laws

State laws requiring sellers to keep a minimum price level for similar products.

predatory pricing

When companies act in a predatory manner by setting low prices to drive competitors out of business.

bait and switch

A pricing tactic a seller uses to lure in, or "bait," customers with a low-priced product. The seller then attempts to persuade the buyer to purchase higher-priced products, perhaps by telling him or her that the low-priced product is no longer available.

By requiring sellers to keep a minimum price level for similar products, **unfair trade laws** protect smaller businesses. Unfair trade laws are state laws preventing large businesses from selling products below cost (as loss leaders) to attract customers to the store. When companies act in a predatory manner by setting low prices to drive competitors out of business, it is a **predatory pricing** strategy.

Similarly, bait-and-switch pricing is illegal in many states. **Bait and switch**, or bait advertising, occurs when a business tries to "bait," or lure in, customers with an incredibly low-priced product. Once customers take the bait, sales personnel attempt to sell them more expensive products. Sometimes the customers are told the cheaper product is no longer available.

You perhaps have seen bait-and-switch pricing tactics used to sell different electronic products or small household appliances. While bait-and-switch pricing is illegal in many states, stores can add disclaimers to their ads stating that there are no rain checks or that limited quantities are available to justify trying to get you to buy a different product. However, car dealers must provide the vehicle identification number (VIN) for extremely low-priced vehicles. Advertisers must offer at least a limited quantity of the advertised product, even if it sells out quickly.

Product Costs

The costs of the product—its inputs and materials—including the amount spent on product development, testing, and packaging required have to be taken into account when a pricing decision is made. So do the costs related to promotion and distribution. For example, when a new offering is launched, its promotion costs can be very high because people need to be made aware that it exists. Thus, the offering's stage in the product life cycle can affect its price. Keep in mind that a product may be in a different stage of its life cycle in other markets. For example, while smart phones are widely adopted (mature stage) in many advanced economies, they are still in the growth stage in many emerging markets. Similarly, if a company has to open brick-and-mortar storefronts to distribute and sell the offering, this too will have to be built into the price the firm must charge for it.

The COVID-19 pandemic led to increased labor, materials, ingredients, and shipping costs, which in turn continued to impact the costs that manufacturers and ultimately consumers pay for products. For example, the rising costs of steel that companies such as Campbell Soup Co. use for canned soup affects the price consumers pay. Lumber prices rose rapidly putting a strain on builders and consumers wanting to remodel. Logistical problems and higher shipping costs have affected most companies and the problem is not likely to improve any time soon.[3]

The point at which total costs equal total revenue is known as the **breakeven point (BEP)**. For a company to be profitable, a company's revenue must be greater than its total costs. If total costs exceed total revenue, the company suffers a loss.

Total costs include both fixed costs and variable costs. **Fixed costs**, or overhead expenses, are costs that a company must pay regardless of its level of production or level of sales. A company's fixed costs include items such as rent, leasing fees for equipment, contracted advertising costs, and insurance. As a student, you may also incur fixed costs, such as the rent you pay for an apartment. You must pay your rent whether you stay there for the weekend or not. **Variable costs** are costs that change with a company's level of production and sales. Raw materials, labor, and commissions on units sold are examples of variable costs. You, too, have variable costs, such as the cost of gasoline for your car or your utility bills, which vary depending on how much you use.

Consider a company that publishes many unique personalized children's story books, where each story features a child's name as well as the names of their friends. Books may be ordered through different retail gift stores, children's clothing stores, and toy stores as well as select retail book stores. The publisher's (manufacturer's) selling price (MSP) is fifteen dollars, which is what retailers pay to order the personalized (custom) books. The retailers then sell the books to consumers for an additional charge. The company has the following charges:

Copyright and distribution charges for books	$150,000
Cover design and illustrations	$10,000
Advertising and promotion costs	$40,000
Printing of books	$5 per unit
Personalization of each book	$1 per unit
Royalties	$1 per unit

To determine the breakeven point, you must first calculate the fixed and variable costs. To make sure all costs are included, you may want to highlight the fixed costs in one color (e.g., green) and the variable costs in another color (e.g., blue). Then, using the formulas below, calculate how many units the manufacturer must sell to break even.

The formula for BEP is as follows:

$$\text{BEP} = \text{total fixed costs (FC)} \div \text{contribution per unit (CU)}$$

$$\text{contribution per unit} = \text{MSP} - \text{variable costs (VC)}$$

$$\text{BEP} = \$200{,}000 \div (\$15 - \$7) = \$200{,}000 \div \$8 = 25{,}000 \text{ units to break even}$$

To determine the breakeven point in dollars, you simply multiply the number of units to break even by the MSP. In this case, the BEP in dollars would be 25,000 units times $15, or $375,000.

breakeven point (BEP)
The amount (in units or dollars) where total revenue equals total costs.

total costs
Fixed costs plus variable costs.

fixed costs
Overhead or costs that remain the same regardless of the level of production or the level of sales.

variable costs
Costs that change with the level of production or service delivery.

Brandon Speweik—GFT

Source: Used with permission, Brandon Speweik

Brandon Speweik is the Head of Industry Sales and Strategy at GFT and graduated with a Bachelor of Science in Marketing from Clemson University. Through his work navigating business leaders through the emerging technology landscape and enhancing their understanding of how emerging technology impacts their business, he's found that Emotional Intelligence is a critical attribute for employees and their interaction with clients. "Specifically, the ability to practice empathy while coordinating different skill sets, motivations, and personalities becomes essential to orchestrate strategies that meet the needs of both the clients and your organization."

Key Takeaway

- In addition to setting a pricing objective, a firm has to look at a number of factors before setting its prices. These factors include the customers whose needs it is designed to meet; demand; the external environment—such as the competition, the economy, and government regulations; the offering's cost; and other aspects of the marketing mix, such as the nature of the offering, the stage of its product life cycle, and its promotion and distribution. In international markets, firms must look at environmental factors and customers' buying behavior in each market. For a company to be profitable, revenues must exceed total costs.

Review Questions

1. What factors do organizations consider when making price decisions?
2. How do a company's competitors affect the pricing decisions the firm will make?
3. What is the difference between fixed costs and variable costs?
4. How were prices of offerings which face material shortages (such as lumber) affected by the COVID-19 pandemic?

15.3 Pricing Strategies

Learning Objectives

1. Understand introductory pricing strategies.
2. Understand the different pricing approaches that businesses use.

Once a firm has established its pricing objectives and analyzed the factors that affect how it should price a product, the company must determine the pricing strategy (or strategies) that will help it achieve those objectives. As previously discussed, firms use different pricing strategies for their offerings. Many times, the strategy depends on the stage of life cycle the offerings are in currently. Products may be in different stages of their life cycle in various international markets. Next, we'll examine three strategies businesses often consider when a product is first introduced and then look at several different pricing approaches that companies utilize during the product life cycle.

Introductory Pricing Strategies

Think of products that have been introduced in the last decade and how products were priced when they first entered the market. Remember when the iPhone was first introduced, its price was almost $700. The price dropped considerably when a new model was introduced. When each new model is introduced; however, it will be priced high initially and the price of the previous model will usually be reduced. The same is true for LCD televisions, digital cameras, other new smartphones, and many high-tech products. As mentioned in Chapter 7, a skimming price strategy is when a company sets a high initial price for a product. The idea is to go after consumers who are willing to pay a high price (top of the market) and buy products early. This way, a company recoups its investment in the product faster. Over time, the price of the product goes down as competitors enter the market and more consumers are willing to purchase the offering.

The easy way to remember a skimming approach is to think of the turkey gravy at Thanksgiving. When the gravy is chilled, the fat rises to the top and is often "skimmed" off before serving. Price skimming is a pricing approach designed to skim that top part of the gravy, or the top of the market.

In contrast to a skimming approach, a **penetration pricing strategy** is one in which a low initial price is set. Often, many competitive products are already in the market. The goal is to get as much of the market as possible to try the product. Penetration pricing is used on many new food products, health and beauty supplies, and paper products sold in grocery stores and mass merchandise stores such as Walmart and Target.

penetration pricing strategy

A strategy in which an organization offers a low initial price on a product so that it captures as much market share as possible.

Another approach companies use when they introduce a new product is **everyday low prices**. That is, the price initially set is the price the seller expects to charge throughout the product's life cycle. Companies like Walmart and Lowe's use everyday low pricing. Lowe's emphasizes their everyday low pricing strategy with the letters in their name plus the letter "t" (Lowest).

everyday low pricing

The practice of charging a low initial price for an offering and maintaining that price throughout the offering's product life cycle.

Discount stores such as Dollar General and Family Dollar provide products at lower prices and often serve smaller communities that do not have a Walmart or large retailer. Other discount stores such as Dollar Tree and Five Below attract customers looking for low prices. While these stores typically offer consistently low prices, rising shipping and product costs are creating challenges and therefore, changes in pricing. For example, at Dollar Tree where every item has always been priced at $1.00, higher prices ($1.25 and $1.50) on different items have been tested in some store formats

(Combo and Dollar Tree Plus) and markets. New products at even higher price points ($3.00 and $5.00) are anticipated.[4]

Dollar Tree Raises Prices on Many Items

Dollar Tree increases prices on some items to $1.25 and $1.50.

View in the online reader

Pricing Approaches

cost-plus pricing

A pricing strategy where a certain amount of profit is added to the total cost of a product to determine its price.

markup

A certain amount of money added to the cost of a product to set the final price.

markdown

The amount (in dollars or percent) taken off the price.

odd-even pricing

A strategy in which a company prices products a few cents below the next dollar amount or a few dollars (for high-cost products such as automobiles) below the next hundred- or thousand-dollar value.

Companies can choose many ways to set their prices. We'll examine some common methods you often see. Many stores use **cost-plus pricing**, in which they take the cost of the product and then add a profit to determine a price. Cost-plus pricing is very common. The strategy helps ensure that a company's products' costs are covered and the firm earns a certain amount of profit. When companies add a **markup**, or an amount added to the cost of a product, they are using a form of cost-plus pricing. When products go on sale, companies markdown the prices, but they usually still make a profit. Potential **markdowns** or price reductions should be considered when deciding on a starting price.

Many pricing approaches have a psychological appeal. **Odd-even pricing** occurs when a company prices a product a few cents or a few dollars below the next dollar amount. For example, instead of being priced ten dollars, a product will be priced at $9.99. Likewise, a $25,000 automobile might be priced at $24,998, although the product will cost more once taxes and other fees are added. One of the reasons for this type of psychological pricing is that people typically read the left digit first and may perceive price as being lower. See the following photo for an example of odd-even pricing.

The charcoal shown in the photo is priced at $5.99 a bag, which is an example of odd-even pricing, or pricing a product slightly below the next dollar amount.

Source: Photo courtesy of Stubb's Legendary Kitchen

Prestige pricing occurs when a higher price is utilized to give an offering a high-quality image. Some stores have a quality image, and people perceive that perhaps the products from those stores are of higher quality. Many times, two different stores carry the same product, but one store prices it higher because of the store's perceived higher image.

prestige pricing

The practice of pricing a product higher to signal that it is of high quality.

Neckties are often priced using a strategy known as **price lining**, or *price levels*. In other words, there may be only a few price levels ($25, $50, and $75) for the ties, but a large assortment of ties at each level. Movies, video games, and music often use price lining. You may see a lot of electronic games priced for sale at either $39.99, $49.99, and perhaps $59.99, but you won't see a lot of different price levels.

price lining

Pricing a group of similar products (e.g., neckties) at a few different price levels (e.g., $25, $50, and $75).

Remember when you were in elementary school and many students bought teachers gifts before the holidays or on the last day of school. Typically, parents set an amount such as five dollars or ten dollars for a teacher's gift. Knowing that people have certain maximum levels that they are willing to pay for gifts, some companies use **demand backward pricing**. They start with the price demanded by consumers (what they want to pay) and create offerings at that price. If you shop before the holidays, you might see a table of different products being sold for five dollars (mugs, picture frames, ornaments) and another table of products being sold for ten dollars (mugs with chocolate, decorative trays, and so forth). Similarly, people have certain prices they are willing to pay for wedding gifts—say, $25, $50, $75, or $100—so stores set up displays of gifts sold at these different price levels. IKEA also sets a price for a product—which is what the company believes consumers want to pay for it—and then, working backward from the price, designs the product.

demand backward pricing

Pricing a product based on what customers are willing to pay for it and then creating the offering based on that price.

Leader pricing involves pricing one or more items low to get people into a store. The products with low prices are often featured on the front page of store ads and "lead" the promotion. For example, prior to Thanksgiving, grocery stores advertise turkeys and cranberry sauce at very low prices. The goal is to get shoppers to buy many more items in addition to the low-priced items. Leader or low prices are legal; however, as you learned earlier, **loss leaders**, or items priced below cost in an effort to get people into stores, are illegal in many states.

leader pricing

A strategy of offering low prices on one or more items as "lead" items in advertisements to attract customers.

loss leaders

Products priced below cost; this is illegal in some states.

Sealed bid pricing is the process of offering to buy or sell products at prices designated in sealed bids. Companies must submit their bids by a certain time. The bids are later reviewed all at once, and the most desirable one is chosen. Sealed bids can occur on either the supplier or the buyer side. Via sealed bids, oil companies bid on tracts of land for potential drilling purposes, and the highest bidder is awarded the right to drill on the land. Similarly, consumers sometimes bid on lots to build houses. The highest bidder gets the lot. On the supplier side, contractors often bid on different jobs and the lowest bidder is awarded the job. The government often makes purchases based on sealed bids. Projects funded by stimulus money allocated by the federal government were awarded based on sealed bids.

sealed bid pricing

The process of offering to buy or sell products at prices designated in sealed bids.

Bids are also being used online. **Online auction** sites such as eBay give customers the chance to bid and negotiate prices with sellers until an acceptable price is agreed upon. When a buyer lists what they want to buy, sellers may submit bids. This process is known as a **forward auction**. If the buyer not only lists what they want to buy but also states how much they are willing to pay, a reverse auction occurs. The reverse auction is finished when at least one firm is willing to accept the buyer's price.

When people think of auctions, they may think of the words, "Going, going, gone." Online auctions use a similar bidding process.

Source: © Shutterstock, Inc.

online auction

Bidding and negotiating prices online with buyers and sellers on sites such as eBay.com until an acceptable price is agreed upon.

forward auction

The process that occurs when a buyer lists what they want to buy and sellers may submit bids.

Going-rate pricing occurs when buyers pay the same price regardless of where they buy the product or from whom. Going-rate pricing is often used on commodity products such as wheat, gold, or silver. People perceive the individual products in markets such as these to be largely the same. Consequently, there's a "going" price for the product that all sellers receive.

going-rate pricing

Pricing whereby purchasers pay the same price for a product regardless of where they buy it or from whom.

Price bundling occurs when different offerings are sold together at a price that's typically lower than the total price a customer would pay by buying each offering separately. Combo meals and value meals sold at restaurants are an example. Companies such as McDonald's have promoted value meals for a long time in many different markets. See the following video clips for promotions of value meals in the United States (when first introduced) and "I'm Loving It" promotions in Greece (quarter pounder) and Japan (Sponge Bob, which remains popular). Other products such as shampoo and conditioner are sometimes bundled together. Automobile companies bundle product options. For example, power locks and windows are often sold together, regardless of whether customers want only one or the other. The idea behind bundling is to increase an organization's revenues.

The pandemic led to some creative bundling options. For example, a few movie theaters tried bundling tickets with concessions. For $25 on weekends and $20 during the week, a movie theater with ten screens offered unlimited concessions with the movie ticket. When fewer customers than anticipated came to the movies, a new plan (separate prices for ticket and all-inclusive-bundled concessions) was implemented. The number of moviegoers decreased dramatically when they reopened after the pandemic. Theater owners are still trying to figure out the best pricing model to get people in the theater and to buy concessions.[5]

price bundling

A strategy of selling different products or services together, typically at a lower price than if each product or service is sold separately.

Captive pricing is a strategy firms use when consumers must buy a given product because they are at a certain event or location or they need a particular product because no substitutes will work. Concessions at a sporting event or a movie provide examples of how captive pricing is used. Maybe you didn't pay much to attend the game, but the snacks and drinks were extremely expensive. Similarly, if you buy a razor and must purchase specific razor blades for it, you have experienced captive pricing. The blades are often more expensive than the razor because customers do not have the option of choosing blades from another manufacturer.

Pricing products consumers use together (such as blades and razors) with different profit margins is also part of **product mix pricing**. Recall from Chapter 6 that a product mix includes all the products a company offers. If you want to buy an automobile, the base price might seem reasonable, but the options such as floor mats might earn the seller a much higher profit margin. While consumers can buy floor mats at stores like Walmart for $30, many people may pay around $300 to get the floor mats that go with the car from the dealer.

Most people have cell phones. Are you aware of how many minutes you spend texting and what it costs if you don't have unlimited data and go over the limits of your phone plan? Maybe not, if your plan involves two-part pricing. **Two-part pricing** means there are two different charges customers pay. In the case of a cell phone, a customer might pay a charge for one service such as a 12 gigabyte (GB) of data, and then pay a separate charge for each gigabyte over 12. Get out your cell phone and look at how much data you have used. Many people are shocked at how much data they have used or the number of messages they have sent in the last month.

Have you ever seen an ad for a special item only to find out it is much more expensive than what you recalled seeing in the ad? A company might advertise a price such as $25, but when you read the fine print, the price is really five payments of $25 for a total cost of $125. **Payment pricing**, or allowing customers to pay for products in installments, is a strategy that helps customers break up their payments into smaller amounts, which can make them more inclined to buy higher-priced products.

Promotional pricing is a short-term tactic designed to get people into a store or to purchase more of a product. Examples of promotional pricing include back-to-school sales, rebates, extended warranties, and going-out-of-business sales. Rebates are a great strategy for companies because consumers think they're getting a great deal. But as you learned in Chapter 11 Section 8, many consumers forget to request the rebate. Extended warranties have become popular for all types of products, including automobiles, appliances, electronics, and even athletic shoes. If you buy a vacuum cleaner for $35, and it has a one-year warranty from the manufacturer, does it really make sense to spend an additional $15 to get another year's warranty? However, when it comes to automobiles, repairs can be expensive, so an extended warranty often pays for itself following one repair. Buyers must look at the costs and benefits and determine if the extended warranty provides value.

We discussed **price discrimination**, or charging different customers different prices for the same product, earlier in the chapter. In some situations, price discrimination is legal. As we explained, you have probably noticed that certain customer groups (students, children, and senior citizens, for example) are sometimes offered discounts at restaurants and events. However, the discounts must be offered to all senior citizens or all children within a certain age range, not just a few. Price discrimination is used to get more people to use a product or service. Similarly, a company might lower its prices in order to get more customers to buy an offering when business is slow. Matinees are often cheaper than movies at night; bowling might be less expensive during non-league times, and so forth.

McDonald's Value Pack

Look at the cost and the amount of food in the original value meal.

View in the online reader

captive pricing

A strategy firms use to price products when they know customers must buy specific replacement parts, such as razor blades, because there are no alternatives.

product mix pricing

Deciding how to price a firm's products and services that go together, such as power options (locks, windows) on a car.

two-part pricing

A pricing strategy in which providers have two different charges for a product, such as the base monthly rate for cell phone coverage and additional charges for extra minutes or texting.

payment pricing

A pricing strategy in which customers are allowed to break down product payments into smaller amounts they pay incrementally.

promotional pricing

A short-term tactic to get people to purchase a product or more of it.

price discrimination

The process of charging different customers different prices for the same product and quantities of it purchased.

Price Adjustments

price adjustment

A change to the listed price of a product.

quantity discounts

Discounts buyers get for making large purchases.

FOB (free on board) origin

A pricing arrangement that designates that a product's title changes at its origin (the place it's purchased), and the buyer pays the shipping charges.

FOB (free on board) destination

A pricing arrangement that designates that a product's title changes at its destination (the place to which it's transported), and the seller pays the shipping charges.

uniform-delivered pricing

A pricing strategy in which buyers pays the same shipping charges regardless of their locations.

trade allowances

Discounts an organization gives its channel partners for performing different functions.

reciprocal agreements

Agreements whereby merchants agree to promote one another's offerings to customers.

bounce back

A discount card or coupon purchasers can use on their next shopping visits during set dates.

Organizations must also decide what their policies are when it comes to making **price adjustments**, or changing the listed prices of their products. Some common price adjustments include **quantity discounts**, which involves giving customers discounts for larger purchases. Discounts for paying with cash for large purchases and seasonal discounts to get rid of inventory and holiday items are other examples of price adjustments.

A company's price adjustment policies also need to outline the firm's shipping charges. Many online merchants offer free shipping on certain products, orders over a certain amount, or purchases made in a given time frame. *FOB (free on board) origin* and *FOB delivered* are two common pricing adjustments businesses use to show when the title to a product changes along with who pays the shipping charges. **FOB (free on board) origin** means the title changes at the origin—that is, when the product is purchased—and the buyer pays the shipping charges. **FOB (free on board) destination** means the title changes at the destination—that is, after the product is transported—and the seller pays the shipping charges.

Uniform-delivered pricing, also called postage-stamp pricing, means buyers pay the same shipping charges regardless of where they are located. If you mail a letter across town, the postage is the same as when you mail a letter to a different state. Postage stamp pricing as well as electronic communications and bill paying, and other shipping such as UPS and Fed Ex, have affected the profitability of the United States Postal Service

Recall that we discussed **trade allowances** in Chapter 11. For example, a manufacturer might give a retail store an advertising allowance to advertise the manufacturer's products in local promotions. Similarly, a manufacturer might offer a store a discount to restock the manufacturer's products on store shelves rather than having its own representatives restock the items.

Reciprocal agreements are agreements in which merchants agree to promote each other to customers. Reciprocal agreements are often very popular with small businesses as well as some larger companies. Customers who patronize a particular retailer might get a discount card to use at a certain restaurant, and customers who go to a restaurant might get a discount card to use at a specific retailer. For example, when customers make a purchase at a local hardware store, they get a discount coupon good to use at a nearby pet store. When customers are at the pet store, they get a discount coupon to use at the hardware store. Previously, as part of a back-to-school promotion, Old Navy and Great Clips implemented similar reciprocal agreements.

A promotion that's popular during weak economic times is called a bounce back. A **bounce back** is a promotion in which a seller gives customers discount cards or coupons after purchasing. Consumers can then use the cards and coupons on their next shopping visits. The idea is to get the customers to return to the store or online outlets later and purchase additional items. Some stores set minimum amounts that consumers have to spend and an expiration date to use the bounce back card/coupon.

Key Takeaway

- Both external and internal factors affect pricing decisions. Companies use many different pricing strategies and price adjustments. However, the price must generate enough revenues to cover costs in order for the product to be profitable. Cost-plus pricing, odd-even pricing, prestige pricing, price bundling, sealed bid pricing, going-rate pricing, and captive pricing are just a few of the strategies used. Organizations must also decide what their policies are when it comes to making price adjustments, or changing the listed prices of their products. Some companies use price adjustments as a short-term tactic to increase sales.

Review Questions

1. Explain the difference between a penetration and a skimming pricing strategy.
2. Describe how both buyers and sellers use sealed bid pricing.
3. Identify an example of each of the following: odd-even pricing, prestige pricing, price bundling, and captive pricing.
4. What is the difference between FOB origin and FOB destination when paying for shipping charges?
5. Explain how trade allowances work.

15.4 Discussion Questions and Activities

Discussion Questions

1. What is the difference between leader pricing and a loss leader?
2. What pricing approaches do you see most often in drug stores?
3. Which pricing approaches do you feel work best long term?
4. When is price discrimination legal?
5. Which pricing strategies have you noticed when you shop?
6. What new products have you purchased in the last two years that were priced using either a penetration or a skimming approach?
7. Do you think prices higher than $1.00 will affect Dollar Tree's loyal customers?

Activities

1. To understand revenues and costs, get a two-liter bottle of soda, ten to twenty cups, and a bucket of ice. Fill each cup with ice and then fill it with soda. Assume each cup of soda sells for at least one dollar and you paid one dollar for the soda and one dollar for the cups. How much profit can you make?
2. Go to a fast food restaurant for lunch. Figure out how much the price of a bundled meal is versus buying the items separately. Then decide if you think many consumers add a soda or fries because they feel like they're getting a deal.

15.5 Case Study: Customers Pay More to Eat Out

Given shutdowns, social distancing, mask mandates, and increasing costs during the COVID-19 pandemic, restaurants have struggled to remain profitable. Not only have food costs risen, but cleaning supplies, personnel, disposable products/containers, and even menu decisions have contributed to lower profit margins. Consumers want to eat out, but often experience sticker shock when they go to restaurants regardless of whether it's fine dining, fast food, or a casual eatery. At times, restaurant owners have sacrificed profits to retain employees.

To counter higher costs, safety issues, and operating challenges, some restaurants added an extra fee to each customer's check while others increased menu prices for every item. Still others reduced the number of menu items, printed menus on single use paper, wrote menus on blackboards, or posted the menu on walls and windows. Carryout and delivery charges increased. While costs and prices went up, restaurant owners did not want their staff to be penalized with lower tips.

You have been asked by a popular, casual, local restaurant to provide input related to higher costs and other issues while trying to improve profitability, attract and retain customers, and provide an enjoyable dining experience.

Case Study Questions

1. What type of price increases do you think customers will accept more willingly? In other words, is it best to raise prices on every item, the most popular items, certain items, or simply add an extra fee to every ticket?
2. What are the best strategies for keeping costs as low as possible? Be specific and explain why strategies are recommended.
3. To counter higher costs, what could restaurants do to increase revenues (ticket price) per customer?
4. What low-cost strategies could be utilized to attract new customers and get customers to return frequently?

Endnotes

1. Norfolk Southern News (2021), "Norfolk Southern reports fourth-quarter and full-year 2020 results," http://www.nscorp.com/content/nscorp/en/news/norfolk-southern-reports-fourth-quarter-and-full-year-2020-resul.html, (January 27).
2. David S. Jackson, John S. Demott, and Allen Pusey (March 7, 1983), "Dirty Tricks in Dallas," *Time*, http://www.time.com/time/magazine/article/0,9171,953755,00.html.
3. Newman, Jesse (2021), "General Mills Says Costs Keep Rising," *Wall Street Journal* (September 23), B3.
4. Weingarten, Rachel (2021), "Dollar Tree is Raising Their Prices—Here's What We Know," https://parade.com/1272553/rachelweingarten/dollar-tree-raising-prices/, (October 3).
5. Simon, Ruth (2021), "Would Moviegoers Pay Up for Unlimited Snacks," *Wall Street Journal* (October 1–2), B1, B2.

CHAPTER 16

The Marketing Plan

The average tenure of a chief marketing officer (CMO) has decreased to about forty months, which is the shortest tenure of any officer in the corporate suite.[1] Why? Because marketing is one of those areas in a company in which performance is obvious. Marketing executives may be seen as "growth" partners," as they focus on growing the business with their strategies. If sales go up, the CMO can be lured away by a larger company or promoted. However, forecasts may be unrealistic and if sales go down the CMO may be fired. The short tenure makes it difficult for many strategies to gain traction, especially if a company is moving more direct-to-consumer.

Indeed, successful marketing experience can be a ticket to the top. At Disney's Hulu, Kelly Campbell became the new CEO after serving as CMO and may move to another executive role.[2] Michelle Peluso, the first-ever CMO at IBM, became the first Chief Customer Officer at CVS in 2021. In addition to the digital, marketing, and brand strategies, Ms. Peluso will also be in charge of "transforming the customer experience."[3]

Creating a great customer experience may be a focal point for an organization's marketing plan. Customer experience (CX) encompasses every touchpoint a consumer has with a brand, which can impact customer loyalty, retention, and word-of-mouth. Relationships and customer service are critical components of CX. To improve CX, companies must listen to customers and get their insights. The marketing plan and strategies may focus on CX and include specific metrics to see how well a company is doing.

Much as firms must set their customers' expectations, CMOs must set their organization's marketing expectations. Marketing plans also help them do that. A well-designed marketing plan should communicate realistic expectations to a firm's CEO and other stakeholders. If CX is a priority, it must be included in the marketing plan. Forecasting plays a role in determining those expectations. Another function of the **marketing plan** is to communicate to everyone in the organization who has what marketing-related responsibilities and how they should execute those responsibilities.

marketing plan

A document that is designed to communicate the marketing strategy for an offering. The purpose of the plan is to influence executives, suppliers, distributors, and other important stakeholders of the firm so they will invest money, time, and effort to ensure the plan is a success.

16.1 Marketing Planning Roles

Learning Objective

1. Identify the people responsible for creating marketing plans in organizations.

Who within an organization is responsible for creating its marketing plans? From our earlier discussion, you might think the responsibility lies with the organization's chief marketing officer (CMO). The reality is that a team of marketing specialists is likely to be involved. Sometimes multiple teams are involved. Many companies create marketing plans at the divisional level. For example, Rockwell International has so many different business areas that each does its own strategic planning. The division responsible for military avionics, for instance, creates its own marketing plans and strategies separately from the division that serves the telecommunications industry. Each division has its own CMO.

Some of the team members specialize in certain areas. For example, the copier company Xerox has a team that specializes in competitive analysis. The team includes an engineer who can take competitors' products apart to see how they were manufactured, as well as a systems analyst who tests them for their performance. Also on the team is a marketing analyst who examines the competition's financial and marketing performance.

Some marketing analyst positions are entry-level positions. You might be able to land one of these jobs straight out of college. Other positions are more senior and require experience, usually in sales or another area of marketing. Marketing analysts, who are constantly updating marketing information, are likely to be permanent members of the CMO's staff.

In some consumer-goods companies with many brands (such as P&G and SC Johnson), product—or brand—managers serve on their firm's marketing planning teams on an as-needed basis. These individuals are not permanent members of the team but participate only to the extent that their brands are involved. Many other members of the firm will also participate on marketing planning teams as needed. For example, a marketing researcher is likely to be part of such a team when it needs data for the planning process.

Key Takeaway

- The CMO of a business unit is likely to be responsible for the final creation and approval of its marketing plan. However, the CMO is generally assisted by marketing professionals and other staff members, who often work on marketing planning teams as needed. Marketing analysts, however, are permanent members of the CMO's staff.

Review Questions

1. Who is involved in the creation of a marketing plan?
2. In addition to marketing analysts, what other members of an organization help create marketing plans?

16.2 Functions of the Marketing Plan

Learning Objectives

1. Understand the functions of a marketing plan.
2. Write a marketing plan.

In Chapter 1, we introduced the marketing plan and its components. Recall that a marketing plan should do the following:

A. Identify customers' needs and wants.

B. Evaluate whether the organization can meet those needs and deliver value in some way that allows for profitable exchanges with customers to occur.

C. Develop a mission statement, objectives, value proposition, strategy, and organization centered on those needs.

1. Create offerings that are the result of meticulous market research.
2. Form operations and supply chains that advance the successful delivery of those offerings.

D. Pursue advertising, promotional, and public relations campaigns that lead to continued successful exchanges between the company and its customers.

E. Engage in meaningful communications with customers on a regular basis.

The Marketing Plan: An Outline

The actual marketing plan you create will be written primarily for executives, who will use the forecasts in your plan to make budgeting decisions. These people will make budgeting decisions not only for your marketing activities but also for the firm's manufacturing, ordering, and production departments, and other functions based on your plan.

In addition to executives, many other people will use the plan. Your firm's sales force will use the marketing plan to determine its sales strategies and how many salespeople are needed. The entire marketing staff will rely on the plan to determine the direction and nature of their activities. The advertising agency you hire to create your promotional campaigns will use the plan to guide its creative team. "The Marketing Plan: An Outline" shows a complete outline of a marketing plan (you may also want to go to More Business for an example). Next, we will discuss the elements in detail so you will know how to prepare a marketing plan.

The Marketing Plan: An Outline

I. Executive Summary

II. The Business Challenge

  a. A brief description of the offering, the mission, objectives, and goals should be included the plan. This section serves as an introduction.

III. The Market

  a. Customers: Who are they, and what do they need?
  b. Company analysis: Your firm's strengths and weaknesses relative to this market and the offering.
  c. Collaborators: Your collaborators could include suppliers and/or distributors or retailers.
  d. Competitors: Who are they, and what are they doing?
  e. Business climate: The business climate includes opportunities and threats created by environmental forces, such as government regulations and legislation, the economy, and social, cultural, and technological forces.

IV. The Value Proposition and Strategy

  a. After understanding the customers and who the target market(s) include, a value proposition should be developed. It may be the same or different for different target markets as noted in Chapter 2.
  b. The strategy: What recommendations and actions are necessary to achieve the goals stated? Review pros and cons of feasible alternatives considered and discarded. Why did you choose the strategy you did?
  c. The offering: Provide details on the features and benefits of the offering as well as its proving options.
  d. The communication plan: How will the offering be launched? What will the ongoing communication strategies be? What media will be used? What is the message, the timing? Why did you decide on specific media, messages, and timing? This section is

likely to be fairly broad and will require collaboration with communication partners such as your firm's advertising agency.

e. Distribution: How will the offering be sold? Who will sell it? Who will ship it? Who will service it?

f. Pricing: How will offering be priced? Will there be price adjustments? Who pays for shipping?

V. Budget

a. Investment: Provide details about the budget needed to launch and maintain the offering.

b. Return: List both the short-term and long-term financial goals of the offering, including its projected sales, costs, and net income.

c. Timing: How much of the budget will be spent during different times of year and offering's life cycle?

d. Other resources required.

VI. Conclusion

The Executive Summary

A marketing plan starts with an executive summary. An executive summary should provide all the information your company's executives need to make a decision without reading the rest of the plan. The summary should include a brief description of the market, the product to be offered, the value proposition, the strategy behind the plan, and the key budget items. Any other important information, such as how your competitors and channel partners will respond to the actions your firm takes, should also be summarized and included as justification for strategy recommendations. Because most executives will be reading the plan to make budgeting decisions, the budgeting information you include in the summary is very important. If the executives want more detail, they can refer to specific strategy details and the "budget" section, which appear later in the plan. The executive summary should be one to two pages long. Most marketing plan writers find it easier to write a plan's summary last, even though it appears first in the plan. A summary is hard to write when you don't know the whole plan, so waiting until the plan is complete makes writing the executive summary easier.

The Business Challenge

In the "business challenge" section of the plan, the planner describes the offering and provides a brief rationale for why the company should invest in it. In other words, why is the offering needed? What is the value proposition? How does it fit in with what the company is already doing and further its overall business goals? In addition, the company's mission statement should be referenced. How does the offering and marketing plan further the company's mission?

Remember that a marketing plan is intended to be a persuasive document. You are trying not only to influence executives to invest in your idea but also to convince other people in your organization to buy into the plan. You are also trying to tell a compelling story that will make people outside your organization—for example, the director of the advertising agency you work with, or a potential supplier or channel partner—invest money, time, and effort into making your plan a success. Therefore, as you write the plan you should constantly be answering the question, "Why should I invest in this plan?" The value proposition answers this question and drives the strategies. Put your answers in the business challenge section of the plan.

Your marketing plan has to convince busy executives and other stakeholders that your idea is worth investing in.

Source: © Shutterstock, Inc.

The Market

The market section of the plan should describe your customers and competitors, any other organizations with which you will collaborate, and the state of the market. We suggest that you always start the section by describing the customers who currently purchase or will purchase the offering. Why? Because customers are central to all marketing plans. After that, discuss your competitors, the climate, and your company in the order you believe readers will find most persuasive. In other words, discuss the factor you believe is most convincing first, followed by the second-most convincing factor, and so on.

Customers

Who is in your target market? Remember the target market consists of current and potential customers. What makes these people decide to buy the products they do, and how do they fulfill their personal value equations? What is their buying process like? Which of their needs does your offering meet?

Break the market into customer segments and describe each segment completely, answering those questions for each segment. When you write your plan, begin with the most important segment first and work your way to the least important segment. The segment(s) you focus on become your target market(s). Include in your discussion the market share and sales goals for each segment.

For example, Progresso Soups' primary market segments might include the following:

- Families in colder regions
- People who need a good lunch but have to eat at their desks
- Busy young singles
- Older, perhaps retired, empty-nesters

These segments would be based on research that Progresso has completed showing that these are the groups that eat the most soup.

Progresso Soups may divide their market into several groups. This family photo might actually represent three different markets: a person who eats lunch at his or her desk at work and needs something quick and filling; a retired but active couple that wants something hot and nourishing; and a busy young family looking for easy meals to prepare.

Source: © Shutterstock, Inc.

The primary market segment(s) and target markets may change over time. Swerve, which was acquired by Whole Earth Brands, Inc. in late 2020, is an all-natural sugar replacement with no artificial sweeteners. Initially, they thought their primary target market was people with diabetes and those seeking better options for their health. While people with diabetes and other health issues are definitely a market, Swerve executives found that people who were willing to spend more money on all-natural products and better options were a stronger market, which they should prioritize. By focusing on both proactive consumers who wanted all-natural ingredients first as well as the reactive consumers with health concerns, Swerve was able to build market share. As the

"Ultimate Sugar Replacement," Swerve grew rapidly and increased their brand equity. As such, the acquisition provided Whole Earth Brands an opportunity to expand its portfolio and grow their consumer packaged goods.[4]

Your discussion of each segment should also include how to reach the customers within it, what they expect or need in terms of support (both presales and postsales support), and other information that helps readers understand how each segment is different from the others. After reading the section, a person should have a good grasp of how the segments differ yet understand how the needs of each are satisfied by the total offering.

Company Analysis

Include the results of your analysis of your company's strengths and weaknesses in this section. How is the company perceived by the customers you described earlier? Why is the company uniquely capable of capitalizing on the opportunity outlined in the plan? This information helps with development of a strong value proposition and provides justification for the strategies. How sustainable is the competitive advantage you are seeking to achieve?

You will also need to identify any functional areas in which your company might need to invest for the plan to succeed. For example, money might be needed for new production or distribution facilities and to hire new marketing or sales employees and train existing ones.

One tool that is useful for framing these questions as well understanding the external environment is the SWOT analysis. SWOT stands for strengths, weaknesses, opportunities, and threats. Strengths and weaknesses are internal, meaning they are conditions of the company. Either these conditions are positive (strengths) or negative (weaknesses). Opportunities and threats are external to the company, and could be due to potential or actual actions taken by competitors, suppliers, or customers. Opportunities and threats could also be a function of government action, changing lifestyle trends, changes in technology, and other external factors.

When working with executives, some consultants have noted the difficulty executives have in separating opportunities from strengths, weaknesses from threats. Statements such as "We have an opportunity to leverage our strong product features" indicate such confusion. An opportunity lies in the market, not in a strength. Remember, opportunities and threats are external and affect all competitors; strengths and weaknesses are internal. Assuming demand (an external characteristic) for a strength (an internal characteristic) is a common marketing mistake. Sound marketing research is therefore needed to assess opportunity.

Other factors that make for better SWOT analysis are as follows.

- **Honest.** A good SWOT analysis is honest. A better way to describe those "strong" product features mentioned earlier would be to say "strong reputation among product designers," unless consumer acceptance has already been documented.
- **Broad.** The analysis has to be broad enough to capture trends. A small retail chain would have to look beyond its regional operating area in order to understand larger trends that may impact the stores.
- **Long term.** Consider multiple time frames. A SWOT analysis that only looks at the immediate future (or the immediate past) is likely to miss important trends. Engineers at Mars (makers of Skittles, M&Ms, and Snickers) visit trade shows in many fields, not just candy, so that they can identify trends in manufacturing that may take a decade to reach the candy industry. In this way, they can shorten the cycle and take advantage of such trends early when needed.
- **Multiple perspectives.** SWOT analyses are essentially based on someone's perception. Therefore, a good SWOT should consider the perspective of all areas of the firm. Involve people from shipping, sales, production, and perhaps even from suppliers and channel members.

The SWOT analysis for a company, or for any organization, is both internal and external in focus. Some of the external areas for focus are collaborators (suppliers, distributors, and others), competitors, and the business climate.

Collaborators

Along with company strengths and weaknesses, identify any actual or potential partners needed for the plan to work. Note that collaborators are more than just a list of suppliers and distributors. Collaborators are those organizations, either upstream or downstream in the value chain, you need to partner with to co-create value.

For example, AT&T collaborated with Apple to develop the iPhone. AT&T is downstream in the value chain, providing the needed cell service and additional features that made the iPhone so revolutionary. At the same time, however, AT&T was a part of the development of the iPhone and the attendant marketing strategy; the partnership began well before the iPhone was launched.

Competitors

Your marketing plan, if it is any good at all, is likely to spark retaliation from one or more competitors. For example, Teradata and Unica operate in the same market. Both sell data warehousing products to companies. Teradata primarily focuses on the information technology departments that support the data warehouse, whereas Unica focuses on the marketing departments that actually use the data warehouse. Nonetheless, Teradata is well aware of Unica's marketing strategy and is taking steps to combat it by broadening its own market to include data warehousing users in marketing departments. One step was to teach their salespeople what marketing managers do and how they would use a data warehouse as part of their job, so that when these salespeople are talking to marketing managers, they are knowledgeable.

Teradata marketing planners also have to be aware of potential competitors. What if IBM or HP decided to enter the market? Who is most likely to enter the market, what would their offering look like, and how can we make it harder for them to want to enter the market? If your company captures their market before they can enter, then they may choose to go elsewhere.

Identify your competitors and be honest about both their strengths and weaknesses in your marketing. Remember that other people, and perhaps other organizations, will be using your plan to create their own plans. If they are to be successful, they have to know what competition they face. Include how quickly you expect your competitors to retaliate and what the nature of that retaliation will be. Will they lower their prices, create similar offerings, add services to drive up the value of their products, spend more on advertising, or a combination of these tactics?

A complete competitive analysis not only anticipates how the competition will react, it also includes an analysis of the competition's financial resources. Do your competitors have money to invest in a competitive offering? Are they growing by acquiring other companies? Are they growing by adding new locations or new sales staff? Or are they growing simply because they are effective? Maybe they are not growing at all. Are there potential entrants or substitute products that may affect your business? To answer these questions, you will need to carefully review your competitors' financial statements and all information publicly available about them. This can include an executive quoted in an article about a company's growth for a particular product or an analyst's projection for future sales within a specific market.

Business Climate

You may have already addressed some of the factors in the business environment that are creating the opportunity for your offering. For example, when you discussed customers, you perhaps noted a new technology they are beginning to use.

A complete coverage of the climate would include the following (the PEST analysis):

- Political climate
- Economic climate
- Social and cultural environment
- Technological environment

A scan of the political climate should include any new government regulations as well as legislation. For example, will changes in the tax laws make for more or less disposable income among your customers? Will the tightening of government regulations affect how salespeople can call on doctors, for example, hindering your marketing opportunity? Will federal policies that affect exchange rates or tariffs make global competitors stronger or weaker? For example, the government encourages the manufacturer of electric vehicles. Automobile manufacturers have set goals for transition to electric vehicles. However, the pandemic has caused chip shortages which are affecting the manufacturing of most vehicles as well as medical devices, phones, and other products.

A marketing summary should include a PEST analysis.

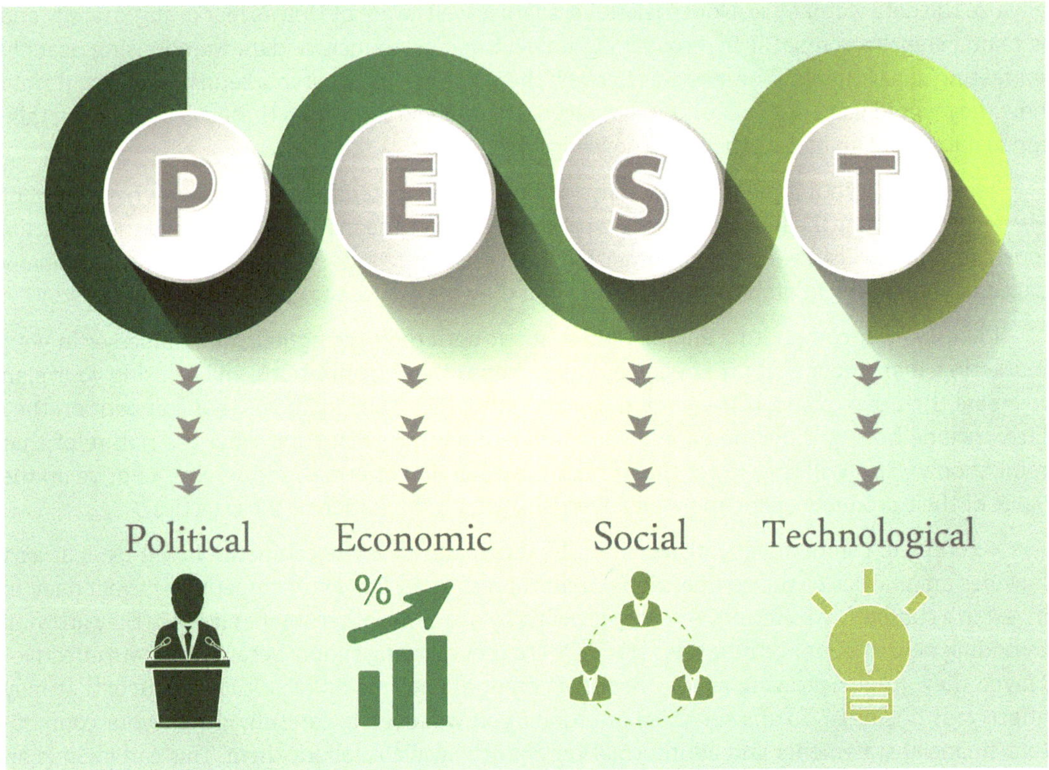

Source: © Shutterstock, Inc.

The economic climate is also important to consider. Inflation and unemployment rates, as well as the exchange rate, may affect your business. During the COVID-19 pandemic, you may remember shortages of goods, high unemployment rates, supply chain problems, and resulting higher prices. Gas prices were low when people stayed home, but increased rapidly once some restrictions were lifted. Housing prices also soared as demand increased and the price of lumber skyrocketed. These factors affected everything from the price of corn to the sales of movie tickets. Such volatility is unusual, but it is important nonetheless to know what the economy is doing.

The housing crisis was caused by a failure in the subprime lending market, an economic condition that affected many other businesses.

Source: © Shutterstock, Inc.

The social and cultural environment is also important to watch. Marketers, for example, may note the rise in the Hispanic population as a market segment, but it is also important to recognize the influence of the Hispanic culture. Understanding the Hispanic culture is important in reaching this market segment with the right marketing mix. In creating marketing campaigns for something such as a financial product, it's very important to understand the history that Hispanics have had with financial institutions in their home countries. Understanding that culturally Hispanics might not trust financial institutions and developing campaigns that generate positive word of mouth, such as refer-a-friend and influencer tactics, can be explosive once the wall has been torn down.

Finally, the technological environment should be considered. Technology is the application of science to solve problems. It encompasses more than just information (computer) technology. For example, when Ted Schulte (profiled in Chapter 13) discusses a pacemaker with a cardiac surgeon, Ted is describing the latest technology available. The new technology could be related to the battery used to power the pacemaker, the materials used in the leads (the wires that connect the pacemaker to the body), or even the material that encases the pacemaker. Understanding the technological environment can provide you with a greater understanding of a product's life cycle and the direction the market is taking when it comes to newer technologies.

Many of the environmental factors we mentioned impact other factors. For example, technological changes are altering the social and cultural environment. Instead of writing letters to one another, families and friends use text, email, and social networking sites to communicate and maintain relationships. Online communication has affected any number of businesses, including the greeting card business and the U.S. Postal Service, which closed many facilities.

Likewise, the economic environment influences the political environment and vice versa. The stimulus payments and forgiveness of some loans and payments during the pandemic provide examples of how the economic environment and the political environment affect each other. Any forthcoming changes in the business climate need to be included in your marketing plan.

Technology encompasses more than just information technology. Produced by Guidant Technology, this pacemaker utilizes information technology to record heart-function data a doctor can read later. But the product might also utilize other new technologies, such as a new battery, materials used to connect the pacemaker to the heart, and the casing for the pacemaker, all of which affect its performance.

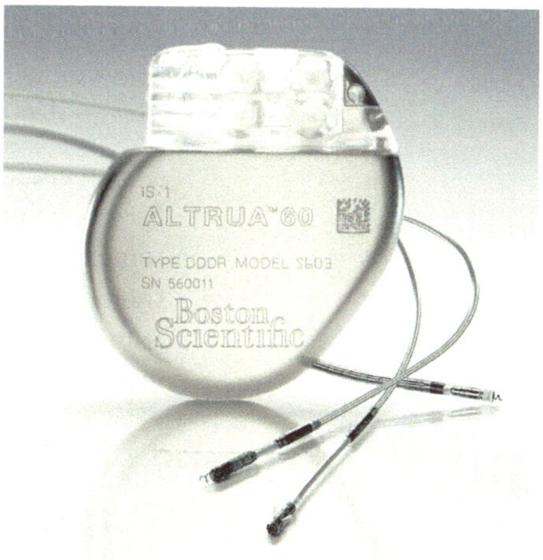

Source: Guidant Technology, used with permission

The Value Proposition and Strategy

The next section of the plan details the value proposition and the strategies your organization will use to develop, market, sell, and deliver the offering. This section is your opportunity to create a compelling argument as to what you intend to do and why others should invest in the strategy. Your reader will be asking, "Why should we adopt this strategy?" To answer that question, you need to include a value proposition (see Chapter 2 Section 1), specifically explaining the benefits for the target customer(s). You may also need to include a brief discussion of the strategic alternatives that were considered and discarded. When readers complete the section, they should conclude that the strategy you proposed is the best one available.

The Offering

Provide detail on the features and benefits of the offering, including pricing options, in this section. For example, in some instances, your organization might plan for several variations of the offering, each with different pricing options. The different options should be discussed in detail, along with the market segments expected to respond to each option. Some marketing professionals like to specify the sales goals for each option in this section, along with the associated costs and gross profit margins for each. Other planners prefer to include a pricing section or wait until the budget section of the plan to provide that information.

The plan for the offering should also include the plan for introducing offerings that will follow the initial launch. For example, when should Progresso introduce new soup flavors? Should there be seasonal flavors? Should there be smaller sizes and larger sizes, and should they be introduced all at the same time or in stages?

Part of an offering is the service support consumers need to extract the offering's full value. The support might include presales support as well as postsales support. For example, Teradata has a team of finance specialists who can help customers document the return on investment they would get from purchasing and implementing a Teradata data warehouse. This presales support helps potential buyers make a stronger business case for buying Teradata's products with executives who control their companies' budgets.

Postsales support can include technical support. In B2B (business-to-business) environments, sellers frequently offer to train their customers' employees to use products as part of their postsales support. Before you launch an offering, you need to be sure your firm's support services are in place. That means training service personnel, creating the appropriate communication channels for customers to air their technical concerns, and other processes.

Prior to launching a new offering, the presales and postsales support personnel for it have to be trained and the appropriate work processes created so that the right level of support is provided. These call center technicians had to first learn the offering's technical processes before it could be launched.

Source: © Shutterstock, Inc.

The Communication Plan

How will the offering be launched? Will it be like Dow Corning's launch of silicone acrylate copolymer, a product used to add color to cosmetics? That product was announced at the In-Cosmetics trade show in Barcelona. Or will you invite customers, media, and analysts from around the globe to your company's offices for the launch, as SAS did with its SAS 9 software product?

In addition to the announcement of the new product, the communication plan has to specify how ongoing customer communications will be conducted. The mechanisms used to gather customer feedback and insights, which can be used to enhance the customer experience, as well as how the offering will be promoted to customers need to be spelled out. For example, will you focus on using social media platforms, create an online community, use traditional advertising such as television, or utilize different media for different target markets?

Some companies may remake successful commercials or use the same promotions many years later. For example, one of the most iconic commercials Coca-Cola ever created was filmed in Italy with people from around the world to promote unity, and originally aired in 1971. The song in the commercial, "I'd Like to Teach the World to Sing," was so popular that it became a top single hit. Years later in 2016, Coca-Cola recreated the same commercial using the same people in the same location. Watch the commercial and see if you and others begin to sing along with the actors.[5]

Remade Version of Coca-Cola's Popular and Successful Commercial

Recreating an iconic commercial.

View in the online reader

The discussion of the communication plan can be fairly broad. You can put additional details in a separate planning document that outlines the product's advertising strategies, event strategies (such as trade shows and special events like customer golf tournaments that will be used to promote the product), sponsorships, and sales strategies.

Distribution

This section should answer questions about delivering value, where and how the offering will be sold. Who will sell it? Who will ship it? Who pays for shipping? How will it be shipped? Who will service and support it with services such as research, credit, and handling? In addition, the distribution section should specify the inventories that need to be maintained in order to meet customer expectations for fast delivery and where those inventories should be kept.

Pricing

Pricing strategies must cover both fixed and variable costs. Information regarding pricing approaches, adjustments, and transportation charges need to be included. If all other information is missing, price indicates quality. What image does the price convey? May customers bundle offerings to save money? What services are included in the price? Remember, price is the only component of the marketing mix that generates revenue. It is the easiest to change and the easiest to copy.

Budget

The budget section is more than just a discussion of the money needed to launch the new offering. A complete budget section will cover all the resources, such as new personnel, new equipment, new locations, and so forth, for the launch to be a success. Of course, these resources have costs associated with them. In some instances, the budget might require that existing resources be redeployed and a case made for doing so.

The first portion of the budget will likely cover the investment required for the launch. The plan might point out that additional funds need to be allocated to the offering to make it ready for the market. For example, perhaps additional beta testing or product development over and above what the firm normally commits to new products is needed. Certainly, marketing funds will be needed to launch the offering and pay for any special events, advertising, promotional materials, and so forth. Funds might also be needed to cover the costs of training salespeople and service personnel and potentially hiring new staff members. For example, Teradata introduced a new offering that was aimed at an entirely new market. The new market was so different that it required a new sales force. Details for the sales force, such as how many salespeople, sales managers, and support personnel will be needed, would go in this section.

The budget section should include the costs associated with maintaining the amount of inventory of the product to meet customers' needs. The costs to provide customers with support services should also be estimated and budgeted. Some products will be returned, some services will be rejected by the consumer, and other problems will occur. The budget should include projections and allowances for these occurrences.

The budget section is also the place to forecast the product's sales and profits. Even though the plan likely mentioned the sales goals set for each market segment, the budget section is where the details go. For example, the cost for advertising, trade shows, special events, and salespeople should be spelled out. The projections should also include timelines. The sales costs for one month might be estimated, as well as two months, six months, and so forth, as Figure 16.1 shows.

Note that Figure 16.1 shows that the product's costs are high early on and then decrease before leveling out. That cost line assumes there is a heavy upfront investment to launch the offering, which is usually true for new products. The sales of the offering should grow as it gathers momentum in the market. However, the market potential stays the same, assuming that the potential number of customers stays the same. That might not always be the case, though. If we were targeting mothers of babies, for example, the market potential might vary based on the projected seasonality in birth rates because more babies tend to be born in some months than others.

FIGURE 16.1 A Marketing Plan Timeline Illustrating Market Potential, Sales, and Costs

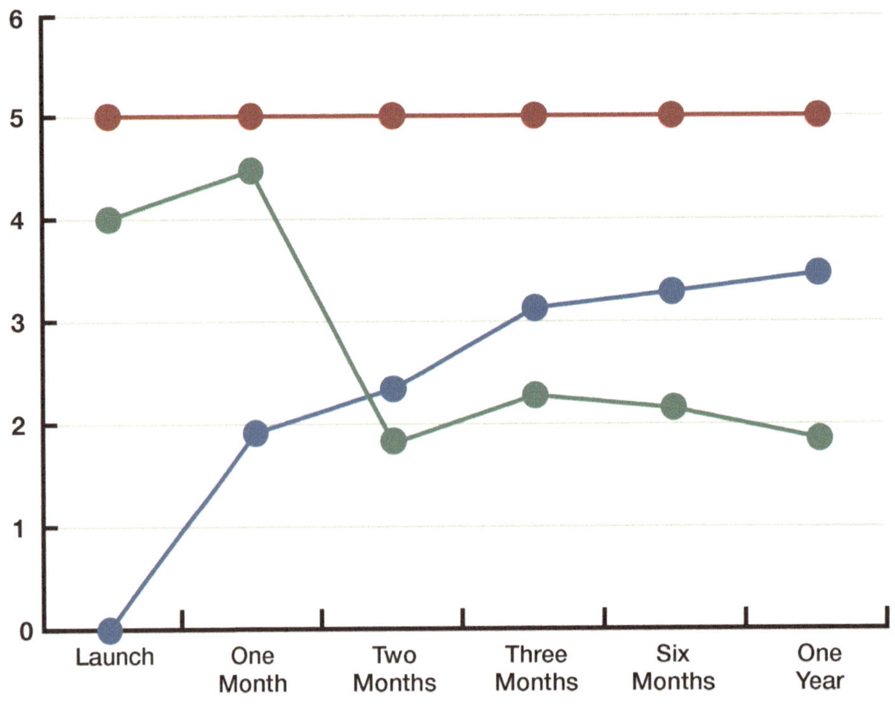

Conclusion

In the conclusion, repeat the highlights. Summarize the target market, the value proposition(s), the offer, the communication plan, distribution plan, and pricing plan. Your conclusion should remind the reader of all the reasons why your plan is the best choice.

Of course, the written plan is itself a marketing tool. You want it to convince someone to invest in your ideas, so you want to write it down on paper in a compelling way. "Tips for Writing an Effective Marketing Plan" offers some tips for effectively doing so. Also, keep in mind that a marketing plan is created at a single point in time. The market, though, is dynamic. A good marketing plan includes how the organization should respond to various scenarios if the market changes. In addition, the plan should include "triggers" detailing what should happen under the scenarios. For example, it might specify that when a certain percentage of market share is reached, then the price of the product will be reduced (or increased). Or the plan might specify the minimum amount of the product that must be sold by a certain point in time—say, six months after the product is launched—and what should happen if the mark isn't reached. The contingency plans also expedite necessary actions in response to unforeseen circumstances. Also, it should once again be noted that the marketing plan is a communication device. For that reason, the outline of a marketing plan may look somewhat different from the order in which the tasks in the outline are actually completed.

Tips for Writing an Effective Marketing Plan

- Be brief—executives are busy.
- Anticipate and answer questions your organization's executives might have.
- Use active (not passive) voice when you write your plan.
- Use visuals and bullet points. Some people are visual learners and others are verbal. Meet the needs of both types of people.
- Read, proofread, and have someone else proofread the plan.

Mplans.com is a website that that has examples of "model" marketing plans for many types of businesses: Everything from outdoor gear designers to bakeries and bowling alleys. You can also build your own marketing plan from scratch using a template on the site.

Key Takeaways

- A marketing plan's executive summary should include a brief summary of the market, the product to be offered, the value proposition and strategy behind the plan, and the budget, as well as any other important information. In this section of the plan, the planner describes the offering and a brief rationale for why the company should invest in it. The market section of the plan should describe a firm's customers, competitors, any other organizations with which it will collaborate, and the climate of the market. Opportunities and threats should be clear. The strategy section details the tactics the organization will use to develop, market, and sell the offering. An organization's strengths should be leveraged to take advantage of appropriate opportunities. When readers complete the strategy section, they should conclude that the proposed strategy is the best one available.
- The budget section of the marketing plan covers all the resources, such as new personnel, new equipment, new locations, and so forth, needed to successfully launch the product, as well as details about the product's costs and sales forecasts. A timeline should be included so expenses can be budgeted.

Review Questions

1. What is a marketing plan, and how is it used?
2. Which section of the marketing plan is most important? Why? The least important?
3. What is the purpose of scenario planning?

16.3 Forecasting

Learning Objectives

1. List steps in the forecasting process.
2. Identify types of forecasting methods and their advantages and disadvantages.
3. Discuss the methods used to improve the accuracy of forecasts.

Creating marketing strategy is not a single event, nor is the implementation of marketing strategy something only the marketing department has to worry about. When the strategy is implemented, the rest of the company must be poised to deal with the consequences. As we have explained, an important component in developing the marketing plan is the sales forecast, which is the estimate of how much the company will actually sell. The rest of the company must then be geared up (or down) to meet that demand. In this section, we explore forecasting in more detail, as there are many choices a marketing executive can make in developing a forecast.

Accuracy is important when it comes to forecasts. If executives overestimate the demand for a product, the company could end up spending money on manufacturing, distribution, and servicing activities it won't need. The software developer Data Impact recently overestimated the demand for one of its new products. Because the sales of the product didn't meet projections, Data Impact lacked the cash available to pay its vendors, utility providers, and others. Employees had to be terminated in many areas of the firm to trim costs.

Underestimating demand can be just as devastating. When a company introduces a new product, it launches marketing and sales campaigns to create demand for it. But if the company isn't ready to deliver the amount of the product the market demands, then other competitors can steal sales the firm might otherwise have captured. Sony's inability to deliver the e-Reader in sufficient numbers made Amazon's Kindle more readily accepted in the market; other features then gave the Kindle an advantage that Sony is finding difficult to overcome.

The marketing leader of a firm has to do more than just forecast the company's sales. The process can be complex, because how much the company can sell will depend on many factors, such as how much the product will cost, how competitors will react, and so forth—in fact, much of what you have already read about in preparing a marketing strategy. Each of these factors has to be taken into account in order to determine how much the company is likely to sell. As factors change, the forecast has to change as well. Thus, a sales forecast is actually a composite of a number of estimates and has to be dynamic as those other estimates change.

market potential

Total industry-wide sales expected in a particular product category for the time period of interest.

A common first step is to determine **market potential**, or total industry-wide sales expected in a particular product category for the time period of interest. (The time period of interest might be the coming year, quarter, month, or some other time period.) Some marketing research companies, such as Nielsen, Gartner, and others, estimate the market potential for various products and then sell that research to companies that produce those products.

Once the marketing executive has an idea of the market potential, the company's sales potential can be estimated. A firm's **sales potential** is the maximum total revenue it hopes to generate from a product or the number of units of it the company can hope to sell. The sales potential for the product is typically represented as a percentage of its market potential and equivalent to the company's estimated maximum market share for the time period. As you can see in Figure 16.1, companies sell less than potential because not everyone will make a decision to buy their product: some will put off a decision; others will buy a competitor's product; still others might make do with a substitute product. In your budget, you'll want to forecast the revenues earned from the product against the market potential, as well as against the product's costs.

sales potential

The maximum total revenue a company hopes to generate from a product or the number of units of it the company can hope to sell.

Forecasting Methods

Forecasts, at their basic level, are simply someone's guess as to what will happen. Each estimate, though, is the product of a process. Several such processes are available to marketing executives, and the final forecast is likely to be a blend of results from more than one process. These processes include judgment techniques and surveys, time series techniques, market tests, spending correlates, and other models.

Judgment and Survey Techniques

At some level, every forecast is ultimately someone's judgment. Some techniques, though, rely more on people's opinions or estimates and are called **judgment techniques**. Judgment techniques can include customer (or channel member or supplier) surveys, executive or expert opinions, surveys of customers' (or channel members') intentions or estimates, and estimates by salespeople.

judgment techniques

Forecasting methods that rely on someone's estimate(s).

Customer and Channel Surveys

In some markets, particularly in business-to-business markets, research companies ask customers how much they plan to spend in the coming year on certain products. Have you ever filled out a survey asking if you intend to buy a car or refrigerator in the coming year? Chances are your answers were part of someone's forecast. Similarly, surveys are done for products sold through distributors. Companies then buy the surveys from the research companies or do their own surveys to use as a starting point for their forecasting. Surveys are better at estimating market potential than sales potential, however, because potential buyers are far more likely to know they will buy something—they just don't know which brand or model. Surveys can also be relatively costly, particularly when they are commissioned for only one company.

Sales Force Composite

A **sales force composite** is a forecast based on estimates of sales in a given time period gathered from all of a firm's salespeople. Salespeople have a pretty good idea about how much can be sold in the coming period of time (especially if they have bonuses riding on those sales). They've been calling on their customers and know when buying decisions will be made.

sales force composite

An estimate of future sales based on the sum of estimates from all of the company's salespeople.

Estimating the sales for new products or new promotions and pricing strategies will be harder for salespeople until they have had some experience selling those products after they have been introduced, promoted, or repriced. Further, management may not want salespeople to know about new products or promotions until these are announced to the general public, so this method may not be useful in situations involving new products or promotions. Another limitation reflects salespeople's natural optimism. Salespeople tend to be optimistic about what they think they can sell and may overestimate future sales. Conversely, if the company uses these estimates to set quotas, salespeople are likely to reduce their estimates to make it easier to achieve quota.

Salespeople are more accurate in their near-term sales estimates, as their customers are not likely to share plans too far into the future. Consequently, most companies use sales force composites for shorter-range forecasts in order to more accurately predict their production and inventory requirements. Konica Minolta, an office equipment manufacturer, has recently placed a heavy emphasis on improving the accuracy of its sales force composites because the cost of being wrong is too great. Underestimated forecasts result in some customers having to wait too long for deliveries for products, and they may turn to competitors who can deliver faster. By contrast, overestimated forecasts result in higher inventory costs.

Executive Opinion

executive opinion

A forecasting method in which an executive or group of executives provides a best estimate of what will be sold or what will happen.

Executive opinion is exactly what the name implies: the best-guess estimates of a company's executives. Each executive submits an estimate of the company's sales, which are then averaged to form the overall sales forecast. The advantages of executive opinions are that they are low cost and fast and have the effect of making executives committed to achieving them. An executive-opinion-based forecast can be a good starting point. However, there are disadvantages to the method, so it should not be used alone. These disadvantages are similar to those of the sales force composites. If the executives' forecast becomes a quota upon which their bonuses are estimated, they will have an incentive to underestimate the forecast so they can meet their targets. Organizational factors also come into play. A junior executive, for example, is not likely to forecast low sales for a product that his or her CEO is pushing, even if low sales are likely to occur.

Expert Opinion

expert opinion

A forecasting method in which the forecast is based on an objective third-party expert's best estimate of what will happen in the market and how that will influence sales.

Expert opinion is similar to executive opinion except that the expert is usually someone outside the company. Like executive opinion, expert opinion is a tool best used in conjunction with more quantitative methods. As a sole method of forecasting, expert opinions are often very inaccurate. Just consider how preseason college football rankings compare with the final standings. The football experts' predictions are not always very accurate.

Time Series Techniques

trend analysis

A group of forecasting methods that base the future period of sales (or another variable) on the rate of change for previous periods of time.

Time series techniques examine sales patterns in the past in order to predict sales in the future. For example, with a **trend analysis**, the marketing executive identifies the rate at which a company's sales have grown in the past and uses that rate to estimate future sales. For example, if sales have grown 3 percent per year over the past five years, trend analysis would assume a similar 3 percent growth rate next year.

A simple form of analysis such as this can be useful if a market is stable. The problem is that many markets are not stable. A rapid change in any one of a market's dynamics is likely to result in wide swings in growth rates. Just think about auto sales before, during, and after the government's Cash for Clunkers program. What sold the previous month could not account for the effects of the program. Consequently, if an executive were to have estimated auto sales based on the rate of change for the previous period, the estimate would have been way off.

The COVID-19 pandemic and shortage of paper towels.

Source: © Shutterstock, Inc.

The paper towel, paper products, hand sanitizer shortages at the beginning of the COVID-19 pandemic, were unusual and created hoarding situations, making it necessary for sellers to limit quantities purchased. Material shortages and shipping delays caused continued shortages. Many products may have wide variations in demand for other reasons. Trend analysis can still be useful in these situations, but adjustments have to be made to account for the swings in rates of change. Two common adjustments are the **moving average**, whereby the rate of change for the past few periods is averaged, and **exponential smoothing**, a type of moving average that puts more emphasis on the most recent period.

moving average

A trend analysis type of forecasting method that estimates sales (or other variable) based on an average rate of change over a group of previous periods of time; the rate changes (moves) as the oldest period is dropped off and the most recent period added in.

exponential smoothing

A method of trend analysis forecasting that weights more recent periods of time more heavily than more distant periods of time.

Correlates and Other Models

A number of more sophisticated models can be useful in forecasting sales. One fairly common method is a **correlational analysis**, which is a form of trend analysis that estimates sales based on the trends of other variables. For example, furniture-company executives know that new housing starts (the number of new houses that are begun to be built in a period) predict furniture sales in the near future because new houses tend to get filled up with new furniture. Such a correlate is considered a **leading indicator**, because it leads, or precedes, sales. The Conference Board publishes an Index of Leading Economic Indicators, which is a single number that represents a composite of commonly used leading indicators. Some of these leading indicators are housing starts, wholesale orders, orders for durable goods (items like refrigerators, air conditioning systems, and other long-lasting consumer products), and even consumer sentiment, or how consumers think the economy is doing.

correlational analysis

A form of trend analysis that estimates sales based on the trends of other variables.

leading indicator

A correlate that occurs before the variable being forecasted (e.g., permits to build new houses is a leading indicator of building material sales because permits are issued before the materials are purchased).

Response Models

Some companies create sophisticated statistical models called **response models**, which are based on how customers have responded in the past to marketing strategies. For example, companies take previous sales data and combine it with customer data gathered from the retailer's website to learn about customers' behaviors. Data can show how many customers are price sensitive and only buy products when they are on sale and how many customers are likely to respond to certain offers. The retailer can then estimate the sales for products by market segment based on the offers and promotions directed at those segments.

response models

Sophisticated statistical models used in forecasting that are based on how customers have responded in the past to marketing strategies.

Market Tests

market test

The test launch of a product's complete marketing plan to ensure that it reaches buyers, gets positive reactions, and generates sales of the product.

A **market test** is an experiment in which the company launches a new offering in a limited market or for a limited time in order to gain real-world knowledge of how the market will react to the product. Since there isn't any historical data on how the product has done, response models and time-series techniques are not effective. A market test provides some measure of sales in response to the marketing plan, so in that regard, it is like a response model, just based on limited data. The demand for the product can then be extrapolated to the full market. However, remember that market tests are visible to your competitors, and they can undertake actions, such as drastic price cuts, to skew your results.

HEB uses Waco, Texas, as a test market, combining data from its loyalty program with sales data to see who buys what and at what price.

Source: © Shutterstock, Inc.

The grocery chain HEB uses Waco, Texas, as a test site. HEB has a loyalty program that enables it to collect lots of data on its customers. When HEB wants to test market a new product, the firm does it in Waco, where individual customer data can be combined with sales data. Testing in Waco tells HEB who is likely to buy the product and at what price, information that makes extrapolating to their larger market more accurate.

Building Better Forecasts

At best, a forecast is a scientific estimate, but really, a forecast is just a sophisticated guess. Still, there are steps that can enhance the likelihood of success. The first step is to commit to accuracy. At Konica Minolta, regional vice presidents are rewarded for being accurate and punished for being wrong about their forecasts, no matter what the direction of them is. As we mentioned earlier, underestimating is considered by Konica Minolta leadership to be just as bad as overestimating sales.

We've also mentioned how salespeople and managers will lower estimates if the estimates are used to set quotas. Using forecasts properly is another factor that can improve forecasting accuracy. But there are other ways to make forecasts more accurate. These begin with picking the right methods for your business.

Pick the Right Method(s) for Your Business and Your Decision

Some products have very short selling cycles; others take a long time to produce and sell. What is appropriate for a fast-moving consumer good like toothpaste is not appropriate for a durable good like a refrigerator. A response model might work for Crest toothpaste in the short term, but longer-term forecasts might require a sophisticated time-series technique. By contrast, Whirlpool might find, for example, that channel surveys are better predictors of refrigerator sales over the long term.

Use Multiple Methods

Since forecasts are estimates, the more estimates generated from various methods, the better. For example, combining expert opinions with a trend analysis could help you understand not only what is happening but also why. Every forecast results in decisions, such as the decision to hire more people, add manufacturing capacity, order supplies, and so forth. The more forecasts you have to make and resulting decisions you have to live with, the better you will get at forecasting.

Use Many Variables

Forecasting for smaller business units first can result in greater accuracy. For example, JCPenney may estimate sales by region first, and then roll that information up into a national sales forecast. By forecasting locally, more variables can be considered, and with more variables comes more information, which should help the accuracy of the company's overall sales forecast. Similarly, JCPenney may estimate sales by market segment, such as women over age fifty. Again, forecasting in a smaller segment or business unit can then enable the company to compare such forecasts to forecasts by product line and gain greater accuracy overall.

Use Scenario-Based Forecasts

One forecast is not enough. Consider what will happen if conditions change. For example, how might your forecast change if your competitors react strongly to your strategy? How might it change if they don't react at all? Or if the government changes a policy that makes your product tax-free? All of these factors will influence sales, so the smart executive considers multiple scenarios. While the executive may not expect the government to make something tax-free, scenarios can be created that consider favorable government regulation, stable regulation, and negative regulation, just as one can consider light competitive reaction, moderate reaction, or strong reaction.

Track Actual Results and Adjust

As time goes on, forecasts that have been made should be adjusted to reflect reality. For example, Katie Scallan-Sarantakes may have to do an annual forecast for Scion sales, but as each month goes by, she has hard sales data with which to adjust future forecasts. Further, she knows how strongly competition has reacted and can adjust her estimates accordingly. So even though she may have an annual forecast, the forecast changes regularly based on how well the company is doing.

Key Takeaways

- A forecast is an educated guess, or estimate, of sales in the future. Accuracy is important because so many other decisions a firm must make depend on the forecasts. When a company forecasts sales, it has to consider market potential and sales potential. Many methods of forecasting exist, including expert opinion, channel and customer surveys, sales force composites, time series data, and test markets.
- Better forecasts can be obtained by using multiple methods, forecasting for various scenarios, and tracking actual data (including sales) and adjusting future forecasts accordingly.

Review Questions

1. Which forecasting method would be most accurate for forecasting sales of hair-care products in the next year? How would your answer change if you were forecasting for the next month? For home appliances?
2. What is the role of expert opinion in all forecasts?
3. How can forecasting accuracy be improved?
4. How can previous sales data and customer feedback be used to improve customer experience and sales?

16.4 Ongoing Marketing Planning and Evaluation

Learning Objectives

1. Apply marketing planning processes to ongoing business settings.
2. Identify the role of the marketing audit.

Our discussion so far might lead you to believe that a marketing plan is created only when a new offering is being launched. In reality, marketing plans may be created or revised frequently—sometimes on an annual basis, or when a new CMO is hired, when market dynamics change drastically and quickly, or a company's CEO wants one. Moreover, as we indicated, a marketing plan should be something of a "living" document; it should contain triggers that result in a company reevaluating its strategies should different scenarios occur. Strategies and results are typically reviewed on a quarterly basis and adjustments are made as necessary.

Lisi Lerch—Lisi Lerch Jewelry

Source: Lisi Lerch, used with permission

Lisi is founder of Lisi Lerch (LisiLerch.com), a company featuring handcrafted jewelry, accessories, and bags. She also founded LibbyKat.com, an online shopping destination for cute clothes. "With a combination of grit, tenacity, kindness and a couple more layers of skin, anything is possible! Go for it!"

Andress Blackwell, President & CEO, Swerve

Andress Blackwell, President and CEO of Swerve, discusses emphasis on quality product.

View in the online reader

Some of those scenarios can occur immediately. For example, when a product is launched, the market reacts. Journalists begin to cover the phenomenon, competitors respond, and regulators may take note. What, then, should happen if the sales goals for the product are substantially exceeded? Should its price be raised or lowered? Should follow-on offerings be launched sooner? What if a competitor launches a similar offering a week later? Or worse yet, what if the competition launches a much better offering? The key to a successful ongoing marketing strategy is twofold: understanding causality and good execution of the marketing plan. Next we discuss each of these aspects.

Causality

causality

The relationship between two variables whereby one variable is a direct consequence of the other.

Causality is the relationship between two variables whereby one variable is a direct consequence of the other. For a scientist in a lab, identifying causality is fairly easy because the causal variable can be controlled and the consequences observed. For marketers, such control is a dream, not a reality. Identifying causality, then, can be a real challenge.

Why is causality so important? Assume you've observed a drop in sales that you think is caused by a competitor's lower price. If you reduce your price to combat the competitor's when, in reality, the poor sales are due simply to seasonal factors, lower prices might give consumers the impression that your product is cheap or low quality. This could send your sales even further downward. Drawing the wrong conclusions about causality can lead to disastrous results.

control

(a) The degree to which you can manipulate an outcome; (b) the degree to which you can separate the effects of a variable on a consequence.

managerial control

The ability to manipulate variables, such as how a marketing plan is implemented.

statistical control

Mathematically removing the influence of a variable on an outcome so as to isolate the cause of a problem.

Control is an important related concept. **Control**, in this context, means not the degree to which you can manipulate an outcome but rather the degree to which you can separate the effects of a variable on a consequence. For example, you have complete control over what the customer pays for the offering. You are able to manipulate that outcome. However, you have no control over seasonal effects. Nonetheless, you can identify what those effects are and account for their influence.

The first type of control is **managerial control**, whereby you have control over how variables in a marketing plan are implemented. You decide, for example, how many stores will carry your product. You can vary that number and have an effect on sales. The second type of control is **statistical control**, whereby you can remove the influence of the variable on the outcome mathematically. For example, you have no control over seasonality. If you are selling a product for babies and more babies are born in August than any other month, then your sales will go up in September. Statistical control allows you to smooth out the seasonal variance on sales so you can then determine how much of the change in sales is due to other factors, especially those you have control over. Statistical control is something you learned in a regression class. However, the numbers in a statistical analysis can be as easily approximated. You don't necessarily need to utilize complicated equations. Consider the following scenario:

1. Over the past five years, you have observed an average decline of 20 percent in sales for the months of June, July, and August, which also happen to be months in which many salespeople and buyers vacation.
2. This year, the decline was 28 percent.
3. You can therefore safely assume that about 20 percent of the decline this year was due to people taking vacations, as they have in years past; you can further assume that the amount of the decline due to factors other than vacations was about 8 percent.

Doing a simple analysis such as this at least gives you some idea that something new is going on that is lowering your sales. You can then explore the problem more completely.

So how do you figure out exactly what *is* the cause of such a decline? In some instances, marketing executives speculate about the potential causes of problems and then research them. For example, if the product's price is perceived to be the problem, conversing with a number of former customers who switched to competing products could either verify this hunch or dispel it. In a B2B environment, salespeople who are aware of a competitor's new lower prices might be the first to identify the problem, rather than marketing executives. Nonetheless, the firm's marketing executives can then try to verify that lower prices led to the sales decline. In consumer-goods markets, there are often many segments of consumers. Rather than asking a few of them what they think, formal market research tools such as surveys and focus groups are used.

The Marketing Audit

Another investigative tool that can be used to research a drop in a company's sales performance is a marketing audit. A **marketing audit** is an examination or snapshot of the state of a company's marketing strategies as they are actually implemented. Here, managerial control becomes important. Was the strategy implemented as intended? Is the strategy working?

marketing audit

A snapshot of the state of the company's marketing strategies as they are actually implemented; an examination of the implementation of a marketing plan to determine if it was implemented properly and if it was successful.

For example, when Xerox launched a new workstation, the company ran a promotion giving a customer who bought a workstation a discount on a copier. Despite the promotion, the overall sales of the workstation failed to meet Xerox's expectations. There were, however, geographical areas in which the sales of the product were quite good. What was up?

Upon closer examination, Xerox's managers learned that the firm's salespeople in these areas had actually developed a much more effective selling strategy: they sold the copiers first and then offered the workstation for free by applying the amount of the discount to the workstation, not the copier. Xerox's marketing quickly revamped the promotion and communicated it effectively to the rest of the sales staff.

A marketing audit is an examination of all of the company's marketing activities. Here, an auditor is looking at actual product displays in a retail store to make sure the product is being displayed and priced properly.

Source: © Shutterstock, Inc.

Fidelity is the degree to which the plan is being implemented as it is supposed to be. In the example of the Xerox workstation, there was substantial fidelity—the plan was being implemented right—but the plan was poor. Usually, though, the problem is that the plan is not executed properly.

fidelity

The degree to which a plan is implemented as intended.

More serious issues require more in-depth study. Metrics such as the win/loss ratios of business deals, the length of time it takes to get a proposal approved and presented to a customer, the number of customers lost, customer complaints, packaging problems, recalls, and sales declines provide examples of problems that can be found during a market audit.

According to the marketing consulting company Copernicus, a marketing audit should assess many factors, but especially those listed below. Does any of the information surprise you?

Top Ten Factors a Marketing Audit Should Assess

1. Key factors that impacted the business for good or for bad during the past year.
2. Customer satisfaction scores and the number and type of customer complaints.
3. The satisfaction levels of distributors, retailers, and other value chain members.
4. The marketing knowledge, attitudes, and satisfaction of all executives involved in the marketing function.
5. The extent to which the marketing program was marketed internally and "bought into" by top managers and nonmarketing executives.
6. The offering: Did it meet the customer's needs as expected, and was the offering's competitive advantage defensible?
7. The performance of the organization's advertising, promotion, sales, marketing, and research programs with an emphasis on their return on the money invested in them.
8. Whether the marketing plan achieved its stated financial and nonfinancial goals.
9. Whether the individual elements of the marketing plan achieved their stated financial and nonfinancial goals.
10. The current value of the brand and customer equity for each brand in the product portfolio.[6]

You were probably surprised by a few items on the list. For example, did your marketing plan include a plan to market the marketing program to important internal parties, such as the company's managers and employees? We discussed earlier that the marketing plan should persuade others to invest in the plan's success. Part of that persuasion process could actually include a plan to communicate the plan! A marketing audit should assess the extent to which the plan was successful in achieving the goal of getting important people and departments within an organization to buy into the plan.

Do you think the "top ten" list above is prioritized correctly? Some people would argue that the first four or five factors that need to be examined are the most important. Other people would argue that only the financial factors (factors 7–10) matter. Which group is right?

The answer really depends on what's important at the time to a company. Declining sales and financial problems are usually the first to prompt a marketing audit.

Many firms don't wait for problems before conducting an audit. Either they hire consultants like Copernicus Marketing Consulting and Research to conduct the audit, or they do the audits themselves. If a firm's budget doesn't allow for a complete audit annually, the company will often focus on one particular area at a time, such as levels of satisfaction among its customers and channel partners. The following year it might audit the company's communications strategy. Rotating the focus ensures that every aspect is audited regularly, if not annually.

Key Takeaway

- The key to a successful ongoing marketing strategy is twofold: understanding causality and good marketing plan execution. Drawing the wrong conclusions about causality, or what actually causes a change in a company's sales performance, can lead to disastrous results. That's why companies investigate the causes by gathering market feedback and conducting market research. Another tool that can be used to research a change in a company's sales performance is a marketing audit. A marketing audit is an examination or a snapshot of the state of a company's marketing strategies as they are actually implemented. Complete and partial audits can be done internally or by a consulting firm in order to find areas for improvement.

Review Questions

1. What is the difference between managerial control and statistical control? How is statistical control used?
2. What should a marketing audit accomplish?

16.5 Discussion Questions and Activities

Discussion Questions

1. In addition to CMOs, why do you believe so many other employees participate in marketing planning?
2. What is the most important part of a marketing plan? Why? What is the least important? Why?

3. Why doesn't the execution of a marketing plan necessarily follow the same order as the plan itself?
4. What is the most important part of a marketing audit? Why? What is the least important part? Why?

Activities

1. Pick a product with which you are very familiar and create a simple marketing plan for it. Focus on one market segment.
2. Conduct an audit of a company's marketing plan as if you were a consultant. Selecting a relatively new consumer product may be easier because it is likely to have more press available that you can use for data.

16.6 Case Study: Lisi Lerch Jewelry and Accessories

After several years working on Wall Street, Lisi Lerch started her company in the Spring of 2001 during her full time job in the recruiting office at Cornell University, while her new husband was getting his MBA. Her brand initially offered classic, Kentucky Derby hats that she was inspired to create due to the lack of affordable women's hats she saw in the marketplace. A few years later she decided to test the waters and dabble in jewelry-making, which became an instant obsession.

As her business grew, so did her family. With her first baby on the way and her husband by her side, Lisi Lerch moved to Philadelphia where her business was a huge success. She expanded her offering to include fabulous wool winter hats in addition to the Kentucky Derby hats that her customers loved. Following this expansion, Lerch was invited to participate in hundreds of trunk shows from New York to Florida.

Although she loved designing hats, they soon became a hassle to travel with due to her growing family. Due to her growing family, Lerch decided to shift gears and focus on creating jewelry, which she discovered was her true passion. Lerch put the hats on the back burner, knowing that one day she would bring them back again. She was completely blown away by how well received her jewelry was (and how much easier it was to transport!). After having her third child, she decided to take her jewelry business to the next level. She started showing at AmericasMart in Atlanta where the management loved her product and soon included her in an exclusive Boutique section. From then on, her jewelry business soared. Lisi Lerch offers apparel and handbags. Lisi Lerch products are sold online and at over 100 boutiques across the United States.

Case Study Questions

1. Outline a marketing plan for the next year including a SWOT analysis, objectives, target market(s), value proposition(s), strategies regarding new and existing products, target markets with communication strategies to reach each target, and any recommended changes to distribution and current pricing.
2. What additional information would attract college students and their mothers to the Lisi Lerch website?

3. What strategies do you recommend to increase awareness and sales of jewelry to college students and their mothers?
4. What strategies do you recommend to increase awareness and sales of other Lisi Lerch products?
5. What strategies do you recommend to increase the number of Instagram followers?
6. Identify competitors and potential market entrants that pose the biggest challenge for Lisi Lerch.

Endnotes

1. Barwick, Ryan (2021), "CMO Tenure Hits New Low," https://www.morningbrew.com/marketing/stories/2021/04/30/cmo-tenure-hits-new-low, (April 30).
2. Deighton, Katie (2020), "Hulu reviews CMO role as Kelly Campbell ascends to president," https://www.thedrum.com/news/2020/02/25/hulu-reviews-cmo-role-kelly-campbell-ascends-president (February 25).
3. Swant, Marty (2021), "IBM CMO Michelle Peluso Joins CVS Health As Company's First Chief Customer Officer," https://www.forbes.com/sites/martyswant/2021/01/06/ibm-cmo-michelle-peluso-joins-cvs-health-as-companys-first-chief-customer-officer/?sh=5d17e34d7f5c (January 6).
4. Whole Earth Brands (2020), "Whole Earth Brands, Inc. Acquires Swerve®, a Rapidly Growing Keto-Friendly & Plant-based Sweeteners & Baking Brand," https://www.globenewswire.com/news-release/2020/11/10/2124260/0/en/Whole-Earth-Brands-Inc-Acquires-Swerve-a-Rapidly-Growing-Keto-Friendly-Plant-based-Sweeteners-Baking-Brand.html, (November 10).
5. Tim Nudd (2016), "Coca-Cola Just Remastered Its Famous 'Hilltop' Ad From 1971, and It Looks Fantastic," https://www.adweek.com/creativity/coca-cola-just-remastered-its-famous-hilltop-ad-1971-and-it-looks-fantastic-170630/.
6. "Marketing Audit: 10 Critical Components," Copernicus Marketing Consulting, http://www.copernicusmarketing.com/our-thinking/blog/2011/07/20/10-critical-components-of-a-marketing-audit/.

Index